# Contents

v

## SECTION III Nutrition in Early Childhood Education 209

# SECTION V Current Issues in Early Childhood Education Safety, Nutrition, and Health 531

# *Preface*

**Working** with children today can be challenging. There has been a societal shift, and the daily lives of children are not the cultural images of a perfect childhood that are often popularized in the media and on children's Web sites. *Safety, Nutrition, and Health in Early Education* includes vital information for those who work with children and addresses the challenges they will encounter in today's diverse world. Adequate preparation in the areas of safety, nutrition, and health is imperative, because even the best child development knowledge for learning and teaching will not be useful if the children are unhealthy, in unsafe environments, or malnourished.

This text focuses on the safety, nutrition, and health of children in early childhood education settings, including family child care homes. The audience for this text are students of child development or early childhood education who are or are preparing to be teachers, paraprofessionals, nannies, family home child care providers, or workers in other jobs that directly relate to young children. My experience teaching a variety of students who became nannies, preschool teachers, elementary teachers, and family home care providers has helped me understand that, although they will have many similar experiences, there will also be differences. This text is organized so that both the similarities and the differences are recognized and discussed.

## ORGANIZATION

The whole child is addressed with respect to safety, nutrition, health, and special topics. All areas of the environment are examined to create policies that emphasize children's status and minimize any risk to children's well-being. *Safety, Nutrition, and Health in Early Education* combines basic information and theory with practical applications, resources, and caregiving skills needed today for working with children, families, and staff. Because the purpose of this book is to help prepare people for a variety of occupations working with children in early education, I have chosen to use the term "teacher," which will apply to all. Regardless of the specific job, all people who work with young children are their teachers. Previously, I referred to "caregivers" but, because more children will be entering early education sites as states offer "preschool for all" or "universal" preschool, that term seems less relevant than before. I have also chosen to replace the term "child care" with "early childhood education," because it relates better today with the circumstances surrounding the early education of children. This includes infant and toddler care, preschools, day care, family child care, state preschools, and the early elementary years.

This book is divided into four sections: safety, nutrition, health, and current issues in early childhood education. This text serves courses that may include all of those subjects, but it was meant to stand alone for each of the subjects as needed. Every college and every instructor has a unique way of organizing the course that corresponds with this text. If one thinks of the sections in terms of modules, it may help both the student and the instructor find the information they need.

## NEW TO THIS EDITION

There are a number of new additions to this text on the recommendations of the reviewers. These new additions include two new chapters. One chapter is the expansion of the nutrition segment and deals specifically with exercise, obesity, malnutrition, and other nutritional challenges. This information will be helpful to the teacher, especially when they are dealing with children that have these nutritional challenges. The other new chapter is on working with children with disabilities and other special needs and has information to help the teacher provide a more optimum environment for these children in the areas of health, safety, and nutrition. The chapter on curriculum has been removed and information on creating curriculum, including project curriculum, is found in chapter one. Specific curriculum is found at the end of every section of the text. By putting emphasis on curriculum for the specific area it will help the teacher to focus on that area. Project curriculum that is introduced will benefit teachers by having another way of presenting their curriculum information.

Also included is the expansion of the goals for providing quality early childhood education from four goals to six goals. The two new goals that are found throughout the text deal with cultural competence and being supportive by creating a caring community for families in the early childhood education environment. By including these goals, teachers will be better able to provide quality early childhood education for the whole child.

New graphics such as the brand new MyPyramid from the new Food Guidance System of the USDA, the Physical Activity Pyramid and the Vegetarian Pyramid are included to help in the greater understanding of nutrition and the issues that surround it. There are new tables and checklists that provide even greater strategies or practical skills for teachers. These include information on Homeland Security; alerts adapted for early childhood education; best practices for menu planning; how to use technology for observation of children; and protective factors for helping families prevent child abuse. Several new Reality Checks are present that include information on bullying; disaster planning for human generated disasters; how America eats; the impact of war and terrorism on children; Autism; Fetal Alcohol syndrome; and being at risk for preventable diseases. Also new to this edition are questions at the end of each Reality Check box, labeled "Checkpoints" which allow readers to think more critically about the information presented.

## INTRODUCTION

Chapter One is an introduction to the text. This edition includes two new goals for quality early childhood education for safety, nutrition and health. These new goals are to practice cultural competence, and to develop partnerships with families to provide a caring community. Information on theories by Uri Bronfenbrenner and Abraham Maslow has been expanded. The NAEYC Code of Ethics as it applies to issues in this text has been included.

## SAFETY

Creating safe early childhood education environments is the major goal of this section of the text. The type of care and the developmental ages of the children are carefully examined in order to produce an appropriate safety plan. Accessories, behaviors, and conditions for safety risk are carefully explained, so that the teacher can anticipate, monitor, and modify any risks to safety in the early education environment.

Both indoor and outdoor environments are examined for common risks such as toys, equipment, traffic, fires, and burns. In addition, interpersonal safety and environmental factors are considered in relation to early childhood education. This edition now includes information on bullying, SAFE playgrounds, and Shelter in Place. It has expanded information on insects. Chapter 5 has a Homeland Security Alert List adapted for early childhood education environments that goes with the new Reality Check about human-generated disasters.

## NUTRITION

Providing nutritional balance in early childhood education is covered in this section of the text. This section has been expanded by one chapter which addresses how to protect nutrition in the early childhood education environment. The new 2005 Dietary Guidelines for Americans and the new MyPyramid Food Guidance System will help teachers to teach children about the importance of good nutrition.

Nutritional needs and feeding practices for infants, toddlers, preschoolers, school-aged children, and children with special needs are examined to help the teacher meet the diverse needs of children in care. The growing concern over childhood obesity in our country is addressed in this section. There is focus on menu planning to create nutritionally balanced meals and snacks for the children whom teachers work with. Food safety, the newest information on supplemental food programs, and the CACFP Guidelines are covered so that the teacher can maximize nutrition and minimize health risks in the early childhood education environment.

Reinforcement of the information is provided through strategies and methods. In addition to the latest Dietary Guidelines and the MyPyramid Food Guidance System, this edition includes a Reality Check on how Americans are meeting their dietary needs. There is expanded information on food jags, a new Vegetarian Pyramid, and a Best Practices for Menu Planning Checklist.

## HEALTH

Strategies for maintaining a healthy early childhood education environment are covered in this section of the text. Tools are provided for observation, assessment, and screening of physical and mental health. A new focus in this area includes how to use technology to observe and record information.

Information on staff health, infection control, and health care will help teachers manage good care in early education with minimum health risks. Methods and strategies for using education, cultural competence, role modeling, and supervision are highlighted for the student to reinforce understanding of the health needs of children in care.

This section includes new information on the Well Care Tracker, administering inhaled medications, medication safeguards, hand hygiene, lice, and managing chronic illness. It also includes a new section on Optimizing Health in Early Childhood Education Environments, which discusses the importance of having medical care for each child and lists the many duties of a health consultant that could help teachers better manage the health of their early childhood education environment.

## CURRENT ISSUES

This section covers topics of special interest to teachers. The chapter on Child Maltreatment has had a title change and includes the latest in statistics and strategies for working with children who have been maltreated. It also includes information on how to work with families that are abusing substances, as well as foster and kinship families that might take on the family role for children of substance abusers. In the Reality Check on Shaken Baby Syndrome, there is very new information on the "Period of Purple Crying." This edition includes a complete new chapter on children with disabilities or special needs in early education environments and a chapter on the linkages that a teacher needs to be successful in the areas of safety, nutrition, and health. These linkages include communication skills, cultural competence, accessing resources, using advocacy for improved early childhood education, creating a caring community for families to maximize the environment for children, and supporting families. As in previous sections, reinforcement is provided through discussion of methods and strategies in education, cultural competence, and supervision.

## SPECIAL FEATURES

Reality Checks address current issues that have an impact on the well-being of children. They bring an *in-depth* approach to some of the more critical areas that are affecting children and early childhood education environments today. Reality Checks include information that is often absent in the popular cultural images found in many textbooks and the media regarding children's development. At the end of each Reality Check there is a Checkpoint question to encourage critical thinking about the information that has been covered. The following are some of the issues discussed in **Reality Checks:**

- effects of war and terrorism on children (NEW!)
- child custody and its impact on early childhood education environments
- kids and guns
- bullying (NEW!)
- neighborhood violence
- dealing with natural disasters in early childhood education environments
- dealing with human-caused disasters in early education environments (NEW!)

- sudden infant death syndrome
- secondhand smoke
- effects of lead poisoning
- effects of poverty on children
- how Americans are eating: do we fulfill our nutritional needs? (NEW!)
- peanut allergy
- effects of advertising on children's food choices
- children of the fast food generation
- helping vulnerable children to become resilient
- lice in early childhood education environments
- otitis media in early childhood education environments
- special care for mildly ill children
- shaken baby syndrome
- domestic violence and its effects on children's lives
- children and attention deficit/hyperactivity disorder
- autism (NEW!)
- fetal alcohol syndrome (NEW!)

**Vignettes** are located throughout each chapter so that the student can "observe" stories based on real-life events.

**Pause for Reflection** allows the student time to reflect on how the information might pertain to his or her own life.

**Case Studies** are placed at the end of each chapter to allow an opportunity for critical thinking on one or more of the subjects that have been covered therein.

## PEDAGOGY

The chapters are organized for ease of use, beginning with an outline of expected outcomes. This outline format is used so the student can easily assimilate the information. In the beginning of each chapter, there are citings of research findings that support the need to learn the information provided in that chapter. Each section of a chapter ends with **Key Concepts**, which summarize the important points of that portion of the chapter.

Case Studies, Pause for Reflection, Checkpoints, and Vignettes reflect practical applications and can help the teacher apply the information from each chapter. Reality Checks enhance the chapter information with an in-depth look at subjects that are affecting children today.

**Important terms** are highlighted in color in the text and defined on the page where they first appear. This allows students to understand the term when they come to it and be familiar with it before they continue. There is also a comprehensive glossary at the end of the text for reference.

Chapters 2 through 15 include **Implications for Teachers.** These chapters help to reinforce the information given and reflect the responsibilities of the teacher to perform the practices, strategies, and methods discussed in each chapter. The information on cultural competency has been expanded in most chapters. Implications for Teachers now includes a "For Families" section

● **Rescue breathing**
*the process of steps to
help a person who is
not breathing resume
normal breathing*

that helps the teacher to create a caring community. Chapter 16 is devoted to issues that directly relate to the teacher's ability to provide the best environment possible for all children in care. In this new edition, information related to curriculum development is dispersed throughout the text. At the end of the body of Chapter 1 is a discussion on "Building Curriculum" that provides an overview of how curriculum may be built. At the end of each section on safety, nutrition, health, and current issues there is curriculum that applies. These are specific examples of how curriculum for a topic might be built. Also included in each section is a list of appropriate children's books for that topic.

The final section of each chapter is entitled **To Go Beyond**. This section gives the instructor ideas for classroom discussion, individual and group projects, and assignments. It also includes questions for chapter review, extensive references, and suggestions for further reading.

Tables, graphs, checklists, figures, and photographs are placed throughout each chapter to help present information in an organized manner. These features reinforce important concepts. For example:

**TABLE 7-6**
*Educational Methods for Nutrition and Nutritional Risk*

| | |
|---|---|
| • Telling | Explaining and providing information |
| • Showing | Role modeling good nutritional habits |
| • Providing resources | Offering handouts and Web site addresses for parents |
| • Questions | Ask children questions to assess their understanding |
| • Practicing | Engaging in physical activity, making healthy food selections |

Adapted from Story, M., Holt, K., Sofka, D., & Clark, E. (Eds.). (2002). *Bright Futures in practice: Nutrition-pocket guide.* Arlington, Va.: National Center for Education in Maternal and Child Health.

## Professional Enhancement Booklet

A new supplement to accompany this text is the Safety, Nutrition, and Health booklet for students. This booklet, which is part of Thomson Delmar Learning's Early Childhood Education Professional Enhancement series, focuses on key topics of interest to future early childhood directors, teachers, and caregivers. Students will keep this informational supplement and use it for years to come in their early childhood practices.

## WebTutor™

The WebTutor™ to accompany *Safety, Nutrition, and Health in Early Education, 3E* allows you to take learning beyond the classroom. This Online Courseware is designed to complement the text and benefits students by enabling them to better manage their time, prepare for exams, organize their notes, and more. Special features include:

- Chapter Learning Objectives: Correlated with textbook chapter objectives.
- Online Course Preparation: A listing of what students should have read or done prior to using online content.

- Study Sheets: Outline the content of each chapter and contain notes. Study Sheets can be printed to help students learn and remember important points.
- Glossary: Provides definitions for terms in each chapter or in the course as a whole.
- Flashcards: Allow students to test themselves on word definitions.
- Discussion Topics: Posted to encourage use as a threaded bulletin board and as assignments to develop critical thinking skills.
- FAQs: Provide questions and answers that students may have about specific content.
- Online Class Notes: Provide additional information about the chapter content.
- Online Chapter Quizzes: Given in various formats including matching exercises, true-false quizzes, short-answer questions and multiple-choice questions with immediate feedback for correct and incorrect answers. Multiple-choice questions also include rationales for right and wrong choices.
- Web Links: Provide students with practice searching the Web for information. Learners choose from a variety of Web links and report findings to their instructor through email.
- Case Studies are provided along with many critical thinking opportunities.

A benefit for instructors as well as students, the WebTutor™ allows for online discussion with the instructor and other class members; real-time chat to enable virtual office hours and encourage collaborative learning environments; a calendar of syllabus information for easy reference; email connections to facilitate communication among classmates and between students and instructors; and customization tools that help instructors tailor their course to fit their needs by adding or changing content.

WebTutor™ allows you to extend your reach beyond the classroom, and is available on either WebCT or Blackboard platforms.

## Online Companion™

Additional resources for this textbook can be found on the Online Companion™ at www.earlychilded.delmar.com. This supplemental material includes extensive chapter quizzes, PowerPoint® outlines, Web links, and various other activities. The site is updated regularly, so you may check back often to receive the latest information about the subjects in each chapter. The author and Thomson affirm that the Web site URLs referenced in this supplement were accurate at the time of printing. However, due to the fluid nature of the Internet, we cannot guarantee their accuracy for the life of the edition.

### Instructor's Manual

An extensive Instructor's Manual is available for this text. This manual includes an outline guide, a test bank, enhancement activities, case studies, a video and film list, and other resources for each chapter. The enhancement activities offer ideas for meaningful projects that include many community links. The case studies will provide opportunities for critical thinking and practical application of the information provided in the text.

### e-Resource

The new e-Resource component is geared to provide instructors with all the tools they need on one convenient CD-ROM. Instructors will find that this resource provides them with a turnkey solution to help them teach by making available PowerPoint® slides for each book chapter, the Computerized Test Bank, an electronic version of the Instructor's Manual, and other text-specific resources.

### Computerized Test Bank

A computerized test bank on the e-Resource CD-ROM allows teachers to create student exams composed of multiple choice, true/false, short answer, and completion questions for each chapter. The CD-ROM provides approximately 1,000 questions in addition to the following features:

- Multiple methods of question selection.
- Multiple outputs (print. ASCII, and Rich Text Format).
- Graphic support.
- Random questioning support.
- Special character support.

## ACKNOWLEDGMENTS

I wish to extend my gratitude to a number of people who continue to make this text a valuable tool for child development professionals. Erin O'Connor, my editor, has been very supportive throughout every edition, and I appreciate her help. Alexis Breen Ferraro also contributed to the process of gathering and organizing the material, sending it out to reviewers, and then getting it back to me. Alexis and Stephanie Kelly both worked hard to put everything together at the end of the process. In addition I appreciate the work of Amber Leith in the production department.

I want to extend my heartfelt thanks to the following reviewers for sharing their expertise with me. Their constructive suggestions and recommendations were very helpful in shaping the final product.

Nancy H. Beaver, M.Ed.
Eastfield College of the Dallas County Community College District
Dallas, TX

Teresa Frazier, Ph.D.
Thomas Nelson Community College
Hampton, VA

Jennifer M. Johnson, M.Ed.
Vance-Granville Community College
Henderson, NC

Ithel Jones, Ed.D.
Florida State University
Tallahassee, FL

Laura Manson, M.A.
Santa Monica College
Santa Monica, CA

Elizabeth Tarvin, M.S.
Orange County Community College
Middletown, NY

## DEDICATION

I would like to dedicate this book to my husband, Dan. His loving and constant support has allowed me the time, energy, and effort to complete this ongoing project. Also, through the years of writing and rewriting this text, I have lost close family members that have influenced my life and would like to remember their contributions to it: my mother, my father, my brother Paul, and my aunt Bernice.

I would like to thank my children, Matt and Annie, and my newly adopted daughter, Madilyn, who at five has brought the real joys of childhood back into our daily lives. My grandchildren—Zarli, Tatiana, Jacob, Jessica, Daniel, and Clay—are works in progress who have helped me rediscover the importance of childhood and how good care and early education can effect it. Having young children in my life again was an important part of my decision to write this text and to continue in my quest to see that all children have what I expect for the children in my life—including a good start through quality early childhood education that cares about the safety, health, and nutritional needs of children.

## THE AUTHOR

Cathie Robertson received her BS and MS degrees from San Diego State University. She teaches courses in Child Development and Family Studies at Grossmont College near San Diego, California. She has taught child development, family studies, and food and nutrition courses, specializing in childhood nutrition, for a number of years. She is the former president of the International Nanny Association and presently serves on several committees for issues that involve early childhood education. She has made numerous national, state, and local professional presentations.

Ms. Robertson has been the recipient of a number of grants, including one for a curriculum and resource guide for working with prenatally substance-exposed children and their families. She is currently working with the Foster, Adoption and Kinship Care Education program in San Diego to teach subjects in the areas covered by this text. Ms. Robertson is married, the mother of three adult children plus one kindergartner, and grandmother to six.

# SECTION I
## Introduction

This section discusses the holistic approach to safety, nutrition, and health in quality early childhood education environments.

1. A Holistic Environmental Approach to Safety, Nutrition, and Health in Quality Early Childhood Education Environments

# A Holistic Environmental Approach to Safety, Nutrition, and Health in Quality Early Childhood Education Environments

**After reading this chapter, you should be able to:**

### 1.1 Holistic Approach

Define a holistic approach to the safety, nutrition, and health of children.

### 1.2 The Environment

Describe an ecological perspective and explain how the environment may affect the safety, nutrition, and health of a young child.

### 1.3 Health Promotion, Protection, and Disease Prevention

Describe and discuss the differences between health promotion, protection, and disease prevention as they apply to early childhood education.

### 1.4 Risk and Risk Management of Children's Well-Being

Define risk and discuss how risk management is crucial to the safety, nutrition, and health of children in early childhood education.

### 1.5 Providing High-Quality Early Childhood Environments for Safety, Nutrition, and Health

Discuss how a teacher can provide high-quality early childhood education for safety, nutrition, and health.

### 1.6 Building Curriculum for Quality Early Childhood Education in Safety, Nutrition, and Health

Design and construct quality curriculum for early childhood education in the areas of safety, nutrition, and health.

## 1.1  HOLISTIC APPROACH

It can no longer be assumed that all of the safety, nutritional, and health needs of children are met at home by parents. The U.S. Department of Labor estimates that more than 13 million children younger than six years of age have mothers in the workforce, and it is expected that these numbers will continue to increase. It is estimated that 75 percent of children younger than 5 years of age and 50 percent of infants are in some form of early childhood education environment on a regular basis (Lucarelli, 2002). By the age of six, 84 percent of children in the United States have received supplemental early childhood education (Child Care Action Campaign, 2001). Public and private center-based early childhood education programs, family child care, homes, and nanny care are providing nonparental care for the majority of children while their mothers are working. These non-parental **teachers** need to help parents meet the health, safety, and nutritional needs of the children in their care. Throughout this text, general reference will be made to "parents." The author recognizes that families have many different compositions, such as single parents, grandparents raising grandchildren, and foster families. The term parents will be used to refer to the primary caregivers who have the responsibility of raising the children. The term "teacher" will be used to describe all those who work in early childhood education, whether they are teachers, family child providers, or nannies.

Teachers, family child providers, nannies, and other nonparental care-givers spend their days working with children to provide intellectual stimulation, social and emotional support, and physical care. Good physical care is of primary importance to support the health, safety, and nutritional well-being of children. Children who are unhealthy or whose physical well-being is **at risk** may have difficulty performing cognitive tasks and relating to others in terms of social and emotional development. Cognitive, social, and emotional deficits as well as physical difficulties may result in poor health. Health should be defined in terms of a person's physical, mental, social, and emotional well-being. These areas are interrelated, and a **holistic** approach allows the effects of all areas of development to be observed for health and well-being.

Good health is the result of reducing unnecessary risk, preventing illnesses, providing sensitive and stimulating care, and promoting the well-being of an individual child. Teachers need to create an atmosphere for children that provides this protective type of environment. In order to accomplish this task, teachers need to focus on three basic areas: safety, nutrition, and health. Lack of good health practices, an unsafe environment, or providing poor nutrition may all contribute to failure in protecting children. The interrelationship of the areas of health, safety, and nutrition will be easier to understand if a holistic approach is used.

The **environment** of children's safety, nutrition, and health in early childhood education is the focus of this text. It is important to remember that early childhood education programs mirror the diversity in society. So, when we look at this ecological interrelationship of health, safety, and nutrition we must also consider culture, families, and the teachers themselves. Each chapter begins with a lead-in paragraph and then points out current research findings that reinforce the need for concern for that issue. The issues presented indicate how children may be put at risk in early childhood education programs as well as family child care and nonparental care given

● **Teachers**
*persons who provide care for children; teachers, family child care providers, nannies*

● **At risk**
*exposed to chance of injury, damage, or hazard*

● **Holistic**
*consideration of the whole being.*

● **Environment**
*all of the conditions, circumstances, and influences that surround and affect the development of an individual.*

to a child in the home. The body of each chapter provides the teachers with the information and strategies needed to deal with these issues.

As an example, the following research findings indicate and support the need for dealing with safety, nutrition, and health in a holistic manner:

- "The whole child has been fragmented"; early childhood educators must have the knowledge, training, and skills to support the development of the whole child (Hyson, 2001).

- Good quality early childhood education where families are involved can help reduce the magnitude of the effects of problems children may encounter such as poverty, violence, and the ability to achieve their whole potential (American Academy of Pediatrics [AAP], 2005; Bronfenbrenner, 2005; Foster et al., 2005).

- Good-quality early childhood education should meet the standards that protect the basic health and safety of children (AAP, 2005; Bassok et al., 2005). It is estimated that two-thirds of licensed child care facilities exhibit a variety of safety hazards (Shepard, 2002).

- "The reality is that only 10 to 15 percent of day care is of high quality . . ." (Greenspan, 2003). Low-income parents who thought their children's care was of good quality were proven wrong in half the cases that were studied (Morris, 2005).

- Children in this country are experiencing a greater number of at-risk difficulties than previously reported. These include psychological problems, emotional disorders, and chronic physical conditions (U.S. Department of Health and Human Services [USDHHS], 2000).

- A holistic approach is needed to address the needs of children who are at risk for severe health problems and school failure (Newman et al., 2000).

- Issues of nutrition and feeding children can affect a child's well-being in both the short term and the long term. We can help to facilitate good nutritional habits (Hayden, 2002).

- Excellence of early childhood education is directly related to compliance with a high standard of care (Hyson, 2002a; Bassok et al., 2005).

- Early childhood education programs can be seen as second homes, and teachers face the challenge of creating safe environments in these challenging times (Gaines & Leary 2004).

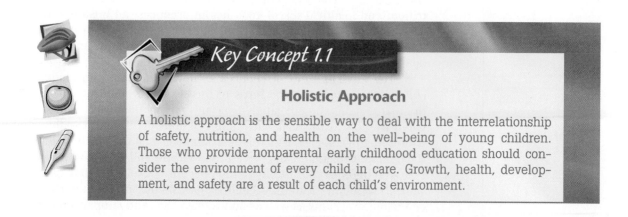

### Key Concept 1.1

#### Holistic Approach

A holistic approach is the sensible way to deal with the interrelationship of safety, nutrition, and health on the well-being of young children. Those who provide nonparental early childhood education should consider the environment of every child in care. Growth, health, development, and safety are a result of each child's environment.

Research findings support the need for dealing with safety, nutrition, and health in a holistic manner.

- We must understand that we are partners with the families of the children in our care. Early education programs are steadily becoming family-centered organizations (Hamilton et al., 2003).

● **Ecological**
*pertaining to the relationship of the individual to the environment*

## 1.2  THE ENVIRONMENT

Environment includes all of the conditions, circumstances, and influences that surround a person. All of the complex factors in the environment can be simplified by using an **ecological** point of view (Figure 1-1). The ecological perspective examines the physical, social and emotional, economic, and cultural environments that affect a child. It relates all of the factors that might influence children's lives in terms of growth, health, safety, development, and well-being. Early childhood education is an essential part of environment for those children who receive nonparental care. Those who are teachers need to be aware of all of the environmental factors. The ecological point of view allows teachers to work with the child, the family, and the community to help provide the best environment possible. Children are best

FIGURE 1-1
Holistic View Ecological
Approach.

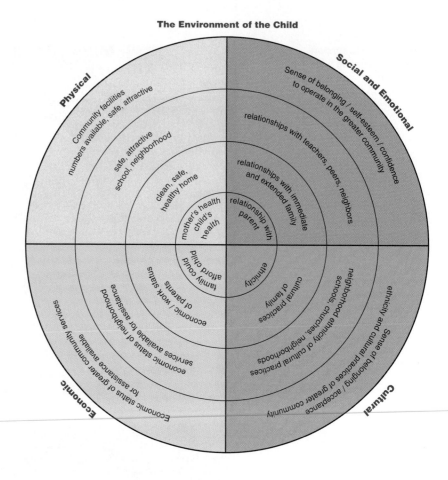

The Environment of the Child

supported and understood when all of these contexts are looked at in the holistic perspective. Bronfenbrenner (1979, 2005) uses the term "bioecological model" to describe how to study the development of the whole child. This is similar to the Holistic Ecological Approach shown in Figure 1-1.

## The Physical Environment

For a child, the physical environment begins in the mother's womb. A child born to a mother who had regular prenatal checkups and proper nutrition during pregnancy is less likely to have physical complications at birth and more likely to experience good health later in life than a child born to a mother who had no prenatal care (USDHHS, 2000). A child whose mother had no prenatal care is more likely to be born at a low birth weight and is far more likely to have physical problems at birth and health difficulties later in life.

Beyond **genetics** and the health of the mother, the physical environment encompasses a number of things. The child's temperament, physical health, and attributes are genetic in nature but can be affected by environment. Environmental factors include the family, home, school, neighborhood, and greater community. Children who are raised in poor

● Genetics
*the origin of features of
an individual*

circumstances are more vulnerable to inadequate nutrition, family violence, and exposure to environmental toxins *and are likely to have diminished physical health* (Zenah et al., 2005). Children who live in neighborhoods where they are protected from harm and are carefully watched are less likely to become injured or victims of violence than children who live in unsafe neighborhoods (Lynch & Cicchetti, 1998). This is significant because in recent years violence, poverty, physical illness, and family stress have increased in the United States.

Another factor in the physical environment is **heredity**. Heredity plays a key role in the health and nutrition of children. In addition to body type and temperament, the propensity for certain diseases may be inherited. The disease may show up at birth or appear later in life.

An example of a disease that shows up at birth is phenylketonuria (PKU). It causes an inability in the child to **metabolize** one type of protein in the normal manner. Left untreated, this condition can cause brain damage and mental retardation. These harmful effects can be prevented if PKU is diagnosed in early infancy and if the proper diet is followed. Hospitals in many states routinely test for PKU at birth. Providing the proper environment through correct diet measures can eliminate the risk.

Diabetes, cancer, obesity, and heart disease are inherited family factors that may appear later in life. These conditions may be prevented or their effects may be reduced through proper diet and exercise throughout life. By managing the environmental factors, the associated risks can be diminished and possibly eliminated.

Children enter early childhood education programs from many different physical home environments. Some children have had good physical environments and are healthy and protected from harm. Other children come from at-risk physical environments. Families may not provide good health practices, or children may have an inherited condition or disease. Some children may be at risk for safety due to abuse or neighborhood violence. Children from at-risk home environments who have access to quality early childhood education greatly increase the likelihood that they will grow up without problem behaviors and will contribute to society rather than becoming violent teens or adults (Newman et al., 2000). Children who attend a good early childhood education environment are more likely to develop properly even if they are considered to be at risk in their own home environments (Foster et al., 2005).

● **Heredity**
*the transmission from parent to child of certain characteristics*

● **Metabolize**
*change occurring by chemical and physical processes in living cells*

Andrea was ten months old when she was diagnosed with diabetes. Her family struggled to control the disease through diet and insulin. Even though several members of the extended family had the disease, none had been as young as Andrea at its onset. At age two and a half, her disease was finally managed with insulin in the morning and careful diet control. When Andrea was three, her mother went back to work part-time, and she put Andrea in a family child care home. Andrea's teacher worked closely with her mother to make sure Andrea's diet was closely monitored. Today, Andrea is a healthy seventeen-year-old high school senior. The cooperation of her early childhood education teacher contributed to maintaining a positive environment for Andrea so that she could be healthy and grow.

A good early childhood education environment using the holistic approach screens for health difficulties, provides good health and safety practices, and promotes proper nutrition. Teachers integrate health, safety, and nutrition into the curriculum and value them as highly as social skills, language, or any other aspects of curriculum. This means that teachers include all of these areas in the program every day. By providing this instruction to children in care, a good quality early childhood education environment can provide the foundation for good health and well-being in adulthood. Early childhood education may offer many children a better chance for an improved physical environment for at least part of the day.

## The Social and Emotional Environment

The social and emotional environment of a child begins with the parent–child relationship. As the child grows, this environment expands to include the family, neighbors, teachers, peers, and other members of the community. Children's mental health and sense of well-being are very important factors in overall health. A family that provides a stable environment and creates the opportunity for a secure **attachment** for a child is more likely to raise a happy, cheerful child. A family that exposes a child to a high-risk situation and fails to form a secure attachment is more likely to produce a child who is at risk for many social and emotional problems (Shonkoff & Meisels, 2000; Sullivan, 2001). Children raised in healthy, functional families are more likely to retain good mental health and be well

● **Attachment**
*the bond that develops between a child and another person as a result of a long-term relationship*

Mary Elizabeth is a four-year-old girl with a healthy appetite, a hearty laugh, and the ability to move from activity to activity with little need for transition. When she was born to a cocaine-addicted mother, the doctors were not sure of her prognosis for growth or behavior. She was briefly removed from her mother's custody and then returned when her mother went into a parent-supportive recovery program. Her mother, Ellen, received help for her addiction as well as help in learning how to parent, including the importance of early bonding in the mother–child relationship. Ellen studied to be a computer operator at a local community college and has been working for the past two years. Mary Elizabeth has been in the same early childhood education program since she was 11 months old.

The staff at the early childhood education program were supportive of Ellen and understood that Mary Elizabeth might need some special help as a result of prenatal substance exposure. When Mary Elizabeth exhibited a high degree of frustration in certain types of play, the staff were able to provide emotional assurance and reduce the stimulation around her while redirecting her behavior. Mary Elizabeth is a good example of what early intervention and a good environment can do for the healthy development of a child at risk. Studies that have followed substance-exposed children from birth have concluded that, in many cases, a secure and supportive environment can overcome most of any possible side effects of prenatal exposure to drugs (Robertson, 1993).

adjusted than those raised in dysfunctional, violent households (Bowlby, 1988; Osofsky, 1999).

The consistency of caregiving and emotional investment on the part of a teacher has a direct relationship to the healthy development of children (Young Children, 2001; AAP, 2005; Zenah et al., 2005). Quality care contributes to children's sense of well-being. A good early childhood education environment is one in which there are good one-on-one relationships between teachers and children in care. Larger early childhood education situations may have to provide a **primary caregiver** for each child to accomplish this optimal type of relationship (USDHHS, 2003). The teacher who relates to the children in care is more likely to be alert and observant. A teacher who has noticed any social or emotional effects of nonparental care can help the child adjust (Shonkoff & Meisels, 2000; Currie, 2000; Zenah et al., 2005). The teacher can also work with families to offer them strategies for providing a home environment that makes a child feel more secure and mentally healthy.

The quality of peer relationships may be a good indicator of a child's mental and emotional health status. A child's ability to cope with new situations, her sense of self-esteem, and her level of confidence affect how a child deals with her peers. The observant teacher will notice these things. A child's sense of self affects how he grows and develops into a member of the greater community as an adult. It is widely recognized that early intervention by a teacher provides a more secure environment for children who are at risk for adjustment difficulties (Zero to Three, 2002; American Public Health Association & American Academy of Pediatrics, 2002).

## The Economic Environment

A child's **economic** environment is established in the home and is influenced by the parents' work history, the economic health of the neighborhood, the community, and the nation. Low income is the primary factor for the majority of childhood health and nutritional risks in this country (Children's Defense Fund [CDF], 2004). Many children who are economically at risk are in child care situations.

Forty percent of the homeless are families. Children in homeless families are at high risk for mental health difficulties (National Mental Health Association, 2005). More children than ever before who are economically at risk are now in early childhood education situations, due to the welfare policy shift that encourages mothers to work outside the home (Loeb et al., 2004, Foster, et al., 2005). One in every six young children in the United States lives below the poverty level. More than three out of four poor children live in a home where one family member was employed at least part of the time. One in three poor children lives in a family where at least one parent is employed full-time, year-round (CDF, 2004). The impact of financial stress on the home environment can affect children's emotions and behavior (Zenah et al., 2005). Financial limitations can also affect children's health. Lack of good medical care, poor nutrition, and an environment in which parental attention is limited can affect children's well-being. Another effect of low income may be the inability to afford quality early childhood education. Poor children are more

● **Primary caregiver**
*the person assigned to be a child's main caregiver throughout the day in order to form a positive attachment bond*

● **Economic**
*the satisfaction of the material needs of people*

at risk for serious illness and death. Some childhood health problems related to poverty are:

- low birth weight
- accidental death
- lead poisoning
- asthma
- lack of immunizations; death due to childhood diseases
- iron deficiency anemia

Economic factors that include lack of preventive care and lack of access to care seriously impair the potential of many children in this country for maximum growth, healthy development, and protection from harm.

The person who provides early childhood education needs to be aware of the impact that the economic environment of families has on the health, safety, and well-being of children. Teachers may be able to improve the impact of the economic environment on children by providing good nutrition and preventive health and safety measures. Teachers can also help families to access resources, create community linkages, and advocate for children. These efforts and collaborations may provide families with critical information on health, safety, and nutritional issues. Teachers who collaborate with the greater community on these issues can improve their community environment.

## The Cultural Environment

● **Cultural**
*related to traits and ascribed membership in a given group*

The child's **cultural** environment includes the framework of beliefs, perspectives, and practices of the family, the neighborhood, and the greater community. It has been estimated that by the year 2030, less than one-half of the U.S. population of children will be of European ancestry (Shonkoff & Meisels, 2000). The United States has become a multiethnic society. With so many cultural traditions, practices, and values present, there may be value conflicts among different cultures. There may be bicultural conflict within families that represents several generations of values. One outcome of these conflicts may be the reinforcement of cultural values within families.

How can an at-risk environment where parental attention is limited negatively affect a child's well-being?

Practices for maintaining traditional cultural values in daily life, such as food choices and child care practices, are seen as meaningful declarations of family heritage. For example, the cultural perspective of a family could have an impact on the type of early education that is chosen for a child (Johnson et al., 2004). It is important that the professional early childhood education teacher support the family cultural values of the children in care (Shonkoff & Phillips, 2000; California Association for the Education of Young Children [CAEYC] 2005). In instances where these cultural values put children at risk, cultural differences and legal practices will need to be addressed.

Characteristics of family health attitudes may relate directly to culture. For example, Latin American families appear to have lower expectations for children's health and therefore may be less likely to use preventive services (Carballo & Nerukar, 2001). The combined impact of social problems due to culture and economic hardship may cause harm to children. Children from these environments are more likely to experience social, emotional, and behavioral problems and to suffer from poor mental health (Duarte & Rafanello, 2001).

It is important for the teacher to be aware of the diversity of the children and families in care (Obegi & Ritblatt, 2005). In 2000, this diversity of children was apparent. Sixteen percent of the population of children were Hispanic, 15 percent were African American, four percent were Asian/ Pacific Islander, and one percent was Native American (*America's Children,* 2001). These numbers are expected to increase in the next three decades, especially in the Hispanic and Asian/Pacific Islander categories. As teachers, we need to go beyond cultural sensitivity or awareness, which calls for responsiveness but go no further. We need to practice **cultural competence** in our interactions with the children in care and their parents so that our relationships are mutually beneficial, even though we may have diverse cultural heritages and practices (Obegi & Ritblatt, 2005). This competence will allow us to better understand ways to communicate information on issues concerning safety, nutrition, and health.

● **Cultural competence** *demonstration of behaviors, attitudes, and policies that allow for cross-cultural effectiveness and valuing of diversity*

The National Association for the Education of Young Children (NAEYC) makes specific recommendations to address cultural competency in early education. For children, teachers should (1) recognize the connection children have to the culture of their language and of their home, (2) be aware that children demonstrate their capabilities in many ways, and (3) realize that learning a second language is not easy. For families, teachers should (1) actively involve families in the early education program, (2) provide support and encouragement for the learning of another language while at the same time valuing the home or first language, and (3) try to honor and support the culture of the children, including the values and norms present in the home (CAEYC, 2005).

*Pause for Reflection*

Consider your own childhood environment. What was the physical environment? What was the social and emotional environment? What was the economic environment? What was the cultural environment? What factors of these influences from your childhood led you to want to work with children? What positive factors from your childhood influences will you have to contribute to the children you work with?

## Environment

An ecological perspective allows one to view the environment of a child. A risk factor in the health and well-being of children can come from any area of the environment. The physical, social and emotional, economic, and cultural environments all influence children's growth and development. Negative conditions from any part of a child's environment may place that child at risk. Poor physical and mental health, injury, or an impaired sense of well-being and self-esteem may prevent the maximum growth potential and development of a child. Using an ecological perspective, the teacher can approach the safety, nutrition, and health of children considering their total environment.

## 1.3  HEALTH PROMOTION, PROTECTION, AND DISEASE PREVENTION

This text deals with the developmental aspects and issues that can help promote and protect children's well-being. The text also illustrates ways to prevent childhood illness, disease, or accident. Teachers should establish and maintain a healthy environment using **health promotion**. Teachers promote health by checking for immunization and encouraging the use of proper hand-washing and diapering techniques. They provide adequate nutrition and arrange for hearing, vision, and dental screening tests. Teachers protect children in care by promoting safety practices such as using child safety seats in travel, checking toys and other equipment for hazards, and providing a low-risk environment.

● **Health promotion**
*the improvement of health conditions by encouraging healthful characteristics and customs*

The holistic approach includes other measures to promote the health, safety, and well-being of children outside the early education environment. Awareness of these outside efforts may help clarify the role of a teacher in terms of the importance of providing good health, safety, and nutrition practices in the early childhood education environment. This knowledge may also help the teacher understand the necessity of community linkages and of advocacy for children. The following sections present several examples of how others are trying to ensure the health and well-being of children.

### Healthy People 2010

*Healthy People 2010: National Health Promotion and Disease Prevention Objectives* is a report that is a product of a national process that has set health objectives for the year 2010. The major purpose of the program is to improve the health and well-being of Americans (Tate & Patrick, 2000). Some of the objectives that affect children are:

- Consider the environmental risks that cause emotional, physical, psychological, and learning problems.

- Provide culturally appropriate educational and support programs for parents in high-risk environments to help reduce child maltreatment and other health problems.

- Increase the proportion of children whose intakes from snacks at school (or in the early childhood education environment) contribute proportionally to overall diet quality.

A teacher can help improve the health and well-being of children in care by addressing these issues. Topics in this text provide the teacher with a base of knowledge to effectively consider the issues.

## National Health and Safety Performance Standards for Child Care

The American Public Health Association (APHA) and the American Academy of Pediatrics (AAP) collaborated and produced *National Health and Safety Performance Standards: Guidelines for Out-of-Home Child Care Programs* (APHA & AAP, 2002). Funding for this project and its in-process update was provided by the Maternal and Child Health Bureau of the Department of Health and Human Services. These guidelines recognize the need for some consistency and guidance to help teachers provide the optimal environment for child health, safety, and nutrition (USDHHS, 2003).

The National Association for the Education of Young Children (NAEYC) is another organization concerned with the well-being of children. Although in agreement with many of the standards set by the APHA and AAP, they encourage teachers to make decisions based on information from several points of view. Teachers must first have the information and an understanding of specific procedures before making any decision regarding the health, safety, and nutritional needs of children in early childhood education environments. Teachers need training to do this (Caulfield & Kataoka-Yahiro, 2001). Another contribution to early education by NAEYC is their Code of Ethical Conduct and Statement of Commitment, which is divided into four parts: (1) for children, (2) for families, (3) for colleagues, and (4) for community and

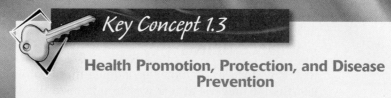

### Health Promotion, Protection, and Disease Prevention

Health promotion, protection, and disease prevention are ineffective if teachers fail to understand the effects of the environment. Clearly, some programs and initiatives try to help parents and teachers promote and protect the health and well-being of children. Teachers play an essential role in the holistic approach to early childhood education environments. They should be able to provide good nutrition and healthy environments that are safe from harm for the children in care. By modeling this environment, teachers can help children feel secure and help parents recognize the value of quality care.

society. The principal responsibility of a teacher to a child is to provide a safe, healthy, and nurturing environment with responsive care. The foremost commitment a teacher has to a family is to bring about collaboration between the school and the home to maximize the potential development of the child. To colleagues, the main responsibility is to provide supportive relationships and productive environments. The teacher's primary responsibility to the community (and to society) is to provide programs that meet its needs and to advocate for children (NAEYC, 1998). A full reference to this document may be found by searching for Code of Ethical Conduct at http://www.naeyc.org. This text was written to help teachers acquire training in the areas of health, safety, and nutrition.

### Other Efforts

Many federal and state programs such as Project Head Start, WIC (the USDA's Supplemental Food Program for Women, Infants, and Children) and Project Healthy Start in Hawaii (El-Kamary et al., 2004) are promoting good health and nutrition habits. Groups such as the Consumer Product Safety Commission promote safety measures that improve the well-being of children.

Many of the initiatives that fund health promotion, protection, and disease prevention operate at all levels of government. There is a clear indication of the need for all entities involved in caring for young children to work together. Some collaborative efforts to promote safety, nutrition, and health for young children include the following:

- improving the health and nutrition of the developing child
- providing health and nutrition instruction for preschoolers
- providing parent education in health and nutrition
- preparing preschool teachers to educate children and parents to use the skills themselves for health, safety, and nutrition issues

There are implications for teachers from these governmental efforts. Teachers need to be prepared to perform the preceding tasks. They also need to understand how to communicate with families and collaborate with others in the community.

## 1.4  RISK AND RISK MANAGEMENT OF CHILDREN'S WELL-BEING

Risk is defined as a chance or gamble that is often accompanied by danger. Risk management is a way to minimize the chance that danger may occur. Risk management takes on specific meaning when it is applied to taking care of children. Results of health risks include illness, infection, disease, mental illness, developmental difficulty, disability, and death. Results of safety risks include accidents, disability, and death. Nutritional risk results include developmental delay, growth retardation, poor health, and lack of resistance to infection or disease.

The opposite of risk in relation to health is well-being. Well-being is measured by wellness, degree of activity, resiliency, proper growth, at-level development, and general vitality. Children who are at risk for problems will display one or more of the risk factors previously discussed.

Joey, a bright, happy two-year-old boy, was small for his age and seemed not to have grown in the six months that he had been at the child care center. Occasionally, he was listless. His teacher was concerned and spoke to Joey's mother, who had noticed the same thing. Joey's mother took him to the doctor for a checkup. The doctor inquired about Joey's diet and discovered that the mother was giving Joey large amounts of fruit juice and not enough milk and other foods. The doctor put Joey on a balanced diet. The mother explained that she had had a problem of being overweight when she was a child and did not want to feed him foods that had too much fat in them. The doctor explained that too much fruit juice may hinder growth and that Joey needed some fat and more milk in his diet. To stay healthy and grow properly, children need a variety of food sources (Bittman, 1994; Briley & Roberts-Gray, 1999).

### Key Concept 1.4

### Risk and Risk Management

Risk management is an effective way to protect, promote, and prevent difficulties regarding children's health, safety, and nutrition. A number of strategies, such as modeling good practices and complying with standards and guidelines, are good risk management tools for teachers.

Proper risk management strategies remove risk factors from children's health, safety, and nutrition. For the teacher, the strategies of health promotion, safety protection, and nutritional education are necessary risk management tools. Modeling good health, safety, and nutrition practices is a positive risk management strategy. The key to managing risk in relation to the well-being of children is to set thorough standards and guidelines for early childhood education environments, including training and staffing.

## 1.5 PROVIDING HIGH-QUALITY EARLY CHILDHOOD EDUCATION ENVIRONMENTS FOR SAFETY, NUTRITION, AND HEALTH

According to Bredekamp and Copple (1997), high-quality early childhood education programs should provide "a safe and nurturing environment that promotes the physical, social, emotional, and cognitive development of young children while responding to the needs of families" (p. 1). In terms of the health, safety, and well-being of children, the teacher needs to have six basic goals in mind to ensure a high-quality early childhood education program:

1. Maximize the health status of the children.
2. Minimize risks to the health, safety, and well-being of the children.

3. Utilize education as a tool for health promotion and risk reduction for both children and adults.

4. Recognize the importance of guidelines, standards, and laws as they apply to the health, safety, and well-being of children.

5. Practice cultural competence.

6. Develop partnerships with families to provide a caring community.

## Goal One: Maximizing Children's Health Status

● **Health status**
*the condition of health of an individual*

A person's **health status** reflects the condition of health of that person. Teachers have the opportunity to provide optimal conditions to maximize the health and sense of well-being of the children in their care. In order to accomplish this goal, a set of objectives for health promotion and the prevention of illness and disease should be planned, carried out, and monitored through the creation of health policies. Regardless of whether care is in an early childhood education program, a family child care home, or the child's own home, many of the objectives are the same. In some instances, the objectives may apply more specifically to the type of setting in which the care is performed (Table 1-1).

**TABLE 1-1**
*Objectives for the Optimal Health and Well-Being of Children*

**For children, all teachers should:**

- Respect the developmental needs, characteristics, and diversity of each child.
- Support a child's development based on current knowledge of the general health and unique characteristics of the individual child. This includes emotional support as well as attention to physical needs.
- Provide and maintain healthy, safe and nurturing environments
- Reduce and prevent the transmission of infectious and communicable diseases.
- Understand the management of ill children, including exclusion policies.
- Use universal health procedures for toileting, diapering, maintaining toys, and handling and storing food.
- Utilize the health status of the staff as an important component of job performance.
- Ensure good nutrition and food safety by following the requirements of the USDA child care component, the Child Care Food Program, and the Code of Federal Regulations.

**For families, all teachers should:**

- Help families understand the importance of developing care routines that contribute to children's sense of well-being.
- Develop relationships with families based on mutual trust

**TABLE 1-1 (Continued)**
*Objectives for the Optimal Health and Well-Being of Children*

- Utilize community health and nutrition professionals to create helpful linkages for children, families, and staff.
- Promote good health and nutrition through education for children, families, and staff.
- Build on the families' strengths and provide support for any improvements that may be needed.
- Provide education and support to parents for the management of infectious illness and disease.
- Respect each family in regard to culture, language, customs, and beliefs.

**For early childhood education programs, all teachers should:**

- Provide a primary caregiver for each child.
- Provide someone to communicate in the children's and parents' first language.
- Provide an atmosphere of mutual respect, trust and cooperation for everyone involved

## Goal Two: Minimizing Risks for Childhood Safety, Nutrition, and Health

Proactive planning to reduce risk for children is an essential element in providing quality early childhood education. The vulnerability of children places them at risk for many problems that can be prevented. Historically, infectious diseases have been perceived as the major risk associated with childhood. The threat of many childhood diseases has been lessened or eliminated with the availability of widespread immunizations to eliminate those diseases. However, these immunizations are effective only if they are administered to children. Other risks for spread of disease could decrease through proper sanitation practices.

Today, in reality, the major risks to children are unintentional injury, child maltreatment and neglect, homicide, lead poisoning, and developmental difficulties. The vulnerability of children at risk for unintentional injuries is influenced by age, cognitive development, motor skills, and the home environment (Centers for Disease Control and Prevention, 1999). The danger of child maltreatment and neglect and homicide has become a major issue in the health and well-being of children in America. Children are more at risk for violence when substance abuse, poverty, and family violence are present in the home environment.

This text includes a number of Reality Checks to help the reader understand the significance of current issues that affect the health, safety, or nutrition of children. The first Reality Check indicates an overview of issues that often go unnoticed due to lack of awareness.

# REALITY CHECK

## Early Childhood Education and Child Care in America: The Reality

Historically, the care, protection, and supervision of children has been performed within families. The shift from family care to nonparental care has taken place mostly in the last half of the last century. Today, 84 percent of children who reach kindergarten age have participated in some form of nonparental early childhood education (CCAC, 2001). Seventy-three percent of infants and toddlers are in nonparental care at least part of the time (Ehrle et al., 2000). Enrollments in early childhood education programs will continue to rise as more mothers enter the workplace for economic reasons (Loeb et al., 2004; Bassock et al., 2005). One reason for increased workplace entry is the change in the welfare system referred to as the Personal Responsibility and Work Opportunity Reconciliation Act of 1996 (PRWORA), which compels people formerly on welfare to enter the workforce. Considering the number of children in care, early childhood education is no longer an option but a necessity for most families. The majority of families must rely on others to provide for the care, protection, and supervision of their children at least part of the time.

Because early childhood education is such an important part of most young children's lives, one would assume that quality care would be the norm. Of children in nonparental care, approximately 30 percent are in center-based care, 23 percent are in family child care, and 5 percent are at home with a nanny or babysitter. Ninety percent of parents rated the early childhood education programs that their children are in as very good. However, trained observers rating the same programs noted that the great majority of care was poor to mediocre (Cost, Quality and Outcomes Study Team, 1995). In fact, many studies on the same subject lead us to believe that quality center-based care

is not the norm, but is available in only 10 to 15 percent of the licensed early childhood education programs in this country (Greenspan, 2003). In addition, many parents cannot afford good-quality early childhood education and must settle for substandard programs in terms of health and safety (Lucarelli, 2002; Moore, 2005). State-run preschools were found to be sadly lacking. In a study of state preschools, it was found that not one state program met any of 10 quality standards (Report on Preschool Programs, 2004). The Cost, Quality and Outcomes study also found that the quality at most early childhood education centers does not meet children's needs for health, safety, and secure attachments. Galinsky et al. (1994) did a similar study on family child care and found that only 9 percent of the homes were rated as good quality. This study also found that 13 percent of the regulated and 50 percent of the nonregulated family child care homes were inadequate in their ability to provide good care to children. In these same homes, only half of the teachers provided secure attachment to the children in their care.

There are approximately 3 million child caregivers in this country who work in 102,458 licensed early childhood education centers and 290,000 regulated family child care homes (CCAC, 2001). The remainder work in nonregulated family child care homes and as nannies in families where no supervision is provided for them. In this country, there is no formal system in place to oversee family child care homes (Shallcross, 1999) or nanny care, and no consistent federal regulations for center-based care. Many states have marginal licensing laws for child care (Gordon, 2000). Regardless of the age or family income of the children in care, consistent state and federal policies for child

*(continues)*

## REALITY CHECK (Continued)

care would help children receive the quality care they deserve (Capizzano et al., 2000).

If we were to have the quality of early childhood education that children deserve, what would it look like? Many people in the fields of child development, health education, and safety education, and others that support children have their opinions. A combination of the best of these would include the following:

- Teachers who have adequate training in the areas of child development, health, and safety, and what provides for the well-being of children (CCA, 2001; Caulfield and Kataoka-Yahiro, 2001; AAP, 2005; Bassok et al., 2005)

- Teachers who provide sensitive, responsive care that allows for secure attachment (Shonkoff & Phillips, 2001; Clark-Stewart et al., 2002; Honig, 2002; Bassock et al., 2005)

- Teachers who have skills to engage parents in communication and who promote parental nurturing for the well-being of the children (Gordon, 2000; Lally et al., 2001; DiNatale, 2002; AAP, 2005)

- Teachers who are competent with diverse cultural and language backgrounds of children (Derman-Sparks, 1999; Hamilton et al., 2003; Obegi & Ritblatt, 2005)

- An environment that allows for good health and safety in early childhood education and provides good working conditions for teachers (Gordon, 2000; Shonkoff & Phillips, 2000; Greenspan, 2003; Bassock et al., 2005)

- Adequate compensation for teachers (Cost, Quality and Outcomes Study Team, 1995; Shonkoff & Phillips, 2000; Gordon, 2000; Greenspan, 2003) so that they will remain on the job and be a stable part of the children's lives

- Adequate teacher-to-child ratio (Gordon, 2000; CCB, 2000b; Shonkoff & Phillips, 2000; CCA, 2001; Greenspan, 2003)

- For care that includes meals and snacks, caution should be taken to provide adequate nutrition and food safety (Briley & Roberts-Gray, 1999; Johnson & Kennedy, 2000; Hispanic PR Wire, 2004; Briley & Roberts-Gray, 2005)

- An environment in which toys and equipment are age appropriate and developmentally appropriate practice is an integral part of the program (Koshansky, 1997; Shonkoff & Phillips, 2000; NICHD, 2003).

The importance of the need for quality early childhood education environments in the United States is overlooked by many people, including legislators and some families who utilize this care, and by some of the people who are performing this care. *It is critical to the development of young children who are in care to be in high-quality early childhood education environments. This type of care best can provide a stable, safe, and consistent environment.* This would allow children of all incomes, ethnic and cultural backgrounds, and family circumstances to have equal opportunities for good child development. This has been proven by several recent studies (Peisner-Feinberg et al., 2000; Shonkoff & Phillips, 2000; Bassock et al., 2005).

There are many ways that high-quality early education and child care can be accomplished (Hyson, 2001; AAP, 2005). It was best summed up by a teacher, Peggy Haack of Madison, Wisconsin, who said, "The key to quality is the person providing it" (Winik, 1999). It is the responsibility of teachers to be caring, consistent, well-educated, and well-trained so that they can support the children in their care with the best of quality available. But, beyond that, we need to educate parents as to what quality care looks like. The public should be made aware that these changes will need legislative guidelines, standards, and regulations, as well as funding to ensure that quality early childhood education is a reality for all children in care.

**CHECK***point:* Imagine you have a three-year-old whom you want to place in a quality early education program. How would you go about finding one in your local area? What five things would top your list as to what to look for in a quality program?

Prevention, recognition, protection, and early intervention are the major tools that teachers can use to reduce risks to children in their care. Table 1-2 lists some risk management objectives for child care safety, nutrition, and health.

**TABLE 1-2**
*Risk Management for Early Childhood Education*

**All teachers should:**

- Require proof of immunizations before admitting children to care.
- Meet immunization requirements personally.
- Follow health and safety licensing guidelines.
- Provide a safe staff-to-child ratio.
- Develop good observational skills.
- Use health appraisals and assessment as risk management tools.
- Follow sanitary guidelines for hygiene and food handling.
- Protect the facility from neighborhood violence.
- Recognize and manage mild childhood illnesses.
- Provide backup or substitute teachers to replace ill teachers.
- Develop an inclusion/exclusion policy for ill children.
- Communicate by written notice about exposure to communicable disease.
- Provide a hazard-free environment.
- Prevent accidents in the indoor environment by following safety guidelines and practices.
- Prevent accidents in the outdoor environment by selection and placement of equipment and by following safety guidelines and practices.
- Create a safety plan for the facility.
- Create a disaster preparedness plan for fire and other dangers.
- Prevent fire by following local fire code standards and practices.
- Post and be ready to allow emergency procedures.
- Have knowledge of pediatric first aid and be able to practice it in case of an emergency.
- Be able to perform cardiopulmonary resuscitation (CPR).
- Detect, prevent, and report child maltreatment.
- Understand and utilize acceptable methods of discipline.
- Arrange the facility so there is no opportunity for isolation or privacy of individual teachers with children.
- Develop a written plan for nutritious meals and snacks.
- Provide nutritious foods.
- Provide relief time for all staff.

**Family child care providers and nannies should:**

- Organize the home for child care.
- Organize for mixed-age child care.

## Goal Three: Education as a Tool for Children's Health Promotion and Risk Reduction

A holistic approach to health promotion and illness and disease prevention is needed because health and well-being cannot be achieved without awareness. An educational component must be present in order to create a safe and nurturing environment for children. The educational component must impact the staff, the children, and the parents involved in the early childhood education program or relationship.

Education and training for quality early childhood education are essential (Gordon, 2000; Burchinal et al., 2002). The teacher should be educated in promotional, preventive, and protective practices to provide the maximum environment and minimum risk for the child (Table 1-3). A fundamental role of the teacher is to pass along knowledge. Modeling good health and safety measures and good food choices teaches children by example. Role modeling also allows children and their parents to see the teacher put this knowledge to practice.

**TABLE 1-3**
*Educational Tools for Teachers*

**A teacher should have knowledge of:**

- Health promotion and the importance of modeling health promotion behavior
- Observational skills
- Immunizations and when they are to be given
- Health appraisals and use of assessment tools
- Mechanisms of communicable diseases and how they are spread
- Universal sanitary practices
- Common childhood illnesses, including management and exclusion policies
- Environmental health and safety hazards
- Safety standards and practices for both indoor and outdoor equipment
- Disaster preparedness
- Emergency response procedures
- Cardiopulmonary resuscitation (CPR) and first aid
- Detection and reporting of child maltreatment
- Prevention of child maltreatment
- Nutritional needs of children
- Good feeding practices for children
- Any special health or nutritional needs of children in care
- Communication skills
- Diversity and how it can affect health, safety, and nutrition
- Advocacy for children
- Access to community resources
- Development of family and community coalitions for improved safety, nutrition, and health

Teaching children about good health and proper nutrition helps them contribute to their own health. Instructing children in preventive and protective measures permits them to participate in their own well-being. The children can pass that information on to others by modeling and through discussion. This may motivate parents to be more receptive to the teacher's modeling and information.

Teachers educate parents by discussing health, safety, and nutrition directly with them and by providing handouts and holding workshops. Teachers can access the help of community groups to aid with this task. Parents who are supported through continual contacts with teachers and educational assistants are better at providing holistic health for their children (USDHHS, 2003).

Knowledgeable teachers who work with children, parents, and the community contribute to a team effort to promote good health, safety, prevention, and nutrition. Creating these linkages allows the teacher to effect a holistic approach to ensure a quality environment for the children.

## Goal Four: Recognizing the Importance of Guidelines, Standards, and Laws for the Health, Safety, and Well-Being of Children

● **Guidelines**
  *statements of advice or instruction pertaining to practice*

● **Standards**
  *statements that define a goal of practice*

● **Laws**
  *rules of conduct established and enforced by authority*

**Guidelines, standards,** and **laws** affecting early childhood education environments have been created for the purpose of protecting children and promoting quality environments for them. Programs in states where there are stringent regulations tend to provide higher quality care than those in states that have less stringent regulations (Child Care Bureau, 2000b). When teachers in all settings comply with standards, there is a lower turnover rate, more sensitive care, and staff with better training, resulting in better-quality early childhood education. NAEYC's position on licensing and regulation states, "The fundamental purpose of public regulation is to protect children from harm, not only threats to their immediate physical health and safety, but also threats of long-term development impairment" (1997). Compliance with minimum standards can affect environmental practices, relationships with parents, and the general attitude of teachers (Grubb, 1993).

● **Regulations**
  *recommendations that are made a requirement by law*

● **Staff-to-child ratio**
  *the number of staff required to provide proper care for the number of children of a certain age group*

Whenever a child is injured or dies in the care of a teacher, the media are quick to report it. Although the sensationalism may hurt the profession at the time, good may come from these unfortunate accidents or poor care. Quality early childhood education seeks to improve health and safety standards as well as provide education for families (Caulfield & Kataoka-Yahiro, 2001). Some legislators in this country are more receptive to recommendations from organizations such as the NAEYC, Children's Defense Fund, the AAP, The National Center for Clinical Infant Programs, The American Dietetic Association, and The American Public Health Association. Those organizations have developed standards and recommended guidelines for teachers to follow concerning the safety, nutrition, and health of young children. These and other groups are helping to effect legislation that originates **regulations** or enacts laws that protect children's well-being. For example, the **staff-to-child ratio** is an issue covered by regulations.

The AAP and the APHA believe that standards and guidelines should be established for all nonparental early childhood education programs. The USDHHS oversees federal regulations that have been enacted to help children. Individual states can enact legislation that creates regulations for early childhood education programs. Many states have strict licensing regulations for child care settings, although some states have few, if any, licensing requirements. These licensing requirements basically relate to center-based care, schools, and family child care. There are virtually no regulations for nannies.

Guidelines, standards, and regulations affect the teacher. They exist to support and promote the health and well-being of children. If guidelines, standards, and regulations exist, they should be followed. In a center-based facility, it is up to the director to ensure that the staff complies with and understands the guidelines, standards, and regulations. In a family child care home, it is the provider who monitors guidelines, standards, and regulations to ensure compliance. A teacher who cares for a child in the child's own home must use common sense and form guidelines based on information from classes and available support such as this text or a network of community resources.

If the state in which the early childhood education environment is located has no regulations, it is imperative that the teacher follow guidelines and standards suggested by the organizations previously discussed in this introduction. Many of the guidelines and standards are reflected in this text. It is basic good early childhood education practice to follow them. The teacher who uses them will be able to provide a healthy, protective environment for the children in care.

## *Goal Five: Practice Cultural Competence*

The United States is becoming more and more diverse, and this diversity is especially noted in the numbers of children. As an example, half of all births reported in California are those of Latino children (Hispanic PR Wire, 2004). A teacher would be remiss if he or she did not consider the cultures of the children present when planning for the safety, health, and well being of those children. For quality early childhood education, the best practice in relation to culture would be that the teacher's practices and the environment reflect the language and culture of the children in care (Duarte & Rafanello, 2001; Obegi & Ritblatt, 2005). It is thought that quality early childhood education is reflected in practices that consider cultural differences (Burchinal & Cryer, 2003). For example, Head Start performance standards for care require a multicultural perspective or approach to the children and families in their program.

By displaying behaviors, attitudes, and policies that allow for cross-cultural effectiveness, teachers are more competent to deal with the diversity found in their early childhood education programs. The National Center for Cultural Competence (NCCC) believes that cultural competence "is achieved by identifying and understanding the needs and help-seeking behaviors of individuals and families" (NCCC, 2004). This may not always be easy to do, because caregiving practices are a reflection of the culture beliefs and history of those performing the care. In order to become culturally competent, a teacher must first examine his or her own cultural background, beliefs, and practices (Obegi & Ritblatt, 2005). This self-assessment can help determine whether there are any biases that need to be addressed. Teachers should also understand that the beliefs and practices of families might be quite different from their own. This is why open and reciprocal communication and respect for each family is vital. We need to accommodate and to help empower children from diverse cultures (Obegi & Ritblatt, 2005; Okagaki & Diamond, 2000).

Cultural values often are reflected in the early childhood education choice of the families (Johnson et al., 2004). The ease with which a child and his family adapt to care will be accelerated if the caregiving practices in the early childhood education environment are similar to those of the home environment. Collaboration or partnering between the teacher and the family are more likely to occur when care is taken to understand the child's cultural background. If inquiry is made to parents as to the family's beliefs, values, and practices, the teacher can help to create a more complementary environment for the child. Cultural competency is more likely to lead to quality early childhood education programs that help keep children safer and healthier and promote a greater sense of well-being.

## Goal Six: Develop Partnerships with Families to Provide a Caring Community

The number of women with young children who work outside the home has continued to increase, and demand for nonparental care is expected to rise another 12 percent by the end of this decade (Neugebauer, 2002). In part, this has been caused by a shift in family policy (Loeb et al., 2004). As a result, more families are using out-of-home care (Greenspan, 2003) and are depending on that care for the benefit of both the children and the family. The recent NAEYC revision of standards for teachers has given high priority to building family and community relationships (Hyson, 2002a). The NAEYC suggests that well-prepared professionals should value, respect, and involve families in order to help a child reach his or her greatest potential. Early childhood education environments that have meaningful family involvement are more likely to reflect quality (DiNatale, 2002). Teachers who invite families to partner for the success of the child and are aware of the families' circumstances and needs are able to be more effective in establishing a caring community for the child (Baldwin et al., 2003). A caring early childhood education community is especially important for the health, safety and well-being of the child.

The teacher–parent partnership is established in numerous ways. First, the families should be offered a real orientation to the early childhood education program. A good orientation for families can relieve concerns and confusion that they may have about what takes place in their children's particular program. This is especially true for "first-time" families that have never accessed the use of early childhood education in any form. An orientation allows the family to know the people involved in the program. Quality early childhood education programs are likely to offer a parent handbook that includes much important information, such as policies and practices and even the program philosophy or mission statement (DiNatale, 2002). An orientation may even include home visits (Baldwin et al., 2003), during which the teacher can gain insights into the child's home environment.

The parent and the teacher should establish a clear and open channel of communication. Any prejudice on the teacher's part about the superiority of his or her knowledge of early childhood education should be dispelled if a relationship is to be established (Ahnert & Lamb, 2003). The parent and the teacher should talk often and begin to know each other. Discussing such topics as parenting practices, child-rearing perspectives, and interactions can help both understand each other. This helps to establish respect and reciprocity between the family and the early childhood education program. A regularly scheduled parent conference should occur several times a year for more in-depth discussion. Good communication can enhance parenting and create a balance between the home and early education programs for children. Another benefit is that, as parents become involved, they become educated about best practices for their children.

Families can also be actively involved by volunteering to help with activities such as field trips or special events or by helping out at home in a number of appropriate ways. This might include helping with a newsletter, sewing, or computer work (DiNatale, 2002).

Special events that involve families and children can also be scheduled. A yearly picnic, an open house for families once or twice a year, and other events such as "nacho" parties or ice cream socials can give families a chance to get to know each other and the teachers better. When everyone is involved, a caring community is the result.

---

## Pause for Reflection

Why are the six goals so important to creating a caring environment for children and families in early education programs? What could you specifically do to prepare to help create this type of environment for the children you work with or will be working with?

---

# REALITY CHECK

## The Reality of War and Terrorism for Young Children in the United States

As we look at safety, nutrition, and health in a holistic manner and think about providing a quality environment for children, we have a new reality to deal with. We are providing early education and care to children who are living in a country that has been attacked by terrorism for the first time on its own soil and, as a result, is now involved in a lengthy war on terrorism. September 11, 2001, was a scary time for all of us because it disrupted our equilibrium. In the days that followed, we all sought to achieve a balance, but the children who experienced this

event via the media or adults talking about it wanted to know all about it. As adults, it was difficult to explain these events to ourselves, much less to children. Terrorism is about putting potential victims in a state of terror that has psychological and emotional repercussions (Schonfield, 2002). This is especially true if the child has experienced the trauma or loss firsthand (National Center for Children Exposed to Violence [NCCEV], 2003). Children express grief from a tragic event in different ways. Some withdraw or become clingy and fearful. Others

(continues)

# REALITY CHECK (Continued)

act out and become more aggressive (Brodkin, 2004). A range of behaviors that may be expressed include the following (North Carolina State University, 2003):

- irritability
- inability to be calmed
- sadness
- fearfulness, including talking about scary things
- anticipation of another bad event
- developmental regression
- anger
- aggressive behavior
- changes in sleep patterns
- clinging behavior
- physical effects such as stomach-aches or headaches
- change in eating habits
- hypersensitivity

When children are fearful, they often want to know all about whatever it is that they are afraid of (Perry, 2003). Many children have fantasies that do not reflect reality. They may ask questions, or they may hesitate to ask questions. Part of each child's reaction to the issue of war and terror depends on his or her age, developmental level, and personality (NCCEV, 2003). Children who are old enough to understand may know enough to be really afraid. Children who have had trauma in their lives before may be more vulnerable than others who have not experienced trauma (NASP, 2003). Children who have been actually involved in a terrorist attack in some manner are three times more likely to suffer from post-traumatic stress disorder than if exposed to some other type of trauma (Mental Health Weekly, 2004).

As teachers, it is important to be truthful with children. On the other hand, we should not offer more information than they need. Listen carefully to what they are asking. Give the best possible answer that deals only with what they are asking. Do not go beyond the simple question they ask. A simple answer is the best. Children may also exhibit nonverbal cues. These might include changes in their normal facial expressions, play behavior, or how they talk (LifeCare, 2003).

One of the things that young children want to know is that everything is okay and that they are safe. War is a concept that children do not fully understand, and part of that lack of understanding may be the fear that war is closer than it really is and that it may come to where the child is. To help children better understand the situation can be difficult because we do not know what will happen, but we can reassure them that we are doing as much as we possibly can to keep them safe and secure. Teachers can let the children know that they are there for the children and they can be counted upon.

War may be a greater reality to a young child if either of her parents is deployed to the war zone. Besides the factor of war, the child is dealing with separation from her parent or maybe both parents. This can cause major changes, such as moving, a change in income for family necessities, or even living with others if both parents have left (Myers-Walls, 2003). These children may need the extra reassurance and familiarity that a teacher can provide.

Children in care look to teachers for stability and security. Teachers are very important in their lives, and children need their help to deal with scary and fearful feelings about what is happening in our world today. The most important thing you as a teacher can do is to provide routine and structure that is familiar in the environment he or she has created. A simple hug or two might be just enough to reassure a fearful child when he is thinking about war or terrorism.

Teachers can help children by letting them deal with some of their fears in their own ways. One of the things that Fred Rogers used to tell children was to look for the "helpers" in any scary situation (Mister Rogers

# REALITY CHECK (Continued)

Neighborhood, 2004). That would have been easy to do on 9/11, with all the firemen and policemen helping. Today, while we are in a war situation, it is easy to find the soldiers, both men and women, who are helping the United States. Finding the helpers can lead to discussions about how these people help to keep the world a safer place to be.

Play is one way that children are able to deal with things they do not understand (AAP, 2003). Unfortunately, much of the play that comes out of the issue of war and terror may be violent play (Levin, 2003a). There has been an increase in play with weapons, which is not surprising considering the circumstances (Perry, 2003). This type of play may lead to unsafe conditions or aggressive behaviors by some children. If the play gets scary or dangerous, intervention may be needed. Play behavior may need to be redirected, and discussions might take place about how people can help or support each other instead of hurting each other. As children play, watch to find out what they are thinking or feeling and what they are worried about. If toys such as rescue vehicles or doctor's kits are available, children might be led into more positive play (Levin, 2003a). Talking about the importance of peace and conflict resolution might lead children into a different mode of thinking (Levin, 2003b). Another consideration is to spend more time outdoors doing gross motor activities; this will help children be active and less involved in thinking about the issues surrounding war and terrorism (Perry, 2003).

Children may feel anger toward a group of people who may be seen as causing this war on terrorism. Children can become prejudiced at a young age. Cultural competency is something a teacher should strive for, and it would be especially important here. An early childhood education environment should model respect for diversity. Provide activities that help children appreciate differences among cultural groups. Help children to learn tolerance and nondiscrimination.

It is also very important to involve families as part of the early childhood education program to deal with the turbulent times we all live in. Be involved with the families of children in your care. Talk often with them. If there are concerns in this area, it might be wise to hold a deeper discussion about what is happening with the child at home in dealing with the unease over war and the threat of terrorism. Work closely with the family to provide consistency between home care and the early childhood education program when it comes to discussions or feelings on this subject. This is especially important if a family member is deployed in the military or other services.

In all, it appears that what a child needs from a teacher in this instance, as in many others, are five fundamental things (Tylenda, 2004):

- structure
- consistency
- predictability
- nonpunitive limit setting
- nurturance

The teacher's job is not an easy one. Trying to maintain the stability of children's lives can be difficult after watching the nightly news reports on deaths of our soldiers or terror attacks around the globe. The task may be even more formidable if we have a loved one in another country fighting for our protection. Teachers need to remember to take care of themselves so they can take care of the children in their care (Tyson, 2003). They should also provide a good role model for coping. One way to do this is to make sure that teachers talk about their feelings with others such as family, friends, and coworkers (Stephens, 2003).

CHECK*point:* What would you specifically do to support a family that has a parent away at war? What protective measures might you offer to the child in your program from this family?

*Key Concept 1.5*

### Providing High-Quality Early Childhood Education

High-quality care should be the objective of every teacher. For good safety, nutrition, and health in early childhood education, the teacher should have six basic goals: to maximize the health status of children; to minimize risks to children; to utilize education as a tool for health promotion and risk reduction; to recognize the importance of guidelines, standards, and laws as they apply to early childhood education, to practice cultural competence, and to develop partnerships with families to provide a caring community.

## 1.6 BUILDING CURRICULUM FOR QUALITY EARLY CHILDHOOD EDUCATION

● **Curriculum**
*course of study that relates to the subject being examined*

**Curriculum** provides the mechanism for teaching children. Teachers provide instruction in safety, nutrition, and health to children every day by role modeling behaviors and actions. However, role modeling does not provide enough information for children so that they may understand, change their actions, and practice healthy and safe behaviors. Other methods are needed to properly inform children and to involve families. Curriculum can be presented in a number of different ways (Table 1-4).

Curriculum must include a number of elements for it to be effective. It should provide a holistic approach to the subject for the children. The developmental abilities of the children should be considered. Curriculum should be developmentally appropriate (Bredekamp & Copple, 1997). Understanding what is appropriate for each age group helps the teacher to use suitable practices for constructing curriculum. Curriculum should also be **anti-bias**. The teacher should consider the diversity of the children and their families, the staff, and the greater community.

● **Anti-bias**
*an approach to curriculum that removes all inequities due to race, gender, and abilities*

Curriculum should offer children several important qualities, including flexibility. This allows for the flow that may involve a child's interest and

**TABLE 1-4**
*Curriculum Design Considerations*

- Does it provide for a holistic approach?
- Is it developmentally appropriate?
- Is the information presented in an anti-biased manner?
- Is it flexible?
- Does it promote positive feelings?
- Do children have choices?
- Can children explore and interact?
- Are a variety of activities or methods used for presenting ideas to children?

attention span. Any curriculum used should promote positive feelings on the part of the children. Curriculum should offer the child choices in how best to learn about a subject. Some forms of learning are more appealing to some children than others. A variety of activities or methods allows a child different ways to explore an idea. This reinforces learning for many children. When children are allowed to explore and interact with others, learning becomes more meaningful.

Designing curriculum for the early childhood education environment is an ongoing task. The class that uses this text will be covering the subjects in safety, nutrition, health, and current issues that form the basis for the curriculum needed to promote good health, safety, and well-being.

In the past decade or so, there has been meaningful dialogue as to how curriculum should be delivered to young children. Heavily scheduled days full of lesson plans and planned activities are giving way to more flexibility on the teacher's part and more involvement on the children's part to help construct the curriculum. In many programs in this country, children are being given more of a voice in what they are interested in learning about. This has been a result of the influence of the Reggio Emilia approach to learning (Stegelin, 2003; Hendrick, 2004). This perspective allows for the investigation of information and gaining of knowledge through project-based learning by doing. The basic tenets of the Reggio approach include the following (Fraser & Gestwicki, 2002):

- The child is competent, full of ideas and imagination that can lead the child to a fuller understanding if allowed to participate to the level that he or she is capable of.

- Environments are designed to facilitate the social construct of understanding.

- The relationships and interactions of children are seen not as in a vacuum but as part of a system of interrelationships with other children, their teachers, and their families.

- Collaboration plays a major role. Everyone works together to create a learning community.

- Documentation is a cornerstone. A visual and written view of children's experiences enhances learning. This also allows for reflection about what was learned and may lead to further investigation or interpretation.

- Flexible planning is used instead of a rigid curriculum full of lesson plans. This allows for the investigation of an idea or subject. Children, teachers, families, and even the larger community collaborate together to seek the answers or knowledge needed.

- The role of the teacher is to listen closely to children and to devise ways or possibilities for investigation of the idea or subject at a deeper level.

- Often referred to as "one hundred languages of children" is the provision of many types of media and materials that encourage the children to explore the many facets of an idea or subject.

- Transparency is a metaphor for openness for ideas from many sources, including many cultures, and making information available to the families and larger community as children and teachers search together to expand their knowledge.

- The result of this process is often called a project (Stegelin, 2003). It can come from children's ideas, or it can be introduced by the teacher. The project idea or base should be one that can be developed over time, maintains the interest of the children, and can be explored in diverse ways.

● Topic web
*graphical representations used for organizing and communicating knowledge about a particular topic*

The project emerges from something that sparks interest from the children in care. It might be an idea from the teacher, something that someone brings to share, or a book or story. Once the topic base has been decided, exploration in the form of a **topic web** or concept map should begin. Exploring the topic starts with information that the children already know and continues with lists of questions that they might want to find answers to. The teacher helps direct this exploration and may help the children think of questions that will lead to more in-depth investigation. At this point, parents are included by letting them know about the project the children are working on. Parents may discuss the project with the children at home. Some parents may have knowledge or expertise that they are willing to share. This is usually thought of as the beginning or first stage of the project.

Development is the second stage of the project. The teacher provides resources for the children. This includes the materials and media that the children need to carry on the investigation. The materials and media might include books, dramatic play materials, music, art supplies, and anything else the teacher feels would contribute to the success of the project. As the project evolves, it is documented through picture taking, journal writing (children dictating to the teacher), and class discussion. Field work may be part of the project. Whether this is done inside the classroom or on the premises or actually leads to a field trip depends on the nature of the project. If it is a project investigating food, the field work could be growing beans or a trip to a pumpkin patch to see how pumpkins grow. The object of the field work is to afford opportunities to understand the project from many views. At the end of each phase of field work, there is discussion, perhaps drawing of pictures, and continued documentation. Another part of the development stage may be inviting "experts" to come and talk with the children. This might be a dental hygienist to talk about brushing teeth or a grocer talking about how food gets to the store. In some cases, these experts come from the families of children in the early childhood education program. The documentation is available for the families to see as the project progresses.

The final stage is the conclusion of the project. Reflection of what was learned is a key component for the children. This wind-up phase often includes sharing the information with others. Parents may be invited to a discussion or presentation of the project. Children can present their experiences in a number of ways, such as art, some form of dramatic play, or in telling it in story form. As the project finishes up, it is important for the teacher to help the children transition from this project to another one.

It is not an easy task to change from routine schedules with lesson plans that are comfortable for the teacher and appear to be well received by the children. However, it has been proven that children are capable of much deeper learning if they are involved in investigation and have on hand a myriad of materials that can allow them to give direction to their own understanding.

This approach may be especially important for children with special needs who have been included in the early childhood education program

(Vakil et al., 2003). Planning for this emergent type of curriculum is a process that begins with consideration of children's actions and conversations. Further education in co-constructive curriculum might include taking a class on the Reggio Emilia approach or doing research or reading one of the many books on the subject. Someone considering this approach could benefit greatly from talking with others who have already adopted this style of building curriculum. This type of curriculum easily qualifies as a holistic approach. The construction of it involves the teacher, the children, the families, and the community. An investigation of hand washing could take the direction of looking at microbes, finding out about germs, the importance of sanitation, seeing how the greater community deals with sanitation, or even talking about how soap is made. A look at food could lead us from the grocery store, to the packer, to the farmer, to the earth, and to a discussion of how vitamins work in our bodies.

For many teachers who have yet to try co-construction of curriculum, lesson plans may be the daily substance of their curriculum. The **theme** or purpose of the lesson plan must be selected. A curriculum unit might have a number of themes to allow the teacher to address the subject. The **objectives** or expected outcomes should be clearly connected to the theme. At least one cognitive objective (what is learned) and one behavioral objective (how it is practiced) should be the goal of each lesson plan. NAEYC takes the position that curriculum content should be "intellectually challenging, varied and responsive to individual, cultural and community characteristics" (Hyson, 2002b). Curriculum goals should be realistic and achievable and should take into consideration the varied ways that children can learn.

According to Zemelman, Daniels and Hyde (1998), the best practices for lesson plan curriculum include seven considerations. First, they should be centered on the children's interests and concerns. Next, they should be experiential, so that children learn by doing. Thematic units that build upon each other lead to holistic understanding. Lessons should be authentic and should give children the opportunity to learn at a deeper level. Children should be allowed opportunities to express their ideas. There should be time for reflection about what they have learned and how it applies to what they knew. Finally, lesson planning should be collaborative. When cooperative learning is used, it can be a powerful tool for learning.

Materials should be provided that are appropriate to the developmental levels of the children. Many different types of materials should be made available; these might include books, equipment, art materials, sensory materials, and dramatic play embellishments. A number of different methods can be used to present curriculum (Table 1-5).

- **Theme**
  *subject being emphasized*
- **Objectives**
  *goals, expected outcomes*

**TABLE 1-5**
*Ways to Present Curriculum*

- Investigation
- Collaboration
- Documentation
- Family involvement
- Dramatic play

*(continues)*

**TABLE 1-5 (Continued)**
*Ways to Present
Curriculum*

- Arts and crafts
- Finger plays
- Tapes
- Stories
- Books
- Sensory experiences
- Bulletin boards
- Cooking experiences
- Gross and fine motor experiences
- Resource people such as a fireman or dentist
- Field trips

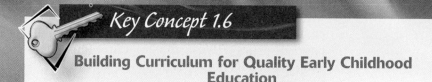

*Key Concept 1.6*

## Building Curriculum for Quality Early Childhood Education

Curriculum requires a number of elements to be effective, and it should provide a holistic approach to the subject for the children. The curriculum should be appropriate to the developmental abilities of the children and should consider the diversity of the children and their families, the staff, and the greater community. It should be flexible and positive and should offer children choices in how to learn. Curriculum should be authentic and should give children the opportunity to learn at a deeper level. Children should be allowed opportunities to express their ideas and should have time for reflection about what they have learned and how it applies to what they know.

## CHAPTER SUMMARY

A holistic approach allows the teacher to view the interrelationships of safety, nutrition, and health for young children. An ecological perspective views the total environment of the child. The physical, social and emotional, economic, and cultural environments all have an effect on the growth and development of children. Risk factors for safety, nutrition, and health for children may come from any or all of these environments.

Awareness of efforts on national, state, and local levels may help clarify the role of the teacher concerning practices that involve safety, nutrition, and health. The ability to recognize signs and symptoms of at-risk issues is key to early intervention.

## CHAPTER SUMMARY (Continued)

Quality early childhood education involves maximizing the health status of children and minimizing risks to safety, nutrition, and health. Using education for health promotion will reduce risk. A teacher who recognizes the importance of guidelines, standards, and laws has the tools to the best possible learning environment.

Practicing cultural competence affords the tools needed to address diversity in early education. Teachers who collaborate with parents and develop a caring community will offer the optimal environment for healthy development of the children they work with. When teachers carefully construct curriculum to meet the needs and developmental levels of children, they can offer the children tools of their own to maintain safety, good nutrition, and a healthy lifestyle.

## TO GO BEYOND

In this section you will find a number of activities that you can use to apply and improve your knowledge of this chapter. There are also thorough online resources that accompany this text and can be found at: http://www.earlychilded.delmar.com (see description at the end of this chapter).

### Chapter Review Critical Thinking Applications

1. Discuss the holistic approach to children's safety, nutrition, and health. Why do you suppose so many people who work with young children fragment or select one portion to look at and do not view the whole child? Does the interrelationship between safety, nutrition, and health affect issues regarding any one of them when applied to early childhood education?

2. Describe the ecological perspective of the total environment. Consider a child whom you know. How does each of these areas affect this child's safety? Nutrition? Health?

3. Discuss the changes in diversity in this country. How might these changes affect early childhood education programs? What could be done to minimize the impact?

### As an Individual

1. Look at your own environment at home. What risks do you see in it? What could you do to minimize those risks? What can be done to maximize the health and safety of your environment? What if your environment were used for an early childhood education environment—would it be a safe and healthy place for children?

2. Write down everything you have eaten for one typical weekday and one typical weekend day. How could you improve your own nutritional status?

3. Observe an early childhood education situation. Look at it with a holistic approach. What are the teacher and the facility doing to contribute to the children's safety, nutrition, and health? How would you improve the program by thinking of the whole child?

4. What are the health and safety standards or licensing regulations for early childhood education programs in your community? Your state? If possible, obtain a copy.

## As a Group

1. Examine the health promotion activities on your own campus. Are you aware of them? Are they adequate? What suggestions for improvement do you have? Remember to consider the whole person.

2. Obtain and analyze the local licensing requirements for health and safety measures in early childhood education environments. Would you consider them adequate? How would you change these requirements to improve the health, safety, and well-being of children? Are those changes practical?

3. Assess your community's environment. Be sure to consider all the elements: physical, social, emotional, economic, and cultural. How would you rate your community in relation to safety, nutrition, health, or a place to raise children? What might be done to improve it? List 10 things that could be done to improve your community.

4. Analyze the quality of early childhood education on your campus. If you do not have a program on-site, choose an off-campus site to evaluate. Compare the quality in relation to items reported in the Reality Check on Early Education and Child Care in America.

5. Design a quality early childhood education environment considering both a holistic approach and the total environment.

## Chapter References

Ahnert, L. & Lamb, M. (2003). Shared care: Establishing a balance between home and child care settings. *Child Development, 74*(4), 1044–1049.

American Academy of Pediatrics (AAP). (2003). Talking about violence and war with young children. *Early Childhood Health Link, 14*(4), 6.

American Academy of Pediatrics (AAP). (2005). Quality early education and child care from birth to kindergarten. Policy statement. *Pediatrics, 115*(1), 187–191.

American Academy of Pediatrics. (2002, June/July). Warning to parents who smoke. *Healthy Kids,* 52.

American Public Health Association & American Academy of Pediatrics. (2002). *Caring for our children: National health and safety performance standards: Guidelines for out-of-home care.* Washington, DC: American Public Health Association.

*America's children: Key national indicators of well-being, 2001.* (2001). Vienna, VA: National Maternal and Child Health Clearinghouse.

Baldwin, V., DaRos-Voseles, D., & Swick, K. (2003). Creating a caring community: The University of Arkansas nursery school experience. *Early Childhood Education Journal, 10*(3), 157–162.

Bassok, D., Stipek, D., Inkelas, M., & Kuo, A. (2005). *Building community systems for young children: Early childhood education.* Building State Early Childhood Comprehensive Systems Series, No. 11. Los Angeles, CA: National Center for Infant and Early Childhood Health Policy. Retrieved October 10, 2005, from http://www.healthychild.ucla.edu/Publications/Documents/ECEFINALfor-publication.pdf

Bittman, M. (1994, March 18). Eating well: Why would a child exasperate his parents by refusing to eat? Maybe he isn't hungry. *New York Times,* B7, C4.

Bowlby, J. (1988). *A secure base.* New York: Basic Books.

Briley, M., & Roberts-Gray, C. (1999). Nutrition standards for child care programs—Position of ADA. *Journal of American Dietetic Association, 99*(6), 981–988.

Briley, M. & Roberts-Gray, C. (2005). Position of The American Dietetic Association: Benchmarks for nutrition programs in child care settings. *Journal of The American Dietetic Association, 105*(6), 979–986.

Bredekamp, S., & Copple, C. (Eds.). (1997). *Developmentally appropriate practice.* Washington DC: National Association for the Education of Young Children.

Brodkin, A. (2004 Jan./Feb). My grandpa died. *Scholastic Early Childhood Today,* 18–19.

Brofenbrenner, U. (1979). *The ecology of human development: Experiments by nature and design.* Cambridge, MA: Harvard University Press.

Brofenbrenner, U. (Ed.). (2005). *Making human beings human: Bioecological perspectives on human development.* Thousand Oaks, CA: Sage Publications.

Burchinal, M., & Cryer, D. (2003). Diversity, child care quality and developmental outcomes. *Early Childhood Quarterly, 18*(4), 401–426.

Burchinal, M., Howes, C., & Kontos, S. (2002). Structural predictors of child care quality in child care homes. *Early Childhood Research Quarterly, 17*(1), 87–105.

California Association for the Education of Young Children (CAEYC). (2005). Linguistic and cultural diversity: Building on America's strengths. *Connections, 3*(2), 20.

Capizzano, J., Adams, G., & Sonenstein, C. (2000). *Arrangements for children under five: Variation across states.* New Federation: National Survey of America's Families Series. Washington, DC: Urban Institute.

Carballo, M., & Nerukar, A. (2001). Migration, refugees and health risks. *Emerging Infectious Diseases, 7*(3), 556–560.

Caulfield, R., & Kataoka-Yahiro, M. (2001). Health training needs of child care professionals. *Early Childhood Education Journal, 29*(2), 119–123.

Centers for Disease Control (CDC). (1999). *Childhood injury fact sheet.* Atlanta, GA: Author. Retrieved May 15, 2002, from http://www.cdc.gov/ncipc/factsheets/childh/htm.

Child Care Aware (CCA). (2001). *Five steps to choosing quality child care.* New York, Author. Retrieved October 10, 2005, from http://www.childcareaware.org/en/5steps.html.

Child Care Bureau (CCB). (2000). *Child care for young children: Quality. Frequently asked questions.* Department of Health and Human Services, Washington, DC: Author. Retrieved May 15, 2002, from http://www.acf.dhhs.gov/programs/ccb/faq/quality.htm.

Children's Defense Fund (CDF). (2004). 2003 Facts on childhood poverty in America. Washington, D.C.: Author.

Children's Defense Fund (CDF). (2005). *Child care basics.* Washington, DC: Author. Retrieved October 24, 2005, from http://www.childrensdefense.org/earlychildhood/childcare/child_care_basics_2005.pdf.

Clarke-Stewart A., Vandell, D. Burchinal, M., O'Brien, M., & McCartney, K. (2002). Do regulable features of child-care homes affect children's development. *Early Childhood Research Quarterly, 17*(1), 52–86.

Cost, Quality and Outcomes Study Team. (1995, January). *Cost, quality and child care outcomes in child care centers.* [Executive Summary] Denver, CO: Economics Department, University of Colorado at Denver.

Currie, J. (2000). *Early childhood intervention programs: What do we know?* Working paper from the Children's Roundtable. Washington, DC: The Brookings Institute.

Derman-Sparks, L. (1999). Markers of multicultural/antibias education. *Young Children, 54*(5), 43.

DiNatale, L. (2002). Developing high-quality family involvement programs in early childhood settings. *Young Children, 57*(9), 90–95.

Duarte, G., & Ratanello, D. (2001). The migrant child: A special place in the field. *Young Children, 56*(2), 26–34.

Ehrle, J., Tout, K., & Adams, G. (2000). *Who's caring for our youngest children: Childcare patterns for infants and children.* New Federation: National Survey of America's Families Series. Washington, DC: Urban Institute.

El-Kamary, S., Higman, S., Fuddy, L., McFarlane, E., & Duggan, A. (2004). Hawaii's Healthy Start home visiting program: Determinants and impact of rapid repeat birth. *Pediatrics, 114*(3), e317–e326. Retrieved October 10, 2005, from http://pediatrics.aappublications.org/cgi/content/full/114/3/e317

Foster, M., Lambert, R., Abbott-Shim, M., McCarty, F., & Franze, S. (2005). A model of home learning environment and social risk factors in relation to children's emergent literacy and social outcomes. *Early Childhood Research Quarterly, 20*(10), 13–36.

Fraser, S. & Gestwicki, C. (2002). Authentic childhood: experiencing Reggio Emilia in the classroom. Clifton Park, N.Y, Thomson Delmar Learning.

Gaines, S., & Leary, J. (2004). Public health emergency preparedness in the setting of child care. *Family and Community Health 27*(3), 260–265.

Galinsky, E., Howes, C., Kontos, S., & Shinn, M. (1994). *The study of children in child care and relative care.* New York: Families and Work Institute.

Gordon, J. (2000). How our field participates in undermining quality child care. *Young Children, 55*(6), 31–34.

Greenspan, S. (2003). Child care research: A clinical perspective. *Child Development, 74*(4), 1064–1068.

Grubb, P. (1993). The quality of regenerated family day care homes and compliance with minimum standards. *Child Welfare, 72*(5), 461–472.

Hamilton, M., Roach, M., & Riley, D. (2003). Moving toward family-centered early care and education: The past, the present and a glimpse of the future. *Early Childhood Education Journal, 30*(4), 225–232.

Hayden, J. (2002). Nutrition and child development. Global perspectives. *Child Care Information Exchange, 145,* 38–41.

Hendrick, J. (2004). *First Steps to Teaching the Reggio Way,* Columbus, OH, Merrill/Prentice-Hall.

Hispanic PR Wire. (2004, September 10). Innovative Spanish language series targeting home-based child care providers to begin airing on PBS stations this week. Retrieved September 17, 2004: http://www.hispanicprwire.com/news.php?l=in&id=28968cha=8

Honig, A. S. (2002). *Secure relationships: Nurturing infant/toddler attachment in early care settings.* Washington, DC: NAEYC

Hyson, M. (2001). Better futures for young children, better preparation for their teachers: Challenges emerging from recent national reports. *Young Children, 56*(1), 60–62.

Hyson, M. (2002a). Preparing tomorrow's teachers: NAEYC announces new standards. *Young Children, 57*(2), 78–79.

Hyson, M. (2002b). Curriculum and assessment in early childhood programs. *Young Children, 57*(3), 56–57.

Johnson, D., Jaeger, E., Randolph, S., Cauce, A., Ward, J., & National Institute of Child Health and Human Development Early Child Care Research Network. (2004). Studying the effects of early child care experiences on the development of children of color in the United States: Toward a more inclusive research analysis. *Child Development, 74*(5), 1227–1244.

Johnson, R., & Kennedy, E. (2000). The 2000 dietary guidelines for Americans: What are the changes and why were they made? *Journal of the American Dietetic Association, 100*(7), 769–774.

Koshanksy, D. (1997). High-quality child care: Luxury options or standard equipment. *Young Children, 52*(2), 80–81.

Lally, J., Lerner, C., & Lurie-Hurvitz, E. (2001). National survey reveals gaps in the public's and parent's knowledge about every childhood development. *Young Children, 56*(2), 49–53.

Levin, D. (2003a). Beyond war and superhero play: Meeting children's needs in violent times. *Young Children, 58*(3), 60–65.

Levin, D. (2003b). *Teaching young children in violent times: Building a peaceable classroom* (2nd ed.). Cambridge, MA: Educators for Social Responsibility.

LifeCare (2003). A LifeCare Guide: Helping children cope during times of war. Retrieved September 17, 2004 from http://www.lifecare.com

Loeb, S., Fuller, B., Kagan, S., & Carrol, B. (2004). Child care in poor communities: Early learning effects of type, quality and stability. *Child Development, 75*(1), 47–65.

Lombardi, J. (2001). It's time to redesign child care to create 21st century early education. *Young Children, 56*(3), 74–77.

Lucarelli, P. (2002). Raising the bar for health and safety in child care. *Pediatric Nursing, 28*(3), 239–242.

Lynch, M., & Cicchetti, D. (1998). An edological-transactional analysis of children and context: The longitudinal interplay among child maltreatment, community violence and children's symptomatology. *Developmental Psychopathology, 98*(10), 235–258.

Mental Health Weekly (2004). Child posttraumatic syndrome symptoms more likely after terror attacks. *Mental Health Weekly 14*(11), 7–9.

Mister Rogers Neighborhood. (2004). Helping children talk about their scary feelings. Retrieved October 10, 2005, http://pbskids.org/rogers/parentsteachers/special/war.html

Moore, T. (2003, November/December). Giving children global views. *Scholastic Early Childhood Today,* 41–48.

Morris, M. (2005, March 30). Purdue researchers find children of working poor need more help. Purdue University News. Retrieved October 10, 2005, from http://news.uns.purdue.edu/html4ever/2005/050330.Elicker.childcare.html

Myers-Walls, J. (2003). When war is in the news. Purdue Extension. Knowledge to go. Retrieved October 10, 2005, from http://www.ces.purdue.edu/terrorism/war%20and%20children%20feb%2003.htm

National Association for the Education of Young Children (NAEYC). (1997). *Position statement: licensing and public regulation of early childhood programs.* Retrieved October 10, 2005, from http://www.naeyc.org/about/positions/pdf/PSLIC98.PDF

National Association for the Education of Young Children (NAEYC). (2005). Code of ethical conduct and statement of commitment (Draft 1). Retrieved October 10, 2005 from http://www.naeyc.org/about/positions/pdf/ethics_rev.pdf

National Association of School Psychologists (NASP). (2003). Helping children deal with tragic events in unsettling times: Tips for parents and teachers. Retrieved October 10, 2005, from http://www.nasponline.org/NEAT/tragicevents.html

National Center for Cultural Competence (NCCC) (2004). Definition and conceptual framework of cultural competence. Washington, D.C.: Georgetown University: Author. Retrieved October 21, 2005. Available online: http://gucchd.georgetown.edu/nccc/framework.html#lc

National Center for Children Exposed to Violence (NCCEV). (2003). Parents' guide for talking to their children about war. Retrieved October 10, 2005, from http://www.nccev.org/docs/children_war.pdf

National Mental Health Association (NMHA). (2005). Children without homes. Retrieved April 11, 2005 from http://www.nmha.org/homeless/childrenandHomelessness.pdf

Neugebauer, R. (2002). Continuing strong demand projected for child care. *Child Care Information Exchange, 145,* 34–36.

Newman, S., Brazelton, T., Zigler, E., Sherman, L., Bratton, W., Sanders, J., & Christeson, W. (2000). *America's child care crisis: A crime prevention tragedy.* Washington, DC: Fight Crime: Invest in Kids.

NICHD Early Child Care Research Network. (2003). Does quality of child care affect child outcomes at age $4^1/_2$? *Developmental Psychology,* (39) 451–469.

North Carolina State University (NCSU). (2003). Recognizing stress in children: Helping children cope with a disaster. Retrieved September 17, 2004 http://www.ces.ncsu.edu/depts/fcs/human/disas1.html

Obegi, A., & Ritblatt, S. (2005). Cultural competence in infant/toddler caregivers: Application of a tri-dimensional model. *Journal of Research in Childhood Education, 19*(3), 199–213.

Okagaki, L., & Diamond, K. (2000). Responding to cultural and linguistic differences in the beliefs and practices with families of young children. *Young Children, 55*(3), 74–80.

Osofsky, J. (1999). The impact of violence on children. *The Future of Children, 9*(3), 33–49.

Perry, B. (2003, April). *Early Childhood Today* talked with renowned expert and ECT author Bruce Perry about young children and the tumultuous times we live in. *Scholastic Early Childhood Today,* 14–15.

Peisner-Feinberg, E., Bruchinal, M., Clifford, R., Culkin, M., Howes, C., Kagan, S., et al. (2000). *The children of the cost, quality and outcomes report go to school: Technical report.* Chapel Hill, NC: Frank Porter Graham Child Development Lab, University of North Carolina.

Report on Preschool Programs. (2004). State-run preschools score "failing" marks for children. *Author: 36*(4), 25.

Robertson, C. (1993). *California community college curriculum and resource guide for working with prenatally substance exposed children and their families.* Sacramento, CA: Chancellor's Office California Community Colleges.

Schonfeld, D. (2002). Almost one year later: Looking back and looking ahead. *Developmental and Behavioral Pediatrics, 23*(4), 1–3.

Shallcross, M. (1999). Family child care homes need health and safety training and an emergency rescue system. *Young Children, 54*(5), 70–73.

Shepard, S. (2002). How safe are your child care programs? *School Planning and Management, 41*(11), 6–9.

Shonkoff, J., & Meisels, M. (Eds.). (2000). *Handbook of early childhood intervention.* New York: Cambridge University Press.

Shonkoff, J., & Phillips, J. (Eds.). (2000). *From neurons to neighborhoods.* The Committee on Integrating the Science of Early Childhood Development. Washington, DC: National Academy Press. Retrieved October 10, 2005, from www.nap.edu/books/0309069882/html/RI.html

Stegelin, D. (2003). Application of the Reggio Emilia approach to early childhood science curriculum. *Early Childhood Education Journal, 30*(3), 163–169.

Stephens, K. (2003). Children need attentive support during wartime. *Child Care Information Exchange, 154,* 17–18.

Sullivan, R. (2001, March 19). What makes a child resilient? *Time Magazine.* Retrieved October 10, 2005, from http://www.time.com/time/archive/preview10,10987,999474,00.html

Tate, M., & Patrick, S. (2000). Healthy People 2010 targets healthy diet and healthy weight as critical goals. *Journal of the American Dietetic Association, 100*(3), 300.

Tylenda, B. (2004). The five fundamental needs of the child. *The Brown University Child and Adolescent Behavior Letter, 20*(5), 8.

Tyson, S. (2003, February). Helping our children cope with terrorism. *State Magazine,* 23–25.

U.S. Department of Health and Human Services (US DHHS). (2000). *Healthy people year 2010: National health promotion and disease prevention objectives.* Washington, DC: U.S. Government Printing Office.

U.S. Department of Health and Human Services (US DHHS). (2003). *Stepping stones to using Caring for Our Children,* 2nd ed. Author: Rockville, MD. Retrieved April 10, 2005 from http://nrc.uchsc.edu/STEPPING/SteppingStones.pdf

Vakil, S., Freeman, R. & Swim, T. (2003). The Reggio Emilia approach and inclusive early childhood programs. *Early Childhood Education Journal, 30*(3), 187–192.

Winik, L. (1999, January 24). Every child deserves the best. *Parade Magazine,* 4–6.

Young Children. (2001). The irreducible needs of children: An interview with T. Barry Brazelton and Stanley Greenspan. *Young Children, 56*(2), 6–14.

Young, K. (1994, May 1). From zero to three. *San Diego Union-Tribune,* G-4.

Zemelman, S., Daniels, H., & Hyde, A. (1998). *Best practice: New standards for teaching and learning in America's schools.* Portsmouth, NH: Heinemann.

Zenah, P. Stafford, B., Nagle, G., & Rice, T. (January 2005). Addressing social-emotional development and infant mental health in early childhood systems. Building State Early Childhood Comprehensive Systems Series, No. 12. Los Angeles, CA: National Center for Infant and Early Childhood Health Policy. Retrieved October 10, 2005 from http://www.healthychild.ucla.edu/Publications/Documents/IMHFinal.pdf

Zero to Three/National Center for Clinical Infant Program. (2002). Caring for infants and toddlers in groups. Arlington, VA: Author.

Additional resources for this chapter can be found by visiting the Online Companion™ at http://www.earlychilded.delmar.com. This supplemental material includes extensive chapter quizzes, PowerPoint® outlines, Web links, and various other activities to help better utilize the material in this chapter. The site is updated regularly, so you may check back often to receive the latest information about the subjects in each chapter.

# SECTION II
# Safety in Early Childhood Education

This section discusses elements of safety in early childhood education.

2. Creating Safe Environments for Early Childhood Education
3. Indoor Safety
4. Outdoor Safety
5. Emergency Response Procedures for Early Childhood Education Environments

## CHAPTER 2

# Creating Safe Environments for Early Childhood Education

**After reading this chapter, you should be able to:**

### 2.1 Safety Policies

Define and discuss safety policies and their use as tools for safety, risk prevention, protection, and promotion.

### 2.2 Structuring Safe Environments

Discuss the importance of safe environments and describe a safe environment for all types of early childhood education.

### 2.3 Management for Injury Prevention

Discuss the factors involved in childhood injury and describe strategies for use in injury prevention.

### 2.4 Constructing a Safety Plan for Early Childhood Education Environments

Explain the development of a safety plan for a child care setting.

### 2.5 Implications for Teachers

Describe the importance of and strategies for education, working with families, supervision, and observation for maintaining a safe environment.

## 2.1  SAFETY POLICIES

Developing safety policies for the teacher to manage risk, provide protection, and promote safety in early childhood education environments is important. Some factors that indicate the need for these safety policies are the following.

- Unintentional injury is now the leading cause of death in childhood (Deal et al., 2000). Injury is the leading cause of death and disability for children in the United States and Canada (Khoury et al., 2005). To ameliorate this fact, safety intervention strategies are needed (King et al., 2005).

- In 1997, about 31,000 children under four were treated in U.S. hospital emergency rooms for injuries that occurred in early childhood education or school settings. At least 56 children have died in early childhood education environments since 1990 (Shepard, 2002). In 2002, 50% of the 2.3 million children treated for injuries due to falls were preschoolers (NCCCHSRC, 2005).

- Sixty-seven percent of parents believe that children's serious injuries are "random acts of fate or accidents" and therefore they do not think in terms of prevention (OEY, 2004). However, two-thirds of parents believe that childhood serious injury accidents are preventable (OEY, 2004).

Because children may lack the capacity to judge whether or not an activity is safe, they must be provided with a secure, safe environment to ensure their well-being and protection.

- We can no longer assume that children are safe in their own environments of home and school (Pless & Millar, 2002).
- Playground design, lack of attention, falls, and choking are common hazards in early childhood education environments. Sudden infant death syndrome (SIDS) as a hazard in early childhood education environments can be prevented if babies are put to sleep on their backs (Aronson, 2001).
- Children's sense of safety may be at risk as a result of what they observe in their world (Levin, 2003a).

Teachers should realize that most injuries to children are preventable. An accident infers a chance occurrence that is accompanied by no control or responsibility. Many injuries that children suffer can be prevented and do carry with them the need for a degree of control for prevention and responsibility for protection. Because of developmental factors that limit children's physical, cognitive, and emotional abilities, they are more vulnerable than adults to injury. Children are natural risk takers who attempt actions for which they may lack skills. Children want to test and master their environments. Children need a sense of trust and security that their environment is friendly and safe. Depending on their developmental level, children may lack the capacity to judge the safety of their environment.

## Designing a Safety Policy

Safety policies should be developed and directed toward the children and staff. They should promote safe practices for the child, the teachers, and the family. Basic safety policies lay the foundation for quality early childhood education.

Policies establish a process, assign responsibility, and offer guidance for action. Safety policies may take the form of checklists, injury reports, guidelines, practices, and strategies to improve risk. When policies are being developed, the following questions should be asked (Aronson, 2002).

- What needs to be done?
- What process will be followed?
- Who is responsible for making sure the process is followed?
- Are there any time parameters or limitations?

The question "What needs to be done?" provides the teacher with information needed to create a specific safety policy for each particular safety hazard that might be present in the early childhood education environment. The teacher needs to know what hazards are addressed by the local licensing regulations and fire board. An example is a state mandate that teachers must report any suspected maltreatment. The teacher then creates a policy for dealing with how, when, and where to make a report of suspected maltreatment. Some local areas have county or city fire regulation and zoning codes that may affect the design of safety policies.

Addressing the process involved in a safety policy helps the teacher understand how the policy should be carried out. The process explains when, and perhaps where, an action should be performed. The teacher should be aware of what safety hazards exist in both the indoor and outdoor environments. Viewing the environment through the eyes of a child will help the teacher find safety hazards and create safety checklists and other policies that offer maximum protection. It is essential that the teacher have knowledge of the developmental abilities of children in early childhood education programs. Developmental level safety checklists are important tools that may be used to manage the environment for risk.

Knowledge of environmental hazards will help the teacher create specific policies for early childhood education. Each type of safety hazard should have a process of actions to be followed to avoid risk. For example, if field trips are to be taken, there should be a definite policy for travel with children. This policy would include actions to be taken before the trip as well as actions needed during the trip.

Time limitations or parameters may be a critical factor in some areas of safety in early childhood education. This is especially true for emergency situations. A child who has fallen and is unconscious for more than a few seconds should have immediate emergency medical care.

The setting determines who is responsible for carrying out the policy. In an early childhood education environment, responsibility may fall to the director or primary teacher (see Chapter 5), or to an assigned safety advocate. In family child care, the responsibility usually falls to the provider. For in-home care, the nanny will probably share the responsibility with the parents. It is important to define the responsible party so that the policy does not go unenforced. A good health policy will have checks and balances for responsibility built into the policy. All staff should be encouraged to understand all safety precautions needed in the early childhood education environment. Every teacher should be encouraged to carry out actions that provide for the greatest degree of safety.

Safety policies should be clearly written and should include guidelines, limitations, and suggested methods of communication to be used. Safety policies help the teacher develop proper practices based on the knowledge of safety, risk prevention, protection, and promotion. Basic policies should be created for safety, nutrition, health, and special topics and should incorporate the six major goals of high-quality early childhood education.

- Maximize health status
- Minimize risk
- Use education as a tool
- Recognize the importance of guidelines
- Practice cultural competence
- Develop partnerships with families to provide a caring community

A responsible teacher helps to encourage safety and safe behaviors. Educating the children and their families so that they also know how to recognize dangers in any setting will ensure further protection. There should be several policies addressing the educational aspects of safety.

General early childhood education safety policies should cover the following.

- **Creating Safe Environments:** practices for creating and managing safe facility-specific environments

● *Injury prevention*
*forestalling or antici-*
*pating injury risk*

- **Injury Prevention Management:** understanding of injury and practices for preventing injury and protecting children
- **Developing a Safety Plan:** strategies for developing guidelines for prevention and protection in early childhood education environments.
- **Implications for Teachers:** methods and practices for conducting education, observation and supervision and working with families to provide safety and minimize risk.

### Key Concept 2.1

### Safety Policies

Safety policies should be planned and executed to prevent unintentional injury, protect the children from harm, and promote the use of safety practices for the teacher, the child, the family, and the people in the environment of the greater community. These policies should be clearly written and should be based on standard safety practices and licensing regulations. The policies should consider developmental stages of the children and should be applicable to the specific early childhood education environment. These safety policies guide the teacher in methods of practicing safety prevention, using protection and promotion to maximize the environment and minimize the risk to children.

## 2.2 STRUCTURING SAFE ENVIRONMENTS

The teacher needs to use all the risk management and **injury prevention** tools available in order to create the safe environment children need to grow to their greatest potential. Knowledge of the ABCs of potential for injury

Something as simple as making sure all footwear is properly worn and tied may prevent an accident from occurring. What are other preventive measures to avoid accidents?

helps the teacher be aware of what is needed to create a protective and secure environment. Safety policies for modifying the environment, modifying behavior, monitoring children, and teacher injury-preventive behaviors helps the caregiver to provide more safety, protection, and prevention in every situation in the early childhood education environment. Most of the practices and behaviors that create a safe environment can be applied to all early childhood education environments. See Table 2-1 for a guide to safe practices and injury prevention. Safety policies can be created from the list.

There may be some variations in early childhood education safety policies that depend on several considerations. How these policies apply to specific safety protection, prevention, and promotion practices may relate to the following:

- In what type of environment are you applying these safety practices?
- What are the ages of the children in care?
- What is the greater community surrounding the early childhood education environment like?
- What is the child's family environment?

## *The Type of Environment*

The type of early childhood education environment has a definite impact on the degree of safety the teacher is able to provide. Protective and preventive measures may differ depending on the type of environment. Early childhood education centers may be able to control for safety more than a family child care home. The level of safety in an in-home care situation may vary widely.

***Early Childhood Education Programs.*** Early childhood education environments are different from homes. In most states, they must follow certain licensing safety codes and practices (APHA & AAP, 2002). These basic codes and practices help the teacher lay the foundation for normal safety practices for that environment. Early childhood education environments generally are

**TABLE 2-1**
*A Teacher's Guide to Safe Practices and Injury Prevention for a Safe Environment*

- Know all applicable safety practices for the early childhood education environment.
- Screen environment for hazards and remove, where possible.
- Use safety devices, where applicable.
- Monitor environment for hazards that are part of the environment.
- Know developmental levels of the children, including capabilities and limitations.
- Promote safety through action, word, and deed.
- Role model safety practices to children and parents.
- Be aware of conditions that contribute to injury.
- Closely observe children, giving special consideration during at-risk conditions.

● **Multi-use facilities**
*child care sites that are*
*used for other functions*

not **multi-use facilities.** A major purpose of early education programs in child care centers is to perform care and to provide a safe environment for the children in care.

Some early education programs are very different due to the location of the center where the programs are held. An early education program in a church-related environment may not be subject to the same safety rules and guidelines as those in the public sector. In addition, the church facility may be used by a number of different groups for different activities, thus introducing a greater degree of safety risk factors.

The same hazardous situation may be true for early childhood education environments that are located in public facilities. Ski resorts, fitness centers, and elementary schools may have early childhood education centers on site. These sites may not be subject to the same licensing safety codes or regulations and may be used for other purposes at other times. Modifying the environment in these unregulated, multi-use facilities can be a challenge for the teacher. Modification is a constant, ongoing process. Environments that are unregulated may make it even more imperative that teachers know safety practices, be a role model, and promote safety through actions, words, and deeds. Teaching the children about these safety risk factors may help provide an added level of monitoring for these environments. The responsibility for maintaining a safe environment rests with the teachers. Some examples of shared space are

- a college or university preschool used in the evenings for classroom space
- a ski lodge that uses a corner of its lounge for early childhood education while parents ski
- a church preschool room, used as a Sunday school and meeting room
- a corporate early childhood education center that is used for meetings and training classes on weekends
- a community recreation center that has child care while parents attend classes

Depending on the environment, different degrees of protective and preventive measures must exist.

*Family Child Care Homes.* Family child care homes are multi-purpose by definition. If the state or local area requires licensing, the home must pass certain safety requirements, such as a fire code. Some states and local jurisdictions do not require licensing for family child care homes. Other states may license only larger family child care homes with 12 or more children. This puts the responsibility of providing safety and protection directly on the provider in whose home the child care takes place. Self-regulation and monitoring of the environment are vital for the prevention of injuries and protection of the children.

There may be local programs available through resource and referral services that help to support the family child care provider. This support can help the teacher create a safe environment using specific safety policies that are similar to licensing regulations in other areas. Another source of help for the family provider is the National Family Child Care Association. This organization offers a program for accreditation that includes safety standards, policies, and practices.

*In-Home Child Care.* An in-home situation in which the nanny comes to the child's home presents different challenges. In both the family child care home and the early childhood education center, the teacher is the person responsible for creating and monitoring the environment for safety. An in-home teacher shares this responsibility with the parents. It would be easy to assume that this is a fairly straightforward task. Unfortunately, this is not always the case. Some parents do not understand the need for making the environment as safe as possible. The environment is the home they have carefully selected and decorated for comfort and style, and it meets their needs.

When an infant arrives in the home, that child makes no demands on the home environment other than a place to sleep. As the child grows older and goes through the developmental stages, the need for modifying the home environment becomes important. Some parents are intent on making these modifications, but others do not see the need because they believe their child is "just going through a phase." It is on the shoulders of the

The caregiver at a home care center with a pool should take all appropriate safety steps to avoid the possible "accident waiting to happen."

Damon was a quiet, curious toddler. Mary Ann, his nanny, was concerned that as he was becoming more mobile Damon would get into unsafe situations. Mary Ann asked Damon's parents to remove the cleaning chemicals from under the sinks in the kitchen and bathroom. She asked that they remove small decorative objects from his reach. Some of these objects had sharp edges, and others were small enough for him to choke on if he put them in his mouth. The parents did not see the need. They felt that Mary Ann should rely solely on monitoring the child and not worry about the environmental hazards.

Mary Ann served her two-week notice when they refused to cooperate. The following weekend, while in the care of his aunt, Damon got under the sink and drank some cleaning solution. He was rushed to the hospital and had his stomach pumped. He was very lucky that the cleaning product he swallowed did not do permanent damage. The aunt felt terrible, the parents realized their mistake, and Damon had to go through a very scary situation. The family begged Mary Ann to stay and offered their full cooperation for childproofing their home.

nanny or in-home teacher to make sure the parents participate in modifying and monitoring the home environment for safety. If the parents choose not to childproof the home environment, it is recommended that the teacher not stay in this situation.

Not all situations like Damon's turn out so well. A home environment needs to be just as safe as any early childhood education environment.

*Pause for Reflection*

Take a minute to think about the safety of your own home environment. Is it a place that might pose risk to children if they were to come visit you? What steps would you have to take if a toddler came to visit? What types of things might you have to anticipate, monitor, and modify to make your home safe?

### The Age of Children in Care

Because of the developmental stages children go through (see Table 2-2, page 51), the age of children in care affects the type of safety policies that are needed (AAP, 2002). If the environment is planned for a particular age group and the children are all at about the same developmental level, as is true in most large early childhood education environments, the safety modifications that the teacher makes will be standardized to fit that age range.

Jean Piaget explained the four cognitive developmental stages that children go through from birth to age 18 (Smith, 1997). The first three of these stages are referred to in the following developmental age categories.

*Infants.* Some early childhood education environments involve caring for infants. This may be a center at which infant care is available, a family child care home that specializes in infants, or a nanny caring for one or two

**TABLE 2-2**
*Piaget's Sensorimotor Developmental Stages*

| Stage | Age | Actions |
|---|---|---|
| 1 | 0–1 month | Mostly sucking and looking. |
| 2 | 1–4 months | Making interesting things happen repeatedly with the body, like kicking legs or sucking a finger. Pleasure from repetition. |
| 3 | 4–8 months | Repeated actions focusing on objects and events. Picking up rattle and shaking over and over. Pleasure from repetition. |
| 4 | 8–12 months | Combine actions to reach a goal. |
| 5 | 12–18 months | Experiments to find new and different ways to solve problems or reach goal. This stage often referred to as "little scientist." |
| 6 | 18–24 months | Beginning of thought using symbols or language to solve problems mentally. |

All children should be provided with a safe environment that accommodates their developmental stage.

- **Cephalocaudal** *development from the top to the bottom of the body or from the head down toward the toes*
- **Proximodistal** *development of the body from the inside toward the outside or the torso through the arms and out to the fingers*
- **Gross motor skills** *physical skills using large body movements such as running, jumping, and climbing*

infants. Infants are totally dependent and therefore very vulnerable to injury if not carefully monitored. Infants develop their motor abilities in the **cephalocaudal** and **proximodistal** directions. Development in the cephalocaudal direction moves from head to toe. As a child grows, development progresses down the body. For example, one of the first milestones for an infant is the ability to lift the head. One of the last infant milestones is the ability to walk. These **gross motor skills** develop earlier than **fine motor skills.** Proximodistal direction motor development works from the center of

● **Fine motor skills**
*physical skills related to small body movements, particularly of the hand and fingers. These skills include using scissors, holding a crayon, or working a puzzle*

the body to the outside. An infant can roll over and use her arms long before she can reach and grasp (see Figure 2-1).

During the first few months of life, infants are not mobile and do not encounter many risks. The major risk that infants of all ages encounter is SIDS. The teacher should use protective and preventive measures to reduce the possibility of a child's being at risk for SIDS (see Reality Check, page 81).

Once an infant rolls over, mobility and thus risk, increases. A child could turn over and fall from a changing table or infant seat set on a counter. As the cephalocaudal motor direction develops, skills and thus mobility, increase. Children who creep and then crawl are apt to get into more and more territory that may pose risk to them. The need for safety devices increases at this stage. This is the time for safety gates on stairs, closed doors to bathrooms, and so forth.

● **Sensorimotor cognitive development**
*first stage of cognitive development that utilizes motor abilities and senses*

Proximodistal motor development allows children to become more agile when using their hands and arms to reach for things and pick up things. Combined with **sensorimotor cognitive development** (see Table 2-2), this can lead to danger. Children who are able to pick up objects usually explore those objects by placing them in their mouths. The agile infant can get into practically any cabinet and may also be able to open containers in those cabinets. Safety latches should be used for cabinets, doors, and so forth. Any cleaning solutions or other chemical hazards should be removed to a high, locked cabinet. All electrical sockets should have safety plugs blocking inspection by curious infants.

*Toddlers.* Once a child has begun walking, both his skills and his ability to access dangerous situations increase. Cephalocaudal development progresses to abilities that include running and climbing. At the beginning of this stage, the balance of the toddler is somewhat unsteady. Being mobile allows the toddler different ways to look at the environment. It can also give the toddler the ability to overcome obstacles that may have previously prevented action.

Proximodistal development leads to greater manipulative abilities. Sensorimotor development presents cognitive abilities in children that will challenge any teacher to keep one step ahead. Children at this stage are

**FIGURE 2-1**
An infant showing proximodistal and cephalocaudal development.

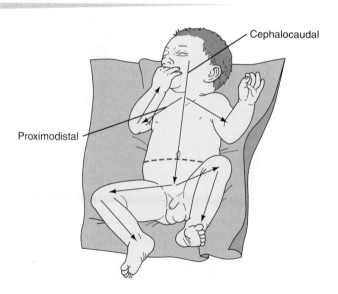

perhaps most at risk for dangerous situations. They are exploring and trying to master their environments, but they do not have the cognitive abilities to understand cause and effect. This can be a deadly combination.

Children in the toddler stage need to be supervised very closely. Their physical abilities and cognitive limitations will have them performing dangerous acts, so they must be carefully watched. All physical and environmental hazards need to be examined. Safety devices should be in place, and all hazards that can be removed, should be.

*Preschoolers.* Preschool children have mastered most of their gross and fine motor skills. They are capable of most physical tasks. Cognitive abilities of children of this age have also developed. They are in the **preoperational stage** (see Table 2-3), which offers some limitations in their thought processes. These limitations cause preschool children to see the world from their point of view. Children of this age may not perceive risk when it is present. For example, a four-year-old may be certain that she can climb to the top of playground equipment, jump off it, and land on the ground without getting hurt because she saw her favorite cartoon character do this very thing.

This age group responds well to role modeling and education. Preschool children are less likely to need safety devices such as stair gates and plastic plugs in electrical sockets, because they understand the perceived risk from these items. Preschool children can be trained to understand many of the risks in their environment. They will need monitoring, but not at the intense level of the older infant and toddler.

*School Age.* School-aged children are at far less risk for safety because they have cognitive abilities that can help keep them out of danger. Children of this age are at the **concrete operational stage** of cognitive development and have the ability to understand most situations that involve safety risks or hazards. Children of this age like to test their abilities to perform. Accidents and injuries involving this age group are often from sports activities

● **Preoperational stage**
*second stage of cognitive development, in which logic is limited*

● **Concrete operational stage**
*third stage of cognitive development in which logical ideas can be applied to concrete or specific situations*

**TABLE 2-3**
*Limitations of the Preoperational Stage*

| Limitation | Meaning |
|---|---|
| Egocentrism | World is centered around "me." Nothing else exists. Sharing is hard. All toys seem to be "mine." |
| Centration | Child focuses only on one aspect of a situation or object. Child sees a toy and heads for it, regardless of what is in the way. |
| Fantasy | Children love to make believe and role play. |
| Irreversibility | Inability to reverse a situation or an action. Difficult for child to retrace steps of thoughts or action. |
| Animism | Everything is "alive" and all objects are capable of human feelings or actions. |
| Transductive Reasoning | Child cannot relate general to specific or a part to the whole. They only relate specific to specific. For example, if Sparky, the dog, is friendly, any dog that is encountered is friendly. |

such as bicycling, skating, or organized sports such as soccer and baseball. Another area of concern for this age group is the curiosity about firearms. Guns are objects that provide great risk to children of any age, but this age group is more likely to be able to access them (Jackman et al., 2001).

School-aged children respond well to education and role modeling. The issue of firearms and the risk they pose should be discussed with these children (Eller, 1998). School-aged children can be excellent examples when they role model safety to other children. Although school-aged children need some monitoring, they can also be their own monitors for safety if they are armed with safety knowledge.

*Multi-age Groups.* If the children in an early childhood education program are of varying ages and thus different developmental levels, the teacher will need to take a different look when planning for safety in the environment. If the environment needs to be designed for multi-age groups, then it should be modified as closely as possible to fit the youngest child's developmental abilities. This may cause some frustration for older children, but safety issues must come first. Role modeling and talking with the older children about the need for safety can help buffer their frustration and lead to greater understanding. Depending on their ages, older children may even help the teacher monitor the potential risks in the early childhood education environment and observe unsafe behaviors that younger children exhibit.

## The Community Surrounding the Early Childhood Education Environment

The safety of the children in early childhood education environments can no longer be taken for granted. It is impossible to consider the environment of early childhood education as only the premises and the surrounding yard or outdoor play area. Early childhood education takes place in the middle of cities, in suburbs, and in rural areas. The holistic approach for child care safety must consider the community area that surrounds the site (Earls & Buka, 2000). No matter where the early childhood education takes place, there are safety hazards, conditions, and behaviors that may affect the situation.

In addition to violence and traffic, discarded drug paraphernalia may be a potential hazard and liability for providers using inner city public playgrounds with their children.

● **Liabilities**
*safety risks or hazards*

It is the teacher's responsibility to be aware of the safety aspects or **liabilities** surrounding the premises. In some inner-city areas violence may be a liability; in other areas, traffic may be the key liability. Rural and sub-urban areas may be isolated, and distance may be a liability in case of an emergency. Rural areas may be more likely to have hazards such as animals in the environment.

It is the teacher's responsibility to understand the risks and liabilities of the surrounding neighborhood. The children should be taught safety and prevention strategies that apply to the surrounding community. The pro-motion of safety should not end at the door of the early childhood education environment.

## The Child's Family Environment

A child's family environment may affect the early childhood education envi-ronment. If the child's home environment is safe and secure, the child trusts that the teacher's is also. A child who is free to explore and master a safe environment at home will also explore the early childhood education envi-ronment. It is essential that the teacher teach the child the rules and limi-tations that will help to keep the child safe while in the early childhood education environment.

A child who comes from an environment that is less safe and secure will also need consideration. Low income or poverty can affect the home environment. Abraham Maslow (1968) tried to explain basic human needs to help us understand why people act as they do. He came up with five lev-els of need (see Figure 2-2). The first level is physiological needs, which include shelter, food, and clothing. The second level of needs involve safety and security. The third level is the need for love and the feeling of belong-ing. The fourth level involves a human being's desire for self-esteem. And finally, at the fifth level is the need for self-actualization, which a person reaches when he or she has achieved his or her potential. If a lower need is not met, it is difficult to go beyond that need. For example if a family is poor, the parents may try to meet the basic needs of the first level and may not have the time or energy to think much about safety and security as an important issue. Ninety percent of Native American children, one-half of African-American children, one-third of Hispanic-American children and one-fifth of Caucasian (white) children live in poverty. Forty percent of

**FIGURE 2-2**
According to Maslow's Hierar-chy of Human Needs, a per-son's needs for such basics as food, shelter, and clothing must be met before higher-level needs can be addressed.

**Maslow's Hierarchy of Human Needs**

Self-Actualization
Self-Esteem
Social
Love, Friendship
Safety and Security
Food, Shelter, Clothing

Imagine being at work in an early childhood education environment when suddenly, a Special Weapons and Tactics (SWAT) team arrives and there is a helicopter hovering above. The children are frightened, and the teachers and director have no idea what is happening. It takes almost an hour to resolve the situation, and even longer to calm the frightened children. This actually did occur, and it was a result of an argument over child custody. The mother of a little girl in the early childhood education program accused the father of a kidnap attempt, and the sheriff's department took it seriously. There was no kidnap attempt, just a mother's anger over the separation from the father. The father had placed the child in the program and regularly brought the child to care and picked her up. The teachers had never even seen the mother. There was no child custody court order for this little girl, because the parents had never married, and when they stopped living together they did nothing about legal child custody. The next day, a child custody policy was established at this center.

Children living in poverty situations may be unaware of the potential safety and health risks their environment presents.

homeless people in the United States today are children (NMHA, 2005). Because of their poverty and homelessness, the basic needs of these children for safety and security may be almost completely unfulfilled and their first-level needs may be challenged by their environments.

Forty percent of the homeless today are families with children, and families are the fastest growing segment of the homeless population. The number of children living in poverty is significant considering the safety risks that may be present. Children from low-income families may need help understanding the need for safety and protective measures. In this case, role modeling and safety promotion will be important tools. Some of these children may also be unfamiliar with a secure environment that allows them to explore and develop a sense of independence. These children will need a predictable, supportive environment so that they can develop a sense of trust.

Violence and child maltreatment are also safety risks that can come from the home environment of some children.

# REALITY CHECK

## Child Custody and the Impact on an Early Childhood Education Program

With the high divorce and cohabitation rates, more children are coming to early childhood education environments with unresolved custody issues. Included with this may be a risk for the child to be taken by a parent who does not have custody, or liability to the center for allowing a child to leave the premises with a parent who has no legal right to remove the child. It is extremely important for every center to have a policy on how to handle the risks involved.

It is helpful to understand exactly what the term "custody" means. There are some common terms in regard to this and they include:

- *Sole legal custody* gives one parent the right to make all decisions regarding the health, education, and welfare of the child. The other parent has no say in these matters (*Types of custody,* 2001).

- *Joint legal custody* gives both parents the ability to participate in the decisions regarding the health, education, and welfare of the child (NCCUSL, 1997).

- *Sole physical custody* gives one parent the sole physical custody of the child and prevents the other parent from having physical custody of the child. This often occurs if a parent has neglected or abused the child or has a drug addiction that prevents that parent from acting responsibly.

- *Joint physical custody* gives both parents the ability to be with the child. Custody as far as days and dates is specified, and a co-parenting plan may be inserted into the custody order.

- *Shared custody* gives an equal share to each parent in the legal and physical custody issues concerning the child. This type of order is issued only if the parents are in full agreement and cooperation about the welfare of the child.

- *Bird's nest custody* allows the child to remain in the family home while the parents take turns moving in and out (*Types of custody,* 2001).

- *Noncustodial parent* refers to the parent who has the child the lesser amount of time, and *custodial parent* refers to the parent who spends more time with the child and with whom the child lives.

- *Child visitation* encompasses the time that the noncustodial parent spends with the child.

Historically, custody rights were usually given to the mother due to the underlying prevalent theory that mothers were better suited than fathers to raise children. When divorce rates began their dramatic rise during the 1960s, the focus shifted to the best interest of the child. Fathers were recognized for their contribution to children's lives. This led to more joint custody situations after divorce. By 1991, more than 40 states included joint custody as a common option (Kelly, 1997).

Divorce often creates anger and animosity between the parents that results in battles over the children in a number of ways. This can filter down to issues that may affect a child or children in the early childhood education environment. The major concern of the teacher should be the protection of the child and keeping the facility free from any safety or liability issues that may be involved.

How does the center or teacher deal with this? If there is a joint custody order and the parents have given the center or teacher a copy of the order, there are clear guidelines for the picking up of children. If there is a sole custody order, there should be clear guidelines as to who is allowed to pick up the child. Joint legal custody does not necessarily mean that both parents have the right to physical custody, and

*(continues)*

## REALITY CHECK (Continued)

the custody order will reflect this (*Joint custody vs. sole custody,* 2001).

The line may become blurred. If a custody order is at hand, and the custodial parent presents a document to the early childhood education center authorizing the noncustodial parent to pick up the child, the center should be able to release the child without liability and without risk to the child. It may be wise to check state law (DivorceSource.com, 2001). If a noncustodial parent tries to pick up the child without authorization, there should be no question that you would not allow the child to go with this parent.

Particular cases should be very clearly defined for the early childhood education program, and a policy may not be needed, other than to follow the court order, unless there is clear authorization from the custodial parent to allow the other parent pick-up rights. This should be more than a phone call. It should be a document that has been notarized and acknowledges that the custodial parent has given this authorization.

In a case in which the child's parents are unmarried and there is no custody agreement order, it is more difficult to determine who has pick-up rights for the child. This situation may also apply to parents who are married but are separated and have no legal document for custody or visitation. If there is no legal document available, some type of policy must be created to deal with this issue.

The early childhood education program should not act as a mediator or judge. In polling a number of programs about this issue, the majority had a policy based on common sense but also considered liability. The consensus was that, unless one parent has indicated the other parent is not to pick up the child, both are allowed to pick up the child. In the case of one-parent pick-up only, a legal document is requested stating that only that parent is authorized. If this is not forthcoming and the "unauthorized" parent picks up the child, the child will no longer be enrolled in the program, and each parent will be so advised. Legally, an early child-

hood education program has no right to withhold a child from a parent unless there is a court document. Although dropping the child from the program may appear to be a harsh response, the centers polled said that this works well. Even though many parents are angry with each other, the child's welfare is still the main concern. These providers stated that, when faced with expulsion of the child from the early childhood education program, the "unauthorized" parent usually does not attempt to take the child.

Whatever the situation, early childhood education providers must be aware of this issue and their role in it. Court documents are the safest and best measure for a policy on child pick-up rights. When the rights for child pick-up are not clear, a policy should be carefully developed.

Another child custody issue for early education programs is joint custody, in which the child moves back and forth between parents. Adjusting to a new situation, a new home environment, and maybe the early childhood education environment itself can take a toll on the child (Tynan, 2004) (See Chapter 10, page 386). This experience can make a child fearful, confused, and sad (Brodkin, 2002). It is important that the teacher do whatever is necessary to make the early childhood education environment as stable and routine as possible. Partnering with the parents, without mediating between them, may help the child to adjust to the new situation. Parents should realize that their child should not be forgotten, but in essence the child should come first (Benedek & Brown, 2001), because a young child lacks the cognitive ability to understand divorce. An open line of communication about the child with both parents is essential. If the child is acting in a way that is different from his or her usual behavior, both parents should be informed. A visit to both homes might also be helpful, so that the teacher can help to bridge the gap between the two homes and the early childhood education environment (Brodkin, 2002). Spending extra individual time with the child might help the child feel a sense of security that she may not be feeling in other realms of her life.

**CHECK***point:* What protective measures could a teacher offer for a child who is involved in joint custody and has two households to live in on a regular basis?

## Key Concept 2.2

### Creating a Safe Environment

Creating a safe environment by using safe practices allow the teacher to provide the sense of security and protection from harm that children need to be free to develop, learn, and grow. Developing safety policies should directly relate to the type of early childhood education that is being provided. Understanding the developmental needs, capabilities, and limitations resulting from the age of children in care helps the teacher to lay a foundation of safety and protection. Knowing about the community and the family will enable the teacher to more adequately prepare the safest environment possible for the children in the early childhood education environment.

## 2.3 MANAGEMENT FOR INJURY PREVENTION

A safe environment for a child is one that provides freedom from harm and offers a sense of security in which to play, develop, and learn. The teacher is responsible for providing this type of environment for the children in care. A major goal for a teacher is to manage the early childhood education environment for injury prevention. Injury prevention promotes safety, protects the child, and minimizes risk. Injury prevention also offers a plan to manage injuries as they occur with the least distress to everyone concerned. The early childhood education environment should be prepared for reducing risk, protecting children from harm, and planning for occurrence of injury. Injury prevention offers children the sense of safety and security they need to develop to the fullest potential.

### ABCs of Childhood Injuries

Every accident has a cause. Accidental injuries generally occur when a risk is taken or a hazard is present in the environment. To avoid unintentional injuries, causal factors must be understood and anticipated.

The injury triad is a valuable tool for injury prevention (see Figure 2-3). When an injury occurs, certain questions can be asked to understand the circumstances.

- What type of injury occurred?
- How did the injury happen?
- Why did the injury occur?
- Where did the injury occur?
- When did the injury happen?

As these questions are explored, a clearer picture may form as to what could have been done to prevent the injury to the child. Table 2-4 provides common factors for childhood injury.

*Accessory.* Accessories that are involved in injuries include physical and environmental hazards and lack of safety devices. Accessories help explain how the injury happened. An accessory is a known factor. A physical hazard

**FIGURE 2-3**
The injury triad is used to understand the circumstances surrounding an injury and to help prevent future injuries.

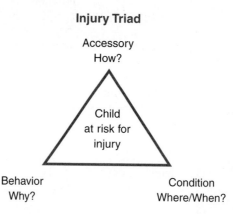

**Injury Triad**

Accessory
How?

Child at risk for injury

Behavior
Why?

Condition
Where/When?

**TABLE 2-4**
*The ABCs of Injury Risk to Children*

| A | = | **Accessory = How** |
|---|---|---|
| | | Physical and environmental hazards |
| | | Lack of safety devices |
| B | = | **Behavior = Why** |
| | | *By Child:* |
| | |   Developmental level |
| | |     Mastery/Exploration |
| | |     Don't know/understand |
| | |     Lack of physical ability |
| | |     Don't grasp cause and effect |
| | |     Lack of fear |
| | |     Inattention |
| | |   Emotions |
| | |   Stress |
| | |   Imitation |
| | | *By Adult:* |
| | |   Inattention, no supervision |
| | |   Lack of knowledge/understanding |
| | |   Lack of communication |
| | |   Lack of safety precautions |
| | |   Emotions |
| | |   Stress |
| C | = | **Conditions = Where or When** |
| | | *Where:* |
| | |   Place |
| | |   Indoor/outdoors |
| | | *When:* |
| | |   Time of day |
| | |   Tired, hungry, in a hurry |

could be an object such as a penny on the floor, a cleaning solution stored under a sink, or a piece of equipment such as a jungle gym. Environmental hazards might include a swimming pool or traffic around the early childhood education environment. Lack of safety devices might include an open electrical outlet without a plug cap or a car without a proper safety seat.

The most effective risk management tool to remove accessories as a risk factor in the injury triad is to use preventive and protective strategies and practice. Because accessories are known factors, the teacher can modify the environment to remove risk caused by them. Modifications might include moving cleaning solutions to a high, locked cabinet or installing electrical outlet plug covers.

*Behavior.* Behaviors contribute action or inaction that leads to an injury. This can help explain why an injury occurred. Behavior bears most of the responsibility for injury. Action of a child is the most common behavior in the injury triad. The majority of behaviors children display are related to their developmental level (Bredekamp & Copple, 1997). The common developmental tasks children perform as they go from stage to stage are the very behaviors that lead them to injury. A child explores his environment, masters his skills and abilities, and uses his cognitive processes to solve problems. These behavioral factors can lead a child into situations that can cause injury.

Knowledge of the developmental levels of children can help alleviate risky situations. Being aware of the developmental stages and situations a child is prone to encounter at a particular age can help the teacher monitor the environment and be a keen observer of the child.

The adult behaviors that can contribute to a child's injury can be active or inactive. In the case of child maltreatment, violence, or an accident such as running over a child with an automobile, the adult behavior is active. In the majority of cases, however, the adult contributes inactive behavior to an injury. Lack of supervision, knowledge, communication, and understanding of a situation are causes of inaction (Shallcross, 1999). Inattention to what is going on around oneself can also be inaction. A teacher who is under stress or experiencing emotional difficulties may not be as attentive as usual. Inaction presents itself as the absence of preventive, protective, and promotional safety measures.

The same risk management tools for safety that are used for children also apply to adult behaviors. A full knowledge of safety practices through

Regardless of the cause, when an injury occurs it must be taken care of properly by a teacher or nurse.

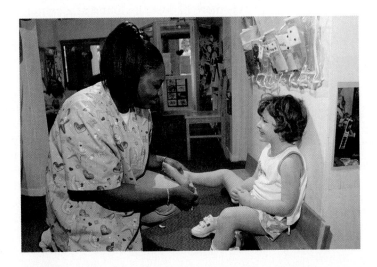

Rodney was a teacher for two-year-olds at an inner city day care center. The two-year-olds shared a large room with the three-year-olds and often played together during free time. Rodney was well aware of the differences between his children and those in the older group. He carefully monitored the free play time. One morning he stopped Joshua from putting a small toy part in his mouth. Kelley, a three-year-old, had brought a small car from home. One of the wheels had fallen off, and Joshua picked it up and attempted to put it in his mouth. Although Rodney had no choice about his group playing with the older children and their toys, he was careful in what he watched for, because he knew the developmental level limitations of his two-year-olds.

education is critical to provide the necessary supervision for a safe and secure environment for children (Aronson, 2001). The teacher also needs to be aware of how stress and emotions can affect the care given to the children. The use of education, promotion, and good role modeling by the teacher can help children learn more safe practices. The teacher should be practical and use good judgment. These risk management tools may also lead children to an earlier understanding of cause and effect and provide them with preventive strategies that can protect them from harm in dangerous situations. Using education, role modeling, and communication, the teacher can also help parents lay the foundation for a safer, more secure environment in the home.

● Condition

*circumstance or situation in which safety is at risk*

*Condition.* The **condition** factor of the injury triad indicates the circumstances around an injury. The questions as to when and where the injury took place are answered as conditions are explored (Smith, 2001). The place, the time, and the situation in which an injury takes place may have contributed to the injury. Injuries take place in early childhood education environments, in homes, on playgrounds, and in many other places.

Certain types of injuries are more likely to happen in certain places (Figure 2-4). For example, falls from equipment such as climbing structures are more likely to occur on playgrounds or in early childhood education environments than in a home environment, because this type of equipment is more likely to be found at a center than in a private home. A child is more likely to have a bicycle accident in the street than on a sidewalk, because streets have traffic and pedestrians, whereas sidewalks contain pedestrians only. Certain types of injuries are more likely to happen indoors, and others more commonly occur outdoors.

Time can be a critical factor that contributes to injury. Children are more likely to get injured in the late morning or late afternoon, when they are tired. If a child or adult is in a hurry, an injury is more likely to occur. A shift in environment or routine can present distractions or conflicts that are stressful and lead to accidents. Developing an awareness that certain conditions in the early childhood education environment contribute to injury can help the teacher be more alert when those conditions are present.

Table 2-5 applies the causal factors from the injury triad to specific situations that may be found in early childhood education environments.

## When Injury Does Occur

Even in the safest environments, injuries do happen. How the teacher handles the injury can contribute to keeping the early childhood education environment as secure as possible. Careful planning prepares the teacher to handle accidents and injuries as they occur with as little stress as possible. This can help reinforce the trust of the children present in an early childhood education environment. Safety policies should include injury response methods and practices to help provide good injury management.

**FIGURE 2-4**
Pie chart with common conditions for childhood accidents.

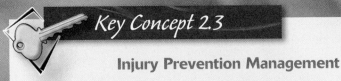

### Key Concept 2.3

#### Injury Prevention Management

Injury prevention is a major responsibility of the teacher. To prevent injury and protect children, the teacher must first understand how injuries occur. A teacher who understands how accessories, behaviors, and conditions contribute to injury will have the ability to anticipate injury. Monitoring the children and modifying the environment allows the teacher to prevent injury and promote safety.

**TABLE 2-5**
*Factors in Childhood Injury*

**Who = Children of all developmental stages and ages**

| What | How | Why | Where | When |
|---|---|---|---|---|
| Motor vehicle accident | Lack of seat belt or safety seat<br>Inattention of driver | Inattention to importance of using safety device | In automobile | Anytime |
| Riding bicycle near cars | Darting in front of car | Inattention<br>Doesn't grasp cause/effect<br>Lack of fear<br>In a hurry | Near home, school, neighborhood | Anytime<br>Unsupervised |
| Fall | Unsafe equipment<br>Mastery<br>Exploration | Lack of safety knowledge<br>Lack of ability<br>Doesn't grasp cause/effect<br>Imitation | Outdoor playgrounds<br>Indoor climbing | Late morning<br>Late afternoon<br>Unsupervised<br>Tired |
| Collision with objects | Mastery<br>Exploration | Hazards in environment<br>Lack of ability<br>Doesn't grasp cause/effect<br>In a hurry<br>Imitation | Anywhere | Anytime<br>Tired<br>Unsupervised |
| Poisoning | Exploration<br>Mastery | Hazards in environment<br>Doesn't grasp cause/effect<br>Imitation<br>Inability to read | Kitchen, bathroom, bedroom, garage, living room, yard | Unsupervised<br>Anytime |
| Choking | Exploration | Hazards in environment<br>Doesn't grasp cause/effect | Anywhere | Unsupervised<br>Anytime |
| Burns | Lack of safety devices<br>Mastery<br>Exploration | No smoke detector<br>Water too hot<br>Doesn't grasp cause/effect<br>Imitation<br>Access to fire device | Anywhere<br>Bathroom<br>Kitchen | Unsupervised<br>Anytime |
| Drowning | Exploration<br>Mastery | Lack of ability<br>Imitation<br>Lack of safety precautions<br>Doesn't grasp cause/effect<br>Hazards in environment | Bathtub<br>Pool<br>Any body of water | Unsupervised<br>Anytime |

**TABLE 2-5 (Continued)**
*Factors in Childhood Injury*

Who = Children of all developmental stages and ages

| What | How | Why | Where | When |
|------|-----|-----|-------|------|
| Child Maltreatment | Parent<br>Someone child knows<br>Stranger | Repeat of cycle of abuse<br>Poverty<br>Dysfunction | Anywhere | Anytime<br>Under stress |
| Violence | Lack of safety precautions<br>Firearms available | Guns and other hazards<br>Inattention to safety | Neighborhood<br>Home<br>School | Anytime<br>Unsupervised |

## 2.4  CONSTRUCTING A SAFETY PLAN FOR EARLY CHILDHOOD EDUCATION ENVIRONMENTS

The safety policy designed for each type of early childhood education environment includes the construction of a safety plan. This plan prevents risk and promotes safety. It consists of the guidelines the teacher develops to promote safety in the early childhood education environment (Aronson, 2002). The guidelines address the areas in which risks are anticipated, and the environment is modified and monitored for safety. These applications lessen risks due to accessories, behaviors, and conditions.

### *Anticipation*

The anticipation process begins with a room-by-room indoor inspection and an overall outdoor inspection for safety with checklists that the teacher creates for that particular early childhood education environment. These checklists apply to the type of early childhood education environment, child care, the ages of the children in care, the surrounding community, and the family environments the children represent.

Teachers should search for the accessories, behaviors, and conditions that affect injury prevention. The teacher should anticipate these factors based on the developmental level of the children who are present in the early childhood education environment. Seeing the environment room by room from a child's eye view helps the teacher to identify risks that an adult-only point of view might miss.

The next step is to anticipate the behaviors that lead to injury that might occur in the teacher's type of early childhood education environment. In order to best meet the needs of the children, the teacher must consider the factors of age, community, and family. Knowledge of behaviors that contribute to injury helps the teacher prepare to promote safety through education and good role modeling. Children who learn safe practices and preventive strategies are less at risk for behavior factors that contribute to injury.

# REALITY CHECK

## Bullying in the Early Childhood Education Environment

Bullying and its effects on children have been a topic of discussion since the shootings at Columbine High School in 1999, Santana High School in 2001, and at Red Lake High School in 2005. These shootings that ended in the deaths of other students have made educators take a better look at the causal factors involved. One major conclusion has been that bullying and the victimization that occurs as a result of bullying were contributing factors. It is estimated that 10% of children are bullied on an ongoing basis, and 50% of children have the experience of being bullied at some point during their school years (Huston, 2003). Bullying is considered a major public health and safety issue. Bullying can be defined as ongoing physical or verbal abuse or persecution between two or more people where the power is unequal (Olweus et al., 1999). Basically, bullies abuse their power by teasing and taunting others (Walls, 2004).

Bullying doesn't begin in high school, nor does it necessarily have its roots in elementary school. Bullying can begin as early as toddlerhood. Young children may push others, bite, grab toys away, or make up rules so that they are in charge (Ucci, 2004). Some of us might think of the character "Angelica" on the Nickelodeon cartoon *Rugrats*. She constantly takes advantage of the power she has being the oldest child in the group.

Very young children whose parents have difficulty in social experiences and are coercive or verbally abusive may have little positive enforcement or social skills in their lives (Goleman, 1995). Parental involvement and warmth may be not be present (Huston, 2003). Another reason for bullying in young children is that parents may not set limits or clear expectations

for behavior, and any behavior on the part of the child may appear to be acceptable to the parent. Children may also be overwhelmed in their lives by a loss or change, such as the divorce of their parents or a move from familiar surroundings. In addition, a recent study found that preschoolers who watch $3^1/_2$ hours of television per day are 30% more likely to exhibit bullying behaviors than children who watch no television (Zimmerman et al., 2005).

One way a child can feel good is to display her anger at her circumstance and find someone who is less powerful, so as to feel powerful in that child's presence (Walls, 2004). Bullying behavior is apt to attract attention, and a child may feel more important when attention is paid to him or her. This type of showing off may get the child exactly what he wants. In addition, a scared, insecure, or angry child may also feel more powerful when he or she is being abusive to other children (NCCCHSRC, 2004).

Some gender differences are evident in bullying. Boys are far more likely to bully, and their victims are more likely to be boys than girls. Boys are likely to use both direct physical and verbal bullying and an indirect, relational form of bullying. Girls are less likely to engage in physical bullying and much more likely to engage in relational bullying toward another girl, such as gossiping about her, slandering her, or engaging in actions to exclude her from her social peer group (Smith & Myron-Wilson, 1998) This can begin at a very young age.

Victims tend to be the more vulnerable children in the group (Bosch, 2003). They may be sensitive or quiet, or they may stand out in some way, such as having a disability or being a child with special needs. Children who are

## REALITY CHECK (Continued)

annoying or appear to be occasionally aggressive due to lack of social skills might also be targeted as victims. Another reason for victimization in preschool is that the bully is jealous of the child or children targeted. In general, those who are targeted as victims may be those less likely or able to defend themselves in this type of situation (Huston, 2005).

Bullying can begin as early as preschool, and teachers who work in early childhood education environments need to anticipate bullying actions and monitor and modify those behaviors immediately. The importance of bul-

lying is sometimes underestimated by adults, but it is a matter of great significance for children, parents, and teachers. It is important for teachers to intervene so that this type of behavior stops before the problem escalates (parenting.org. 2005). They must set behavior limits and ensure that there are consequences for unacceptable behavior. Teachers can create an early childhood education environment that is safe and developmentally appropriate (Ucci, 2004). Adults can be role models for positive, warm relations and can help children by mediating disputes at any age.

**CHECK***point:*  What are some of the reasons a child may become a bully at a young age? Name three preventive measures that a teacher might take when faced with bullying behavior.

Conditions that contribute to injury must be anticipated next. Creating a plan for safety and careful observation during times when children are more likely to be injured will help to reduce the possibility of injury. The teacher who understands the common conditions and times associated with injuries, will be especially alert when faced with those circumstances.

Children who come to early childhood education from conditions that place them at greater risk for injury can especially benefit from efforts to help them understand safety and prevention. Children need a supportive and caring environment in which they can explore yet be protected from harm. Children from at-risk environments may not feel this protection at home. Children in violence-prone neighborhoods may feel especially vulnerable. For these children, the early childhood education environment or school may serve as a safe haven. Giving these children tools of safe practices and a sense of security in the early childhood education environment may help them to be more resilient in their home environment (Levin, 2003b) and more alert in their community environment (Levin, 1999).

Communicating with parents about conditions, such as stress, that contribute to injury may help them avoid situations that can lead to injury. Role modeling for safety under stressful conditions delivers the message to the parent that injury can be prevented and that a safer environment can be created for children.

### Modifications

Carefully screening the environment for hazards, removing the hazards, and placing safety devices where needed are simple tasks that a teacher can perform to ensure a safe and secure physical environment for children. The use of checklists can assist the teacher in this process.

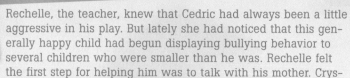

Rechelle, the teacher, knew that Cedric had always been a little aggressive in his play. But lately she had noticed that this generally happy child had begun displaying bullying behavior to several children who were smaller than he was. Rechelle felt the first step for helping him was to talk with his mother. Crystal, Cedric's mother, explained that circumstances at home had changed. Her sister and two children, a two-year-old girl and a six-year-old boy, had moved in with them while her sister recovered from knee surgery. Crystal explained that the little girl was always getting into Cedric's things and that the older boy, Ethan, was jealous of Cedric and constantly taunted him. She herself was at her wit's end. Rechelle and Crystal devised some strategies to help Cedric both at home and at school. Crystal arranged to set aside some time every day for Cedric to play and talk just with her, and she spoke with her sister about Ethan's behavior. As a result, her sister enrolled Ethan in a soccer league to help him. Crystal also got several containers so she could place Cedric's special toys out of reach of the two-year-old. Rechelle explained to Cedric that the younger, smaller children in class were not his two-year-old cousin and he did not have to be afraid that they would mess up his work or play with the things he was playing with. She also counseled him about not making other children feel like his cousin Ethan made him feel. Rechelle also decided to put a blow-up clown in the outdoor play area so that a child could hit the clown to help with aggressiveness. In about two weeks, both Rechelle and Crystal noticed that Cedric was happier and back to being himself again. Involving Cedric's family was a key to this solution.

Teachers can role model safe behaviors, and they can talk with the children about how to be safe in particular situations.

Behaviors can be modified through teaching and exhibiting safe, protective, and preventive practices. The teacher's safety plan should use the most applicable and suitable models of communication for the early childhood education environment. Injury prevention can be taught at all levels, to some extent. Preschool children are more receptive and have greater capabilities than toddlers or infants. School-aged children are very receptive to safety behaviors and practices. There are several steps that the teacher can use to help children of all ages modify their behaviors to protect themselves and prevent injury. The three most important teaching tools for promoting behavior change are

- feedback
- modeling
- role playing through practice drills

**Feedback** about safety can include **positive reinforcement** for good safety behavior practices, **diversion** away from unsafe situations and practices, and a two-way communication channel about both safe and unsafe practices.

Modeling can include role modeling by the teacher, the use of safety posters and signs, and the use of videos, stories, and other modes of communicating about safety and how it is achieved.

Role playing helps prepare children to act in unsafe or dangerous situations. It is a preventative tool that allows children to be better equipped in a real emergency. Drills for fires, earthquakes, and other types of disasters are practiced on a regular basis in many early childhood education environments. Role playing is often recommended for other types of dangerous situations, such as prevention of child maltreatment, gun safety, and neighborhood safety.

Modification works well when it is applied to the factor of condition. The teachers cannot change the time of day when injuries are most likely to happen. However, they can teach the children to avoid certain activities when they are tired. Teachers can also modify activities at times when children are more prone to injuries, such as making a climbing apparatus off limits during high-injury times such as late morning. The teacher might also make that a time when children gather together to relax over stories, instead of playing outside. If a mixed age group is present, while younger children nap, older children might play with toys that are not appropriate for the younger children. These would be put away once the younger children awaken (Blythe-Saucier, 2000).

Role modeling and communicating about safety conditions offer children greater protection. Older children who are able to learn safety practices and understand certain conditions that can lead to injury can have a greater sense of safety and security.

## Monitoring

Monitoring the physical environment of the early childhood education environment for accessories is an ongoing process. Change is a constant process. A teacher should develop an intuition for the changes, but the monitoring process should be formalized. The use of checklists allows the teacher to evaluate changes and check for hazards.

**Feedback**
*a technique for encouraging desired behaviors in children through communication*

**Positive reinforcement**
*reward given in response to a particular behavior that increases the chance of that behavior occurring again*

**Diversion**
*something that changes the focus of attention*

**Key Concept 2.4**

## Constructing a Safety Plan for Early Childhood Education Environments

Constructing a safety plan for early childhood education environments is a process that involves anticipation, modification, and monitoring. The three-step process considers the accessories, the behaviors, and the conditions that lead to injury or lack of safety and protection of the children in care. Some of the tools for the process include checklists, feedback, modeling, practice drills, education, and other promotional techniques. Other effective tools include careful observation, active listening, and communication.

Monitoring the early childhood education environment for behaviors includes observing whether safety practices have changed. This involves keeping track of whether injuries have decreased or increased and examining the behaviors present in the environment. Regularly scheduled weekly examination of injury reports is a good idea, because it helps the teacher to recall any incidence of lack of safety precautions in the environment while they are still fresh in mind. The early childhood education environment should be reviewed for changes on a monthly basis. Changes can occur with the arrival of new children, in the developmental levels of the children in care, in the community, or in family situations. Monitoring helps the teacher manage change by once again anticipating and modifying the environment.

Careful observation under conditions that lead to injury is the foremost activity of monitoring. Mishaps can be prevented through observation. Ongoing evaluation for conditions that lead to injury will help identify changes. Use of monitoring tools such as convex mirrors on corners to increase visibility and baby monitors to listen for safety might lessen risk (Aronson, 2001). If changes in conditions occur, this type of evaluation can lead to early intervention to prevent injury and protect the child. Evaluation of conditions is accomplished through observation, active listening, and communication.

## 2.5  IMPLICATIONS FOR TEACHERS

The teacher should use preventive and protective measures to prepare and maintain a safe early childhood education environment. The risk-management tools that will help the teacher to provide a good measure of safety include role modeling, education, observation, and supervision.

### Role Modeling

Children like to imitate the adults in their lives. Safety and protection of children from harm can be influenced by teachers who role model good safety practices and create a safe, secure environment.

**TABLE 2-6**
*Role Modeling Behaviors for Safety*

- Verbalizing safety actions to the children
- Teacher safety actions in the early childhood education and community environments
- Presence of safety devices such as smoke alarms and electrical outlet plugs
- Teacher being attuned to unsafe conditions
- Teacher safety behaviors during practice drills and role playing
- Good teacher/parent communication level about safety measures
- Daily routines for safety checklists
- Removal of hazards to ensure a safe physical environment
- Promotion and education on safety issues and practices
- Teacher predictability and support given the importance of safety in the early childhood education environment

A safety policy for role modeling should reflect those behaviors the teacher wishes to instill in the children. Some of the knowledge and practices the children should be able to observe the teacher role model are listed in Table 2-6.

## Education

Safety education should involve the teacher, the children, and the parents. To provide safety in the early childhood education environment, the teacher must be aware of strategies and methods to reduce risk (Aronson, 2001). The teacher must develop a keen awareness of the risks posed by the accessories, behaviors, and conditions of the particular early childhood education environment.

Children can learn safe practices as they watch the teacher model safe practices and behaviors. The teacher can talk to the children about safety and share books and videos that promote safety and safe behaviors.

Educational materials provided for the parents can help them understand the importance of safe practices and behaviors for children in all environments. A parent who is aware of conditions or behaviors that may put a child at risk for safety is able to offer an extra measure of protection and prevention.

## For Families

One item that teachers could provide for families is a checklist to examine the early childhood education environment for safety. The checklist would include the following:

- The staff-to-child ratio is safe. These ratios are available from the licensing agency in the state in which the early childhood education program is located.
- Teachers have training and continue to educate themselves about issues of safety in early childhood environments.
- There is careful supervision of all children, and teachers focus on the children, not on other adults.

- Teachers act in a way that is developmentally appropriate for the children they are with.
- Teachers avoid conflict between children and create a peaceful classroom.
- Toys are safe and developmentally appropriate.
- All equipment is maintained for safety.
- All cleaning materials are locked away.
- Outdoor areas are safe, developmentally appropriate, and well maintained.
- Emergency numbers and an emergency exit plan are posted.
- There is an "open door" policy that welcomes parent visits. Some parents may prefer a "nanny cam" at the facility so that they can watch their children from work.
- The facility is licensed and maintains licensing standards, if applicable.

When parents have a list to check for safety in the early childhood education environment, it might cause them to think about their own home safety situation. The teacher might want to have a brief discussion about safety when handing the checklist to the parent, before the decision is made to sign the child up for the program. It is critical that parents understand the entire issue of safety that teachers are trying to provide.

## Observation

A teacher can use observation to protect children from risk and to prevent risk to safety. Observing for accessories, behaviors, and conditions keeps the teacher aware of all areas of injury risk management. The teacher should watch for safety risks from hazards and equipment. He or she should observe for the need for safety devices. Behaviors of both children and adults should be observed for safe practices and risk of injury. The teacher should observe the conditions in the environment that are known to lead to risk of injury and reduction of safety.

## Supervision

Using the ABCs of injury risk management helps the teacher offer the greatest degree of constant supervision in order to maintain the safest possible early childhood education environment. Supervision can also help ensure that all strategies and practices that promote safety, prevent risk, and offer protection are used.

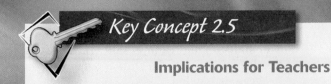

### Key Concept 2.5

#### Implications for Teachers

The teacher needs to use all tools at her disposal to help promote safety, prevent injury, and offer protection. Role modeling, education, observation, working with families, and supervision provide the practices, strategies, and methods needed to provide these for the children in care.

## CHAPTER SUMMARY

Safety policies that manage risk and prevent injury promote and protect the safety of the early childhood education environment. Teachers should be aware of environmental hazards such as accessories, behaviors, and conditions in their particular early childhood education program. It is most important that children's developmental levels be understood and considered when addressing safety in the environment. Teachers need to learn to anticipate, modify, and monitor the environment for injury prevention. Role modeling is a key to promoting safe practices. Education for both the children and the parents helps the teacher to maintain a safer environment. Supervision adds another level of safety to early childhood education programs.

## TO GO BEYOND

In this section you will find a number of activities that you can use to apply and improve your knowledge of this chapter. There is also an online resource that accompanies this text that can be found at: http://www.earlychilded. delmar.com (see description at the end of this chapter.)

### Chapter Review Critical Thinking Applications

1. Discuss the interrelationship of accessories, behaviors, and conditions of safety applied to early childhood education environments.

2. Describe how the anticipation, modification, and monitoring process occurs in a typical early childhood education environment. Compare that to a family child care home. Compare that to an in-home care situation. What are the commonalities? What are the differences? Select the five most important elements for any early childhood education situation.

3. How does developmental level affect the risks for injury? What are some common injuries in infancy? In toddlerhood? For a four-year-old?

4. What are some of the issues for early childhood education environments that deal with child custody? How would you handle the case of a noncustodial parent arriving to pick up a child?

5. Why is bullying a problem even with young children?

### As an Individual

1. Interview a teacher in your community, preferably at the early childhood education program. Ask the person how risk and injury prevention are managed in his or her program. Was the teacher aware of developmental levels? How were these applied to risk management? Were any modifications made to the early childhood education environment in relation to developmental levels? How might you personally improve your own risk management in relation to early childhood education?

2. Go to a local park and observe the community surrounding the park. Would you consider this a safe environment for children?

Would there be any risk to an early childhood education program or family child care home if the park were nearby? Record your observations and conclusions.

3. Find someone you know who is divorced, separated, or never married and has preschool-aged children. Is there a child custody order for the children? If not, find out why. What arrangements have been made for picking the child up at the early childhood education program? Does the early childhood education program have a child custody policy? Compare the answers to the information in the Reality Check on Child Custody.

## As a Group

1. Watch *Setting Up for Health and Safe Care,* an AAP video. What safety measures were observed? If you do not have access to this video, go as a group to an early childhood education environment and observe for safety. Discuss two indoor and two outdoor risk management measures that were promoted. Compare those measures to the measures from other groups in your class. Have the entire class select the two most important indoor and outdoor safety measures that will lessen risk in the early childhood education environment.

2. In a small group of four to five people, create a safety checklist that could be used in an early childhood education environment. Compare the lists. Select the 10 most important items.

3. Divide the class into three smaller groups. Have one group write a safety policy for indoor safety, one group a policy for outdoor safety, and one group a policy for child custody. Review the policies with the whole class and make any suggested changes.

4. Survey a local early childhood education program for the diversity of its population. Estimate the largest non-English-speaking group at the site. Obtain the three safety policies that are considered most important in that program. Enlist the help of parents from that program who represent that population to help translate the three center safety policies. Present these translations to the early childhood education program.

## Case Studies

1. Late on Monday morning, because of special morning activities, Luwanda and Kelly are sharing the outdoor play area with their two classes. Luwanda is the teacher for the four-year-olds, and Kelly is the teacher for the two-year-olds. They are good friends, and both had exciting weekends that they want to share with each other. What risks for accessories, behaviors, and conditions might an observer find in this scenario? What might Luwanda and Kelly do to reduce the potential risk?

2. Kyle is the first teacher to arrive at the church preschool on Monday morning. Since the last preschool session, the activities room that he teaches in has hosted a number of events including a quilt-

ing bee, preparation for a wedding, Sunday school, Bible study, and baby-sitting for attendees of the evening service. How should he proceed before the children arrive? What types of accessories might he find left in this shared space?

3. Mary Ellen is the director of an early childhood education program in the downtown area of a major city. It is a convenient site for many parents who either live or work in the local area. The center is very near to a city park and an inner-city high school. She is concerned about the safety of the neighborhood surrounding her early childhood education environment. What steps might she or her teachers take to maximize the safety of the children in care?

4. Grace is a teacher of four-year-olds in a state preschool. Henry is a robust four-year-old boy who just started school a few weeks ago. It appears that he is trying to intimidate Marcus and Leon when they go out to play. Henry is trying to make up rules and coerce the other boys into playing what he wants to play. How should Grace handle this potential bullying? What direction should she take?

## Chapter References

American Academy of Pediatrics and American Public Health Association (APA & APHA). (2002). *Caring for our children: National health and safety performance standards. Guidelines for out-of-home care.* Washington, DC: American Public Health Association.

American Academy of Pediatrics (AAP) (2005). Quality early education and child care from birth to kindergarten. Policy Statement. *Pediatrics, 115*(1), 187–191.

Aronson, S. (2001). Reducing the risk of injury in child care. *Child Care Information Exchange, 3,* 64–66.

Aronson, S. (2002). *Healthy young children: A manual for programs.* (4th ed.). Washington, DC: NAEYC.

Benedek, E., & Brown, C. (2001). *How to help your child overcome your divorce: A support guide for families.* New York: Newmarket Press.

Blythe-Saucier, S. (2000). Toy safety. *Healthy Child Care, 3*(1). Retrieved September 28, 2005, from http://www.healthychild.net/articles/sf13toys.html

Bosch, K. (2003). Bullying—How to stop it. Cooperative Extension, Institute of Agriculture and Natural Resources, University of Nebraska-Lincoln. Retrieved October 21, 2005. Available online: http://ianrpubs.unl.edu/family/nf309.htm

Bredekamp, S., & Copple, C. (1997). *Developmentally appropriate practices in early childhood education programs* (Rev. ed.) Washington, DC: NAEYC.

Deal, L., Gomby, D., Zipporli, L., & Berhman, R. (2000). Unintentional injuries in childhood: Analysis and recommendations. *The Future of Children, 10*(1), 4–22.

Earls, F., & Buka, S. (2000). Measurement of community characteristics. In S. Meisels & J. Shonkoff (Eds.), *Handbook of early childhood intervention* (2nd ed., 309–324). New York: Cambridge University Press.

Eller, D. (1998, August). It's shocking how many people you know own a gun and how easy it is for kids to get their hands on one. *Parents Magazine,* 62–65.

Goleman, D. (1995). *Emotional Intelligence.* New York: Bantam.

Huston, J. (2003, August). Children and bullying: A guide for parents. Montana State University Extension Service *Montguide* MT200307HR. Retrieved April 12, 2005 from http://www.montana.edu/wwwpb/pubs/mt200307.html

Jackman, G., Farah, M., Kellerman, A., & Simon, H. (2001). Seeing is believing. What do boys do when they find a real gun? *Pediatrics, 107*(6), 1247–1250.

Kelly, J. (1997). *Determination of child custody in the USA.* The World Wide Legal Information Association. Retrieved May 15, 2002, from http://www.futureofchildren.org/information2826/information_show.htm?doc_id=75568

King, W., Leblanc, J., Barrowman, N., Klassen, T. Bernard-Bonnin, A., Robitaille, Y., Tenenbein, M. and Pless, B. (2005) Long term effects of a home visit to prevent childhood injury: Three year follow up of a randomized trial. *Injury Prevention, 200*(2), 106–109.

Levin, D. (1999). Changing needs, changing responses: Rethinking how we teach children. *Child Care Information Exchange, 99*(7), 46–49.

Levin, D. (2003a). Beyond war and superhero play: Meeting children's needs in violent times. *Young Children, 58*(3), 60–65.

Levin, D. (2003b). *Teaching young children in violent times: Building a peaceable classroom* (2nd ed.). Cambridge, MA: Educators for Social Responsibility.

Maslow, A. (1968). *Toward a psychology of being.* New York: Van Nordstrom.

National Coalition for the Homeless. (2001, June). *Homeless families with children.* NCH Fact Sheet 7. Retrieved September 28, 2005, from http://www.nationalhomeless.org/families.html

National Conference of Commissioners of Uniform State Laws (NCCUSL). (1997). *Uniform child custody jurisdiction and enforcement act.* Chicago, IL: Author. Retrieved May 15, 2002, from http://www.law.upenn.edu/bll/ulc/uccjea/chldcus2.htm

National Mental Health Association (NMHA) (2005). Children without homes. Retrieved October 8, 2005. Available online: http://www.nmha.org/homeless/childrenhomelessnessfacts.cfm

North Carolina Child Care Health and Safety Resource Center (NCCCHSRC) (2004). Bye-bye-bully. *North Carolina Child Care Health and Safety Bulletin, 4*(4), 3.

Olweus, D., Limber, S., & Mihalic, S. (1999). *Blueprints for violence prevention, book nine: Bullying prevention program.* Boulder, CO: Center for the Study and Prevention of Violence.

Ontario Early Years (OEY), (2004, Fall). Preventing injuries: What parents think. *Safety Never Hurts Bulletin,* 2. Retrieved from http://www.londonsafecommunities.com/SNH-Fall2004-Eng.pdf

Parenting.org (2005, January 3). Biting, bullies and other bad behavior at preschool. Retrieved April 12, 2005 from http://www.parenting.org/archive/precious/education/2001-02/Sep02_bad_behavior.asp

Phelan, K., Khoury, J. Kalkwarf, H. & Lanphear, B. (2005). Residential injuries in U.S. children and adolescents. *Public Health Report, 120*(1), 63–70.

Pless, B., & Millar, W. (2002). *Unintentional injuries in childhood: Results from Canadian health surveys.* Retrieved September 28, 2005, from the Public Health Agency of Canada Web site. http://www.phac-aspc.gc.ca/dca-dea/publications/unintentional_e.html

Shallcross, M. (1999). Family child care homes need health and safety training and an emergency rescue system. *Young Children, 54*(5), 70–73.

Shepard, S. (2002). How safe are your child care programs? *School Planning and Management, 41*(11), 6–9.

Smith, C. (2001). Safe spaces for infants and toddlers. *Healthy Child Care, 4*(4), 7–10. Retrieved September 28, 2005, from http://www.healthychild.net/articles/sf22safeplaces.htm

Smith, L. (1997). Jean Piaget. In N. Sheehy, A. Chapman, & W. Conroy (eds). *Biographical dictionary of psychology.* London: Routledge.

Smith, P., & Myron-Wilson, R. (1998). Parenting and school bullying. *Clinical Child Psychology and Psychiatry, 3*(3), 405–417.

Tynan, W. D. (2004, December). Helping your child through a divorce. Retrieved September 28, 2005, from the Nemours Foundation Web site: http://www.kidshealth.org/parent/positive/talk/help_child_divorce.html

*Types of custody.* (2001). Retrieved September 28, 2005, from http://www.nolo.com/encyclopedia/articles/div/pc18.html

Ucci, M. (2004, Jan.). Bullying and the young child. *Child Health Alert Newsletter.* Retrieved April 13, 2005 from http://www.childhealthalert.com/hottopics. htm#Bullying%20And%20The%20Young%20Child

Walls, L. (2004). What makes a bully? Committee for Children. Retrieved April 12 from http://www.cfchildren.org/articlef/walls1f/what

Zimmerman, F., Glew, G., Christakis, D. & Katon, W. (2005). Early cognitive stimulation, emotional support and television watching as predictors of subsequent bullying among grade-school children. *Archives of Pediatric Adolescent Medicine, 159*(4), 384–388.

Additional resources for this chapter can be found by visiting the Online Companion™ at www.earlychilded.delmar.com. This supplemental material includes extensive chapter quizzes, PowerPoint® outlines, Web links, and various other activities to help better utilize the material in this chapter. The site is updated regularly, so you may check back often to receive the latest information about the subjects in each chapter.

## CHAPTER 3

# Indoor Safety

**After reading this chapter, you should be able to:**

### 3.1 Indoor Safety Policies

Describe and discuss safety policies for indoor environments as tools for risk prevention, protection, and promotion.

### 3.2 Indoor Safety Guidelines

Indicate and discuss specific guidelines for making any indoor early childhood education environment free from risk and protected for safety.

### 3.3 Indoor Equipment Safety

Relate and discuss the safety hazards of indoor equipment in early childhood education environments.

### 3.4 Toy Safety

Describe and discuss the importance of safe, risk-free toys for infants, toddlers, and preschoolers.

### 3.5 Interpersonal Safety

Describe and discuss clear rules for consequences of behavior and appropriate methods of conflict resolution.

### 3.6 Poison Control

Indicate the methods and means of poison control and risk prevention in early childhood education environments.

### 3.7 Fire and Burn Prevention

Describe and discuss methods of fire and burn prevention in early childhood education environments.

### 3.8 Implications for Teachers

Indicate the need for education, observation, and supervision to maintain a safe indoor environment.

## 3.1  INDOOR SAFETY POLICIES

The safety risks of indoor and outdoor environments vary widely. Because the variation is so widespread, we will look at these environments separately. The indoor early childhood education environment can include many physical hazards that pose risk through choking, interpersonal violence, poisoning, burns, lead poisoning, and other means. The following factors indicate the need for policies to cover indoor safety:

- Two-thirds of early childhood education programs were reported as unsafe in a study conducted in 300 centers throughout the United States (Shepard, 2002).

- Toys and equipment provided for children should be checked and maintained to prevent toy related injuries (Hood & Smith 2005; Walsh, 2005).

- Falls are the most common source of injury in the early childhood education setting (Zavitkovsky & Thompson, 2000).

One very important safety measure for early childhood education environments with infants is to make sure they are put down for naps on their backs to help prevent SIDS.

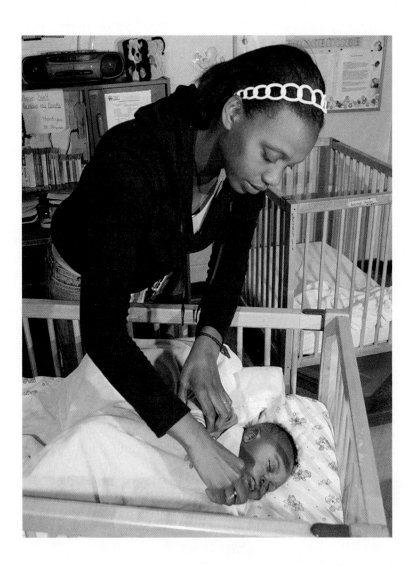

- In 2001, 1.2 million poisonings occurred in children younger than six years of age. Preventing poisoning is a critical component in making early childhood education environments safe (Sutton, 2004).
- Children four years of age and younger account for more than 70,000 toy-related injuries and more than 75 percent of deaths related to toys (National Safe Kids Campaign, 2001).
- Sixty percent of the products used in fall zones for indoor equipment in early childhood education environments do not meet national standards (American Academy of Pediatrics, 2003a).
- Using violence to solve interpersonal problems has become common for children (Levin, 2003a).
- "Biting causes more upset feeling than any other behavior in child care" (Oku, 2002).
- Teachers should model the values of compassion and kindness to children for interpersonal safety skills (Moore, 2004).

The indoor environment includes a multitude of levels that can pose risk. Hazards come from household items, toys, animals, stoves and other kitchen equipment, children's furniture, foods, firearms, fireplaces, paint, ceramics, medications, plants, and electrical outlets and cords, among others. Other indoor risks include unsafe teacher practices, unmonitored conditions, and children's behavior based on developmental levels, physical abilities, and emotional health. The teacher must have an awareness of all accessories, behaviors, and conditions that may lead to an accident or injury. The teacher must also be in compliance with all regulations affecting the safety in care, such as those from licensing and fire boards.

Indoor environment risk management process should include the following:

1. *Indoor Early Childhood Education Environments:* understanding indoor safety practices and applications for risk management as they apply to specific early childhood education environments
2. *Indoor Equipment Safety:* practices for preventing injuries and managing safety on indoor equipment
3. *Toy Safety:* practices for preventing injuries, removing unsafe toys, and managing selection of toys for children in care
4. *Interpersonal Safety:* strategies for developing guidelines for interpersonal safety and conflict management for the children in care
5. *Poison Control:* strategies for developing guidelines for poison prevention and protection in early childhood education
6. *Fire and Burn Prevention:* educational and promotional strategies to model good fire and burn prevention behaviors and practices
7. *Implications for Teachers:* methods and practices of conducting education, supervision, observation, and use of outside resources

## Key Concept 3.1

### Safety Policies

Safety policies should be planned as a tool for prevention of injuries, the protection of children, and the promotion of safe practices in the early childhood education indoor environment. These policies should consider the specific environment and should be applicable to the accessories, behaviors, and conditions present indoors. Use of these policies minimizes risk to children and maximizes the early childhood education environment for safety.

## 3.2 INDOOR SAFETY GUIDELINES

Some hazards are common to all early childhood education environments. The most common indoor childhood accidents are related to

- falls
- choking
- burns
- drowning
- poisoning

Screening the environment for these risks to safety should be done in an organized fashion. In 1999, the Consumer Product Safety Commission (CPSC) conducted a national study of safety hazards in 200 licensed early

## REALITY CHECK

### Sudden Infant Death Syndrome

Sudden Infant Death Syndrome (SIDS) describes the sudden death of an infant younger than one year of age that cannot be explained even after thorough investigation by medical and police authorities (Stubbs-Wynn et al., 2004). It claims more child deaths between the ages of one month and one year than cancer, child maltreatment, AIDS, cystic fibrosis, muscular dystrophy, and heart diseases combined (SIDS Network, 1996). It is estimated that there are as many as 2500 deaths per year from SIDS

(States seek ways, 2004). SIDS strikes without warning to children of all racial, ethnic, and economic groups. It has been found that SIDS rates are higher for American Indian and African-American infants than for white infants (National SIDS/Infant Death Resource Center [NSDRC], 2004). The hours that children are in care in early education programs or facilities are the hours when SIDS strikes most commonly (Aronson, 2003). Twenty percent of SIDS deaths occur in care outside the home (Moon et al., 2003).

*(continues)*

## REALITY CHECK (Continued)

The medical community still cannot explain what causes SIDS. Speculation includes a vulnerability period early in infancy, a birth defect, stress caused by infection and/or failure to develop (SIDS Network, 1996). Several risk factors that contribute to SIDS have been previously identified. These risk factors include:

- Sleeping on the stomach in the prone position
- Pre- and post-natal exposure to cigarette smoke
- Sleeping materials that are too soft
- Overheating of the baby

In October 2005, the American Academy of Pediatrics came out with additional, specific recommendations to reduce the risk of SIDS that had been supported by research. These new recommendations for risk reduction include:

- Not having the infant share a "family bed"
- Side sleeping (putting a child to bed on its side) is no longer acceptable
- Pacifiers should be used at naptime and bedtime for the first year of life except for a breastfeeding child, who needs to establish the breastfeeding routine. The use of a pacifier for those babies is recommended at one month.

In addition, the AAP recommends that parents not use commercial devices marketed to reduce the risk of SIDS, nor count on monitors as a deterrent to SIDS. The teacher can help reduce risk by offering protective measures for the majority of these risks.

A major discovery has revolutionized how parents, teachers and other caregivers should put babies down to sleep. Studies in Europe in the 1980s found that babies who were put to sleep on their stomachs in the prone position, were twice as likely to die from SIDS as children placed on their sides. Since 1992, the American Academy of Pediatrics has recommended that all babies be put down to sleep on their backs or sides and not on their stomachs. More recently, it has been found that children placed on their sides are likely to roll onto their stomachs, thus increas-

ing risk, so the American Academy of Pediatrics removed their suggestion to place babies on their sides (AAP, 2005). It was also found that the combination of infection and being put to sleep on their sides greatly increases the risk.

Today, only 24 percent of American infants sleep on their stomachs, compared with 70 percent in 1992. This change alone has contributed to a 40 percent reduction of SIDS deaths from 5000 to 3000 per year (NSDRC, 2004). This reduction applies to full term and preterm babies, as well as low birthweight babies (Malloy & Freeman, 2000). It is hoped that not putting babies on their sides will further decrease risk and contribute to a reduction in numbers of deaths due to SIDS.

Despite this success, it has been found that people in early childhood education centers continue to place infants in the prone position. It is estimated that 20 to 25 percent of early childhood education centers continue to place infants on their stomach (Moon & Oden, 2003). One reason cited for the discrepancy was that as many as 43% of teachers were unaware of the relationship between prone sleep and SIDS. To help ameliorate this discrepancy, the Healthy Child Care America "Back to Sleep" campaign was launched in 2003 (NSDRC, 2004). Another reason cited for why many teachers did not put children to sleep on their back is that they believed it was more likely to increase illness, cause trouble sleeping, or cause choking problems if infants vomited while on their back. These excuses have been proved wrong (Aronson, 2003). It has been found that infants who are placed on their back for sleeping until the age of six months actually have fewer reports of illness or doctor's visits.

Cigarette smoke is considered to be the second greatest risk factor for SIDS. It is believed that this risk factor may account for 20 to 40 percent of SIDS cases (DiFranza & Lew, 1995). An infant exposed to cigarette smoke may be at 200% increased risk for SIDS (Wisborg et al., 2000). If babies are also exposed in utero, they are three times more likely to die of SIDS

## REALITY CHECK (Continued)

(Anderson & Cook, 1998). Smoking is still not prohibited in 15.6% of early childhood education care centers in 45 states (Moon et al., 2003).

Babies should sleep on firm, flat mattresses to lessen the risk of entrapment or heavy covering (Kemp et al., 2000, AAP 2000a). Parents, teachers and other caregivers should avoid placing infants on beanbags, sheepskins, synthetic pillow and foam pads, either alone or covered with a comforter. All stuffed animals should be removed from the crib or sleeping area (Gorman, 2001).

Overheating is another important factor. Too much bedding, clothing that is too heavy, and an environment that is too warm can contribute to SIDS (AAP, 2000a). Overheating may occur when babies have a cold and efforts are made to keep them warm. Babies who are overheated exhibit sweating, damp hair, heat rash, rapid breathing, and fever. It is recommended that the indoor temperature be kept at 70 degrees Fahrenheit or less (SIDS Network, 1996).

Several recent studies have found that bedsharing increases risk in infants under 11 weeks of age (Carpenter et al., 2004; Tarpin et al., 2005). This risk is increased if there are multiple bed sharers, a smoker who shares the bed, or has a bed sharer that had alcohol before

going to bed. Room sharing, without being in the same bed, has appeared to reduce risk because of the proximity (AAP, 2005).

Another factor that appears to reduce risk is the use of a pacifier (Arnestad et al., 2001; AAP, 2005). The use of a pacifier during naptime and bedtime is recommended after one month in breast fed babies and from birth for bottle fed babies. To further reduce risk the AAP also recommends that when placing a child to sleep, foreign objects should be checked for by sweeping the mouth using clean hands.

Research has also shown that SIDS cases are more likely to be reported in the fall and winter than at any other time of year and that boys are more likely to die of SIDS than are girls (NSDRC, 2004). A more recent suspected factor has been dispelled. The relationship between multiple doses of vaccines and SIDS was investigated, and the conclusion was that the evidence was insufficient to link the two (Stratton et al., 2003). The use of preventive measures can reduce risk, but nothing can guarantee that SIDS will not strike. Parents and teachers should remember this. A SIDS death disrupts the sense of normalcy and security regardless of where it occurs.

**CHECK*point:*** What are the four most protective factors for preventing SIDS in early childhood education environments? How would you pass this information on to parents?

childhood education settings. They were looking for safety hazards in these product areas: cribs, soft bedding, playground surfaces, surface maintenance, window blind cords, drawstrings in children's clothing, and recalled children's products. This investigation found that two-thirds of these settings had at least one safety hazard present. Applying the ABCs of injury risk (see Table 2-4) allows the teacher to anticipate, modify, and monitor the early childhood education environment. This chapter provides indoor safety checklists that can be used as a basis to help prepare to minimize risk.

### Environmental Hazards

The great majority of children's time is spent indoors, including in early childhood education programs. Indoor screening should include environmental hazards such as secondhand smoke, lead, asbestos, chemicals, and anything else that might be a risk in the environment, even though it may not be within a child's reach. Other irritants to a child's air quality environment should also be thought through. Examples of irritants may include air fresheners, plug-in fresheners, and perfumes used by teachers. All environmental hazard risks should be removed or modified wherever possible.

*Ventilation.* Inadequate ventilation is a safety risk that is considered an environmental hazard. Air needs to move sufficiently so there is no gathering of fumes, germs, or other safety risks to children. Children inhale two to three times more air than adults, so adequate ventilation is necessary (Rosenblum, 1993). APHA and AAP standards can be found in *Caring for Our Children: National Health and Safety Performance Standards: Guidelines for Out-of-Home Child Care Programs* published by the APHA. The quality of air can be polluted from a number of sources including molds, secondhand smoke (see Chapter 10), and carbon monoxide (NCCCHSRC, 2004). Carbon monoxide is a deadly gas that cannot be smelled or seen. It is important that a carbon monoxide detector be placed in the early childhood education environment and that all gas appliances such as furnaces and water heaters be checked regularly.

*Pets or Animals.* Pets or animals in the environment can also provide safety risks through injury, infection, and allergic reactions. Any animal that is present should be friendly and healthy. The American Society for the Prevention of Cruelty to Animals (ASPCA) has reported that half of all children are bitten by a dog by the time they are twelve years old, usually by a familiar male dog (AAP, 2003b). For young children, most bites occur around the neck and head. Any animal bite should be reported to the authorities

Family pets, although vaccinated and clean, may still be a conceivable safety and health risk to children in family child care. Animals must be supervised and monitored regularly to avoid unpleasant incidents.

because of the possibility, if only slight, of transmission of rabies (Palmer, 2003). Some diseases carried by cats and dogs are catscratch fever, salmonella, scabies, and ringworm. Puppies and kittens can carry infections that cause a variety of serious diseases in children. Dogs and cats should be fully immunized and under a veterinarian's care for flea, tick, and worm control. Flea collars for either animal may pose risk to children and their developing nervous systems (Colino, 2003).

Never allow turtles, parrots, or lizards to be handled by children because these types of pets often carry diseases that are transmitted by direct contact (French, 1999). Do not allow other wild or aggressive animals such as ferrets to be present in an early childhood education environment (Zamani, 1999). If pets are present, they should be kept in a supervised and confined area of the facility and regularly checked for disease by a veterinarian. Pet living quarters should be cleaned often, and animal waste should be kept to a minimum. Children should always wash their hands immediately after handling pets. Follow the AAP/APHA guidelines for animals present in the early childhood education environment.

Another risk factor that pets may present is allergic reactions. Some children may be allergic to certain pet hair or dander. Parents may be unaware of the allergy if there are no pets in the home environment. The teacher should observe children for any reactions to the pets in the early childhood education environment.

**FIGURE 3-1**
Teachers should teach children the meaning of the poison sign.

***Cleaning and Other Supplies.*** Cleaning supplies are a risk to children whether or not they are poisonous. These items can cause burns or rashes and other possible problems. All cleaning supplies or chemicals that might present danger to children should be kept at a level where children cannot reach them. Paints and some craft supplies may present a risk if a child ingests them. Anything that might be poisonous should be kept at a high level in a locked cabinet. These items should be well labeled with the poison sign. The teacher can teach the children about the danger that is present when they see the sign (Figure 3-1). This may not help the toddler or crawling infant, but it will help older children.

## Safety Devices

Safety devices should be present wherever applicable in the indoor early childhood education environment. All wall sockets should be covered with difficult-to-remove plastic plugs. All drawers that can be pulled out and fall onto a child's head or upper body should have safety latches in them that

Safety latches and electric outlet covers are just two of the numerous safety devices available. As with any device, these must be properly installed and used to be truely effective.

make them childproof. All doorways that might lead to danger should be shut and lockable. Safety gates should be installed for doorways without doors that may lead to danger or risk. All stairways where infants and toddlers are present should have safety gates to prevent the children from crawling up or falling down the stairs. The teacher should check local hardware stores and early childhood education catalogs for safety devices.

## Developmental Level

Prevention is the single most significant factor in risk management for safety. The teacher begins this process by defining the boundaries for indoor safety and screening the environment for hazards with the developmental levels of the children in care in mind (Centers for Disease Control and Prevention [CDC], 1999). Safety hazards can be broken down by developmental age and vulnerabilities associated with that particular stage, as shown in Table 3-1.

**TABLE 3-1**
*Indoor Safety Hazards*

| Age | Hazards | Prevention Tips |
|---|---|---|
| 0–6 months | Scalds | Set hot water temperature to 120°F or less and always test bath water before immersing baby. |
| | Falls | Never leave infant alone on bed or table. |
| | Choking/Suffocation | Buy toys larger than two inches in diameter. Keep crib free of plastics or pillows. Crib slats should be less than $2\frac{5}{8}$ inches apart, and space between mattress and slats should be less than 2 fingers wide. |
| | Toys | Should be larger than $1\frac{1}{2}$ inches in diameter and should have smooth round edges and be soft and flexible. |
| | Drowning | Never leave child in bath unattended |
| 6 months–1 year | Burns and scalds | Check water temperature (see above). Keep hot foods and liquids out of reach. Put guards around hot pipes, radiators, and fireplaces. |
| | Poisons | Store household products, cosmetics, and medicines in high, preferably locked cabinets. Post poison control number by phone. |
| | Choking | Check floors and reachable areas for small objects such as pins, coins, buttons. Avoid raw vegetables, nuts, hard candy, popcorn, and other foods that are difficult for child to properly chew and swallow. |
| | Toys | Should be large, unbreakable, and smooth. |
| | Drowning | Always carefully supervise when bathing. |
| 1–2 years | Falls | Put toddler gates on stairways and keep any doors to cellars, attics, and porches locked. Remove sharp-edged furniture from child's frequently used area. Show child proper way to climb up and down stairs using handrails. |
| | Burns | While cooking, turn pot handles to back of stove. Keep electric cords out of reach. Use shock stops to cover used and unused outlets. Teach child the meaning of the word *hot* and talk about different types of hot. |

**TABLE 3-1 (Continued)**
*Indoor Safety Hazards*

| Age | Hazards | Prevention Tips |
|---|---|---|
| 1–2 years<br>—cont'd | Poisons | Keep poisons locked in high cabinets. Have child tested for lead poisoning during regular checkup. |
| | Drowning | Always supervise child's bath. |
| | Choking | Remove small objects. |
| 2–3 years | Poisons | Teach child about the difference between food and nonfood and what is not good to eat. Watch child during art projects so he does not put art supplies in mouth. Keep poisons locked in high cabinets. |
| | Burns | Keep matches, lighter, and cigarettes out of reach and sight of children. Put screen around fireplaces and wood stoves. Reinforce the meaning of *hot*. |
| | Toys | Check for sharp edges, hinges, and small parts that could be swallowed. Remove toy chest lids. |
| | Drowning | Always supervise. |
| | Guns | Keep any firearms unloaded and locked away out of reach. |
| 3 years and up | Burns | Teach child "drop and roll" to prepare for clothing catching fire. Practice fire drills with escape route, meeting place, and sound of smoke alarm. Train to bring found matches to adult. |
| | Tools and equipment | Teach child safe use of scissors. Keep sharp knives out of reach. |
| | Guns | Keep firearms unloaded and locked. Teach safety precautions about guns, by telling an adult immediately when they see a gun and not to touch! Discourage use of toy guns or violent play. |

*Infants.* Young infants are relatively helpless and must be carefully watched to protect and prevent risks. Older, more mobile infants develop new motor skills at a rapid rate that lead them into an increasing number of hazardous situations. Children at this stage are particularly at risk for choking on small objects that they can mouth. The environment should be constantly and carefully monitored for small objects if infants are present, and expanding hazards should be anticipated. The early childhood education environment should frequently be updated and checked for any Consumer Product Safety Commission recalls of toys or infant equipment that might pose risk (CPSC, 2004).

*Toddlers.* Toddlers probably represent the developmental group with the most potential for unsafe practices. They are at a cognitive level that allows them new ways of thinking and solving problems, but they do not understand cause and effect. Toddlers try to stretch their limits and test their environment, which they now have the physical ability to accomplish. Toddlers like to explore places that may not be in view. Poisons and chemicals that are kept in cabinets, drawers, or on shelves are a major risk for this age group. Toddlers need careful, constant monitoring and potential hazards need to be constantly anticipated. Therefore, the environment should be modified as needed (Figure 3-2).

*The Preschooler.* Preschool-aged children have more physical and cognitive abilities and are beginning to understand cause and effect. Indoor falls pose risk to these children. Although they know about cause and effect, physical mastery often takes precedence over thought processes. Besides monitoring the conditions and safety risks, the teacher can teach preschool children preventive measures and help them to anticipate hazards. Children of this age can be good helpers to monitor the indoor environment for hazards.

Most children younger than three years of age are not developmentally ready to use scissors. Even children who are three or older should be regularly monitored for safety reasons.

**FIGURE 3-2**
Common indoor hazards.

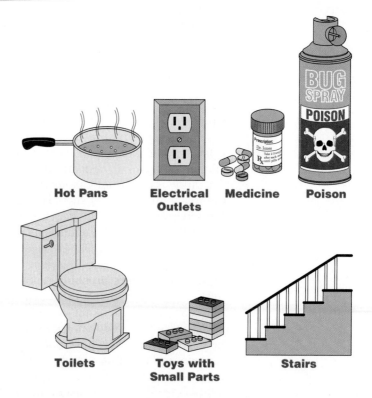

Hot Pans    Electrical Outlets    Medicine    Poison

Toilets    Toys with Small Parts    Stairs

Adequate floor space in a clear and organized environment aids in the prevention of injury.

***School Age.*** School-aged children are much less prone to indoor safety hazards than children who are younger. Firearms may be the greatest threat to school-aged children. This age group has intense curiosity about things they see in movies and on television. They may not understand the danger guns pose. It is important, if guns are present in an early childhood education environment, such as a family child care home, that they be stored unloaded and locked up. Children of this age can learn preventive measures and can help the teacher monitor the environment and the younger children.

## Space

Specific early childhood education environments present unique conditions and circumstances that can lead to environmental hazards. There should be adequate space to move around the equipment and not have to compete for space with other children. Most early childhood education centers, Head Start programs, and state preschools are licensed and do comply with spacing required by the licensing agencies.

Recommended indoor space is 35 square feet per child of play space, which does not include kitchen, bathroom, closet, laundry, or staff facilities (APHA & AAP, 2002). This space usually translates to 50 square feet per child when furnishings are included. Family child care homes that are informed try to keep to this standard. Unlicensed or license-exempt sites also need to follow this standard for space.

Adequate floor space is essential. How the teacher sets up the environment in the space available is a critical factor in prevention of injury. Enough space should be provided for crawling, keeping separate play areas for infants/toddlers and older children. Teachers should not have barriers that impair their ability to watch all the children at the same time. These considerations need to be remembered as the early childhood education environment is planned and organized. Planning should include the arrangement of interest areas of the classroom with the interest of safety in mind (Figure 3-3).

**FIGURE 3-3**
How to set up an early childhood education environment—Do's and Don'ts.

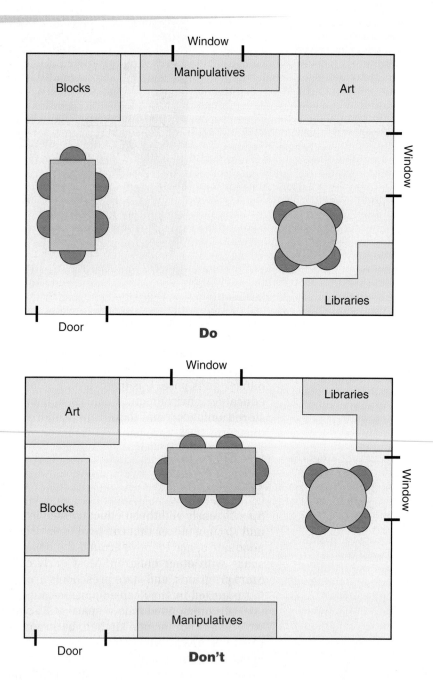

## Shared Space

Another indoor environmental hazard for early childhood education may be shared space. Some early childhood education environments are located in areas that have multiple uses. These shared spaces may carry risks that the teacher must anticipate, continually assess, and be prepared to eliminate (see Table 3-1).

Whenever spaces are shared, safety risks can occur. Multiple-use facilities need thoughtful anticipation for possible hazards, and the environment should be carefully screened before resuming early childhood education in a shared space that has been used for another purpose.

Screening a shared space may require coming to the site 15 to 30 minutes before the children arrive. Using a shared facility checklist created for the particular multiple uses helps organize and speed up this process. Table 3-2 contains a checklist for a family child care home's morning check that could also be used by a nanny on arrival at a child's home.

It was Monday morning at the church preschool. Monica, the teacher, was pleased to see that someone had filled the juice pitchers for her and had them ready in the refrigerator. The children had come to school either tired or still excited from a busy summer weekend, so Monica really appreciated the extra help.

Lorraine, the director, had a habit of taking time to sit with the children at their morning snacks on Mondays to see how they were doing and to hear about their time on the weekends. She sat down after the snacks had been handed out and the juice had been poured. Lorraine took one sip of the juice and commented to the children, "You know this juice doesn't taste quite right, let's all throw it out and get some new juice." Lorraine had a very organized reaction to drinking punch with alcohol that had been left over from a wedding at the church over the weekend.

It turns out that the people cleaning up didn't want anything to go to waste, so they saved the punch in the only containers available—the preschool pitchers. Monica should have checked to see what it was first, and fortunately Lorraine had the presence of mind to solve the problem before anyone had a chance to take more than a sip of juice.

**TABLE 3-2**
*6 A.M. Checklist*

## ✓ CHECK FOR:

**Remove:**

- ☐ All food, beverages, and dirty dishes
- ☐ Scissors, knives, or other sharp items
- ☐ Pesticides, medications, or other products that might be poisonous
- ☐ Standing water left around in buckets or other containers
- ☐ All craft supplies, game pieces, and so forth
- ☐ All breakable objects
- ☐ All matches or flammable items
- ☐ Any small toys or other objects that could cause a child to choke
- ☐ Any object that attracts a child to climb, such as a stepladder or stool

**Replace as needed:**

- ☐ Safety latches
- ☐ Safety gates by stairways
- ☐ All other safety devices
- ☐ All doors, gates, and other openings that could cause safety hazards

It is also helpful to post signs in the shared facility about hazards so that others who use the facility are aware of safety risks to the early childhood education environment (Figure 3-4). Speaking with the person in charge of the other uses helps to keep the risks at a minimum. People who are responsible for the cleaning and care of the facility should be encouraged to cooperate and watch for the possible safety hazards, to keep the children from undue risks. Parents should also be trained and utilized as environmental scanners whose extra eyes can help check for risks when they drop off their children.

---

*Pause for Reflection*

Have you ever considered that indoor space might be a safety issue? Consider the early childhood education facilities you have seen or worked in. Was care taken to make the area as safe as possible and to meet the standards discussed? Shared space is even more likely to present risk. Have you experienced a shared-space early childhood education program that had particular risks that would not have been there if the space had not been shared?

---

**FIGURE 3-4**
Sign for shared use facility.

### Please Remember
### Child Care Takes Place Here!

- Pick up all small objects.

- Put any dangerous objects out of reach.

- Check electrical outlets for safety covers.

- Lock all cabinets that contain nonchildproof objects.

*Key Concept 3.2*

### Indoor Safety Guidelines

Examining the indoor environment for safety hazards allows the teacher to provide protection for the children and may help prevent unnecessary accidents. Indoor environmental hazards include ventilation, cleaning and other supplies, and pets. Safety devices can be used to prevent risk. The environment should be screened to meet the risk in relation to the developmental levels of the children in care. Adequate space and setup for indoor early childhood education are factors that should be considered to prevent undue risk. Shared spaces pose many risks and need extra supervision to promote safety and prevent risk.

**Safety gates and latches should be routinely used.**

## 3.3 INDOOR EQUIPMENT SAFETY

Equipment used in early childhood education environments shall be sturdy and free of sharp points or corners, splinters, protruding nails or bolts, loose rusty parts, hazardous small parts, or paint that contains lead (APHA & AAP, 2002). Furniture should be durable, easy to clean, and, where appropriate, child-sized. Equipment should be placed so that children have enough freedom of movement to prevent accidents and collisions with equipment and each other. Refer to Figure 3-3 for improper equipment placement and proper placement of the same equipment.

Some infant equipment is regularly tested and must comply with certain standards (APHA & AAP, 2002). Cribs, high chairs, strollers, and safety gates fall into this category. For information regarding the specifications of the standards, the teacher can write to:

> The American Society for Testing and Materials
> 1916 Race Street
> Philadelphia, PA 19103

Cribs should be made of wood, metal, or plastic and should have non-lead-based paint. Cribs should also have

- slats that are no more than $2\frac{3}{8}$ inches apart.
- a mattress that is fitted so that no more than two fingers can be wedged between the mattress and the crib side
- a minimum height of 36 inches between the top of the mattress and the top of the crib
- secure latches, which, when the sides are dropped, shall hold the sides in the raised position. The latches should be inaccessible to the child in the crib

Never leave a large stuffed toy in a crib. Children can use such toys to climb out of the crib. Never place a crib near a window because children can fall out of windows, hurt themselves on broken glass, or get caught up in cords from window shades or curtains. Bumper pads should be securely tied to the crib. There should be a minimum of six evenly placed tie strings that prevent children from crawling into an opening and suffocating. Make sure the tie strings are less than 12 inches so that children do not strangle in them (NCCCHSRC, 2004). Make sure that blinds or curtains do not have a looped cord, as the cord could cause strangulation (CPSC, 2004).

When high chairs are used in early childhood education environments, they should have a safety strap that goes between the legs and around the waist. The legs should have a wide enough base so the high chair will not tip over. If paint is used on the high chair, it should be lead-free. Strollers should clearly display the ASTM seal of compliance with the number F833. Safety gates should display the seal with the number F406 (APHA & AAP, 2002).

If the teacher is using a changing table, it should have a lip around it that discourages a child from rolling off the changing table. The changing table should have a safety strap, and the strap should always be used. The child should never be left unattended when being changed.

## Preventing Falls

Falls are one of the most common injuries related to indoor equipment. Childhood falls account for 2.3 million emergency room visits per year (CDC, 2003). A child's changing abilities to move about and manipulate the environment are major contributors to causing safety risks with indoor equipment. A tiny baby can wiggle and move and push. An older baby can roll over, crawl, and creep. Changing tables vary greatly and can be the cause of an infant's fall if the infant is left unattended, even if the safety strap is used. Although infant walkers are tested, they are the cause of more injuries than any other infant equipment, so the AAP recommends against their use.

Toddlers can climb to get to places that were formerly inaccessible. Discouraging climbing on furniture and other equipment helps prevent risk. Falls from windows injure more than 4000 children per year (Smith & Hendricks, 2005). Using a safety device such as a window guard helps to prevent falls. These should be checked regularly to make sure they are working properly. If windows are low enough for children to reach them, a barrier should be put in front of them.

Preschoolers are coordinated enough and fast enough to do almost any physical activity. Using only safe, sturdy equipment that is in good repair also helps protect children from falls. Table 3-3 presents a list for checking indoor equipment to help prevent falls.

## Indoor Water Safety

Water safety is also a consideration in the use of indoor equipment. Under any condition, direct adult supervision is necessary any time water play is introduced into the early childhood education environment (Sutton, 2003).

**TABLE 3-3**
*Checklist to Prevent Falls in the Indoor Environment*

### ✓ CHECK FOR:

- ☐ Use infant and child equipment that is in good repair and inspected for safety.
- ☐ Use durable, balanced furniture that will not tip over easily.
- ☐ Do not allow climbing on furniture, stools, or ladders.
- ☐ Place safety gates at stairways.
- ☐ Remove all objects from stairs.
- ☐ Repair or remove frayed carpeting or other flooring.
- ☐ Install window guards on upstairs windows.
- ☐ Secure all window screens.
- ☐ Clean up spills quickly.
- ☐ Avoid highly waxed floors and stairways.
- ☐ Do not use loose throw rugs.
- ☐ Keep toys picked up as often as possible.
- ☐ Never leave a baby alone in a high place.

Drowning can occur in a relatively small amount of water, such as a bucket of standing water that someone forgot to clean up and put away. A curious infant or toddler could look into the bucket, fall in, and drown. Toilets, tubs, and sinks also pose risk for drowning. Toilet lids should always be closed. Some early childhood education environments do not have lids for toilets, in which case, the area should have a door that shuts and should be carefully monitored. Water should never be left standing in tubs or sinks.

Hot water faucets also pose risk. Hot water can cause burns by scalding. All hot water heaters should be set at 120°F (Figure 3-5). Children should never be left unattended near hot water faucets. When turning on water for children, always turn on the cold water first.

Toilets and water tables may also carry germs that put children at risk. To promote indoor water safety, the basic rules in Table 3-4 should be followed.

**FIGURE 3-5**
Hot water heaters should be set to 120°F to prevent burns.

**TABLE 3-4**
*Indoor Water Safety Guidelines*

- Any equipment that uses water, such as toilets, sinks, tubs, and buckets, should be carefully monitored and cleaned often.
- Keep hot water temperature at 120°F.
- Never leave standing water unattended.
- No child should ever be left unattended in a tub or other device used to bathe a child.
- Where toilet lids are present, keep them down, if possible.
- In a family child care home, keep the door to the bathroom closed when not in use, if very young children are present. Keep a set of jingle bells on the door so that it can be heard opening and closing.
- Keep lid on diaper pail securely fastened.
- Keep lid on water table when not in use.

Equipment that uses water, such as toilets and sinks, should be carefully monitored and cleaned often, and children and staff should be encouraged to wash hands often.

## Key Concept 3.3

### Indoor Equipment Safety

Using safe, sturdy indoor early childhood education equipment can help eliminate some risk. Safety devices, safety practices, and good supervision will help the teacher add a greater degree of protection for the children. Some indoor equipment that involves water poses risks. The risk of drowning and of burns from scalding water can be reduced through safe practices and supervision.

## 3.4 TOY SAFETY

● *Age appropriateness consideration of the developmental abilities of a particular age group in the selection of toys, materials, and equipment*

Toy-related accidents cause more than 118,000 children to be injured each year. Approximately 70 percent of deaths for children three years of age and younger are caused by toys and other children's products (CDC, 2001c). Other typical toy-related accidents involve inhaling balloons, toy chest lids falling on or pinching a child, projectile toys piercing the body, and strangulation on toys with ropes or strings. These accidents may be avoided if the toys are examined for **age appropriateness** of the children playing with them (CHA, 2003a). Art supplies may also pose risk to children and should be checked for safety and age appropriateness. Toys should also be separated by age group so that younger children are not exposed to toys that may endanger their safety. Toys should be inspected for any small parts, broken pieces, or sharp surfaces. They should also be checked for cords or strings that could cause strangulation or entanglement (Walsh, 2005). Projectile toys should be eliminated from early childhood education programs if they pose risk for eye injuries.

## Choking and Suffocation Hazards

Choking and suffocation are major hazards to very young children who still mouth things such as toys, foods, and small objects in their environment. The developmental level for that mouthing, along with new cognitive abilities to master the environment can lead children to risk their safety (Table 3-5).

Ensuring that small toys and other objects are too large for mouthing is important to prevent choking and suffocation hazards (Figure 3-6). As

**TABLE 3-5**
*Choking and Suffocation Hazards for Young Children*

### Toys

| | |
|---|---|
| Marbles | Game pieces |
| Balloons | Jacks |
| Dress-up jewelry | Toy chest with no air holes |
| Plastic bags | Toys with strings or cords long |
| Any toy less than 1½ inches in diameter | enough to encircle a child's neck |
| Game tokens | |

### Food

| | |
|---|---|
| Hot dogs | Peanuts |
| Grapes | Popcorn |
| Gum | Olives |
| Lollipops | Hard candy and cough drops |
| Carrots, celery, and other raw vegetables | |

### Small Objects

| | |
|---|---|
| Pins and safety pins | Crayons |
| Toothpicks | Nails |
| Tacks | Pencils and pens |
| Jewelry | Staples |
| Coins | Small cuplike objects such as spray can lids, measuring cups, and small bowls |

**FIGURE 3-6**
Device for measuring small parts to prevent choking. Notice that the domino gets caught in the tube, but the die passes through the tube, indicating a choking hazard.

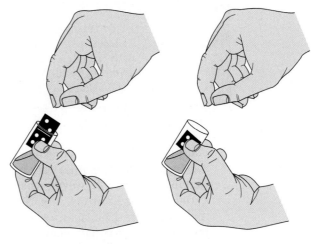

**Pass**                    **Fail**

Children in the oral stage need to be carefully watched and provided with a safe environment free of small toys and objects.

Marty had been a family child care provider for about six months. She had children in care from four months old to five years old. The older children were very active and helpful. Diana, the older four-year-old, and Holly, the five-year-old, really liked to do things that were grown-up. They especially enjoyed helping Marty. Marty appreciated their help and liked to give them little tasks to do. One of those tasks was to help her go through the child care setting looking for any safety risks. The girls often caught things that Marty might have missed because they explored the environment from a child's level.

One day Ramsey, a toddler, was chewing something. Holly went to Marty and brought her to Ramsey right away. Even though they had all searched for hazards that morning, they had missed a playing piece from a Monopoly game. The safety consciousness in this early childhood education environment helped save Ramsey from a hazard that could have caused a real problem.

consumers, we are probably more conscious of foods and small objects causing choking hazards than we are of toys. One purchases a toy and expects that toy to be safe. However, what is safe for a five-year-old may be very dangerous to a two-year-old. The CPSC has a small-parts standard that prohibits manufacturers from marketing toys with small parts to children younger than three years of age. Their toll-free telephone number is 1-800-638-2772.

## Age Appropriateness

The age group for which a toy is intended is often included on the package. However, contents of the package, including small parts, are not always listed, and safety precautions are often not included in the packaging or instructions. If a teacher fails to see the package, or if she does not understand other safety precautions that should be taken with the toy, she may put the children in care at risk for injury.

Consumer awareness of toy safety is imperative, especially in early childhood education environments where there is a population of children of mixed ages. Age appropriateness is one of the most important tools for removing hazardous toys from the environment. Table 3-6 shows age-appropriate toy suggestions.

The teacher needs to check the environment for the age appropriateness of toys, because different developmental levels affect the way children play with toys. Table 3-7 gives teachers a checklist for toy safety.

**TABLE 3-6**
*Age-Appropriate Toys*

| Age | Toys |
| --- | --- |
| Up to 6 months | Squeeze toys, colorful mobiles, large pictures of faces or simple patterns, and nonbreakable mirrors |
| 6 months to 1 year | Cradle gyms, sturdy books, drums, manipulative toys, toys that make noises, and busy boards |
| 1 year to 18 months | Stacking toys, balls, large blocks, pounding toys, push-pull toys, books, simple puzzles, and tapes with simple stories or music |
| 18 months to 3 years | Large blocks, crayons, puzzles, trucks, dolls, dramatic play toys, musical instruments, outdoor climbing equipment, sandboxes, sand toys, and water toys |
| 3 years to 6 years | Dramatic play toys, puppets, playhouses, art materials, chalkboards, tricycles, bicycles, balls, simple games, books, simple board games |

**TABLE 3-7**
*Toy Safety Checklist*

### ✓ CHECK FOR:

- ☐ Age appropriateness for the children playing with toy.
- ☐ Set safety rules for mixed-age groups to keep toys for older children out of younger children's reach, and secure a place in the care environment where the older children can use these toys.
- ☐ No toys or toy parts smaller than $1\frac{1}{2}$ inches.
- ☐ Check for sharp parts, points, rough edges, pinch points, and loose small parts.
- ☐ Check toys for durability—if it is easily broken, it is dangerous.
- ☐ Examine toys for construction, including stuffed animals that might have seams that could open easily or eyes that could be pulled off and swallowed.

*(continues)*

**TABLE 3-7 (Continued)**
*Toy Safety Checklist*

## ✓ CHECK FOR:

- ☐ Throw out all pieces of broken toys, crayons, and games.
- ☐ Regularly check pacifiers that children use, for nipples that resist pulling and for guards that cannot fit inside a child's mouth.
- ☐ Check instructions for art and craft supplies and make sure that they are nontoxic, washable, and environmentally safe.
- ☐ Check toys that are mouthed but too large to be swallowed to make sure they are washed after use.
- ☐ Check paint on toys to make sure it is lead-free.
- ☐ Toys with projective parts are not present.
- ☐ Toy chests with lids are not present.
- ☐ All toys are flame resistant.
- ☐ Mobiles and other hanging crib toys are not used after infants are able to sit up.
- ☐ Toys are cleared and put away when not in use.
- ☐ Toys with pull strings are restricted to use when an adult is present.
- ☐ Play areas are away from electrical cords and other cords, such as telephone wires.

## Art Supplies

Art supplies present some potential hazards. The hazards may be from inhaling lead or other dangerous substances or from mouthing the various materials used for art. The Federal Arts Materials Labeling Act took effect in 1990. Hazard-free art products should be labeled CP or AP. Products that may be potentially toxic should carry a health label that indicates caution or warning. Table 3-8 will help the teacher lessen risk to safety when using art supplies. If there is any question regarding art supplies, contact the manufacturer and ask for a copy of the Material Safety Data Sheet. This will give information about ingredients and toxicity.

Common household products are often used to make art materials. Examples of these are play dough, cornstarch clay, and goop. If these items are used in the early childhood education environment, children should be instructed in how to use them. Children should not mouth these materials, and toddlers should be well monitored when these materials are used.

Other products such as beans and seeds may be dangerous to children. Kidney beans, apple seeds, morning glory and four-o'clock flower seeds are toxic (Sutton & Slattery 2004). It is also important to choose a well-ventilated area for indoor art and craft projects. Fumes from certain safe art supplies can build up. Cleaning up as you go in art projects is a good safety measure to avoid needless injuries such as a fall caused by spilled paint.

## Other Factors

Recent reports indicate that children can suffocate other than from choking (CHA, 2003b). A condition called "cupping" can occur when the child puts a small cuplike object over the mouth and nose. When the child's breathing creates a vacuum, the object attaches tightly enough to cause suffocation. Another issue that has caused concern about children's toy safety is the use of polyvinyl chloride (PVC) in toys that children may mouth. There can be chemicals called phthalates that are toxic in PVC. Although most toy manufacturers are removing this from teething toys, it may still be present in other toys. For a list of toy products that are unsafe, go to http://www.toysafety.net/.

**TABLE 3-8**
*Keeping Art Safe*

- Avoid using any art supplies, such as tempera paint and clay, that are dry and could be easily inhaled.

- Avoid using any materials that contain lead or other hazardous substances that can cause poisoning if ingested.

- Use poster paints, liquid paints, and water-based paints that are nontoxic.

- Do not use rubber cement, epoxy, or instant glue. Use glue sticks, double-sided tape, paste, or school glue. These should have the AP or CP label. Use only water-based glues, glue sticks, and paste.

- Do not use permanent markers. Use only washable markers, and avoid using scented markers that tempt children to put them in their mouths.

- Avoid using empty film canisters for art projects, as the lids can be mouthed and have the potential hazard for choking.

- When using small items such as beans, rice, or small Styrofoam shapes for projects, always keep special watch, because children may mouth their art materials and might choke on them. It is better to use these items only with older children.

- Avoid the use of glitter, which is metallic and can cause eye damage if it gets into the eye.

 *Key Concept 3.4*

## Toy Safety

The teacher needs to supply toys and other play materials that are safe and as risk-free as possible. Toys should be examined for hazards. By using such tools as the choking hazard checklist and the toy safety checklist, the teacher can eliminate those toys that may present risk. Knowledge of age-appropriate toys will help the teacher select toys that are safe for the care environment. If the environment is mixed age, supervision and safety practices should be used to make certain younger children are not playing with toys that may present risk to them. Art materials may pose risk. The teacher should be aware of these risks and do whatever is necessary to minimize them.

## 3.5 INTERPERSONAL SAFETY

Injuries to children by other children such as biting, kicking, scratching, and fighting are common in early childhood education settings. Teachers need to be prepared to intervene when behaviors that threaten interpersonal safety occur. They need to understand the background for such behavior and know strategies for eliminating that behavior and utilizing conflict resolution. The NAEYC's position statement on violence reflects this.

Of all these behaviors, biting is the most upsetting. It is also common for children younger than three years of age. There are a number of reasons why children bite. Among these are using their mouths to explore, not having language to express themselves, teething, and attention getting. Many teachers ask parents if the child has had a biting problem before entering care. If so, they can be alert. It is important that quick, proper action be taken when biting occurs, because it is disturbing to the child who is bitten and may be dangerous (Oku, 2002; Biting, bullies and other bad behavior, 2005) (Table 3-9).

### *Exposure to Violence*

Violence as a means of handling conflict has filtered down into early childhood. Children are seeing violent behavior modeled on television, on the streets, in their neighborhoods, and even in their homes (Levin, 2003). This is especially true when war and terrorism are being talked about and shown on television. When children or angry, tired, or upset they may resort to behaviors that reflect their exposure to violence in our society. They may also act out their need to feel strong and powerful as they have seen portrayed in the media. There are a number of toys today that are

These children may be playing cooperatively in this manner, but if they are not, this type of behavior could reflect the beginnings of bullying.

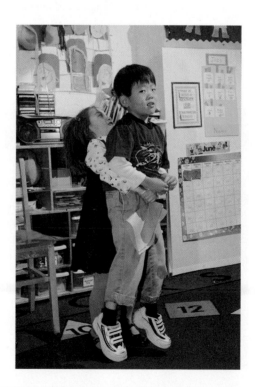

**TABLE 3-9**
*Biting in Child Care*

Develop a policy for biting and inform parents on entry of the child into care. Try to create an atmosphere that reinforces positive behaviors to avoid biting in the first place.

**If biting does occur, find out:**

- When (under what conditions) did it happen?
- Who was involved?
- Why did the child bite? (Is there a pattern?)
  - —Teething
  - —Exploring
  - —Inability to express frustration or anger verbally
  - —Overstimulation
  - —Jealousy
  - —Insecurity
  - —Recent changes in child's life
  - —Asserting independence

**Immediately after biting occurs:**

- Intervene
- Never bite the child back
- Talk to child who bit
  - —Tell the child that biting is not okay
  - —Explain that food is for biting, not friends
  - —Encourage the child to help the child she bit
- Talk to the child who was bitten and give her reassurance
  - —Encourage the child to tell the biter that "that hurt me"
- Give immediate first aid (see Chapter 5)

**Follow-up**

- Alert the staff
- Fill out injury report
- Tell parents of both children what happened
- If it is not the first incident, sit down with the parents of the biter and work out a plan for changing the behavior
- Examine the early childhood education environment for any actions, behaviors, or conditions that might be modified to lessen risk

linked to violent media (Levin, 2003b). Action figures, guns, and video games can depict or recall violent stories or violent behavior.

Interpersonal behaviors that threaten safety include biting, fighting, kicking, hitting, stealing, screaming, spitting, hard pushing, and threatening violence. These behaviors show aggression that may indicate a child has personal problems that may have to be addressed if the behavior continues.

Research has shown that children who have witnessed or been direct victims of violence can suffer from posttraumatic stress disorder. This disorder can be displayed by reliving the violence in play (Groves et al., 2000). Children who display especially violent behavior may need special help, including psychological referrals. A conscientious teacher can often handle violent behavior by observation, communication, and redirection (Poole, 2004).

The amount of violence shown on television is increasing. It can be harmful to children and may cause children who watch it to be more aggressive with other children (Thornburg, 2002). The use of guns has escalated even among young children. Real firearms, not just toy guns, are a threat to many young children in their neighborhoods and their homes. Thirty-four percent of U.S. children, or 22 million children, live in homes with at least one firearm (Rand Corporation, 2001).

## Strategies to Promote Positive Interaction

Teacher awareness of unsafe behavior is the primary tool for safety promotion and prevention of injury in interpersonal relations among the children. Children learn best when appropriate behavior is modeled for them.

Strategies that the teacher can use to promote positive social interaction and conflict resolution are listed in Table 3-10. The use of these strategies will be helpful to ensure a greater degree of interpersonal safety in the early childhood education environment.

**TABLE 3-10**
*Strategies for Promoting Interpersonal Safety*

- Help children recognize the difference between appropriate and inappropriate behaviors.
- Help children recognize that violence and antisocial behavior cause problems.
- Provide limits and consistent behavior.
- Acknowledge needs, fears, and wants of children.
- Realize negative behavior may indicate unmet needs of a child.
- Verbally redirect children's behavior.
- Model a full range of emotions in acceptable ways.
- Allow, identify, and react to a child's expression of emotion.
- Label expressions of emotions so that children learn to identify those emotions.
- Use play, role playing, conversation, books, and pictures to explore and help the child express a range of feelings.
- Do not allow the use of toy guns.
- Avoid storing firearms in the early childhood education environment, if possible. If present, the guns must be locked up and ammunition stored in a separate location.
- Support and encourage cooperation among the children during play.
- "Catch them being good" by acknowledging positive behaviors.
- Encourage those behaviors that promote conflict resolution.

Kevin lived in a neighborhood where he saw much violence. His early childhood education center was in an inner city area. Jacob, Kevin's primary teacher, noticed that Kevin seemed to become more and more aggressive in his play. One day Jacob decided to track Kevin's behavior. He counted four physical confrontations with friends, two biting incidents, and several threats. Jacob did not know what might have occurred to change Kevin's usually good behavior. Jacob spoke to Kevin's mother, Mona, and found that Kevin's older brother had been beaten up and Kevin had witnessed it. Jacob decided to try several things to help Kevin deal with his emotions.

First, Jacob talked to Kevin about his brother and what had occurred. He explained to Kevin how violence did not solve problems and that talking out feelings was better than acting on them. Jacob knew that this was not always easy. He decided to bring in a punching bag and placed it in a corner of the early childhood education center so that using it would not put children at risk.

Jacob showed Kevin how to use the bag and he instructed Kevin to come and use it whenever angry feelings started to grow. Kevin began using it the next day. In fact, he spent a lot of time punching the bag. After a week or so, Kevin's behavior was noticeably improved, as was the interpersonal safety of the other children. Jacob noticed an interesting result in helping Kevin. Without discussing it, many of the children began using the punching bag when they were angry.

# REALITY CHECK

## Kids and Guns

Kids and guns cause a serious safety issue for this country. Approximately 1.2 million children older than six years of age have access to guns in their homes. One in every three households contains a gun (Rand Corporation, 2001). Forty-four million Americans own a total of 192 million guns. More than 60 percent of these guns do not have trigger locks. In 13 percent of homes with children and guns, the guns are either unlocked and loaded or unlocked and stored with ammunition available. Approximately one-third of the guns owned are handguns (Eller, 1998). In the United States, 10 children die every day from gunshot wounds (CDF, 2002). In 1998, more children died from gunshot wounds than from a combination of HIV-AIDS, cancer, asthma, influenza, and pneumonia.

The majority of families that own guns feel their guns are hidden and stored safely. A study showed otherwise. As many as 80 percent of children whose families had guns knew where those guns were by the time they were in the first or second grade (NSKC, 2001). Even more revealing was a study whose subjects were 8- to 12-year-old boys. Findings showed that even though 90 percent of these boys had had gun safety training, when they found a handgun in a safe environment, all of them picked up the gun and played with it, and many pulled the trigger (Jackman et al., 2001).

(continues)

# REALITY CHECK (Continued)

Children are witnessing violence in increasing numbers on the streets, in their homes, and on television. Even very young children who see a violent act are deeply affected by it (ACT, 2001). Because children's minds develop rapidly in these early years, behavior learned in these years can affect development and adult personality (Palmer, 2000). Witnessing violence may threaten a child's basic sense of trust in people. Some children who witness violence may turn their feelings outward toward others (Groves et al., 2000).

Often the witnessing of violence occurs while viewing television. By the time a child completes elementary school, he has witnessed some 8000 murders on television. Commercial television for children is 50 to 60 times more violent than adult prime-time television (Osofsky, 1999). Children may learn that handling violence with aggression is acceptable. Violence and the use of firearms are often treated humorously in cartoons. Some cartoons average 80 violent acts per hour.

Children need a sense of trust and safety so they can grow and develop to their potential. Children are witnessing the fact that they may not be safe or protected in many of their life situations.

> Children need to feel that they can direct part of their existence, but children who live with violence learn that they have little say in what happens to them. Beginning with the restrictions on autonomy when they are toddlers, this sense of helplessness continues as they reach school age. (Wallach, 1994)

As they grow up, many children exposed to violence may begin to carry guns in order to feel safe and protected.

Children's curiosity about guns and how they work is encouraged by the violence they see on television. In the nightly news they can view terrorism and war (Levin, 2003b). They are also tempted by manufacturers of children's toys. Guns are everywhere. They are in poor neighborhoods as well as middle-class schools. The events at Columbine and other schools reinforce this fact. Many children are at risk for safety because of guns.

The teacher can do several things to protect children from guns. The best thing would be to have no guns in the environment, so that no children are at risk (AAP, 2000b). However, some family child care homes and some early childhood education centers in high-risk neighborhoods may have guns. The teacher can ensure that any firearm present is kept out of sight, locked away, separate from the ammunition (Health and Human Services Administration, 2004). Teachers can provide children with alternative forms of handling disagreements in a prosocial manner by teaching them to resolve their conflicts (Levin, 2003a). Teachers can insist on a peaceable classroom, with no toy guns and no pretending other toys such as Legos or blocks are guns. Teachers can also provide a sense of community in their early childhood education environment so that children learn that contributing toward peace in a community is a valuable thing (Levin, 2003b). Teachers can also educate parents about the dangers of guns and that no child is immune from playing with a firearm if it is around. If television is available in the early childhood education environment, programs may be monitored and violent programs should be turned off. Teachers should also model appropriate behaviors in how they handle conflict, anger, and stress (Poole, 2004).

**CHECK**_point:_ Under what situations might guns be available in an early childhood education program? What could a teacher do to educate a child about how to prevent violence in the home and community?

### Interpersonal Safety

The early childhood education environment may have situations involving behaviors that put interpersonal safety of those present at risk. Biting, kicking, and other aggressive behaviors can pose threats to other children and the teacher. The effect that television and other media have on how children behave in relation to violence needs to be addressed. Some types of early childhood education environments may have guns present that would pose great risk if children were to gain access to them. It is very important that the teacher use all of the strategies for positive social interaction to resolve conflict and protect the interpersonal safety of those present in the early childhood education environment.

## 3.6  POISON CONTROL

The most common emergency involving children is accidental poisoning. Ninety percent of poisonings occur in the home, and of these more than one-half involve children younger than six years of age (CDC, 2001b). Children younger than two years old are especially at risk. Family child care and nanny care operate out of a home environment, so they are more likely to

Knowledge of poisonous substances could prevent a dangerous situation here. Apple seeds can be poisonous, so this innocent-looking art project could actually put children at risk.

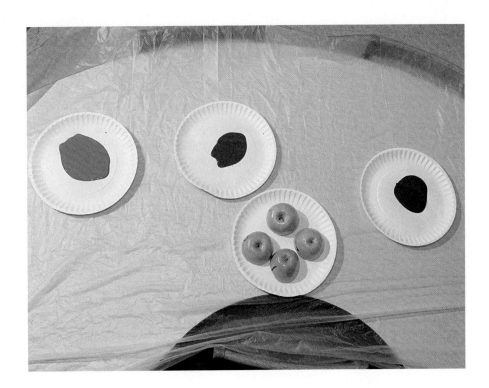

be at risk than center-based care. Regardless of the type of early childhood education environment, the teacher must employ prevention as the primary means of poison control.

The first order of prevention is vigilance in monitoring the children in care. This is effective only if the environment has been modified for safety. Removing all hazards and risks for exposure to poisons provides a protected environment.

## Examining the Environment

Poisoning occurs from many common items found in a household or early childhood education environment. Cleaners, medicines, laundry supplies, cosmetics, plants, pesticides, garden supplies, automobile fluids, and certain foods can poison a child who ingests them. The teacher should make a room-by-room inspection for poisons in the early childhood education environment. If the care is performed in a home, special care should be taken to inspect the entire environment. Bathrooms, bedrooms, kitchens, and garages are full of poisonous substances that may go unnoticed in daily life, if children are not present. Table 3-11 gives the teacher a list of common substances that are poisonous to children and are found in the home. For more information contact the American Association of Poison Control at 1-800-222-1222 or visit their Web site at http://www.aapcc.org/findyour.htm.

> ## Pause for Reflection
>
> Use Table 3-11 to think about what poisons might be in your own home environment. In your mind's eye, go through your home by room as the table indicates. What items did you think of? Were there more than were on the table? What could you do to make your own home safer from poisons?

## Strategies for Removal of Risk from Poisons and Toxins in the Early Childhood Education Environment

The teacher who anticipates, modifies the environment, and monitors children carefully should be able to avoid risk due to poisoning. Poisonings can occur in five ways.

1. ingestion
2. contact
3. inhalation
4. animal, insect, or reptile bites
5. injection

*Ingestion* is swallowing the poison. Children are attracted to bright, colorful packages, pills, and odd shapes. They often encounter containers that have been used for food or drink that now contain poisonous substances.

*Contact* occurs when poisonous substances or plants come in contact with the skin. This type of poisoning is indirect; the poison is absorbed through the skin into the bloodstream.

**TABLE 3-11**
*Common Hazardous Substances Found in the Home*

### Bathrooms

| | |
|---|---|
| Prescription drugs | Antacids |
| Over-the-counter medicines, creams, and lotions | Hair care products |
| Peroxide, alcohol, mercurochrome, and other medications for injuries | Makeup and skin care products |
| | Nail products such as polish and polish remover |
| Vitamins, iron pills, and other dietary supplements | Hair removal products |
| Cleaning solutions | Electric blow dryers, curling irons, and radios |

### Bedroom

| | |
|---|---|
| Birth control pills, foams, and so forth | Hair care products |
| Body lotions products | Makeup and skin care |

### Kitchen

| | |
|---|---|
| All-purpose cleaning products | Alcoholic beverages |
| Detergents | Bleach |
| Polishes for silver, brass, chrome, and so forth | Oven cleaning products |
| Baking sprays and oils | Waxes and other appliance care products |
| Insecticides | Floor care products |
| Kidney beans, apple seeds | |

### Garage

| | |
|---|---|
| Gasoline | Laundry products |
| Motor oil, lubricants, and other engine care products | Solvents |
| | Paint and paint removal products |
| Waxes, detergents, and other car care products | Glue |
| Insecticides and pesticides | |

*Inhalation* occurs when children breathe fumes from pesticides, certain types of art materials, or dust that may contain lead. The exchange of air in the lungs allows the poison to come in direct contact with the lungs, after which it enters the bloodstream.

*Animal and insect bites* can cause allergies in children. Some allergic reactions are very toxic and can lead to death. Certain insect bites can cause health and safety risks. These include the bites of ticks, which can transmit Lyme disease or Rocky Mountain spotted fever. Reptiles such as rattlesnakes and copperhead snakes can bite children and cause the poison to enter the bloodstream. Other diseases such as cat scratch fever, rabies,

Some common indoor plants such as the philodendron are poisonous. To protect the children in their care, teachers need to know which plants are poisonous and keep them out of the children's reach. (Courtesy of Interior Plantscape division of ACLA).

and salmonella can come from bites or other types of direct contact with animals.

*Injection* occurs when there is a puncture wound. The danger may come from the substance that was injected or remnants of tetanus on the item that caused the puncture. Today there is an extra threat of children finding needles that have been used to inject drugs. An accident like this can cause the child to be exposed to HIV.

Table 3-12 includes teacher strategies for promoting poison control protection in the early childhood education environment.

## Plants that Pose Risk

Plants are another poisonous hazard found in the indoor environment. The teacher should be familiar with the types of plants that may be present. All plants should be out of reach of children. Any plants that are potentially hazardous to children should be removed from the early childhood education environment. Table 3-13 lists indoor plants that pose risk for poisoning. In the past it was recommended that syrup of ipecac be given to a child who swallowed poisonous material. That policy changed in 2003, and the American Academy of Pediatrics is no longer recommending that syrup of ipecac be used at all (Sutton, 2004).

**TABLE 3-12**
*Strategies for Promoting Poison Control*

- Always supervise children in care.
- Keep poisons out of sight and reach of children and in a locked cabinet.
- Keep medicines, household cleaners, and laundry products in their original containers. Never store nonfood items in food containers.
- Use childproof safety caps.
- Use safety latches or locks on all storage cupboards.
- Never call medicine candy, and do not take medicine in front of children—they love to imitate.
- Inspect the early childhood education environment location from a child's eye view—on your hands and knees—to check the environment for poison risks.
- Determine that all the plants in your environment are nonpoisonous.
- Keep pets in a regulated environment.
- Keep the environment free of insects.
- Teach poison prevention to the children and to the teachers who are in the early childhood education facility.
- Keep the local poison control center number on your phone.
- Keep parents informed about poison control.
- When prevention fails, learn to act immediately in an educated manner.

**TABLE 3-13**
*Common Indoor Plants that Pose Risk for Poisoning*

| Plant | Reaction |
|---|---|
| Philodendron Schefflera Pothos | Burning and irritation of the lining of the mouth, tongue, and lips. Can be fatal. May also cause skin reaction. |
| Diffenbachia Elephant ear | Intense burning and irritation of the lining of the mouth and tongue. If tongue swells, it may cause blockage to air passage and result in death. |
| Hyacinth Narcissus Daffodil | These bulbs are often found indoors in late winter and early spring. Nausea, diarrhea, and vomiting. Can be fatal. |
| Castor bean Rosary pea | Fatal. A single pea or bean is enough to kill a child. |
| Poinsettia | Nausea, skin reactions |

### Key Concept 3.6

#### Poison Control

Poison control is an essential task of the teacher. The environment should be examined for poisons. Safety risks from poisons in the early childhood education environment can be reduced through removal, proper storage, supervision, and using as few poisonous products as possible. Good safety practices and supervision help prevent accidents involving poisoning. Plants in the environment should be nonpoisonous and should be kept away from children.

## 3.7 FIRE AND BURN PREVENTION

Children are very susceptible to fires and burns because they are so curious and do not yet recognize dangers. Injuries from these accidents are the third leading cause of death among American children (CDC, 2001a). Thirty-five percent of all burn injuries happen to children; scalding is the chief cause of burns to children of preschool age. Fires caused by playing with matches and lighters are the number one cause of fire-related deaths among young children (Figure 3-7). The concept of cause and effect is not operational enough to help children protect themselves unless they are repeatedly taught fire and burn prevention and safety.

### Environmental Hazards

The teacher must be aware of all the things in the early childhood education environment that can present hazards and fire and burn risks. Table 3-14 gives an overview of typical environmental hazards that may be present.

In second-degree burns, such as shown here, the outer and inner skin layers are burned and usually blister. If nerve endings are exposed to air or are affected by swelling, the injury can be very painful.

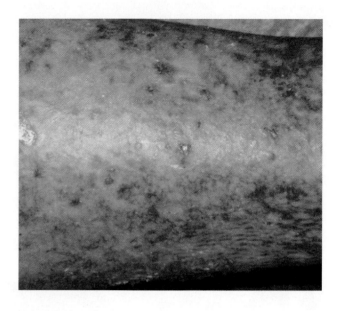

**FIGURE 3-7**
First-, second-, and third-degree burns.

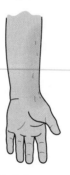 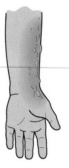 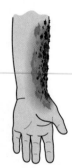

First degree, superficial

Second degree, partial thickness

Third degree, full thickness

## Strategies for Fire and Burn Prevention

It is up to the teacher to help the children be aware of hazards that can cause fires or burns. Children should regularly be taught to avoid matches and lighters. These items should be stored out of sight and not used unless necessary. Children should also have regular practice drills for fire evacuation. They should be familiar with "Stop, Drop, Roll," "Go Tell a Grown-up," and "Crawl Low under Smoke" (Cole et al., 2004). Safety devices such as fire extinguishers and smoke alarms should be present and in working condition. As with any safety hazard, the teacher is ultimately responsible for keeping children safe. One of the best things one can do is to lower the hot water heater to 120 degrees or less so that there is no chance for scald burns in the sink. Modeling preventive behaviors will reinforce fire and burn accident prevention. Table 3-15 gives the teacher some strategies that will help prevent fires and burns in the early childhood education environment.

**TABLE 3-14**
*Environmental Hazards for Burns*

**Scalding**
- Boiling liquids or food on or off stove
- Steam
- Hot coffee or cocoa
- Hot bath water or water out of tap hotter than 120°F

**Electrical**
- Sticking a foreign object into an electrical outlet
- Touching a live wire
- Water contact with an electrical appliance

**Contact**
- Hot pan on stove
- Touching fire in fireplace
- Candles or candle wax
- Cigarettes, cigars, or pipes
- Matches, lighters
- Flammable clothing or sleeping materials

**Chemical**
- Strong household chemicals
- Automobile chemicals
- Lawn and garden chemicals

**TABLE 3-15**
*Strategies for Fire and Burn Prevention*

- Use only correct size fuses in the fuse box.
- Install and regularly check smoke detectors. Change batteries frequently.
- Teach children to "Stop, Drop, Roll, Cool, and Call." Be sure to include keeping their faces covered with their hands during the Roll portion.
- Keep a fire extinguisher on hand, know how to use it, and refill it immediately after use.
- Place and maintain barriers around fireplaces, heaters, radiators, and hot pipes.
- Try not to use matches or lighters around children. If matches are present, store them out of sight in a locked cabinet or drawer.
- Teach children to bring you any matches they find. If they find a lighter, have them immediately tell you so that you can pick it up.
- Use safety devices to cover electrical outlets.
- Inspect and clean heating systems, including stoves and fireplaces, once a year.
- Make sure there are sufficient outlets for all appliances to prevent overloading electrical wiring.

*(continues)*

**TABLE 3-15 (Continued)**
*Strategies for Fire and Burn Prevention*

- Place smoke alarms around the child care environment and check the batteries on a regular basis.
- Keep extension cords exposed; do not run them under furniture or rugs.
- Keep all flammable liquids stored in safety cans and out of reach of children.
- Keep furnaces, heating equipment, and chimneys and flues cleaned regularly.
- Never allow children in food preparation area without supervision.
- Do not drink or carry anything hot when close to a child.
- Test hot food before giving it to a child.
- Never warm a bottle in the microwave.
- Set water heaters to no higher than 120°F
- Never bathe a child in water you have not tested.
- Never leave children unattended in the bath or near a faucet. They might turn on the hot water.
- Turn pot handles in toward center or rear of stove and only cook on rear burners when possible.
- Never use portable, open-flame, or space heaters.
- Never smoke around children.
- Never store flammable liquids such as gasoline near the child care environment.

## Key Concept 3.7

### Fire and Burn Prevention

The teacher should actively practice fire and burn prevention. Burn hazards to children come from many areas. Children can be burned from scalding hazards, electrical hazards, hazards that are directly contacted with heat or fire, and chemical hazards. The teacher needs to use all strategies available to protect the children in early childhood education environments from any hazards that might cause fires or burns.

## 3.8 IMPLICATIONS FOR TEACHERS

The teacher should use observation, supervision, and education to provide a safe indoor environment. These risk management tools provide preventive and protective measures for the early childhood education environment.

Table 3-16 shows a safety policy for the teacher to prevent choking and suffocation. This measure uses all of the risk management tools previously mentioned.

**TABLE 3-16**
*Preventing Choking and Suffocation in Early Childhood Education*

- Remove loose parts from toys.
- Use a choke testing device on small toys. Always do this before adding a questionable toy to the environment.
- Keep diaper and other pins, toothpicks, and nails out of your mouth.
- Do not wear dangle-type jewelry such as necklaces and earrings.
- Check toys, games, and art supplies for broken pieces and throw them away.
- Teach children not to run with anything in their mouths.
- Teach children to chew well, and so not allow playing when eating.
- Never prop a baby bottle.
- Never use Styrofoam cups—children like to chew them.
- Regularly hand out consumer toy alerts as you find them. Newspapers and magazines carry this information, particularly around Christmas.

## Observation

Observation for accessories, behaviors, and conditions offers the teacher the awareness needed to prevent risk in the indoor environment. Knowledge of hazards in equipment, toys and craft supplies, and poisons helps the teacher remove these items and reduce risk. Observation adds another layer of protection. The teacher needs to also be aware of unsafe interpersonal behavior practices. This may help the teacher to stop or redirect action before it causes injury. The early childhood education environment should also be inspected for fire and burn hazards. Children should be carefully observed to avoid burns or fires.

## Supervision

The greatest concern for supervision is the constant monitoring of children for safety in all situations. In addition, all safe practices, methods of prevention, and means of promotion should be monitored by the teacher (Aronson, 2001). This will ensure that every measure possible is being used to provide a safe environment. Careful observation for anticipation, monitoring, and modifying is necessary at all times. Never let conversation or anything else distract from the safety of children in care. Checking for compliance with licensing standards, local fire safety guidelines, and other safety-related ordinances is another way to monitor the environment for safety. Communication is a tool that the teacher can use to make sure safe practices are being used by all adults in the early childhood education environment.

## Education

Prevention of safety risks is promoted through education of teachers, children, and their parents. The more tools everyone has for becoming aware of hazards, developmental limitations, and the early childhood education environment, the greater the opportunities that are available to prevent accidents and injuries.

Children can be taught many safe behaviors through a number of methods and curriculum. Visitors such as firefighters and police officers can show children how to keep safe. Teachers can be role models of safe behaviors every day. They can read books and provide videotapes that will help children become aware of the need for safe practices. Teachers can conduct regular drills for fire and other safety threats. They can practice "Stop, Drop, Roll, Cool, and Call" with children on a regular basis. Teachers can talk with children about appropriate and inappropriate interpersonal behaviors.

## For Families

Teachers can provide families with information about safety by handing out information sheets or handouts supplied by agencies such as fire departments, poison control centers, and police departments. They can request parents and children to practice fire drills at home on a regular basis. Teachers can also provide indoor information on a bulletin board, in a newsletter, or by having workshops on safety for families. They can point out safety measures that are being used and help families to understand the importance of safety.

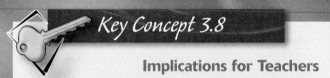

### Key Concept 3.8

#### Implications for Teachers

The teacher should use all measures possible to protect the children and prevent injury. Tools such as observation, supervision, education, and working with families can provide practices for the teacher to ensure safety through promotion, prevention, and protection.

## CHAPTER SUMMARY

There are a number of threats to indoor safety, including indoor equipment, toys, interpersonal behaviors, poisons, and fires and burns. Safety policies are necessary for the teacher to monitor and protect the environment. An understanding of the developmental levels of the children present is essential. The teacher should use checklists to monitor and modify the early childhood education environment. All items, including cleaning supplies, pets, plants, and art supplies, should be examined for safety and removed if they present risk. Through the use of observation, supervision, education, and working with families, teachers can promote and practice safe behaviors in the early childhood education environment.

## TO GO BEYOND

In this section you will find a number of activities that you can use to apply and improve your knowledge of this chapter. There are also thorough online resources that accompany this text that can be found at http://www.early childed.delmar.com. (See description at end of this chapter).

### Chapter Review Critical Thinking Applications

1. Compare and contrast the safety policies for the indoor environment found in an early childhood education center and a family child care home. How are these policies affected by the ages of children?

2. Discuss the need for safe, risk-free toys.

3. Relate how age appropriateness affects toy selection for early childhood education. What are some of the potential risks if inappropriate toys are selected?

4. Discuss the importance of conflict resolution for interpersonal safety in the early childhood education environment.

### As an Individual

1. Visit an early childhood education center and survey it for indoor safety. Write down the risks observed and bring it back to class to share. Compare your list with what others observed.

2. Take the list of indoor plants found in this chapter to a local nursery or flower shop and identify poisonous indoor plants that you find there. Have you seen any of these plants in a household that has children in it? Share your results in a discussion in class.

3. Search the World Wide Web for two sites that directly relate to kids and guns. Write a synopsis of the sites. Share these sites with your classmates in class.

### As a Group

1. List the developmental-level risks for an 18-month-old toddler in an indoor environment at an early childhood education center, then a family child care home. Compare and contrast the two lists.

2. In groups of four or five students, design an early childhood education room for two-year-olds that includes all the amenities, while being at low risk.

3. In groups of four or five students, have the group choose among the following topics and design a safety policy.

   - fire safety
   - play dough
   - art projects
   - interpersonal safety
   - poison control
   - indoor water safety

4. As a class, discuss sudden infant death syndrome. List the major risk factors. Design a safety policy that would work for early childhood education environment from this list.

5. Visit a fire station and have the firefighters give the class the same demonstrations they would give to preschoolers. Assess the presentation for developmental appropriateness. Have students discuss what they learned from this demonstration.

## Case Studies

1. Travis is a gregarious, feisty three-and-a-half year old who has been at the early childhood education center for about six weeks. He has two much older brothers, one of whom may be in a gang. Mallory, his teacher, has been concerned about Travis' behavior. He seems to have a number of disagreements with his classmates, and now he has started biting other children. What actions should Mallory take? What supportive measures could she offer to Travis, while still protecting the other children in her care? How should she approach Travis' mother about this problem?

2. Marnie has worked as a nanny for the Wilson family for ten months. The Wilson's have two children Josh, age six years, and Jocelyn, age fourteen months. They have a two-story house, and it took Marnie several weeks of begging to get them to install a safety gate for the stairs. Her concern now is the kitchen and the bathroom, where there are hazardous substances within Jocelyn's reach. The Wilsons' answer to her plea to remove these items was, "Josh lived through this stage and never bothered a thing." They don't seem inclined to reduce the risk factors. What should Marnie do?

3. Madelyn is a family child care provider who has generally specialized in infant care. She has decided to continue with the three infants for whom she now cares as they grow older. One of them is approaching twelve months, and Madelyn feels that she needs to safety-proof her home to allow for the change in developmental levels of the children she is caring for. You are a friend who provides early childhood education for a multi-age group of children. What advice would you give her to inspect her environment, to anticipate actions and behaviors, and to monitor and modify her child care environment for safety risks to toddlers?

## Chapter References

Adults and Children Together (ACT). (2001). *Violence prevention for teachers of young children.* Retrieved May 15, 2002, from http://www.actagainstviolence.org/class.html.

American Academy of Pediatrics (AAP). (2000a). Changing concepts of sudden infant death syndrome: Implications for infant sleeping environment and sleep position. *Pediatrics, 105*(3), 650–656.

American Academy of Pediatrics (AAP). (2000b). Firearm-related injuries affecting the pediatric population. *Pediatrics, 105*(4), 888–895.

American Academy of Pediatrics (AAP). (2003a). Indoor active play equipment need safe surfacing too. *Early Childhood Health Link, 14*(4), 6.

American Academy of Pediatrics (AAP). (2003b). Teach kids how to be safe around dogs. *Early Childhood Health Link, 14*(4), 5.

American Academy of Pediatrics (AAP). (2005). The changing concept of sudden infant death syndrome: Diagnostic coding shifts, controversies regarding sleeping environment, and new variables to consider in reducing risk. Policy statement, Task Force on Sudden Infant Death Syndrome. *Pediatrics, (116),* 1245–1255.

American Public Health Association & American Academy of Pediatrics (APHA & AAP). (2002). *Caring for our children: National health and safety performance standards: Guidelines for out-of-home care.* Washington, DC: American Public Health Association.

Anderson, H., & Cook, D. (1998). Review: Maternal smoking associated with an increase risk for SIDS. *Evidence-Based Medicine.* Retrieved May 15, 2002, from http://www.acponline.org/journals/ebm/julaug98/maternal.htm.

Arnestad, M., Andersen, M., Vege, A., & Rognum, T. (2001). Changes in the epidemiological pattern of sudden infant death syndrome in southeast Norway, 1984–1998: Implications for future prevention and research. *Archives of Disease in Childhood, 85,* 108–115.

Aronson, S. (2001). Reducing the risk of injury in child care. *Child Care Information Exchange, 101*(3), 64–66.

Aronson, S. (2003). Sudden Infant Death Syndrome—SIDS. *ChildCareExchange.com.* Retrieved October 15, 2005, from http://www.ccie.com/resources/view_article.php?article_id=5015367

Biting, bullies and other bad behavior at preschool. (2005, January 3). Retrieved October 11, 2005, from http://www.parenting.org/archive/precious/education/2001-02/Sep02_bad_behavior.asp

Carpenter, R., Ingens, I. & Blair, P. (2004). Sudden unexplained infant death in 20 regions in Europe case control study. *Lancet, (363),* 185–191.

Centers for Disease Control (CDC). (1999). *Childhood injury fact sheet.* Atlanta, GA: Author. Retrieved May 15, 2002, from http://www.cdc.gov/ncipc/factsheets/childh.htm.

Centers for Disease Control (CDC). (2001a). *Fire safety.* Atlanta, GA: Author. Retrieved May 15, 2002, from http://www.cdc.gov/safeusa/fire/firesafe.htm.

Centers for Disease Control (CDC). (2001b). *Poisonings Factsheet.* Atlanta, GA: Author. Retrieved October 11, 2005, from http://www.cdc.gov/ncipc/factsheets/poisoning.htm.

Child Health Alert (CHA) (2003a). Selecting appropriate toys for children. *Child Health Alert, (21),* 1064.

Child Health Alert (CHA) (2003b). And suffocation from unexpected products. *Child Health Alert (21),* 1065.

Children's Defense Fund Reports. (1994). Violence: Every two hours a gun kills a child. Washington, DC: Children's Defense Fund.

Children's Defense Fund. (2002). *Violence touches the lives of too many children.* Washington, DC: Author.

Cole, R., Crandall, R., & Kourofsky, C. (2004). We CAN teach young children fire safety. *Young Children, 59*(2), 14–18.

Colino, S. (2003). Are these 7 dangers hiding in your home? ER doctors and other health experts reveal the things—from irons to exercise equipment—that put children in serious danger. *Redbook, 200*(3), 184–185.

Consumer Product Safety Commission (CPSC) (2004). *Be sure your childcare setting is as safe as it can be.* Washington, DC: Author.

DiFranza, J., & Lew, R. (1995). Effect of maternal cigarette smoking on pregnancy complications and sudden infant deaths. *Journal of Family Practice, 40*(4), 385–394.

Eller, D. (1998, August). It's shocking how many people you know own a gun and how easy it is for kids to get their hands on one. *Parents Magazine,* 62–65.

French, L. (1999). Children and pets in childcare. *Healthy Child Care, 2*(5). Retrieved October 11, 2005, from http://www.healthchild.net/articles/sf11pets.html.

Groves, B., Lieberman, A., Osofsky, J., & Fenichel, E. (2000, April/May). Protecting young children in violent environments: A framework to build on. *Zero to Three, 5,* 9–13.

Health and Human Services Agency (HHSA) (2004). *Family child care.* Publication 72. Sacramento: State of California. Department of Social Services.

Hood, A. & Smith, C. (2005). Safe toy play for toddlers. *Healthy Child Care, 8(1).* Retrieved October 11, 2005, from http://www.healthychild.net/articles/sf43toys.html

Jackman, G., Farah, M., Kellerman, A., & Simon, H. (2001). Seeing is believing: What do boys do when they find a real gun? *Pediatrics, 107*(6), 1247–1250.

Kemp, J., Unger, B., Wilkins, D., Psara, R., Ledbetter, T., Graham, M., Case, M., & Thach, B. (2000). Unsafe sleep practices and an analysis of bedsharing among infants dying suddenly and unexpectedly: Results of a four-year, population based, death-scene investigation study of sudden infant death syndrome and related deaths. *Pediatrics, 106*(3), 41.

Levin, D. (2003a). *Teaching young children in violent times: Building a peaceable classroom.* (2nd edition). Cambridge, MA: Educators for Social Responsibility.

Levin, D. (2003b). Beyond war and superhero play: Meeting children's needs in violent times. *Young Children, 58*(3), 60–65.

MacDorman, M., Cnattingius, S., Hoffman, H., Kramer, M., & Haglund, B. (1997). Sudden infant death syndrome and smoking in the United States and Sweden. *American Journal of Epidemiology, 146,* 249–257.

Malloy, M., & Freeman, D. (2000). Birth weight- and gestational age-specific Sudden Infant Death Syndrome mortality: United States, 1999 versus 1995. *Pediatrics, 105*(6), 1227–1231.

Moon, R. & Oden, R. (2003). Back to sleep: Can we influence child care providers? *Pediatrics, 112*(4), 878–882.

Moon, R., Weese-Mayer, D., & Silvestri, J. (2003). Nighttime child care: Inadequate Sudden Infant Death Syndrome risk factor knowledge, practice and policies. *Pediatrics, 111*(4), 795–799.

National Institutes of Health (NIH) (2003, February 28). *Higher SIDS risk found in infants placed in unaccustomed sleeping position.* National Institute of Child Health and Human Development [Press Release]. Retrieved October 11, 2005, online: http://www.nichd.nih.gov/new/release/infant_sids_risk.cfm

National Safe Kids Campaign (NSKC). (2001). *Why kids are at risk.* Retrieved May 15, 2002, from www.safekids.org.

National SIDS/Infant Death Resource Center (NSDRC) (2004). *What is SIDS?* [Brochure.] Washington, D.C. Health Resources and Services Administration.

North Carolina Child Care Health and Safety Resource Center (NCCCHSRC) (2005). Humpty Dumpty safe on a wall. *North Carolina Child Care Health and Safety Bulletin, 7*(2), 1.

Oku, C. (2002). Biting in the childcare setting. *Healthy Child Care, 5*(1). Retrieved October 11, 2005, from http://www.healthychild.net/articles/sf25biting.html

Osofsky, J. (1999). The impact of violence on children. *The Future of Children, 9*(3), 33–49.

Palmer, D. (2000). Violence prevention: What childcare providers can-must!-do about it. *Healthy Child Care, 3*(6). Retrieved May 15, 2002, from http://www.healthchild. net/Articles.

Palmer, D. (2003). Zoonoses: Diseases from Animals. *Healthy Child Care, 6*(2). Retrieved October 11, 2005, from http://www.healthychild.net/articles/sh32200noses.html

Poole. C. (2004, January/February). How children learn through conflicts. *Scholastic Early Childhood Today,* 29–31.

Rand Corporation (2001, March). Guns in the family: Firearm storage patterns in U.S. Homes with Children. Retrieved October 11, 2005, from http://www.rand.org/publications/RB/RB4535/

Rosenblum, G. (1993, November). Is your house making your children sick? *Sesame Street Parents,* 68–72.

Shepard, S. (2002). How safe are your child care programs? *School Planning and Management, 41*(11), 6–9.

SIDS Network. (1996). *Reducing the risks for SIDS: Some steps parents can take.* Retrieved October 11, 2005, from http://sids-network.org/risk.htm

Smith, C. & Hendricks, C. (2005). Window wonders. *Healthy Child Care, 8*(3). Retrieved October 11, 2005, from http://www.healthychild.net/articles/sf45windows.html

States seek ways to stop infant SIDS deaths. (2003, October). *State Legislatures Magazine, 29*(9). Retrieved October 10, 2005, from http://www.ncsl.org/programs/health/sidsfr.htm

Stratton, K., Almario, D., Wizeman, T. & McCormick, M. (Eds.) (2003). *Immunization safety review: Vaccinations and sudden unexpected death in infancy.* Washington, DC: The National Academies Press.

Stubbs-Wynn, Karjicek, M., Hamilton, B., Collins, S., & Torrey, V. (2004). SIDS risk-reduction language in state childcare regulations as of July 2002: Lessons learned. *Journal for Specialists in Pediatric Nursing, 9*(1), 32–36.

Sutton, A. (2003). Water play safety. *Healthy Child Care, 6*(5). Retrieved October 11, 2005, from http://www.healthychild.net/articles/sf35water.html

Sutton, A. (2004). Ipecac policy change. *Healthy Child Care, 7*(3). Retrieved October 11, 2005, from http://www.healthychild.net/articles/sf39ipecac.html

Sutton, A. & Slattery, A. (2004). Arts and crafts the safe way. *Healthy Child Care, 7*(6). Retrieved October 11, 2005, from http://www.healthychild.net/articles/sfartscrafts.html

Tappin, D., Ecob, P., & Brooke, H. (2005). Bed sharing, room sharing and sudden infant death syndrome in Scotland. A case-controlled study. *Journal of Pediatrics, (147),* 32–37.

Thornburg, L. (2002). Exporting TV violence—What do we owe the world's children. *Young Children, 59*(2), 6–7.

Wallach, D. (1994). *Violence and young children's development.* ERIC Digest. Champaign, IL: Eric Clearinghouse on Elementary and Early Childhood Education.

Walsh, E. (2005). Toy safety for young children. *Child Care Health Connections, 18*(1), 3.

Wisborg, K., Kesmodel, U., Henriksen, T., Olsen, S., & Secher, N. (2000). A prospective study of prenatal smoking and SIDS. *Archives of Diseases in Childhood, 83,* 203–206.

Zamani, R. (1999). *Pets in the child care setting.* California Child Care Health Program. Health and Safety Notes. Retrieved May 15, 2002, from http://www.childcare health.org.

Zavitkovsky, A., & Thompson, D. (2000). Preventing injuries to children: Interventions that really work. *Child Care Information Exchange, 100*(1), 54–56.

Additional resources for this chapter can be found by visiting the Online Companion™ at www.earlychilded.delmar.com. This supplemental material includes extensive chapter quizzes, PowerPoint® outlines, Web links, and various other activities to help better utilize the material in this chapter. The site is updated regularly, so you may check back often to receive the latest information about the subjects in each chapter.

# Outdoor Safety

**After reading this chapter, you should be able to:**

**4.1 Safety Policies for the Outdoor Early Childhood Education Environment**

Describe and discuss safety policies for outdoor environments as tools for risk prevention, safety protection, and safety promotion.

**4.2 Examining Early Childhood Education Environments for Outdoor Hazards**

Indicate and discuss specific guidelines for making the early childhood education playground environment free from risk and protected for safety.

**4.3 Playground Equipment Safety**

Relate and discuss the safety hazards of outdoor equipment as they relate to early childhood education situations and general safety.

**4.4 Traffic and Transportation Safety**

Relate the guidelines for safe transportation and traffic involved in early childhood education environments.

**4.5 Water Safety**

Describe and discuss the water safety hazards in outdoor early childhood education.

**4.6 Implications for Teachers**

Indicate the need for education, observation, cultural competency, working with families, and supervision to maintain a safe outdoor environment.

## 4.1  SAFETY POLICIES FOR THE OUTDOOR EARLY CHILDHOOD EDUCATION ENVIRONMENT

Unintentional accidents and risks to safety are more likely to occur in the outdoor environment than indoors. Some risks may be similar, such as drowning, falling, choking, and poisons. Other hazards, such as automobiles and bicycles, are responsible for a large number of childhood injuries and deaths each year. The following factors indicate a need for outdoor safety policies:

- Falls from playground equipment are the leading cause of injury in early childhood education environments. Head injuries cause most of the disabilities and fall-related deaths (North Carolina Child Care Health and Safety Resource Center [NCCCHSRC], 2005).
- Playgrounds should provide both play value and safety for health development (Frost, 1994).
- Approximately 3 million thefts and violent crimes occur near public schools each year (Levin, 2003). Many early childhood education centers and family child care homes are close to schools and therefore are at risk for safety.

Behavior in the form of lack of attention is one of the reasons children may be at risk in outdoor situations. The child looks contemplative, but there may be another child ready to come down the slide, and she might not realize it and could be hurt.

- Motor vehicles cause most accidental deaths of children. More than 70 percent of the fatalities could be prevented with the use of a safety seat restraint (National Safe Kids Campaign [NSKC], 2004a).
- Almost 300,000 children each year are treated in an emergency room for bicycle-related injuries (NSKC, 2004b).

Safety policies for the outdoor environment need to cover a wide range of areas. Not all of the policies in this chapter will apply to all early chidhood education environments. Vulnerability to safety involves a number of risks. These risks may come from playground equipment, travel, traffic, bicycles, bodies of water, and the nearby neighborhood. Some of the hazards are related to accessories such as improper equipment or lack of proper cushioning under equipment. Behaviors such as lack of attention or a child trying a physical act he is not capable of performing may present risks. Conditions such as the child being tired or the teacher talking to another adult can cause risk.

Policies should cover monitoring accessories, conditions, and behaviors. They should comply with local licensing regulations and suggestions for accreditation, if applicable. Planning and promoting safe practices should be based on children's physical and developmental abilities as well as their emotional needs. Safety policies should include the following:

1. *Outdoor Early Childhood Education Environments:* understanding outdoor safety practices for the early childhood education environment and applications for risk management as they apply to the type of outdoor environment

2. *Playground Equipment Safety:* practices for preventing injuries and managing safety on playground equipment

3. *Travel and Traffic Safety:* practices for preventing injury, promoting safety, and strategies for developing guidelines for travel and traffic as it applies to early childhood education environments

4. *Water Safety:* practices for removing hazards, promoting safety, and preventing injury as it applies to water in the early childhood education environment

5. *Implications for Teachers:* methods and practices for conducting education, supervision, and observation and working with families for safety in the outdoor environment

## Key Concept 4.1

### Outdoor Safety Policies

The outdoor environment offers a large degree of risk for early childhood education environments. Outdoor safety policies should begin with examining the care environment. Policies should be created for playground equipment, traffic and travel safety, water safety, and implications for the teachers.

## 4.2 EXAMINING EARLY CHILDHOOD EDUCATION ENVIRONMENTS FOR OUTDOOR HAZARDS

Outdoor environments may vary greatly from one early childhood education environment to the next, but they all have common features that contribute to outdoor childhood accidents. These relate to

- falls
- motor vehicle and other transportation accidents
- poisons
- equipment

The environmental screening for safety should address the ABCs of injury risk (refer back to Table 2-4). The teacher must anticipate problems, modify the environment, and monitor the children in care for unsafe practices. The teacher must also be aware of conditions and behaviors that lead to injury in the outdoor environment.

### Outdoor Environmental Hazards

The early childhood education outdoor environment should be free of hazards. Protective measures and preventive practices can help reduce the risk that accessories may provide in the outdoor environment. General environment hazards include lack of barriers, poisons, insects, and extremes of temperature. Other considerations may also present risk in the outdoor environment.

*Barriers.* The play area should have a fence or other barrier that surrounds it and is at least four feet high. A fence should separate the play area from all automobile traffic and any hidden corners of the outdoor area that may go unobserved if a child wanders into that corner. Fences should be constructed of safe materials and kept intact and in working order. Gates should fasten securely and should have latches high enough to be out of the reach of children or should have a safety latch that is childproof.

*Poison Control.* Poison control in the outdoor environment is essential. Toxic plants are the most common hazard for poison in the outdoors. Table 4-1 has a comprehensive listing of toxic outdoor plants.

Other poison hazards include pesticides, insecticides, other gardening materials, and barbecue supplies. If these are in the environment, they should be placed up high and in a locked cabinet (NSKC, 2004c). If a garage or workshop is present on the site where automobile repair fluids and gasoline are present, this area should be off limits and fenced off or have a locked door as a barrier to this area.

Keep the outdoor area as free from pollutants as possible. Use insect sprays sparingly and only when children are not present. If lawns are sprayed with weed killers or fertilizers, wait several days before allowing children to play on them (Fournier, 2004). Also, keep the environment free of poison ivy, poison oak, and sumac, which can cause rashes that may spread on contact. Remove these plants from the environment but do not burn them, because the fumes can damage the lining of a child's lung.

**TABLE 4-1**
*Common Outdoor Poisonous Plants*

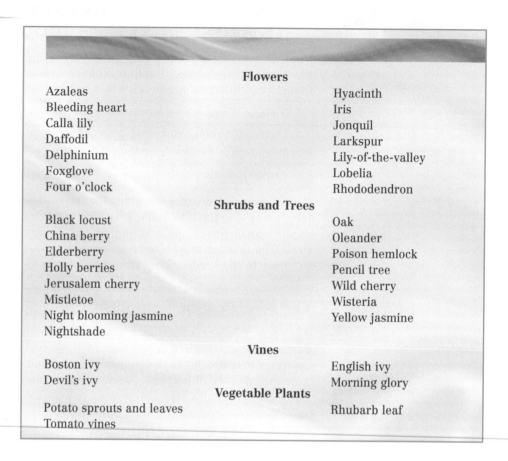

### Flowers

| | |
|---|---|
| Azaleas | Hyacinth |
| Bleeding heart | Iris |
| Calla lily | Jonquil |
| Daffodil | Larkspur |
| Delphinium | Lily-of-the-valley |
| Foxglove | Lobelia |
| Four o'clock | Rhododendron |

### Shrubs and Trees

| | |
|---|---|
| Black locust | Oak |
| China berry | Oleander |
| Elderberry | Poison hemlock |
| Holly berries | Pencil tree |
| Jerusalem cherry | Wild cherry |
| Mistletoe | Wisteria |
| Night blooming jasmine | Yellow jasmine |
| Nightshade | |

### Vines

| | |
|---|---|
| Boston ivy | English ivy |
| Devil's ivy | Morning glory |

### Vegetable Plants

| | |
|---|---|
| Potato sprouts and leaves | Rhubarb leaf |
| Tomato vines | |

*Insects.* Insect safety is important (American Academy of Pediatrics [AAP], 2004a). Although bites and stings do not normally cause serious harm to a child, some children may be especially sensitive. If the teacher knows that a child is sensitive to bee stings, he or she should be prepared to deal with this situation. (See Chapter 5.) The outdoor environment should be inspected and rid of insect infestation and anthills. The U.S. Environmental Protection Agency suggests that places where children gather such as early childhood education environments, should rely less on spraying for insects and more on what is referred to as insect pest management or IPM (Fournier, 2004). This method has the teacher doing a thorough investigation of the outdoor area of the early childhood education environment and managing it for pest control. For example, standing water is especially critical for keeping down the population of mosquitoes that can carry the West Nile virus (AAP, 2002). Checking for standing water includes flower pots, buckets, old tires, water tables, and bird baths (Palmer, 2004). Those things that hold water, such as the bird baths and water tables, should be changed frequently to avoid giving mosquitoes the opportunity to breed. Another consideration is to inspect buildings for structural gaps where wasps could gather.

To keep children as protected as possible from stings and bites, there are several things the teacher can do:

- Do not use scented soaps or lotions.
- Make sure children wear shoes and socks.

Outdoor areas should have a good source of shade to prevent risk from the sun.

- Teach children what wasp's and bee's nests look like.
- Have children wear light-colored, long-sleeved clothing.
- Reduce outdoor activities in the early morning and late afternoon hours, when pests are more likely to gather, especially in spring and summer.

Some recommend the use of DEET, which is effective against mosquitoes. However, there are several drawbacks. These products should not be used with children younger than three years of age, and, if used with children, they should contain no more than 30 percent DEET or they can be harmful to children (AAP, 2002). Palmer (2004) recommends using a DEET product that has a concentration of 10 percent, which he says is effective. The AAP recommends that DEET should be applied to the clothing rather than skin (Colino, 2003). Regardless, before a teacher would ever apply insect repellent with DEET in any way, the parents should give permission.

Some areas of the country have problems with ticks that can transmit Lyme disease. In these areas, children should be dressed in high socks, and their clothing should be checked for ticks before they come indoors. In fact, it is recommended that children wear light colors and long sleeves for greatest protection (Bush, 2003, Focus on Health, 2004). Another recommendation is to avoid sitting on the ground. Remind parents to check children during bath time. If pets are in the early childhood education environment, inspect them daily and remove any ticks that are found.

*Temperature.* Extremes of temperature are potential hazards for children. Protection from heat stroke or heat exhaustion is a major consideration for outdoor play areas. Shade should be present in the outdoor area. Try to schedule your outdoor activities before 11 A.M. and after 3 P.M., because these are the hours when sun exposure is the most damaging or the heat is at its hottest (Norris Cotton Cancer Center [NCCC] 2002). If it is not naturally available, provide a shade structure. Children need the relief from the sun and heat to prevent overheating. All facilities should also have a safe outdoor source of drinking water to protect children from overheating or becoming dehydrated. It is a good idea to make sure children drink water before they go outside and drink some water every 20 minutes while they are outdoors to keep well hydrated (Colina, 2003). For more information see *Reality Check: Sun Safety.*

Freezing temperatures and snow on outdoor equipment may result in slippery surfaces that cause children to fall more easily. Before going outdoors in these conditions, check equipment surfaces to make sure they are safe and not slippery. Children should be dressed warmly when playing outdoors in the cold. Ask parents to not dress their children with bulky clothing and instead to layer lighter clothing on cold days. This allows warm air to be trapped and keeps the child from getting chilled sooner (Koontz, 2003).

*Other Considerations.* Other safety considerations for the outdoor area include keeping bushes and trees trimmed so that children do not run into branches and injure themselves. Trimming trees also discourages or prevents climbing. If there is dirt in the environment, make sure it is not so fine that it will cause breathing problems for some children. Always check the outdoor environment after storms, high winds, and heavy rains.

Sand in a sandbox is another outdoor safety issue. The best type of sand to use is play sand or "natural sand" that has been sterilized and that is specifically made for use by children. It does not contain any harmful materials such as asbestos that is found in some other types of sand. Sand in an outdoor area should be replaced every two years (Sutton, 2003). When playing in sand, children should always be well supervised to make sure they are not eating or throwing sand. Make sure to follow the same steps for sand toys as for indoor toy safety. Plastic toys are best; wooden or metal toys should be avoided because they can splinter or rust with time.

Some family child care backyards or shared facilities may have barbecues present. This implies potential for harm from lighter fluid, barbecue utensils, and the barbecue itself. Other common hazards in these two environments are gardening tools and equipment. All of these hazards should be kept in a garage, barn, or out of the reach of children.

Items such as toxic fumes, gases, and air conditioner units should not be present in the outdoor environment. Early childhood education environments should not be less than 30 feet from high-voltage power stations, railroad tracks, or electrical substations. The facility should be maintained in a safe condition by removing any sharp rocks, building supplies, or dilapidated structures. The outdoor area should be free of unprotected ditches, cesspools, wells, and utility equipment (APHA & AAP, 2002). Abandoned appliances should not be present in the early childhood education environment.

Limit children going barefoot to areas where the surfaces are safe. Confine pets to certain areas during child care and remove animal feces often. Treat the feces as you would disposing of a diaper (see Chapter 12) as in Table 10-6 on page 387.

# REALITY CHECK

## Sun Safety

Skin cancer from sun exposure begins in early childhood. Scientists believe that two things can predispose a person to skin cancer: (1) a lifetime exposure and (2) severe sunburns (NCCC, 2002). It may only take one severe sunburn as a child to cause melanoma in adulthood. Because children do play so much outdoors, and the outdoor environment in early childhood education is so important to children's development, it is critical that children be kept sun safe (Mathe, 2005).

Protecting children from the hazards of the sun on hot and sunny days is very important. It is recommended that the teacher access the climate prediction center and find out the degree of ultraviolet exposure for that day (http://www.cpc.ncep.noaa.gov/ U.S. Environmental Protection Agency [EPA], 2001). On days where the ultraviolet exposure is highest, plan activities that keep you out of the sun.

Other suggestions to help keep ultraviolet exposure for children at a minimum include:

- Keep infants out of direct sunlight (AAP, 1999).
- Avoid exposure of children to the sun between the hours of 10 A.M. and 4 P.M., if possible (Mathe, 2005).
- If that is not possible, make sure children play in a shady area, such as under a tree, a permanent shade structure, or a cloth canopy. Teach children how to seek out these areas for themselves (US EPA, 2001).
- Make sure children wear protective clothing if going out into the sun, such as hats and long-sleeved shirts, pants, and socks. Teachers should model this behavior (Buller & Farina, 1999). Explain to parents that on hot sunny days, dressing children in lightweight clothing that will cover their body offers more protection.
- When taking children out into the sun, use a sunscreen of SPF 15 or higher for children over the age of 6 months, 30 minutes before going outside (Mathe, 2005). Staff should also do this. The AAP has recommended that, if there is no shade for infants under 6 months, a sunscreen could be used (AAP, 1999). You may want to ask parents to provide the sunscreen for their child or children. Some states require a physician's statement allowing the use of application of sunscreen. Be sure to check on the requirements for child care facilities in your state.
- Plan field trips for sunny days where shade is available (Buller & Farina, 1999).
- Educate parents and children about sun safety.

**CHECK**point: Why is it important to keep children sun safe? What do you do on a regular basis to keep yourself protected from the harmful rays of the sun? How could you be a better role model for children?

## Developmental Level

The impact that behavior has on risk for safety is especially crucial in an outdoor environment. The majority of accidents happen outdoors. Children's developmental behaviors such as lack of fear, curiosity, inattention, and going beyond physical capabilities can easily put them at risk for injury. Teachers may not be paying adequate attention or may not properly communicate the risk of certain outdoor hazards.

Using developmental levels to define the boundaries of the outdoor environment will help the teacher screen for accessories, behaviors, and conditions that lead to injuries. Prevention is the key to risk management. Planning and evaluating the environment based on the vulnerabilities of the children in care will help increase protection. Developmental levels of the children in care should be used as the starting point for screening the outdoor environment for hazards. Table 4-2 indicates the relationship of outdoor safety hazards to the

**TABLE 4-2**
*Outdoor Safety Hazards by Developmental Levels of Age*

| Age | Hazards | Prevention Tips |
|---|---|---|
| 0–6 months | Motor vehicle | Infant should always be in rear-facing infant safety seat in backseat. |
| 6 months–1 year | Motor vehicle | Continue using safety seat; switch to toddler seat when able to sit up by self; keep child in backseat. |
| | Poisons | Watch child for mouthing of objects. Check area for poisonous plants. |
| | Choking | Watch child for mouthing of objects. |
| | Drowning | Keep pool covered, fenced, and lock gate. |
| 1–2 years | Motor vehicle | Continue using safety seat; keep child in backseat. |
| | Falls | Carefully watch while climbing on outdoor equipment. Teach child safe play practices. |
| | Equipment | Check playground equipment for rough edges, rust, loose parts. Wood chips or soft sand are best ground coverings under play equipment. |
| | Poisons | Place all outdoor chemicals, and so forth, in high place, preferably locked. Check area for poisonous plants. |

**TABLE 4-2 (Continued)**
*Outdoor Safety Hazards by Developmental Levels of Age*

| Age | Hazards | Prevention Tips |
|-----|---------|-----------------|
| | Drowning | Cover, fence, and lock gate to pool. Always supervise child when playing near pool or any body of water. |
| 2–3 years | Motor vehicle | Keep child away from streets and driveways using supervision, fences, and firm discipline. Role model pedestrian behavior such as crossing street. Role model wearing seat belt; use safety seat for child; keep child in backseat. |
| | Falls | Carefully supervise when on equipment. Reinforce safe behavior on equipment. |
| | Poisons | Keep poisons up high and locked. Check for poisonous plants. |
| | Drowning | Always supervise when near any body of water. Begin to teach water safety, including role modeling. Cover, fence, and lock gate to pool. |
| | Equipment | Check equipment for hazards. Supervise and role model safety. |
| 3 years and up | Motor vehicle | Use safety seat or seat belt; keep child in backseat. Teach pedestrian and traffic safety rules. Role model this behavior. |
| | Equipment | Reinforce safe play habits. Supervise when using tools. Check equipment for hazards. |
| | Drowning | Children should have swimming lessons if they are in care near a body of water. Teach water safety. |
| | Violence | Teach children neighborhood safety, including safe houses and familiarity with law enforcement. |

developmental levels by age. This chart also indicates the greatest threats to safety at particular ages.

When the teacher realizes the hazards that make children at risk by age level, it will be much easier to carry out safe practices, appraise risks, and avoid potentially dangerous situations.

As the teacher inspects the outdoor environment, age appropriateness should be kept in mind. If there are children of different ages and they play

Children should always be carefully observed in the outdoor environment. Many times, children are overconfident about their abilities and can get in situations like this that present a safety risk.

at the same time, the teacher will need to provide low barriers that prevent infants and toddlers from using equipment intended for older children. These barriers provide the teacher more time to watch the children for safety and less time for worry.

*Infants and Toddlers.* The outdoor play area for infants and toddlers should consist of flexible materials that offer no hazards due to the common "mouthing" of children of this age. The emphasis for this age group is sensory motor activity, so the outdoor equipment for this age group should reflect that need. These children will be exploring and mastering their environment, so it is imperative that there be a safe place for them to investigate.

*Preschool.* As the teacher looks at the environment with preschool children in mind, the task is to see if whether space has been provided for the children to be as active as this age group is likely to be. Are there areas for exercise play, construction play, and dramatic play, as well as solitary play? Are the climbers and swings at appropriate heights, or are they too high or too low? Does this inappropriate height level provide risk? The APHA & AAP standard for children six years old and younger is that no structure shall be more than $5\frac{1}{2}$ feet tall. When structures are taller than that, research indicates that injuries are more serious. Do the climbers, swings, and slides have appropriate cushioning materials under them? Are these structures free of loose or rusty parts? A complete checklist for these pieces of equipment is found in Table 4-3 later in this chapter. The teacher should ensure that the children have been given guidelines for the use of swings, slides, and climbing equipment and should remind them on a constant basis of proper use.

*School Age.* Children of this age have good coordination and are physically capable of most activities. The teacher should provide equipment that will offer children the ability to use their skills. Is there enough equipment available so that children do not become bored and find inappropriate activities to engage in that may pose risks? Does the equipment provide options for degree of difficulty for children of different ability levels? For example, does the climbing structure provide different heights, a number of exits, and areas that challenge skills yet do not threaten the safety of a child with less physical abilities? Managing risks by age appropriateness minimizes the risk and provides greater protection.

## Space

Early childhood education facilities vary greatly. Each facility's outdoor area is unique and presents conditions that may be unsafe or lead to risk. Adequate outdoor space is important to prevent crowding of children and equipment. Space must also be provided to allow safety zones around large equipment so there is no encroachment by other equipment or potential for collision with other children playing in the area. The rule of thumb is a clearance of 9 feet around stationary equipment and 15 feet around equipment with moving parts, such as swings.

The outdoor play area should provide 50 square feet of space for each child. If equipment areas are figured in, this generally translates to about 75 square feet per child (APHA & AAP, 2002). If this is not possible in the early childhood education environment but there is a large indoor activity area such as a gym available, then that area can be used for some outdoor types of activities and space is less likely to be a risk factor.

The total outdoor play area may not be utilized by all the children at once, so the total area need not reflect space for all children present. The general standard in that situation is that there should be enough space for one-third of the children in care to play at any one time and that the outdoor scheduling should accommodate all children over a period of time without space being an issue. If the entire play area is utilized at the same time then space becomes a more critical issue.

This playground provides children with a safe environment: children are visible to the teacher at all times, swings are not in a walking area, and the entire playground is fenced to keep strangers out while protecting children from wandering.

The outdoor space should be arranged so that all play areas are visible to the teacher at all times. This allows for prevention of injury and abuse and gives children a more secure feeling. Bathrooms should be close enough to the outdoor play area so that the teacher can keep an eye on the children in the outdoor area and the child who is using the toilet facilities.

## Shared Space

A shared space facility can present a distinctive set of dangers that need to be managed for risk. The outdoor environment of these facilities may not meet early childhood education safety standards. Close inspection and constant observation are vital to the children in care under these situations.

Using a list similar to Table 3-2, the outdoor environment should be inspected every morning before it is used. Remove all debris, trash, and anything else that may have been discarded in the play area. Inspect the area for animal droppings.

For public multiuse facilities in inner-city areas, particular caution should be taken to inspect for sharp objects such as broken glass, razors, and needles from syringes. Also inspect the area for discarded condoms, clothing, and so on, that may pose risk for infectious diseases.

In cases where the facility includes a swimming pool or other body of water, particular care should be taken to make sure that all safety devices are in place, including shutting the gate to this area of the facility before children are allowed outside to play.

When the multiuse facility is a family home in the evenings and on the weekends, the provider should routinely inspect the outside for hazards that might remain after normal family use. For example, if there are pets, a check for animal feces should be a regular morning event, or if someone barbecued the night before, a check for matches and lighter fluid might be necessary.

## Time of Day

Many outdoor accidents can occur at any time of day. Poisoning, choking, drowning, and burns occur because of the potential hazards in the environment. Many accidents and injuries occur because children cannot understand cause and effect. This may relate to developmental level.

Maureen and Sara were two teachers at an inner-city early childhood education center. One Monday morning they decided to take the children to the park next door. Several of the children were excited and really wanted to get on the slide, the swings, and the climbing structure. The children had seen their teachers go through an inspection process before, but they rarely found any hazards. Several of the children voiced displeasure about the inspection, but Maureen and Sara insisted that the children wait. On this morning they were very surprised to find razor blades placed on the slide. The teachers showed the children this hazard and explained what might have happened. The children never complained about the safety inspection again.

Some accidents seem to occur at particular times of day, when children are tired or hungry and are not concentrating on what they are doing. The teacher should be aware of the times in the early childhood education environment when a child appears to be tired or indicates that she is hungry. For example, more active play injuries occur in summer and fall during midmorning and midafternoon (Aronson, 2001). Monitoring can help prevent risk. The teacher can modify the environment by changing the schedule to avoid the outdoor environment at the times of day that seem to pose a higher risk.

## The Neighborhood

The neighborhood contributes to the early childhood education environment. It may offer conditions that support the care of the children, or it may offer risks to them. The teacher needs to be aware of the neighborhood and plan for safety accordingly.

A supportive environment is one that has little traffic, has no noise pollution, and poses little risk for the safety of children. It may be a neighborhood where people know and support each other and the safety of the area. There may be community resources such as a park or recreation center that pose no risk for violence or injury.

Many neighborhoods do not offer an environment that supports safety (Shonkoff et al., 2000). A number of risks may come from the neighborhood where the early childhood education environment is situated. There may be traffic, people who do not belong coming in and out of the area, and noise pollution. There may be community resources that are not safe areas for children. It is up to the teacher to determine what the risks are in the neighborhood. Once these risks are determined, the teacher should do everything possible to minimize the risk to the children in care.

**FIGURE 4-1**
Continuum of Violence in Children's Lives. Reprinted with permission from *Teaching Young Children in Violent Times: Building a Peaceable Classroom,* by Diane E. Levin © 1994. Published by Educators for Social Responsibility. (For more information, call 800-370-2515.)

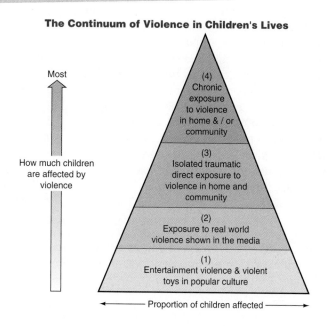

# REALITY CHECK

## *Neighborhood Violence*

Someone is raped, murdered, assaulted, or robbed every 16 seconds in the United States (Moyers, 1995). Children are often victims of violence and may react by being instruments for violent behaviors themselves (Osofsky, 1999). Many children are finding that the world is no longer a safe place. It is dangerous and people use violence to hurt other people (Groves, 2003). Poor neighborhoods, where violence may be a way of life, can have severe impacts on a child's and family's well-being (Shonkoff et al., 2000). Exposure to neighborhood violence is particularly common in low-income inner-city areas. In New Orleans, it was found that 90 percent of elementary children surveyed had witnessed violence in their community and 40 percent of those children had seen a dead body. It is estimated that 10–20 percent of homicides in Los Angeles are witnessed by children (Groves, 2001).

Exposure to neighborhood violence can put children at risk for safety as well as for good mental health. Neighborhood violence can have indirect effects on development, if mothers feel they need to restrict their children's ability to interact with their environment (Shonkoff & Phillips, 2000; Benson, 2004). Even very young children may remember and have been known to play out traumatic events they witnessed as infants. Some children may be exposed to so much violence that they become desensitized to it (Linares, 2001). Children may lose perspective on what is right and what is wrong. When neighborhood violence is the norm, children may be at risk for performing violent crimes themselves, later in life (Groves et al., 2000; Groves, 2003).

Violence is becoming a standard in our society (see Figure 3-1). Although known to permeate neighborhoods in the inner cities, it has reached the suburbs and rural areas as well. Neighborhood violence is severely affecting the children in this country (CDC, 2000b). More children than ever before are reported to have posttraumatic stress disorder (Groves et al., 2000). Many of the victims and perpetrators of violence may be the parents of young children (Osofsky, 1999). If children perceive a threat from the people around them, they are less likely to interact with them (Haberman, 1994).

Children's ability to cope with violence and the resulting trauma may depend on several factors: (1) age, (2) developmental stage, (3) the availability of resources to help them, and (4) the ability of the children to use those resources (Groves et al., 2000).

Teachers can offer children a safe haven from neighborhood violence (Osofsky, 1999). They can monitor their neighborhood environment for safety on a constant basis. They can access resources such as police and public help to offer children a greater degree of protection. Teachers can encourage children to become less violent and more gentle (Haberman, 1994; Levin, 2003). A good teacher can help children recognize and acknowledge their feelings (Meltz, 2004). When children become angry, teachers can show them appropriate ways to express their anger (Massey, 1998). Teachers can offer children a person they can trust and relate to (Gaensbauer, 2004; Zenah, 2005). For a part of every day, neighborhood violence can be eliminated from children's lives.

**CHECK***point:* How could you as a teacher create a more peaceable community in your early childhood education environment? What might your early childhood education program do to encourage a more peaceable community in the neighborhood or the surrounding locality?

## Key Concept 4.2

### Examining the Outdoor Environment for Safety

The outdoor environment should be examined for safety on a regular basis. Hazards that pose risk may be items such as lack of barriers, poisons, insects, temperature, and others. Developmental behaviors and mixed-age play may pose risk. Lack of space or space not properly organized can pose risk through collisions and falls. Shared space allows certain conditions such as debris or trash that may cause danger to children. The neighborhood may pose risk for outdoor safety and should be carefully monitored.

## 4.3 PLAYGROUND EQUIPMENT SAFETY

Playground equipment is a major source of childhood accidents. Falls are responsible for 70 percent of playground injuries (Scott, 2004). The greatest number of these injuries are the result of falls to the ground, onto other children, or onto other equipment. Thirteen percent of injuries to young children on playgrounds occur during early childhood education programs (Tinsworth & McDonald, 2001). Recent trends have all but removed swings from public playgrounds, because they have been the source of the greatest number of falls.

### SAFE Playgrounds

The National Program for Playground Safety (NPPS) has surveyed a number of playgrounds and has identified four components for a "SAFE" playground.

**Supervision,** the first component, begins with the design of the playground so that all areas of safety are considered. Play areas should be divided into zones that reflect the type of activity that is involved in order to promote safety and reduce accidents (Olsen et al., 2004). These areas might include a playground zone, a gross motor zone, a quiet play zone, and a sand area zone. There might also be an area for riding, such as a blacktop zone. These areas should be free of visual barriers.

**Appropriate** developmental design is the next component. It has been found that playgrounds that are designed for age appropriateness reduce the number of playground accidents (NPPS, 2001). Playground equipment for two- to five-year-olds should be designed closer to the ground. Playgrounds for children of this age could include the following:

- Low platforms with a few access points
- Crawl areas
- Ramps with pieces for grasping
- Low tables for water, sand, and manipulation
- Tricycle paths
- Sand area with covers
- Shorter slides

- Play areas to play alone or with other children
- If swings are included, they should be low to the ground

**Falls** are the third component to consider. The major consideration for falls is the surfaces where falls may occur. The first factor to consider is the suitable materials that will be used under equipment. All playground equipment should have energy-absorbing, resilient surfaces under and around them to cushion falls and prevent serious injury. Materials such as soft, loose sand; pine or bark mulch; or pea gravel are **shock absorbers** and should have a minimum depth of 12 inches. Asphalt, grass, and dirt are more dangerous and should not be used around play equipment. The surface material should be raked every few days to keep it from getting compacted and therefore losing some of its shock absorbency.

The final component of SAFE playgrounds is **Equipment** maintenance. This should be a consideration when equipment is purchased. Equipment made with wood may dry out over time and begin to splinter. A recent concern about wood equipment is the use of pressure-treated wood to create outdoor structures. This green-tinted wood has been found to contain arsenic, which can leech out onto the surface and wash down into the materials beneath when it gets wet (Dolesh, 2004). It has been recommended that structures made with pressure-treated wood built before 2003 be immediately disposed of because of the poisoning hazard they pose. Pressure-treated wood treated after 2003 no longer contains the arsenic in the treatment. Metal equipment can rust and may cause serious cuts if it breaks. Plastic equipment has been found to be the safest over time. In addition to inspecting equipment for general hazards, climbing equipment, slides, and swings, if they are present, must meet standards set by the U.S. Consumer Product Safety Commission. Figure 4-2 shows areas to check on this equipment.

Play equipment that is properly designed, well maintained, and correctly placed can help minimize risk and provide greater protection from serious injury. Using a general inspection list is a good idea for the teacher to review the safety of the playground equipment. The list in Table 4-3 is

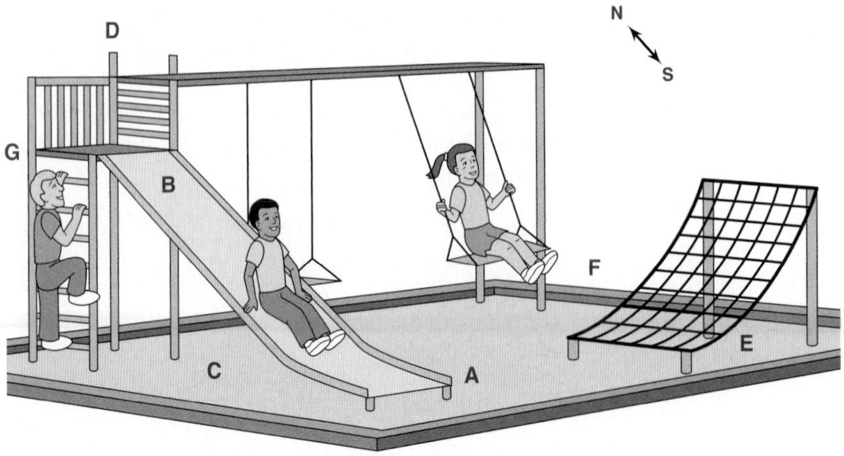

● **Shock absorbers**
*materials that lessen the force of a fall*

**FIGURE 4-2**
Potentially harmful areas on a playground:
**A.** The end of the slide is too close to the border.
**B.** The slide faces south and will get hot during the warm months. Locating the slide in a shaded area will minimize the risk of burns for children wearing shorts.
**C.** The structure is built on asphalt, whereas rubber, sand, pea gravel, wood chips, bark, or turf cushions falls.
**D.** Decks above 3 feet need a safety barrier to prevent falls.
**E.** The climbing net and posts are too close to the main structure and maximize the risks of collisions and injury during accidental falls.
**F.** The border is too close to the swing area; children jumping from the swings are likely to fall against the border.
**G.** Openings such as in rails or between ladder rungs should be less than 3.5 inches or more than 9 inches in order not to trap children. Guardrails should surround elevated platforms and should be at least 29 inches high for preschoolers.

**TABLE 4-3**
*General Inspection for Outdoor Equipment*

### ✔ CHECK FOR THE PRESENCE OF THE FOLLOWING HAZARDS:

- ☐ Lack of supervision; children cannot be seen at all times
- ☐ Inadequate fall zone
- ☐ Protrusion and entanglement hazards
- ☐ Insufficient equipment spacing
- ☐ Age-inappropriate activities
- ☐ Platforms with no guardrails
- ☐ Equipment, such as swinging exercise rings and trapeze bars, not recommended for public playgrounds
- ☐ Broken, cracked, bent, or warped surfaces
- ☐ Sharp parts or edges
- ☐ Squeaky parts in need of lubrication
- ☐ Loose nuts and bolts
- ☐ Rotting wood, splinters
- ☐ Defects in moving parts
- ☐ Broken or missing parts
- ☐ Peeling paint, rust
- ☐ Tripping hazards
- ☐ Too little depth of loose fill under equipment
- ☐ Too small a zone of loose fill or shock-absorbent surface around equipment
- ☐ Worn out parts
- ☐ Open tubes or pipes that need to be capped
- ☐ To get a playground safety report card that you can use to rate your playground with, go to http://www.idph.state.ia.us and search for the report card.

Adapted from U.S. Consumer Product Safety Commission, (1997). *Handbook for public playground safety.* Publication 35. Washington, DC: Author.

suggested as a tool for regular inspection. If an accident does occur, it is important to be prepared by having a first aid kit available in the outdoor environment so that any injury can be tended to immediately.

## Riding Toys

Toys that children ride should be sturdy, have a low center of gravity, and be well balanced. These toys should also be age-appropriate. There should be no sharp edges and pedal and hand grips should be in good condition. The area for riding should have a flat, smooth surface and not be slippery.

There should be barriers protecting this space from other play areas as well as from traffic and walkways.

## Sandboxes

Sandboxes should be kept clean and raked at least once a week. If the sandbox is in a shared use facility, it should be carefully checked and raked daily for broken glass and other sharp objects. If possible, the sandbox should have a cover in place when it is not being used. A sandbox also tends to attract cats that may use it as a litter box. Cats' feces can pose risk. Surfaces around the sandbox should be swept often to prevent falls. If standing water remains in sandbox after a rain, it should be removed as soon as the rain stops.

## Other Hazards

Seesaws and trampolines are not recommended as regular equipment in early childhood education environments. If a seesaw is present, it should be designed so that children are protected from parts that can pinch. If a trampoline is present, it should have a protective surface underneath and surrounding it, just like other large pieces of equipment. Only one child should use the trampoline at a time, and only when there is an adult observer present who is dedicated to that one task.

All equipment, including equipment assembled or made at home, must meet the basic criteria of the standards set for manufactured equipment. Close inspection and adaptation to U.S. Consumer Product Safety Commission standards will lessen risk. If someone donates equipment to an early childhood education facility, follow the same procedure. Proceed with caution, because one can never assume that playground equipment is safe. One factor that should always be carefully observed with outdoor equipment is that children should never wear hoods or drawstrings that could get caught on equipment and cause a choking hazard (National Safety Council, 2004).

### Key Concept 4.3

### Playground Equipment Safety

Playground equipment safety is essential in the early childhood education environment. Risk is posed if the equipment has not met national safety standards. Climbing equipment, swings, and slides should be properly placed to prevent accidents. There should be shock-absorbing material beneath this equipment. Riding toys should be sturdy and not tip over easily. If seesaws and trampolines are in the environment, they should be closely observed and have rules for use. All equipment should be regularly inspected to keep the playground safe.

## 4.4  TRAFFIC AND TRANSPORTATION SAFETY

In 2002, 227,000 children under the age of fourteen years were involved in motor vehicle accidents (NSKC, 2004a). Of those, 1579 died from their injuries. In the United States, motor vehicle accidents are the number one killer and crippler of children younger than four years of age. Motor vehicle injuries to children occur in three ways:

1. when children are pedestrians and are hit by an automobile
2. when children are riding in a car that stops suddenly or crashes
3. when children are riding bicycles and crash into or are run into by a car

To protect the children in care, safety policies should be developed for each case.

### Pedestrian Safety

Children being let off at and picked up from school account for the great majority of pedestrian accidents. Pedestrian injury is the second leading cause of death (after cancer) for children ages five to nine years (Childhood pedestrian injury, 2002). There should be a plan devised for safe dropping off and picking up of children. Pick-up and drop-off points for children should be located in an off-street area or directly at a curb near the early childhood education facility under an adult's supervision. In the majority of cases, this adult would be the parent bringing the child to school or taking him home. Parents should be reminded of the importance of close supervision of their children in a traffic situation. The outdoor play area should be as far away from traffic as possible and should be fenced.

### Motor Vehicle Safety

Transporting children involves major safety concerns for early educators and for the families of the children in care (National Association for the Education of Young Children [NAEYC], 2002). All drivers, chaperones, and assistants need instruction in safety precautions. At least one adult who either drives or accompanies the children needs to have training by a professional who is knowledgeable in safety and child development (U.S. Department of Health and Human Services [US DHHS], 2003). Car travel and field trips are likely to be special events and not common occurrences in most early childhood education situations. Planning for these events should be well organized and use accessories, behaviors, and conditions as the guidelines for safety. Some early childhood educators regularly transport children to and from home and pick up older children after school. If this is the case, as much risk management as possible should be considered. Head Start is an example of this. Beginning in January, 2004, any transportation service involving Head Start vans must ensure that any vehicle used to transport children is equipped with child restraint systems that consider the height and weight levels of children (AAP, 2004b). Any child weighing less than 50 pounds must use this system. Another example of safety precautions for early childhood education transportation is the Tennessee law that requires child safety monitoring systems in all early childhood education vans (Tennessee Lawmakers, 2004).

*The Vehicle.* The accessories in motor vehicle travel are the vehicle itself and the safety seats utilized. Vehicles should be in good working order and should be cleaned and inspected inside and out on a regular basis. Special care should be taken to see that brakes, lights, and other safety features of the car are working properly.

Vehicles should have heating and air conditioning features working in locations where temperatures go below 50°F and over 75°F. Children are susceptible to cold and heat and need to have the vehicle climate controlled.

*Safety Seats.* Safety seats are very important to the prevention of serious injury in motor vehicles. Children are safest when they ride in the age/weight-appropriate safety seats. Although there are laws in every state that require a child riding in a car to be safely restrained, many drivers still do not follow the "buckle up" rule. About fourteen percent of children younger than fourteen years of age rise unrestrained, and of those children who are restrained, about 82 percent are riding in safety seats that are either not correctly installed or used incorrectly. When safety seats are used correctly, they can reduce deaths of children from ages one to four by 54 percent and deaths of infants by 71 percent (NSKC, 2004a). Drivers should become familiar with the manufacturer's installation instructions for each safety seat used by children in care.

Each child should be in an appropriate safety seat, harness, or seat belt that corresponds to the child's weight and age. These features shall be approved in accordance with federal safety seat standards and used in compliance with the manufacturers' directions. All children younger than one year of age and weighing 20 pounds or less should ride in the backseat in a rearfacing safety seat (National Highway Traffic Safety Administration [NHTSA], 2002). Children who are more than one year old or weigh more than 20 pounds may ride forward facing and should ride in a safety seat with full harness until they reach the weight of 40 pounds. Booster seats can be used for children who weigh more than 40 pounds but are younger than 8 years of age unless they are more than 4 feet 9 inches tall (NHTSA, 2002).

The safest place for children in a motor vehicle is riding in the backseat and in an approved, secured car seat.

Seat belts shall be provided for all children who are too old for the safety seats. For more information on transportation, bicycle, and traffic safety go to http://www.nhtsa.dot.gov/. If a small bus or van is used, seat belts shall be provided for all children. The teacher should always model safety by using a seat belt.

*Pretravel Guidelines.* Safety behaviors are necessary in the preplanning stage as well as in actual travel in the motor vehicle. In planning for the field trip or other reason to travel, make sure the destination itself is safe (Walsh, 2005). A good way to make sure is to take a visit to the site before the trip is even planned. This will ensure that the site can be looked at for all safety hazards before trip planning continues. Begin pretravel planning by using the guidelines in Table 4-4.

*Travel Guidelines.* If the pretravel guidelines have been met, the next step is to follow the travel guidelines in Table 4-5. These guidelines are to help the teacher be prepared for all contingencies and offer a greater degree of protection for a safe journey for the children in care.

*Travel Conditions.* Try to plan any travel with the children for a time when the conditions are optimal. Avoid high traffic times or times when children will be most tired or hungry and less alert. If the weather is bad,

**TABLE 4-4**
*Pretravel Safety Guidelines*

**Teacher:**
- Obtain permission slips for all children participating in travel. Check your insurance coverage.
- Make sure driver is licensed, is familiar with vehicle, and knows how to drive defensively.
- Carefully plan out route, including placement of emergency care facilities along the way.
- Explain route to children and point out highlights.
- Prepare children for travel by explaining why buckling up and safe passenger behavior are important.
- Arrange for backup vehicle in case of car emergency.
- Understand safety precautions and child supervision for travel.
- A second set of emergency contact forms should be brought on any excursion.
- Know how to handle emergency situations, and be certified in pediatric first aid and cardiopulmonary resuscitation (CPR).
- Make sure the vehicle is in good working condition. This check should include checking the gas, oil, and tires.

**Children:**
- Understand the importance of travel safety, including buckling up.
- Practice safe travel behaviors, including hands inside the car.
- Understand rules for play in car, including no yelling or screaming.

**TABLE 4-5**
*Early Childhood Education Travel Safety Guidelines*

**Teacher:**
- Have trip authorization forms in your possession for all children present.
- Provide the proper ratio of adults to children and assign specific children to each adult.
- Do not allow loud music or tapes.
- Stop and pull off road to calm children down if they are unruly and noisy.
- Do not be under the influence of drugs or alcohol, including prescription or over-the-counter medications that could make you drowsy.
- Provide soft books or toys and conversation and songs for children so driver can concentrate on traffic safety.
- Provide a first aid kit to carry in each vehicle.
- Make sure everybody buckles up, and never allow children out of seat restraints while car is moving.
- Pay special attention to traffic and the children when exiting and entering the vehicle.
- If the trip is more than a few minutes, have juices and snacks for children allowing them to keep their focus on safety and not on being hungry or thirsty.
- Do not allow children to ride up front in vehicles that have passenger airbags.

**Children:**
- Observe car safety rules.
- Buckle up.
- Ride quietly, keeping hands to yourself.
- Be extra alert for traffic when exiting and entering vehicle.

it is best to postpone the trip until it improves. Prepare a backup activity that will excite the children to lessen the disappointment if the trip is postponed.

Make sure children are constantly under supervision during travel. At a minimum, keep to the proper adult–child ratio, but it is a good idea to ask for volunteers to accompany the teacher and children. If travel is by walking and away from the neighborhood or across streets, the ideal ratio would be one adult for three to five children, depending on age. The teacher must prepare any volunteers with rules of supervision by giving them handouts and talking to them several days before the trip so that they understand what is expected of them. It is also helpful to remind them of basic travel safety before leaving, so that they will be fresh in their minds when the trip begins.

The teacher should always leave a **travel information sheet** with a responsible person left at the early childhood education site. This sheet should include the following:

- date and time of trip, including approximate return time
- destination, including address, telephone number, and contact person

● **Travel information sheet**
*check-off sheet that monitors all conditions for travel safety*

- planned route; be specific: "Main Street to Laurel Ave., left on Center Circle, right on Pine two miles to Fourth"
- names of children participating
- names of teachers and parents providing supervision

*Pause for Reflection*

Do you remember taking a field trip as a child? Do you remember any safety precautions taken before or during the trip? Have you ever taken a field trip with children as an adult? What was the experience like? What might have been done to make it a more safe and pleasant experience?

## Bicycle Safety

School-aged children in family home child care, nanny care, or after school care should be taught about bicycle safety. Every year more than 135 children are killed in bicycle related crashes (NSKC, 2004b). Almost 300,000 other children are injured. The majority of these crashes involve head trauma. Using bike helmets can reduce the risk of injury by 85 percent and the risk of brain injury by 88 percent (NSKC, 2004b). Unfortunately, it is estimated that only 25 percent of children between five and fourteen years of age wear helmets. If all children used helmets, 75 percent of fatal bicycle head injuries could be averted.

*Helmets.* Practicing safety by using bike helmets for children riding tricycles and small bicycles in the early childhood education environment can reduce risk while riding the vehicles in the outdoor environment (Figure 4-3). It can also help prepare children for a future of greater safety by being in the habit of wearing a helmet. The Consumer Product Safety Commission sets mandatory standards for helmets, so the teacher must make sure the helmets provided meet these standards.

These boys look like they are having a good time on sturdy bikes, but more safety risk would be eliminated if they were wearing helmets.

*Riding Safety.* Helping children learn proper tricycle behaviors can begin in the early childhood education environment, using the same rules as for the riding toys. The skills and precautions in Table 4-6 will help the teacher set guidelines for teaching children bicycle safety.

The riding safety guidelines will help the teacher set up the early childhood education environment to minimize risk. If children all ride in the same direction, the number of crashes or collisions with other riders will be reduced. Keeping nonriders out of the area also reduces the number of collisions. A teacher who observes the children for speed, reckless riding, and two hands on the handlebar can prevent accidents and ensure a safer experience for them. Risk will also be reduced by checking the riding toys for proper working order.

*Other Riding Conditions.* Optimizing the conditions in the outdoor environment should not be too difficult. Creating a riding area in which riders have a flat, nonslick surface is important. Enforcing the rule that riders only go in one direction will be a matter of changing habits; most children will readily adapt and will change direction when reminded, but others may need more effort.

Setting the time of day when children are most alert for outdoor riding activity decreases risk. Providing necessary and active supervision will also help offer greater protection to the children in the outdoor environment.

**FIGURE 4-3**
Bicycle helmets are available in various sizes.

**TABLE 4-6**
*Guidelines for Safe Bicycle Riding*

- Always ride in the same direction so all traffic goes the same way and not against each other.
- Always be careful of other people and other traffic in the riding area.
- Keep hands free to hold handlebars with both hands. Never carry anything with your hands.
- Never show off, fool around, or ride recklessly.
- Do not ride too fast, so if you do see someone or other traffic you can slow down or stop to avoid colliding with them.
- The tricycle, bicycle, or other riding vehicle is appropriate for the age of the rider.
- The riding vehicle is in good working order.
- Stay clear of pedestrians.

## Key Concept 4.4

### Traffic and Travel

Traffic and travel pose risk for children in and out of the early childhood education environment. Children should be protected and learn good travel safety practices. Pedestrians, motor vehicles, and bicycles are the three areas where there should be safety promotion and prevention from risk. Checklists, guidelines, use of safety devices, travel information sheets, and using optimum conditions will help the teacher set up the environment for travel and traffic safety.

Gates that enclose a pool should be self-closing and have locks that are at least 55 inches high.

## 4.5  WATER SAFETY

Water safety presents its own set of challenges to the early childhood education environment. Bathtubs pose the biggest drowning hazard to infants, and pools are the greatest drowning hazard to toddlers, preschoolers, and school-aged children (Zavitkovsky & Thompson, 2000). Eighty-eight percent of children who drown are supposedly being supervised by an adult (Sullivan, 2004). Two-thirds of all drownings occur in the outdoor environment in standing bodies of water such as swimming pools, wading pools, hot tubs, ponds, and ditches. Covers for these items that are left with standing water after a rain become potential drowning hazards even though they may have originally been meant to protect. Popular belief is that a child in danger of drowning screams for help. In reality, drowning can be a silent event, which means that constant adult supervision is necessary whenever there is any body of water around children. These bodies of water also have the potential for spreading disease.

## Water Hazards

Safety precautions must be taken to keep the water in the early childhood education environment as risk-free as possible (NCCCHSRC, 2004). Any body of water can pose a threat, so screening the outdoor environment for hazards that may lead to the risk of drowning should be thorough. Young children can drown in as little as one inch of water. It is also important to remember that even small standing bodies of water make good breeding grounds for both mosquitoes and germs.

Water hazards in the outdoor environment must be secured to prevent children from reaching them (NCCCHSRC, 2004). Drownings occur in surprisingly short periods of time. Children have been seen playing indoors or outdoors away from a water source, and adults have been present nearby, yet these children have still drowned. Table 4-7 lists ways to childproof the early childhood education environment from the hazards that may lead to drowning. Other hazards may include furniture outside the fence that children could climb on and having riding and other non-water toys around a pool.

**TABLE 4-7**
*Water Safety Guidelines*

- Any hazard should be enclosed with a fence that is at least five feet tall and that is not easy to climb. A door or sliding glass door is not a safe substitute for a fence.
- Gates should have locks that are at least 55 inches high and should be self-closing. Keep gate keys in a safe place away from children.
- Remove chairs and objects children can use to climb over fences or gates or into spas.
- All bodies of water that are man made, such as swimming pools, hot tubs, and cesspools, should have rigid covers to protect children from falling in, if they get past the gate.
- If an inground pool is present in the early childhood education environment, a nonskid surface should surround the pool to prevent slipping and falling.
- Always drain standing water from pool or spa covers.
- Do not use floating spa or pool covers. Children can slip underneath and out of sight.
- Avoid the use of floating devices that can give children a false sense of safety.
- Remove all toys from pool after children are out of pool.
- If a portable wading pool is used in the early childhood education environment, it should be filled with water, used immediately, and drained and put away as soon as children leave the pool.
- Always carefully supervise children if there is a body of water present in the outdoor environment. *Never leave children without adult supervision, even for a few seconds.* Maintain visual contact with children.
- Keep a rescue device such as a long pole right next to the pool.
- Have telephone access to pool for emergencies.

Reprinted with permission of Children's Hospital of San Diego.

## Children's Behavior Around Water

Children themselves pose a threat when a body of water is present in the outdoor environment. They move fast, are curious, and do not understand cause and effect. They may lack fear or overestimate their physical abilities. Adults may underestimate children's abilities to manipulate their environment and therefore get into trouble. The majority of drownings occur within a very short period of time after a teacher has seen a child. It is imperative that the teacher *never* leave a child alone, even for a moment, when there is a body of water in the outdoor environment.

The children should be taught safe practices for swimming and playing in the water to further protect them if they will be using the pool or wading pool. Table 4-8 offers guidelines for teaching safe behavior around and in the water.

When outdoors and near the water, always reinforce safety for the children. If the children are allowed to play in water, plan the time of day for this activity for when they are least tired and most alert. Always be sure there is adequate supervision and maintain a sufficient ratio of adults to children. *Anyone attending children in the water should know how to swim and be competent in CPR.*

**TABLE 4-8**
*Water Safety Behaviors for Children*

- Do not run, push, or play around swimming areas.
- Do not swim with anything in your mouth.
- Be on the lookout for other children who may be having difficulty.
- Only swim in warm water. Cold water increases risk of drowning.
- Never go near a pool unless supervised.
- Always walk around a pool, never run.
- Wait at least an hour after eating before entering water.
- Do not roughhouse or fool around in water.
- Do not scream for help unless you mean it.
- Always have a buddy with you; never swim alone.

## Key Concept 4.5

### Water Safety

Water in many forms poses risk for children in the outdoor environment. Swimming pools, ponds, or any type of standing water may cause safety to be endangered. The teacher needs to understand water hazards and how to eliminate them, if possible. Children's behavior poses risk, and teachers should be prepared to promote and teach children water safety behaviors.

## 4.6  IMPLICATIONS FOR TEACHERS

Outdoor safety poses a number of risks to children in the early childhood education environment. The risks may come from different areas of hazards, such as environmental hazards, playground equipment, traffic and travel, and water. The risk may come from specific hazards, behaviors, and conditions. The teacher should provide observation, supervision, and education that promote safe behaviors and prevent risks.

### Observation

There are many areas of outdoor safety for which observation is the best method of prevention of accident and injury. Learning to use the ABCs of safety as it applies to outdoor accessories, behaviors, and conditions can help the teacher. A teacher who understands specific risks can be on guard for those risks.

### Supervision

Children need to be constantly supervised in the outdoor environment. The teacher should supervise all aspects of the environment for risks posed by accessories, behaviors, and conditions. These are effective tools for managing outdoor risks to children.

Supervision also supplies the teacher with methods and practices that provide a checks and balances system where there is more than one teacher. This is especially important to remember, because a teacher may view outdoor time as "break time," and it is essential to avoid that mentality. Communication about outdoor safety should be a regular occurrence between the teachers. Constant supervision can also reinforce that outdoor safety training and promotion take place on a regular basis.

### Education

Teachers, children, and parents can be educated for outdoor safety. The teacher should access training that will provide the knowledge and awareness needed. The teacher who has a knowledge base of outdoor safety can maximize the environment to protect the children.

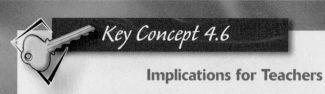

### Key Concept 4.6

#### Implications for Teachers

The teacher can promote and protect for outdoor safety in a number of ways. Observation for safety risks can prevent injury. Supervision for making sure safe practices are followed can promote safety and provide protection. Education for teachers, children, and families can provide extra measures of protection.

Children can be taught safe behaviors and items or conditions to look for that may pose risk. The children can be encouraged to use safety devices that will protect them. Having signs around that spell out cautions such as "Stop," "Danger," "Walk," and "Ride in One Direction" can help children learn, even though they might not be able to read the signs; they can remember the warning the sign poses (Smith, 2002). Communicating with children on a regular basis and reminding them about outdoor safety can offer a greater degree of protection both in and out of the early childhood education environment. The teacher can use educational methods such as reading books, showing videos, and circle time to reinforce safety measures and methods.

## For Families

Parents can be helped to understand the safety risks present in the outdoor environment. Methods such as an outdoor safety awareness week with handouts, videos to borrow, and a group meeting that families attend allows the teacher to provide education. This education will provide families with greater awareness about the importance of outdoor safety, which in turn can lead to more protective outdoor environments at home for the children.

## TO GO BEYOND

In this section you will find a number of activities that you can use to apply and improve your knowledge of this chapter. There are also thorough online resources that accompanies this text that can be found at http://www. earlychilded.delmar.com/ (see description at end of this chapter).

### Chapter Review Critical Thinking Applications

1. Discuss the relationship between outdoor activities and risk to safety.

2. Describe some of the safety hazards that might be found in a shared space environment. How do these differ from an early childhood education environment that does not share space? Compare and contrast the two types.

## CHAPTER SUMMARY

Risks for accidents are great in the outdoor environment even though less time is spent there. Risks can occur on playgrounds, in backyards, on bicycles, in cars, on streets, and in water. Teachers should monitor both the environment and the children for safety and make modifications using checklists. Safety devices such as helmets and safety car seats should always be used. Teachers can use observation, supervision, and education to protect and promote safety in their environment. They can work with families to ensure a higher degree of awareness of the importance of safety in the outdoor environment.

3. How can SAFE concepts improve playground safety in the early childhood education environment?

4. You are organizing a field trip to a pumpkin patch. Describe the steps you will follow and some of the hazards you may encounter.

## As an Individual

1. Find an early childhood education setting in the local area that reflects shared space, such as a church preschool, an early childhood education program at a gym, or a community center. Observe the environment and record your observations.

2. Visit an elementary school playground. Observe the equipment and the surface under it. Do these meet the safety standards discussed in the text?

3. Locate a park in your area. Assess it for the degree of shade it would provide for children on a hot day. What might you do to improve it?

## As a Group

1. In groups of four to five people, make a safety checklist for a shared-space environment at a church preschool. Use the information collected as individuals to compile this list. Compare the lists of the whole class.

2. Collect handouts from community resources that deal with outdoor safety. These might include an auto club, a poison control center, and the American Red Cross.

3. Think of a local neighborhood that is often in the news for the violence that occurs in it. What are the characteristics of that neighborhood? Research what might be done to make the neighborhood safer for children. List the local agencies that might be enlisted to help with this project.

## Case Studies

1. A teacher, Dan, notices that there appear to be a number of bees in the outdoor play yard. On further inspection, he comes upon a beehive. What course of action should he take to protect the children and eliminate the risk of bees?

2. Deborah is a family child care provider who has been in business for ten years. Her family has saved for many years to put in a pool so that her own children can enjoy the swimming and other water sports they love. The pool has been installed, and she has put up a seven-foot fence around the pool. What else should she do to protect the toddlers and young children in her care?

3. Marilou is in the process of setting up an early childhood education program with limited funds. A friend offers to donate his children's homebuilt play equipment because they have outgrown it. Should she accept this gift? How should she proceed to check for the safety of this equipment?

## Chapter References

American Academy of Pediatrics (AAP). (1999). Ultraviolet light: A hazard to children. *Pediatrics, 104*(2), 328–333.

American Academy of Pediatrics (AAP). (2002). West Nile virus. *Early Childhood Health Link, 13*(3), 1–2.

American Academy of Pediatrics (AAP). (2004a). Insect bites. *Early Childhood Health Link, 15*(4), 4.

American Academy of Pediatrics (AAP). (2004b). New Head Start transportation regulations. *Early Childhood Health Link, 15*(1), 4.

American Public Health Association & American Academy of Pediatrics (APHA & APA). (2002). *Caring for our children: National health and safety performance standards: Guidelines for out-of-home care.* Washington, DC: American Public Health Association.

Aronson, S. (2001). Reducing the risk of injury in child care. *Child Care Information Exchange, 101*(3), 64–66.

Benson, L. (2004, September 27). Can early ed close the gap? Minnesota Public Radio. Retrieved October 14, 2004 from http://news.minnesota.publicradio.org/features/2004/09/20_bensonl_gapbeforek/

Buller, M., & Farina, A. (1999). Becoming a sun-safe child care center. *Child Care Information Exchange, 99*(5), 69–71.

Bush, V. (2003). Summer safety: Protecting kids against sunburn, ticks and other hazards. *Essence, 34*(2), 208–209.

Centers for Disease Control, (CDC). (2000). Youth violence: Factsheet. Retrieved October 11, 2005, from http://www.cdc.gov/ncipc/factsheets/yvfacts.htm.

Childhood pedestrian injuries are preventable tragedies. (2002, November 18). *Health and Medicine Week,* 13.

Colino, S. (2003). Summer dangers: Is your child at risk? *Redbook, 200*(6) 176–177.

Dolesh, R. (2004). Arsenic and your playground. National Parks and Recreation Association. Retrieved October 15, 2004 from http://www.nrpa.org/content/default.aspx?documentld=1025.

Fournier, A. (2004). Outdoor pest problems. *Healthy Child Care. 7*(4). Retrieved September 19, 2004 from http://www.healthychild.net/volume7.html

Frost, J. (1994, April). Preventing playground injuries and litigation. *Parks and Recreation,* 53–60.

Gaensbauer, T. (2004). Telling their stories: Representation and reenactment of traumatic experiences occurring in the first year of life. *Zero to Three, 24*(5), 25–31.

Groves, B. (2001). *Children who witness violence.* Family Communcations. Retrieved October 11, 2005, from http://www.fci.org/early_care/violence_witness_article.asp.

Groves, B., Lieberman, A., Osofsky, J., & Fenichel, E. (2000, April/May). Protecting young children in violent environments: A framework to build on. *Zero to Three, 5.*

Groves, B. (2003). *Children who see too much: Lessons from the child witness to violence project.* New York: Houghton Mifflin.

Haberman, M. (1994, Spring). Gentle teaching in a violent society. *Educational Horizons,* 131–135.

Hudson, S., Thompson, D., & Olsen, H. (2004). How safe are our playgrounds: New report card shows significant improvement, but still room for more change. *Parts & Recreation Magazine, 39*(4), 52–59.

Koontz, K. (2003, Feb.). Weather safety: How to keep your child toasty—and protected all winter long. *Parenting Magazine (XVII)* page 37.

Levin, D., (1999, July). Changing needs, changing responses: Rethinking how we teach children. *Child Care Information Exchange, 99*(1), 46–49.

Levin, D. (2003). *Teaching young children in violent times: Building a peaceable classroom.* (2nd edition). Cambridge, MA: Educators for Social Responsibility.

Linares, L. (2001). Community violence: The effects on children. Retrieved October 11, 2005, from http://www.aboutourkids.org/articles/communityviolence.html.

Massey, M. (1998). *Early childhood violence prevention.* ERIC Digest. Champaign, IL: Eric Clearinghouse on Elementary and Early Childhood Education.

Meltz, C. (2004, September 16). Validating fears helps students to face them. Boston Globe. Retrieved October 11, 2005, from http://www.boston.com/yourlife/family/articles/2004/09/16/validating_fears_helps_students_to_face_them/

Moyers, B. (1995, January 8). There is so much we can do. *Parade Magazine,* 4–6.

Mathe, T. (2005). Sun safety. CAEYC Connections, 33(3).

National Association for the Education of Young Children (NAEYC). (2002). FYI: Child passenger safety. *Young Children 57*(4), 49.

National Program for Playground Safety (NPPS). (2001). *Age-appropriate design guidelines for playgrounds.* Cedar Falls, IA: School of Health, Physical Education and Leisure Service University of Northern Iowa.

National Safety Council (NSC). (2004, April 26). *Playground safety fact sheet.* Itasca, IL: Author. Retrieve October 11, 2005, from http://www.nsc.org/library/facts/plgrdgen.htm

National SAFE KIDS Campaign (NSKC). (2004a). *Motor vehicle occupant injury fact sheet.* Washington, DC: Author.

National SAFE KIDS Campaign (NSKC). (2004b). *Bicycle injury fact sheet.* Washington DC: Author.

National SAFE KIDS Campaign (NSKC) (2004c). *Poisoning fact sheet.* Washington DC: Author.

National Highway Traffic Safety Administration (NHTTSA). (2002). *Occupant protection for children safety information.* Washington, DC: U.S. Department of Transportation. Retrieved October 11, 2005 from http://www.nhtsa.dot/gov/CPS/safetycheck/MinuteChecklist/

Norris Cotton Cancer Center (NCCC). (2002). The Sunsafe Project: Preschool/childcare curriculum. Hanover, NH: Dartmouth Medical School. Retrieved 10/14/04. Available online: http://www.dartmouth.edu/~sunsafe/preschool.htm.

North Carolina Child Care Health and Safety Resource Center (NCCCHSRC). (2005). Humpty Dumpty safe on a wall. *North Carolina Child Care Health and Safety Bulletin, 5*(2), 1.

North Carolina Child Care Health and Safety Resource Center (NCCCHSRC) (2004). Managing water outdoors. *North Carolina Child Care Health and Safety Bulletin, 4*(2), 3.

Olsen, H., Hudson, S., & Thompson, D. (2004, June). Building a safe outdoor environment. *School Planning and Management Magazine.* Retrieved October 11, 2005, from http://www.peterli.com/archive/spm/695.shtm.

Osofsky, J. (1999). The impact of violence on children. *The Future of Children, 9*(3), 33–49.

Please be car-seated. (1994, Winter). *Scholastic Parent and Child,* 6.

Palmer, D. (2004). West Nile virus. *Healthy Child Care, 7*(4). Retrieved October 11, 2005, from http://www.healthychild.net/articles/mc40westnile.htm

Scott, J. (2004, September 7). Safety rules retiring playground standby. Arizona Daily Star. Retrieved October 11, 2005, from http://www.dailystar.com/dailystar/dailystar/377739.php

Shonkoff, J., Phillips, J. (Eds.), & The Committee on Integrating the Science of Early Childhood Development. (2000). *Neurons to neighborhoods.* Committee on Integrating the Science of Early Childhood Development, Board of Children, Youth and Families. Washington, DC: National Academy Press. Retrieved October 11, 2005, from http://www.nap.edu.

Shonkoff, J., Phillips, D., & Keilty, B. (Eds.). (2000). *Early childhood intervention: Views from the field: A report of a workshop.* Committee on Integrating the Science of Early Childhood Development. Washington, DC: National Academy Press. Retrieved October 11, 2005, from http://www.nap.edu.

Smith, C. (2002). Teaching health and safety through outdoor activities. *Healthy Child Care, 5*(4). Retrieved October 11, 2005, from http://www.healthychild.net/articles/sf28outdoor.html.

Sullivan, D. (2004). Water smarts. *Parenting 18*(6), 37–38.

Sutton, A. (2003). Sand sanitation and safety. *Healthy Child Care, 6*(4). Retrieved October 11, 2005, from http://www.healthychild.net/articles/sh34sand.html.

Tinsworth, D. & McDonald, J. (April 2001). *Special study: Injuries and deaths associated with children's playground equipment.* Washington, D.C.: U.S. Consumer Product Safety Commission.

Tennessee lawmakers pass child-care van safety, lending, litigation tax bills. (2004, May 11). Retrieved 9/16/04. Available online: Knight-Ridder/Tribune Business News (NRTBN) at http://web5infotrac.galegroup/itw/infomark/495/798/53269167w5/purl=rc1_ITOF_0

U.S. Department of Health and Human Services (US DHHS). (2003). Stepping stones to using *Caring for Our Children,* 2nd Edition. Rockville, MD: Author. Retrieved October 11, 2005, from http://nrc/uchsc.edu/STEPPING/SteppingStones.pdf.

U.S. Consumer Product Safety Commission (CPSC). (1997). *Handbook for public playground safety.* Publication 35. Washington, DC: Author.

U.S. Environmental Protection Agency (EPA). (2001). *Sun safety action steps.* Washington, DC: Author. Retrieved October 11, 2005, from http://www.epa.gov/sunwise/actionsteps.html.

Walsh, E. (2005). Field trip safety tips. *Child Care Health Connections. 18*(1), 6–7.

Zavitkovsky, A., & Thompson, D. (2000). Preventing injuries to children: Interventions that really work. *Child Care Information Exchange, 100*(1), 54–56.

Zenah, P., Stafford, B., Nagle, G. & Rice, T. (2005, January). *Addressing social-emotional development and infant mental health in early childhood systems.* Building State Early Childhood Comprehensive Systems Series, No. 12. Los Angeles, CA: National Center for Infant and Early Childhood Health Policy.

Additional resources for this chapter can be found by visiting the Online Companion™ at www.earlychilded.delmar.com. This supplemental material includes extensive chapter quizzes, PowerPoint® outlines, Web links, and various other activities to help better utilize the material in this chapter. The site is updated regularly, so you may check back often to receive the latest information about the subjects in each chapter.

CHAPTER **5**

# Emergency Response Procedures for Early Childhood Education Environments

**After reading this chapter, you should be able to:**

### 5.1 Safety Policies for Emergency Response

Describe and discuss safety policies for response to childhood accidents and injuries.

### 5.2 Identifying an Emergency

Define and discuss the differences between what constitutes an emergency and what necessitates only basic first aid.

### 5.3 Basic Emergency Response Procedures

Indicate the steps to go through in addressing the proper responses to a real emergency and how it is to be performed.

### 5.4 Basic Cardiopulmonary Resuscitation and First Aid

Define, discuss, and summarize the methods of basic cardiopulmonary resuscitation (CPR) and first aid to infants and children.

### 5.5 Emergency Planning for Children with Special Needs

Discuss methods and practices for emergency care of children with special needs.

### 5.6 Disaster Preparedness

Define, discuss, and summarize the basic methods of disaster preparedness for early childhood education.

### 5.7 Implications for Teachers

Indicate the need for supervision, observation, education, cultural competence, and working with families for basic response procedures for childhood injuries and accidents.

## 5.1  SAFETY POLICIES FOR EMERGENCY RESPONSE

Emergencies occur in many situations. Automobiles, playground equipment, and natural disasters all pose risk for accidental injury that might be classified as an emergency. A chronic illness or a childhood disease might manifest as an emergency situation. It is important that the teacher in any early childhood education situation be prepared to handle emergencies. The following show the need for preparedness for emergency response in early childhood education:

- In a survey of more than 300 early education environments, two-thirds were considered to be at risk for safety (Shepard, 2002).
- Teachers of young children should be prepared to treat bleeding, poisoning, convulsions, sprains and fractures, head injuries, and dental and mouth injuries (Reeves, 2003).
- Broken bones, often the result of falls are the fourth most common injury in preschool-aged children (North Carolina Child Care Health and Safety Resource Center, 2005a).
- During a disaster, teachers should be able to provide safe, competent care to the children in care for several days, regardless of whether it is the regular early childhood education setting or an evacuation site (LeMay, 2004).
- Parents of children in early education environments expect that their teachers should be able to handle emergencies (Gaines & Leary, 2004).
- When emergencies do happen in early childhood education environments, it is necessary to know how to take proper action (Pennsylvania Chapter of the American Academy of Pediatrics [PAAAP], 2003).
- It is essential that at least one teacher in an early childhood education program be trained for emergency, life-threatening situations such as breathing difficulties, head injury, or poisoning (Sokol-Gutierrez, 1999).
- Early education environments should be prepared for all levels of disaster alerts (Federal Emergency Management Agency [FEMA], 2002).

Teachers need to avoid emergencies by providing prevention and protection in the care environment. They do this with constant supervision and by anticipating, modifying, and monitoring for accessories, behaviors, and conditions that pose risk. These proactive behaviors reduce risk.

To provide the maximum protection in the early childhood education environment, the teacher needs to be prepared for the possibility that an emergency may occur. The teacher needs to plan for emergencies, be prepared to handle emergencies, and be equipped with the training necessary to deal with life-threatening emergencies as they occur.

In order to carry this out, the teacher needs to plan for policies in the following areas:

1. *Defining an Emergency:* understanding what constitutes an emergency situation
2. *Basic Emergency Response Procedures:* understanding of methods and practices for response to emergencies in early childhood education environments

3. *Basic CPR and First Aid:* understanding when and how to use basic CPR and first aid to handle emergencies in early childhood education environments

4. *Emergency Planning for Children with Special Needs:* methods, practices, and understanding of how to handle emergencies for children in care with special needs

5. *Disaster Preparedness:* methods and practices for preparing for disasters such as fire, weather disasters, and earthquakes

6. *Implications for Teachers:* methods and practices for preparing the early childhood education environment to deal with emergencies through education, observation, and supervision

## Key Concept 5.1

### Safety Policies for Emergency Procedures

Even though much risk may have been reduced, accessories, behaviors, and conditions can cause situations that constitute an emergency. The teacher needs to be prepared to respond to any emergency in the early childhood education environment. The preparation includes defining an emergency, how to respond to an emergency, awareness of basic CPR and first aid, and how to prepare for disaster. The implications for the teacher to carry out these preparations are to provide for education, observation, working with families, and supervision in the early childhood education environment.

## 5.2 IDENTIFYING AN EMERGENCY

In order to understand how to prepare for an emergency, the teacher must first understand what constitutes an emergency. There are common factors that indicate an emergency exists. The teacher needs to be able to identify these factors, to help determine if an emergency is occurring. Three major factors have been used to indicate that an emergency is taking place.

### Breathing, Bleeding, and Poison

The three basic factors that always indicate an emergency exists are breathing, bleeding, and poison. These emergencies are fairly easy to recognize. They are also rapidly life-threatening and must be acted upon quickly. There may not even be time to call 911 right away if there is only one person present besides the victim. Any of these three factors could occur in the early childhood education environment, and the teacher should be prepared to recognize them and act immediately and appropriately.

● **Profusely**
*pouring forth freely or abundantly*

A person who is bleeding **profusely** may die if the bleeding is not stopped. Stopping the bleeding is of foremost importance, and first aid is needed immediately. If someone else is present, that person can call the emergency number (usually 911).

If a person has difficulty breathing, brain damage can occur in a matter of a few minutes and the heart may stop with death following. Anything that interferes with a child's breathing is life-threatening (Aronson, 2001). Offering **rescue breathing** may be the only alternative. Calling an emergency number is also vital, if possible.

● **Rescue breathing**
*the process of steps to help a person who is not breathing resume normal breathing*

When someone has ingested poison, has contacted it directly through the skin, or has inhaled it, emergency procedures should begin immediately. Call Poison Control Central (800-222-1222) to get help for the victim. In most cases, the person who answers will walk the rescuer through the exact method of treating the particular poison. Be aware that the use of syrup of ipecac to make a victim vomit up any poison that may have been swallowed is no longer recommended (Sutton, 2004).

## Other Emergency Indicators

There are a number of other indicators that show when an emergency may be present. The American Red Cross suggests that using one's senses is a good tool to help recognize when an emergency may exist. Hearing, seeing, smelling, and feeling can all be tools of recognition, as listed in Table 5-1.

When any of the conditions in Table 5-1 are present in the early childhood education environment, an emergency may exist and the teacher

Emergency numbers, such as the local poison control number, should be located next to the phone for immediate use.

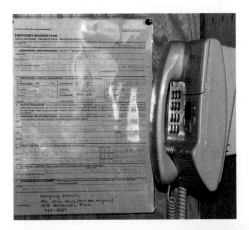

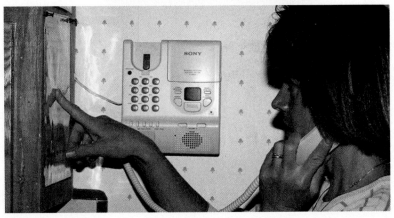

**TABLE 5-1**
*Indicators of Emergencies*

Your senses may help tell you whether or not an emergency may exist. Below are some examples of what might indicate an emergency using four of the five senses.

### Hearing

- Screams
- Loud bangs or pops, possibly from a gun
- An explosion
- Breaking glass
- A car crash
- Someone choking

### Smelling

- Chemicals
- Smoke
- Strong odors
- Vomit

### Seeing

- Unusual appearances or behaviors
- An unconscious person
- Smoke
- Bleeding
- A broken bone
- Profuse sweating

### Feeling

- High fever
- Broken bone

Courtesy of the American Red Cross. All Rights Reserved in All Countries.

**FIGURE 5-1**
Illustration of indicators of emergencies.

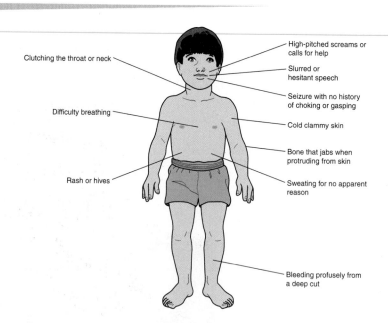

Clutching the throat or neck

Difficulty breathing

Rash or hives

High-pitched screams or calls for help

Slurred or hesitant speech

Seizure with no history of choking or gasping

Cold clammy skin

Bone that jabs when protruding from skin

Sweating for no apparent reason

Bleeding profusely from a deep cut

should act promptly (Figure 5-1). The teacher should follow through with any unusual sights, sounds, smells, and sense of touch. The follow-up may prove that nothing was out of order; on the other hand, it may establish that an emergency is taking place. The teacher needs to remain calm, act quickly, and follow emergency procedures.

There are a number of human-caused and other risks that regularly contribute to childhood injuries and must be prepared for. These risks can be found in Table 5-2.

**TABLE 5-2**
*Contributors to Early Childhood Education Emergencies*

- Garage door injuries (family child care)
- Choking from toys and other hazards
- Falls from playground equipment
- Firearms, poisons, and bodies of water
- Burns from fires, scalding, or electric wires
- Natural disasters such as floods, earthquakes, hurricanes, and tornadoes
- Human-caused disasters such as hostage-taking, bomb threats, terrorism, and random acts of violence.

### Key Concept 5.2

#### Identifying an Emergency

The teacher needs to identify what constitutes an emergency. Difficulty breathing, profuse bleeding, and ingestion or direct contact with poison always present emergency conditions that need prompt action. Other emergency indicators may be observed through the use of the senses of sight, hearing, smell, and touch. Once the teacher has observed a questionable condition, follow-up can eliminate or determine the need for emergency response procedures.

These children are in the garage of their family child care home, where there are many dangerous items. To lessen risk, there should be a way to block children from entering this area.

## 5.3 BASIC EMERGENCY RESPONSE PROCEDURES

The teacher should be prepared for an emergency at all times. In order to lessen risk as an emergency occurs, the teacher should be prepared with proper planning, organizing, and responses based on knowledge and training. Bright Horizons (2003) suggests that all teachers be prepared with an emergency response plan. The following is a suggested list of emergencies that should have a response planned:

- Medical emergencies
- Evacuation procedures and process
- Survival mode sheltering/sheltering in place
- Natural disasters (hurricane, tornado, severe storms)
- Utility disruption
- Fire/smoke emergencies
- Hazardous materials
- Bomb threat
- Suspicious articles
- Potentially violent situations
- Random acts of violence
- Disgruntled impaired parents/guardians or parent's/guardian's authorized representatives
- Hostage situations
- Missing child

## Organization for Emergency

When an emergency occurs, the teacher should remain calm and act immediately. This is hard enough to do under normal conditions, but it is even more difficult in emergencies if one is not prepared to follow emergency procedures. There are a number of ways to prepare for the possibilities of emergencies and organize the early childhood education environment to cope with them.

The procedures in Table 5-3 should be followed to prepare the environment for emergencies.

**TABLE 5-3**
*Emergency Preparedness Procedures*

- All teachers should have basic training and certification for first aid for children, including how to offer help to a choking victim. There should be one teacher on site in the early childhood education environment who is certified in basic CPR, and all other teachers should be trained in rescue breathing.

- All emergency information forms and health records should be readily available for each child and teacher in the early childhood education environment. It would be helpful to have a second set in a box that is easy to carry in case of evacuation. A Rescue Registration form for everyone in the early childhood education environment should be filled out and turned in to the nearest fire rescue department.

- Emergency numbers should be posted next to each phone. In addition, a list of vital information that the emergency operator will need should be posted.

TABLE 5-3 (Continued)
*Emergency Preparedness Procedures*

- Have a list of backup helpers in case the teacher must accompany a child to the hospital, away from the early childhood education environment.

- In case of fire, natural disaster, or other major human-caused emergency, an evacuation plan should be prepared. An evacuation place should be predetermined, such as a local school or place the American Red Cross has designated as a shelter-in-place for evacuations. If the designated spot is not available at the time of the evacuation, other shelters in the local area should be considered. The shelter should be considered accessible and safe under all conditions. A transportation plan should be developed for this.

- In case of natural disaster, chemical spill, or other human-caused disaster, a survival mode or shelter-in-place plan should be prepared.

- Have available a first aid kit that is comprehensive enough for most emergencies.

- Copies of the emergency response plans should be placed throughout the early childhood education environment.

- One person should be designated to be a "team" leader for emergencies.

- Check all emergency supplies on a monthly basis.

- Have regular fire drills and other evacuation practices.

- Post a map that includes emergency exit routes and locations of all utilities that might need to be turned off, such as water, electricity, gas, furnace, and control panels for the telephone and any alarm controls. Clearly label all emergency exits and utility shut-off areas.

- Develop a code word or words for use in human-caused emergency situations. All the teachers should understand the meaning of the words so that, if they are said, the person who hears the words will understand that an emergency exists.

- Notify families of the evacuation procedures you have planned and prepare a list of family phone numbers, including cell phone numbers, so the families can be notified when a large-scale emergency exists.

***Basic Training.*** All teachers should have basic training for and certification in first aid for infants and children, including how to offer help to a choking victim. This training should be updated as required by certification and the follow-up training should be recorded to keep track. Any new teachers should have this training before they start. One teacher at the early childhood education site at all times should be trained in basic CPR and should renew that certification yearly. All other teachers should know how to perform basic rescue breathing.

All teachers should be familiar with the procedures to be followed for first aid and rescue breathing for both infants and children. Keep reminders of this training available in a notebook or on the wall where it is readily available. Posting pictures that depict emergency responses are helpful as reminders. These reminders can be invaluable in a real emergency. Reference books for this training should also be available for the teacher to look at on a regular basis to help keep current.

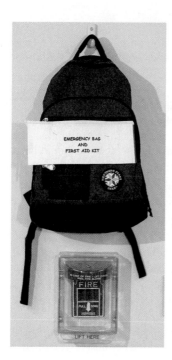

**A.** Emergency and first aid kits should be readily available. This one is located above the fire alarm, so it is easily seen and convenient. **B.** Emergency response plan posted at an early childhood education program.

A

B

*Emergency Information.* All emergency information forms and health records should be readily available in a file for each child in care. These forms include:

- emergency information forms filled out by parents including health information, the parents' work, cell, and home phone numbers, emergency phone numbers of other people listed by the parents in case of an emergency, the physician's phone number, the name of the hospital that has a treatment release on file, and any allergic reaction information
- a parental release form to treat the child in case of an emergency
- all "ouch" or injury reports filled out for the child
- all health records, including immunizations
- a master log of injuries that occurred in the early childhood education environment

Another part of organizing emergency information would be submit a "Rescue Registration Form" (see page 165) to the local or closest fire rescue department, so that if an emergency does occur they have adequate information to help them in arriving as quickly as possible. It would also help them to have knowledge of the early education environment where the children are located (Shallcross, 1999). Although these forms were intended for family child care, they would work equally well for any early education environment.

Family Child Care Rescue Registration Form. (Courtesy of Mary Ann Shallcross Smith, Ed.D. Child Care Connection.)

# FAMILY CHILD CARE RESCUE REGISTRATION FORM

**(Send one copy to your nearest fire/rescue station. Keep one copy for your files.)**

Date of Registration _____

Provider's Name _____

Street Address _____

City/Town_____ State _____ Zip Code _____

Phone _____

Licensed Family Child Care Home?   Yes _____ No _____

License # (if Applicable) _____

Hours of Operation _____

Maximum Number of Children (Including Own Children) in Home at Any Time _____

Age Range of Children in Child Care _____

Employee(s)/Assistant(s) Present: Yes _____ No _____ If Yes, What Are Their Hours? _____

Language Commonly Spoken in Home _____

Describe where exactly in your home you provide child care. Include as much information as possible, including the type of home (single, multifamily, etc.), which floors and rooms you use. Describe entrance to child care and any additional entrances, etc. _____

_____

_____

_____

_____

Other important information, such as special needs children/adults, animals, etc.

_____

_____

_____

**DESIGNED AND PREPARED BY DR. MARY ANN SHALLCROSS-SMITH, CEO**
**25 BLACKSTONE VALLEY PLACE**
**LINCOLN, RI 02865**
**PHONE NUMBER 401-727-8982**
**WWW.CHILDCARECONNECT.COM**

*Emergency Numbers.* Emergency numbers should be posted next to each telephone. In addition, a list of vital information that the emergency operator will need should be posted as a reminder of what the teacher needs to provide. This emergency information includes

- teacher's name and address
- type of emergency (e.g., burn, fall)
- where and how accident occurred
- child's (or children's) name, sex, age, and condition
- directions to the early childhood education site
- assistance already given to child
- always stay on the line until the emergency operator hangs up

The teacher should be informed about the local area emergency system. Knowing where the emergency care is coming from, how it is dispatched, and the location of the nearest hospital emergency room are helpful bits of information that may come in handy in an actual emergency.

A list of emergency contact numbers for all children in care should also be posted by each phone. These will be readily available and can be grabbed if an evacuation takes place or a field trip is planned.

*Emergency Backup.* A list of backup helpers should be available in case the teacher must accompany a child to the hospital, away from the early childhood education environment. The backup person could be an off-duty teacher, a substitute, a friend, neighbor, or volunteer to the early childhood education environment. It is essential that these people are familiar with the early childhood education environment and have been introduced to the children. A familiar person adds a sense of protection to the children who may already be very upset. Leaving the children with a stranger would be more upsetting. If the teacher must leave with an injured or ill child, she should have the peace of mind that the children are in familiar good hands.

*Shelter-in-Place or Survival Mode Plan.* In case of natural disaster, or some human-caused disasters such as a chemical spill, it might be best to stay at the early childhood education site. This is also a major topic and will be discussed later in this chapter.

*Emergency Response Plan.* In case of fire, natural disasters, or other major emergencies, an evacuation plan should be prepared. This is a major topic and will be dealt with later in this chapter. A copy of this plan should be available in a number of easily accessed locations. This might include the director's office, the staff room, and the classroom. In the case of a family child care home or nanny care at home, it should be in several easily accessible places. One person in care should be designated the "team leader" of the plan, and this person should be prepared to take charge in case of emergency in a calm manner. This person would obviously be the family child provider or nanny in those modes of care, but in a center it might be the director, a teacher or another designated person.

*Practice Drills.* Drills for fire and other evacuation emergencies should be practiced on a regular basis. Children should know what is expected of them, and teachers should be very familiar with the procedure. It might be helpful to practice evacuating to another site once a year to get the feel of how it would be.

*First Aid Kit.* A first aid kit that is comprehensive enough for most emergencies should be available. The kit should be easy to access and at the same time should be out of reach of the children. It should include the items found in Table 5-4. The first aid kit should accompany the teacher and children on any outings (walking) or any field trips (automobile). In addition to the kit, there should be ice or bags of frozen vegetables available for fast ice packs.

## Supplies

There are also specific supplies (see Table 5-11) that will be needed in case of a shelter-in-place mode of emergency. The first aid kit and these supplies should be checked on a monthly basis to make sure that everything is in place and adequate to cover an emergency.

## Signage/Maps

All exit routes out of the classroom or early childhood education environment should be clearly posted, as should the locations of all turn-off valves for water, gas, electrical panels, and the furnace. If there is a telephone control panel or alarm controls, those too should be clearly signed. An exit route and emergency shut-off map should be posted throughout the care facility and in the classrooms. This information should also be available in a family child care home or a home where a nanny works.

## Communication

Develop an emergency communication plan for the early education environment. This includes having a list of parents' phone numbers for work, cell, and home phones. Parents should have previous notice of what type of evacuation or shelter-in-place plan you have devised. Included with this notice should be the telephone numbers of the early childhood education center, including at least one dedicated cell phone line that can be called should an emergency arise. Another essential communication piece is the selection of a code word or sentence that could be used in case of potentially threatening situations where other people are involved. If a situation arises in which a person or persons pose risk, the word or sentence could be used (for example, "Doctor Jones sent his regards"). If it is a medical emergency only, a detailed injury report should be filled out and a copy given the parent.

---

*Pause for Reflection*

Have you ever been in an emergency situation such as an earthquake, fire, blizzard, or hurricane? What emergency precautions were taken, and what steps were used to recover from this emergency? How was communication handled?

A first aid kit should accompany the teacher and children on any outings or field trips (Photographs courtesy of Masuen.)

TABLE 5-4
*Emergency First Aid Kit Checklist*

## ✓ CHECK FOR:

☐ Emergency and contact numbers for all children and adults present

☐ Cellular phone or change for pay phone if out of cellular range

☐ Special items needed for all children with disabilities, special needs or allergies such as an inhaler or Epipen with emergency instructions

☐ Instant ice packs

☐ Adhesive bandages of assorted sizes

☐ Sterile gauze pads and a roll of sterile gauze

☐ Butterfly bandages

☐ Triangular bandages or something to use as a sling

☐ Safety pins

**TABLE 5-4** (Continued)
*Emergency First Aid Kit Checklist*

## ✓ CHECK FOR:

- ☐ 1 roll of athletic or adhesive bandage tape
- ☐ Ace bandages (2″, 3″, and 4″)
- ☐ 1 pair each scissors and tweezers
- ☐ 1 bottle of tincture of benzoin or antiseptic wound wipes
- ☐ 1 tube cortisone ointment
- ☐ 1 tube antibiotic ointment
- ☐ 1 microshield for giving CPR
- ☐ Charcoal suspension for poisoning, used only as advised
- ☐ 1 bee sting kit and insect preparation stick
- ☐ Hand sanitizer and antibacterial hand soap
- ☐ Pads for eye injuries
- ☐ Eye wash (saline wash)
- ☐ Unbreakable thermometer
- ☐ Bottled water
- ☐ 2 or 3 large black plastic trash bags
- ☐ Duct tape
- ☐ First aid guide and CPR instruction card

## Order of Response

The early childhood education environment that is organized for possibilities of an emergency situation will be better prepared to respond to an emergency when it actually occurs. If an emergency does occur, the following responses are recommended by the National Association for the Education of Young Children (NAEYC) for the teacher to attend to the emergency:

1. Act immediately and remain calm.
2. Stay at the scene, giving help and reassurance to the victim and other children present. If another teacher is present, assign him the task of keeping the other children calm.
3. Assess the child with a head-to-toe check as if using Figure 5-1 and the senses check in Table 5-1.
4. Do not move a seriously injured child unless in a life-threatening situation, such as immediate danger from fire. If you must move the child, you should drag her by the legs in order not to compromise the neck and spine if an injury is present.
5. If necessary, call for emergency help. In most areas of the country this is accessed by dialing 911. The emergency numbers will be posted by the phone. If for some reason the early childhood education environment's phone is out, send someone to the nearest pay phone, car phone, or cellular phone. A portable or cellular

phone serves as an extra precaution for emergencies in an early childhood education environment.

6. Notify parents and agree on a plan of action. If the agreement is to meet at the emergency care site because it is closer, call for backup help for the early childhood education site. If the parent is unavailable, call other emergency contacts and let the child's physician know what has happened. Call for backup teacher.

● **Shock**
*an imbalance of the circulatory system as a result of injury that includes a decrease in blood pressure, a rapid pulse, and possible unconsciousness*

7. Treat child for **shock**, if indicated. Cover the child with a blanket and keep her warm.

8. Stay with the child until parents or emergency help arrives. Accompany child if parents are to meet the child at the emergency care site. Have backup teacher stay with children. If parents have not arrived and there is no other teacher present and the backup teacher is unavailable, the teacher must stay with the children who remain in the early childhood education environment. Try to reassure the child that he will be taken care of by the emergency technicians. If the teacher knows that a parent or other emergency contact is going to be at the emergency care site, let the child know that someone will be with him soon.

9. After the incident is over, fill out a report. Study it carefully to see if the incident could have been avoided through better safety practices or greater compliance with health practices.

These procedures are easy to follow if they have been reviewed frequently and are posted in several places throughout the early childhood education site. Good planning and preparation will help the emergency situation go more smoothly.

## Key Concept 5.3

### Basic Emergency Response Procedures

Knowledge of and training in basic emergency response procedures are essential for the teacher. All teachers should have training in basic first aid and rescue breathing, and at least one teacher per site must be certified in CPR. The teacher should organize for emergencies and plan accordingly. Emergency numbers and information should be posted and easily accessible. Every early childhood education program should have a comprehensive first aid kit that travels with the group if they leave the site for an outing or field trip. Every teacher should have an understanding of the 10 steps for emergency response and be able to respond in the right order.

## 5.4 BASIC CARDIOPULMONARY RESUSCITATION AND FIRST AID

Breathing emergencies are always life-threatening. Regular breathing is effortless and comfortable. When breathing becomes an effort, causes pain, or makes unfamiliar noises, these are indicators that a breathing emergency may be occurring. If a child is found unconscious, it probably indicates a breathing problem. Every teacher should be able to recognize the symptoms and be able to perform rescue breathing. Once the determination is made to perform rescue breathing, the ABCs of rescue breathing should be put into place. This memory tool makes it easier to follow the correct steps to help someone who may need immediate assistance. The **A** stands for **airway,** the **B** represents **breathing,** and the **C** represents **circulation.** If a disabling condition such as fracture or bleeding may be present, then a **D** should be added to this list. *The following paragraphs are informative and are not meant to replace the needed CPR and first aid training.*

## Basic CPR and First Aid for Infants

If an infant is found unconscious, the teacher should check the victim (Figure 5-2) and have someone call for emergency assistance. If no one else is present, then wait until rescue breathing has been attempted for several minutes before calling for emergency assistance. Carefully look, listen, and feel for breathing, and pat the child's feet or tap the shoulder to see if there is a response.

Check to see if the tongue or something else is obstructing the **airway (A).** Infants often put things in their mouth that could cause an airway obstruction. If there appears to be an obstruction, lay the infant along your forearm with his face down, making sure that his head and neck are lower than his torso. Be sure to support the head with your hand on the jaw and rest the forehead on your thigh. Using the heel of your free hand, give the baby four or five rapid blows to the back between the shoulder blades, which should take about four to five seconds (Figure 5-3). Once the first set of back blows have been done, turn the infant over, supporting the body on your free forearm and the head and neck with your free hand and fingers, while enclosing the child between your two arms. Now that the infant is well supported on the back and head, place your forearm on your thigh for further support. Now, using the middle and index fingers of the other hand, give four quick chest thrusts in the center of the infant's breastbone with a

**FIGURE 5-2**
If an infant is found unconscious, the victim should be checked while someone calls for emergency assistance, if possible.

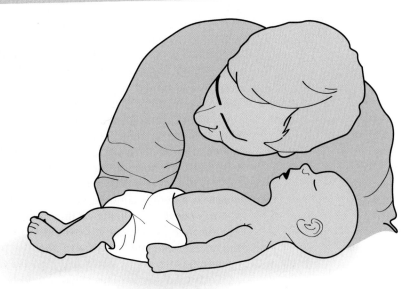

**FIGURE 5-3**
Using the heel of your free hand, give the baby four or five rapid blows to the back between the shoulder blades.

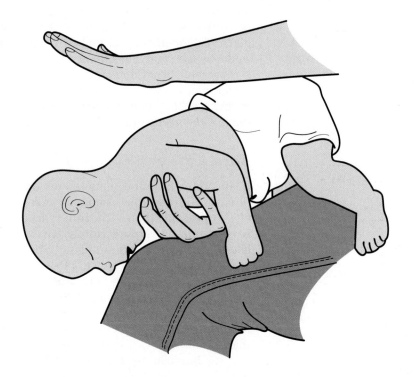

steady, jabbing motion (Figure 5-4). Once one set of back blows and chest thrusts has been completed, continue several more times. In the case of children a finger sweep might be performed, but this is not usually done because of the size of the infant's mouth. A finger check in an infant may actually push an obstruction further down the throat. The exception might be if you can see the object and believe that you can get hold of it to remove it carefully, so as not to push it further down the air passage.

If there appears to be no obstruction, then infant rescue **breathing (B)** should be performed. In infants it is very important not to tilt the head back too far. An infant's air passage is very narrow and pushing the head back too far may actually shut the airway. Once the neck is in position, the teacher should cover the infant's nose and mouth with her mouth and use a gentle puff of air that is blown from the cheeks, not the lungs (Figure 5-5). This ensures that it is the right amount of air for the infant. The infant should expel the air you have breathed in on his own. As this is occurring, watch the chest and listen to see whether breathing has resumed. Repeat this process several times.

If the infant does not resume breathing, then a check for **circulation (C)** should be performed. This is done by checking the brachial artery near the arm pit, between the elbow and shoulder. Place the middle and index finger with light pressure on this artery and wait four to five seconds (Figure 5-6).

If no pulse is felt, then it is necessary to perform compression on the chest. In a gentle manner, place the middle three fingers in the center of the victim's chest, visualizing an imaginary line between the infant's two nipples. Tilt the neck back, as you would with rescue breathing. Lifting the index finger, exercise gentle pressure about $1/2$ to $3/4$ inch deep on the chest with the remaining two fingers. This is done for five times, then a rescue breathing puff is administered. This cycle should be repeated 20 times before checking for breathing and pulse. It should continue until help arrives.

**FIGURE 5-4**
Support the neck and head with your hand and fingers, then using the middle and index fingers of the other hand, give four quick chest thrusts in the center of the infant's breastbone with a steady jabbing motion.

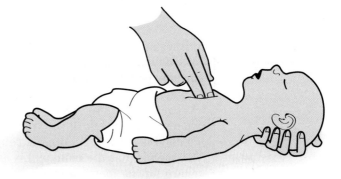

**FIGURE 5-5**
Cover the infant's nose and mouth with your mouth and use a gentle puff of air blown from the cheeks.

**FIGURE 5-6**
Check the brachial artery near the arm pit between the elbow and shoulder using the middle and index finger with light pressure on this artery and wait 4 or 5 seconds to feel pulse.

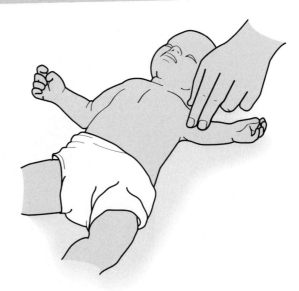

## *Basic CPR or Rescue Breathing for Children*

If a child is found unconscious, the teacher should check the victim (Figure 5-7) and emergency assistance should be called. Figure 5-8 shows a teacher administering rescue breathing.

If a child appears to be choking, the **airway (A)** for breathing may be partially or totally blocked. Choking in children can happen during eating or when a child puts an object in her mouth that is small enough to swallow and get caught. The usual recognized sign that a child is choking is when she grasps her throat with one or both hands. Another sign of a choking child is coughing. Forceful coughing usually indicates partial blockage. This means that the child still is able to get air in the lungs. The best procedure for the moment is to encourage the child to continue coughing and try to cough up the object. The child should be attended by a teacher. If nothing comes out in a short time, call for emergency assistance.

Weak coughing usually indicates the blockage is more complete. A choking child can stop breathing and lose consciousness rapidly. The

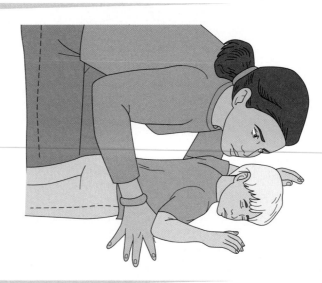

**FIGURE 5-7**
Check the victim.

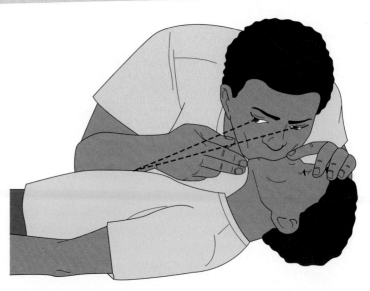

**FIGURE 5-8**
Give rescue breathing.

teacher should give abdominal thrusts until the object is coughed up or the child becomes unconscious. Have someone call for emergency assistance.

If a breathing emergency exists and none of the other methods work, then the teacher who is qualified in CPR should begin performing CPR while someone calls for emergency assistance.

The first part of performing the rescue **breathing (B)** is similar to the steps used for an infant, but in this case the head is tilted back further (Figure 5-8). The teacher should pinch the child's nose using two fingers and place his or her mouth over the child's. If it is a small child, the teacher might be able to place his mouth over both the nose and mouth of the child. Give two shallow breaths, making sure the child's stomach does not distend or protrude. If the breath is too deep, it could cause the child to vomit. If this happens, turn the child's head on the side and use your finger to sweep all obstruction away.

If rescue breathing has been performed once and the child still does not appear to be breathing, you will need to check the **circulation (C).** To feel for the pulse, apply two fingers to the carotid artery with slight pressure for between five and ten seconds. If there is no heart beat, then compression thrusts will need to be performed. To find the right place, the teacher should place two fingers of one hand on the child's sternum and then place the other hand on top of those fingers. Once placed, use the top hand to hold the head back for rescue breathing between the compression thrusts. If the child is small, the compression pressure should be less. Counting aloud, press down five times, then do one breath. Repeat this for 20 times. Check the carotid artery for a pulse. Continue this process until help arrives.

## First Aid Procedures

There are many minor emergencies, such as scraping a knee or bumping a head, that can be taken care of easily by first aid. Other emergencies, such as a broken bone, a cut that needs stitches, or a burn that is beyond first degree, will need prompt first aid and then have the parent take the child to his own physician for further treatment. It is essential that the teacher know how to perform basic pediatric first aid procedures. The American Red Cross and other organizations perform a service to the community by providing this training. The following are reminders for the teacher of signs, symptoms, and responses.

*Bites.* There are a number of common ways that a child can suffer bites in an early childhood education environment. These include bites from insects, animals, or other children. Insects may bite or sting a child. These commonly come from bees, wasps, ants, and ticks. Some of these bites may cause an allergic reaction in some children. When the teacher observes those signs, the emergency medical services should be called immediately. Table 5-5 reflects those signs. (See Chapter 13 for the use of an Epipen in the case of a severe reaction to an insect bite or sting.)

**TABLE 5-5**
*Signs of Allergic Reaction to Insect Bites or Stings*

| | |
|---|---|
| • Pain | • Swelling of the throat |
| • Itching | • Difficulty breathing |
| • Hives or red rash | • Partial loss of consciousness |

If a child is stung and the stinger remains, the teacher should try to remove it with tweezers. The area around the stinger must not be scraped or squeezed after removing the stinger; the teacher must wash the area with soap and water and apply an ice pack. The same procedure is followed with an insect bite. If the early childhood education program is located in an area of the United States where ticks, scorpions, black widow spiders, or brown recluse spiders live, the teacher should have first aid information regarding them. For further information on ticks, see Chapter 4. In addition to first aid, if it is suspected that a child was bitten by a scorpion, black widow, or brown recluse spider, he or she should see a physician immediately.

There are a number of poisonous snakes throughout the United States and Canada. If a snake bites a child, remove the child from the area of the snake immediately. Get a good description of the snake for medical purposes. Have the child lie down, and elevate the place where the bite occurred, if possible. Call 911 for emergency assistance.

For a bite from another child or an animal, the teacher should wash the wound immediately with soap and water. If the bite breaks the skin, the child should be taken to his or her physician for a follow-up. The wound should be covered with a sterile gauze bandage. If heavy bleeding is caused by the wound, emergency assistance must be called.

If a child is bitten by a dog or cat, it should be reported immediately to public health officials or a physician, because bites from animals could carry rabies. Another reason to report it to a physician is that animal bites can also carry infection. It is important that the area is washed well with soap and water and bandaged to keep it clean. If it is a serious animal bite, call 911 for emergency assistance. Animal bites can also cause emotional trauma, and this should be carefully watched for.

*Cuts and Other Injuries to the Skin.* Cuts and other injuries to the skin occur when children play, collide with objects, or take risks. The type of cut or degree of injury to the skin determines whether emergency assistance is necessary. If the cut is bleeding profusely or is jagged, torn, or deep, emergency assistance will be needed. Table 5-6 indicates the type of cut and the degree of injury.

Before emergency assistance arrives, it is important to stop the bleeding of a deep or severe cut. If possible, elevate the wound above the level of the heart. The teacher should use a clean cloth that is folded to firmly apply

Some cuts and wounds require stitches.

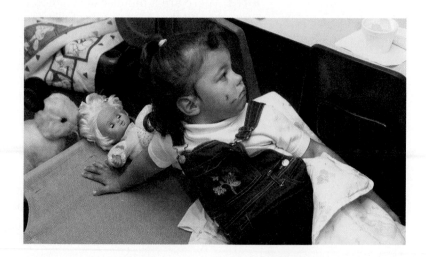

**TABLE 5-6**
*Types of Cuts and Wounds*

*Abrasion.* A scrape caused by contact with hard surface such as pavement or carpet. Common childhood cut.

*Incision.* A sharp, even cut caused by glass, knives, and other sharp objects. The depth or length of wound determines the blood flow and the degree of seriousness.

*Laceration.* A jagged or torn cut caused by objects with uneven edges or by force. Tissue damage may be great.

*Puncture.* A hole in the skin caused by sharp objects such as a nail, thorn, or splinter.

*Bruise.* A discolored area of the skin caused by contact with an object, usually by force, such as falling or colliding with another object.

Adapted from American Red Cross.

Head injuries should be carefully evaluated before they are determined serious.

pressure. If this cloth becomes soaked with blood, do not remove it, but instead add another cloth on top of it. Keep applying this pressure for at least 7 minutes or as long as 10 minutes. If emergency help has not yet arrived, find a pressure point that is closest to the wound and apply pressure with the heel of the hand. It is important to avoid the use of tourniquets.

Cuts and wounds not needing emergency medical treatment should be washed with soap and water and covered with a bandage. Cuts that are more than an inch long and those that involve a large or deep wound that could cause scarring may require stitches. If there is an indication for stitches, the child should be sent to his or her own physician as soon as possible.

**Injuries Involving the Head, Mouth, and Nose.** Injuries involving the head are common in early childhood education because of falls from outdoor equipment and collisions with objects or other children. These injuries may be internal or external. External injuries may involve cuts or scratches. Internal injuries may involve bruising of the brain or blood vessel damage to the skull (NCCCHSRC, 2005b). Head injuries may be minor or they may be more serious. Sometimes it is difficult to tell immediately if the injury is serious when the child remains conscious. Table 5-7 lists the symptoms of a serious head injury.

For many children, the result of a fall will be a bruise and swelling where contact was made. Have the child lie down for a while with an ice pack. Carefully observe the child's behavior for at least one hour.

Injuries to the mouth and nose can happen easily. Injuries to the mouth can be to the gums, teeth, tongue, or lips. If there is unusually heavy bleeding, emergency assistance must be summoned. Otherwise bleeding is controlled by direct pressure by holding a sterile piece of gauze where the injury has occurred. Once the bleeding has stopped for a while, have the child rinse out the mouth with water. If the injury is outside the mouth, wash the area with soap and water. In case of swelling, apply an ice pack. If a child loses a tooth, find the tooth and clean it off with water. Place the tooth in a jar of milk and have the parents take the child to his or her dentist immediately.

Nose injuries most commonly involve nosebleeds. This is usually handled by pinching the child's nostrils together between the teacher's thumb and forefinger. Do not tilt the head back. Have the child sit quietly. Talk quietly to the child while this is being done. Explain the procedure and ask the child if he or she has any questions. It normally takes approximately ten minutes for a nosebleed to stop. If it does not stop after ten minutes, the child's physician should be consulted. Some children have a history of nosebleeds that may take longer to stop. The physician can offer further advice.

***Burns.*** Burns come from a number of sources, such as heat, steam, chemicals, or electrical sources. The different degrees of burns are listed in Figure 5-9.

If the burn is a third-degree burn, emergency medical assistance must be called immediately. There are three basic steps to care for burns. First, the burning must stop, which may entail putting out a fire and removal from the area. Never pull off clothes that are stuck to the skin. Second, cool the burn by flushing it with water. Do not use ice unless it is a very minor burn, because ice could damage the tissue. Flush the skin or layer cool, wet cloths on the burn. Third, when the burn has cooled down, cover with a dry, clean, and

**TABLE 5-7**
*Symptoms of Serious Head Injury*

| | |
|---|---|
| • Vomiting | • Change in pulse rate |
| • Shock | • Cold, clammy skin |
| • Confused behavior | • Loss of consciousness |
| • Unevenly dilated pupils | • Bleeding or clear fluid coming from nose, ear, or mouth |
| • Seizure | |
| • Dizziness | • Weakness or paralysis |
| • Change in breathing rate | |

FIGURE 5-9
Burn Institute Burn Depth
Categories *(Courtesy of the
Burn Institute)*

# BURN DEPTH CATEGORIES

| DEGREE | APPEARANCE | PAIN LEVEL |
|---|---|---|
| **1st** | Pink<br>Red | Uncomfortable |
| **2nd** | Pink - Pale<br>May blister<br>Moist | Marked<br>discomfort |
| **3rd** | Pale - White<br>Charred<br>Dry | Painless<br>Some pain |

# WHEN TO CALL FOR MEDICAL HELP:

√ If the burn is on the face, hands or feet.
√ If the victim is an infant, child, sick or elderly person.
√ If swelling or infection develops.
√ If there is marked discomfort or the burn is painless.
√ If a third degree burn is suspected.
√ If there is any doubt about how serious the burn is.
  Burns are often more serious than they first appear.

# FOR BURN EMERGENCIES
# (619) 543-6503

UCSD Regional Burn Center, 24 hours a day

or **911**

**Burn Institute**

3702 Ruffin Rd, Ste.101, San Diego, CA 92123 (619) 541-2277
© 1996

sterile dressing. If the burn appears to be more serious than a first-degree burn, have the parents take the child to his or her physician.

*Temperature.* Both extremes of temperature can have an effect on children in an early childhood education environment. Children can get easily overheated. They may get cramps from the heat or heat exhaustion. The cramps occur in the leg muscles and the stomach. These are usually the first warning signs of trouble with heat. Heat exhaustion involves nausea, headache, dizziness, and flushed skin. Both conditions are treated by placing the child in a cool place and having him drink lots of liquids. Sometimes applying a cool cloth to the face makes the child think he feels cooler (Figure 5-10).

Exposure to cold may involve frostbite, but the normal conditions of early childhood education would preclude this from occurring. However, if the teacher observes the signs, he or she should act accordingly. Frostbite is indicated by a lack of feeling in an area where the skin is cold and may appear discolored or look waxy (Figure 5-11). To render first aid, warm the area by soaking it in warm (not hot) water. Keep doing so until the area appears red and feels warm. Bandage the area with a light sterile dressing. Have the parents take the child to her physician.

Hypothermia is another winter risk for very young children. A young child usually loses heat faster than an adult and with the larger head in proportion to the body a child is more likely to lose heat from the head area. It may be easy for children to ignore this condition because they are cold and may not know when it is time to go inside. Hypothermia usually comes on gradually, and the first sign is shivering. Other signs include slow rate of breathing, pale skin and slurred speech. If you see these signs, move the child out of the cold, remove any wet clothing, give him something warm to drink and share body heat if necessary. Breathing should be monitored. Do not apply direct heat or massage/rub the child. Either of those measures can have serious or even fatal consequences.

*Poisoning.* Poisoning can occur in four ways: by ingestion, by inhalation, by absorption, and by injection such as snake venom. Under any poisoning circumstance, the first step in first aid is to call the **poison control center** in your area. Closely follow the instructions given. These instructions will include the age of child and the evidence of poisoning that has been observed. As indicated by poison control, call for emergency assistance where applicable. Table 5-8 indicates the symptoms of poisoning by ingestion, inhalation, and absorption. The symptoms in Table 5-5 are the same symptoms that may appear after injected poisoning.

The child must not have anything to eat or drink unless instructed. If the poison has been absorbed through the skin, flush the skin with water until help arrives. If the child appears to have inhaled a poison, provide fresh air or put the child in a well-ventilated room with an open window.

● **Poison control center**
*a resource available through a phone call in case of poisoning*

**FIGURE 5-11**
Frostbite results when cold temperatures freeze body cells. Hypothermia results when, over time, the body's temperature drops.

**TABLE 5-8**
*Symptoms of Poisoning*

**Ingested**
- Nausea and/or vomiting
- Diarrhea
- Change in breathing
- Unconsciousness

**Inhaled**
- Headache
- Dizziness
- Difficulty breathing
- Unconsciousness

**Absorbed**
- Irregular breathing
- Headache
- Abnormal pulse
- Skin or eye irritations

## Key Concept 5.4

### Basic CPR and First Aid

It is important for the teacher to know basic CPR and first aid techniques because they may help save a child's life. Knowing what an emergency is and when to call for help is vital. There may be other situations in which basic first aid techniques will satisfactorily solve the situation and enable the teacher to take care of the child's injury. Having information about illness or injury due to bites, cuts, head injuries, temperature, burns, and poisons allows the teacher to provide a greater degree of protection for the children in care.

## 5.5 EMERGENCY PLANNING FOR CHILDREN WITH SPECIAL NEEDS

Many early childhood education situations today include one or more children with special needs such as a chronic medical condition or allergy that may call for emergency response. The teacher should be very familiar with what emergency might arise for each child who has special needs.

Every child with special needs should have a written emergency management plan that includes the child's diagnosis, as well as routine measures that keep that child healthy and at less risk (Sokol-Gutierrez, 1999). It should also include emergency signs to watch for, emergency procedures that should be followed, and who should be contacted when this occurs. A duplicate copy of this plan should be kept in the first aid kit. This information should be updated regularly (AAP, 1999).

If medication is part of the emergency response, it should also be included in a separate first aid kit. This might include inhalers for children with asthma, epinephrine for children with peanut or other allergies, and insulin for a diabetic child. It would be helpful for the teacher to speak to the physicians of children with special needs in order to better understand how to protect them and be prepared to handle emergency situations that can arise when children with special needs are in care (Sailors, 2004a). Parents will need to authorize the release of this information.

### Key Concept 5.5

**Emergency Planning for Children with Special Needs**

It is essential for a teacher to be prepared to handle emergency responses for children with special needs. An emergency management plan should be written for each child in care who has special needs. The teacher should be prepared to respond in the proper manner. These responses may include the administering of special medications that will help a child to recover from the emergency.

## 5.6 DISASTER PREPAREDNESS

Disaster preparedness is an essential element in addressing emergency response procedures. No teacher ever expects a disaster to occur. However, for the safety of the children in care, it should be planned for, and the environment should be organized to cope with a disaster, should it occur.

Disasters have normally been associated with acts of nature, such as tornadoes, floods, earthquakes, or fires. Fires may also be caused by human carelessness. Other potential disasters might include a gas leak or noxious fumes from a chemical spill. Procedures for a chemical emergency spill or release should be prepared and posted (Bright Horizons, 2003). Another potential for a disaster might be blackouts of electricity, whether they are rolling or otherwise. Lack of electricity could affect heating, air conditioning, and refrigeration. These may be critical factors for some children with special needs. An example might be a child who needs to be on a nebulizer for which electricity is needed. Lack of refrigeration could put the food that is stored in the freezer or refrigerator at risk for growing bacteria that could cause illness. A plan for dealing with blackouts should be discussed if the early childhood education program is located in an area where they are an issue.

Early childhood education programs may also be impacted by an intentional human act of violence, meant to harm. The recent destruction of the World Trade Center Twin Towers in New York City greatly affected the on-site early childhood education program. Quick action and an evacuation plan by teachers allowed all children in care to escape safely. The bombing of the Federal Building in Oklahoma City included an on-site early childhood education center, and there was much loss of life, including children. Early childhood education centers have also been threatened with violence involving guns. For example, an incident in the late 1990s in Granada Hills, California, occurred when a man invaded an early childhood education environment and shot a number of children.

A planned response to violence should be talked about and agreed upon before it occurs. A code phrase such as "Ground Hog Day" should be known to all teachers so that they can be alerted to danger without causing fear to the children (Sailors, 2000). If you are a family home teacher who is all alone with no one to assist you, you should respond by calling 911 or the rescue number in the local area.

Just as it has been suggested to all Americans that we be vigilant in our awareness of our surroundings for terrorists, the same should hold true for an early childhood education situation. As teachers we are protectors of children and should do our utmost to keep their environment safe from any type of violent act, including terrorism. See Figure 5-12 for the Homeland Security Alert List, adapted for early childhood education environments.

The disaster most likely to occur is fire, because it is more common than all of the other disasters combined. Fire can happen any time, any where, and under a number of circumstances. Because it is a common disaster, all teachers should prepare the environment to deal with a fire should it take place.

The location of the early childhood education environment has an impact on the type of natural disaster that may occur. Tornadoes are more likely to occur in the mid-America sector, whereas hurricanes are more likely to occur on the southern coastal areas. Earthquakes are more apt to happen in California. Floods occur near rivers, lakes, dams, and other bodies of water. Snow, with blizzard potential, occurs throughout the country. Knowledge of the particular disasters that are likely to occur in the location of the early childhood education environment is a good way to begin preparations.

## Evacuation Procedures

● **Evacuation**
*removal of persons from a site where a disaster or emergency exists*

● **Survival procedures**
*preparation and steps to follow to stay in place in case of disaster or weather emergency*

Most disasters can be divided into two categories. The first is a disaster that requires **evacuation** and the second type of disaster calls for **survival procedures**. These survival procedures are usually referred to as "shelter-in-place": instead of leaving the site, you would remain in place for the greatest safety. Many types of disaster such as fires, floods, tornadoes, and hurricanes may require evacuation. Evacuation procedures are basic. Since evacuation may be necessary in the case of fire, all teachers should be prepared with evacuation procedures and policies that help to reinforce them.

Every early childhood education environment should have a written plan that includes a diagram about emergency evacuation. Figure 5-13

**FIGURE 5-12**

Recommended action for early childhood education environments.

**Risk of Attack**

Develop an emergency plan for the environment
Develop policies for the type of emergency
Create an emergency supply kit for shelter-in-place
Create an emergency supply kit for evacuation
Know how to turn off utilities in the environment
Have all emergency information and phone numbers of families gathered and available
Have an emergency packet for each child with a letter, picture of the family and a special toy
Make sure at least one person in the environment has first aid and CPR training
Send home emergency plan information including communication system that will be used
Have a cell phone available for emergency calls

**Green**
Low Risk

Review all steps at level green
Check emergency supplies and replace outdated items
Conduct emergency drills
Be alert to suspicious activity and report it to proper authorities
Send emergency information home to families
Send reminder of emergency and communication plan home

**Blue**
Guarded Risk

Complete recommended steps from level green and blue
Update emergency information and phone numbers as necessary
Develop alternative routes to and from early childhood education site
Be more vigilant and alert to suspicious activity and report it to authorities

**Yellow**
Elevated Risk

Complete recommended steps from levels green, blue, and yellow
Review emergency plan and policies
Be prepared to handle concerns from children and families
Survey the neighborhood for emergency assistance
Be more vigilant and alert to suspicious activity and report it to authorities

**Orange**
High Risk

Complete recommended steps at all other levels
Listen to emergency information and stay tuned to radio or television for instructions
Be prepared to shelter-in-place or evacuate
Close early childhood education site if recommended
Be extremely vigilant about strangers in the environment or unusual situations

**Red**
Severe Risk

**Information Adapted from Homeland Security Advisory System**

**FIGURE 5-13**
A diagram of the early childhood education center is an important tool to have during emergencies, particularly if the center must be evacuated.

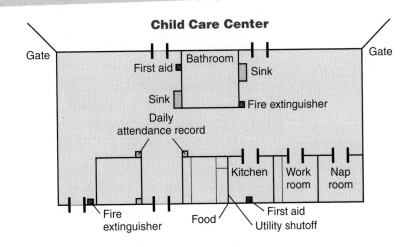

shows a diagram of a typical early childhood education center. Included on the diagram are the exit doors and windows, location of first aid kits, daily attendance records and fire extinguishers, utility shutoff, and location of food, clothing, and tools. Each of these items may need to be accessed.

It is essential that there be an evacuation plan that everyone concerned with the early childhood education program understands. This includes teachers, children, and their parents. Teachers will need to know what emergency records might have to be accessed. It is a good idea to keep copies of all children's emergency information in a fireproof, portable file, because this allows the teacher access to information about emergency contacts and so forth. If a child has a specific health challenge such as an allergy or other special needs, his or her records should be copied and placed in the portable file. A teacher should be designated in charge of this file, including keeping the information current and updated.

A teacher should be responsible for keeping daily attendance checklists for the children in care. The checklist should be frequently checked throughout the day for accuracy. This information may be needed if evacuation occurs and confusion ensues. Having a checklist will help to bring order. The teacher should also be familiar with emergency phone numbers and should follow the organization for emergencies.

The teacher should plan for emergency evacuation using several proactive strategies. These are included in Table 5-9.

The teacher should discuss emergency procedures with parents so they are familiar with the practice and drills the children are performing. Inform parents of the emergency evacuation plans. The teacher should let the families know where the children will be taken in case of an emergency. Having a safe emergency shelter is important, and it is equally important that the parents know the location.

The teacher should prepare the children for an evacuation emergency by having them practice fire drills, using and understanding exits. They should participate in group discussions about what to do and should understand about a meeting point outside if the building does have to be evacuated. These drills should be held once a month.

**TABLE 5-9**
*Proactive Strategies
for Evacuation*

- Plan two exit routes from the building. Post these throughout the building.
- Test smoke and fire alarms once a month.
- Plan a fire drill once per month.
- Plan exit strategies for removing infants and toddlers. These may be using a wagon, crib, and so forth, that can carry several children at a time and will go through a door.
- Be familiar with and post information concerning the shut-off switches for gas, water, electricity, and other utilities that may pose a safety risk.
- Know how and when to use a fire extinguisher.
- Prepare children to handle emergencies by drills, discussion, and use of diagram.
- Teach children "Stop, Drop, Roll, Cool, and Call" techniques and practice with them.
- Keep a fireproof, portable file with emergency and health information for special needs of children in care.
- Choose a safe emergency shelter spot and prearrange for its use during an emergency.

Teachers should conduct fire drills once each month. In this case, children are practicing walking out of a building through a darkened area.

The teacher should practice drills with infants and toddlers who may not walk or not walk well yet. These exit drills would take place in a wagon or crib, just as they would under emergency conditions. Children should also be taught several catch phrases. These include "Stop, Drop, and Roll," "Go Tell a Grown-up," and "Crawl Low Under Smoke" (Cole et al., 2004). See Figure 5-14 as an example of a sign that children could recognize and that would help them learn. They should practice it regularly on the day of a fire drill.

**FIGURE 5-14**
Children should be taught to "Stop, Drop, Roll, Cool, and Call." (Courtesy of the Burn Institute.)

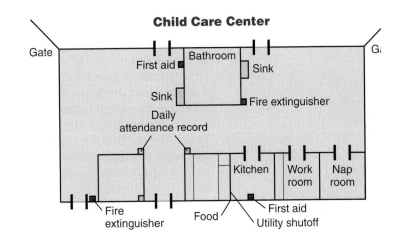

Children should regularly practice the "Stop, Drop, and Roll" procedure.

## Shelter-in-Place Procedures

Other disasters such as an earthquake or blizzard may call for everyone to remain in the early childhood education environment. This isolation may last a few hours or several days. The survival mode or shelter-in-place procedure may need to be applied in this instance. If the early childhood education environment is in a location that has potential for the need for survival, then the teacher must be organized and properly prepared. Another reason for survival mode might be a countywide school lockdown due to gunfire or an intruder in the local area (American Red Cross [ARC], 2001b). Certo (1995) suggested that a "pretend" emergency day be held so that children and staff are prepared to function should that emergency occur. Table 5-10 shows a sample schedule explaining the functions that can take place when simulating an emergency due to an earthquake.

Table 5-11 shows an emergency survival supplies list that should be kept on hand in case of a survival mode emergency.

In case of an earthquake, it may be safer if the teacher carries out the survival mode outdoors. The supplies kept on hand might just be moved outside. It is important to have a designated area in which care will take place.

It is very important that the teacher do whatever possible to protect health during this time (Sailors, 2004b). Having a clean supply of water is essential. Enough bottled water should be available for drinking. To stop the spread of disease, frequent hand washing is critically important for this time. If a chemical spill or other contamination compromises the water, then use alternatives to hand washing such as antibacterial hand wash. Contaminated water can be used to flush toilets. Make sure that plenty of

**TABLE 5-10**
*Sample Schedule for an Earthquake Emergency*

| Time | Activity |
| --- | --- |
| 8:15 A.M. | Pretend quake. Children get under tables. Staff supervises then gets in doorways. Staff then simulates damage and blocks off some areas. Staff tries to keep children calm and quiet. |
| 8:25 A.M. | Go to center of room. Count children, check attendance list. Discuss plan and assign every child a partner. Give first aid with masking tape. Simulate shutoffs of gas, electricity, and water. |
| 8:35 A.M. | Gather emergency survival kit (see Table 5-11) and emergency information. Pretend cleanup with children helping with smaller items. |
| 8:45 A.M. | Try to resume normalcy by having children play in small groups away from windows. Simulate aftershock. Children go under tables, staff into doorways. Try to calm and quiet children again. |
| 9:00 A.M. | Children wash up (simulate, using very little water). Have snack bar from emergency survival kit. Drink juice. Talk about quake and plans for further survival mode. |
| 9:15 A.M. | End of drill. |

Adapted from "Helping Children and Staff Cope with Earthquakes," by D. Certo, March 1995, *Child Care Information Exchange.*

**TABLE 5-11**
*Emergency Survival Supplies Checklist*

## ✓ CHECK FOR:

☐ Fire extinguisher

☐ First aid kit

☐ Flashlights and extra batteries

☐ Crescent or pipe wrench to turn off gas/water, if needed

☐ Shovel, screwdriver, 20-foot length of rope

☐ 1 gallon of water per child, 2 gallons per adult, and iodine tablets

☐ Duct tape and one package plastic sheeting

☐ Portable radio and batteries for emergency broadcasts

☐ Three- to four-day supply of dry or canned food per person, hand (non-electric) can opener; include energy bars and juice boxes. Also include some comforting foods for all, such as tinned cookies, candies, and tea and/or coffee for the staff.

☐ Paper plates, plastic utensils, paper cups, and paper towels

☐ Alternate cooking source, matches

☐ Blankets and extra clothing (Most early childhood education sites already keep extra clothing for children.)

☐ Extra newspapers to wrap waste and trash

☐ Large plastic trash bags for trash and waste

☐ Three- to four-day supply of toilet paper

☐ Infant supplies—diapers, formula, food—for three to four days

☐ Three- to four-day supply of food and water for any pets present

☐ Essential medications needed for children with special needs (e.g., inhaler for asthmatic)

☐ Safe alternate heat source (nonelectric) and fuel for it; this might be wood for a fireplace or kerosene for a room heater

☐ Copies of class lists, medical records, and release form for children

☐ Maps with evacuation exits, if needed later, and shut-off sites for utilities, etc.

☐ Large plastic bucket with lid, a child's potty chair, and toilet paper

☐ One gallon of bleach and a bottle of liquid soap

☐ Several bottles of antibacterial hand wash

☐ Work gloves

☐ Personal hygiene items

☐ Whistle to signal for help if needed

toilet paper, diapers, and diaper wipes are readily available to sustain a three-day shelter-in-place. If the water supply is cut off due to broken pipes, then use a plastic bucket with a lid or a child's potty chair as alternatives (Sailors, 2004b). Having plenty of bleach on hand will be important for sanitizing the environment.

## Helping Children Cope with Disaster

The first rule of any disaster is for the teacher to behave in a calm manner. If the teacher is in a total panic, the children's behavior will reflect this (ARC, 2001b). Therefore, although the teacher may feel upset or panicky, he or she should try not to show it. When disasters are planned for and practiced, physical safety is easier to cope with and handle.

Adults often tend to ignore the emotional needs of a child, once safety has been established. Children often have emotional consequences as a result of being in an emergency situation. Children are often very afraid and may not be able to verbalize it. This may be especially true in situations such as earthquakes, when aftershocks occur, or tornadoes, when the wind might still be blowing. The University of Illinois Cooperative Extension (UIE) has a helpful pamphlet *Children, Stress and Natural Disasters* that may help you to help the children as they try to cope with any type of disaster that has occurred (UIE, 1998).

# REALITY CHECK

## Creating an Emergency Natural Disaster Plan for Your Early Childhood Education Environment

Natural disasters are more widespread than one might think. In 2000, there were 44 major disasters in 32 states in this country. These disasters included tornadoes, tropical storms, severe winter and spring storms, hurricanes, floods, and wildfires. Each area has liabilities for certain natural disasters (Riopelle et al., 2004). Floods, wildfires, severe thunderstorms, and earthquakes have occurred in every state. Hurricanes occur from Texas to Maine on the Gulf and eastern seaboard. Hailstorms happen in the midwest, and tornadoes take place in 38 states. Weather-related disasters seem to be increasing due to changes in the weather pattern and ozone layer (Institute for Business and Home Safety, 1998).

Mitigation is the preparation to protect people and structures from risk for natural disasters (Disaster Training International [DTI], 2001). This should occur in early childhood education environments, because risk is everywhere and children may be more vulnerable to injury. Lack of adequate preparation for disaster could cause the need to replace equipment or repair buildings, requiring a program to be shut down for a time. It could also mean injury or loss of life to children or teachers.

An example of an early childhood education environment using mitigation measures took place in Washington State, when Federal Emergency Management Agency (FEMA) officials helped Little Church on the Prairie Learning Center, which was in a seismic zone, prepare for earthquakes. The measures, such as bolting cribs to walls and strapping water heaters in place, prevented any children from getting injured on February 28, 2001, when a quake hit (FEMA, 2001a). The project was funded in part by FEMA Hazard Mitigation funds and the rest by local businesses.

To adequately prepare for a natural disaster in your local area, there are certain steps to consider. The first step would be to identify the hazards that are typical in your area (ARC, 2001b). There are several ways to do this. You could talk with emergency management people in the local area to find out the possible hazards they have dealt with, or you could look

# REALITY CHECK (Continued)

at the history of weather for the past 100 years for that area. The American Red Cross has a place on their Web site that identifies the typical disaster state by state: http://www.redcross.org. FEMA's Web site, http://www.fema.gov/, has storm watches and other information to help determine risk in your area. The national weather bureau's site, http://www.noaa.gov/, includes a large amount of information on weather, as well as forecasts for hurricanes and tropical storms.

The next step would be to develop an outline for each hazard you have found to be present in your area.

- How often does this hazard occur?
- How bad might it get?
- Where is it likely to happen?
- How long might it last?
- Is it seasonal?
- How fast might it occur?
- Will there be a warning?

You may live in an area where an earthquake has occurred once in 50 years, so it would not be a hazard for which you might develop a disaster plan. On the other hand, if you live in an area where there are severe snowstorms or tropical storms on a regular seasonal basis, you might need to be better prepared for them than you have been.

The third step would be to put together the information you have gathered as to risk for each hazard and then look to your early childhood education center or family child care home for answers to possible consequences should that hazard occur. For example, if your center or family child care home is in a valley near a river and the greatest potential risk you found was flooding, your location points to greater degree of risk than if you were located on a hillside. To fully examine this step, you should ask the following questions:

- What are the geographical features that might put you at risk (DTI, 2001)?

- Are there any features of your property that might cause risk or offer protection? For example, are there telephone or electrical wires directly above your building?
- What are the available communication systems between your facility and the parents? Do you have a cell phone, and which parents have cell phones or pagers?
- How many children are in care, and what are their developmental levels (i.e., can they walk or do they have to be carried)?
- What local resources do you have that could help in an emergency and help you plan for one?

As those questions are answered, the information will be combined with the information gathered in the first two steps and used to prioritize risk for the local area and specifically for the early childhood education center or family child care home.

The last step is to think about possible scenarios for the risks that you found. What would the impact of each hazard be, and how would you deal with it? At this point, you can list the needed actions and resources that would be available to help you mitigate the potential damages at your early childhood education center or child care home to prepare for disaster. This might be a complex preparation, or it could be simple. For example, if earthquakes were a great risk, then mitigation similar to the example in Washington State would have to be performed. You would also talk about earthquakes, conduct earthquake drills for "stop, drop, and hold" with children, and find the "safe place" in every room. Adequate preparation for survival mode should take place (Copeland, 1996).

However, if the greatest risk in your area were thunder and lightning storms, the mitigation would be to be aware that a storm might be coming and to take the necessary precautions. Lightning kills approximately 100 people each year in this country; and another 300 are injured by it (Lay, 2001). You could talk to the children about lightning and read books about how it

*(continues)*

# REALITY CHECK (Continued)

occurs (FEMA, 2000b). You could also look at the FEMA Web site for kids: http://www.fema.gov/kids (FEMA, 2001c). You will know that when you hear thunder you need to move children inside immediately, even before it rains (Lay, 2001).

As you create a plan or plans for the natural disasters in your area, remember that children learn a lot by seeing and talking about events. You can better prepare them to deal with natural disasters if you talk about them, read books about them, look at Web sites, and discuss how to keep safe. Do not scare the children, but treat these disasters as the natural occurrences that they are and help

the children to understand them before they happen.

At this time there are two excellent sources that deal with disaster preparedness specifically for early childhood education environments. These are the Head Start Disaster Preparedness Workbook from UCLA's Center for Public Health and Disaster, available online at http://www.cphd.ucla.edu/headstart, and the Pennsylvania Chapter of the American Academy of Pediatrics (PAAAP) Daycare Facilities Emergency Planning Guide, available online at http://www.pema.state.pa.us. These are both comprehensive and would be of assistance in developing a disaster plan.

**CHECK***point:* What is the most likely natural disaster in your local area? What steps would be needed to prepare for an emergency should it occur? Do you know an early childhood education program that is prepared? Do you know one that should take greater safety measures for an emergency?

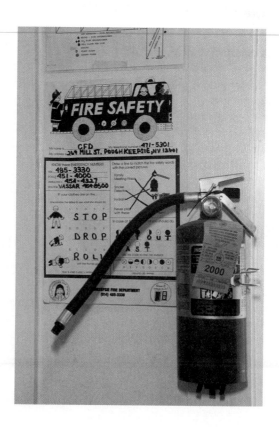

Fire extinguishers should be visible, and all emergency exits should be clearly marked.

Because children need reassurance, the teacher must explain as clearly as possible, without speculation, what has occurred and the facts that are known about it. The teacher should encourage the children to talk and express their concerns and fears. Listening to what others say about their fears and about how they feel and think about what has happened can help the children realize that this shared experience affected everyone. When things settle down, it is important for the teacher to establish a routine. Routines give children a sense of comfort and some predictability.

It is important for the teacher to understand that children may go through stages similar to the bereavement process in dealing with *any* disaster. The first stage occurs during and immediately after the disaster and can bring anxiety and disbelief. The second stage can appear several days or several weeks after disaster strikes. This is when the most disturbing behavior may occur and children may need the most reassurance. Boys are more likely to take a longer time to recover and to display more aggressive behaviors, whereas girls may be more distressed and more verbal about how they feel (Saylor, et al., 1994). The last stage may occur months later, and this is the time when the children come to terms with the disaster. It is important for teachers to understand that they may feel extra stress and strain in dealing with distressed children and need to take care of themselves, as well as the children in care (Giosa, 2004).

Some children may act more clingy or revert to an earlier stage of behavior. Often children are afraid of being left alone, and this may escalate because they are not with their families. Continued reassurance will help. In most disasters, help arrives quickly and the children are likely to be reunited with their families in a short period of time.

If the disaster that the children are reacting to is as a result of an act of violence or terrorism, it is especially important that they get extra help in trying to cope with this disaster. There are crisis counselors available through both public and private agencies who are trained to deal with this type of traumatic event, for both children and adults. You may be having difficulty yourself, coping with your own reactions. Do not try to do this alone. Both you and the children in your care may need professional help, so do not be afraid to seek this outside support.

# REALITY CHECK

## Human-generated Disasters

In Chapter 1, in a Reality Check, war and terrorism and the effect it has on children was discussed. Unfortunately, in the world we live in today, we must be vigilant not only for natural disasters but also for those that are generated by humans. Some of these disasters may be unintentional, such as a chemical spill or a wildfire that starts with a careless camper. However, many of the human-generated disasters that teachers need to think about and be prepared for are intentional. These include chemical and biological terrorism, bomb blasts, radiological

*(continues)*

## REALITY CHECK (Continued)

releases, and hostage-taking. The world was made very aware of how terrorism can affect an entire community in 2004 when a school in Beslan, Russia, was invaded by terrorists and hundreds of people, many of whom were children, were taken hostage. That situation ended badly, with several hundred people dying, with half of them children. This situation left the world wondering what was next. If terrorists were so motivated to make their mark here with so many children present, where would they stop? One difficulty with that situation was the lack of planning and organization on the part of the government and the community for an act of this kind. Today, many schools all over the world are thinking about preparing for this type of a human-generated disaster.

It is much more difficult to do a risk assessment for human-generated disasters than for natural ones, because they will come without warning. It is possible, though, to examine the area that you live in for the possibility of a human-generated disaster and begin preparation from there (Riopelle, et al., 2004). This is best done by examining your community for risk. Is there a nuclear plant or dam nearby? Does your community have a railroad, or is it near a shipping port? Are there any military bases nearby? Are you close to a government building or other government installation? A teacher can help to understand what the local risks are by doing a resource assessment of local agencies to see what risks they may be preparing for. The local Red Cross, fire or police departments, or hospitals may have a plan in place and may offer specific training. Public schools may also have plans prepared. Because many early childhood education environments are privately owned and operated, there is no public plan of action in place for these facilities. It is important to partner with these public agencies to seek some help in planning for a human-generated disaster. It would be helpful for at least one teacher in each early childhood education program be trained in disaster preparedness. A teacher may also look to early childhood education organizations for information on planning for this type of disaster.

It is important to maintain awareness of what is going on in the world. The U.S. Department of Homeland Security issues a color-coded alert. Figure 5-12 presents the preparation steps adapted for early childhood education environments. Review this list to see how it applies to your particular facility. Besides risk assessment and knowledge of the potential types of disaster, it is important that plans assess the particular early childhood education environment and the possible impact that each disaster might have. The next step is to consider the possible scenarios that might exist and how they would affect an early childhood education environment.

Vigilance is key to avoiding the effects of disaster in every community. It is important to watch for unusual persons or items, such as suspicious items left outside the early childhood education facility. If there appears to be someone loitering around the facility for no particular reason, this should be a red-flag warning. It is important to enforce the security that is present in the early childhood education environment. This is the daily signing in and out, having a record of who is and who is not allowed to pick up children, and basic awareness of who is coming and going. It is a good idea to know the neighbors and the neighborhood near the early childhood education environment. Many areas are organized for a Neighborhood Watch; it would be helpful to be part of such a group.

If someone comes into your facility and is armed, the first thing to do is call for help. This may mean calling 911 or calling out the code word or sentence so that someone else can call 911. The children should be gotten to safety, either in an area of the early childhood education facility that can be locked or through evacuating the building and going to a safe place previously agreed upon that the parents are aware of. If confronted by this situation, try to remain calm before the intruder and do what you can to calm him or her. Pay attention and remember details (PAAAP, 2003).

## REALITY CHECK (Continued)

Any suspicious-looking package outside the early childhood education environment should be treated as if it were dangerous. Evacuation should take place as soon as the outside area is surveyed to see if it is safe. A package or a bomb threat that causes evacuation could be a ploy for hostage-taking. Threats from a bomb can also occur via the phone. Get the details, including the distinctive sound of the voice, the apparent age of the caller, and the threat (PAAAP, 2003).

Hazardous substances or materials include chemicals, radioactive materials, and biological agents. If chemicals are manufactured in the local area or if there is a nuclear plant nearby, local fire and other emergency departments have knowledge about the materials. When an incident occurs, there is usually a warning by local police or fire departments (PAAAP, 2003). You may be evacuated from your facility, or it may be determined that it is better to shelter-in-place. If evacuated, before returning, an all-clear signal should be given by authorities. If sheltering-in-place, it may be necessary to use the duct tape and plastic sheeting in your disaster kit to close off all outside ventilation and keep the radio on for further instructions (ARC, 2001b).

As discussed in the Reality Check on war and terrorism and how they affect children, it is important to be truthful with children. On the other hand, do not offer more information than they need. The teacher will need to have practice drills for evacuation and shelter-in-place. Children will want to know what they are doing. Listen carefully to what they are asking. Give the best possible answer that deals only with what they are asking. Don't speculate, and be sure to tell them that preparing for unexpected events may lessen risk. Above all, remember that the main objective is to keep the children and staff safe. Whenever possible, call the emergency resources in the local area.

**CHECK***point:* Have you ever wondered what you would do in a situation that was prompted by terrorism? What do you think you might personally need to be prepared for in your local area?

Fire is just one of the destructive natural disasters that can occur in any region of the country. (Courtesy of Palm Harbor Fire Department.)

## Key Concept 5.6

### Disaster Preparedness

Teachers should be prepared to handle a disaster. Although chances for disasters are slim, preparation will allow for the physical safety of the children to be carried out in an organized manner. Disasters come in many forms and may be natural or manmade. Regardless of the source, disasters can be prepared for by defining what type of disaster might be likely to occur in the early childhood education environment. All teachers should prepare for evacuation, because fire is the most likely disaster to occur. Children should practice fire drills and know all exits. Teachers in locations where the survival mode might be needed should be prepared to handle taking care of children for several days. Teachers should also be prepared to help children with their emotions throughout the disaster, as well as protecting their physical safety.

## 5.7  IMPLICATIONS FOR TEACHERS

Providing prevention and protection should be a part of everyday early childhood education. The teachers should be prepared as best as possible to handle emergencies as they arise. In order to promote protection and prevention in the early childhood education environment, the teacher can act in several ways.

### Education

The beginning step for the teacher is training and education to be prepared to handle an emergency. All teachers should know basic pediatric first aid and rescue breathing. At least one teacher per early childhood education site should have basic CPR training for infants and children. The teacher should know how to organize for and respond to an emergency, including disasters.

Children should be educated in evacuation procedures, should understand exit routes, and should know how to respond. The teacher should arrange for the fire department to visit several times a year and explain about fires and the procedures to respond to them.

Fire drills should be offered monthly. Evacuation and shelter-in-place drills should take place several times a year. It is important to prepare and practice. The drill should be so routine that all children and teachers can be evacuated in minutes, if necessary. Children should also be taught about falls and collisions and how to avoid them. They can also be informed about how to avoid poisons in any environment. Children in areas where survival mode may be a possibility should be given practice drills in survival mode emergency situations.

## For Families

Parents and other family members should be educated in preventing and responding to emergencies as well. The teacher should provide written information to parents that explains about evacuation procedures, a safe place to meet, and how the early childhood education environment will respond to emergencies. The teacher can hold a workshop on how to make a family emergency plan for the household in order for children to have a more protective environment at home as well. This would include an evacuation plan that can be practiced at home every six months. Fire safety information is readily available and can be provided to families. Most fire stations are happy to provide a speaker, and it would be beneficial for families to hear about fire emergencies and evacuation plans from a professional.

## Supervision

Supervision plays a major role in keeping the environment prepared to respond to emergency situations. The emergency forms should be accurate, current, copied, and ready for fast response by being in a fireproof file. Emergency information should be posted by each phone. The teacher should make sure that everyone in the early childhood education environment is prepared to make a call if necessary. Everyone should understand the information needed in an emergency. The teacher should make sure that the backup list for people to help in emergencies is updated and kept current. These backup teachers should be contacted on a monthly basis to maintain the currency of the list.

The first aid kit should be checked regularly to make sure that it is kept up-to-date. As items are used, they should be replaced. If there is a supervising teacher, he or she should make sure that all teachers have the basic first aid and rescue breathing procedure training, and follow up to make sure everyone is kept current in their training. The teacher should be prepared for evacuation or survival mode disasters. The evacuation plan should be regularly reviewed. The survival mode supplies should be periodically checked and replaced if needed.

## Cultural Competence

Emergencies are unsettling to everyone. Emergencies need understanding and adequate preparation. The teacher should provide families of children whose first language is not English with all the written emergency information in their native language whenever possible. The teacher may need to find someone who can translate by using resources such as the local chapter of the NAEYC or the National Family Child Care Association. Arming people with knowledge can prevent panic in emergency situations. The families can reinforce the information that the teacher has given the children by discussing it at home.

If there are families who are recent immigrants or refugees, they may have left their home environments in emergency situations. Because of the trauma they suffered, these children may need extra support during emergencies.

## Key Concept 5.7

### Implications for Teachers

Teachers need to be prepared to handle emergencies in the early childhood education environment. This requires education for both the teacher and the children, working with families, supervision, and cultural competence to get the information across. Education takes place by preparing the teacher to be trained in basic first aid, rescue breathing, and organization for and response to emergencies. Teachers need to prepare children for emergencies by providing training through drill and practice techniques for emergency response. Teachers also need to provide written information to families and communicate with them about the emergency response procedures that will be used, if needed.

Supervision should be provided to update and keep current the emergency information for everyone in the early childhood education environment. This includes having a backup teacher list, a first aid kit, an evacuation plan, and the shelter-in-place supplies needed. Cultural competence should be practiced by having emergency information translated into native languages so that all families are prepared to help their children respond to emergencies.

## CHAPTER SUMMARY

An important part of being a teacher in an early childhood education environment is knowing how to respond in an emergency. In order to be prepared for this response, the teacher needs to understand what constitutes an emergency and what types of injuries will necessitate first aid. The teacher needs to establish an understanding of what steps should be taken for proper action and how they are performed and be able to perform them if an emergency occurs. Basic CPR and rescue breathing are summarized. Disaster preparedness is explained, and the differences between evacuation procedures and shelter-in-place procedures are given. Strategies for teachers on education, working with families, supervision, and cultural competence are discussed.

## TO GO BEYOND

In this section you will find a number of activities that you can use to apply and improve your knowledge of this chapter. There are also thorough online resources that accompanies this text that can be found at http://www.early childed.delmar.com (see description at end of this chapter).

### Chapter Review Critical Thinking Applications

1. Describe the three factors that always indicate an emergency. Relate these to other indicators that an emergency is present.

2. Discuss the importance of preparing for an emergency. How might this preparation have helped the teachers at the World Trade Towers on-site early childhood education program?

3. Compare and contrast the evacuation and shelter-in-place modes of disaster preparedness.

4. Compare and contrast natural disasters with human-generated disasters. How are the preparations similar, and how are they different?

## As an Individual

1. Assemble a list of emergency numbers for your local area.

2. Create an emergency contact form for the early childhood education program.

3. List the items that you would have in an emergency survival mode kit for the type of natural emergency most likely to occur in your local area.

## As a Group

1. Discuss the items that should be kept in the early childhood education environment to prepare for disaster.

2. Break into smaller groups and identify and list at least five things that should be done in the early childhood education environment to prepare children for an emergency.

3. Role play different emergency situations, taking turns being the injured and the teacher who finds them. Have the group evaluate the actions of the teacher during the exercise.

4. Formulate a plan and safety policy that would help you deal with a gun-carrying irate ex-husband of one of your teachers. Compare and contrast that plan to one you might have for a gun-carrying upset parent in a child custody suit.

5. What might be done in an early childhood education environment to help children and families who do not speak English prepare for an emergency?

## Case Studies

1. There is a lot of rain in your area, but lately there has been much more than normal. Your early childhood education program is located on a hill in a suburban area that is close to a river. The center would be in no danger of flooding if the river were to rise, but the lower-lying area might flood enough to isolate you and the children. How might you prepare for this possibility?

2. Mei Lee is a director for an infant/toddler center. A teacher notices smoke coming from the water heater area of the early childhood education environment and rushes to tell Mei Lee about it. Before she can investigate, smoke and flames come pouring out of the water heater closet. How should she proceed? What directions should she give her teachers? What might she have done to prepare her early childhood education environment for this type of emergency?

3. Sam and Kevin, both three years old, have just collided while riding their bikes on the bike path at their early childhood education environment. Sam scraped his knee; Kevin hit his forehead really hard, and there is swelling and some bleeding. What procedures would you take to treat both boys?

## Chapter References

American Academy of Pediatrics (AAP). (1999). Emergency preparedness for children with special health care needs. *Pediatrics, 104*(4), 53.

American Red Cross (ARC). (2001a). *Facing fear: Helping young people deal with terrorism and other tragic events.* Washington, DC: Author.

American Red Cross (ARC). (2001b). What types of disaster do you need to prepare for? Retrieved May 15, 2002, from http://www.redcross.org/services/disaster/keepsafe/map.html.

American Red Cross (ARC). (2001c). *Terrorism: Preparing for the unexpected.* Washington, DC: Author.

American Red Cross (ARC). (2002a, August). *Homeland Security advisory system recommendations: Schools.* Washington, DC: Author:

American Red Cross (ARC). (2002b). *First aid fast.* Washington, DC: Author.

American Red Cross (ARC). (2004). *Children and disasters.* Washington, DC: Author. Retrieved October 14, 2005, from http://www.redcross.org/services/disaster/0,1082,0_602_,00.html

Aronson, S. (2001). Reducing the risk of injury in child care. *Child Care Information Exchange, 101*(3), 64–66.

Aronson, S. (2002). *Model child care health policies.* Rosemont, PA: Healthy Child Care Pennsylvania.

Bright Horizons (2003). Ready to respond emergency preparedness plan for early care and education centers. Retrieved October 14, 2005, from http://www.brighthorizons.com/talktochildren/docs/emergency_plan.doc

Certo, D. (1995, March). Helping children and staff cope with earthquakes. *Child Care Information Exchange, 95*(3), 9–12.

Cole, R., Crandall, R., & Kourofsky, C. (2004). We CAN teach young children fire safety. *Young Children, 59*(2), 14–18.

Copeland, M. (1996). Code blue! Establishing a child care emergency plan. *Child Care Information Exchange, 96*(7), 17–21.

Disaster Training International (DTI). (2001). Emergency plans for centers. Retrieved October 14, 2005, from http://www.disastertraining.org/EmergPlan.htm.

Federal Emergency Management Agency (FEMA). (2001a, May/June). Taking earthquake mitigation steps in Washington state keep youngsters safe. *FEMA Impact, 4*(1), 8. Retrieved May 15, 2002, from http://www.fema.gov/about/hqnltr/downloads/may01.pdf.

Federal Emergency Management Agency (FEMA). (2001b). Helping children cope with disaster. Retrieved May 15, 2002, from http://www.fema.gov/pte/children.htm.

Federal Emergency Management Agency (FEMA). (2001c). FEMA for kids. Retrieved October 14, 2005, from http://www.fema.gov/kids/.

Federal Emergency Management Agency (FEMA). (2002). Are you ready? An in-depth guide to citizen preparedness. Washington, DC: Author. Retrieved October 15, 2005, from http://www.fema.gov/areyouready/

Gaines, S. & Leary, J. (2004). Public health emergency preparedness in the setting of child care. *Family and Community Health 27*(3), 260–265.

Giosa, R. (2004). Stress in an emergency. *Healthy Child Care, 7*(3). Retrieved October 14, 2005, from http://www.healthychild.net/articles/hy38stress.html

Institute for Business and Home Safety (IBHS). (1998). *Protecting our kids from disaster. Non-structural mitigation for child care center.* Tampa FL: Author. Retrieved October 15, 2005, from http://www.ibhs.org/publications/downloads/461.pdf

Lay, K. (2001). Natural disasters: Are you prepared? *Healthy Child Care, 4*(1). Retrieved October 14, 2005, from http://www.healthychild.net/articles/sf19disaster.html

LeMay, S. (2004). Emergency planning tips. *Healthy Child Care, 7*(2). Retrieved September 19, 2004. Available online: http://www.healthychild.net/volume7.html

North Carolina Child Care Health and Safety Resource Center (NCCCHSRC). (2005a). Humpty Dumpty safe on a wall. *North Carolina Child Care Health and Safety Bulletin, 7*(2), 1.

North Carolina Child Care Health and Safety Resource Center (NCCCHSRC). (2005b). Bumps, bruises and broken bones. *North Carolina Child Care Health and Safety Bulletin, 7*(2), 2–3.

Pennsylvania Chapter of the American Academy of Pediatrics (PAAAP). (2001). *Situations that require immediate medical attention.* Retrieved October 16, 2004 from http://www.paaap.org/pdf/ecels/immediatemedical.pdf

Pennsylvania Chapter of the American Academy of Pediatrics (PAAAP). (2003, August). *Day care facilities emergency planning guide.* Retrieved October 16, 2005 from http://www.pema.state.pa.us/pema/lib/pema/day_care_facilities_planning_guide.doc.

Reeves, D. (2003). First aid training. *Healthy Child Care, 6*(2). Retrieved September 19, 2004. Available online: http://www.healthychild.net/volume6.html

Riopelle, D., Harrison, K., Rottman, S., & Shoaf, K. (2004). Head Start disaster preparedness workbook. Los Angeles: Center for Public Health and Disasters. Retrieved October 17, 2004. Available online: http://www.cphd.ucla.edu/headstart/Final%20Workbook/Complete%20Workbook.pdf

Sailors, J. (2000). Preparing for emergencies: Information and training. *Healthy Child Care, 3*(2). Retrieved October 14, 2005, from http://wwwhealthychild.net/articles/sf14emergprep.html.

Sailors, J. (2004a). Managing medications in an emergency. *Healthy Child Care, 7*(3). Retrieved October 14, 2005, from http://www.healthychild.net/articles/mc38manage.html.

Sailors, J. (2004b). Staying healthy during a crisis. *Healthy Child Care, 7*(3). Retrieved October 14, 2005, from http://www.healthychild.net/articles/sh38stayheal.html.

Saylor, C., Swenson, C., & Stokes, S. (1994). *Psychosocial issues for children and families in disasters: A guide for the primary care physician.* Elk Grove Village, IL.: American Academy of Pediatrics.

Shallcross, M. (1999). Family child care homes need health and safety training and an emergency rescue system. *Young Children, 54*(5), 70–73.

Shepard, S. (2002). How safe are your child care programs? *School Planning and Management, 41*(11), 6–9.

Sokol-Gutierrez, K. (1999). Being prepared: The first aid kit. *Healthy Child Care, 2*(6). Retrieved October 14, 2005, from http://www.healthychild.net/articles/mc12firstaid.html.

Sutton, A. (2004). Ipecac policy change. *Healthy Child Care, 7*(3). Retrieved October 14, 2005, from http://www.healthychild.net/articles/sf39ipecac.html.

University of Illinois Cooperative Extension (UIE). (1998). *Children, stress and natural disasters: A guide for teachers.* Urbana-Champaign, IL: Author. Retrieved May 15, 2002, from http://www.ag.uiuc.edu/~disaster/teacher/csndres2.html.

Additional resources for this chapter can be found by visiting the Online Companion™ at http://www.earlychilded.delmar.com. This supplemental material includes extensive chapter quizzes, PowerPoint® outlines, Web links, and various other activities to help better utilize the material in this chapter. The site is updated regularly, so you may check back often to receive the latest information about the subjects in each chapter.

### SAFETY CURRICULUM SUPPLEMENT

Sample lesson plans and topic maps for subjects that concern safety are provided in the next few pages for the teacher to help reinforce the information that is being modeled by teachers and learned by the children in the early childhood education environment. In addition to the sample curriculum there is a list of children's books and sources for further information. Some of this information may include songs or finger plays. This sample group is presented to help the teacher design his or her own curriculum by adding to the information provided.

**LESSON**_plan_
CHAPTER **5**

### LESSON PLAN **1**
***Unit:*** Children's Environment
***Suggested Themes:*** My Neighborhood, My Family: Where Do You Live?
***Theme:*** Where Do You Live?
***Objectives:*** Helping children become familiar with their physical environment.
***Materials:*** Books about different lifestyles: living in the country, the city, and the suburbs. Dramatic play materials to play house or farm. Bulletin board with pictures depicting different lifestyles. Magazines for children to cut out pictures.
***Lesson:*** Talk about different lifestyles and read the book, *A Crack in the Wall.* Discuss how the boy who lived in the city brought happiness to his environment by changing how he viewed the crack in the wall. Talk about what life is or might be like to live in a city. Ask how living in the country would be different.
***Follow-Up:*** Provide dress-up materials for playing house in the city or the country. Have children cut out pictures of houses, apartments, and so forth, in cities and in the country. Have them circle those places that represent their own lifestyles. Put a note on the bulletin board about what was discussed today. Read *Come Home with Us* later in the day. Talk about how people in different places in the city live. Discuss different ways families do things. Compare differences and similarities.
***Age-Appropriate:*** Preschoolers.

**LESSON**_plan_
CHAPTER **5**

### LESSON PLAN **2**
***Unit:*** Safety
***Suggested Themes:*** Injury Prevention, Practicing Safe Behaviors, Hazards in My Environment.
***Theme:*** Practicing Safe Behaviors.

**Objectives:** Children should be able to understand and practice safe behaviors.

**Materials:** Books. Pictures from magazines. Paper in the shape of a badge and crayons. Police officer badges and hats. Stop sign, stop light. Box of items to sort for safety.

**Lesson:** Talk about safe behaviors to practice on a daily basis like crossing the street, staying away from medicines or poisons, using seat belts, staying away from strangers, not playing with matches or guns, and so forth. Talk about people who help keep us safe, like police officers, firefighters, and so on. Have a box of items. Show them one at a time and have children sort those items that promote safety, such as a stop sign, from those that may cause problems, such as a cigarette lighter. Sort them into two boxes. Talk about things that may keep young children safe in the early childhood education environment. Take a safety walk around the indoor and outdoor environment. Point out the things that help keep the children safe.

**Follow-Up:** Have safety books available in the library. Read *Dinosaurs Beware: A Safety Guide.* Observe dramatic area for play with props such as police badges, uniforms. Offer badge-shaped paper to color on. Hand out parent information sheet about safe practices.

**Age-Appropriate:** Preschoolers.

## LESSON*plan*
### CHAPTER 5

LESSON PLAN **3**

**Unit:** Safety

**Suggested Themes:** Fire Safety/Stop, Drop, Roll, Cool, and Call; Poison Safety; Indoor Water Safety; Toy Safety; Electrical Safety.

**Theme:** Fire Safety.

**Objectives:** Children should be able to protect themselves by understanding fire safety and fire safety strategies.

**Materials:** Fire hats, uniforms, and other props for dramatic play area. Books. Cut shapes of a smoke alarm to color. Bulletin board featuring STOP! DROP! ROLL! COOL! and CALL!

**Lesson:** Visit a firestation or firehouse. A firefighter will show a uniform, including full gear. Talk about how important it is to listen to firefighters if they are trying to rescue us. Have a firefighter show the fire engine and other equipment and how it works. If the children are not allowed in the fire station, have the firefighter come to you. This varies from area to area.

Have a firefighter demonstrate stop, drop, roll, cool, and call. If possible, have children practice now. Otherwise, practice when children have returned to care.

**Follow-Up:** A great number of books are available in the library. Read *Fire Diary.* Observe dramatic play area for firefighter/fire station play. Talk about safe behaviors that help support firefighters. Talk about smoke alarms and how they work. Listen to one. Put out smoke alarm cutouts for coloring.

Talk about how to get out of fires. Talk about fire drills. Hand out information sheets for parents. Include a request to have them diagram home

and create a fire drill for evacuation, then practice it. Several days later, have a fire drill.
**Age-Appropriate:** Preschoolers.

**LESSON***plan*
CHAPTER **5**

**LESSON PLAN 4**
**Unit:** Safety
**Theme:** Using Traffic Signs and Signals to be Safe.
**Objectives:** Children will learn how signs and signals help them to be safe.
**Materials:** A standing pretend stoplight. A flannelboard and flannel cutouts. A hand-held stop sign. A whistle. A bulletin board about traffic safety. Block area set up for street, street signs, and cars.
**Lesson:** Tell a flannelboard story about Bobby and the traffic signs to children in group time. Ask children when they see these signs in their environment.

Practice what red lights, green lights, and yellow lights mean, using the standing stoplight. Repeat several times. Show the stop sign and ask them what it means. Demonstrate the whistle and talk about traffic guards and how they help children. Ask the children what signs are around when they cross the street. Talk about crossing safety.

- Always cross the street in a crosswalk.
- Stay on the curb and look both ways.
- When there is no traffic or the traffic is stopped, it is safe to cross.
- Look both ways again and then cross.

Discuss how this would be different in the case of a stoplight. Practice traffic light crossing safety by playing "Red Light, Green Light" for several minutes to reinforce the idea.
**Follow-Up:** Have traffic lines drawn outside on playground surface. Take out the traffic signal and traffic sign. Children can get on trikes and wagons and practice traffic safety. Whistles are available for guiding traffic. A handout to parents requesting they practice the traffic safety procedures that are included.
**Age-Appropriate:** This may be presented to mixed age or preschoolers only. Toddlers may not grasp idea by themselves, but may model behaviors of older children.

**LESSON**plan
CHAPTER **5**

**LESSON PLAN 5**
*Unit:* Safety
*Suggested Themes:* Poisonous Plants, Car Travel Safety, Bicycle or Riding Toy Safety, Water Safety, Playground Safety, Neighborhood Safety. Choose only those that are appropriate to care site.
*Theme:* Car Travel Safety/Buckle Up.
*Objectives:* Children should understand how to be safe when in a car, truck, or bus.
*Materials:* Chairs set up in dramatic play area to simulate a four- or six-passenger car with a steering wheel for the driver. Books. Bulletin board on travel safety. Toy cars to paint on paper. Toy cars, buses, and trucks. Outside, a gas station set up for trikes and wagons. Magazines for pictures of vehicles.
*Lesson:* During group time, read *When I Ride in a Car*. Talk about safety in the car. Always buckle up, no hands out the windows, speak with indoor voices, and so forth. Talk about how safety might be different in a bus or in a truck. Compare behaviors.
*Follow-Up:* Go on a field trip in a car or bus. Practice what children learned. Observe children in dramatic play area playing car or bus. Put books about vehicles in library. Encourage children to play gas station in outdoor area and have them practice safe behaviors while on their "vehicles."

Have children use toy cars for painting. Have children cut pictures of vehicles out of magazines. Discuss safety while they are doing the task. Give parents an information sheet on travel safety. Include a few tips on how to survive travel with children.
*Age-Appropriate:* Preschoolers.

**LESSON**plan
CHAPTER **5**

**LESSON PLAN 6**
*Unit:* Safety
*Suggested Themes:* First Aid, Disaster Preparedness, Fire Drills, Earthquake, Tornado, Hurricane.
*Theme:* Fire Drills.
*Objectives:* Children will learn the importance of fire drills and how to protect themselves in case of fire.
*Materials:* A fire drill bell or buzzer. Clearly marked exits. Sign or poster that shows stop, drop, roll, cool, and call concept. A bulletin board with fire safety, fire drill information. A safe place outdoors to meet during the fire drill.
*Lesson:* Invite a firefighter to talk about fires and how they destroy things and hurt people. Talk about how things can be replaced, but that people cannot. Discuss the importance of getting out of a fire. Have students practice a fire drill. Have fireman demonstrate stop, drop, roll, cool, and call. Children will practice stop, drop, roll, cool, and call. At one point during the

day, have a random fire drill so children can practice while the ideas are fresh in their minds.

***Follow-Up:*** Read the book *When There Is a Fire, Go Outside.* Give parents information about home fire drills and ask them to practice at home. Once a month conduct a random fire drill in the early childhood education environment.

**Topic Map for Interpersonal Safety**

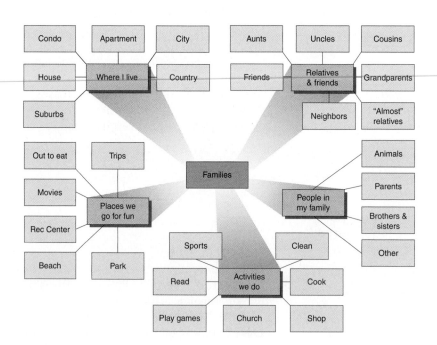

**Topic Map for Fire and Fire Safety**

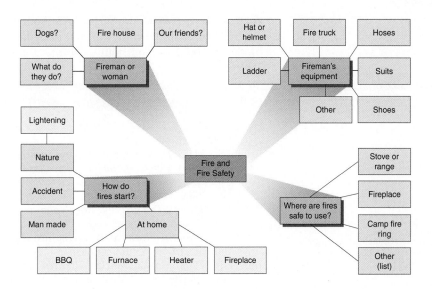

**Topic Map for Natural Disasters**

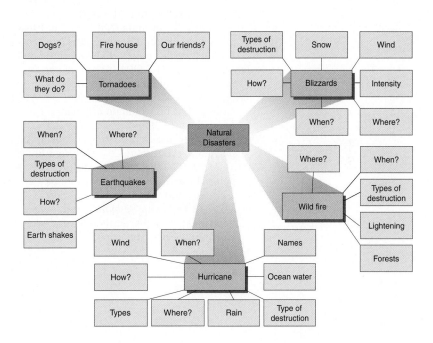

*Age-Appropriate:* Toddlers, preschoolers, and school-aged children are all capable of understanding this information at some level. Toddlers may model the behavior without understanding it, but that modeling could save their lives.

## Children's Books on Safety and Environment

Bajaj, V., & Bates, I. (2004). *How many kisses do you want tonight?* A book about bedtime rituals. New York: Little, Brown

Braun, S. (2004). *I love my daddy.* New York: HarperCollins.

Braun, S. (2004). *I love my mommy.* New York: HarperCollins.

Cuyler, M., & Howard, A. (2001). *Stop drop and roll* (A Book about Fire Safety). New York: Simon and Schuster.

DeCock, N. (2003). *The girl and the elephant.* A book about friendship. Berkeley, CA: Tricycle Press.

Gross, P. (1996). *Stranger safety.* Adventure with a Kangaroo and stranger safety. Gulfport, FL: Roo Publications.

Harris, R. (2003). Go! Go! Maria: What It's Like To Be 1. The tale of a one-year old's life in her family. Macmillan, NY: Margaret K. McElderry.

Hill, M. (2003). *Signs on the road.* Book about reading street signs. Connecticut: Children's Press.

Kotke, J. (2000). *A day with firefighters.* Danbury, CT: Children's Press.

Kotke, J. (2000) *A day with paramedics.* Danbury, CT: Children's Press.

Kotke, J. (2000). *A day with police officers.* Danbury, CT: Children's Press.

Pendziwol, J. & Gourbault, M. (2001). *No dragons for tea: Fire safety for kids (and dragons).* Tonawanda, NY: Kids Can Press.

Ross, M., & Long, S. (2004). *Snug as a bug.* This book follows different bugs and how they are made snug . . . like different families. San Francisco: Chronicle Books.

Ryder, J., & Sweet, M. (2004). *Won't you be my kissaroo?* Journey of a sheep through town watching many families kissing their children. New York: Gulliver Books.

Wallace, J., & Horse, H. (2004). *Anything for you.* At bedtime the baby promises his mother that he would do anything for her because he loves her so much. New York: HarperCollins.

White, A., & Morales, Y. (2004). *Sand sister.* About a lonely girl and her imaginary playmate. Cambridge, MA: Barefoot Books.

Willems, M. (2003). *Don't let the pigeon drive the bus.* This book follows a pigeon going through his emotions much like a preschooler's emotion and getting what he wants. New York: Hyperion.

Willems, M. (2004). *Knuffle bunny.* Follows a very young girl around her neighborhood looking for her stuffed bunny, when she finds him she says her first word. New York: Hyperion.

# SECTION III
# Nutrition in Early Childhood Education

This section discusses nutrition and how it impacts children:

6. Basic Nutrition in Early Childhood Education Environments
7. Protecting Good Nutrition in Early Childhood Education Environments
8. Providing Good Nutrition in Early Childhood Education Environments

These topics relate nutritional needs to health promotion and risk management tools that will enable the student to design nutritional policies that work well in early childhood education settings.

## CHAPTER 6

# Basic Nutrition in Early Childhood Education Environments

**After reading this chapter, you should be able to:**

## 6.1 Nutrition Policies

Define and discuss nutrition policies and their use as tools for the nutritional well-being of children.

## 6.2 Understanding Nutritional Guidelines

Describe the importance of the Dietary Guidelines for Americans, the MyPyramid Food Guidance System, Daily Recommended Intakes, and other measures that provide guidelines for nutritional well-being.

## 6.3 Basic Macronutrients

Define the three basic macronutrients in the diet and discuss their importance to overall well-being.

## 6.4 Basic Micronutrients

Define the three basic micronutrients in the diet and discuss their importance to overall well-being.

## 6.5 Implications for Teachers

Indicate the need for education, working with families, supervision, and role modeling for proper nutrition to promote health and well-being.

## 6.1  NUTRITION POLICIES

Policies that ensure proper nutrition for early childhood education are important to the overall well-being and development of children in care. Children are at risk for poor nutrition under most circumstances. Indicators of the need for nutrition policies include the following:

- There are 13 million children in early childhood education every day, 46 percent of whom are infants and toddlers. All of these children get a significant part of their weekday nutrition from the early childhood education environment (Padget et al., 2005; Hayden, 2002).

- Parents should consider the nutritional program of a center before choosing an early childhood education program. This includes meals and snacks as well as the environment for eating and the nutrition education program (Nicklas, 2001).

- Many children fail to consume enough vegetables, bread, cereal, pasta, and rice while in care (Briley & Roberts-Gray, 2005; Soanes, 2004).

- The low degree of staff nutritional knowledge has a direct effect on menu planning, food selection, and role modeling (Cobb & Solera, 2004).

- One study found that fewer than 50% of children two to five years of age in early childhood education environments ate the recommended amounts of grains, fruits, and dairy products, and about 30% did not meet the recommended amounts of vegetables and meat in their diets. Overall, these children were lacking zinc, calcium, iron, folate, and vitamin E in sufficient amounts (Padget et al., 2005).

- Early good milk-drinking habits in girls help them to get enough calcium to keep their bone health good as adults (USDAARS, 2005).

- The Dietary Guidelines for Americans 2005 recommends an increased intake of whole grains, fruits and vegetables, and low-fat milk and milk products (Zamani, 2005).

All teachers should have a basic knowledge of nutrition. This information may be used to model proper food selection, create menus to serve the children, or teach nutrition to children and their parents. Food and nutrition should be an integral part of the promotion of health.

Teachers need to create nutritional policies that will support the growth, health, and well-being of the children in their care. The six major goals for nutritional policies are similar to the policies for health and safety. They include:

1. maximizing nutritional status
2. minimizing nutritional risk
3. using nutritional education as a tool
4. recognizing the importance of nutritional guidelines
5. practicing cultural competence
6. developing partnerships with families to provide a caring community

Nutritional policies may include menu planning guidelines, food selection, and preparation practices. These policies should be clearly written and should reflect nutrition as part of the promotion of health.

Nutritional policies should encompass the following:

- *Nutritional Guidelines:* understanding nutritional guidelines for optimum nutritional well-being
- *Basic Macronutrients:* understanding the basic **nutrients**, their sources, and the problems related to deficiencies
- *Basic Micronutrients:* understanding basic micronutrients, their sources, and the problem related to their deficiencies
- *Implications for Teachers:* methods and practices for promoting good nutrition through education, role modeling, and supervision to provide minimum nutritional risk and maximum health

● Nutrients
*substances found in foods that provide for the growth, development, maintenance, and repair of the body*

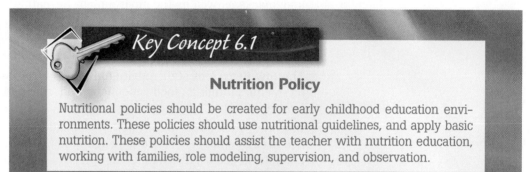

## Key Concept 6.1

### Nutrition Policy

Nutritional policies should be created for early childhood education environments. These policies should use nutritional guidelines, and apply basic nutrition. These policies should assist the teacher with nutrition education, working with families, role modeling, supervision, and observation.

## 6.2 UNDERSTANDING NUTRITIONAL GUIDELINES

Adequate nutrition during childhood is necessary to maintain overall health and to provide for growth. A number of nutritional guidelines or strategies for good health have been established to help accomplish this task. In the past, the responsibility for following these recommendations fell to the parents, because young children ate most of their meals at home. The past 20 years have presented major societal shifts in the number of working mothers and the number of single-parent families. As a result the number of children in early childhood education has risen dramatically. In the United States, teachers are helping to meet at least part of the nutritional needs of 60 percent of children younger than five years old, as well as millions of school-aged children (Briley & Roberts-Gray, 2005).

Although some families of school-aged children depend on the children to care for themselves, the majority of these children are in some form of care. It is essential that the teacher understand nutrition regardless of whether the care is center based, school based, family child care, or nanny care. Because so many children are cared for by others, the transfer of responsibility for adequate nutrition has at least partially shifted from the home to the early childhood education environment. The more hours the child is in care, the greater the teacher's responsibility for providing adequate nutrition for growth and maintenance of health. Established nutritional guidelines help the teacher plan for adequate nutrition in menu selection. These guidelines and good nutritional practices can be shared with the children and their parents.

## Dietary Guidelines for Americans

Dietary Guidelines for Americans forms the basis for nutrition policies in the United States. It is considered an important part of the standard for any federal program that deals with food and nutrition. The guidelines were completely revised in 2005. Table 6-1 highlights the basic guidelines. This 2005 version is not without some controversy, because the item about moderating intake of sugar has been eliminated. It has been found that sugar and fruit juice intakes in preschoolers have increased over the past 25 years (Kranz et al., 2005). This suggests that, although the suggestion for moderation of sugar has been removed, it is still important to consider.

**TABLE 6-1**
*Dietary Guidelines for Americans: The ABCs of Nutritional Recommendations*

### Aim for fitness

- Aim for a healthy weight by balancing calories from foods and beverages with calories expended
- Engage in at least 60 minutes of physical activity on most, preferably all, days of the week

### Build a healthy base

- Meet recommended intakes within energy needs by adopting a balanced eating pattern, such as the USDA MyPyramid Food Guidance System.
- Consume a variety of nutrient-dense foods and beverages within and among the basic food groups while choosing foods that limit the intake of saturated and *trans* fats, cholesterol, salt, and added sugars.
- Consume a sufficient amount of fruits and vegetables while staying within energy needs.
- Children two to eight years of age should consume 2 cups per day of fat-free or low-fat milk or equivalent milk products.
- Keep foods safe to eat.

### Choose sensibly

- Choose a variety of fruits and vegetables each day. In particular, select from all five vegetables subgroups (dark green, orange, legumes, starchy vegetables, and other vegetables) several times a week.
- Consume whole-grain products often; at least half the grains should be whole grains.
- Keep total fat intake between 20 and 35 percent of calories, with most fats coming from sources of polyunsaturated and monounsaturated fatty acids, such as fish, nuts, and vegetable oils.
- When selecting sources of protein, make choices that are lean, low-fat, or fat-free.
- Choose fiber-rich fruits, vegetables, and whole grains often.

## MyPyramid Food Guidance System

The U.S. Department of Agriculture (USDA) introduced a new tool, entitled MyPyramid Food Guidance System, in April of 2005 (see Figure 6-1). This tool replaces the Food Guide Pyramid that had been used for more than 12 years (USDA, 2005). This new system is also designed to help Americans make good food choices that fall within the Dietary Guidelines for Americans (Federal Register, 2004). This system is designed to help people meet nutritional standards as set in those guidelines, but it is also supposed to help people make better choices in areas where there is excess.

It emphasizes fruits, vegetables, whole grains, and fat-free or low-fat milk and milk products. In accord with the Dietary Guidelines for Americans, it focuses on lower fat or lean meats, poultry, and fish and includes beans, eggs, and nuts as acceptable sources of protein. This system also accentuates lowering saturated fats, *trans* fats, cholesterol, salt, and added sugar. The recommendations of the system are interrelated and direct the individual toward an increased intake of dietary fiber, vitamins and minerals, and other essential nutrients. It is hoped that this new system will help people to lower intakes of saturated fats, sugars, *trans* fats, and sodium, as well as increase the amounts of micronutrient-dense foods that are consumed by Americans.

The system is divided into two levels: (1) individualized daily food intake recommendations and (2) information to help individuals make better food choices. MyPyramid Food Guidance System uses Daily Food Intake Patterns that will help consumers identify suitable choices for foods and amounts to eat. These choices are based on activity level, sex, and age. Chapter 8 includes some of this information for children from ages two to eight years. MyPyramid Food Guidance System is designed to be interactive and to allow individuals to work with their own information to create their most appropriate food and activity pattern. The System can be accessed at http://www.mypyramid.gov. Included on this site is a Food Tracker, with which one can place age, sex, and activity level into "My Plan" and get dietary recommendations that include 7 days of menus for the recommended calorie intake.

MyPyramid Food Guidance System is created in a manner to help consumers improve their food intake choices and amounts to eat that will help them meet nutritional guidelines. Four dominant themes are presented in MyPyramid: variety, proportionality, moderation, and activity. *Variety* reminds people to eat from all food groups and subgroups. *Proportionality* prompts people to eat more of some foods that are healthier for us and to eat less of foods that are not as healthy or are full of calories but few nutrients. *Moderation* focuses on choosing foods that limit intake of sugars, cholesterol, salt, saturated fats, and *trans* fats. *Activity* addresses physical activity, or energy expenditure, as part of the way to look at the food we consume and balance it with the energy we expend.

MyPyramid Guidance System uses the Daily Food Intake Patterns that will help consumers identify suitable choices for foods and amounts to eat (Federal Register, 2004). These pattern choices are based on activity level, sex, and age. MyPyramid separates the list of intake patterns into five major food group categories and the subgroups that fall under them. Those categories are grains, vegetables, fruits, milk and milk products, and meat and beans. There is a minor category of oils, but it is not focused upon. See MyPyramid (Figure 6-1).

MyPyramid Food Guidance System: Overall view of the Pyramid

# MyPyramid.gov
## STEPS TO A HEALTHIER YOU
### MyPyramid.gov

| GRAINS | VEGETABLES | FRUITS | MILK | MEAT & BEANS |

The Grain group on MyPyramid suggests that half of an individual's intake should be of whole grains every day (see Figure 6-2). The system divides grains into two groups: refined grains and whole grains. This group includes any food made from wheat, rice, oats, cornmeal, barley, or other cereal grains. We receive our grains from breads, pastas, cereals, tortillas, and other products made from them. Whole grains include the entire kernel of grain, including the bran and germ. Refined grains have been milled, and the bran and germ have been removed. Milling also removes many nutrients such as iron and vitamin B and dietary fiber. Often, these products are "enriched," which means that the nutrients taken out are added back after processing. But this enrichment does not include the dietary fiber many people are missing from their diets. By looking at the list, consumers can make better food choices on a daily basis.

The Vegetable group on MyPyramid suggests that people eat more dark green and orange vegetables and have dry peas and beans on a regular basis (see Figure 6-3). This group is divided into five different areas based on their nutrient content: dark green vegetables, orange vegetables, dry beans and peas, starchy vegetables, and "other" vegetables, which includes tomatoes,

**FIGURE 6-2**
MyPyramid Food Guidance System: Foods in the Grain group.

## Grain Group
Make half your grains whole

**MyPyramid.gov**

**What foods are in the grain group?**

Any food made from wheat, rice, oats, cornmeal, barley or another cereal grain is a grain product. Bread, pasta, oatmeal, breakfast cereals, tortillas, and grits are examples of grain products.

Grains are divided into 2 subgroups, **whole grains** and **refined grains.**

Whole grains contain the entire grain kernel—the bran, germ, and endosperm. Examples include:

- whole-wheat flour
- bulgur (cracked wheat)
- oatmeal
- whole cornmeal
- brown rice

Refined grains have been milled, a process that removes the bran and germ. This is done to give grains a finer texture and improve their shelf life, but it also removes dietary fiber, iron, and many B vitamins. Some examples of refined grain products are:

- white flour
- degermed cornmeal
- white bread
- white rice

Most refined grains are *enriched.* This means certain B vitamins (thiamin, riboflavin, niacin, folic acid) and iron are added back after processing. Fiber is not added back to enriched grains. Check the ingredient list on refined grain products to make sure that the word "enriched" is included in the grain name. Some food products are made from mixtures of whole grains and refined grains.

Some commonly eaten grain products are:

| **Whole grains:** | **Refined grains:** |
|---|---|
| brown rice | cornbread* |
| buckwheat | corn tortillas* |
| bulgur (cracked wheat) | couscous* |
| oatmeal | crackers* |
| popcorn | flour tortillas* |
|  | grits |
|  | noodles* |
| *Ready-to-eat breakfast cereals:* |  |
| whole wheat cereal flakes |  |
| muesli | *Pasta** |
|  | spaghetti |
|  | macaroni |

**FIGURE 6-2 (Continued)**
MyPyramid Food Guidance System: Foods in the Grain group.

whole grain barley

whole grain cornmeal

whole rye

whole wheat bread

whole wheat crackers

whole wheat pasta

whole wheat sandwich buns and rolls

whole wheat tortillas

wild rice

*Less common whole grains:*

amaranth

millet

quinoa

sorghum

triticale

pitas*

pretzels

*Ready-to-eat breakfast cereals:*

corn flakes

white bread

white sandwich buns and rolls

white rice

*Most of these products are made from refined grains. Some are made from whole grains. Check the ingredient list for the words "whole grain" or "whole wheat" to decide if they are made from a whole grain. Some foods are made from a mixture of whole and refined grains.

Some grain products contain significant amounts of bran. Bran provides fiber, which is important for health. However, products with added bran or bran alone (e.g., oat bran) are not necessarily whole grain products.

**FIGURE 6-3**
MyPyramid Food Guidance System: Foods in the Vegetable group.

Vegetable Group
Vary your veggies
MyPyramid.gov

**What foods are in the vegetable group?**

Any vegetable or 100% vegetable juice counts as a member of the vegetable group. Vegetables may be raw or cooked; fresh, frozen, canned, or dried/dehydrated; and may be whole, cut-up, or mashed.

Vegetables are organized into 5 subgroups, based on their nutrient content. Some commonly eaten vegetables in each subgroup are:

**Dark green vegetables**
bok choy
broccoli
collard greens
dark green leafy lettuce
kale

**Starchy vegetables**
corn
green peas
lima beans (green)
potatoes

*(continues)*

mesclun
mustard greens
romaine lettuce
spinach
turnip greens
watercress
**Orange vegetables**
acorn squash
butternut squash
carrots
hubbard squash
pumpkin
sweetpotatoes
**Dry beans and peas**
black beans
black-eyed peas
garbanzo beans (chickpeas)
kidney beans
lentils
lima beans (mature)
navy beans
pinto beans
soy beans
split peas
tofu (bean curd made from soybeans)
white beans

**Other vegetables**
artichokes
asparagus
bean sprouts
beets
Brussels sprouts
cabbage
cauliflower
celery
cucumbers
eggplant
green beans
green or red peppers
iceberg (head) lettuce
mushrooms
okra
onions
parsnips
tomatoes
tomato juice
vegetable juice
turnips
wax beans
zucchini

onions, and celery. Any vegetable or 100% vegetable juice counts as a member of this group. Vegetables can be served cooked, raw, frozen, canned, or dehydrated.

The Fruit group on MyPyramid suggests that people focus more on fruit and eat a variety of fruits on a daily basis (see Figure 6-4). It also cautions us to go easy on fruit juice and to choose fresh, frozen, canned, or dried fruit instead. All fruits and 100% juices are considered part of this group. The list of commonly eaten fruits includes everything from apples to melons and citrus to berries.

Milk is the next major group on MyPyramid (see Figure 6-5). This group encourages people to get calcium-rich food and to choose low-fat or fat-free types. The recommendation for lower fat intake would not apply to children younger than two years of age. MyPyramid also suggests that people who cannot or do not consume milk should choose lactose-free products or other sources of calcium. The Milk group includes all fluid milk products and many foods that are made from milk. This would include milk-based desserts such as pudding or ice cream, cheese, and yogurt.

The last major category on MyPyramid is Meat and Beans (see Figure 6-6). The MyPyramid System suggests going lean on protein. It focuses on making low-fat or lean choices of meats and poultry. Preparation of meats should focus on broiling, grilling, or baking. The System also suggests that protein choices should include more fish, beans, peas, nuts, and seeds. One reason for this is to include healthy oils from these products in the diet. The Meat and Beans category is divided into six areas: meats, poultry, eggs, fish, dry beans and peas, and nuts and seeds.

A minor category, but an important one in the MyPyramid Food Guidance System, is Oils (see Figure 6-7). This category suggests that people

**FIGURE 6-4**
MyPyramid Food Guidance System: Foods in the Fruit group.

# Fruit Group
## Focus on fruits

**MyPyramid.gov**

### What foods are in the fruit group?

Any fruit or 100% fruit juice counts as part of the fruit group. Fruits may be fresh, canned, frozen, or dried, and may be whole, cut-up, or pureed. Some commonly eaten fruits are:

Apples
Apricots
Avocado
Bananas

*Berries:*
  strawberries
  blueberries
  raspberries
  cherries

Grapefruit
Grapes
Kiwi fruit
Lemons
Limes
Mangoes

*Melons:*
  cantaloupe
  honeydew
  watermelon

*Mixed fruits:*
  fruit cocktail

Nectarines
Oranges
Peaches
Pears
Papaya
Pineapple
Plums
Prunes
Raisins
Tangerines

*100% Fruit juice:*
  orange
  apple
  grape
  grapefruit

know sources of fats so that they can make the most of the fat sources for healthier choices from fish, nuts, and vegetable oils. The system suggests that people limit their intake of solid fats such as butter, stick margarine, shortening, and lard. One reason for this focus on limiting solid fats is to limit *trans* fats. Dietary food labels will be required to reveal the amount of *trans* fats in foods beginning in 2006.

MyPyramid Food Guidance System is intended to simplify the original USDA Food Guide Pyramid information in order to help people make better choices. One major difference is the focus on an individual's needs. This new system fosters several key factors that were recommended by the American Academy of Pediatrics (AAP) in 2003 to help control the epidemic of overweight children that the United States is experiencing today (AAP, 2003). In the past three decades, the number of overweight two- to five-year-olds has more than doubled, to more than 10% of children (Nicklas & Johnson, 2004). The number of overweight children ages six to eleven has tripled in that

FIGURE 6-5
MyPyramid Food Guidance System: Foods in the Milk group.

**Milk Group**
Get your calcium-rich foods

**MyPyramid.gov**

## What foods are included in the milk, yogurt, and cheese (milk) group?

All fluid milk products and many foods made from milk are considered part of this food group. Foods made from milk that retain their calcium content are part of the group, while foods made from milk that have little to no calcium, such as cream cheese, cream, and butter, are not. Most milk group choices should be fat-free or low-fat.

Some commonly eaten choices in the milk, yogurt, and cheese group are:

**Milk***
All fluid milk:
  fat-free (skim)
  low fat (1%)
  reduced fat (2%)
  whole milk

flavored milks:
  chocolate
  strawberry

lactose reduced milks
lactose free milks

**Milk-based desserts***
Puddings made with milk
ice milk
frozen yogurt
ice cream

**Cheese***
Hard natural cheeses:
  cheddar
  mozzarella
  Swiss
  parmesan

soft cheeses
  ricotta
  cottage cheese

processed cheeses
  American

**Yogurt***
All yogurt
  Fat-free
  low fat
  reduced fat
  whole milk yogurt

**\*Selection Tips**

Choose fat-free or low-fat milk, yogurt, and cheese. If you choose milk or yogurt that is not fat-free, or cheese that is not low-fat, the fat in the product counts as part of the discretionary calorie allowance.

If sweetened milk products are chosen (flavored milk, yogurt, drinkable yogurt, desserts), the added sugars also count as part of the discretionary calorie allowance.

For those who are lactose intolerant, lactose-free and lower-lactose products are available. These include hard cheeses and yogurt. Also, enzyme preparations can be added to milk to lower the lactose content. Calcium-fortified foods and beverages such as soy beverages or orange juice may provide calcium, but may not provide the other nutrients found in milk and milk products.

**FIGURE 6-6**
MyPyramid Food Guidance System: Foods in the Meat and Beans group.

## Meat & Bean Group
### Go lean with protein
**MyPyramid.gov**

### What foods are included in the meat, poultry, fish, dry beans, eggs, and nuts (meat & beans) group?

All foods made from meat, poultry, fish, dry beans or peas, eggs, nuts, and seeds are considered part of this group. Dry beans and peas are part of this group as well as the vegetable group.

Most meat and poultry choices should be lean or low-fat. Fish, nuts, and seeds contain healthy oils, so choose these foods frequently instead of meat or poultry. (See Why is it important to include fish, nuts, and seeds?)

Some commonly eaten choices in the Meat and Beans group, with selection tips, are:

**Meats***
*Lean cuts of:*
  beef
  ham
  lamb
  pork
  veal

*Game meats:*
  bison
  rabbit
  venison

*Lean ground meats:*
  beef
  pork
  lamb

*Lean luncheon meats*
*Organ meats:*
  liver
  giblets

**Poultry***
  chicken
  duck
  goose
  turkey
  ground chicken and turkey

**Eggs***
  chicken eggs
  duck eggs

**Dry beans and peas:**
black beans
black-eyed peas
chickpeas (garbanzo beans)
falafel
kidney beans
lentils
lima beans (mature)
navy beans
pinto beans
soy beans
split peas
tofu (bean curd made from soy beans)
white beans

*bean burgers:*
garden burgers
veggie burgers
tempeh
texturized vegetable protein (TVP)

**Nuts & seeds***
almonds
cashews
hazelnuts (filberts)
mixed nuts
peanuts
peanut butter
pecans
pistachios
pumpkin seeds
sesame seeds
sunflower seeds
walnuts

**Fish***
*Finfish such as:*
catfish
cod
flounder
haddock
halibut
herring
mackerel
pollock
porgy
salmon
sea bass
snapper
swordfish
trout
tuna

*Shellfish such as:*
clams
crab
crayfish
lobster
mussels
octopus
oysters
scallops
squid (calamari)
shrimp

*Canned fish such as:*
anchovies
clams
tuna
sardines

(continues)

**FIGURE 6-6 (Continued)**
MyPyramid Food Guidance System: Foods in the Meat and Beans group.

**\*Selection Tips**

Choose lean or low-fat meat and poultry. If higher fat choices are made, such as regular ground beef (75 to 80% lean) or chicken with skin, the fat in the product counts as part of the discretionary calorie allowance.

If solid fat is added in cooking, such as frying chicken in shortening or frying eggs in butter or stick margarine, this also counts as part of the discretionary calorie allowance.

Select fish rich in omega-3 fatty acids, such as salmon, trout, and herring, more often.

Liver and other organ meats are high in cholesterol. Egg yolks are also high in cholesterol, but egg whites are cholesterol-free.

Processed meats such as ham, sausage, frankfurters, and luncheon or deli meats have added sodium. Check the ingredient and Nutrition Facts label to help limit sodium intake. Fresh chicken, turkey, and pork that have been enhanced with a salt-containing solution also have added sodium. Check the product label for statements such as "self-basting" or "contains up to __% of __", which mean that a sodium-containing solution has been added to the product.

Sunflower seeds, almonds, and hazelnuts (filberts) are the richest sources of vitamin E in this food group. To help meet vitamin E recommendations, make these your nut and seed choices more often.

**FIGURE 6-7**
MyPyramid Food Guidance System: What are "oils"?

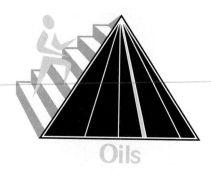

Oils

MyPyramid.gov

**What are "oils"?**

Oils are fats that are liquid at room temperature, like the vegetable oils used in cooking. Oils come from many different plants and from fish. Some common oils are:

- canola oil
- corn oil
- cottonseed oil
- olive oil
- safflower oil
- soybean oil
- sunflower oil

Some oils are used mainly as flavorings, such as walnut oil and sesame oil. A number of foods are naturally high in oils, like:

- nuts
- olives
- some fish
- avocados

**FIGURE 6-7 (Continued)**
MyPyramid Food Guidance
System: What are "oils"?

Foods that are mainly oil include mayonnaise, certain salad dressings, and soft (tub or squeeze) margarine with no *trans* fats. Check the Nutrition Facts label to find margarines with 0 grams of *trans* fat. Amounts of *trans* fat will be required on labels as of 2006. Many products already provide this information.

Most oils are high in monounsaturated or polyunsaturated fats, and low in saturated fats. Oils from plant sources (vegetable and nut oils) do not contain any cholesterol. In fact, no foods from plants sources contain cholesterol.

A few plant oils, however, including coconut oil and palm kernel oil, are high in saturated fats and for nutritional purposes should be considered to be solid fats.

Solid fats are fats that are solid at room temperature, like butter and shortening. Solid fats come from many animal foods and can be made from vegetable oils through a process called hydrogenation. Some common solid fats are:

- butter
- beef fat (tallow, suet)
- chicken fat
- pork fat (lard)
- stick margarine
- shortening

Nutrition education includes having graphics around the classroom, as well as providing dramatic play materials for the children to play what has been modeled to them.

same period, to more than 15% of that age group. The AAP recommendations include dietary practices that emphasize moderation in energy-dense foods and encourage making healthy food selections along with regular physical activity. The USDA also released a children's version of MyPyramid in 2005. It is suitable for use by children in grades 1–6 (ages 6–11 years).

The American Dietetic Association (ADA) has published a position paper that deals with the nutritional intakes of children age two to eleven years in the United States (Nicklas & Johnson, 2004). They found that there has been an increase in the consumption of foods that are higher in sugar content, such as fruits, fruit juices, and sweetened beverages, while at the same time a decrease in the consumption of foods such as milk, vegetables, and grains and breads has been reported. The ADA concluded that the food choices of most children in the United States do not meet the recommended nutritional guidelines. The ADA also introduced a position paper on nutrition in early childhood education programs (Briley & Roberts-Gray, 2005). The basic premise of this position is that children's nutritional needs must be met, and done so in ways that model healthy dietary patterns. Use of the MyPyramid Food Guidance System is intended to help children and teachers meet the recommended guidelines on both of these ADA positions.

> *Pause for Reflection*
>
> How do your dietary habits hold up to this MyPyramid Food Guidance System? For a real look at your own habits, go to MyPyramid Plan at http://www.mypyramid.gov and find out. What could you do to improve your dietary habits to better fit MyPyramid?

## Daily Reference Intake

The U.S. Daily Reference Intake values (DRIs) are the suggested amounts of essential nutrients such as protein, vitamins, and minerals that should be consumed in foods daily to ensure good health (Baylor College of Medicine, 2004). The Daily Reference Values (DRVs) have been established for **macronutrients**, cholesterol, sodium, and potassium.

● **Macronutrients**
*major nutrients needed for the body, such as fats, protein, and carbohydrates*

DRIs are most commonly found on food labels (Figure 6-8) on packaged products where manufacturers are required to list nutrition facts. The information is broken down on a per-serving basis. Calories and amounts of fat, cholesterol, carbohydrates, protein, vitamin A, vitamin B (thiamine, riboflavin, and niacin), vitamin C, vitamin D, sodium, and other essential minerals such as calcium and iron are listed. The Daily Values shown on the label help one to understand the general contribution of nutrients that particular food makes toward the daily diet (Mydlenski, 2004).

## Healthy People 2010

Many of the objectives included in Healthy People 2010 are aimed at decreasing the prevalence of overweight in both adults and children, increasing intake of fruits and vegetables, and decreasing intake of sodium, sugar, and fat. It also addresses reducing growth retardation and iron deficiency in children (Nicklas & Johnson, 2004).

## Child and Adult Care Food Program

The Child and Adult Care Food Program (CACFP) of the USDA enables family child care homes as well as nonprofit early childhood education centers to be reimbursed for creating menus and serving meals that meet dietary guidelines established by this program. These dietary guidelines are based

**FIGURE 6-8**

Sample Nutrition Facts label for Macaroni and Cheese. Beginning in 2006, the amount of *trans* fat will be included on the label.

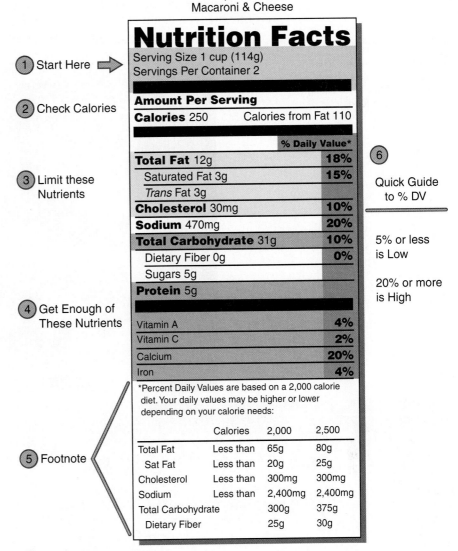

Sample label for Macaroni & Cheese

# The Serving Size

| Serving Size 1/2 cup (114g) | (#1 on sample label) |
| Servings Per Container 4 | The first place to start when you look at the Nutrition facts is the serving size and the number of servings |

in the package. Serving sizes are standardized to make it easier to compare similar foods; they are provided in familiar units, such as cups or pieces, followed by the metric amount, e.g., the number of grams.

on the DRIs and the Dietary Guidelines for Americans. Recommended meal patterns are provided by CACFP.

Early childhood education programs and regulated family child care homes that participate in the CACFP are required to follow meal pattern guidelines (see Table 9-1 in Chapter 9), engage in some training, and utilize food and nutrition handbooks. Investigations in the past have shown that as many as 90 percent of observed participating centers fell short of the recommended CACFP standards (Briley, Roberts-Gray, & Rowe, 1993). More recent studies have found early childhood education centers falling short of nutrients compared to the Food Guide Pyramid, which has been used until recently (Padget, et al., 2005). ADA has stated that no extensive evaluations have been done to assess the effectiveness of CACFP.

Even at a young age, children can be taught good nutritional habits for eating and selecting foods.

# REALITY CHECK

## How is America Eating: Do We Fulfill Our Nutritional Needs?

There has been a great deal in the news recently about how obesity has taken hold in all ages of the population in the United States. Almost 60 percent of the country is overweight (Cox, 2003). That leads to the questions: (1) What are we eating? and (2) How does this match with our basic nutrient needs? In a comparison of how Americans ate in 1909 and how they ate in 2000, Gerrior et al. (2004) found some interesting data. First, we are eating a lot more fat today than one hundred years ago, although cholesterol lev-

els of the foods we eat are lower. We are eating more fat, but less fat from animal sources. Our total consumption of meat is slightly up recently from the past years, but consumption of beef is down, and we are eating more chicken than ever before, which is good because it is leaner. So, how do we eat more fat than ever before, but less cholesterol? One answer to this is that we are eating more snacks such as potato chips and crackers and more desserts. These all have quite a bit of fat, especially *trans* fats, in them. Another reason

## REALITY CHECK (Continued)

is that we are super-sizing, not only while eating out, but at home too (Cox, 2003).

We have also changed our consumption of carbohydrates. During much of the twentieth century we were eating fewer grains, but today we are eating more grains than we have for a number of years; however, it still does not come close to our consumption of one hundred years ago (Gerrior et al., 2004). Many of the grain items we are eating today are highly processed flours, rice, and pastas, or they have added sugar, such as cereals. The bran and germ have been removed from processed foods, so many of the positive factors in grains have also been removed. This has lowered the dietary fiber in our diets. We have become consumers of lots of sugar and sweetened beverages and other foods. The consumption of sugar or sweetening products went up more than 20% between 1980 and 1994. At that time, each American was eating an average of almost 150 pounds of sugar and other sweeteners, such as corn syrup, each year in the foods we consumed.

We are eating more protein than in 1909, but we are getting it from other sources. Almost two-thirds of the protein diets in those days was from animal sources. Today it is a balance of 50% from animal sources and 50% from vegetable sources. The animal sources include dairy products such as milk, yogurt, and cheese. There has been a large increase in the use of cheese. We are using it in many Mexican food products and items such as pizza, and this has increased our consumption of cheese over recent years (Cox, 2003). Other protein sources include beans, peas, and soy products. Protein appears to be something that we eat adequate amounts of but do not overconsume as much as we do other nutrients.

It is a little difficult to compare consumption of vitamins and minerals, because these were not really understood until partway through the twentieth century, and these items only began getting tracked for consumption in 1949 (Gerrior, et al., 2004). Since then, our knowledge of vitamin and mineral requirements has radically changed, because we are understanding

more about their functions and how much of each vitamin and mineral is needed for the body to operate efficiently. Most levels of consumption for vitamins and minerals are higher today than in the past. This may be partially due to the enrichment of many food products, which puts back the minerals and vitamins taken out during processing. It is also due to the use of daily vitamins and minerals in pill form. However the levels of Vitamin $B_{12}$ and potassium consumption are lower today, perhaps due to a lower consumption level of eggs and organ meats and plant foods such as potatoes.

Consumption of water has increased greatly. Of the 17.6 eight ounces servings of beverages that are drunk every day by the average American, 6.1 servings are water. Of the 6.1 servings of water, 2.3 are bottled waters. (Saint John & Barricella, 2001). Bottled water is the sixth most popular drink in the United States, and it is projected to be the second most popular drink by 2010 (Saint John & Barricella, 2001). The Coca-Cola Company has complained that bottled water is beginning to erode the consumption of soft drinks.

Where do we eat? In 1909, there were few places outside the home to eat. Today there are food venues everywhere, including school cafeterias with branded kiosks of pizza, burgers, and fries (Ebbin, 2002). We are eating more and more meals away from home, and many of these meals are fast foods and therefore also high-fat foods. Average consumption of commercially prepared meals has increased to a total of 53.5 billion meals per year (Enns, 2002). That is an average of almost 4 meals per week, per person, eaten out. It was also found that only 14 meals were prepared at home per week and an average of more than 2 meals per week were skipped. Another way to look at this is that 57% of Americans, on any given day, eat away from home (Tippett et al., 1999). The most likely meal eaten away from home is lunch, which represents about half of the commercially prepared meals consumed. Approximately 85 percent of Americans do eat breakfast, and about 20 percent of them are getting breakfast out at

*(continues)*

# REALITY CHECK (Continued)

least once a week (Tippett et al., 2000). Coffee and milk are the most popular foods at breakfast. Processed cereals are also popular.

We have looked at the general population, but how do these trends compare to how children are eating? There has been a large increase in the consumption of soft drinks and a decrease in the consumption of milk by children (Enns et al., 2002). Children ate more grains in 2002, but these were in the form of crackers, popcorn, pretzels, and corn chips. They are eating more fried potatoes, noncitrus juices, cheese, candy, and fruit drinks. The consumption of noncitrus juices rose by 280 percent over the last twenty years (Tippett et al., 2000). Children are eating less bread, green peas, corn, beef, pork, and eggs.

In 2000, the most recent Healthy Eating Index was compiled. It was found that the mean score was about 64 percent, meaning that we were meeting about that much of our dietary needs. Another way to look at this is that we were failing to meet those needs by 36 percent. If we look at the overall habits, we find that 16 percent of the population have poor diets, 74 percent of the population needs improvement in their diets, and only 10 percent of American diets are considered good (Basiotis et al., 2004). If we look at the quality of children's diets, we find that only 9% were poor, and 72% were needing improvement, but 19% of children's diets were good (Lino et al., 2002) That is generally better than for adults, but the majority of Americans could use some improvement in their diets.

Dieticians, physicians and other experts are telling us that we need to change some of our diet habits. One change is that we should eat more whole grains. The new MyPyramid Food Guidance System (2005), prepared for the general population by the USDA and experts representing all areas of nutritional concern, tells us that we should make whole-grain choices half the time. It also indicates that we should eat more vegetables, especially dark green and deep yellow ones. We should eat more fruits, both citrus and noncitrus, and we should consume more legumes. These same recommendations were also made specifically for children by the USDA in 2002 (Enns, et al., 2002).

**CHECK***point:* How well are you eating? Do you share some of the issues that are of concern in how Americans eat? What might you do to improve your own diet?

## Key Concept 6.2

### Nutritional Guidelines

An increasing number of children rely on early childhood education programs to provide a good portion of their nutritional needs. Teachers should be knowledgeable about nutritional guidelines as they plan menus and provide food to the children in care. The MyPyramid Food Guidance System is easiest to understand and will help the teacher educate children and their parents about nutrition. Dietary Guidelines for Americans, the Daily Reference Intake, Healthy People 2010, and the Child and Adult Care Food Program also provide helpful information for the teacher.

## 6.3  BASIC MACRONUTRIENTS

Each source of nutrients performs specific functions. The two major functions by which nutrients can be categorized are the macronutrients and the micronutrients.

The first major group of nutrients is the energy nutrients, or macronutrients. Macronutrients that produce energy are carbohydrates, fats, and proteins. Energy is needed to maintain life, for growth, to regulate the body, and to perform voluntary activities. We measure energy in terms of **calories**. The number of calories each body needs depends on the **basal metabolism**, **metabolism** of food, growth and physical activity, and the age of that body. Calories are supplied to the body from three major nutrients:

- fats, which supply 9 calories per gram
- carbohydrates, which supply 4 calories per gram
- proteins, which supply 4 calories per gram

Carbohydrates, fats, and protein provide the energy needed to run the body and provide materials to help the body grow and maintain its functions. Although trends have been toward more energy intake from carbohydrates and less from fats, children are still not eating the balance suggested for these categories (Padget et al., 2005; Enns et al., 2002).

### Carbohydrates

Carbohydrates are the first source of energy the body uses, and they are the major source of energy for the central nervous system. Carbohydrates are made up of carbon, hydrogen, and oxygen. Carbohydrates, protein, and fats provide energy to the body in the form of calories. If our bodies do not have carbohydrates, we cannot properly use the other energy sources of protein and fat. Carbohydrates provide a slow, steady source of energy necessary for utilization of other nutrients in the body. For example, carbohydrates supply energy so that protein can be used for growth and maintenance of body cells.

Carbohydrates come in two forms, simple and complex. Simple carbohydrates include the sugars, and complex carbohydrates are made up of strings of sugars in the form of starch or fiber. Simple carbohydrates are found in various forms including lactose, which is found in milk. Lactose from breast milk or formula supplies the major source of carbohydrates for infants. Complex carbohydrates are generally found in the Grains group in MyPyramid, which includes cereal, rice, bread, and pasta. They are also found in the Fruits category and Vegetables category, as well as the Meat and Beans category.

It is important that a child's diet have an adequate amount of carbohydrates. Many adults are on diets that stress low amounts of carbohydrates, but these diets do not have adequate amounts of carbohydrates for children to function as they should. Having children participate in these types of diets should be discouraged. A diet with insufficient amounts of carbohydrates causes the body to use fats or proteins for the energy it needs, thus robbing it of the functions these two nutrients provide. Having children participate in these types of diets should be discouraged. Growth and maintenance of the

---

● **Calories**
  *the unit of measurement for the energy found in foods*

● **Basal metabolism**
  *the amount of energy used by the body while at rest*

● **Metabolism**
  *chemical changes that take place as nutrients are taken into the blood, processed and absorbed by the blood, or eliminated from the body*

These children are eating a healthy lunch of pizza, milk, and applesauce and they look happy. With a little effort, meals in the early childhood education environment can cut down on too many foods that are high in fat and still supply the fat needed for normal growth and development.

body will be at risk. A child needs carbohydrates to fuel the work of muscles. If a child appears listless and tired, it may be that his or her carbohydrate level is low. This fuel is especially important to get the day started, so a breakfast that includes complex carbohydrates is a good source to start the day with energy.

### Fats

Fats are considered to be the body's second source of energy. Fat also supplies essential fatty acids that are critical for proper growth of children. Other functions include cushioning of organs, maintaining body temperature, promoting healthy skin, and helping fat-soluble vitamins be carried throughout the body. Fat is in the membrane of every cell in the body. Fats also help regulate the metabolism of **cholesterol** in the body. Body fat also provides a good energy reserve.

● Cholesterol
*a steroid or fatty alcohol found in animal fats that is produced by the liver of the animal*

Intake of fat is an important part of every child's diet. However, it should be carefully monitored to fall within the range of 20 to 35 percent, as recommended in the Dietary Guidelines in relation to children ages two to eight years. Fat is an essential part of promoting brain development and growth in infants and young children. Infants and children younger than two years of age need greater amounts of fat than the guidelines recommend. The AAP and the Dietary Guidelines for Americans both advise against the restriction of fat in the diet for the first two years of life (AAP, 1998; Johnson & Kennedy, 2000).

The major source of fats are the categories of Meats and Beans and Dairy, and they are highly represented in the minor category of Oils. Sources are both plant and animal. Primary animal sources include red meats, fish, poultry, eggs, and milk products, which account for about 58 percent of the fat in our diets. Plant sources such as corn, safflower, canola, palm, and coconut oils provide the remaining 42 percent of the fat found in a typical diet. Table 6-2 lists the different types of fats.

The Daily Reference Intake for fat consumption takes into consideration the risk of excess fat. Saturated fats are of particular concern because they contribute to high blood cholesterol, which influences the development of coronary heart disease. All animal fats are saturated; most vegetable sources of fat are either polyunsaturated or monounsaturated. To help lower the fat in the diet, it is important to choose vegetable sources of fat more often than animal fats (see Figures 6-9 and 6-10).

Another source of concern about fat are *trans* fatty acids, also known as *trans* fats. These *trans* fats occur when vegetable oils are saturated as a result of the heat and hydrogenation in order to process these oils into margarine or shortening. Major sources of *trans* fats include baked goods and snack foods that are made with vegetable shortening or partially hydrogenated vegetable oils. *Trans* fats can also occur naturally in animal products such as dairy foods.

## Protein

Protein, the third source of energy, is the major building block in our bodies. It is found in every cell and is necessary for growth and maintenance. Any new tissue is put together from proteins. Any growth or regeneration needs proteins to accomplish the task. Protein builds new cells and aids in the repair of damaged tissue. It is used to form **enzymes** that aid in digestion and **hormones** and **antibodies** that increase resistance to infection.

● **Enzymes**
*organic substances produced in body cells that can cause changes in other substances through catalytic reaction*

● **Hormones**
*chemical substances formed in one organ of the body and carried to another organ or tissue where they have specific effects*

● **Antibodies**
*proteins produced in the body to react with or neutralize antigens in order to protect the body*

**TABLE 6-2**
*Types of Fats*

- Polyunsaturated fats

  Function: Lowers blood cholesterol, decreases tendency of blood to clot

  Sources: Plants and plant oils (sunflower, corn, canola) and fish

  DRI: 10 percent or less of total calories

- Monounsaturated fats

  Function: Neutral—neither raises nor lowers blood cholesterol

  Sources: Olives, peanuts, nuts, avocado

  DRI: 10 percent of total calories

- Saturated fats

  Function: Raises blood cholesterol, increases tendency of blood to clot

  Sources: Animals, animal fats, butter, shortening, nuts, cheese, coconut, coconut and palm oil, ice cream

  DRI: 10 percent or less of total calories

- *Trans* fats

  Function: Raises blood cholesterol

  Sources: Shortening or margarine, snack foods, baked goods, and some dairy products

  DRI: To be included on food Nutrition Facts label, beginning in 2006.

# Comparison of Dietary Fats

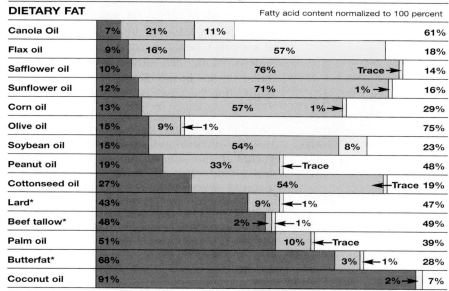

| DIETARY FAT | | | | Fatty acid content normalized to 100 percent |
|---|---|---|---|---|
| Canola Oil | 7% | 21% | 11% | 61% |
| Flax oil | 9% | 16% | 57% | 18% |
| Safflower oil | 10% | 76% | Trace → | 14% |
| Sunflower oil | 12% | 71% | 1% → | 16% |
| Corn oil | 13% | 57% | 1% → | 29% |
| Olive oil | 15% | 9% | ←1% | 75% |
| Soybean oil | 15% | 54% | 8% | 23% |
| Peanut oil | 19% | 33% | ←Trace | 48% |
| Cottonseed oil | 27% | 54% | ←Trace | 19% |
| Lard* | 43% | 9% | ←1% | 47% |
| Beef tallow* | 48% | 2% → | ←1% | 49% |
| Palm oil | 51% | 10% | ←Trace | 39% |
| Butterfat* | 68% | 3% | ←1% | 28% |
| Coconut oil | 91% | 2% → | | 7% |

*Cholesterol Content (mg/Tbsp): Lard 12; Beef tallow 14; Butterfat 33. No cholesterol in any vegetable-based oil.
Source: POS Pilot Plant Corporation, Saskatoon, Saskatchewan, Canada June 1994   Printed in Canada

■ SATURATED FAT (Bad)        POLYUNSATURATED FAT (Essential)
                             ☐ Linoleic Acid
■ MONOUNSATURATED FAT (Good)  ☐ Alpha-Linolenic Acid
                               (An Omega-3 Fatty Acid)

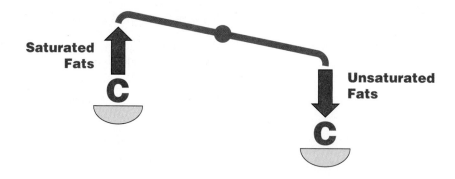

Saturated fats in your diet raise the level of cholesterol in your blood.
Unsaturated fats lower it!

- **Amino acids**
  *organic compounds containing carbon, hydrogen, oxygen, and nitrogen; the key components of proteins*
- **Complete protein**
  *protein that contains all essential amino acids*

Enzymes, some hormones, and antibodies are all examples of proteins. Enzymes promote certain chemical reactions in the body, such as breaking down starches to aid in digestion. Hormones such as thyroxin help the body to regulate itself. Antibodies aid the immune system to prevent invasion of bacteria and other threats.

Protein is made of **amino acids**, nine of which are essential for tissue growth, repair, and maintenance. There are 21 different types of amino acids present. For a food to be considered **complete protein**, it must provide all of the nine essential amino acids. Foods from animal sources are the only complete proteins by themselves.

To obtain adequate protein with the essential amino acids in a vegetarian diet, foods can be combined to provide complete protein. For example, a grain food would be combined with a legume food. Additions of egg or milk products help to provide complete protein in a vegetarian diet. Vegetarian diets should be carefully monitored to ensure adequate intake of nutrients.

A diet that is deficient in protein causes stunted growth in children and makes them easily fatigued and irritable. Lack of protein also makes children susceptible to infection and slow to recover or repair a wound. It is recommended that diets have 12 percent protein to be sufficient.

### Basic Macronutrients

Foods provide the basic nutrients needed for the body to grow, repair, regulate, and maintain itself. The macronutrients that provide energy are carbohydrates, fats, and protein. These nutrients provide needed energy through calories that help to run the body. Macronutrients also provide the materials needed for growth and maintenance of the body. Protein is the major building block for the body. A diet that follows the MyPyramid Food Guidance System and considers the DRIs should provide the basic macronutrients needed.

## 6.4  BASIC MICRONUTRIENTS

● **Micronutrients**
*supporting nutrients,*
*such as vitamins, minerals, and water, needed*
*by the body*

The macronutrients depend on the helper nutrients, or **micronutrients**, to perform their functions and to regulate the body's metabolism. Micronutrients, which are classified as vitamins, minerals, and water, must be present in sufficient quantities for the macronutrients to perform properly. Micronutrients do not contain calories. They each perform specific functions and are found in many foods. It is important for teachers to realize that children in early childhood education programs often fall short of intakes of calcium, iron, and zinc (NR, 2000). An awareness of the need for micronutrients will help the teacher to prepare menus that provide adequate amounts.

### Vitamins

Vitamins are essential nutrients needed by the body in small amounts and are categorized into two groups. Fat-soluble vitamins attach to fats to travel throughout the body and can be stored in the body. Water-soluble vitamins travel easily through the body with water and cannot be stored in the body, so they must be replaced daily (see Figure 6-11).

The fat soluble vitamins are vitamin A, vitamin D, vitamin E, and vitamin K. These are stored in the body in the liver and build up over time, so too much can produce toxic effects.

Vitamin A

- Vitamin A is important for good vision, healthy skin and membranes in the body, and strong bones.
- Lack of vitamin A can cause poor bones and tooth enamel growth, rough skin, and night blindness.

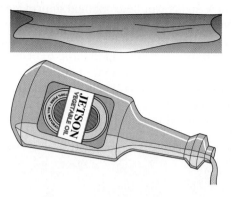

FIGURE 6-11
Fat and Water-Soluble
Vitamins.

**Water-Soluble Vitamins**
Vitamin B
Vitamin C

**Fat-Soluble Vitamins**
Vitamin A
Vitamin D
Vitamin E
Vitamin K

- Vitamin A is most commonly found in foods in the form of retinol and carotene.
- Retinol is most commonly found in the fat of animal products such as fish, milk, eggs, and liver.
- Carotene is most commonly found in yellow, orange, and green leafy vegetables and yellow and orange fruits.
- Carotene, also known as beta-carotene, is considered to be an antioxidant that strengthens the immune system and might be a deterrent to cancer.

**Vitamin D**

- Vitamin D is needed to help calcium make strong bones and teeth.
- Vitamin D is produced naturally in the skin when it gets sunshine and is often referred to as the "sunshine" vitamin.
- Vitamin D is produced by a reaction of the ultraviolet rays with cholesterol in the skin.
- To ensure vitamin D consumption is adequate in all parts of the country at all times of the year, vitamin D is added to most milk.
- Vitamin D is also found in fatty fish, liver, eggs, and butter.
- Insufficient amounts of vitamin D can lead to rickets, a disease in children that stunts bone growth.

**Vitamin E**

- helps preserve cell tissues
- protects red blood cells and the lungs
- is considered an antioxidant
- can be found in whole grain cereals, vegetable oils, and a wide variety of foods so most people get enough
- there are no known effects of vitamin E deficiency

**Vitamin K**

- is needed for normal blood clotting.
- lack of vitamin K has been known to cause hemorrhaging
- is found in dark green leafy vegetables and whole grains, and is also made in our bodies

Water-soluble vitamins include the B vitamins and vitamin C. There are numerous B vitamins, but the most important ones for children are thiamin ($B_1$), riboflavin ($B_2$), niacin, and folicin, more commonly known as folic acid. These B vitamins work with the enzymes in the body to release the energy from food.

### Thiamin

- Thiamin is essential for carbohydrate metabolism so that energy can be released and used.
- Thiamin contributes to the normal functioning of the nervous system.
- Good sources of thiamin are lean pork, nuts, grains, and green leafy vegetables.
- Fatigue and irritability may be signs of a lack of thiamin in the diet.

### Riboflavin

- Riboflavin is essential for the metabolism of all the energy sources.
- Riboflavin promotes healthy skin and eyes and clear vision.
- Good sources of riboflavin include milk products, eggs, legumes, liver, and leafy vegetables.
- Lack of riboflavin can cause skin and digestive disturbances, as well as sensitivity to light.

### Niacin

- Niacin is needed for release of energy from all the energy sources, as well as helping fat synthesis and tissue respiration.
- Niacin helps promote healthy nerves and skin and aids in digestion.
- Meat, poultry, fish, peanuts, liver, whole grains, enriched cereals, and green leafy vegetables are good sources of niacin.
- Insufficient amounts of niacin can cause conditions known as pellagra or the Four Ds: dermatitis, diarrhea, dementia, and death.

### Folic Acid

- Folic acid is required for normal growth, helps prevent anemia, and is an important factor in reproduction.
- Folic acid helps to form red and white blood cells and is necessary for proper cell division.
- During pregnancy, infancy, and early childhood, when rapid cell division is occurring, a sufficient amount of folic acid is crucial. In pregnant women, it can help to prevent neural tube defects or damage to the fetus.
- Good sources of folacin include dark green leafy vegetables, legumes, liver, and nuts.
- Anemia might be the result if there is insufficient folic acid in the diet.

### Vitamin C

- Vitamin C is an antioxidant that helps fight disease and protect the body by preventing oxidation of molecules that could help create free radicals.

- Vitamin C assists with the formation and maintenance of collagen, which that gives support and shape to the body.
- Vitamin C helps in healing wounds and maintaining healthy blood vessels.
- Vitamin C prevents scurvy in humans.
- Vitamin C stimulates the immune system to prevent infections.
- Good sources of Vitamin C are citrus fruits, cabbage, kale, brussels sprouts, broccoli, bell peppers, black currants, and turnip greens.

## Minerals

Minerals help the metabolic process and regulate body fluids. There are 25 minerals that help the body to perform. The minerals that are especially important for children are calcium, phosphorous, iron, sodium, magnesium, potassium, fluoride, and zinc.

### Calcium

- Calcium is the most important mineral because it is present in all bones and teeth. Because the childhood years are also the bone-forming years, it is critical to have enough calcium.
- Calcium helps to regulate the body systems, promotes normal nerve transmission, and functions in normal muscle contraction and relaxation.
- Major sources of calcium are milk and dairy products and dark green, leafy vegetables.

### Phosphorous

- Phosphorous is combined with calcium in the bones and teeth.
- Phosphorous helps to transport fat and provides enzymes for energy metabolism.
- Phosphorous is found in milk products, meat, poultry, fish, whole grain cereals, and legumes.

### Iron

- Iron combines with protein to form red blood cells and carry oxygen to the blood.
- Iron helps the immune system resist infection and helps enzymes release energy to the body.
- Liver, green leafy vegetables, whole grains, legumes, meats, and dried fruits are good sources of iron.
- A deficiency of iron causes anemia and fatigue.
- Anemia among children is one of the major health problems in the United States.

### Sodium

- Sodium is important for fluid balance in the body. This balance occurs between the inside and outside of the body's cells.

- Sodium contributes to the stimulation of nerves and muscle contraction.
- Sources of sodium are salt, baking soda, celery, milk, eggs, meats, poultry, and fish. Canned foods are another source. Even if we never used salt on our foods, our diets would have sufficient amounts of sodium from all the foods that have it.

### Magnesium

- Magnesium is present in bones and teeth.
- Magnesium is important for the release of energy from the macronutrients.
- Magnesium helps transmit nerve impulses and helps muscles contract.
- Magnesium is found in milk, meat, green leafy vegetables, whole-grain cereals, nuts, seafood, and legumes.

### Potassium

- Potassium is important for the metabolism of protein and carbohydrates.
- Potassium helps maintain water balance in the body and transmits nerve impulses.
- Potassium is the critical factor in maintaining heartbeat.
- During exercise or in hot weather, when sweating occurs, potassium loss can result, so it should be replaced through food or drink.
- Sources of potassium are vegetables, fruit juices, and fruits, especially bananas and tomatoes, and is also in meats and cereals.

### Fluoride

- Fluoride helps to promote strength of bone and tooth structure and is important in preventing tooth decay.
- Fluoride is found in fish and fluoridated water. Many water systems in the United States add fluoride to the water to help prevent tooth decay.
- Some fluoridated water is too high in fluoride for many young children. Overfluoridation can cause pitting and discoloration of teeth.

Milk is a primary source of calcium, an important mineral for bone and teeth development.

Encourage children to drink water when they are thirsty. This will make them more likely to turn to water instead of sugary fruit drinks.

### Zinc

- Zinc is necessary for healing of wounds, fetal development, proper growth, and to help the body properly use vitamin A.
- Zinc can be found in whole grains and meats and meat products.
- Zinc seems to be one of the DRIs that early childhood education programs have a difficult time providing in sufficient amounts (Padget et al., 2005)

## *Water*

Water is necessary to sustain life and is the most indispensable nutrient we have. It comprises about 70 percent of the body and transports nutrients and oxygen. Water also protects organs, regulates temperature, and helps to eliminate waste products. How much water a body needs on a daily basis depends on body metabolism, age, and outside temperature.

Most of the water loss in the body is due to urination or evaporation from the skin or respiratory tract. A small amount of water is lost through fecal elimination. Larger than normal losses, such as may occur with increased sweating from exercise or heat, can be dangerous. This is especially important for infants and young children. Loss of water from fever, diarrhea, or vomiting can occur quickly and cause the infant or child to become dehydrated. This condition can turn serious very quickly, so children should be monitored for their water intake. Early signs of fluid loss include fewer wet diapers, less urination, or dark urine. The tongue may also be coated with a film instead of looking moist. There may also be nausea, clammy skin, and muscle cramping. If these occur, medical attention should be sought.

Water is present in most foods found in nature. Fruits and vegetables have it in large amounts. Fruit juices can be a major source of water for older infants and young children. Fruit juice intake should be limited to four to six ounces per day for children under six and between eight and twelve ounces for older children (AAP, 2001). Children should be encouraged to drink water on a regular basis (How much Water, 2004). Extra water may be needed during physical activity or in times of hot weather. Children who learn to drink water at an early age are more likely to turn to water to quench their thirst instead of sugary drinks.

## Key Concept 6.4

### Basic Micronutrients

Foods provide the basic nutrients needed for the body to grow, repair, regulate and maintain itself. The micronutrients are vitamins, minerals, and water. These nutrients provide help to the macronutrients to run the body. Micronutrients also provide the materials needed to regulate the body's metabolism. A diet that follows the MyPyramid Food Guidance System and considers the DRIs should provide the basic micronutrients in sufficient quantities.

## 6.5  IMPLICATIONS FOR TEACHERS

Nutrition education of children and their parents is one of the most powerful tools that a teacher has to promote and protect the health and well-being of children. Good nutrition can help a child maintain health and fight off infections, colds, and other communicable diseases. It allows children to grow adequately and develop to the best of their potential. Nutrition information shared with parents and other family members can lead to a healthier, more protective environment for the families.

### Education

Children can learn about basic nutrition and food selection early. Nutrition education activities should be prepared with the children's developmental level in mind (Plum et al., 1998). Good role modeling, providing healthy food selections, and discussions about the MyPyramid Food Guidance System can send children positive messages about good nutrition. Children can learn that they play a role in their nutritional well-being.

### For Families

Many families are unaware of the importance of an adequate diet. Because of the pace of life in this country, regular family mealtimes are losing ground as part of a daily routine. Use of convenience foods, fast foods, and take-out meals is increasing and taking a toll on the general diet of Americans. Children in urban areas may obtain more than half of their calories outside the home.

Families that are aware of basic nutrition can work to supplement the foods offered in the early childhood education environments on the days that their children are in them (Padget et al., 2005). Teachers can help families do this by posting menus or having them available in handout form or in a newsletter for parents. They can also observe what children have eaten during a day and let the parents know what foods that the child might have avoided. Table 6-3 offers more suggestions.

Children may be bombarded by messages about food through visits to fast food restaurants, watching television ads, and looking at food labels in

**TABLE 6-3**
*Good Nutrition Practices for Parent Education*

- Monitor your child's growth in height and weight.
- Help children understand the difference between hunger and other needs.
- Provide only good, nutritious food choices that will lead to a well-balanced diet.
- Observe the amount and type of food consumed.
- Do not use food as a reward—choose other methods of rewarding a child.
- Help children learn to interact with others.
- Role model exercise and encourage children to exercise.
- If a child's nutritional health seems to be at risk, seek nutritional counseling.

Children learn about nutrition from the adults in their lives. This teacher is selecting healthy foods for her own meal. This will help her to demonstrate good role modeling to the children she teaches.

the supermarkets. The messages carried by these foods make it hard for children to understand that good nutrition is not present in all foods. Children may see poor food selections at home or in early childhood education environments due to convenience and the time crush. It is important to talk about food and nutrition with children often. Early childhood education has an impact on children's developing food habits (Fuhr & Barclay, 1998).

## Role Modeling

Nutrition and food selection are integral to achieving good health and well-being. This is an area where many centers and family care homes fall short. Nutrition is often disregarded as an important part of early childhood education. Recent studies have shown a majority of early childhood education programs do not meet the nutritional needs of the children they serve (Briley et al., 1999; Padget et al., 2004; Soanes, 2004). Some common practices that role model poor nutrition and food selection are included in Table 6-4.

**TABLE 6-4**
*Observed Practices for Role Modeling Poor Nutrition*

- There was little variety in the food presented; the same foods and menus were repeated often.
- Vegetables were generally ignored.
- Foods that were high in fats and low in fiber were served often.
- Sweets such as sugar, jelly, and honey were used moderately to liberally.
- Teachers encouraged children to eat but rarely discussed the importance of a food and why the child should eat it.
- There was not enough food served to meet the DRI requirements for energy during the time the children were in the early childhood education environment.
- Menus did not reflect the cultural diversity of the groups they served.
- Food served did not provide adequate amounts of niacin, iron, zinc, and vitamin $B_6$ needed in a child's diet.
- Convenience seemed to drive menu planning and included using a majority of foods that were canned or frozen.
- Staff in some centers ordered fast food instead of eating the same foods prepared for the children.

Teachers who sit and eat with children and engage them in conversation can make mealtimes pleasant and can keep children on task. This measure could help with increasing the intake of good foods, hence improving nutrition.

These poor role modeling practices show a need for nutrition education and training in menu planning and food selection. A good background in basic nutrition and nutritional guidelines provides the knowledge for good role modeling strategies and practices. Some of the basic role modeling for good nutritional practice is included in Table 6-5.

**TABLE 6-5**
*Basic Practices for Role Modeling Good Nutrition*

- Provide menus and food selections that follow USDA, DRI, and CACFP guidelines, taking into consideration the number of meals and snacks a child will consume while in care. Match this consideration to the percentage of daily diet that the teacher provides for the child. Plan the menus accordingly.
- Select a variety of foods for snacks and meals while planning menus.
- Use a large number of fresh fruits and vegetables to provide more vitamins, minerals, and fiber.
- Select low-fat foods and preparations.
- Eat with the children, eating the same foods and discussing the importance of individual foods in the children's diet. This is a good place to use the MyPyramid Food Guidance System.
- Plan menus that take into consideration the regional and cultural diversity of the population at the early childhood education site. This includes children, teachers, and parents.
- Establish good communication with parents about nutrition and why it is an integral part of overall health and well-being.
- Promote and provide nutrition education for children, their parents, and staff.
- Provide parents sack lunch guidelines for the children who bring their lunch from home. The guidelines should include acceptable food selections and suggestions for meeting the child's nutritional needs. Combined with healthy snacks provided by the teacher this will provide the child an adequate diet while in care.

## Cultural Competence

Cultural competence is something to be considered when trying to impart information about basic nutrients to both children and their families. One must have a basic understanding of the foods offered in the cultures the children come from. Traditional foods may be very important to families in helping continue their culture where they are now living. Food patterns may be difficult to understand, but the teacher should try to gather information so that the early education environment can augment foods prepared at home to provide good basic nutrition throughout the day. Basic nutrition information should be presented to parents in their native language as much as possible.

## Supervision

Supervision ensures that the process of parent education, child education, and role modeling occurs. It is also helpful in examining whether the early childhood education facility, family child care home, or in-home site is practicing good nutrition habits and offering healthy food choices.

Marylou, a center director, has a basic knowledge of nutrition. When the center was small, Marylou planned the menus, but as it grew she got further away from menu planning and food selection. Several years ago the center became involved with the Child and Adult Care Food Program (CACFP), which allowed it to be reimbursed for providing meals that met CACFP program guidelines. CACFP provided training and technical assistance and gave the center a handbook to help in menu planning and food selection. With staff turnover, menus changed only gradually and the same foods appeared over and over—sometimes two or three times a week. When a local college dietetics class evaluating menus at several centers and family child care homes in the area asked Marylou's center to participate in their study, Marylou accepted, because the staff felt they were doing an adequate job.

They were surprised to learn that not only was their menu not well balanced, but it did not even comply with the directives of the CACFP. In addition, Marylou's staff had not considered the cultural diversity of the children now attending the center when planning menus. The staff looked carefully at the problems and decided to hold in-service nutrition workshops periodically and to put into practice the suggestions made by the college class. Marylou and her staff also took greater advantage of the CACFP handbook and technical assistance. The staff involved the parents in menu planning and asked for recipes that reflected the cultures present in their center.

When the center participated in the same college study the following year, the staff got a glowing report and the center was cited in the local press as being a good example of healthy nutritional practices in early childhood education.

## CHAPTER SUMMARY

An increasing number of children rely on early education environments to provide a good portion of their nutritional needs. Nutritional policies that include the use of nutritional guidelines such as the Dietary Guidelines for Americans, MyPyramid Food Guidance System, and the CACFP standards should be created for early education environments. Teachers should have an understanding of basic macronutrients and micronutrients and be able to use this information along with MyPyramid Food Guidance System and CACFP standards to plan menus. Teachers should monitor children for growth and provide nutrition education. They should work with families for greater nutritional awareness so that children can have the same protective factors at school and at home. Teachers can use role modeling and supervision to manage risk and practice good nutrition.

## TO GO BEYOND

In this section you will find a number of activities that you can use to apply and improve your knowledge of this chapter. There are also thorough online resources that accompany this text that can be found at http://www.early childed.delmar.com (see description at end of this chapter).

## Chapter Review Critical Thinking Applications

1. Discuss the interrelationship between nutrition and health.
2. Bring four food labels in to class and analyze by serving size, DRIs, and calories. What would be the difference if this food were prepared fresh and/or from scratch?
3. As a teacher, why would you have to be careful to meet the needs of a vegetarian child in your care?

## As an Individual

1. Record and chart your diet for three days, including one weekend day. Analyze by comparing it to the MyPyramid Food Guidance System. What could you do to improve your overall diet? What steps should you take?
2. Find a local early childhood education center that serves all the meals to children. Ask to look at their menus and evaluate them. How well do they do? What might you do to improve those menus, if you worked at the center?

## As a Group

1. Examine and discuss practical ways to encourage children to try different kinds of foods.
2. Gather nutritional information available in your local community. Make sure that there are enough copies for your entire class, and compile into a portfolio for each class member to keep.
3. Separate students into smaller groups. Have each group plan a one-day menu for children in care. Next have them go to a grocery store and pick out, but not purchase, the products they selected for the menu. Have them evaluate the cost per serving and try to determine the total DRI of the foods they placed on the menu.

## Case Studies

1. Karen teaches in the four-year-old class at an early childhood program. The program serves breakfast and snack, but the children bring their lunches. Karen has noticed several children in her group have been bringing food items that are mostly empty calories. She does send reminder notes to parents, but they occasionally forget. What can she do to ensure that children get a more balanced diet at lunch than they are presently?
2. Jain is a new family child care provider who is trying to make sure the children in her care get proper nutrition. What suggestions would you have for her so that she can ensure the children in care have good nutrition.

## Chapter References

American Academy of Pediatrics (AAP). (1998). Cholesterol in children. *Pediatrics, 101*(1), 141–147.

American Academy of Pediatrics Policy Statement (AAP). (2001).The use and misuse of fruit juice in pediatrics. *Pediatrics, 107*(5), 1210–1213.

American Academy of Pediatrics (AAP) (2003). Prevention of pediatric overweight and obesity. *Pediatrics, 112*(2), 424–430.

Basiotis, P., Carlson, A., Gerrior, S. Jua, W., & Lino, M. (2004). Trends in food and nutrient intakes by children in the United States. *Family Economics Review, 16*(1), 39–48.

Baylor College of Medicine. (2004). How do the Daily Values found on food labels compare to the nutritional recommendations of children? Houston, TX: USDA/ARS Children's Nutrition Research Center at Baylor College of Medicine. Retrieved October 24, 2005, from http://www.bcm.edu/cnrc/consumer/archives/percentDV.htm

Briley, M., & Roberts-Gray, C. (2005). Position of The American Dietetic Association: Benchmarks for Nutrition Programs in Child Care Settings. *Journal of The American Dietetic Association, 105*(6), 979–986.

Briley, M., Roberts-Gray, C., & Rowe, S. (1993). What can children learn from the menu at the child care center? *Journal of Community Health, 18*(6), 363–377.

Cobb, K., & Solera, M. (2004). Are we failing our children and our future? *Topics in Clinical Nutrition, 19*(1), 28–33.

Cox, A. (2003, January 23). Study: Americans super-sizing at home, too. Retrieved October 26, 2005, from the CNN.com Web site: http://www.cnn.com/2003/HEALTH/diet.fitness/01/21/portion.sizes/

Ebbin, R. (2002, November). America's dining out habits. *Restaurants USA.* Retrieved 4/21/05 from http://www.restaurant.org/research/magarticle.cfm?ArticleID=138

Enns, C., Mickle, S., & Goldman, J. (2002). Trends in food and nutrient intakes by children in the United States. *Family Economics and Nutrition Review, 14*(2), 56–68.

Federal Register (FR) (2004). Center for nutrition policy and promotion; Notice of proposal for food guide graphic presentation and consumer education materials; opportunity for public comment. *Federal Register, 69*(133), 42030–42033.

Fuhr, J., & Barclay, K. (1998). The importance of appropriate nutrition and nutrition education. *Young Children, 53*(1), 74–80.

Gerrior, S., Bente, I., & Hiza, H. (2004). *Nutrient contents of the U.S. food supply 1909–1997. Home Economics Research Report No. 56.* U.S. Department of Agriculture, Center for Nutrition Policy and Promotion.

Hayden, J. (2002, May). Nutrition and child development: Global perspectives. *Child Care Information Exchange,* 38–41.

How much water should children drink each day? (2004). *Child Health Alert, 22*(4).

Johnson, R, & Kennedy, E. (2000). The 2000 Dietary Guidelines for Americans: What are the changes and why were they made? *Journal of the American Dietetic Association, 100*(7), 769–774.

Krantz, S, Siega-Riz, A., Herring A. (2004). Changes in the diet quality of American preschoolers from 1977 to 1998. *American Journal of Public Health, 94*(9), 1525–1530.

Lino, M., Basiotis, P., Gerrier, S., & Carlson, A. (2002). The quality of young children's diets. *Family Economics Review, 14*(1), 52–61.

Mydelenski, P. (2004). Demystifying food labels. *Healthy Child Care, 7*(1). Retrieved October 26, 2005, from http://www.healthychild.net/articles/hy37labels.htm

Nicklas, T. (2001). Consider nutrition when choosing day care. *Nutrition and Your Child, 2,* 1, 3.

Nicklas, T., & Johnson, R. (2004). Position of the American Dietetic Association: Dietary guide for healthy children ages 2 to 11 years. *Journal of the American Dietetic Association, 104*(4), 660–677.

Padget, A., Briley, M., Gillham, M., Peterson, F., & Willis, R. (2005). Dietary intakes at childcare centers in Central Texas fail to meet Food Guide Pyramid recommendations. *Journal of The American Dietetic Association, 105*(5), 790–793.

Plum, J., Hertzler, A., Brochetti, D., & Steward, D. (1998). Games to assess nutrition concepts of preschool children. *Journal of the American Dietetic Association, 98*(7), 1168–1171.

Saint John, N., & Barricella, M. (2001). The volume of bottled water consumption. Retrieved October 26, 2005, from http://hypertextbook.com/facts/2001/NaomiSaintJean.shtml

Soanes, R. (2002). Child care nutrition and eating practices. *Nutridate, 13*(2), n.p.

Tippett, K., Enns, C., & Moshfegh, A. (2000). Food consumption surveys in the U.S. Department of Agriculture. In F. J. Francis (Ed.), *Encyclopedia of Food Science and Technology* (2nd ed., pp. 889–897). New York: Wiley.

U.S. Food and Drug Administration. (1999). *The Food Label.* Retrieved October 26, 2005, from http://www.fda.gov/opacom/backgrounders/foodlabel/newlabel.html.

United States Department of Agriculture (USDA) (2005). Steps to a healthier you. Washington, D.C.: Author. Retrieved on April 19, 2005 from http://www.mypyramid.gov/

Additional resources for this chapter can be found by visiting the Online Companion™ at http://www.earlychilded.delmar.com. This supplemental material includes extensive chapter quizzes, PowerPoint® outlines, Web links, and various other activities to help better utilize the material in this chapter. The site is updated regularly, so you may check back often to receive the latest information about the subjects in each chapter.

## CHAPTER 7

# Protecting Good Nutrition in Early Childhood Education Environments

**After reading this chapter, you should be able to:**

### 7.1 Specific Nutritional Policies

Define and discuss the nutritional challenges that pose risks for children in the early childhood education environment and the creation of policies to address these risks.

### 7.2 Hunger and Malnutrition

Define and discuss nutrition in regard to the challenges of hunger and malnutrition as they apply to children in early childhood education.

### 7.3 Obesity

Define and discuss childhood overweight and obesity in regard to the impact it may have on the provision of food to children in the early childhood education environment.

### 7.4 Physical Activity and Exercise

Define and discuss the importance of including physical activity and exercise as part of the diet in early childhood education environments.

### 7.5 Food Allergies

Define and discuss the issue of food allergies and how the risks for those allergies may be dealt with in the early childhood education environment.

### 7.6 Other Childhood Nutritional Challenges

Define and discuss the challenges of dental caries, iron deficiency anemia, cardiovascular disease, and hypertension and how to minimize risk for those conditions in the early childhood education environment.

### 7.7 Implications for Teachers

## 7.1 SPECIFIC NUTRITIONAL POLICIES

Specific policies to prevent risk for poor nutrition and nutritional challenges are important for good health and well-being of the children in early childhood education environments. Indicators for the need to provide protective nutritional policies include the following:

- Early childhood education environments have difficulty achieving nutrition standards (Briley & Roberts-Gray, 2005; Padget et al., 2005; Rolls, Engell & Birch, 2000).

- Almost 11 percent of households in the United States are food insecure. Children in single-parent households are six times more likely to feel this food insecurity (Nicklas & Johnson, 2004). Infants and toddlers who are from food-insecure homes are 90 percent more likely to be in poor or fair health and to have health problems (Infants, toddlers in food-insecure homes, 2004).

- More than 10 percent of children aged 2 to 5 years and 15 percent of children age 6 to 11 are overweight (Ogden et al., 2002). Those figures double when the number of children at risk for overweight is considered (The role of media in childhood obesity, 2004). Prevention of obesity is critical to the long-term health of children (American Academy of Pediatrics [AAP], 2003).

- A child's developmental outcomes can be negatively affected even if his or her nutrition is only slightly less than required (Struble & Aomari, 2005). Only 27 percent of children in the United States between the ages of 2 and 5 years have what is considered a good diet (Marcon, 2003).

- In the United States, more than 50 percent of children's daily intake is made up of foods with low nutrient density (Miller, 2004). Children need structure and support from the adults in their life so that they eat the right amounts of the foods that they need (Satter, 2005).

- Low physical activity and obesity in young children can increase risk for hypertension and early heart disease (Sutterby & Frost, 2002; NIH, 2003).

- Children in care are susceptible to food intolerance or allergy because of their young age and the fact that their immune and digestive systems are not yet mature (Holland, 2004).

Social changes such as increase in one-parent families, dual-career families, and homelessness have had a negative impact on food selection and nutrition of children in this country. Nutritional challenges that pose risks can be related to malnutrition or misnutrition, in which a person is either overnourished in low-density nutrients or undernourished in high-density nutrients (Marcon, 2003). These imbalances may appear in the form of growth retardation, hunger, obesity, iron deficiency anemia, and cardiovascular disease (Nicklas & Johnson, 2004). When children drink a lot of juices and eat sugared foods, they are at risk for dental caries. Diets high in sodium and fat can lead to the development of hypertension and high levels of cholesterol later in life. Other risk factors found in childhood are food allergies and lack of physical activity.

Some of the societal changes affecting the family are related to the lack of environmental support needed for proper growth. More than one-fourth of the children in the United States are living in single-parent households.

Hunger is six times more prevalent in those households (Nicklas & Johnson, 2004). There are 500,000 children born each year to teenage mothers and more than 70 percent of those mothers are unmarried. More than half of the children in single-parent families are living at the poverty level (Children's Defense Fund, 2001).

Other children may be at the poverty level or homeless due to unemployment or underemployment. Families with children represent the fastest growing portion of the homeless population. Children represent 39% of the total homeless population (National Coalition for the Homeless, 2002). It is estimated that more than 125,000 children are homeless every day. Half of these children are reported to be younger than six years of age.

During the past three decades the number of working mothers has greatly increased. More than 13 million children younger than six years of age have mothers who work outside the home. These families are turning to early childhood education for their children in increasing numbers (Niklas, 2001). Early education environments often fail to meet the nutritional needs of children (Padget et al., 2005).

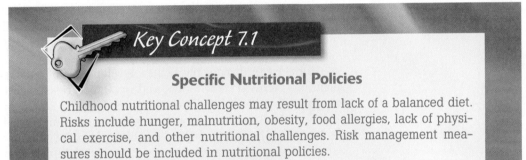

## Key Concept 7.1

### Specific Nutritional Policies

Childhood nutritional challenges may result from lack of a balanced diet. Risks include hunger, malnutrition, obesity, food allergies, lack of physical exercise, and other nutritional challenges. Risk management measures should be included in nutritional policies.

Starvation and malnutrition is not something that happens only in other parts of the world. Children in U.S. cities are especially at risk as the number of single-parent families below the poverty level continues to increase.

## 7.2 HUNGER AND MALNUTRITION

Hunger is defined as a chronic shortage of necessary nutrients. According to that definition, more than 3 million children in the United States are experiencing hunger. In 2002 in the United States it was found that 11% of children were experiencing food insecurity, which means that they did not always have access to enough food to meet basic needs. More than one-third of those households experiencing food insecurity were experiencing it with hunger. The prevalence of food insecurity and hunger varies throughout the United States. The states of the West Coast, the Southwest, and Southernmost edge of the country, as well as the District of Columbia, have the highest levels of hunger (Nord et al., 2003).

Malnutrition, on the other hand, means more than being hungry or not having enough food available. Malnourished children do not receive the energy needed from food in the form of macronutrients (Torpy, 2004). Weight loss may occur. Children can also suffer from micronutrient malnutrition, which occurs when the body is lacking in micronutrients, the nutrients that are needed to support the functions of the energy consumed (see Basic Micronutrients in Chapter 6). The most common micronutrient that is lacking worldwide is iron (discussed later). When children have diets that are too high in fats, sodium, and sugars, they may be misnourished and might even suffer from micronutrient malnutrition because of the way they eat or the foods they are fed.

Hunger can disrupt the health development of children. It can lead to weight loss, growth retardation, and weakened resistance to disease, and it can cause cognitive difficulties (Olson & Holben, 2002). Malnutrition from hunger or food insecurity can be especially harmful to children in the first years of life, when their bodies and brains are developing rapidly (Marcon, 2003). Research has shown that the effects of malnutrition on brain development of very young children can be reversed (Brown & Pollitt, 1996). These studies also found that the health of children older than two years of age can be adversely affected if they become malnourished. This reverses the former theory that malnourishment to children younger than two years old is always permanent and that these are the only years to be concerned about.

If a child's growth is stunted by malnutrition or plagued by misnutrition, problems in other aspects of physical growth may result. These changes in physical growth can have an effect on brain growth and social development. If a child has poor nutrition in the first three years of life, his or her mental development can be compromised (Core, 2003). This failure to thrive typically leads children to become impassive and cranky. Marcon (2003) made three points when discussing how the social development of children could be affected when malnutrition causes physical growth to be below the norm:

1. Undernourished children may reduce their social and exploratory activities because they do not have the energy to play and interact.

2. If a child is not very active, teachers may change the way they behave toward that child.

3. Children who are smaller and grow more slowly may be treated as if they were younger than they actually are.

Other risk factors for social development and mental health may be present for food-insecure children. Higher levels of internalizing behavior problems as well as anxiety and depression have been linked to children who were experiencing hunger (NMHA, 2005; Weinreb et al., 2002). Other adverse consequences from food insecurity and hunger in children are higher levels of aggression, hyperactivity, and difficulty getting along with other children (Center on Hunger and Poverty, 2002). Children who are homeless are twice as likely to experience hunger (NMHA, 2005).

Children with chronic health conditions, physical handicaps, or developmental delays may be at increased risk for hunger and growth retardation due to inadequate nutrition. These children may have physical feeding difficulties, alterations in bodily functions, or poor feeding behavior. Nutrition expectations and growth patterns must be carefully monitored for such children to prevent malnutrition.

Poor nutrition may occur because parents or teachers lack the time, knowledge of nutrition, or ability to prepare nutritious meals. They may rely on fast foods and convenience foods to feed their children (Briley et al., 1999). Children whose daily intakes are too low in high-nutrient-density foods and too high in calories and low-nutrient-density foods will be at risk for misnutrition. These children are not likely to have adequate amounts of vitamins and minerals in their diets. Children who are poorly nourished are more vulnerable to infection and disease, including frequent colds, ear infections, anemia, tuberculosis, and environmental toxins such as lead poisoning.

Prevention strategies for malnutrition and undernutrition include nutrition education, a balanced diet with a selection of healthy foods, and healthy food preparation methods. Because many children eat twice a day in early childhood education environments, teachers should examine their menus and compare them with the Dietary Guidelines and MyPyramid Food Guidance System to see how the selections meet the standards. Children who eat well and see good food in early childhood education environments may change their outlook on food selection as well as their nutritional status. Teachers can provide regular exposure to nutritious foods and encourage children to choose a greater variety of those foods. Children who understand that food is fuel that makes their bodies work properly may make better food choices when offered the opportunity, especially if the food is enjoyable and appetizing.

Ruth, a nanny, went to work for a family when the child, Mark, was two months old. She had no problems with Mark's diet until he was eleven months old and ready to begin eating a regular diet without baby food. His parents ate all their meals away from home and were not used to keeping regular food at home. The only things they normally had in the refrigerator were salad dressing, olives, and leftovers from their latest takeout meals.

Fortunately, Ruth was a trained nanny who had taken a childhood nutrition class and was therefore aware of what Mark needed in his diet. She was able to educate the parents as to the importance of Mark's diet. They asked her to provide them with a shopping list and they bought the foods she requested. The nicest reward for Ruth was that the entire family began eating better and the parents started preparing family meals at home to share with Mark. They were grateful to Ruth for making them realize how their habits may have caused Mark problems.

## Key Concept 7.2

### Hunger and Malnutrition

Hunger and malnutrition provide risks to children in early childhood. Poor nourishment lacking in the necessary nutrients may alter the growth pattern and the health, physical, and social development of children. With the increasing numbers of children in early childhood education environments and significant numbers of children experiencing food insecurity in this country, it is necessary for teachers to be aware of the importance of providing a balanced diet with healthy food selections. Teachers can help to educate children about how their bodies work and how to make better selections in their foods.

Children who are allowed to self-select and serve themselves are less likely to be hungry and less likely to overeat.

## 7.3 OBESITY

Childhood obesity is now the most prevalent nutritional disease in children 18 years of age and younger (Peters, 2004). Childhood obesity is measured by the Body Mass Index (BMI), which compares weight to height. The Centers for Disease Control and Prevention (CDC) classifies children in the 95th percentile and higher as obese and children in the 85th to the 95th percentile as overweight. The percentage of children who are obese has doubled in the last 20 years (CDC, 2001). Data suggests that 15% of children ages 6 to 11 years of age and more than 10% of children ages 2 to 5 years are overweight (Ogden et al., 2002). New data suggest that another 15% of children older than six years of age are heading in the direction of being overweight (Brody, 2005). One might conclude that a similar increase would occur in children ages 2 to 5 years. It is considered to be an epidemic that relates to both the health of these children today and to their increased risk for adult morbidity and mortality (Dwyer et al., 2000).

In May of 2005, former President Bill Clinton and his foundation joined with the American Heart Association to try to cut down on childhood obesity in this country. They developed a Web site for older children, aged 9 to 14 years, to help them understand the seriousness of this problem. Obese children may have a three- to five-year shorter lifespan due to the effects of their weight. This interactive Web site can be found at http://www.americanheart.org/

Obesity is especially prevalent among Hispanic, African American, and Native American children (Dennison et al., 2002; The role of media in childhood obesity, 2004). This condition has recently been linked to television viewing, sugary soft drinks, and portion size (Ludwig et al., 2001; Cox, 2003). In fact, The Kaiser Family Foundation reported that television advertising, time spent watching television instead of being engaged in physical activity, and snacking while watching television correlated with obesity in a number of recent studies. See Table 7-1 for reasons for obesity in children.

Another study found that about one-fourth of children's daily food intake occurred while they watched television (Matheson et al., 2004). A very strong correlation between television in a child's room and obesity was also found (Dennison et al., 2004). Sugary drinks appear to be replacing milk as a beverage in many children's diets, and this appears to relate to later weight gain (Splete, 2004). Fisher et al. (2003) found that serving bigger portion sizes in preschools led to children's consuming 25% more of the entrée and 15% more than if self-selection had been offered.

There are a number of other reasons for childhood obesity, as shown in Table 7-1. It is likely that childhood obesity results from a combination of familial, nutritional, physical, and psychological factors. One of the major nutritional factors is the fast food consumed away from home, including at restaurants, schools, and even early childhood education environments. There has been a movement afoot for fast food outlets, schools, and early childhood education environments to stop providing so many low-nutrient-density foods and begin offering more healthy selections (Green, 2005). This movement does have opposition from the soft drink and vending machine industries.

Excess weight is basically a problem created by energy imbalance. The amount of energy taken in through foods is metabolized and then released through the body's work, including involuntary bodily functions such as breathing and voluntary functions such as movement and exercise. If more energy is taken in than is put out, an imbalance results, and the excess energy is stored in the body fat.

A child who weighs more than 10% above the normal weight as shown on a standard growth chart is considered overweight. A child who weighs more than 20% over the normal weight for corresponding height on the growth chart is considered obese.

**TABLE 7-1**
*Common Reasons for Obesity in Children*

- Dietary excesses in foods containing fats, cholesterol, and sugar
- Poor infant or child feeding practices
- Lack of sufficient exercise
- Watching too much television
- Family genetic predisposition
- Using food as a comforting device or for emotional support
- Weight gain during critical developmental periods

Childhood obesity can cause pediatric hypertension and diabetes mellitus. Stress on the weight-bearing joints is one physical problem that may result. Mentally and emotionally, obesity lowers self-esteem (Strauss, 2000) and has a powerful effect on peer relationships and social acceptance.

Prevention is the key to curing childhood obesity. However, a problem in perception may result in difficulty initiating preventive measures. Many mothers of preschool children who are obese do not perceive their children as obese (Baughcum et al., 2000). Many mothers believe that if they are overweight, their children will be too, regardless of preventive measures (Jain et al., 2001).

The problem of childhood obesity can be improved by an increase in physical activity, diet management, and behavior modification. Physical activity alone does not seem to be effective, but the addition of diet and behavior modification contributes to successful weight loss in obese children.

Diet management should include both a doctor-recommended modified caloric intake and nutrition education. Modifying caloric intake reduces dietary fat intake, and nutrition education encourages children to make better choices in food selection. Families should be included in the behavior modification process, which should include problem-solving techniques. Early intervention that uses the whole-child approach has been especially effective in helping obese children lose weight and improve their level of self-esteem. The best way to help prevent childhood obesity is good parental education.

Teachers can help obese children by providing a well-balanced diet that is not high in fat. They can also provide self-selection or age-appropriate portion sizes for all the children in their care to prevent overeating (McConahy et al., 2004). Teachers can help children select high-nutrient-density foods and teach them about limiting selection of low-nutrient-density foods. They can help children to understand external food cues and opportunities to snack and to make better food choices when the occasion arises. Children need structure and support for mealtimes. If a child eats only at mealtimes

Children who are not physically active and take in too many calories can be headed for overweight and possibly obesity.

and is not allowed to "graze," it is much easier to control nutritional input (Satter, 2005). It is suggested that children have three meals and two snacks per day and be allowed to eat as much as they want during those times, but eat only during those times. Teachers should also provide children with plenty of activity and exercise throughout the day, so that they have adequate opportunities to burn calories.

## Key Concept 7.3

### Obesity

Childhood obesity poses significant risk to children in the early education environment. The number of young children who are obese has doubled in the past 20 years. Some factors that pose risk for obesity include over-consumption of fats and sugars and an increase in sedentary activities. Teachers can help children to make more healthy selections of food, help them read their own inner food cues and provide foods that encourage and provide structure and support at mealtimes for children to follow the MyPyramid Food Guidance System.

*Pause for Reflection*

Could your weight be improved? What types of things might you do as far as diet and exercise to improve it? What suggestions do you have for an overweight four-year-old to help him?

## 7.4 PHYSICAL ACTIVITY AND EXERCISE

In 2000, a new guideline was added to the Dietary Guidelines for Americans, reflecting the fact that physical activity is needed to balance food intake (Johnson & Kennedy, 2000). Healthy People 2010 has included increased physical activity as one of its top 10 priorities (Tate & Patrick, 2000). The new MyPyramid Food Guidance System has a component of finding balance between food intake and physical activity and encourages greater physical activity among Americans. Even though they may not think their children are overweight, mothers generally understand that their children need to be physically active (Jain et al., 2000).

When we consider the problem of obesity, overweight, or even fitness in children we often focus on diet alone. Programs need to be offered in schools to teach children how to choose healthy physical activity as well as foods (Schmidt, 2003). As a result of the need to include physical activity as a priority for children, the University of Missouri Extension designed a poster for physical activity intended to help children easily understand how to select appropriate activities to help them keep fit. This figure is included here as Figure 7-1. This Kid's Activity Pyramid gives children activities that they should cut down on and activities they can do by themselves or with their friends and family. If children are given goals for physical activity that are reachable, it is much easier to expect them to achieve a healthy level of activity as part of their diet (Borra et al., 2003). It is much easier to prevent obesity and overweight than it is to correct it. Allowing time for physical activities and exercise is a necessary part of creating nutritional policies to protect children's health and well-being. Time spent in physical activity can also help create neural connections in the brain (Rampmeyer, 2000).

Preschool and school-aged children are active on a daily basis. Large motor activities offer them the exercise they need. The preschool years are especially important for motor development. Running, throwing, catching, kicking, climbing, and jumping are motor activities that come naturally to young children. They enjoy practicing these new abilities.

It is important that children have at least one hour of unstructured active play every day. Infants should not be inactive for longer than one hour unless they are sleeping. Toddlers should be provided with 30 minutes of structured play every day, and preschoolers should have at least one hour of structured play that allows for movement and physical activity. If children in early childhood education programs are active, the teacher should encourage them to remain that way. Free play is best for active children. If some of the children are interested only in sedentary activities such as quiet play with dolls or puzzles, these children should be encouraged to be more active by providing interesting activities that use their large motor skills. Music and movement are wonderful ways to get children involved. Playing games together to the playground is another way to get these sedentary children involved and active.

The Kellogg Company provided the funding in 2003 for a booklet on young children's physical fitness activities, entitled "Kids in Action," which can be accessed online at http://www.fitness.gov. It has good suggestions for

**FIGURE 7-1**
Physical Activity Pyramid. From Children's Activity Pyramid, by Barbara Willenberg, Associate State Food and Nutrition Specialist, University of Missouri Extension.

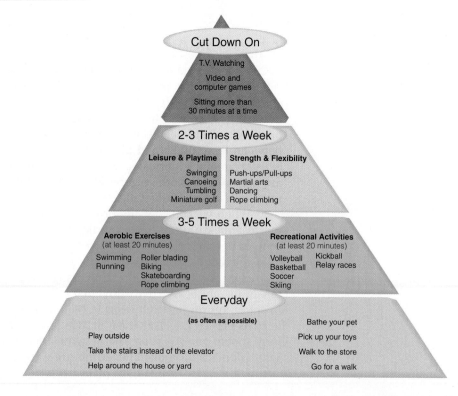

A good amount of physical activity should be worked into every early childhood education environment. An evaluation of the general activity level of the class and of specific children can help the teacher identify which activities are best.

activities to do with infants, toddlers, and preschoolers to help them meet their physical fitness needs. Table 7-2 is a summary of The President's Council on Physical Fitness' *10 Tips to Healthy Eating and Physical Activity.* Although this list was originally meant for 9- to 15-year-olds, it can easily be adapted for younger children. Children are able to burn more calories in outdoor activities than they are in indoor activities (Sutterby & Frost, 2002). Have children consider adapting movement activities that are normally done inside to the outdoors.

When children have more room to move their bodies they can be more physically active. Encouraging children to take an active part in playground play is a good way to ensure that children get enough exercise. Providing both free and structured activities, such as taking a walk or playing a game, should be part of the daily routine.

If the weather is inclement, indoor play should be planned for and used as a way for children to get exercise. If adequate room is not available and there is a nearby school, gymnasium, or community center available for use, this would be a good alternative. Having on hand or checking out a simple exercise video from the library and having the children try to perform the exercise may be another fun way to exercise indoors on occasion. If there are school-aged children in the early childhood environment, the teacher can have them help lead the exercises. These children also might really enjoy demonstrating exercises they have learned in school.

**TABLE 7-2**
*Ten Tips to Healthy Eating and Physical Activity*

- Start your day with breakfast—we all operate better with proper "fuel"
- Get moving! Fit physical activities into a daily routine—make sure you are active for at least 30 minutes per day.
- Snack smart—choose a variety of nutrient-dense foods
- Work up a sweat—include some aerobic exercise each day, such as running or dancing.
- Balance food choices—be smart about food selections and make most of them healthy foods that are nutrient dense.
- Get fit with friends or family—activities are more fun when they are done with others.
- Eat more grains, fruits and vegetables—they provide energy that we need to be active and vitamins and minerals needed to support growth, maintenance, and repair of the body.
- Participate in physical activities at school—structured activities help us to stay physically fit.
- Foods aren't good or bad—balance a low-nutrient-density food at one time of day with high-nutrient-density foods at another time of day.
- Make healthy eating and physical activities fun—be adventurous!

Based on information from the President's Council on Physical Fitness 10 Tips to Healthy Eating and Physical Activity available online at http://www.fitness.gov.

Children should be active and should watch television in early childhood education environments only when it is something educational. Television use should be kept to a minimum.

The teacher can also remove temptations to inactivity, such as television. This may enhance greater exercise and movement for the children in early childhood education environments. Children who watch a lot of television are likely to be less physically fit and more overweight and to have a distorted knowledge of nutrition. Use television sparingly and only for educational viewing.

# REALITY CHECK

## Television and Its Effects on Children's Diet and Exercise

Television has a great impact on the health and nutritional status of young children in this country. Hunger/malnutrition, obesity, dental cavities, iron deficiency anemia, lack of physical exercise, cardiovascular disease, and food allergies are basic nutritional challenges facing children. All but food allergies may be affected by television viewing.

Children between the ages of two and five years watch about 27 hours of television per week (Hindin et al., 2004). This means that children are watching about three hours of advertising every week. It is estimated that children are now watching about 40,000 advertisements per year (The role of media in childhood obesity, 2004). Of those, 45 percent are ads for food. Eighty percent of Saturday morning television ads are for foods of low nutritional quality (Consumers International, 2001). See Figure 7-2 to compare the Food Guide Pyramid to a Saturday Morning Pyramid. Thirty-two percent of all children's ads are for candy, thirty-one percent are for sugared cereal, and nine percent are for fast food. This means that more than 70 percent of these ads are for low-nutrient-density foods.

Food commercials continue to encourage the consumption of highly sugared and high-fat foods that are low in fiber. This is a concern to many health professionals and nutritionists. The food that is advertised is not healthy food. In 2001, 44 percent of ads were for the top of the pyramid, and no fruits and vegetables were represented at all. Only 4 percent of the ads were for milk and yogurt, 2.5 percent for the meat group, and 37 percent for breads and grains (Kotz & Story, 1994). Of the breads and grains, the majority of the ads were for sugared cereals. The ads for fast foods (9 percent) were mostly for hamburger and pizza restaurants, which are known to serve foods high in fat, sodium, and sugar.

For many years, the Food Guide Pyramid was the measuring tool for our diets. It was in use until the spring of 2005, when it was replaced by the MyPyramid Food Guidance System. Figure 7-2 shows how diets would be if we went by the information for Saturday morning food ads (Kotz & Story, 1994). Aronson reported in 2000 that 16 percent of children were not meeting any of the needs in any category of the Food Guide Pyramid. A more recent study found that only 10 percent of children met the Dietary Reference Intake (DRI) for the two-thirds of the day that they were in early education environments (Padget et al., 2005).

Television viewing is a significant source of misinformation about nutrition (Byrd-Bredbenner, 2002). Advertisers use vibrant colors and packaging that lures children to want to purchase the product (Texas A&M University, 2003). This leads children to make unhealthy choices when it comes to food selection.

Food advertising geared to children usually has a particular "hook" or appeal that makes them want to purchase a product. Children's ads have an identifiable character to relate to more often than adult ads do. These characters may be cartoon or real-life heroes. Children's advertising often has jingles or corporate logos that help children identify with those ads (Borzekowski & Robinson, 2001). The number of times children request things seen on television may be an indicator of the effect of these ads. In a recent study, parents reported that after watching television ads, almost half of their children requested a food item and 57 percent requested to go to a restaurant or store that was advertised (Borzekowski & Robinson, 2001).

Much of the advertising for breakfast cereals includes the phrase "part of a balanced breakfast," but this may be erroneous, considering the amount of sugar present in the cereal.

*(continues)*

# REALITY CHECK (Continued)

Young children do not have the knowledge or sophistication to be discerning consumers. The appearance of the hooks of happiness, being cool, or getting good taste or a toy may cause children watching these ads to desire many items of low nutritional quality. Cereals that are marketed specifically to children usually contain more sugar per ounce than a Hostess Twinkie (Texas A&M University; 2003). These cereals are usually placed at children's eye level in the supermarket.

Many products that are labeled as "fruit," such as "fruit snacks," "fruit ropes," or "fruit leather," are highly sugared and may have as much as 50 percent of their content in sugar of some form. These frequently advertised "fruit" products also have intense colors that attract children.

Besides the advertisement of food products on television, there is also a significant amount of food present in television shows. Many of the characters present in television shows geared to children are depicted as eating snacks instead of sitting down to a meal with other people (The role of media in childhood obesity, 2004). These snacks tend to be sweet or salty. Very little consumption of fruits and vegetables is shown. Modeling of good food choices is not common.

One major effect that television viewing has on children is a risk to both nutrition and health. It discourages exercise, so children may become "couch potatoes." Body metabolism for watching television is actually 14.5 percent less than for lying down in bed. Many young children are spending more and more time watching television, which is a sedentary activity. This increases the risk for overweight or obesity.

Children who have a television in their room are even at more risk for obesity (Dennison et al., 2002). It has been found that in one week's time children eat more than one-fourth of their daily food intake in front of a television (Matheson et al., 2004). This may be in the form of snacks or even meals with foods such as pizza, salty snacks, and sodas, which tends to decrease the intake of fruits, vegetables, and juices (Coon et al., 2001). The consumption of soft drinks has increased 500 percent in the last 50 years, and much of this rise may be due to television advertising. All of these dietary habits may lead to obesity, and television viewing has been directly related to increased obesity in this country (The role of media in childhood obesity, 2004).

Teachers can promote good nutrition by using the MyPyramid Food Guidance System to make healthier choices to serve to children. They can provide age-appropriate portions or allow children to self-select. Teachers can provide guidance to children on how to select appropriate food choices, how to snack with nutrient-dense healthier foods, and how to choose activities that are less sedentary. They can also offer support and structure for mealtimes and omit "grazing" behaviors (Satter, 2005). Teachers can also talk about food advertisements and help children understand that although they are appealing, the food is not healthy and should be limited in their diets. Teachers can also help children by reading food labels so that they can become more discriminating in their food choices (Johnson & Kennedy, 2000). Another effort to help children is to teach them how to read their own internal cues as to when they are hungry, and not to eat just because the television is on (Johnson & Kennedy, 2000).

**CHECK***point:* Considering all the information given in the Reality Check, do you personally feel that television does influence children's food choices? How about food selections when they are at the grocery store?

**FIGURE 7-2**
The Food Guide Pyramid compared to the Saturday Morning
Pyramid. From Kotz, K., &
Story, M. (1994). Food advertisements during children's Saturday morning television programming. Are they consistent
with dietary recommendations?
*Journal of the American
Dietetic Association, 94,*
1296–1300.

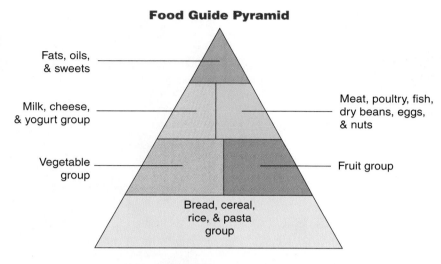

**Food Guide Pyramid**

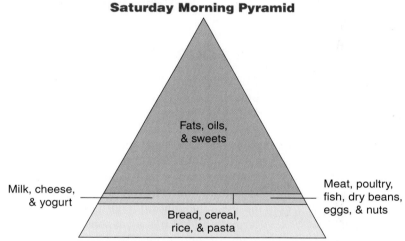

**Saturday Morning Pyramid**

Although the Food Guide Pyramid is no longer the tool used by the U.S. Department of Agriculture, this comparison gives one a good idea of how the typical Saturday Morning Diet compares to healthier, more balanced selections.

## Key Concept 7.4

### Physical Activity and Exercise

Using physical activity and exercise as a component of diet is an important preventive measure that a teacher can provide children in early
childhood education environments. Children are increasingly more involved in sedentary activities. A teacher who encourages exercise in the
daily early education program provides a broad base for reducing nutritional risk. Encouraging all children to be physically active and providing
daily large motor activities to ensure this allows the teacher to protect
good health and well-being.

Lactose intolerance is a common allergic reaction to lactose, the simple sugar found in milk. Good communication between teachers and parents regarding a child's food allergies should be maintained.

## 7.5 FOOD ALLERGIES

If a child cannot eat or properly metabolize a food with important nutrients, he may be at risk for malnutrition and undernutrition. The response to food allergies may range from skin rashes and difficulty breathing to gastrointestinal problems. Foods that commonly bring on allergic reactions are milk, eggs, peanuts, tree nuts, wheat, fish, soybeans, and shellfish (Holland, 2004). The difference between an allergic reaction to a food and intolerance to a food involves the immune system. A child who has food intolerance has an abnormal response to a food, but it does not compromise the general health and well-being of the child. A child with an allergy to a food has a response that is triggered from the immune system; such a reaction may bring about a serious medical condition or may be life-threatening.

● **Lactose intolerance**
*inability of body to process lactose found in milk and milk products*

A reaction to milk is most often apparent as **lactose intolerance**. Lactose is the simple sugar found in milk. When someone is unable to metabolize lactose properly, she experiences gastric distress such as diarrhea or vomiting. Infants who exhibit lactose intolerance are put on soy-based or lactose-free formulas. Care should be taken when putting a child on a soy-based formula, because soy is another product that children are commonly allergic to. Lactose intolerance is fairly common in the United States. As many as 90 percent of Asian Americans and 75 percent of Hispanic Americans, African Americans, and Native Americans may exhibit lactose intolerance (Lactose intolerance, 2003).

When an allergic reaction occurs, most often it includes itching or hives and swelling of the lips. In more serious cases, an anaphylactic reaction may occur. These symptoms appear quickly and include difficulty breathing, rapid heart beating, loss of consciousness, and cardiac arrest. The following paragraph discusses treatment for this type of reaction, and Figure 7-3 shows the EpiPen that would be used. If a child is suspected of having an allergic reaction to a food, use of that food should be halted immediately, and the child should be taken to a physician for

**FIGURE 7-3**
The EpiPen automatic intra-muscular injection device. It is used to inject epinephrine for the emergency treatment of anaphylaxis or shock.

diagnosis. Sixty-three percent of teachers may have a child in care with a food allergy (Wachter, 2004). For children with known allergies, a teacher should have a Food Allergy Action Plan. This plan should include the symptoms or signs to look for in case an allergic reaction occurs, as well as the most common areas where these signs of allergy may occur, such as the mouth and throat (Chang, 2004). Very young children may pull or scratch at their tongue or put a hand in their mouth when they are having a reaction (Child Health Alert, 2004). Older children might tell you that the food is too spicy or that their tongue feels prickly or strange.

The action plan should also include the steps to be taken if a serious anaphylactic reaction does occur. A medically appropriate measure, such as using an EpiPen, might be necessary. Figure 7-3 shows what an EpiPen looks like. It is important for the teacher to know how to use this device. There are trainer EpiPens available from the Food Allergy and Anaphylaxis Network (telephone 1-800-929-4040). If there is a child in care, who is at risk for this type of emergency, then a regular supply should be provided by parents of the children with food allergies. It is important to regularly check the EpiPen to make sure it is not outdated. When an emergency arises, the use of an EpiPen may be critical to saving a child's life.

Parents should inform teachers, and teachers should ask whether a child suffers from a food allergy during the orientation. Parents should describe the exact reaction that they have previously observed, so that the teacher can be on alert for those signs. Teachers should post reminders of food allergies of the children in care on the refrigerator and other in obvious places seen during both food preparation and serving. If there is an allergy to foods that might be used in art projects, such as placing peanut butter on a bird feeder that is made, it is important to limit those projects to children who are not allergic. At least one teacher in the early education environment should have training in the use of equipment such as the EpiPen and be able to follow directions in the Food Allergy Action Plan. Teachers should advise parents of all children in the early education program of any food allergies present. This will help avoid foods that cause allergic reactions being brought in as special foods or class treats (Department of Health and Human Services, 2003). A copy of the Food Allergy Action Plan and medication for allergic reaction should be carried on all field trips that include a child with food allergies, in case of exposure to allergenic foods, so that an emergency can be handled correctly. For better management of food allergies in the early education environment, Holland (2004) suggested the guidelines in Table 7-3.

**TABLE 7-3**
*Guidelines for Risk Management of Food Allergies in Early Childhood Education Environments*

- Develop written policies.
- Establish written emergency procedures, using the Food Action Plan.
- Plan menus that consider food allergies and intolerances present in the children in care.
- Make meals and snacks safe—do not allow any of the offending foods near an allergic child, and do not encourage sharing of the offending food.
- Review recipes, plans, and labels for activities such as cooking projects and art projects.
- Adopt a team approach—have everyone in care help to monitor for food allergies.

Based on information from Holland, M. (2004). "That food makes me SICK!": Managing food allergies and intolerances in early childhood settings. *Young Children, 59*(2), 42–46.

## Key Concept 7.5

### Food Allergies

Food allergies may pose great risk for some children in the early childhood education environment. It is important to identify those children with food allergies and take steps to make sure there is no exposure of those foods to the children who are allergic. Risk management measures also include awareness of any form of exposure, learning how to use an EpiPen, and being prepared to handle an emergency, should it exist.

# REALITY CHECK

## Peanut Allergy

In recent years, greater media focus and information has been available on allergy to peanuts. The prevalence of peanut allergy in American children doubled from 1997 to 2002 (Sampson, 2004). It is estimated that allergy to peanuts and tree nuts affects more than 3 million people in this country. Peanut allergy is an important issue for early childhood education environments for three reasons. The first reason is that the most common time for food allergies is between infancy and three years of age. This allergy occurs in approximately 5 percent of that age group of children. In fact, the allergy to peanuts represents 28 percent of food allergies; it occurs before one year of age in 46 percent of cases, and

## REALITY CHECK (Continued)

before age 15 years in 93 percent of cases (Moneret-Vautrin et al., 1998). The second reason is that many early childhood education environments often rely on peanut butter and peanut products to provide a less expensive form of protein in snacks and lunches. Other products used in daily food preparation may contain peanut oil or other peanut derivatives. The third reason is that more than 25 percent of children who are allergic to peanuts have not been identified (Sicherer et al., 2003). In addition to exposure to an actual food product containing peanuts, exposure to peanut dust or skin contact with someone handling a peanut product can bring on a reaction.

Peanut allergies bring about more severe symptoms than any other food allergies. Approximately one-third of all emergency room visits for **anaphylaxis** are due to the allergic reaction to peanuts. It is also more likely to cause death than many other food allergies. A recent study found that a peanut allergy was responsible for 55 percent of deaths due to food anaphylaxis (Bock et al., 2001). Anaphylactic shock occurs when one is hypersensitive to a substance and is exposed to the substance; the result is an attack that sometimes causes collapse and death. Often this type of shock includes the constriction of the airway and consequent loss of the ability to breathe.

Parents of children with a peanut allergy should inform the teacher immediately on entering their child into early childhood education environments (Salmon, 1999). If an early childhood setting has a child with this allergy, a plan for preventing exposure and follow-up if exposure does occur should be carefully organized and adopted, including the following points:

● Work with the child's parent to develop a Food Allergy Action Plan for that child that includes information as to the severity of the allergy.

● Inform everyone on staff, including volunteers, that this child has an allergy to peanuts and educate them as to what they are to do in case of emergency.

● Post this child's name and allergy wherever food is prepared, served, or in any place where a child could come in contact with foods, to remind staff, as a precautionary reminder.

● Understand how to read food labels and avoid products that include peanuts and their derivatives, so they are not served. If this is too difficult an issue, the teacher may wish to ask the child's parents to provide the child's lunch or snack. The teacher would still read labels and would try to keep exposure as low as possible.

● Have all food handlers wash their hands after food preparation and handling.

● As a safety precaution, have all staff and children wash their hands immediately after eating, to avoid skin contact possibilities.

● After snacks and meals, wash the tables with warm soapy water so that any residue is removed.

● Notify all parents of the children in care, so that, if they provide lunch or snacks, they can cut down or avoid peanut products. You might want to include a list of "safe" foods and snacks that do not contain peanuts or peanut products. This list may need to be updated periodically, as ingredients change.

● A written emergency action plan, provided by the child's physician, should be on file. This will be the base of the Food Allergy Action Plan that is created for the child.

● An epinephrine auto-injector such as the EpiPen should be readily available, and there should be someone on staff at all times who understands how to administer it.

● If a field trip is planned, be aware of any possible exposure in the surroundings. Make sure the allergic child brings his or her own snack. Have the epinephrine auto-injector available, just in case.

*(continues)*

## REALITY CHECK (Continued)

● Guidelines about developing a food allergy plan for a child in school can be found at The Food Allergy Network, http://www.foodallergy.org

It is important to understand this allergy and be prepared to act on it, even if you do not know that there are any children in care who have it. Many reactions to peanuts and their derivatives comes on first exposure to them (Sicherer et al., 2001).

Serving a balanced variety of foods makes eating a pleasant and comfortable experience for young children. Color variety has also been shown to stimulate children's interest in food. What other ways can the early childhood education environment make meals more appealing to children?

## 7.6  OTHER CHILDHOOD NUTRITIONAL CHALLENGES

Other nutritional challenges that pose risk for children in care include dental caries, iron deficiency anemia, cardiovascular disease, and hypertension. These conditions may pose risks due to the shifts in children's diets (e.g., juice or sugared drinks replacing milk) and the prevalence of high-fat or highly sugared foods offered as snacks, advertised on television, and being predominant in fast food restaurants. More than 30 percent of a child's daily diet comes from low-nutrient-density foods (Miller, 2004).

### Dental Caries

Dental caries, or cavities as they are commonly known, affect almost everyone in the population. Low-income African-American and Hispanic mothers see dental caries as one of three major health problems affecting their children (Pestano-Binghay et al., 1993).

Increase in soft drink consumption has greatly contributed to the increasing risk of dental caries (Shenkin et al., 2003). It has been recommended by the American Association of Pediatrics that children limit the amount of juice consumed daily to 4 to 6 ounces of 100% juice, and that other sugared beverages be restricted to occasional use (PAAAP, 2004). They also encouraged children to have two or more servings of dairy foods per day.

● **Anaphylaxis**
*sensitivity to an allergen that causes an attack that can result in collapse or death*

Teeth brushing can be a fun and informative activity that teachers can add to their nutrition education program. Giving children the opportunity to brush after meals is another way to encourage good dental hygiene.

There may be other social reasons that children in early childhood education programs are not having their dental caries attended to. Some parents do not understand the importance of oral health for their children. Other parents may not have insurance available. And in some cultures, dental care is accessed only when it is deemed necessary, and not as a preventive measure (Frank, 2004).

Foods that are high in carbohydrates and sugar promote the formation of cavities. Carbohydrates in the form of starches break down as sugars, which change rapidly to acid when mixed with the microorganisms commonly found in the plaque present in the mouth. The acids produced break through the natural protective barrier and form cavities. When sugar is ingested, the acid formation process lasts for about 25 minutes. Sticky items that contain sugar, such as honey, soft drinks, raisins, and bananas, lengthen the acid formation process. This is also true of sugars found in milk and fruit juices.

Fluoride use is the most effective method of preventing dental caries. Fluoride is added to many water supplies in the United States. If the teacher lives in an area that has fluoridated water, she should encourage children to drink the water. If fluoride is not in the water supply, then the family dentist should prescribe fluoride supplements. Many family doctors include fluoride in the vitamin and mineral supplements given to babies. Other prevention methods include brushing the teeth after eating a meal and using only water in a baby bottle at bedtime. Baby bottle tooth decay is a leading cause of dental caries for children younger than three years of age (Kidsource.com, 2000). This can come from either milk or juice in the bottle. When milk or juice is given in a bottle at bedtime, the fluid pools in the child's mouth and increases the incidence of cavities. If a baby needs a bottle to go to sleep, the baby should be fed a bottle of formula or should be nursed before going to bed, thus allowing for adequate nutrition. Introducing a child to a cup at about the age of one year can help support the prevention of baby bottle tooth decay.

Twenty-five percent of U.S. children account for 75 percent of dental caries. Children who live in areas without fluoridated water, those who live in rural areas, and those who are members of minority groups are more likely than other children to have dental caries (Skinner et al., 1999). Teachers can make sure that the early childhood education environment is using good practices to prevent dental caries. They can do this by providing foods with plenty of protein, calcium, and vitamins that support good oral health (Zamani, 2005). Supporting children with meals and snacks that do not contain much sugar and eliminating "grazing" or open eating also help (AAP, 2004). Campbell (2005) suggested that children should be encouraged to brush their teeth at least once a day while in the early childhood education environment. Each child should have his or her own toothbrush that is stored properly to prevent cross-contamination and buildup of bacteria.

Table 7-4 gives teachers some guidelines for helping protect children in care from dental caries.

## Pause for Reflection

How many soft drinks do you drink in a week? Were you aware that each 12 ounces of a soft drink contains about 10 teaspoons of sugar? Considering the amount of soft drinks you consume in a week, how much sugar have you consumed? After knowing that answer, do you intend to cut down on soft drink consumption?

### Iron Deficiency Anemia

Iron deficiency anemia is the most prevalent nutritional problem in childhood. It is two times more likely to occur among poor children than among those whose families are not poor. Older infants and young children are more likely to become at risk for iron deficiency, because the iron stored in their bodies when they were born diminishes over time. Anemia due to iron deficiency may cause a shortened attention span, irritability, and fatigue. Children with iron deficiency anemia may have trouble concentrating, which may later affect their cognitive development and IQ (Evers, 2000).

**TABLE 7-4**
*Reducing Risk of Dental Caries in Early Childhood Education Environments*

- Encourage a mother who breastfeeds to continue
- Never let a baby fall asleep with a bottle still in his mouth
- Introduce a "tippy" cup to a baby before the age of 8 months
- Help to wean a baby from the bottle by the first birthday
- Encourage children to drink water instead of juice
- Encourage children to brush their teeth
- Have children rinse their mouths out with water after snacks and meals
- Provide healthy meals and snacks
- Provide oral health information to parents
- Provide simple oral health education to children

An adequate supply of iron must be provided in a growing child's diet, but frequently it is not. Teachers should try to ensure that children get enough of this essential mineral in the meals that are served in early childhood education environments.

The only way to avoid iron deficiency and the anemia that results from it is to get adequate supplies of iron in the diet or to supplement the diet with a doctor-recommended vitamin compound containing iron.

Infants receive most of their nutrients from formulas or breast milk. Most formulas provide the necessary iron (PageWise, 2001). Breast milk provides iron also, but after about four to five months of age, infants need more iron than their mothers can provide. Therefore, doctors recommend vitamin supplements that include iron to prevent iron deficiency. Baby cereals are fortified with iron to help provide the necessary iron in the diet.

As a child grows, more sources of iron, such as meats, fish, poultry, green leafy vegetables, and whole grains, are necessary to prevent iron deficiency. However, many children do not eat balanced diets. When quality of diets was investigated, Stanek et al. (1990) found that one-fourth of the children's diets studied were iron deficient. Menus at early childhood education environments were found to be lacking in foods that could help children meet their need for iron (Briley et al., 1993). Iron deficiency in poor children has been linked to poor compliance with feeding practices, due possibly to inadequate funds or lack of parental understanding of the importance of diet.

The best way to prevent iron deficiency and the resulting anemia is through education of the parents, the teachers, and the children themselves. Menus at early childhood education programs were found to be lacking in foods that could help children meet their need for iron (Padget et al., 2005). Teachers who are aware of the importance of iron can provide more balanced diets with better food selections. In cases where supplementation is necessary, iron-fortified breads and cereals should be used.

## Cardiovascular Disease and Hypertension

The diet of many Americans contains too many calories, too much fat, and too much cholesterol. It is also high in sodium. The Bogalusa Heart Study is an ongoing research project focusing on **cardiovascular disease** risk factors present in children's lives (Perry, 2004). The National Cholesterol Education Program (NCEP), sponsored by the U.S. Department of Health and Human Services, is also concerned with the issue of children's diet and cardiovascular risk.

● **Cardiovascular disease** *disease resulting from impaired function of the heart and/or surrounding arteries*

● **Coronary**
  **atherosclerosis**
  *disease of the heart re-*
  *sulting in degeneration*
  *of the walls of arteries*
  *due to fat buildup*

● **Coronary heart disease**
  *disease of the arteries*
  *that feed the heart*
  *muscle*

● **hypertension**
  *very high blood pressure*

**FIGURE 7-4**
Risk factors for
cardiovascular disease.

**Risk Factors**
High cholesterol
Being male
Diabetes mellitus
High blood pressure
Obesity
Cigarette smoking
Vascular (blood vessel)
  disease
Family members with
  CHD before age 60

Children have their food interests on what tastes good,
not nutritional value. Many
of children's favorite foods
contain too much fat, salt,
or sugar.

Early elevated levels of cholesterol can lead to the development of early **coronary atherosclerosis**. The combination of diet and genetic risk factors can trigger a higher incidence of this disease than in the normal population. Higher blood cholesterol levels can also lead to **coronary heart disease** (CHD), which is the number one cause of death in this country. Children who eat diets with excess calories and too much fat tend to be overweight. This is another risk factor in CHD (see Figure 7-4). One recent study found that hypertension among children has increased over the past decade due to overweight (Munter et al., 2004). This is especially true for African-American and Mexican-American children. As children's weight continues to increase over time, physicians are worried that hypertension will rise too.

Excess weight and high sodium intake contribute to **hypertension**. The Bogalusa Heart Study found that almost all children younger than 10 years of age consume more than the DRI levels of sodium. High sodium intake can be linked to the later development of high blood pressure. Convenience foods and fast foods are high in sodium. Some of children's favorite foods contain too much salt, including chips, hot dogs, lunch meats, canned soups, and store-bought breads. Menus in early childhood education programs often feature these foods. The average daily intake of sodium for preschoolers was found to exceed the DRI (Padget et al., 2005).

The best way to improve the risk factors for cardiovascular diseases and hypertension is to modify the diet. Following the recommendations of the Dietary Guidelines for Americans, children's fat intake, containing between 25 and 35 percent of total calories as saturated, depending on age, should be decreased to less than 10 percent of total calories, and sodium intake should be decreased. See Figure 7-4.

Children should also eat diets higher in carbohydrates, which means more fruits, vegetables, and grain products (Padget et al., 2005). The MyPyramid Food Guidance System recommends that, when choosing

grains, at least half should be whole-grain choices. It also recommends that there be more selection of dark, green leafy, and yellow vegetables. Promoting healthy eating habits by offering a well-balanced selection of foods that are lower in cholesterol, fat, and sodium can help as prevention measures. Helpful guidelines for following these recommendations are found in Table 7-5.

## 7.7  IMPLICATIONS FOR TEACHERS

Nutrition education of both children and parents can help the teacher to protect children from the nutritional risks that are posed in childhood. Having nutritional policies that provide protective measures and manage risk

**TABLE 7-5**
*Guidelines to Decrease Fat and Sodium Intake*

- Provide plenty of fresh fruits and vegetables.
- Serve whole grain breads and cereals.
- Use only lean meats, poultry, and fish.
- Choose low-fat dairy products.
- Choose fats from vegetable sources such as margarine and canola oil. Limit the intake of these fat products.
- Select cooking methods that are lower fat alternatives to frying such as grilling or baking.
- Avoid high-sodium foods such as hot dogs, lunch meats, and chips; if these foods are occasionally used, do so in moderation.
- Carefully select menu items that are lower in fat and sodium at fast food restaurants.
- Moderate the use of frozen, packaged and canned foods.
- Use margarine products made with unsaturated vegetable oils instead of saturated vegetable oils such as coconut and palm kernel oil.
- Set a good example by eating healthy foods.

### Key Concept 7.6

#### Other Childhood Nutritional Challenges

Dental caries, iron deficiency anemia, cardiovascular disease, and hypertension also pose risks to the health and well-being of children in early childhood education environments. Teachers should provide healthy food selections that include lower fat and lower sugar choices, as well as foods that are rich in iron. Teachers can also offer children an opportunity to brush their teeth. They can role model good eating for children in the early childhood education environment.

are very important. Providing well-balanced meals full of healthy food selections is one excellent tool for risk management. In planning physical activity, a teacher can make sure that it is age-appropriate and that some of this activity is vigorous, so that children have the opportunity to be as active as possible. A teacher should understand the issue of food allergy, know which children have allergies to certain foods, and continually survey the environment to prevent any compromise to their well-being. Nutrition information shared with everyone in the early childhood education environment can lead to a more protective environment that will protect children's health and well-being.

## Education

Children may be bombarded by messages about food through visits to fast food restaurants, watching television ads, and looking at food labels in supermarkets. These messages make it hard for children to understand that good nutrition is not present in all foods. Children may see poor food selections at home or in the early childhood education environment due to convenience and the time crush. It is important to talk about food and nutrition with children often. An early childhood education environment has an impact on children's developing food habits (Fuhr & Barclay, 1998). Looking at labels and discussing the nutrition of the food being eaten should occur regularly, so that children begin to understand the importance of good food in their diets. There are a number of ways that the teacher can help to educate children and parents about nutritional risk. Table 7-6 suggests some methods to help the teacher educate families about nutrition and nutritional risk.

## For Families

Families can play a major role in prevention of nutritional risks to children. Parents play a major role in the prevention of inadequate nutrition or obesity in their children. If parents have the knowledge of some prevention methods, then children are more likely to follow good dietary practices.

Offering children books concerning food and good food choices is a good way to educate them about nutrition

**TABLE 7-6**
*Educational Methods for Nutrition and Nutritional Risk*

| | |
|---|---|
| • Telling | Explaining and providing information |
| • Showing | Role modeling good nutritional habits |
| • Providing resources | Offering handouts and Web site addresses for parents |
| • Questions | Ask children questions to assess their understanding |
| • Practicing | Engaging in physical activity, making healthy food selections |

Adapted from Story, M., Holt, K., Sofka, D., & Clark, E. (Eds.). (2002). *Bright Futures in practice: Nutrition-pocket guide.* Arlington, Va.: National Center for Education in Maternal and Child Health.

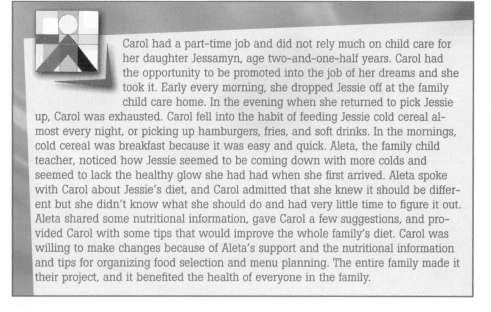

Carol had a part-time job and did not rely much on child care for her daughter Jessamyn, age two-and-one-half years. Carol had the opportunity to be promoted into the job of her dreams and she took it. Early every morning, she dropped Jessie off at the family child care home. In the evening when she returned to pick Jessie up, Carol was exhausted. Carol fell into the habit of feeding Jessie cold cereal almost every night, or picking up hamburgers, fries, and soft drinks. In the mornings, cold cereal was breakfast because it was easy and quick. Aleta, the family child teacher, noticed how Jessie seemed to be coming down with more colds and seemed to lack the healthy glow she had had when she first arrived. Aleta spoke with Carol about Jessie's diet, and Carol admitted that she knew it should be different but she didn't know what she should do and had very little time to figure it out. Aleta shared some nutritional information, gave Carol a few suggestions, and provided Carol with some tips that would improve the whole family's diet. Carol was willing to make changes because of Aleta's support and the nutritional information and tips for organizing food selection and menu planning. The entire family made it their project, and it benefited the health of everyone in the family.

Some preventive practices for nutrition are listed in Table 6-3 to help teachers educate parents about their role in providing children good nutrition. Parents should be involved in planning menus in early childhood education environments and should work at home to complement what children are eating in care (Briley & Roberts-Gray, 1999; Briley et al., 1999).

## Role Modeling

Role modeling takes place in numerous ways. First, by eating with children and making healthy selections from the food served, the teacher indicates that this is an acceptable way to eat. When physical activity is structured, the teacher should be a role model for participating in the activity and should show enthusiasm for movement and working toward fitness.

If television is used at all in the early childhood education environment, it should be used sparingly. Discouraging eating while the television is on is another way to model to children that this is not a healthy thing to do.

## *Cultural Competence*

Cultural competence may prove to be a key to managing nutritional risk such as obesity, dental caries, and physical activity. Understanding that food and culture are clearly related is a good starting point. In some cultures, traditional foods are a mainstay and may represent more than just something to eat. Food patterns may be difficult to change, but providing information on healthier selections or food preparation methods might help a family make some shifts away from nutritional risk. As much as possible, this information should be presented to parents in their native language.

Another method of helping reduce nutritional risk is to introduce the families to the foods that children are eating in care. Some cultures are likely to adapt to the feeding practices that they see being used by people they trust. Others are less likely to do so, because of family food traditions, but they can still see that their children can enjoy other selections when outside the family environment.

A specific issue that is of concern to dieticians in the United States is the parental practice in Latino cultures of encouraging children to eat, even if they say that they are full. The controlling of a child's food intake appears to encourage children to become overweight (Melgar-Quinonez & Kaiser, 2004). Latino children are more likely to be overweight than children from other ethnic backgrounds. This issue was found to be related to a number of things, including food insecurity in the past and high fat content in food preparation. Making sure that food is given in age-appropriate portions or allowing children to self-select may be helpful. If children are encouraged to eat only until they are full, they may be given the tool to turn down food once they are satiated.

Cultural sensitivity is important when considering encouragement of the consumption of dairy products in early childhood education environments. A number of cultures do not regularly consume dairy products. These cultures may also tend to replace the consumption of milk with beverage selections that are sugary, such as juices or sodas. Children can learn to make healthier

Cultural competence should be practiced, not only in the selection of meals, but in the discussions that go on while eating. This is a good time to talk to children about nutritional challenges.

beverage selections if their parents do not want them drinking milk. By offering water as an alternative to sweetened beverages or excess amounts of juice, a teacher may be lessening risk for obesity and dental caries.

## Supervision

Supervision is a key to helping the teacher to manage nutritional risk. By observing children and their food choices, modifying the menu for healthier food selections, and making sure children participate in the right amount of physical exercise can help reduce risk. Being aware of a child's growth pattern can help a teacher to assess whether a child appears to be either too lean or too overweight. Table 7-7 provides some key indicators of nutritional risk adapted from *Bright Futures in practice: Nutrition-pocket guide* (Story et al., 2002). It is important to involve the family in helping to assess risk.

Cost may be an issue for some families in their selection of foods or the way they are prepared. Some families in care may be struggling to make ends meet. Talking to families about their food selections may help the teacher understand whether there is a need. If that is the case, then the teacher can help the family connect to resources providing services or foods that allow families to lessen risk for food insecurity at home.

Supervision is also necessary for children with food allergies. Making sure the guidelines in Table 7-3 are followed will greatly lessen risk for reactions to food allergies. Having everybody in the environment involved in creating a protective environment for the children in care will provide good risk management for food allergies.

**TABLE 7-7**
*Key Indicators of Nutritional Risk*

If the child
- Consumes fewer than 2 servings of fruit daily
- Consumes fewer than 3 servings of vegetables daily
- Consumes fewer than 2 servings of dairy foods daily
- Consumes fewer than 2 servings of meat or meat substitutes daily
- Exhibits poor appetite
- Has food jags
- Eats at a fast food restaurant more than 3 times per week
- Has a BMI of less than 5%
- Has a BMI of more than 85%
- Is physically inactive
- Has dental caries
- Has iron deficiency anemia
- Has a chronic disease or a condition that might compromise nutrition
- May be food insecure due to inadequate financial resources for food

Adapted from Story, M., Holt, K., Sofka, D., & Clark, E. (Eds.). (2002). *Bright futures in practice: Nutrition-pocket guide.* Arlington, Va.: National Center for Education in Maternal and Child Health.

## CHAPTER SUMMARY

Protecting good nutrition in early childhood education environments is necessary to help children avoid problems such as hunger and malnutrition, obesity,
lack of physical activity and exercise, food allergies, and other nutritional risks.
Nutritional policies should be created that help the environment support the
child with protective nutritional practices. Teachers can use education, work with
families, provide role modeling, and supervise to manage risk.

## TO GO BEYOND

In this section you will find a number of activities that you can use to apply
and improve your knowledge of this chapter. There are also thorough online resources that accompany this text that can be found at http://www.
earlychilded.delmar.com (see description at the end of this chapter).

### Chapter Review Critical Thinking Applications

1. Assess how nutritional challenges affect the teacher.
2. Define and discuss the issue of obesity and the impact it has on a
   child's health and emotional well-being.
3. Define and discuss the positive aspects of physical activity on the
   diet of a young child.

### As an Individual

1. How does hunger affect the children in your local area? Research
   the issue and relate the special programs that help these children.
   What agencies might you contact if this issue involved children in
   your early childhood education environment?
2. Survey several local preschools and observe what they do to include physical activity, both structured and unstructured, in the
   daily routine of care.
3. Further research the issue of peanut allergy, and create a nutritional policy to prevent risk to a child who might be allergic to
   peanuts and is in your care.
4. Observe Saturday morning television for one hour. Count the number
   of food commercials you see. Choose two of the commercials and list
   the methods they use to get a child to purchase the foods advertised.

### As a Group

1. Evaluate the impact that a child with a peanut allergy might have
   on the entire early childhood education environment.
2. Separate into smaller groups and discuss childhood obesity. Each
   group should make five suggestions that would help an obese child
   improve her weight. Compare these with the entire class and list
   the seven most important strategies.
3. Hold a class potluck with students bringing foods from diverse cultures that represent people in your local area. Compare the tastes,
   possible nutritional values, and cooking methods, and share ideas
   for healthier adaptations of the same foods.

## Case Studies

1. Mario is an overweight, inactive four-year-old in your program. You notice that he eats sporadically at school, usually heading for meats and sweet foods first. He doesn't seem to like vegetables at all. His mother comes to you concerned about Mario's inactivity, which she feels does not help his ability to get along with other children. She asks for your help. What do you suggest?

2. Heidi notices that few children in her class of three-year-olds seem to enjoy vegetables. What activities could she plan that might increase the children's interest in eating vegetables? What else might she do?

## Chapter References

American Academy of Pediatrics. (2004). *Pediatrics nutrition handbook* (5th ed.). Elk Grove, Ind.: Author.

American Academy of Pediatrics. (2003). Prevention of pediatric overweight and obesity. *Pediatrics, 112*(2), 424–430.

Aronson, S. (2000, July). Updates on healthy eating and walkers. *Child Care Information Exchange,* 30.

Baughcum, A., Chamberlin, L., Deeks, C., Powers, S., & Whitaker, R. (2000). Maternal perceptions of overweight preschool children. *Pediatrics, 106*(6), 1380–1386.

Bock, S., Muniz-Furlong, A., & Sampson, H. (2001). Fatalities due to anaphylactic reactions to foods. *Journal of Clinical Immunology, 107*(1), 191–193.

Borra, S., Kelly, L., Shirreffs, M., Neville, K., & Geiger, C. (2003). Developing health messages: Qualitative studies with children, parents, and teachers help identify communications opportunities for healthful lifestyles and the prevention of obesity—Perspectives in practice. *Journal of the American Dietetic Association, 103*(6), 721–728.

Borzekowski, D., & Robinson, T. (2001). The 30-second effect: An experiment revealing the impact of television commercials on the food preferences of preschoolers. *Journal of the American Dietetic Association, 101*(1), 42–46.

Briley, M., Jastrow, S., Vickers, J., & Roberts-Gray, C. (1999). Can ready to eat cereal solve common nutritional problems in child care menus? *Journal of the American Dietetic Association, 99*(2), 341–342.

Briley, M., & Roberts-Gray, C. (1999). Nutrition standards for child care programs—Position of ADA. *Journal of American Dietetic Association, 99*(6), 981–988.

Briley, M., & Roberts-Gray, C. (2005). Position of The American Dietetic Association: Benchmarks for nutrition programs in child care settings. *Journal of the American Dietetic Association, 105*(6).

Briley, M., Roberts-Gray, C., & Rowe, C. (1993). What can children learn from the menu at the child-care center: A grounded theory approach. *Journal of the American Dietetic Association, 99*(3), 276–281.

Brody, J. (2005, Apr. 5). Sparing extra calories won't spoil your child. KidsCare.com. Retrieved October 2, 2005, from http://www.kids-care.com/Discussions/sparing_the_calories.htm

Brown, J., & Pollitt, E. (1996, February). Hunger in the U.S. *Scientific American,* 38–43.

Byrd-Bredbenner, C. (2002). Saturday morning children's television advertising: A longitudinal content analysis. *Family and Consumer Sciences Research Journal, 30*(3), 382–403.

Campbell, M. (2005). Toothbrushing in childcare. *Healthy Child Care, 8*(2) Retrieved October 2, 2005, from http://www.healthychild.net/articles/mc44toothbrush.html

Center on Hunger and Poverty (2002). The consequences of hunger and food insecurity for children: Evidence from recent scientific studies. Author. Retrieved on October 2, 2005, from http://www.centeronhunger.org/pdf/ConsequencesofHunger.pdf

Centers for Disease Control and Prevention (CDC). (2001). More American children and teens are overweight. Press release. Retrieved October 2, 2005, from http://www.cdc.gov/od/oc/media/pressrel/r010312b.htm

Chang, J. (2004). No for nuts. *Healthy Child Care, 7*(3). Retrieved October 2, 2005, from http://www.healthychild.net/articles/na39nuts.html

*Children without homes.* (n.d.). Retrieved October 2, 2005, from the National Mental Health Association Web site: http://www.nmha.org/homeless/childrenhomelessnessfacts.cfm

Children's Defense Fund. (2001). *The state of America's children: Yearbook 1996.* Washington, DC: Author.

Consumers International. (2001). A spoonful of sugar: Television food advertising aimed at children. An international comparative study. Retrieved May 15, 2002, from http://www.consumerinternatin.org/campaign/tvads.

Coon, K., Goldberg, J., Rogers, B., & Tucker, K. (2001). Relationships between use of television during meals and children's food consumption patterns. *Pediatrics, 107*(1), e7.

Core, J. (2003). Nutrition's role in feeding children's brains. *Agricultural Research, 51*(12), 15–17.

Cox, A. (2003, January 23). Study: Americans super-sizing at home, too. *CNN.com.* Retrieved October 2, 2005, from http://www.cnn.com/2003/HEALTH/diet.fitness/01/21/portion.sizes/

Dennison, B., Erb, T., & Jenkins, P. (2002). Television viewing and television in bedroom associated with overweight risk among low-income preschool children. *Pediatrics, 109*(6), 1028–1025.

Department of Health and Human Services. (2003). Stepping stones to using *Caring for Our Children,* 2nd Edition. Rockville, Md.: Maternal and Child Health Bureau, DHHS. Retrieved October 2, 2005, from http://www.nrc.uhchsc.edu/STEPPING/SteppingStones.pdf

Dietz, W. (1999). Childhood obesity: Causes and prevention. *Feeding Kids Newsletter, 22.* Retrieved October 2, 2005, from http://nutritionforkids.com/emlnews/FK-JanFeb99.htm

Dwyer, J., Stone, E., Yang, M., Webber, L., Must, A., Feldman, H., et al. (2000). Prevalence of marked overweight and obesity in a multiethnic pediatric population: Findings for the Child and Adolescent Trial for Cardiovascular Health (CATCH) study. *Journal of the American Dietetic Association, 100*(10), 1149–1154.

Evers, C. (2000, January/February). Teaching kids about hunger. *Feeding Kids Newsletter, 28.* Retrieved October 2, 2005, from http://nutritionforkids.com/emlnews/FK-JanFeb2000.htm

Fisher, J., Rolls, B., & Birch, L. (2003). Children's bite size and intake of an entrée are greater with large portions than with age-appropriate or self-selected portions. *American Journal of Clinical Nutrition, 78*(2), 215–220.

Frank, R. (2004). Overcoming barriers to oral health care. *Child Health Care Connections Newsletter, 17*(5), 9.

Fuhr, J., & Barclay, K. (1998). The importance of appropriate nutrition and nutrition education. *Young Children, 53*(1), 74–80.

Green, A. (2005, April 4). Bill aims to reduce junk food in schools. The Oregonian, OregoniaLive.com. Retrieved April 4, 2005 from http://www.oregonlive.com/printer/printer.ssf?/base/news/1112608621175340.xml

Hinden, T., Contento, I., Gussow, J. (2004). A media literary nutrition education curriculum for Head Start parents about the effects of television advertising on their children's food requests. *Journal of the American Dietetic Association, 104*(2), 192–198.

Holland, M. (2004). "That food makes me SICK!": Managing food allergies and intolerances in early childhood settings. *Young Children, 59*(2), 42–46.

In their own words: How children might describe an allergic reaction. (2004, February). *Child Health Alert, 22,* 1064.

Infants, toddlers in food-insecure homes more likely to have health problems. (2004, June). *Economic Opportunity Report, 39*(15), 115.

Jain, A., Sherman, S., Chamberlin, L., Carter, Y. Powers, S., & Whitaker, R. (2001). Why don't low-income mothers worry about their preschooler's weight? *Pediatrics, 104*(5), 1138–1146.

Johnson, R., & Kennedy, E. (2000). The 2000 Dietary Guidelines for Americans: What are the changes and why were they made? *Journal of the American Dietetic Association, 100*(7), 769–774.

Kotz, F., & Story, M. (1994). Food advertisements during children's Saturday morning television programming: Are they consistent with dietary recommendations? *Journal of the American Dietetic Association, 94,* 1296–1300.

*Lactose intolerance.* (2003, March). NIH Publication No. 03-2751. Retrieved October 2, 2005, from The National Digestive Diseases Clearinghouse Web site: http://digestive.niddk.nih.gov/ddiseases/pubs/lactoseintolerance/index.htm

Ludwig, D., Peterson, K., & Gortmaker, S. (2001). Relationship between consumption of sugar-sweetened drinks and childhood obesity: A perspective observational analysis. *Lancet, 357*(9255), 505–508.

Marcon, R. (2003). Growing children: The physical side of development. *Young Children, 58*(1), 80–87.

Matheson, D., Killen, J., Wang, Y., Varady, A., & Robinson, T. (2004). Children's food consumption during television viewing. *American Journal of Clinical Nutrition, 79*(6), 1088–1094.

McConahy, K., Smickilas-Wright, H., Mitchell, D., & Picciano, M. (2004). Portion size of common foods predicts energy intake among preschool-aged children. *Journal of the American Dietetic Association, 104*(6), 975–979.

Melgar-Quinonez, H., & Kaiser, L. (2004). Relationship of child-feeding practices to overweight in low-income Mexican American preschool-aged children. *Journal of the American Dietetic Association, 104*(7), 1110–1119.

Miller, K. (2004). Low-nutrient-density food consumption by children. *American Family Physician, 69*(6), 1525.

Moneret-Vautrin, D., Kanny, F., Rance, G., Olsewski, A., Gueant, J., & Dutaul, G. (1998). Food allergy to peanuts in France—evaluation of 142 observations. *Clinical and Experimental Allergy, 28*(9), 1113–1119.

Munter, P., He, J., Cutler, J., Wildman, R., & Whelton, P. (2004). Trends in blood pressure among children and adolescents. *Journal of the American Medical Association, 291*(17), 2107–2113.

National Coalition for the Homeless (2002). *Who is homeless?* Fact Sheet #3. Washington, D.C.: Author. Retrieved online 10/30/04. Available online: http://www.nationalhomeless.org/who.pdf

National Institutes of Health (NIH) (2003, Feb. 10). Study suggests schools lacking in exercise programs for children. Washington, D.C. *NIH News Release.*

National Mental Health Association (NMHA) (2005). Children without homes. Author. Retrieved April 11, 2005 from http://www.nmha.org/homeless/childrenhomelessnessfacts.cfm

Nicklas, T. (2001). Consider nutrition when choosing day care. *Nutrition and Your Child. 2,* 1, 3.

Nicklas, T., & Johnson, R. (2004). Position of the American Dietetic Association: Dietary guide for healthy children ages 2 to 11 years. *Journal of the American Dietetic Association, 104*(4), 660–677.

Nord, M., Andrews, M., & Carlson, S. (2003, October). *Household food security in the United States, 2002.* Food Assistance and Nutrition Research Report No. (FANRR35). Retrieved October 2, 2005, from the Economic Research Service, U.S. Department of Agriculture Web site. http://www.ers.usda.gov/publications/fanrr35/

Ogden, C., Flegal, K., Carrol, M., & Johnson, C. (2002). Prevalence and trends in overweight among U.S. children and adolescents, 1999–2000. *Journal of the American Medical Association, 288*(14), 1728–1732.

Olson, C., & Holben, D. (2002). Domestic hunger and inadequate access to food. *Journal of the Dietetic Association, 102*(12), 1840–1847.

Padget, A., & Briley, M. (2005). Dietary intakes at childcare centers in Central Texas fail to meet Food Guide Pyramid recommendations. *Journal of The American Dietetic Association, 105*(5), 790–793.

PageWise. (2001). Iron deficiency anemia in infants and young children. Retrieved October 2, 2005, from http://www.allsands.com/Kids/Health/anemiainchild_bsy_gn.htm.

Pennsylvania Chapter American Academy of Pediatrics (PAAAP) (2004). Dental caries: Watch what you drink. *Early Childhood Health Link, 15*(4), 4.

Perry, P. (2004, Jan/Feb). Bogalusa's big heart. *Saturday Evening Post.* Retrieved April 4, 2005 from http://www.satevepost.org/issues/2004/0102/bogalusasbigheart.shtml

Pestan-Binghay, E., Reis, J., & Walters, M. (1993). Nutrition education issues for minority parents: A needs assessment. *Journal of Nutrition Education, 25*(3), 144.

Peters, J. (2004). Social change and obesity prevention: Where do we begin? *Nutrition Today, 39*(3), 112–117.

Powers, M. (2004). Sociocultural challenges of feeding infants and small children. *Human Ecology, 32*(1), 21–23.

Rampmeyer, K. (2000). *Appropriate practices in movement programs for young children ages 3–5.* A position statement of the National Association for Sport and Physical Education Development by the Council on Physical Education for Children. Retrieved October 2, 2005, from http://www.aahperd.org/naspe/peappropriatepractice/Appropriate%20Practices%20for%20Young%20Children.pdf

Rolls, B., Engell, D., & Birch, L. (2000). Serving portion size influences 5-year-old but not 3-year-old children's food intakes. *Journal of the American Dietetic Association, 100*(2), 232–236.

Salmon, D. (1999, April). Living with a food allergy. *Child Magazine,* 60–63.

Sampson, H. (2000). What should we be doing for children with a peanut allergy? *Journal of Pediatrics, 137*(6), 741.

Sampson, H. (2004). Update on food allergy. *Journal of Allergy and Clinical Immunology, 113*(5), 805–819.

Satter, E. (2005). *Your child's weight.* Madison, Wisc.: Kelcy Press.

Schmidt, C. (2003, Oct.). Obesity a weighty issue for children. *Environmental Health Perspectives, 111*(13). Retrieved October 2, 2005, from http://ehp.niehs.nih.gov/members/2003/111-13/EHP111pa700PDF.PDF

Shenkin, J., Heller, K., Warren, J., & Marshall, T. (2003). Soft drink consumption and caries risk in children and adolescence. *General Dentistry, 51*(4), 302–303.

Sicherer, S., Furlong, T., Munoz-Furlong, A., Burks, A. & Sampson, H. (2001). A voluntary registry for peanut and tree nut allergy: Characteristics of the first 5149 registrants. *The Journal of Allergy and Clinical Immunology, 108*(1), 128–132.

Sicherer, S., Munoz-Furlong, A., & Sampson, H. (2003). Prevalence of peanut and tree nut allergy in the United States determined by means of a random digit dial telephone survey: A 5-year follow-up study. *The Journal of Allergy and Clinical Immunology, 112*(6), 1203–1207.

Skinner, J., Carruth, B., Houck, D., Bounds, W., Morris, M., Cox, D., et al. (1999). Longitudinal study of nutrient and food intakes of white preschool children aged 24 to 60 months. *Journal of the American Dietetic Association, 99*(12), 1514–1521.

Splete, H. (2004). Low preschool dairy intake linked to later weight gain: Parents: Get milk (or yogurt or cheese). *Family Practice News, 34*(7), 15.

Story, M., Holt, K., Sofka, D., & Clark, E. (Eds.). (2002). *Bright Futures in practice: Nutrition-pocket guide.* Arlington, Va.: National Center for Education in Maternal and Child Health.

Stanek, K., Abbott, D., & Cramer, S. (1990). Diet quality and the eating environment of preschool children. *Journal of the American Dietetic Association, 90*(11), 1582–1584.

Strauss, R. (2000). Childhood obesity and self-esteem, *Pediatrics, 105*(1), e15.

Struble, M., & Aomari, L. Position Statement of the American Dietetic Association: Addressing world hunger, malnutrition and food insecurity. *Journal of the American Dietetic Association, 103*(8), 1046–1057. Retrieved October 2, 2005, from http://www.eatright.org/Public/GovernmentAffairs/92_aworldhunger.cfm

Sutterby, J., & Frost, J. (2002). Making playgrounds fit for children and children fit on playgrounds. *Young Children, 57*(3), 36–41.

Tate, M., & Patrick, S. (2000). Healthy People 2010 targets healthy diet and healthy weight as critical goals. *Journal of the American Dietetic Association, 100*(3), 300.

With children's nutrition, all that glitters is not gold. Retrieved October 2, 2005, from the Ascribe Higher Education Web site: http://www.highbeam.com/library/doc0.asp?DOCID=1G1:100191449&num=1&ctrInfo=Round9%3AProd1%3ASR%3AResult&ao=

*The role of media in childhood obesity.* (2004, February). Publication No. 7030. Program for the Study of Entertainment Media and Health. Retrieved October 2, 2005, from The Henry J. Kaiser Family Foundation Web site: http://www.kff.org/entmedia/7030.cfm

Torpy, J. (2004). Malnutrition in children. *Journal of the American Medical Association, 292*(5), 648.

Tulane Center for Cardiovascular Health (TCCH). (2001). The history of the Bogalusa Heart Study. New Orleans, La.: Author. Retrieved May 15, 2002, from http://www.som.tulane.edu/cardiohealth/bog.htm.

Wachter, K. (2004). Many caregivers ill prepared to respond to food-allergy emergency: Parent's don't provide meds. *Family Practice News, 34*(5), 104.

Weinreb, L., Wehler, C., Perloff, J., Scott, R., Hosmer, D., Sagor, L., & Gundersen, C. (2002). Hunger: Its impact on children's health and mental health. *Pediatrics, 110*(4), 816.

Zamani, A. (2004). Tooth decay: One of the most common childhood diseases. *Child Care Health Connections Newsletter, 17*(5), 5.

Zamani, A. (2005). Good nutrition is the key to healthy smiles. *Child Care Health Connections Newsletter, 18*(1), 5.

Additional resources for this chapter can be found by visiting the Online Companion™ at http://www.earlychilded.delmar.com. This supplemental material includes extensive chapter quizzes, PowerPoint® outlines, Web links, and various other activities to help better utilize the material in this chapter. The site is updated regularly, so you may check back often to receive the latest information about the subjects in each chapter.

## CHAPTER 8

# Providing Good Nutrition in Early Childhood Education Environments

**After reading this chapter, you should be able to:**

### 8.1 Specific Nutritional Policies
Define and discuss the need for nutrition policies that address growth and development to prevent risk, provide protection, and promote nutritional well-being.

### 8.2 Early Feeding and the Infant in Care
Discuss breastfeeding, bottle feeding, and the introduction of solids into the infant's diet, including the developmental implications and practices for the teacher.

### 8.3 Feeding the Autonomous Toddler
Discuss the impact of development on the feeding behavior of the toddler and describe strategies for the teacher to redirect that behavior.

### 8.4 Food and the Preschooler
Discuss the food behaviors of the preschooler and the strategies for the teacher to guide the child to behaviors that foster well-being.

### 8.5 School-Age Nutrition
Discuss the nutritional needs of the school-aged child and the strategies for the teacher to meet these needs that may be compromised by outside influences.

### 8.6 Nutrition and the Child with Special Needs
Explain how special needs might affect the nutrition and feeding of a child and discuss specific strategies to meet the child's nutritional challenges.

### 8.7 Implications for Teachers
Describe and discuss methods for education, supervision, and role modeling to ensure good nutrition for children in care.

## 8.1 SPECIFIC NUTRITIONAL POLICIES

The importance of providing good nutrition in early childhood education environments cannot be stressed enough. Greater numbers of children are relying on their teachers to provide a significant portion of their nutritional needs. Teachers play a significant role in the nutritional well-being of children. Creating policies to meet the changing nutritional needs of the children in care is a vital risk management tool that can affect the way children grow and learn. The following indicators reveal the need for those policies:

- Children who are in the early childhood education environment for eight hours should receive at least one meal and two snacks. Food should be available at least every three hours (Nicklas, 2001).
- Teachers are being asked to take on the role of nutritional gatekeeper for children (Penn State News, 2003; Briley et al., 1997).
- Seventy-eight percent of children are not consuming the recommended amount of vegetables, and 63 percent are not consuming the recommended amount of fruits (Nicklas & Johnson, 2004).
- Children who are in the early childhood education environment eight hours or more should receive foods that provide 50 to 67 percent of their nutritional needs (Nicklas, 2001; Briley & Roberts-Gray, 2005).
- Providing a pleasant eating environment helps set the stage for good nutritional habits (Satter, 2005; Murray, 2000).
- It is important to recognize a child's developmental abilities in respect to feeding him (Butte et al., 2004).

Many children are in early childhood education environments for more than eight hours a day, yet their nutritional needs may not be met by the teacher. The teacher may be unaware of nutritional standards or may not know how to plan menus to meet those standards (Briley & Roberts-Gray, 2005). The teacher's perceptions about what a child will or will not eat may also influence food choices. For example, some teachers may believe that children do not like vegetables and prefer foods that are like fast foods, so they may create menus that they think children will like and eat. These factors can have a negative effect on menu planning choices for food and the balance of the nutrition provided by that food.

Cost is always a factor when trying to balance care with the business of caregiving. Many teachers watch for sales, buy in bulk, and look for other opportunities to cut back on cost. Saving should never be so important as to sacrifice the children's well-being. Early childhood education centers and family child care homes may be eligible to participate in funded food programs that will help to defray the costs for children from low-income families.

Convenience may also be a factor in food selection in early childhood education environments. Menus in these centers have typically been in use a long time with few updates and are limited by lack of nutritional knowledge on the part of the staff (Padget et al., 2005). If the effort is not made to change menus or to learn more about nutrition, then choices may be limited.

Culture may also affect food choices in early childhood education environments. The teacher may have a cultural background that influences cooking and menu selection and may even limit choices available (Story et al., 2000; Johnson & Nicklas, 1999). Culturally competent teachers have the skills to work with diverse populations (Obegi & Ritblatt, 2005). This would include knowing the diversity of children in care and foods that represent that diversity. Children may or may not eat foods from cultural backgrounds that are different from their own. Children may have family cultural influences that limit what they will eat. Television and fast food commercials may have an effect on what the teacher fixes and what children will eat.

The early childhood educator who serves the family in their home may have an added difficulty providing proper nutrition. Many families who hire nannies are so busy and have their focus elsewhere that food for themselves and their children may be more of an irritant than an issue. Some parents may eat all of their meals away from home and only provide what they consider are the necessities for the child or what they think the child will eat, with no regard to nutritional value. Parents may have no knowledge about nutrition and how it can affect the growth and development of a child. This can make caring for the nutritional needs of a child a challenge to a nanny.

Another factor that should be considered is the purpose of the early childhood education environment. Briley et al. (1994) pointed out that there are three perspectives on the purpose of early childhood education. *(1) to promote the well-being of the child, (2) to provide a service to the community, and (3) to provide a living for the provider.* If the early childhood education environment is focused on the second or third perspective, the nutritional well-being of the child may be at risk.

Children have specific nutritional needs at each stage of their growth and development. It is essential that the teacher be aware of these nutritional needs and create policies that will help to meet the specific needs of the children as they grow and develop.

Nutritional policies that will help the teacher meet the specific needs of the children in care are:

- *Early Feeding and the Infant:* understanding the changing needs of infants, including breastfeeding, bottle feeding, and the introduction of solid foods

- *Establishing the Feeding Behavior of the Toddler:* understanding the impact of development and changing needs on the behavior of the toddler regarding food and eating

- *Food and the Preschool Child:* understanding the food behaviors and changing needs of the preschooler

- *School-Age Nutrition:* understanding nutritional needs and how these needs are threatened by outside influences, including school food programs

- *Nutrition and the Child with Special Needs:* understanding how special needs might affect the diet and feeding of a child

- *Implications for Teachers:* understanding the need for education, supervision, support, and role modeling to ensure good nutrition

This child is serving himself milk family-style and, if needed, he can get some help from his teacher. This is an excellent way for children to self-select the foods they eat.

### Key Concept 8.1

#### Nutritional Policies

Every teacher should practice good nutrition in the early childhood education environment. Many teachers are not meeting the nutritional needs of children in their care. Nutrition for the early childhood education environment is approached by each teacher with that person's own perspective based on background, food practices, culture, and what the children eat or will not eat. The teacher should have nutritional policies that cover early infant feeding, food and the toddler, the preschool child, school-age children, and special needs. The implications for the teacher include education, role modeling, and supervision.

## 8.2 EARLY FEEDING AND THE INFANT IN CARE

The birth weight of a healthy baby will double in the first four months of life, and nutritional needs will change as a child grows and develops. An infant grows faster during the first year than at any other time of her life. This growth rate is due to the growth patterns of all the internal organs. An infant's nutrition should be able to supply the nutrients, including energy, for this rapid growth.

The growth and development of an infant is directly related to nutrition. In the first four to six months of life, the only form of food an infant's body can accommodate is liquid breast milk or formula that provides the necessary nutrients. The changes in the organs provide the ability to digest and assimilate solid foods as the infant grows.

At birth, newborns cannot chew or use their tongues to push food. Their kidneys are too immature to handle the wastes of solid food. Digestive systems are not yet mature enough to handle the nutrients from solid foods. Allergic reactions, cramping, and crying are common results of introducing solid foods before the baby can assimilate them into the body.

### *Breastfeeding*

Historically, infants were breastfed. This changed when technology was developed to provide sanitation for bottle feeding and formulas on which babies could survive and thrive. Doctors saw bottle feeding as a way to measure the amount of milk a baby was drinking. The trend for bottle feeding of infants increased until the early 1970s, when research showed that breastfeeding offered more nutrition and immunity than bottle feeding. In the United States, 70 percent of mothers begin breastfeeding when their children are born, and only one-third are still breastfeeding after three months (MacDonald, 2004). Today, the American Academy of Pediatricians (AAP) is

Breast milk contains all of the nutrients that babies need during the first six months of life. Teachers should work to accommodate the mother who wants to continue breastfeeding while her child is in care.

involved in an effort to increase the number of babies who are breastfed, and to have those babies breastfed for the first 12 months of life (AAP, 2000).

Current knowledge shows that breastfeeding is the preferable form to provide infants proper nutrition, protection from bacteria, and immunity from diseases. There is also good cause to believe that breastfeeding actually optimizes cognitive development (AAP, 2000). See Table 8-1 for the benefits of breastfeeding.

The teacher may be called upon to help the breastfeeding mother with quality support (Calo, 2002; U.S. Department of Health and Human Services [US DHHS], 2001). This offers advantages to everyone concerned. The baby will benefit as Table 8-1 indicates, and the mother and the teacher will both benefit because a breastfed baby is less likely than a bottle-fed baby to become sick when left in care (Jones & Matheny, 1993). Increasing breastfeeding is also a goal of the Special Supplemental Food Program for Women, Infants and Children (WIC) because babies receive so many health benefits from it (Carmichael et al., 2001; Ahluwalia et al., 2000).

Mothers can help the teacher by collecting and storing breast milk to use while they are not with the baby. Breast milk will last up to 48 hours in the refrigerator or can be frozen for two weeks. The teacher can help the nursing mother by allowing the mother to nurse the baby in the early childhood education environment. This may occur as the baby is dropped off, picked up, and even at lunch time if the mother is close enough to visit her child during the lunch break. This type of support will help mothers continue to breastfeed for the recommended time for optimum health and well-being for the infant. It is helpful to provide a quiet place for the baby to nurse and to time the baby's feedings to the mother's schedule (Calo, 2002). A sign should be posted that indicates breastfed babies are welcome in your early childhood environment (Aird, 2002). It is helpful to include fathers and others in the infant's life to help support the mother's decision to breastfeed. When a mother feels that everyone is happy about her breastfeeding decision, she is more likely to continue (USBC, 2002). A mother should be discouraged from breastfeeding if: (1) the mother has a communicable or chronic disease such as AIDS; (2) she is taking medication that is harmful to the baby; or (3) she is a drug or alcohol abuser.

Breastfed babies usually need to be fed every two to three hours. Breastfed babies may have more trouble accepting the bottle because they are used to sucking the breast. Using a breast-shaped nipple or a soft nipple

**TABLE 8-1**
*Benefits of Breastfeeding*

- Protein is suited to baby's metabolism.
- Provides antibodies to combat bacteria.
- Provides immunological protection from illness and disease.
- Fat and iron in breast milk are easily absorbed and digested by the baby.
- Convenient—right temperature, sterile, and changes composition as baby's needs change.
- Psychological advantages—bonding with mother, tactile stimulation.
- Fosters optimum cognitive development.

may help the baby get more milk (Figure 8-1). It may take several tries before the right nipple is found. The teacher should not give up!

To really reinforce support for breastfeeding it might be helpful to create a nutritional policy for breastfed infants so that you can share it with expectant parents and new mothers who are breastfeeding. One thing to include on this policy is a discussion on recent findings about how breastfed babies may not be getting enough vitamin D and may need a nutritional supplement (Gartner & Greer, 2003; Butte et al., 2003). In the effort to keep babies and young children from the sun's rays, they may become vulnerable to vitamin D deficiency.

The teacher should apply good sanitary practices and food safety procedures when using breast milk, as listed in Table 8-2.

## Bottle Feeding

Although breastfeeding is the preferred form, many children are fed formula from the beginning or are switched to formula for a variety of reasons. Mothers may find this is easier when they work, and it allows anyone, including fathers, to participate in the feeding of the baby. A child may also be on a combination of breast and bottle feeding; for example, breast milk may be fed in the morning and at night and bottled formula during the day.

Formulas are easy to prepare and come in several forms. Powdered and liquid concentrate formulas are meant to have sterile water added to the exact directions on the can. This is very important because if the formula is incorrectly mixed, it can be harmful to the infant. The other kind of formula is ready-to-feed and merely needs to be put into the bottle.

**FIGURE 8-1**
Types of nipples.

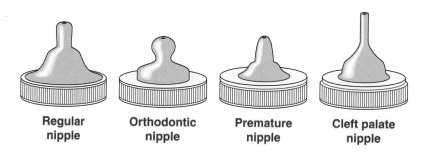

| Regular nipple | Orthodontic nipple | Premature nipple | Cleft palate nipple |

**TABLE 8-2**
*Safe and Sanitary Practices for Breastfeeding*

- Breast milk that has been stored unfrozen should be thrown away if not used within three days.
- Expressed milk should be stored in single portion feedings with date and child's name clearly labeled.
- Thaw frozen milk in the refrigerator or under cold running water. Never heat in the microwave.
- Shake refrigerator thawed milk to mix cream into all the milk.
- Do not refreeze thawed breast milk.
- Dispose of any unused milk left in the bottle immediately after feeding.

If a baby appears to be spitting up a lot or having diarrhea after being fed formula, it may indicate that the baby is intolerant to the formula. Discuss this with the family and make a determination as to how to proceed. The family may want to talk to their physician before changing formulas. Another thing that the family may want to discuss with the physician is the possibility of vitamin D deficiency if the formula is not fortified with vitamin D.

Many manufacturers make soy-protein formulas for infants who are born with lactose intolerance. These infants may suffer from diarrhea, gas, and bloating. An infant may also be allergic to the soy formula, in which case there is a formula available with the proteins already broken down by enzyme action to prevent the allergic reaction.

Formulas try to copy breast milk as closely as possible. Formula manufacturers start with nonfat cow's milk as a base, then add vegetable oil, lactose, vitamins, and minerals to approximate the energy and nutrients available from human milk. Commercially prepared formulas are heavily regulated to keep infants safe from harm.

For proper food safety and sanitation, the measures in Table 8-3 should be commonly practiced in bottle preparation using formula.

*Feeding Pattern.* Whether the baby is being breastfed or bottle fed, there is an important factor to keep in mind. Even at this young age, the child should be able to control his own eating pattern. To accomplish this, the teacher must be aware of the cues the baby gives when a break is needed or when he is full. These cues include drawing the head away from the nipple, releasing it, spitting it out, or biting it. The infant may also stop sucking or shut his mouth tightly. Changing posture or being attentive to the surroundings and not the feeding are also cues that the child may not need any more breast or bottle feeding. A baby should be fed according to his own body's schedule of food energy needs instead of an imposed routine.

**TABLE 8-3**
*Safe and Sanitary Practices for Bottle Feeding*

- Wash hands with liquid soap and hot water before beginning the sterilization process.
- Wash bottles, nipples, and caps in hot, soapy water, using a bottle brush for hard-to-reach places. Rinse thoroughly in hot, clean water.
- Sterilize all bottle parts in a pan of water. Boil for 5 to 6 minutes. Remove from pan with tongs and fill immediately.
- Always buy cans of formula that are intact and have current use dates.
- Wash the tops of formula cans before opening them.
- Prepare formula exactly to manufacturers' instructions. If formula is diluted too much, malnutrition may result. If an insufficient amount of water is added, the child's digestive system may be strained.
- Use clean, sterile bottled water rather than tap water, because some tap water may cause digestive upsets in some infants.
- Pour formula into sterilized bottles and top with nipples, caps, and rings if the bottle is being stored in the refrigerator. Use up all the prepared formula. Prepared bottles should be stored no longer than 24 hours.

Babies should be held in a slightly elevated, reclined position when feeding, to avoid choking and ear infections. These early feedings contribute significantly to the basis of the child's later eating habits.

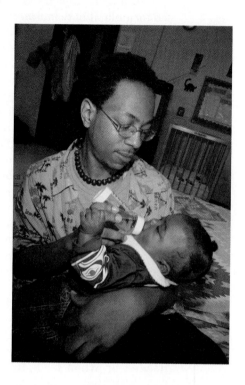

It is important that a child is held correctly when being bottle fed. The baby should not be flat on her back but should be in a semireclining position (Lyles, 2003). When feeding begins, make sure that the nipple is full of formula so that it does not get too full of air. Always burp a baby between one-third and one-half of the way through the feeding, and then again after the feeding is finished. After bottle feeding a baby a few times, the teacher should know the baby's burping "pattern." Try to always hold a baby when feeding her. Never prop a baby's bottle, and avoid getting her a bottle in the crib or on the floor, where she would be lying flat.

Infant-controlled feeding requires the teacher to be attentive to the infant's behavior and to allow the quantity eaten to vary depending on the infant's needs. It also requires that the teacher communicate with the family about how the baby is feeding at home, including during the night (Walker, 2005). The teacher can identify the infant's cues by allowing time for pauses. This may be a good time to see if the baby needs to be held upright to pass a gas bubble. If the baby is fussy during a feeding, it is wise to find the source of the discomfort instead of interpreting the fussiness as a sign that the baby is done eating. Helping the infant to develop a healthy feeding relationship helps to establish good eating habits later in life (Satter, 2000).

## Introducing Solid Foods

Solid foods should not be introduced into a baby's diet until the baby is at least four months old, and not until six months if she does not show signs of readiness. This is about the time it takes for the fine, gross, and oral motor skills to develop so that the child is ready to eat solid food. If foods are introduced in a child's diet too early, it can make the baby vulnerable to food intolerance or food allergies (Calder, 2004). The normal pattern of development and ability of the body to accept solid foods and the nutrients they supply are listed in Table 8-4. As can be observed in Table 8-4, a young baby is unable to sufficiently process the food in her digestive track, even if she could swallow the food.

*Feeding Patterns.* When the infant is demonstrating developmental readiness, then solid foods should be introduced. Until this point, the protein needed for brain growth has been provided by the breast milk or formula. There is a common pattern for the introduction of this type of food, and the pattern has been developed with good reasons. The teacher should start the introduction of solid food slowly, serving only one or two servings of the food at the beginning. One new food is introduced at a time, and the teacher should wait five to seven days before introducing another new food. This waiting period allows the teacher to identify whether the food causes allergies or digestive complications such as diarrhea, gas, rashes, vomiting, or unusual fussiness. If this does not occur, move on to the next new food. It is much better to feed babies commercially prepared foods that do not have any added

**TABLE 8-4**
*Pattern of Developmental Skills for Eating Solid Foods*

- Birth: Baby is only capable of sucking.
- 6 weeks: Baby can smile and has the ability to extrude or push things out of the mouth with the tongue.
- 8 weeks: Baby can use the tongue against the palate and can swallow semisoft food, but cannot digest the food itself.
- 3 months: Baby's gastrointestinal system is sufficiently developed for digesting starch.
- 4 months: Baby shows signs of being ready for solid foods: drinks 40 or more ounces of milk, can swallow instead of suck, and drools, indicating teeth will soon appear. Should be double his birth weight. If formula fed, iron stores may be depleted and baby will need iron from other food sources.
- 4 to 6 months: Baby can control head movements and can keep food in the mouth instead of pushing it out with the tongue.
- 5 months: Baby is a social creature and may be more interested in people and surroundings than in eating. May demonstrate interest in other people's food and open the mouth to show this interest.
- 6 months: Baby can sit up in a high chair and can be easily spoon fed. If breastfed, iron stores may be depleted and baby will need iron from other food sources.
- 6–9 months: Teeth begin to appear, as does the munching movement of the jaw and the pursing of the mouth. This allows for more biting and chewing, making it easier to eat coarser pieces of food and to begin cup feeding.
- 8 months: Baby can grasp soft finger foods with hands and put them in the mouth.
- 10 months: Baby should be able to grasp cup with both hands.
- 12 months: Baby should be able to hold an age-appropriate spoon.

sugars or sodium. This food is prepared in a sanitary manner and has had precautions taken to prevent bacterial growth. This is not true for homemade baby food, which should be avoided because it is not as safe for the baby.

As the teacher starts the solid food routine, there are several things to keep in mind that will help the baby learn how to eat in a safe way. Utensils used to feed the baby should be small and age appropriate (Briley & Roberts-Gray, 2005). To begin with, only small amounts of food should be offered on the tip of the spoon. As the baby progresses, the amount should be increased to two or three tablespoons at a feeding. The food the teacher serves should be placed in a small bowl or custard cup with only enough for one serving, and any unfinished food should be discarded. Returning food to the jar might contaminate the food remaining in the jar and make it unsafe for the baby to eat. Table 8-5 contains the introduction pattern for solid foods.

*Cereals.* The first food normally introduced is iron-fortified rice cereal. Rice is a good food to begin the introduction pattern, because it is easily digested. The teacher should mix the cereal with some formula until it is somewhat runny. It will be easier for infant to assimilate this experience if it is not totally dissimilar from her liquid diet. This food should be fed to the child on a spoon, not from a bottle. It is common practice among certain cultures, including Hispanics, to introduce this food mixed with formula in a bottle in which the nipple has been cut to allow the cereal to come out. Developmentally, this puts the child back to sucking and swallowing rather than using the developing oral skills that will be needed later.

Cereals are normally fed for the first month or two of the introduction of solid foods. The child should not be fed mixed cereals or wheat-based cereal because of possible allergic reactions. It is difficult to tell which ingredient in mixed cereal may be the culprit, and wheat is often the basis for allergy among infants.

*Vegetables.* The next food to introduce is vegetables, one at a time. Infants may show preference for flavors and may totally reject a food. This is one reason vegetables are introduced before fruits, since sweet flavors are preferred to savory flavors. This gives the child the opportunity to learn to

**TABLE 8-5**
*Solid Food Introduction Pattern*

| Age | Include | Exclude |
|---|---|---|
| 0 to 4 months | Formula or breast milk | Solid foods, cow's milk |
| 4 to 6 months | Add iron-fortified cereals | Honey, meat, eggs, sugar, powdered sweetened drink mix, cow's milk |
| 6 to 9 months | Add vegetables, fruits, soft finger foods, yogurt, cheese, unsweetened fruit juices, beans | Same as above plus soft drinks |
| 9 to 12 months | Add meats, egg yolks, breads, crackers, cottage cheese, pasta, rice | Egg whites, all sugared products, honey, peanuts, popcorn, low- or nonfat milk, hot dogs, high sodium meat products |
| 12 months | Add whole eggs | |

This child is making the transition from being fed to trying to feed herself. She is going beyond being fed baby cereal and baby food from jars and is attempting to master the spoon herself.

enjoy vegetables before being introduced to fruits. It is a good idea to stick with dark green and yellow vegetables, because they are good sources of vitamin A. Spinach and beets can cause allergic reactions, so the teacher may want to avoid these in the beginning.

If the child rejects a food several days in a row, the teacher should respect this dislike and discontinue it. The teacher may try introducing the food again in a few months. Vegetables should be strained or pureed at this stage. The teacher may use commercially prepared baby food or make it. Remember that infants do not need salt, spices, or other enhancements to make their food palatable. It is a good habit to get a child to accept food in its natural form, so that the particular food will be acceptable later on in many forms. Infants cannot digest spices, and sweetening foods or adding salt may cause food preferences that may make it difficult for the child to follow the MyPyramid Food Guidance System when he is older.

*Fruits.* Fruits are introduced next, one at a time. Many fresh fruits can be easily mashed. This is a good time to introduce soft finger food such as bananas. Most infants respond well to the majority of fruits, but certain textures such as those in pears may cause the child to reject trying a particular food. If the child rejects a food, the teacher can add the food to the list of things to try again later. When exposed to a food 8 to 10 times, children may develop an increase in preference for that food. By exposing them to new and different foods, teachers can provide opportunities for children to learn to like a variety of nutritious foods (Johnson & Nicklas, 1999).

The toddler is ready to self-feed soft finger foods such as cheese and cooked vegetables.

Yellow fruits such as apricots and peaches are good sources of vitamin A. The teacher must be watchful when introducing items such as fresh strawberries and citrus fruits, because, although they are excellent sources of vitamin C, they also can cause allergic reactions. Fruit juices are another good source of vitamins, but the teacher should use unsweetened juices. This is the perfect time to introduce a cup to a baby. It is preferable to feed a child juice from a cup, not from a bottle. Fruit juice in a bottle can lead to baby bottle tooth decay.

When choosing a cup, the teacher should find one that is unbreakable and weighted at the bottom. It is better when first trying a cup to use one with at least one handle so that the baby has something to grasp. These cups usually come with a lid, but if the baby seems to have difficulty with the sipping action, the lid may be removed. Try a sip at a time, beginning with a small amount and using a bib to protect baby from spills.

*Other Foods.* At this time, most children have enough teeth to be able to do some chewing. Soft finger foods such as cheese are good beginner foods to help the child learn to feed himself. Cheese and yogurt are good sources of calcium and protein, and both are easily digestible by now.

At nine months, meat such as chicken, beef, lamb, and fish can be added. Wait awhile for pork, because it can cause allergic reactions. If the child has enough teeth, the meat can be chopped into very small pieces so she can pick up the pieces and feed herself. Egg yolks can also be added now, but it is best to avoid egg whites and whole eggs until the child is at least one year old. Cottage cheese is another addition that will offer a good source of calcium and protein.

This is the time when other finger foods such as toast and crackers can be added. They are good sources of carbohydrates, as are rice and pasta.

These items can be chewed and easily digested by now. The pasta and rice should be fairly plain, not highly seasoned. The teacher should avoid serving finger foods that are not soft or will not soften in the mouth, such as carrots or celery.

### Teacher Guidelines

There are some guidelines for infant feeding, as shown in Table 8-6. As the teacher helps to establish the eating behavior of an infant as he or she goes from breast or bottle feeding to solid foods, these guidelines may assist in successful infant feeding.

**TABLE 8-6**
*Guidelines for Successful Infant Feeding*

- Use a small spoon and age-appropriate cup.
- Watch for cues that baby is full.
- Never use food as bribery, diversion, or reward.
- Offer an assortment of healthy foods.
- Try new foods at baby's best time of day.
- Respect the child's food likes and dislikes.
- Infants may not be able to eat a great deal at a time, so serve smaller meals throughout the day.
- Make mealtime pleasant, not distracting.
- Avoid serving foods that may choke an infant.
- Only serve foods that are soft or will become soft in the mouth.

## Key Concept 8.2

### Early Feeding and the Infant in Care

Infancy is a critical time for forming the pattern to meet the nutritional needs of a child. Whether the baby is fed by breast milk or formula, a teacher can manage health risk by using food safety behaviors. Being aware of the cues that an infant gives when he is full will help the teacher allow the infant to gain control of his own feeding behavior. The introduction of solid foods brings nutritional challenges that can be easily met if the teacher is knowledgeable about the pattern of introducing these foods. Understanding how to accommodate the infant's physical and psychological needs will allow the teacher to encourage the infant to go at his own pace. The teacher plays an important role in helping the infant and his family to establish good nutrition and providing the groundwork for good feeding behaviors.

## 8.3 FEEDING THE AUTONOMOUS TODDLER

● **Autonomy**
*a child's quest from
ages one to two to
develop a sense of self
and self-rule*

The transition from infant to toddler is most apparent in a child's eating behavior. This is the first place a child begins to show her independence and need for **autonomy**. Good nutrition allows a child to grow, learn, and play. The challenge for this period is to maintain good nutrition while helping the child establish good food habits with her independence intact. As a child develops her sense of autonomy, it can also lead to frustration and a contest of wills . . . her will versus the adult's will. Creating a framework for forming good food habits is one of the most important things the teacher can do for a child to ensure good health and well-being. To help the child establish good eating behaviors, the teacher must understand how growth patterns and developmental changes affect a toddler's actions (see Table 8-7).

### Food as an Issue of Control

Adults feel responsible for a child's eating habits. If the child is not eating right, we may cajole, coerce, bribe, or beg the child to eat. Without realizing it, adults have just drawn the line for the battle over food being used as an issue of control between a well-meaning adult and an independence-seeking toddler. As a child recognizes the adult's concern over the consumption of food, the child may figure out creative ways to utilize food as a weapon in the quest for independence.

Ellyn Satter, dietitian and author of several books (1987, 2000, 2005) on the subject of feeding behavior problems, has offered some specific guidelines to help alleviate the struggle for control between the adult and the child concerning food.

**TABLE 8-7**
*Common Patterns of
Toddler's Growth and
Development That
Affect Eating Actions*

- Child wants and needs to be independent; child wants to control own eating.
- Child learns to say "no" even to favorite foods.
- Appetite is sporadic as growth slows.
- Child learns by doing—wants to feed self.
- Child has food likes and dislikes. Child may develop food jags for favorite foods.
- Child is gaining more control over large motor skills and can lift food to the mouth. Because large muscle control is still developing, the child will sometimes drop or spill food.
- Child is gaining more control over fine motor skills and is able to use a spoon.
- Child is learning to manipulate objects and likes to touch and play with food.
- Child may be teething and have difficulty chewing; she will spit out or remove food from mouth.
- Child wants to master the job of eating and be successful, even if it means hiding food under plate or in a pocket to show she is done.
- Child is learning to be a social creature and may entertain others with food antics.

The teacher and the parent should work together in communicating the child's eating habits at school and at home and decide how best to meet the child's nutritional needs.

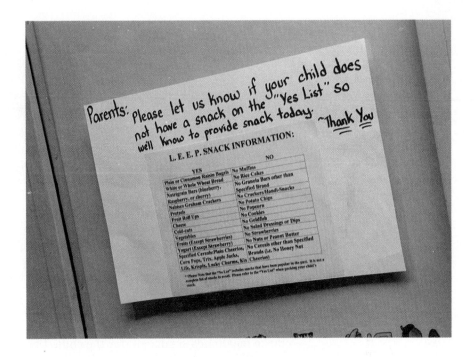

- The adult is responsible for controlling what food comes into the house and how it is presented to the child.
- The adult is also responsible for making sure the child is at a meal, keeping the child on task, making sure the child behaves well, and regulating the time for meals and snacks.
- The child is responsible for how much he eats, whether he eats, and how his body turns out.

Careful examination of these areas of responsibility will change the battle into a cooperative venture.

The way that an adult treats a child at the table may very well be a reflection of how the adult treats the child elsewhere. The adult can help regulate the food consumption behavior in numerous ways. Training the child to be on task in the eating of satisfying and well-prepared foods is a good first step. When a child realizes that food can be enjoyable he is more likely to be agreeable with the idea of eating and less likely to balk at the task at hand. If the child does not eat, the adult should learn to relax and stay calm. Erratic food intake is normal; it will support the child's growth because over time the proper balance will be achieved. Branen et al. (1997) found that when children in early childhood education environments were allowed to select foods, the consumption pattern was not significantly different from being served preselected foods. The one difference they found was that although children did not waste more food, some cases they tended to eat more because they were able to regulate their own intake. A conclusion of their study was that self-selection may help to regulate dietary intake in early childhood education environments and may offer a more healthy alternative to preselection. Studies have shown since then that this idea of self-selection may actually cut down risk for obesity (Melgar-Quinonez & Kaiser, 2004; Powers, 2004).

Eating can often become a power struggle between the adult and the child. Keeping the child on task and making mealtime enjoyable are ways that the adult can help to regulate the child's food consumption without causing undue stress.

Another strategy for helping a child develop good eating habits is to make mealtimes significant for the child. Understanding the temperament of the child, his capabilities, and his tempo will help the teacher prepare for mealtime. The teacher should give the child time, attention, and awareness when meals are served. Sitting and talking with children while they are eating makes this time special. The teacher should reinforce desirable behavior by paying attention, recognizing, and acknowledging good behavior. It is important to be flexible with the amount of time "scheduled" for the children to eat (Lucich, 2003). Some children need more time to eat than others.

The teacher can contribute to regulating eating habits by managing the eating environment. Setting limits makes eating more important and worthwhile. When feeding a child a snack or a meal, the teacher must make sure that eating is the only activity going on (Miller, 2004). The teacher should also limit eating to one or two appropriate places. That may be in a kitchen or patio in a home situation, not in front of a television. In center-based care, eating may occur in the classroom or on tables near the playground. The teacher should spend some time getting the child ready to eat. The transition time from another activity should be quiet and calming, to prepare children for eating time.

A child should come to the table at mealtime ready to eat. If the child is disinterested or not hungry, the teacher should not force the issue, but should have the child stay at the table a few minutes before excusing her. This removes the temptation for the child to entertain or act out. If the child complains about being hungry a few minutes later, the teacher can remind her that snack time is just a few hours away. The child made the choice not to participate and maybe next time will make a different choice. This reinforces the fact that the child made the decision and the teacher supported it. The teacher should not change the eating pattern for meals and snacks to accommodate whims. Children in early education environments should not be allowed to "graze" or to eat at anytime they want. Instead, there should be meals and scheduled snacks only (Satter, 2005). In general, a child should have three meals and two snacks per day, so the

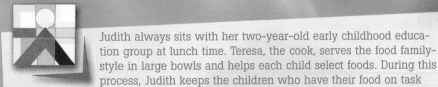

Judith always sits with her two-year-old early childhood education group at lunch time. Teresa, the cook, serves the food family-style in large bowls and helps each child select foods. During this process, Judith keeps the children who have their food on task and talks with the children who have not been served yet. When everyone is served, the group discusses the food and talks about how things taste. Judith also talks with the children about the morning activities and explains some of the things Roberta, the afternoon teacher, has planned for them. This helps the children prepare for the transition and helps them remember what they have done that day. Another significant thing Judith does daily is to eat the same food for lunch that the children are eating. She is role modeling that the food served is just as acceptable to her as it is for the children. Judith's pet peeve is teachers who bring in fast food to eat in front of children and who do not practice what they are trying to enforce—good eating habits.

amount of these available in the early education environment would depend on the time the child is present. Some younger children may need to be fed more often.

One of the issues that may be faced during this toddler stage is called a "food jag." This occurs when a child gets the idea that she wants to eat only a certain food. It might be peanut butter sandwiches, macaroni, or just about anything. These food jags occur for a number of reasons. One reason might be that very young children are much more sensitive to flavor. A child could also be bored with the foods commonly served in care and be holding out for what she enjoys. A teacher may also be tested to see how he reacts to the child's demand for the one food. This is a common task in reaching for self-rule. Some children are afraid to try new things and may need many exposures to a food before it becomes acceptable (Wardle et al., 2003). Less adventurous children may have less adventurous parents when it comes to feeding patterns (Cathey & Gaylord, 2004).

Food jags are just one type of picky eating that toddlers may display (Tessmer, 2004). Picky eating is characteristic of this stage of development and it may well be a definite preference for certain tasting foods. Some foods have a chemical referred to as PTC or phenylthiocarbamide in them (Gamble, 2004). This can cause a bitter taste in the mouth of a very young child. Foods that have this compound include citrus, strawberries, green beans, apples, bacon, and broccoli. Children's preferences come as a result of trial and error (Cathey & Gaylord, 2004). The best advice is to be patient, because this is a normal stage of development (Butte et al., 2004). A teacher could monitor a child's growth, but normally picky eating is not a threat to health. It is important not to make food an issue of control (Satter, 2005).

The teacher should keep food out of sight when eating is not the activity. Seeing food can make children think they need to eat when they are not really hungry. Age-appropriate foods and utensils should be chosen. Finger foods and foods that are easy to eat should help toddlers to learn to manipulate more successfully. Foods such as popcorn, grapes, carrots, and celery can cause a child to choke and should be avoided. The teacher must use

The teacher can promote good eating habits by managing the eating environment. The teacher should also limit eating to one or two appropriate places.

utensils that a toddler can grasp easily, and small plates and cups that look as though they are full when the serving of food is placed on them.

Although it may be difficult to accommodate in some center or school schedules, child care homes and nannies can tailor the serving of food to when children need to eat. The teacher should try to be as reliable and regular as possible in feeding the children, and not wait until they are really hungry and have behavior difficulties because of it. The teacher should not feed children if they do not feel hungry at the moment.

These actions allow the teacher to establish trust in relationship to food and children. Children will act more responsibly when they can trust their teacher to provide the food and atmosphere that make them successful eaters.

Table 8-8 lists some key points about using food as nutrition and not as a battleground.

## Nutritional Considerations

Whether it is served as a meal or as a snack, food should be satisfying and meet the children's nutritional needs. The ideal meal or snack would include a protein food, a carbohydrate food, and some fat. When planning meals or snacks, the teacher must treat empty-nutrient, high-calorie foods that have too much sugar or fat with respect. Snacks should be taken seriously and used as part of the day's nutrition. If someone has a birthday and brings cupcakes, enjoy them. The teacher should model how the food should be savored and serve it with milk or some other nutritious food so that all is not lost.

The teacher should recognize that there will be a variation in food consumption. A child may refuse to eat foods from a particular food group

**TABLE 8-8**
*Food as Nutrition, Not Control*

- The modeling of your actions and attitudes toward food will affect how the children feel about food.
- Stay calm; do not react to negative behavior.
- Realize pressure does not work—forcing and withholding are both ineffective.
- Do not use food as a punishment or as a reward.
- Outside influences, including cultural influences, can affect your good intentions about children and their food behavior.
- Respect cultural eating differences. Expose children to foods from many cultures.
- Children learn from feeding, their first attempt at independence, what to expect from the world.
- If they are successful, the world is a beautiful place. If they fail, they may withdraw or act out.

or may eat only one food to the exclusion of others. This is common. If it continues for longer than a short period, such as a week, this food should be offered only at snack time and the teacher must make sure other foods are served at regular mealtimes.

Milk is a food and should have its proper place. Children older than six months of age should not drink formula to the exclusion of other foods. Toddlers should not drink so much milk that they lose their appetite for other foods. Toddlers who use milk as the main source of energy and nutrients may have a condition called milk anemia, which is an iron deficiency caused by lack of proper food and too much milk. A toddler should drink no more than 24 ounces of milk a day. Children older than one year can have cow's milk, but they should never be served nonfat milk, because they need the fat content for growth and development. Some children may not want to drink milk alone at this stage. The teacher will need to substitute yogurt, cheese, and other dairy products to be sure the child receives the necessary amounts of calcium and other minerals.

According to recent studies, overconsumption of juice can cause a child to not keep pace with the growth and development of children of the same age (Aby-Valestrino, 2001; Cathey & Gaylord, 2004). When juice was not served, all of the children observed began putting on weight again. As previously stated, the teacher should serve juice only in a cup and should use it to enhance a meal but not to replace other foods. If a child is thirsty, water is the best alternative. Some guidelines for the teacher to maximize the eating and nutritional needs of the toddler are listed in Table 8-9.

Teachers should use whatever methods are available to encourage the toddlers in care to eat good foods and be well-nourished. It is the teacher who sets the tone for the toddler and how he patterns his food behaviors in care. Following their lead, children can be helped to learn their own body cues as to when they are hungry or full. Seigman-Grant (2003) suggested making a game of this called "Tummy Talk," where toddlers and preschoolers learn to listen to what their tummies are telling them.

Active toddlers may get hungry more often and may need to be served smaller meals or snacks more frequently than older children. Lucich (2003) and others have suggested that children this age need to eat six times per day. If the teacher offers an additional snack, it should not be served too close to a meal.

**TABLE 8-9**
*Guidelines for Forming Good Food Habits for Toddlers*

- Make food easy to eat.
- Cut finger food into bite-size pieces.
- Make sure some of the foods served are soft and moist.
- Serve food at room temperature. Toddlers shy away from foods that are too cold or too hot.
- Toddlers are sensitive to texture and may not eat foods that are lumpy or stringy. Try these foods, and if they will not eat them, try again later.
- Toddlers like colorful foods and often prefer vegetables that are raw or undercooked because they are brighter in color and crisp.
- A typical toddler may like her food in different or specific shapes. Carrots may need to be cut in coins before cooking so the toddler will eat them.
- Toddlers like fun foods such as faces on pancakes or sandwiches or other foods cut into unusual shapes.
- Provide toddlers with suitable equipment—small utensils, plastic cups, and plates with a lip so the food won't slip off.
- Children are still learning to control their muscle movement and need plenty of space in which to operate when eating.
- Model appropriate food behaviors and choose healthy options.
- Offer foods so that children can practice both gross and fine motor skills, such as pouring, spreading, cutting, tearing, and spearing.
- Offer age-appropriate serving sizes or help children learn how to self-select foods.
- Help children learn to read their own cues as to when they are full.
- Never coerce or force a child to eat a food she refuses.

## Key Concept 8.3

### Feeding Behavior of the Toddler

The toddler is growing and developing in many ways. A number of these growth characteristics have an impact on the toddler's food behavior. If the teacher understands this, food is less likely to be an issue of control. There are a number of strategies a teacher can employ to help make mealtimes pleasant and encourage the child to eat, thus meeting the toddler's nutritional needs.

The toddler and preschooler are growing and developing, becoming more active and autonomous. The toddler's behavior at the table also reflects these changes and, when identified, can aid the teacher in helping the child develop good eating habits.

## 8.4  FOOD AND THE PRESCHOOLER

As children reach the preschool stage, a number of developmental changes have occurred that make feeding and nourishing a much easier task. A child of three knows that he is a separate person and understands acceptable and appropriate behavior. He is capable of being patient and can control impulses. If the preschooler whines, complains, or begs for food not on the table, he is capable of understanding that this behavior is unacceptable and he may be asked to get down from the table.

### *Outside Influences*

Preschoolers are social beings who like eating with others. Preschool children are ready to learn and are willing to change and try new things when they are together, so they are probably more likely to eat more servings of the basic food groups (Levy & Cooper, 1999). The preschooler learns much from observation and role play. She is likely to feel good about herself and enjoys cooperating. The preschooler probably has food preferences that may have been influenced by others. Messages children receive at home from their parents and television have a great deal of influence on their attitude about food (Cathey & Gaylord, 2004; Borzekowski & Robinson, 2001).

Preschoolers can also be influenced by teachers and friends at school. They feel secure eating familiar foods, but if encouraged to explore, they may try new foods. Often a preschooler may eat a food at school that she would not eat at home. This willingness to eat at school and not at home may be a result of negative messages or reinforcement about the particular food. A

Encouraging children to accept new foods can be a difficult task. Serving new foods with familiar foods or having other children introduce the new foods are some methods for encouraging this exploration.

child whose parent says squash is "icky" or makes the comment, "Jerry won't eat squash," may be keeping that behavior a fact at home. In one study, children who were offered new foods in a simple manner were more likely to try them than if they were offered a reward to do so (Wardle et al., 2003).

Children of this age are easily influenced by television advertising of food products that are poor nutritional choices (Hinden et al., 2004). More than one-half of all the advertisements on television are for food products, and the majority of these are for heavily sugared products. The cereal aisle of the grocery store contains an abundance of these foods. A parent may find it difficult to get through this aisle without a confrontation or without giving in to the child's demands. The cereal aisle is one of the best examples of **positive reinforcement** of negative behavior for young children. An adult who gives in to the demands for a certain sugared cereal seen on television allows the child to feel that television is right about the claims made. A better alternative for the adult, be it parent or teacher, is to make positive use of the television ads and have the child help investigate the claim by reading the label.

● **Positive reinforcement**
*reward given in response to a particular behavior that increases the chance of that behavior occurring again*

### Creating a Positive Environment

Just as in toddlerhood, preschool children need help in creating a positive environment that will help them eat, support their growth, and make it a time that will nourish all parts of their development. When meals are served family style and children are allowed to select their foods, they feel more competent. If they can use their muscles in activities such as pouring juice and spooning from a large bowl onto their own plates, they feel more independent. When children are taught to understand cues that their own bodies give them as to whether they are full or hungry, the teacher is providing a skill they can use throughout their lives (Seigman-Grant, 2003). If the teacher sets the tone with a good transition time before the meal, children

Dawn is a teacher of older four-year-olds in a community college preschool. The majority of children in her class have parents in the college. There is a real mixture of family types and income range. The children bring their lunches from home, and Dawn spends time every day with each child investigating the lunches.

Kristin had a juice box that was full of sugar but not much juice. After reading the label with Dawn, Kristin informed her mother that it was not really juice and enlisted her help in finding a better drink for her lunch.

Zarli's dad was new to the lunch-making business, and the first few weeks were a struggle. But after Dawn helped Zarli investigate her lunches, Zarli became aware enough to encourage her dad to read the labels and learn about good food. Her lunches became more interesting and encouraged both child and parent to try to understand more about healthier eating. Her father often asked Dawn for advice on new ideas for lunches. He got to be very creative.

Rashid was from a different cultural background and often had foods that Dawn did not recognize. She did recognize the drink in his lunches as a highly advertised sugared drink and helped Rashid investigate the label. Dawn explained it to Rashid and he in turn helped explain it to his mother who spoke limited English. This exchange led to a wonderful dialogue between Rashid, his mother, and Dawn discussing the foods that Rashid brought. Dawn learned how the foods were prepared and what healthy ingredients they had in them. Rashid and his mother learned not to believe everything one sees on television.

will come to the table more ready to participate. Miller (2004) suggested that the teacher play soothing music at this time to help set the tone of a pleasant experience. When this time is used to sit down and connect with children, they may have some of their social and emotional needs met (Murray, 2000). Pleasant conversation can allow both the teacher and the children in care to get to know each other in different ways than the normal classroom time might allow.

## Participation

The teacher can foster good nutrition by involving preschoolers with the selection of foods and helping with food preparation. Encouraging preschool children to be part of the process can empower them with the knowledge and awareness necessary to make better nutritional choices. Activities that are enjoyable give children confidence to try new foods and different ways of preparation. Children should have the opportunity to learn about food, nutrition, and food preparation and how they are linked to health. Reading books about new foods can pave the way for greater understanding. Letting preschoolers help prepare foods and experiment with new foods helps children develop skills that will widen their food horizons. Mealtime offers genuine opportunities for conversations about food and eating behavior. This is a good time to discuss, practice, and model good nutrition and correct eating behavior (Satter, 2005; Levy & Cooper, 1999). These strategies will help the teacher positively impact the preschooler's nutritional well-being.

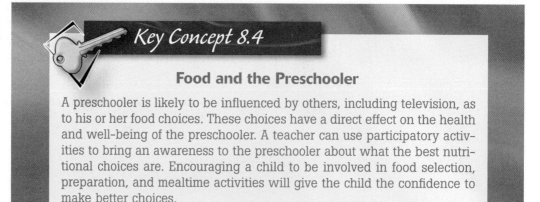

*Key Concept 8.4*

### Food and the Preschooler

A preschooler is likely to be influenced by others, including television, as to his or her food choices. These choices have a direct effect on the health and well-being of the preschooler. A teacher can use participatory activities to bring an awareness to the preschooler about what the best nutritional choices are. Encouraging a child to be involved in food selection, preparation, and mealtime activities will give the child the confidence to make better choices.

Breakfast is a very important meal for children and has been proven to improve cognitive skills. Many schools and centers now provide this meal, which should be high in protein.

## 8.5 SCHOOL-AGE NUTRITION

Teachers who work in early childhood education environments may or may not be involved in care of school-aged children; it depends on what age range the program or school serves. Family child caregivers and nannies are commonly involved with school-aged children before and after school and during school vacations. The needs of school-aged children, ages five to eleven years, vary greatly from those of the infant, toddler and preschooler.

Growth is slower during this period and is not as observable as the earlier infant-toddler growth spurt or the adolescent growth spurt that will occur later. However, the vigorous activity level that most school-aged children experience makes the need for adequate nutrition important. In addition, good nutrition will help the school-aged child maintain resistance to infection and will help ensure adequate stores for the building materials and nutrition needed for the adolescent growth spurt.

Children of this age are not totally capable of planning a well-balanced diet each day. They may eat for social reasons, such as television viewing, when they are not really hungry. Children of this age may have fluctuating appetites and may become finicky in their eating habits. These changes may be attributed to the consumption of more and more foods that are low in nutrients and high in calories.

Snacking is easier because school-aged children are capable of preparing a variety of snacks. High-fat or sweetened foods or beverages are easy to prepare and serve. If these are available, children will probably eat them.

Fast food has a tremendous influence on the school-aged child. These children are more mobile and they may have their own money that allows these purchases. Many school lunch programs serve fast-type foods in order to get the children to eat what is served and cut down on waste. Some elementary school campuses even have fast food outlets as part of their lunch programs. Most fast foods are high in calories or low in nutrients.

Good dietary habits should be focused on and practiced. Teachers can perform a number of functions that will help school-aged children practice better nutritional habits. The first thing the teacher can do is provide healthy, nutritious foods for the children to eat. If children have choices that are good foods, the choices will be limited and good nutrition will be more readily available.

Supervising school-aged children in planning their own menus and preparing good food will show children that they can affect their own nutritional well-being. If the early childhood education environment includes breakfast, the teacher can give children a good start by preparing a meal that includes some protein. Children who have a good breakfast are better at performing cognitive skills.

If the teacher's job includes preparing or helping the child prepare a sack lunch, there are several important considerations. Children who help prepare their own lunches are more likely to eat the lunch. Typical brown bag lunches contain more sugar, sweets, and sweetened beverages and less meat, poultry, or fish than do school lunches prepared by cafeteria staff (Gordon & McKinney, 1995; Wohlleb, 2004). One school in Kentucky helped to solve this problem by having the children bring their lunch boxes or sacks to school in the morning empty. The cafeteria workers would then fill them with healthy selections of food and the children would pick up their lunches when it was time to eat (Wohlleb, 2004). Sack lunches usually do not contain enough fruits and vegetables and have too many convenience-type foods. Packing good food may be a challenge, especially if food safety is taken into consideration. The teacher should use imagination and safe food practices. Some suggestions are found in Table 8-10.

Snacks are likely to be the main foods that most teachers will provide for most school-aged children. It is important that these foods are readily available when the child arrives at the site if this is an after-school care situation. Children are usually very hungry after a long school day. Offering foods prepared by the teacher as well as items that are simple for the child to prepare will help the child appease hunger and build self-confidence.

**TABLE 8-10**
*Packing Healthy Foods for Brown Bag Lunches*

- Pre-cut fruits and vegetables can be stored in the refrigerator and packed in the morning.
- Sandwiches can be prepared the afternoon before, so they get thoroughly chilled in the refrigerator and will last longer in the lunches.
- Choose low-fat cuts of meat. Cut the sandwiches into interesting shapes.
- Leftovers can be frozen in small containers and packed in the morning.
- Use only 100 percent fruit juices or have the parent provide money to purchase milk.
- Forego chips and other high-calorie, low-nutrient foods; substitute pretzels or other low-fat snack foods.
- Provide fruits that are in season and have the child select the fruit.
- Use "Blue Ice" or other devices that will help keep the lunches cool.

## Key Concept 8.5

### School-Age Nutrition

Many care situations do not have school-aged children. Those teachers who do care for school-aged children face nutritional challenges that are different from those of infants, toddlers, or preschoolers. The teacher needs to keep in mind the school-aged children's activity levels in order to provide them with adequate nutrition. The teacher is practicing nutritional risk management by purchasing healthy foods, preparing them, and supervising the children in meal or snack preparation.

# REALITY CHECK

## Children of the Fast Food Generation

The older children get, the more they eat away from home (Lin et al., 1999b). By 1997, almost half of family food expenditures were for food purchased away from home (Lin et al., 1999a). In one study, it was reported that more than 30 percent of food consumed in a day was fast food (Linn, 2004).

Bowman et al. (2004) reported that more than 10 percent of the energy from food consumed by children was from fast food. Americans spent more than $110 billion on fast food in 2000, compared with $6 billion in 1970. Fast food has become a major player in the diet patterns of children in this country (Schlosser, 2001).

## REALITY CHECK (Continued)

### Fast Food Kids Meals Nutritional Breakdown

| | Calories | Fats (g) | Protein (g) | Sodium (mg) | Carbohydrates (g) |
|---|---|---|---|---|---|
| Daily Total | 2000 | 65 | 24 | 2400 | 300 |
| **Burger King (Source: Burger King Corporation)** | | | | | |
| Hamburger | 275 | 11 | 15 | 510 | 28 |
| French Fries | 227 | 13 | 3 | 161 | 24 |
| Cola | 190 | 0 | 0 | 20 | 16 |
| Total | 692 | 24 | 18 | 691 | 68 |
| **McDonald's (Source: McDonald's Corporation)** | | | | | |
| Cheeseburger | 305 | 13 | 15 | 725 | 30 |
| French Fries | 220 | 12 | 3 | 110 | 30 |
| Orange Drink | 230 | 0 | 0 | 30 | 59 |
| Total | 755 | 18 | 18 | 865 | 119 |
| **Taco Bell (Source: Taco Bell Corporation)** | | | | | |
| Taco | 183 | 11 | 10 | 276 | 11 |
| Cinn. Twists | 231 | 11 | 3 | 316 | 32 |
| Lemon-lime | 190 | 0 | 0 | 90 | 48 |
| Total | 604 | 22 | 13 | 682 | 91 |
| **Kentucky Fried Chicken (Source: Kentucky Fried Chicken Corporation)** | | | | | |
| Nuggets | 276 | 17 | 17 | 840 | 13 |
| Kentucky Fries | 377 | 18 | 5 | 215 | 18 |
| Root Beer | 244 | 0 | 0 | 45 | 16 |
| Total | 897 | 35 | 22 | 1100 | 46 |

Children's favorite fast foods include french fries, pizza, hamburgers, fried chicken, and ketchup. It is beginning to appear that a correlation is present between fast food consumption and television viewing (Kaiser Foundation, 2004). In 2002, in the United States, McDonald's Corporation spent more than $1.3 billion and Pepsico spent more than $1.1 billion on advertising (Linn, 2004). The fast food industry has grown, in part, because so many mothers are in the workforce. The eating of fast food may reflect the dietary patterns of families who rarely sit down to eat dinner together (Bowman et al., 2004).

Fast food is available in malls, on main streets, in bowling alleys, at theme parks, on airplanes, and on cruise ships. Fast food is even available at some schools, where the fast food chains and soft drink manufacturers "sponsor" the school in return for marketing their prod-

ucts on campus. There is a trend beginning that is trying to stop these practices in schools (Stang & Beyerl, 2003; Green, 2005). Levin (2004) stated, "There is a growing awareness that consumer culture influences the ideas children develop about what is good and bad. . . ." Nutritional advocates are trying hard to fight the presence of fast foods in schools.

The rise in obesity in children, in part, is attributed to less play and more consumption of fast foods (Ebbeling et al., 2004). Fast foods' most clever marketing has been directed toward children (Borzekowski & Robinson, 2001). Every month 90 percent of America's children between the ages of three and nine visit a McDonald's restaurant (Spake, 2001).

In 2004, a movie came out titled *Supersize Me.* It was about a man living solely on McDonald's food items for 30 days. As the

(continues)

## REALITY CHECK (Continued)

movie progresses, the man gets sicker and sicker, and it becomes apparent that a diet of fast food is not healthy and can even be dangerous. As a result of the movie and the discussion surrounding it, McDonald's and other fast food chains have been offering some healthier selections, especially in children's meals. Children may now choose apples with caramel dip, salad, or mandarin orange sections instead of fries at several chains. They can also choose milk or apple juice as their beverage instead of soft drinks. There is also a growing trend away from "super-sizing." Many chains have dropped their half-pound size of french fries and their 48 ounce and 64 ounce size soft drink options. Some chains are no longer asking if you want to be "super-sized."

A typical fast food meal for children can provide as much as 36 percent of their caloric needs for a day, but fall short of basic nutrients. The most typical meal a child eats at a fast food restaurant is the kid's meal that includes a main item, fries, and a soft drink. Occasionally these meals include a dessert and they almost always include a toy, which draws many children to this type of meal. On the previous page are some typical kid's meals with nutritional breakdown.

As this table reflects, children are getting an over-abundance of fat and sodium and a large number of calories for the nutrients present in these meals. To further view nutritional breakdowns, check the fast food chain Web sites: http://app.mcdonalds.com; http://www.bk.com; http://www.kfc.com; and http://www.tacobell.com.

Because children are eating out so often, it is even more important for the teacher to provide nutritious meals in the early childhood education environment. It is important to refrain from getting caught in the fast food challenge. Children prefer highly flavored, high fat meals, so this may be a challenge. However, teachers can discuss this with children and help them select better choices when they do go out. For example, helping a child choose milk instead of a soft drink will bring the nutrients in the meal more in balance (Ludwig, Peterson, & Gortmaker, 2001).

**CHECK***point:* How would you conduct a discussion about fast foods with four-year old children? What suggestions might you have to help them choose more wisely?

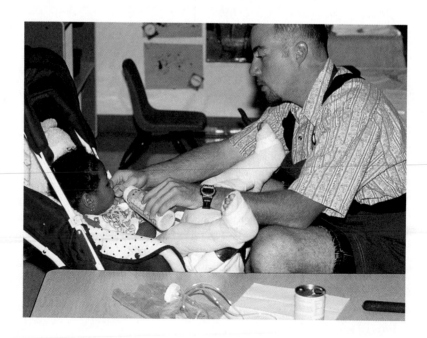

Feeding practice may have to be altered for children with special needs. In this picture, the child is reclined in her chair instead of being cradled. Teachers need to be accommodating and sensitive to these needs.

## 8.6  NUTRITION AND THE CHILD WITH SPECIAL NEEDS

● **Developmental disabilities**
*physical or mental incapacities that interfere with normal progress of development*

Some teachers care for children who have special needs. Many of these children have **developmental disabilities** or chronic illnesses that affect feeding skills, nutritional needs, or equipment needed. Some children require special feeding procedures and some require special foods or diets. Teachers caring for children with special needs may face more challenges at snack time and meal time than they would with a child who is developing in a typical manner (Holland, 2005).

Children who have cerebral palsy, Down syndrome, a cleft lip or palate, or other developmental abnormalities may have physical difficulties eating or feeding themselves. Children with metabolic disorders such as cystic fibrosis, diabetes, phenylketonuria (PKU), and maple syrup urine syndrome have special dietary limitations that prevent them from eating certain types of food and make the MyPyramid Food Guidance System less useful. Some children have conditions that require modifying their intake of sodium, protein, carbohydrates, or fats. Others may have allergies or food intolerances. Certain medical conditions may call for dietary restrictions or requirements (Healthy Child Care, 1998). Children with special needs may require more time to eat. Eating may be a real struggle and cause more mess than normal (Holland, 2005).

The Individuals with Disabilities Act (1990) requires certain early childhood education environments and family child care homes to accommodate children with special needs as best they can. That Act also has a provision that requires states to provide early intervention services to infants and toddlers. Nutrition services are included in this early intervention (Yadrick & Sneed, 1994).

There are many children with special needs who can be accommodated easily and whose nutritional needs may not be difficult to meet. Chairs, tables, and eating utensils may need to be modified for some children. These accommodations can be made by the teacher without great expense or effort.

Some children with special needs offer challenges that the teacher really is not prepared or trained to accommodate. The nutritional needs of some children with chronic illness or developmental disabilities are complicated and may be compounded by eating difficulties. The average teacher should not be expected to provide this type of accommodation without outside assessment, intervention, and help. Some accommodations such as the use of a gastric tube may be something that a teacher could easily train for and would help many children who have feeding difficulties.

The disabilities act provides the vehicle for the nutrition services the teacher may need. Contacting the state child nutrition staff is a good place to begin. Local school districts may be involved in early intervention assessment, and local regional centers may also provide some of this assessment. The American Dietetic Association supports the participation of its members in providing nutrition services to early childhood education programs that include children with disabilities and chronic illnesses. Parents of these children may be good sources of information and may be able to help the teacher to link up with the community services needed to support the care of these children.

Access to these services may not provide a teacher with the skills and special handling that some children with special needs require. A referral for the child to a special care program or regional center may be all that the teacher is able to do to help the families of these children.

For the child with special needs that can be accommodated, it is important to remember to respect the child's food preferences and hunger level, just as with every other child. The eating pace may be slower, so more time may be necessary (CCCHP, 2003). Food textures may be an issue with many children with special needs, so the teacher should be sensitive to that and with the simplest texture, working through to the ones that are more difficult. Food allergies or food intolerance may be more likely to occur in a child with special needs, so care must be taken to observe for this.

Depending on the child's specific condition, a special diet may be needed. Nutritional goals for the child should be discussed with the family. The teacher should keep accurate records of feeding and should communicate often with the family. Being supportive of the family is important. The teacher will be acting as a role model for food and eating practices (Holland, 2005). All of those considerations make it important that the teacher or the early childhood education environment have nutritional policies that deal with those children with special needs who are in care.

## Key Concept 8.6

### Children with Special Needs

The Individuals with Disabilities Act may require that some early childhood education environments and some family child care homes accommodate children with special needs as best they can. Some children with disabilities or chronic illnesses may be easily accommodated in their nutritional needs and feeding levels. Others may require special early intervention nutritional services. Those services may not be adequate to provide the level of care some children with special needs may require. Special nutritional policies for children with special needs should be developed if such children are present in the early childhood education environment.

## 8.7 IMPLICATIONS FOR TEACHERS

Nutrition education is an important tool for the teacher to help parents and children better understand their role in proper nutrition for good health and well-being. Education can break down barriers, provide awareness of the effects of growth and development on feeding habits, and offer strategies to parents who want to make sure their children are getting a healthy start. Education can make children aware of their food selections and how their behavior has an effect on health and well-being. It can empower them to make better choices and participate in their own nutritional well-being. Role modeling can help the teacher carry out educational strategies. Cultural sensitivity may be essential for the teacher who has a diverse group in care. Supervision helps the teacher to carry out good nutritional practices.

### Education and Role Modeling

Teachers and parents have a great influence on what children learn to eat. Modeling healthy eating to children of all ages can help children develop healthy eating habits themselves (Briley & Roberts-Gray, 2005). The kinds of food that are provided for children help to determine how the child will eat and grow. Parents and teachers model food selection and acceptability to the children in their lives. If these selections are healthy choices, a child will have a positive perspective about good foods. If the selections are poor choices, this sends a negative message about good nutrition.

One of the greatest contributors to good health is good food habits. A child is capable of learning this through practice and observation from a very young age. Children are strongly influenced by what they see and hear. Parents and teachers are sources of behavior and information that children model and remember. Children have an influence on the shopping habits of parents. Children's food preferences appear to mirror the television advertising that they see (Borzekowski & Robinson, 2001). Children have a large influence over parents' purchasing habits (Hinton et al., 2003).

The teacher should take time out, on a regular basis, to go over the MyPyramid Food Guidance System with the children in care. The nutritional information about what each person should be eating in a day can be assimilated over time. Regular intervals of repetition help the children to understand and remember. This practice also helps the teacher keep good nutritional information in action.

Enlisting children's help with food selection and preparation encourages them to try new foods and new ways of food preparation. Preparing children to help can be accomplished in several ways. The educational experience can be enhanced by reading books on certain foods, watching a video about foods, having circle time about what is going to be prepared, or telling a flannelboard story about the food or activity.

*For Families.* Families and teachers have the power to establish positive, supportive environments that allow children to develop good feeding behaviors and attitudes toward food. The teacher can help the parent understand this by providing good role modeling and some positive nutrition information. The teacher needs to be aware that there may be some barriers to accepting this information (Briley et al., 1998). There may be environmental constraints to good nutrition for some of the families. Cost of food, access and availability of good food, and storage space are factors that may limit the family's ability to make a wide range of good food choices.

Poverty or low income may prohibit the selection of many foods including fresh fruits and vegetables and dairy products. These families may need help in accessing food programs that help families meet their food needs. The teacher may also be able to provide the parents with information on food selections as well as recipes that use low-cost fresh foods. Consequently, the teacher may find there is great interest on the part of the family to help improve their nutritional intake.

Another influence on food selection may be convenience of preparation of some foods. Some adults find it easier to open a can or a box than to prepare fresh foods. Other adults might select fast foods as a further measure of convenience (see the Reality Check: Children of the Fast Food Generation). These behaviors are an enormous barrier with middle and upper income families who can afford the convenience of packaged or fast foods. Having the children help prepare foods may help interest the parents in preparing more fresh food. Role modeling and providing recipes as well as activities for the families to do together may encourage this behavior.

Another perceived barrier may be related to the role the adult plays as a parent. The parent may not understand the stages and phases of growth and development as well as the teacher does. This may make a parent unsure

When four-year-old Amy came to Head Start, her mother reported that Amy did not like and would not eat most foods. Tanya, Amy's teacher, observed Amy at snack and lunch time for several weeks. She watched as Amy refused to try new things for the first two weeks. The foods that she was most vocal about were vegetables and fruits. Of the fruits and vegetables offered to her, Amy would eat only canned applesauce and corn. Other children were eating most of the foods that Amy was refusing. One day Joelle, another four-year-old, encouraged Amy to try some green beans. Amy tried them and ended up eating all of her beans and asked for more. Several days later, the preschoolers picked some carrots and cherry tomatoes at a cooperative garden they toured near their school. The vegetables were brought back to school and the children helped wash them and prepare them for a snack. Amy ate both the carrots and tomatoes. She loved the carrots and was mildly interested in the tomatoes.

Tanya reported these breakthroughs to Amy's mother, who had a hard time believing Amy was eating vegetables. She explained that Amy's father, who was no longer living with them, had hated vegetables and did not even want them in the house. Amy's mother got used to serving only applesauce and canned corn. Her budget was also tight so this wasn't a sacrifice on her part. Tanya spent some time explaining the MyPyramid Food Guidance System and why a balanced diet was important. She also pointed out that there were some plots available in the community garden, so it did not have to cost too much money to increase the variety of fresh produce in the family's diet. Once Amy's mother realized the importance of a balanced diet, she signed up for a plot in the nearby cooperative garden and she started trying to add more variety to the menu at home.

Children learn many of their behaviors by watching the adults in their lives. For this reason, one of the most effective ways to teach children about good eating habits is for the teacher to model these behaviors by sitting with the children and eating with them. In what other ways can teachers model good nutrition habits?

as to how to proceed. It may also influence the parent to feed the child as he or she was fed. Childhood food memories may influence selection or rejection of certain foods or food behaviors. A parent may model behaviors that are not productive to helping the child widen his or her food selections.

Adults may not realize that the social environment that is provided at mealtimes has a direct relationship to the dietary quality of their children. Children need a positive atmosphere, companionship, and the opportunity to view appropriate adult food-related behaviors to achieve good nutrition. The children in care may be the best educators for this barrier (Briley & Roberts-Gray, 1999). The teacher can help parents by explaining the different stages of growth and development and encouraging parents to observe their child's behavior. Parents may then try different ways to support their children's eating behavior.

The results of companionship at mealtimes and the positive social atmosphere that can be created will be apparent through food selections and observation of behavior. Modeling these behaviors with the children in care will help the teacher provide this information to the families.

The level of written nutritional information may be another barrier for the teacher and the parent. Not all adults are literate. Approximately 60 million adults in the United States have not completed high school. Those who have completed high school may not read at the 12th grade level. In order to be effective, the nutritional information provided to the parent should be at the level that he or she is capable of understanding (Busselman & Holcomb, 1994).

## Cultural Competence

Cultural influences may present an obstacle to proper nutritional balance. The teacher may face a challenge in helping parents select good food choices. Providing food and nutrition for children from diverse backgrounds can be a real task, but it can also be rewarding. Culture influences how food is prepared, seasoned, and even how or when it is eaten. There may be

This teacher is using a flannelboard story to discuss with children the benefits of good eating habits and the risks of making poor food choices.

taboos or certain cultural traits to consider, such as the high percentage of lactose intolerance among the Asian population.

Understanding the cultural influence on food is important if the teacher is going to help the families provide optimum nutrition for their children when they are not in care. Asking parents to share their culture's foods and food habits with the children in care is a good way for the teacher to find out the extent of this obstacle. Adapting food selections to cultural influences may help increase the selection of foods available to the family. As the teacher understands the dietary or food limitations of a family, he or she may need to call on outside help, such as a nutritionist (Padget et al., 2005).

Another issue in cultural competence may be the teacher's own cultural perspective on the selection of foods. Not all children like foods that are different from the ones they are used to eating. These differences may be in the manner in which the foods are prepared or in the way they are seasoned. It is important for the teacher to be sensitive to the needs of the children. The teacher needs to present a balance of foods that represent the food selections of children from a number of other cultures. Awareness of one's own culture in addition to the other cultures present in the early education environment is necessary (Obegi & Ritblatt, 2005). That in combination with good communication skills to discuss nutrition and food choices with families and children can help the teacher provide optimal nutrition for all.

*Pause for Reflection*

What is your own cultural background? How does your cultural background relate to the foods you eat? If you feel you don't have a particular cultural background, are there favorite family foods that are used in celebrations such as birthdays? Do you often eat foods from other cultures? If so, what foods and what cultures?

## Supervision

A teacher is likely to serve one or more meals per day to the children in the early childhood education environment. Supervision of mealtime requires a number of skills. If the teacher provides meals to the children, the first area of supervision needed will be for the selection of healthy food choices. Regardless of whether the food is prepared by the teacher or by someone else, planning the meals should focus on healthy food choices and preparation forms. Food safety and sanitary practices should be used.

If the child brings meals from home, the teacher may have to supervise what are acceptable food selections and what are not. She may also need to determine proper storage so the food remains safe. Sending a sheet of acceptable food choices for the early childhood education situation may help remind the parents that the teacher is there to provide optimum care for their children. If a child brings unacceptable foods, these foods can be set aside to eat only after the good choices have been finished. Reading labels with children can help make them aware of what foods contain. This can be a powerful tool to help influence the parents to make better food selections.

Direction or redirection of mealtime behaviors helps to establish good eating habits and feeding behaviors. Observing the behaviors of children will be made easier when growth and developmental levels are understood. Good role modeling of mealtime practices is essential. The teacher has a great deal of influence on how the children in her care behave. Understanding the teacher's level of responsibility and the child's responsibility about eating will help alleviate any issue of control over food. This helps the teacher to provide a foundation of good feeding behaviors and eating practices.

### Key Concept 8.7

### Implications for Teachers

The teacher has an opportunity to provide positive food practices, good food selections, and an atmosphere conducive to eating. Application of information, strategies, and practices found in this chapter and the previous chapter enables the teacher to do this. Opportunities to educate the children about nutrition will occur on a daily basis. Every time there is a meal or snack, the teacher can sit with the children and role model good eating practices and have a dialogue about the food. Awareness of family conditions and nutritional knowledge can help the teacher be prepared to assist families in several ways. They can provide education as well as connect families to resources for better nutrition for their children. Practicing cultural sensitivity can help remove any barriers about food selection and choices. Acknowledging diverse food habits and preparing foods to reflect this can help break down barriers. Supervision provides the teacher with the tools needed to make sure that proper nutritional habits are being formed and practiced in the early childhood education environment.

# CHAPTER SUMMARY

Every teacher should practice good nutrition in the early childhood education environment. Many teachers are not meeting the nutritional needs of children in their care. Teachers may approach nutrition with their own perspective based on background, food practices, culture, and what the children eat or will not eat. Teachers should have nutritional policies that cover early infant feeding, food and the toddler, the preschool child, school-aged children, and special needs.

The teacher who understands how to accommodate the infant's physical and psychological needs will encourage the infant to go at his or her own pace. A teacher who understands that the developmental characteristics of a toddler influences how he or she deals with food is less likely to make food an issue of control. Teachers should use participatory activities to help the preschooler develop an awareness about the best nutritional choices. Teachers can provide adequate nutrition for school-aged children by keeping in mind their activity levels.

Some children with disabilities or chronic illnesses can be easily accommodated in their nutritional needs and feeding levels. Others may require special early intervention nutritional services or may not be able to be in the early childhood education situation.

The implications for the teacher include education, working with families, role modeling, and supervision. Opportunities to educate and role model good nutrition to the children and adults occur on a daily basis. Cultural sensitivity can break down barriers to food selection. Supervision provides the teacher with the tools needed to make sure that proper nutritional habits are being formed and practiced in the early childhood education environment.

## TO GO BEYOND

In this section you will find a number of activities that you can use to apply and improve your knowledge of this chapter. There are also thorough online resources that accompany this text that can be found at http://www.early childed.delmar.com (see description at end of this chapter).

### Chapter Review Critical Thinking Applications

1. Discuss how developmental levels relate to nutritional needs of children of different ages. How do the developmental levels affect the eating process for children?

2. Examine the benefits of breastfeeding. Compare and contrast these benefits to those of bottle feeding. List suggestions as to how a breastfeeding mother might be supported to continue to breastfeed her baby.

3. Describe how you would introduce solid foods to an infant.

4. Analyze how food is used as an issue of control by toddlers and their parents. How would you avoid this in an early childhood education situation?

## As an Individual

1. Using "Rate Your Plate" found in Chapter 9, rate your own diet. How does this differ from the three-day charting you did the previous week? Compare and contrast the two nutritional evaluations of your diet.

2. Observe children and their parents in a grocery store. How do they act in the cereal aisle? How do these interactions reflect positive rewards for negative behavior? How might food be an issue of control in these situations?

3. Observe Saturday morning television for one hour. Count the different fast food companies and the number of commercials they represent. Choose one of the commercials and list the methods they choose to get a child to come to one of their outlets.

## As a Group

1. During a weeklong period, observe patterns of people eating, including children and cultural patterns. Discuss these patterns in class. List the patterns observed by all students in class. How would you use this information to talk to children about eating and food? How might you use this information to adapt to the different cultures in your local area?

2. Collect menus from early childhood education centers, family care homes, and elementary schools in your area. Evaluate them and determine whether they meet the nutritional needs of children. How might these menus be changed to better meet the needs described in the MyPyramid Food Guidance System?

3. Break up into small groups and each group write three general policies for nutrition in the early childhood education environment. Come back as a large group and discuss. Choose the three most important policies. Discuss why these three policies were chosen.

## Case Studies

1. April is a new mother who must return to work when her son, Henry, is 10 weeks old. She has really enjoyed the breastfeeding relationship with Henry and she has been pumping milk and getting him used to a bottle. As his teacher, what specific things can you do to support April? Why is it important that you offer this support?

2. Drew is a 15-month-old toddler. His mother still has him drinking formula out of a bottle and prefers to hand-feed him toddler food from a jar because it is less messy than letting him feed himself. He wants the bottle and does not attempt to eat much of the food that you prepare for him. Drew seems to catch more than his share of colds and does not seem to be as active as he was when he was younger. How do you handle this problem? What could you say to his mother to enlist her help?

## Chapter References

Aby-Valestrino, M. (2001). Too much juice? *Healthy Child Care, 4*(4), 201. Retrieved October 26, 2005, from http://healthychild.net/articles/na22juice.html.

Ahluwalia, I., Tesssaro, I., Grummer-Strawn, L., MacGowan, C., & Benton-Davis, S. (2000). Georgia's breastfeeding promotion program for low-income women. *Pediatrics, 105*(6), e85.

Aird, L. (2002, May). Breastfeeding promotion in child care. *Child Care Information Exchange,* 46–48.

American Academy of Pediatrics (AAP). (2000, Spring/Summer). Breastfeeding saves lives, reduces illness and fosters optimum child development and parenting. *Breastfeeding: Best for Baby and Mother Newsletter,* 2.

Borzekowski, D., & Robinson, T. (2001). The 30-second effect: An experiment revealing the impact of television commercials on the food preferences of preschoolers. *Journal of the American Dietetic Association, 101*(1), 42–46.

Bowman, S., Gortmaker, S., Ebbeling, C., Periera, M., & Ludwig, D. (2004). Effects of fast-food consumption on energy intake and diet quality among children in a national household survey. *Pediatrics, 113*(1), 112–118.

Branen, L., Fletcher, J., & Myers, S. (1997). Effects of pre-plated and family style food service on preschool children's food intake and waste at snacktime. *Journal of Research in Childhood Education 12,* 88–95.

Briley, M., Jastrow, S., Vickers, J., & Roberts-Gray, C. (1998). Dietary intake at child-care centers and away: Are parents and care providers working as partners or at cross-purposes? *Journal of the American Dietetics Association, 99*(8), 950–954.

Briley, M., Jastrow, S., Vickers, J., & Roberts-Gray, C. (1999). Can ready to eat cereal solve common nutritional problems in child care menus? *Journal of the American Dietetic Association, 99*(2), 341–342.

Briley, M., McBride, A., & Roberts-Gray, C. (1997). Banking on nutrition. *Texas Child Care, 21*(3), 2–5.

Briley, M., Roberts-Gray, C., & Simpson, D. (1994). Identification of factors that influence the menu at child care centers: A grounded theory approach. *Journal of the American Dietetic Association 94*(3), 276–281.

Briley, M., & Roberts-Gray, C. (2005). Position of The American Dietetic Association: Benchmarks for nutrition programs in child care settings. *Journal of The American Dietetic Association, 105*(6), 979–986.

Busselman, D., & Holcomb, C. (1994). Reading skill and comprehension of Dietary Guidelines by WIC participants. *Journal of the American Dietetics Association, 94*(6), 622–625.

Butte, N., Cobb, K., Dwyer, J., Graney, L., Heirdl, W., & Rickard, K. (2003). The Start Healthy feeding guidelines for infants and toddlers. *Journal of the American Dietetic Association, 104*(3), 442–454.

Calder, J. (2004). Infant feeding: When to introduce new foods. *Child Care Health Connections Newsletter, 17*(1), 2.

California Child Care Health Program (CCCHP). (2003). Gastric tubes in the child care setting. *Child Care Health Connections Newsletter, 16*(6), 6.

Calo, R. (2002). How you can support breastfeeding mothers and infants. *Child Care Health Connections Newsletter 15*(5), 4.

Cathey, M., & Gaylord, N. (2004). Picky eating: A toddler's approach to mealtime. *Pediatric Nursing, 30*(12), 101–109.

Carmichael, S., Prince, C., Burr, R., Nakamoto, F., & Vogt, R. (2001). Breast-feeding practices among WIC participants in Hawaii. *Journal of the American Dietetic Association, 101*(1), 7–62.

Ebbeling, C., Sinclair, K., Pereira, M., Garcia-Lago, E., Feldman, H., & Ludwig, D. (2004). Compensation for energy intake from fast food among overweight and lean adolescents. *Journal of the American Medical Association 291*(23), 2828–2833.

Gamble, A. (2004). *Toddler nutrition: Building a healthy relationship with food.* Retrieved October 26, 2005, from http://toddlerstoday.com/resources/articles/nutrition.htm.

Garnter, L., & Greer, F. (2003). Prevention of rickets and Vitamin D deficiency: New guidelines for Vitamin D intake. *Pediatrics, 111*(4), 908–910.

Gordon, A., & McKinney, R. (1995). Sources of nutrients for students. *Journal of Clinical Nutrition, 61*(1), 232–240.

Green, A. (2005, April 4). Bill aims to reduce junk food in schools. *The Oregonian,* OregonianLive.com. Retrieved April 4, 2005 from http://www.oregonlive.com/printer/printer.ssf?/base/news/1112608621175340.xml

Healthy Child Care (HCC). (1998). Special dietary concerns in the childcare setting. *Healthy Child Care, 1*(4). Retrieved October 26, 2005, from http://www.healthychild.net/articles/na4specialdiet.html.

Hinden, T., Contento, I., & Gussow, J. (2004). A media literacy nutrition education curriculum for Head Start parents about the effects of television advertising on their children's food requests. *Journal of the American Dietetic Association, 104*(2), 192–198.

Holland, M. (2005). Feeding children with special needs. *Healthy Child Care, 8*(2). Retrieved October 26, 2005 from http://www.healthychild.net/articles/na44specialneeds.html.

Johnson, R., & Nicklas, T. (1999). Dietary guidance for healthy children aged 2 to 11 years: Position of ADA. *Journal of the American Dietetic Association, 99*(1), 93–101.

The Kaiser Foundation (KF) (2004, February 24). The role of media in childhood obesity. Retrieved October 26, 2005, from http://www.kff.org/entmedia/022404pkg.cfm.

Levin, D. (2004, September/October). From "I Want It" to "I Can Do It": Promoting healthy development in the consumer culture. *Childcare Information Exchange,* 34–37.

Levy, P., & Cooper, J. (1999). Five a day, let's eat and play: A nutrition education program for preschool children. *Journal of Nutrition Education, 31*(4), 235B.

Lin, B., Frazao, E., & Guthrie, J. (1999a). *Away-from-home foods increasingly important to quality of American diet.* Agricultural Information Bulletin No. 749. Washington, DC: US Department of Agriculture and U.S. Department of Health and Human Services.

Lin, B., Guthrie, J. & Frazao, E. (1999b). Quality of children's diets at and away from home: 1994–1996. *Food Review, 22*(1), 2–10.

Linn, S. (2004, Sept./Oct.). Food marketing to children undermines their health. *Childcare Information Exchange,* 44–47.

Lucich, M. (2003). Best practices for feeding young children in group settings. *Child Care Health Connections Newsletter, 16*(6), 3.

Ludwig, D., Peterson, K., & Gortmaker, S. (2001). Relationship between consumption of sugar-sweetened drinks and childhood obesity: A prospective, observational analysis. *Lancet, 357*(9255), 505–508.

Lyles, K. (2003). Infant bottle-feeding. *Healthy Child Care, 6*(6). Retrieved October 26, 2005, from http://www.healthychild.net/articles/na36infantfeed.html.

MacDonald, S. (2004). Which milk is best for babies? *Early Childhood Health Link, 15*(3), 8.

Melgar-Quinonez, H., & Kaiser, L. (2004). Relationship of child-feeding practices to overweight in low-income Mexican American preschool-aged children. *Journal of the American Dietetic Association, 104*(7), 1110–1119.

Miller, S. (2004, January/February). Tips for happy, healthy snack times. *Scholastic Early Childhood Today,* 4.

Murray, C. (2000). Learning about children's social and emotional needs at snack time—Nourishing the body, mind and spirit of each child. *Young Children, 55*(2), 43–52.

Nicklas, T. (2001). Consider nutrition when choosing day care. *Nutrition and Your Child, 2,* 1, 3.

Nicklas, T., & Johnson, R. (2004). Position of the American Dietetic Association: Dietary guide for healthy children ages 2 to 11 years. *Journal of the American Dietetic Association, 104*(4), 660–677.

Obegi, A., & Ritblatt, S. (2005). Cultural competence in infant/toddler caregivers: Application of a tri-dimensional model. *Journal of Research in Childhood Education, 19*(3), 199–213.

Padget, A., Briley, M., Gillham, M., Peterson, F., & Willis, R. (2005). Dietary intakes at childcare centers in Central Texas fail to meet Food Guide Pyramid recommendations. *Journal of The American Dietetic Association, 105*(5), 790–793.

Penn State News (2003, June 11). Day care lunch monitors vital in successful programs. Retrieved November 2, 2004 from http://www.psu.edu/ur/2003/daycarelunch.html.

Powers, M. (2004). Sociocultural challenges of feeding infants and small children. *Human Ecology, 32*(1), 21–23.

Satter, E. (1987). *How to get your kid to eat . . . But not too much.* Palo Alto, CA: Bull Publishing Company.

Satter, E. (2000). *Feeding with love and good sense.* Palo Alto, CA: Bull Publishing Company.

Satter, E. (2005). *Your child's weight.* Madison, WI: Kelcy Press.

Schlosser, E. (2001). *Fast food nation.* New York: Harper Perennial.

Seigman-Grant, M. (2003). Tummy talk. *Healthy Child Care, 6*(4). Retrieved October 26, 2005, from http://www.healthychild.net/articles/na34tummytalk.html

Spake, A. (2001, January 22). How Mcnuggets changed the world: The story of fast food: Yes, you are what you eat. *USNews.Com.* Retrieved October 26, 2005, from http://www.usnews.com/usnews/culture/articles/010122/archive_006787.htm.

Stang, J., & Beyerl, C. (2003). Position of the American Dietetic Association: Child and adolescent food and nutrition programs. *Journal of the American Dietetic Association, 103*(4), 887–893.

Story, M., Holt, K., & Sofka, D. (Eds.). (2000). *Bright futures in practice: Nutrition.* Arlington, VA: National Center for Education in Maternal and Child Health.

Tessmer, K. (2004). Food jags. Discovery Health Channel. Retrieved October 26, 2005, from http://health.discovery.com/encyclopedias/illnesses.html?article=1905&page=1

United States Breastfeeding Committee (USBC). (2002). *Breastfeeding and child care.* [issue paper], Raleigh, N.C.: Author. Retrieve October 24, 2004 from http://www.usbreastfeeding.org/Issues_Papers/Childcare.pdf

U.S. Department of Health and Human Services (US DHHS). (2001). Blueprint for action on breastfeeding. Rockville, MD: US DHHS, Office on Women's Health.

Walker, K. (2005). Infant feeding issues in child care. *Child Care Health Connections Newsletter, 18*(2), 4.

Wardle, J., Herrera, M., Cooke, L. & Gibson, E. L. (2003). Modifying children's food preferences: The effects of exposure and reward on acceptance of an unfamiliar vegetable. *European Journal of Clinical Nutrition, 57*(3), 341–348.

Wohlleb, K. (2004). Hardin County students gobble up 'handy' meals. Kentucky School Boards Association. Retrieved October 26, 2005, from http://www.ksba.org/KSA1003HardinCo.htm.

Yadrick, K., & Sneed, J. (1994). Nutrition services for children with developmental disabilities and chronic illness in education programs. *Journal of the American Dietetic Association 94*(10), 1122–1128.

Additional resources for this chapter can be found by visiting the Online Companion™ at http://www.earlychilded.delmar.com. This supplemental material includes extensive chapter quizzes, PowerPoint® outlines, Web links, and various other activities to help better utilize the material in this chapter. The site is updated regularly, so you may check back often to receive the latest information about the subjects in each chapter.

# Menu Planning and Food Safety in Early Childhood Education Environments

**After reading this chapter, you should be able to:**

### 9.1 Nutritional Policies

Define and discuss nutritional policies in relation to menu planning and food safety in the early childhood education environment.

### 9.2 Guidelines for Food Programs

Discuss the guidelines for subsidized food programs available for early childhood education environments.

### 9.3 Menu Planning for Early Childhood Education Environments

Indicate the importance of proper menu planning for children's well-being, including strategies for planning healthy breakfasts, snacks, and lunches.

### 9.4 Food Safety in Early Childhood Education Environments

Summarize the need for food sanitation and safety and practice strategies for providing it in the early childhood education environment.

### 9.5 Implications for Teachers

Relate the strategies for providing safe and healthy meals in the early childhood education environment through education, observation, cultural sensitivity, and supervision.

# 9.1  NUTRITIONAL POLICIES

An increasing number of children are being cared for in early childhood education environments. These environments appear to be the places where many children are learning their food habits, because they are spending much of their day in care. In order to meet the nutritional needs of the children in care, teachers must be prepared to plan healthy menus that children will enjoy and eat. Teachers must also be prepared to protect the children from disease by practicing food safety. The following are indicators of the need for sound nutritional policies for menu planning and food safety:

- A study by the Child and Adult Care Food Program (CACFP) showed that very few of the early childhood education facilities met the guidelines for food portion size or food quality 100 percent of the time. It also found that only the meat standard for lunch and the milk standard for breakfast were consistently served (Kuratko et al., 2000).

- Early childhood education professionals need to develop skills in maximizing the nutritional value of food so that they can appropriately select, prepare, and cook for the greatest nutritional value (Hayden, 2002; Nicklas & Johnson, 2004).

- Teachers should understand what age-appropriate portion sizes are for maximizing nutrition while children are in care (McConahy et al., 2004).

- Seventy percent of children consume more than the Daily Recommended Intake (DRI) of total and saturated fats (Nicklas et al., 2001). The Dietary Guidelines for fat are rarely met at early childhood education facilities (Spark et al., 1998).

- Research has shown that only one-half of teachers know food sources of nutrients and portion sizes for children (Briley & Roberts-Gray, 1999).

- Menus should be planned to meet guidelines if the early childhood education program is participating in the CACFP (Oakley & Carr, 2003b; Stang & Beyerl, 2003). By 2002, there were 2.9 million children in care participating in CACFP (Food and Nutrition Services Online, 2004).

- It is recommended that teachers provide two-thirds of the recommended daily intake for children who are in care for long hours (Briley & Roberts-Gray, 2005).

- Early childhood education centers should have good food safety and sanitation practices, provide staff training, and promote healthy eating patterns (Nicklas, 2001).

- Keeping food safe to eat is one of the Dietary Guidelines for Americans (Federal Register, 2004).

Early childhood education centers have a number of teachers on staff. In some centers, one of them may double as the food preparer and menu planner. The director may plan the menus, while a food preparation person is hired specifically for the job of cooking. In some cases, there may be a centrally located kitchen, or food may be catered, and pre-prepared food is distributed to several early childhood education centers. These menus may be provided by a dietician hired exclusively for that task.

Many family child care providers and nannies are also responsible for menu planning and food preparation, in addition to child care responsibilities.

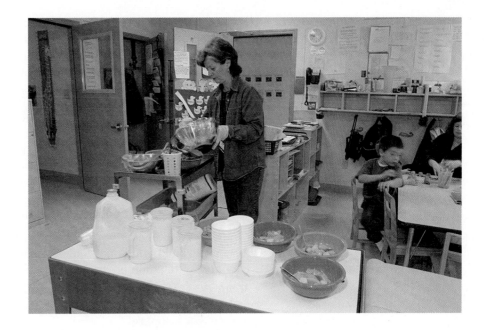

Proper nutrition needs to be taught and reinforced at all levels.

The family child care provider and the nanny are probably the menu planner and food preparer. This task, in addition to caring for children, may appear to be burdensome. With proper training in menu planning and food safety, the teacher may find that awareness and knowledge often make a job easier to perform.

Recently, the early childhood education program has been examined for its ability to provide good nutritional practices and safe food handling techniques. This can be improved through a more thorough understanding of the meals provided in care and the necessity for good menu planning, as well as proper food sanitation and safety practices. Teachers will need to use education, cultural sensitivity, observation, and supervision to carry out this task.

It is recommended that policies be created for the following areas:

- *Guidelines for Food Programs:* understanding how the subsidized food programs' guidelines should affect the food selection in early childhood education environments
- *Menu Planning:* understanding how to plan menus that meet children's tastes and nutritional needs, as well as being cost-effective and easy to prepare
- *Food Sanitation and Safety:* understanding the methods and practices for food sanitation and safety in early childhood education environments
- *Implications for Teachers:* understanding how education, cultural sensitivity, and supervision can help the teacher plan for adequate nutrition and food safety in early childhood education environments

## Key Concept 9.1

### Nutritional Policies

More than five million children are eating meals in early childhood education environments on a daily basis. Nutrition and food safety have been found to be inadequate in many of these environments. It is up to the teacher who plans and/or prepares meals for children to be adequately trained. The teacher needs to have an understanding of how breakfast, snacks, and lunches affect a child's nutritional needs. The teacher should know how to select healthy foods, plan adequate menus, and prepare food that is safe. By using education, cultural sensitivity, observation, and supervision the teacher ensures that the early childhood education environment is providing for the nutritional needs of the children in care.

## 9.2 GUIDELINES FOR FOOD PROGRAMS

There are a number of food programs that teachers and families can use to meet the nutritional needs of children. Several of these affect the early childhood education program directly. The CACFP, the Food Distribution Program,

The main goals of organized food programs is to provide nutritious foods for children in need.

the school Milk Program (SMP), and the Summer Food Service Program for Children (SFSPC) help to provide foods for early childhood education environments that meet the criteria. The CACFP and the Expanded Food and Nutrition Education Program (EFNEP) provide nutrition information and training for teachers, food service personnel, and children.

Programs that help families include the Special Supplemental Food Program for Women, Infants, and Children (WIC), the USDA's Food Stamp Program, the National School Lunch Program, and the School Breakfast program. WIC provides formula and other foods to families with children younger than three years of age. The Food Stamp Program provides more food to children and their families than any other source. A great majority of the people who receive food stamp monies are families with children (Stang & Beyerl, 2003). Teachers should be informed about these resources in case they need to make referrals to families to help them provide adequate nutrition to their children when not in care (Stang & Beyerl, 2003).

## The Child and Adult Care Food Program

The CACFP provides funding for children to age twelve years. To be eligible to participate in this program and receive funds, the early childhood education center or home must be a

1. nonprofit licensed or approved public or private early childhood education center
2. family child care home that belongs to a sponsoring agency
3. for-profit private program that receives funding for more than one-fourth of the children present in care through Title XX of the Social Security Act

In 2002, 2.9 million children were served two meals and one snack while in care with CACFP funding (RPP, 2004).

Funding for the CACFP is made possible through the USDA's Food and Nutrition Service. Eligible early childhood education sites may be funded for up to two meals and one snack per day or two snacks and one meal. A sliding scale is applied at the early childhood education site that indicates how much to charge a family for meals depending upon their income. Many children receive free meals as a result of the application of the scale.

The family child care home must have a sponsoring agency that administers the program. This may be a local early childhood education resource and referral agency, a public agency such as a USDA cooperative extension service, or other local agencies willing to provide financial administration. The state child care licensing agency can provide the teacher with this information. Recently, the numbers of these family child care homes has decreased by 21 percent. This may be due to the fact that the 1996 Welfare Reform Act states that for a family child care home to be eligible, it must be in a low-income area. This new provision only allows about 25 percent of children in family child care homes to participate in CACFP today (Report on Preschool Programs, 2004).

The CACFP provides funding for meals and nutritional training and menu planning for the teachers. In return, the teacher must meet the nutritional guidelines set by the CACFP. These are included in Table 9-1.

**TABLE 9-1**
*CACFP Nutritional Guidelines*

**Infants—***Birth to Three Months*
**Breakfast, Lunch, and Snack**

4–6 oz. formula or breast milk

*Four to Seven Months*

**Breakfast**

4–8 oz. formula or breast milk

**Lunch, and Snack**

4–8 oz. formula or breast milk
0–3 Tbs. iron-fortified infant cereal (not snack)
0–3 Tbs. vegetables or fruits (not snack)

**Snack**

4–8 oz. formula or breast milk

*Eight to Eleven Months*

**Breakfast and Lunch**

6–8 oz. formula
2–4 Tbs. iron-fortified infant cereal
1–4 Tbs. fruit or vegetables

**Lunch or Supper**

6–8 oz. formula or breast milk
2–4 oz. iron-fortified infant cereal *or*
1–4 Tbs. meat, fish, poultry, egg yolk, or dried beans *or*
   1–4 oz. cottage cheese, cheese spread, or cheese food *or*
   $^1/_2$–2 oz. cheese

**Snack**

1–4 Tbs. fruit or vegetables or both
2–4 oz. formula or milk or full strength fruit juice
2 crackers or $^1/_2$ slice bread

**Children—***One to Two Years*
**Breakfast**

$^1/_2$ cup milk
$^1/_4$ cup fruit juice, fruit, or vegetable
Bread and/or cereal or grains ($^1/_4$ cup cereal, $^1/_2$ slice bread, $^1/_4$ cup grain)

**Lunch or Supper**

$^1/_2$ cup milk
Meat or meat alternate (1 oz. meat or cheese, 1 egg, 2 Tbs. peanut butter,
   $^1/_4$ cup cooked dry beans or peas, or 4 oz. yogurt)
$^1/_4$ cup (total) vegetables and/or fruits (more than one choice)
$^1/_2$ slice bread or $^1/_4$ cup pasta, noodles, or grains

**Snack (Select two of four components)**

$^1/_2$ cup milk
$^1/_2$ oz. meat or meat alternate (cheese, egg, beans, peanut butter,
nuts/seeds), *or*
   2 oz. plain yogurt or $^1/_4$ cup flavored yogurt *(do not serve yogurt and
milk at same snack)*

**TABLE 9-1 (Continued)**
*CACFP Nutritional Guidelines*

**Snack (Select two of four components) (Continued)**

$\frac{1}{2}$ cup fruit juice, fruit or vegetable

Bread and/or cereal ($\frac{1}{2}$ slice bread, $\frac{1}{2}$ roll, or equivalent grain such as $\frac{1}{4}$ cup cold cereal, hot cereal, or pasta)

*Three to Five Years*

**Breakfast**

$\frac{3}{4}$ cup milk

$\frac{1}{2}$ cup fruit juice, fruit, or vegetable

Bread and/or cereal ($\frac{1}{2}$ slice bread, $\frac{1}{2}$ roll, or equivalent grain such as $\frac{1}{3}$ cup, cold cereal or $\frac{1}{4}$ cup hot cereal or pasta)

$\frac{1}{2}$ cup fruit juice, fruit or vegetable

**Lunch or Supper**

$\frac{3}{4}$ cup milk

Meat or meat alternate ($1\frac{1}{2}$ oz. meat, poultry, cheese, *or* 1 egg, *or* $\frac{3}{8}$ cup cooked dry beans or peas *or* 3 Tbs. peanut butter *or* $\frac{3}{4}$ oz. nuts or seeds or 6 oz. yogurt)

$\frac{1}{2}$ cup (total) vegetables and/or fruits (more than one choice)

Bread and/or cereal ($\frac{1}{2}$ slice bread, $\frac{1}{2}$ roll, or equivalent grain such as $\frac{1}{3}$ cup cold cereal or $\frac{1}{4}$ cup hot cereal or pasta)

**Snack (Select two of four components)**

$\frac{1}{2}$ cup milk

$\frac{1}{2}$ oz. meat or meat alternate *or* 2 oz. yogurt or 2 Tbs. nut butter or $\frac{1}{2}$ oz. nuts or seeds

$\frac{1}{2}$ cup fruit juice or fruit or vegetable

Bread and/or cereal ($\frac{1}{2}$ slice bread, $\frac{1}{2}$ roll, or equivalent such as $\frac{1}{3}$ cup cold cereal, or $\frac{1}{4}$ cup hot cereal or pasta)

*Six to Twelve Years*

**Breakfast**

1 cup milk

$\frac{3}{4}$ cup fruit juice, fruit or vegetable

Bread and/or cereal (1 slice bread, 1 roll, or equivalent grain such as $\frac{3}{4}$ cup cold cereal, $\frac{1}{2}$ cup hot cereal or pasta)

**Lunch or Supper**

$\frac{3}{4}$ cup fruit juice, fruit or vegetable

Bread and/or cereal (1 slice bread, 1 roll, or equivalent grain such as $\frac{3}{4}$ cup cold cereal or $\frac{1}{2}$ cup hot cereal or pasta)

2 oz. meat or meat alternates (cheese, egg, dry beans or peas, peanut butter or nuts/seeds) or 8 oz. yogurt

**Snack (Select two of four components)**

1 cup milk

$\frac{3}{4}$ cup fruit juice, fruit or vegetable

Bread and/or cereal (1 slice bread, 1 roll, or equivalent grain such as $\frac{3}{4}$ cup cold cereal or $\frac{1}{2}$ cup hot cereal or pasta)

1 oz. meat or meat alternates (cheese, egg, dry beans or peas, peanut butter or nuts/seeds) or 4 oz. yogurt

*Note:* All juices must be full-strength. Breads, cereal and grains must be whole grains or enriched or fortified. Yogurt may be plain, sweetened or unsweetened.

## Other Programs

The other program that may be of help to early childhood education environments in supplying food is the USDA Food Distribution Program. It is organized to distribute surplus foods such as cheese, grains, and canned goods. An early childhood education site that participates in the CACFP program will automatically receive an application to participate in this program as well. Other licensed early childhood education programs are also eligible to apply. If the program is selected to participate, it can receive commodity foods or cash supplements for the surplus food.

The Summer Food Service Program for Children supplies children from low-income families nutritious foods when their regular schools are on summer vacation. Early childhood education and family child care programs that provide care to school-aged children while on summer break may be eligible for these funds.

These teachers are receiving nutrition education to help them teach children about nutrition.

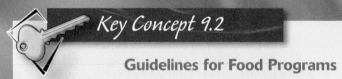

## Key Concept 9.2

### Guidelines for Food Programs

There are a number of nutritional programs that offer assistance to early childhood education centers or sites by providing funding or educational information. Other programs help children and their families to access nutritional foods at no or low cost. The program that helps many early childhood education sites is the CACFP. It provides specific guidelines for the food to be served, and it offers menu planning and nutritional information to teachers. In return, teachers agree to follow the guidelines and provide nutritious meals to children in care. Other programs that offer education support, training, and instructional materials are the Expanded Food and Nutrition Education Program and the National Food Service Management Institute.

The School Milk Program is available to nonprofit private residential child care programs as long as they do not participate in any other Federal child nutrition meal service programs. The Expanded Food and Nutrition Education Program is run by cooperative extension. Extension professionals train others to teach food and nutrition to children and their families as well as food purchasing, safety, sanitation, and menu planning for early childhood education environments. The National Food Service Management Institute at the University of Mississippi has a resource center for early childhood nutrition. The Web site for this is found at: http://www.nfsmi.org.

## 9.3  MENU PLANNING FOR EARLY CHILDHOOD EDUCATION ENVIRONMENTS

The American Dietetic Association has set recommended standards for early education programs, that is that the early childhood education environment should provide two-thirds of the nutritional needs for all children present for a full day (Briley & Roberts-Gray, 2005). The Food and Nutrition Service suggests that child nutrition programs should offer meals low in fats and cholesterol; plenty of fruits, vegetables, grains, and milk products; sugar and salt only in moderation; and a variety of foods (Food and Nutrition Service, 2001). These guidelines follow the most recent Dietary Guidelines for Americans.

### Building a Menu

There are a number of considerations in menu planning and food preparation (Figure 9-1). The best base for good menu planning is knowledge of nutrition and children's nutritional needs and developmental stages (see Table 9-1). A teacher with nutritional knowledge is more likely to create a better atmosphere for good nutrition practices, including the planning of menus (Spark et al., 1998). The menu should be the focal point for nutrition education and should reinforce healthy eating habits.

This first level of menu planning also includes understanding the MyPyramid Food Guidance System, the Dietary Guidelines for Americans, and any regulations that may accompany a food program in which the early childhood education program may participate. It should be prepared to meet state licensing procedures. This level should also consider appetizing presentations. Offer a variety of flavors, textures, and temperatures in the foods that are served. Young children prefer foods that they can identify. The teacher will need to be able to apply this information to help create menus that are healthy and meet the children's nutritional needs as well as fit their developmental level.

The second level involved in menu planning is based on accessibility to healthy food choices. A number of factors influence this level. The cost of food and the economics of providing adequate nutrition heavily influence the food that is purchased or the subsidized food programs that the early childhood education program may access. Spark et al. (1998) found that financial incentives in the form of a salary bonus were given to cooks for coming in under their budget for food.

Another consideration at this level is the culinary skills of the teacher or the food preparer who will cook the meals planned in the menu. Someone with limited skills will have fewer choices and may rely

FIGURE 9-1

Factors involved in menu planning in the early childhood
education environment.

**Factors Involved in Menu Planning in the Early Childhood Education Environment**

**Level One**

Knowledge of Nutrition

Children's Nutritional Needs

A Child's Developmental Stages

Dietary Guidelines for Americans

MyPyramid Guidance System

**Level Two**

Accessibility

for Health Choices

Cost      Convenience      Storage

Culinary Skills      Economy

Seasonal Food Considerations

**Level Three**

Environment

Goal of Child Care

Personal History

Cultural Diversity

Perceptions of

Child Food Choices

Best Practices

on more convenience-type foods that may be less nutritional and more expensive. The literacy level of the person preparing food and the inability to follow a recipe may also provide a barrier and guide that person to the use of convenience foods (Aumann et al., 1999).

Convenience itself may be a factor. Time is often limited, especially if there is only one teacher present in the early childhood education environment. This convenience factor may limit accessibility to the healthiest choices.

Access to healthy food is also affected by seasons. Foods that are in season are much more moderate in price and are more readily available. Fruits, vegetables, and occasionally meats are affected by seasonal availability.

The last factor at this level is the amount of storage available for foods. This includes both room in a refrigerator and room in a pantry or kitchen cabinet. Maintenance of proper food temperature has been found to be a problem at many early childhood education sites (Kuratko, 2000). Early childhood education environments with good storage facilities are able to buy in bulk and save money. These child care environments can also purchase more fresh foods at one time and plan for more frequent use of these foods.

The third level of influence on menu planning is the environment, including the goal of the early childhood education environment. The goal will affect food selection. The menu in a setting where the goal is the well-being of children will be different from the menu in a setting where the goal is to provide an income for the staff.

The cultural diversity of the early childhood education environment often has an influence on menu planning. The diversity may be reflected in the teacher's cultural background and may limit choices in the menu items for planning. Cultural and regional food preparations that are deep-seated

This lunch menu in an early childhood education environment reflects the recommended standards for early childhood education programs.

### WEEK of April 3, 2006

|  | MONDAY | TUESDAY | WEDNESDAY | THURSDAY | FRIDAY |
|---|---|---|---|---|---|
| Breakfast | Milk<br>Cereal<br>Fresh Fruit | Milk<br>Eggs<br>Tortillas<br>Fresh Fruit | Milk<br>Toast & Jelly<br>Fresh Fruit | Milk<br>Cereal<br>Fresh Fruit | Milk<br>Eng. Muffin<br>Fresh Fruit |
| Lunch | Milk<br>Rotelli<br>Turkey<br>Meatballs<br>  Marinara<br>Broccoli<br>Fresh Fruit | Milk<br>Beans<br>Cheese<br>Rice<br>Tortillas<br>Green Beans<br>Fresh Fruit | Milk<br>Tuna/Turkey<br>  Sandwiches<br>Zucchini w/Ranch<br>  Sauce<br>Fresh Fruit | Milk<br>Japanese<br>  Vegetables<br>Teriyaki Chicken<br>Steamed Rice<br>Fresh Fruit | Milk<br>Cheese Pizza<br>Turkey Cubes<br>Carrots w/Ranch<br>  Sauce<br>Fresh Fruit |
| Snack | Cheese<br>Crackers | Fresh Fruit<br>Cookies | Yogurt<br>Cookies | Juice<br>Crackers | Cottage Cheese<br>Fresh Fruit |

week 1

### WEEK of April 10, 2006

|  | MONDAY | TUESDAY | WEDNESDAY | THURSDAY | FRIDAY |
|---|---|---|---|---|---|
| Breakfast | Milk<br>Cereal<br>Fresh Fruit | Milk<br>Cornbread<br>Fresh Fruit | Milk<br>Pancakes<br>Fresh Fruit | Milk<br>Cereal<br>Fresh Fruit | Milk<br>Bagel w/Cream<br>  Cheese<br>Fresh Fruit |
| Lunch | Milk<br>Hamburger<br>  on a bun<br>French<br>  Fries<br>Broccoli<br>Fresh Fruit | Milk<br>Macaroni &<br>  Cheese<br>Turkey cubes<br>Peas & Carrots<br>Fresh Fruit | Milk<br>Grilled Cheese<br>  Sandwich<br>Cucumbers<br>  w/Ranch Sauce<br>Fresh Fruit | Milk<br>Chicken Noodle<br>  Soup<br>Egg Salad<br>  Sandwich<br>Carrots<br>Fresh Fruit | Milk<br>Chicken Nuggets<br>Rolls<br>Corn<br>Fresh Fruit |
| Snack | String<br>  Cheese<br>Crackers | Pretzels<br>Juice | Cookies<br>Fresh Fruit | Yogurt<br>Fresh Fruit | Cheese<br>Crackers |

week 2

habits may be difficult to ignore. Attempts to change these habits by outside forces (e.g., a director) may be looked upon as a threat to the person preparing the food (Spark et al., 1998). A positive process occurs when the menu selection is influenced by the diversity of the children in care.

Another influence at this level is the personal history of the teacher, menu planner, or food purchaser, who in many cases will be the same person. The person who creates the menu and/or prepares the food is going to be influenced by her own food memories, prejudices, and preferences. If she hated lima beans as a child, they will probably never appear on the menu. It is important to discuss and understand why certain types of food or food preparations might be excluded or used in lesser quantities. It is vital that the teacher receive some type of nutritional training. With basic nutritional knowledge, it will be easier for the teacher to provide a menu

Convenience foods do not have to be unhealthy, as this teacher shows with bananas.

that reflects good nutrition and not food prejudices. If food preparation staff is unfamiliar with recommended foods included in the guidelines, they may be resistant to including these foods or may prepare them in a less than acceptable manner. It is also important for the teacher to recognize the fact that the minority population is growing, so cultural preferences of the children in care should also be considered (Briley & Roberts-Gray, 1999). To help the teacher meet these needs, parents should be involved in the planning of menus in some way.

Some teachers have a perception of what foods children will or will not eat. Many menus are planned and are limited by the choices that a teacher "knows" are the ~~only things a child~~ will eat. Food preparation staff should not stereotype the foods they think children would not eat, or be prejudiced against foods because of their own backgrounds (Skinner et al., 1998). Children will accept 80 percent of the food offered to them at first, and with repeated exposure, they will eat most foods.

Oakley and Carr (2003a), in *Steps to Success,* have created a series of checklists for "Best Practices for Quality Nutrition" that will help early childhood education facilities that are tied to CACFP measure whether they are performing up to the level they should. This list is a good measure of how any early childhood education program is doing in how they provide food and nutrition to the children they serve. There are two Web sites connected to this. The best practices checklists for center care and the checklists for family child care homes can be found at http://www.nfsmi.org. Table 9-3 shows a menu planning checklist for early childhood education environments.

Considering the influences at every level, the teacher can begin planning a menu. Care should be taken to remove all prejudices, preferences, and perceptions or any other factor that may be a barrier to good menu planning. The teacher should also remove any barriers to the accessibility of the healthiest food selections. This may involve applying for subsidized food programs, taking cooking lessons, and looking for easier ways to cook nutritious fresh foods.

The teacher should be equipped with the necessary nutritional knowledge and influences of the developmental stages by reading and referencing this text. If the teacher feels more information would be helpful, further training and education in nutrition may be the next step.

Menu planning should be done on a regular basis, such as every two weeks or once per month. The menu should be reviewed and revised on a regular basis. Some child care centers have had the same menu for 15 years (Briley et al., 1993). It is important to keep the menu updated and to change it so a variety of foods can be offered and seasonal availability can be accessed.

By applying the meal guidelines found in Table 9-1, or following specific meal guidelines supplied by a child care licensing agency, the teacher can create menus that meet the needs of the children. Using MyPyramid individual plan, available at http://www.mypyramid.gov, one can rate his or her own nutritional needs. Several other considerations should also be kept in mind.

Many early childhood education menus fail to meet the energy needs of the young child. They also fail to provide enough fresh fruits and vegetables and often do not meet the daily requirements for iron and niacin. Early childhood education menus have often been found to provide too much fat, sugar, and salt.

Another method of making sure the menu is planned properly is to use a checklist (Table 9-2). A sample menu is found in Table 9-3.

## Breakfast

Breakfast may well be the most critical meal of the day. USDA recommends that 25 percent of DRI should be offered at breakfast (Fox et al., 1997). It has been reported that eating breakfast affects cognition, strength, attitude, and endurance (Evers, 1999; Brown & Marcotte, 1999). Children who skip breakfast do not make up for the nutritional loss over the rest of the day (Nicklas et al., 2004). People who eat breakfast are less likely to be obese because their nutritional needs are spread throughout the day. Poor nutrition among children in the United States is in part a result of skipping breakfast.

As reflected in Table 9-1, breakfast should consist of milk, bread/cereal, and fruit. Breakfasts can be built around traditional breakfast foods such as cereal, toast, fruit, milk, and so forth. Breads, cereals, and grains in adequate quantities are consistently missing from early childhood education environments (Briley et al., 1999). Cold cereal that has been fortified with iron has been suggested as an easy way to increase this food group (Briley et al., 1997). These food choices can be enhanced by making them more attractive. Fruits or nuts can be put on hot or cold cereals. A bagel can have cream cheese or cottage cheese and fruit on it. The teacher will have to understand the food habits of the children in care. Some children do not like mixing foods.

**TABLE 9-2**
*Menu Planning Checklist*

### ✓ CHECK FOR:

☐ Menu fits budget.

☐ Food is seasonally available.

☐ Culinary skills are available to prepare foods selected.

☐ There is adequate time and labor to prepare food.

☐ Personal history barriers are removed.

☐ Different methods of preparation are used.

☐ There is adequate storage for the food.

☐ Cultural and ethnic diversity are considered.

☐ Meal pattern meets CACFP guidelines or the Best Practices Quality Programs Checklist for Menu Planning.

☐ A few new foods are tried every menu planning period.

☐ Few foods are offered that have high fat, high sodium, or high sugar content.

☐ A source of vitamin C is served daily.

☐ A source of vitamin A is served three to four times per week.

☐ Whole-grain breads and grains are offered.

☐ Raw vegetables and fruits are served often.

☐ The food is chosen for sensory appeal considering texture, color, and shape.

Other children may be affected by cultural tradition or practices regarding breakfast choices.

Other nontraditional food choices for breakfast are available, such as dried fruits, peanut butter, burritos, pizza, fruit salad, and fruit smoothies, all of which offer good nutrition and might encourage children to eat better at breakfast. Foods from other cultures, such as stir-fried rice, may be served as an alternative to the traditional choices.

### Snacks

Snacks are an essential part of a child's nutritional day. Snacks should provide adequate nutrition and should be served at a sufficient time between meals for the children to be hungry but not too hungry (Niklas & Johnson, 2004). Snacks are a good time to begin to reflect the cultural diversity of the children in care. It is also the best time to introduce new foods. If children do not like the food, their nutritional needs for the day will be less at risk. This is also a time to help create food memories. Children enjoy food preparation and it gives them a better attitude toward new foods (Sigman-Grant, 2005). If fruit juice is used in the menu, it should always be 100 percent juice (AAP, 2001). Children under the age of six years should have no more than 6 ounces and children under the age of twelve years should have no more than 12 ounces of fruit juice in a day (Skinner & Carruth, 2001).

**TABLE 9-3**
*Sample Menu for an Early Childhood Education Environment*

|  | Breakfast | Snack | Lunch | Snack |
|---|---|---|---|---|
| Monday | Cheerios<br>Banana<br>Milk | Rye crisp<br>Cheese<br>Apple juice | Spaghetti with meat<br>  sauce<br>Salad & fruit<br>Milk | Quesadillas<br>Orange juice |
| Tuesday | French toast<br>Applesauce<br>Milk | Carrot sticks<br>Saltine crackers<br>Fruit juice | Chicken and vegetable<br>  soup<br>Grilled cheese sandwich<br>Melon slice<br>Milk | Corn muffins<br>Milk |
| Wednesday | Cinnamon whole<br>  wheat tortillas<br>Peaches<br>Milk | Popcorn<br>Cheese cubes<br>Water | Fettucini with cheese<br>  sauce<br>Carrot rounds<br>Fruit cup<br>Milk | Banana bread<br>  with cream<br>  cheese<br>Grape juice |
| Thursday | Yogurt<br>Strawberries<br>Wheat toast | Rice cakes with<br>  peanut butter<br>Fruit juice | Chicken chow mein over<br>  crisp noodles<br>Orange wedge<br>Milk | Cranberry<br>  muffins<br>Yogurt<br>Water |
| Friday | Granola<br>Pears<br>Milk<br>Water | Yogurt dip with<br>  vegetable sticks<br>  & tomato<br>Milk | Beef tostado with beans,<br>  rice, lettuce<br>Milk | Bread sticks<br>Orange<br>Water |

*Pause for Reflection*

What types of childhood food memories do you have? Did you ever help prepare foods when you were a young child, and do you remember those experiences?

As shown in Table 9-1, snacks should consist of a milk or meat/meat alternate choice such as yogurt, and a bread/grain or fruit choice. Some licensing standards dictate that there be pure fruit juice served at one snack and milk at the other snack. Ideally, there should always be a protein source either from milk, a meat, or a meat alternate. An example of this is peanut butter on celery or crackers. Protein should be spread throughout the day for optimum benefit. The fat in the meat or milk will offer satiety and help to fill up the child. Using a bread, grain, or fruit will provide bulk and flavor, and help the children meet the MyPyramid guidelines.

Typical snacks might include bagels, tortillas, crackers, milk, yogurt, string cheese, and fresh fruit such as apples, bananas or oranges, or applesauce. Snacks may occasionally be more unusual, such as a vegetable soup,

A nutritious breakfast or snack consisting of milk, bread/cereal, and fruit is just one way to provide a healthy start for children.

a yogurt sundae, a cheese crisp, a bread pudding, a fruit smoothie, or a frozen banana pop with peanut butter and coconut. The type of snack may be affected by food preparation time and cost.

## Lunches

Lunches in the early childhood education environment may provide the greatest amount of nutrition in the child's day. The child's lunch should consist of milk, a meat, or meat alternate, fruits and/or vegetables (minimum of two), and a bread or grain. School lunches contain more than the average amount of fats and saturated fats (Nicklas et al., 2004). It is important to address this issue when planning menus.

Some teachers limit the lunches they prepare to those things children are familiar with or those things that may resemble fast food that children will eat. Menu items such as peanut butter sandwiches, burritos, pizza, hamburgers, spaghetti, fish sticks, tacos, macaroni and cheese, and hot dogs may appear often and in some cases may be the rotating menu. Infrequent exposure to many foods as young children may limit children's range of acceptable food choices later in life. Several of these items may contribute more fat at one meal than is desired. This is a practice that should be examined and changed to better meet the nutritional needs of the children.

Teachers who provide lunches for children should keep a menu in mind that offers less fat and a greater variety of food over time. Children who are involved in helping prepare lunches may be more likely to eat a wider variety of foods. Foods such as stir fries, baked chicken or fish, hearty soups, pita pockets, quesadillas, and different pastas can add variety and flavor to the menu. Most children will eat these foods.

**Lunches from Home.** Lunches may present a unique problem if they are not prepared at the early childhood education site. When children bring their own lunches to school, they are more likely to consume sugar, sweets, and sweetened beverages. They are also less likely to eat vegetables, drink milk, or have adequate amounts of meat or meat alternatives (Gordon & McKinney, 1995; Wohlieb, 2004). Many licensed programs prohibit the presence of these less desirable foods. Teachers should have a policy about

Children who bring their lunches from home may not always bring the most nutritious foods. It is a good idea to set standards for acceptable nutritious foods brought from home.

foods brought from home, including a parent handout of unacceptable food choices such as high-density fat, sugar, and calorie-laden foods that offer little food value. That policy should also include the fact that foods from home should (1) be properly labeled with name, date, and type of food; (2) be refrigerated, if necessary; and (3) not be shared with anyone.

## Children on Vegetarian Diets

Some children in care may be from families that are vegetarians. There are four types of vegetarians: vegans, whose diets consist only of plant foods—grain, legumes, fruits, vegetables, nuts, seeds, and fats from vegetable sources; lacto-vegetarians, whose diets consist of those same foods but with the addition of milk and milk products; ovo-vegetarians, who eat eggs in addition to the plant foods; and lacto-ovo-vegetarians, who eat both milk products and eggs in addition to the plant foods. It is not difficult to meet the nutritional needs of lacto, ovo, or lacto-ovo-vegetarian children because good sources of nutrients such as protein, iron, and calcium include milk, milk products, and eggs. Planning the menu for a vegan child can be more challenging. Well-planned vegan diets can meet the nutrient needs of children (AAP, 1998) (see The Vegetarian Pyramid in Figure 9-2). You may

**FIGURE 9-2**
The Vegetarian Pyramid.

**Vegetarian Food Pyramid**

| (Green) | (Red) | (Purple) |
|---|---|---|
| Vegetables | Fruits | Meat Substitute |
| Dark green leafy, orange | Fresh, frozen, canned | Dry beans, nuts, |
| starchy, other, dry beans | Dried or 100% juice | seeds and eggs |

| (Orange) | (Yellow) | (Blue) |
|---|---|---|
| 50% whole grains | Oils | Milk Group |
| 50% refined grains | Oils, fats | Milk, yogurt |
| Bread, ceral, rice | | cheese, milk-based |
| Pasta | | desserts |

Note: If vegan, with no sources of calcium from the milk group be sure to have other sources of calcium such as broccoli and other rich calcium vegetables, tofu, soy and soy protein sources. Increased consumption of nuts, dried beans, and sources of soy will also help replace eggs.

See http://www.nutrispeak.com and
http://www.vrg.org

Information found in this figure is adapted from MyPyramid Food Guidance System and information from the above two websites.

want to consult a dietician to help with menu plans for a vegan child (Messina & Mangels, 2001). Another solution may be to ask the parent of the vegan child to help in the planning of the menu, or have them supply the snacks and lunches for that child.

Vegan children should consume a wide variety of fruits and vegetables, including green leafy vegetables, which can be a good source of calcium and iron. Dried beans, peas, lentils, and soy products are good sources of protein and iron. Soy milk that has been fortified with calcium and vitamin D is a good source to help meet the child's daily intake of calcium. Nuts and seeds help give the child the protein and essential fats that they need for energy and to help metabolize the fat-soluble vitamins. In addition, cooking with vegetable oil and using vegetable margarine spread can help children meet their dietary need for fat.

## Key Concept 9.3

### Menu Planning

Menu planning begins with building a foundation of knowledge and eliminating barriers to accessing healthy food choices and background influences. Guidelines for meeting nutritional needs should be followed, and a variety of foods, including fresh vegetables and fruits, should be provided. Teachers can look at each area of menu planning and relate it to the entire day's menu choices. They should use a checklist to examine whether all criteria for food menu planning are met. A teacher who understands the importance of breakfast, snacks, and lunch will plan more carefully to meet the needs of the children in care.

## 9.4  FOOD SAFETY IN EARLY CHILDHOOD EDUCATION ENVIRONMENTS

Preventing foodborne illness should be a primary task of the teacher who is planning and preparing meals for children in care (Kuratko et al., 2000). Food safety involves proper food purchasing, food storage, handling, and cooking. These practices and strategies for providing protection from risk and prevention of foodborne illnesses should be carefully monitored. It is recommended that the teacher responsible for food purchasing, storage, handling, and cooking use the Food Safety Checklists (Tables 9-4 to 9-7) to periodically monitor the early childhood education environment for food safety.

### Food Purchasing

Food purchasing is the starting point of making sure the food in the environment is safe. Food should be of good quality, fresh, and undamaged. To ensure quality, the purchases should be made from reputable wholesalers, markets, butchers, and others who provide food to the early childhood education environment. These businesses should meet proper local and state health and sanitation codes as well as keep up with any federal regulations that may apply to them.

Buy fresh products before the "sell by" or "use by" dates. Any products that need to be refrigerated should be stored in that section of the store. Do not purchase foods that need to be refrigerated but are not. Avoid fresh products such as fish and poultry that have the label "frozen, defrosted." It is difficult to tell how long these items have been frozen or how long they have been sitting defrosted, or the manner in which they were defrosted.

When buying poultry and other meats, keep them away from fresh fruits, vegetables, and other foods that will not be cooked. This will avoid cross-contamination. Always purchase perishable and fresh foods last. When having food packed, store fresh and frozen foods together to keep them cold.

Do not buy canned goods that are dented or otherwise compromised. The few cents that may be saved could be very costly later. Buy prepackaged foods only if the package is intact. A tear or a rip can allow the food to be contaminated. Table 9-4 lists some guidelines to ensure food safety when purchasing food.

## Food Storage

Proper food storage is a key to keeping food safe. This involves proper wrapping, proper labeling, temperature, and arrangement of the food that has been purchased.

Foods need to be protected from contamination by insects, rodents, dust, coughing, sneezing, dirty utensils, and improper temperature while being stored. Proper temperature maintenance is primary. Improper temperature is responsible for 85 percent of cases of foodborne illness. Germs multiply rapidly in lukewarm foods.

***Refrigerated Foods.*** Meats, poultry, and fish should be well wrapped so they do not contaminate other foods in the refrigerator. Placing the store package in a waterproof plastic bag works well. If these foods are being frozen, freezer bags or aluminum foil will help protect them from freezer burn and quality loss. It is essential that all food in the early childhood education environment be labeled by date of purchase to prevent waste and avoid risk.

**TABLE 9-4**
*Food Safety Purchasing Checklist*

### ✓ CHECK FOR:

☐ Buy from sources that are inspected for health and sanitation.

☐ Buy only good quality, fresh, and undamaged foods.

☐ Buy perishable food before "sell by" date.

☐ Perishable foods are refrigerated.

☐ Do not purchase "frozen, defrosted" foods.

☐ Purchase fresh foods last.

☐ Keep poultry and meats away from other foods.

☐ Do not buy damaged canned or packaged goods.

All refrigerated products should be refrigerated immediately. Quickly freeze all frozen foods. If they have thawed, they must be used within 24 hours. This avoids any contamination. Eggs should be stored in the refrigerator, preferably in their cartons.

Clean utensils must always be used if storing the food. Food must be refrigerated or stored in covered, shallow containers within two hours after cooking. Containers should be less than 2 inches high. If the food is planned for later use, they should be put immediately in the refrigerator. *Never store food in its cooking container!* There is a short period of time to cool the food to avoid contamination.

Cooked food should always be dated, so it will be used while still good and not be wasted or present risk. The teacher should always reheat cooked foods to a minimum of 160°F and make sure runny foods like soups have come to a full rolling boil before serving.

The refrigerator should be maintained at a temperature of less than 40°F and the freezer should be maintained at less than 0°F. This inhibits growth of bacteria that can cause foodborne illnesses. There is a danger zone for contamination of foods above 40°F. Bacteria multiply rapidly between 40° and 125°F.

The refrigerator should be arranged so that there is adequate circulation of cold air. A refrigerator that is too full may not keep the proper temperature and foods may be at risk for contamination.

*Unrefrigerated Foods.* All unrefrigerated products should be stored in clean, rodent-free areas, preferably with doors to cover the storage area. These areas should also be a minimum of 8 inches above the floor. Foods should be stored so that those items that were purchased first will be used first. First in storage, first out of storage is the recommendation. This avoids waste and risk. Nonperishable items such as flour, sugar, and so forth, should be stored in airtight containers once the package is opened. A food safety storage checklist can be found in Table 9-5.

## Food Handling

Anyone who has any signs of illness or infectious skin sores that cannot be covered should not be handling food. It is also preferable that the food handler not change diapers. This is more practical in a center situation where there are a number of teachers. In a family child care home or in the child's own home, the single teacher must perform many roles. In these cases, extra care should be taken, including the use of disposable non-latex gloves. In any case, it is important to remember a key to proper sanitation is good hand washing techniques.

Teachers can avoid many risks for foodborne illnesses by handling food properly. Use of sanitary practices and healthy habits for handling food (see Table 9-6) can avoid food contamination and growth of bacteria. Food may be handled in its raw form, or it may be frozen or cooked. *Never* thaw any food at room temperature. Thawing should take place in the refrigerator, in the microwave oven, or by placing the item in a waterproof plastic bag and submerging it in cold water, changing the water every 30 minutes. When handling cooked foods, always wash hands.

**TABLE 9-5**
*Food Safety Storage Checklist*

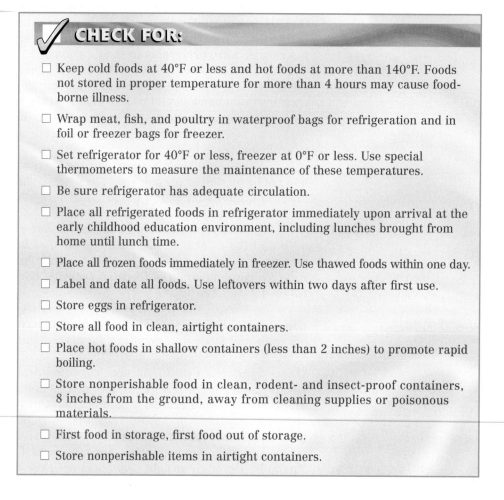

## ✓ CHECK FOR:

☐ Keep cold foods at 40°F or less and hot foods at more than 140°F. Foods not stored in proper temperature for more than 4 hours may cause food-borne illness.

☐ Wrap meat, fish, and poultry in waterproof bags for refrigeration and in foil or freezer bags for freezer.

☐ Set refrigerator for 40°F or less, freezer at 0°F or less. Use special thermometers to measure the maintenance of these temperatures.

☐ Be sure refrigerator has adequate circulation.

☐ Place all refrigerated foods in refrigerator immediately upon arrival at the early childhood education environment, including lunches brought from home until lunch time.

☐ Place all frozen foods immediately in freezer. Use thawed foods within one day.

☐ Label and date all foods. Use leftovers within two days after first use.

☐ Store eggs in refrigerator.

☐ Store all food in clean, airtight containers.

☐ Place hot foods in shallow containers (less than 2 inches) to promote rapid boiling.

☐ Store nonperishable food in clean, rodent- and insect-proof containers, 8 inches from the ground, away from cleaning supplies or poisonous materials.

☐ First food in storage, first food out of storage.

☐ Store nonperishable items in airtight containers.

Proper food handling is essential to avoid risks for foodborne illnesses, sanitary practices and developing healthy habits for handling food can prevent food contamination and growth of bacteria.

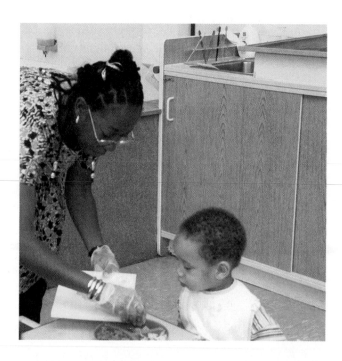

The food handler's clothing should be clean, and use of a clean apron will help maintain a higher cleanliness standard. Other food handling safety measures are included in Table 9-6.

An excellent way to ensure that food is handled properly is to have the person who is preparing and serving food take a food handler's course that is offered in most communities.

Always remember that the kitchen needs to be kept clean and sanitary. The food preparation and dishwashing areas should be kept completely separate from other centers of activity such as where children play, where diapers are changed, and toileting areas (Kunitz, 2003). All surfaces in the kitchen should be clean and free of cracks. Serving dishes should not have any cracks or chips. Dishcloths to clean these areas should be for these areas only and not used in other parts of the environment. After the food has been cleared and stored properly, all areas of the kitchen and eating area should be checked for cleanliness.

**TABLE 9-6**
*Healthy Food Handling Tips*

- Always wash hands.
- Use non-latex gloves to improve sanitation.
- Always prepare food-handling environment using sanitary practices. This includes countertops, bread boards, and can openers.
- Keep nails well-trimmed and clean.
- Keep hair tied back, in a hat, or in a net.
- Wash all fruits, vegetables, and tops of cans prior to use.
- Do not thaw frozen foods at room temperature.
- After cutting poultry, meat, or fish, follow sanitary cleaning procedures for cutting boards and hands.
- Never let meat, poultry, or fish juices get on other foods.
- Check internal temperature of meats using a meat thermometer before serving. This is extremely important to prevent *E. coli* or salmonella bacteria from contaminating food. Follow temperature gauge for proper meat temperatures.
- Always reheat food to a minimum of 160°F, or if runny food like soup, bring to a full rolling boil.
- Refrigerate all cooked foods within two hours or foods for freezing immediately.
- Never reuse a spoon that has been used for tasting.
- Never reuse leftover food from serving bowls used on the table, except when the food is packaged and will not spoil.
- Never prepare food when you are ill.
- Do not help children with toileting, diapering, or blowing noses while preparing food.
- Keep cloth for wiping up food for that purpose only, or use disposable cloths.
- Wash dishes and preparation tools in hot, soapy water. Rinse. Dip for one minute in bleach solution that is at least 75°F. Let air dry. Do not use a dish towel to dry.
- If using a dishwasher, thoroughly rinse dishes first, then utilize hottest, sanitizing cycle. Allow to dry before removing.

## Cooking Foods

Safe, sanitary, and healthy practices should always be used when preparing foods for cooking. As the foods are being cooked, other measures help to provide further protection. Poultry and meats should always be cooked to an internal temperature of 160° to 180°F. The minimum temperature of 160°F protects the food from causing foodborne illnesses. This is especially important for children. Recent outbreaks of *E. coli* bacteria have caused concern about the internal temperature of meats meeting the minimum degree criteria.

If a crockpot or slow cooker is used for cooking foods, several precautions should be taken to provide protection. The cooker should never be more than two-thirds full with plenty of liquid. If using meat, the pieces should be small and uniform, and the internal temperature must be checked before serving to make sure it meets the 160°F requirement.

If cooking foods in the microwave, the teacher should make sure the foods are cooked through and allowed to sit for a short period so the cooking process may finish. Using a microwave probe or a meat thermometer ensures all meats are at an internal temperature of 160°F. Table 9-7 contains a checklist for food safety.

**TABLE 9-7**
*Food Safety When Cooking*

### ✓ CHECK FOR:

- ☐ Always cook meats to an internal temperature of 160 to 180°F.
- ☐ If using a crockpot, never fill more than two-thirds and always use plenty of liquids.
- ☐ For a crockpot, cut meat pieces small and uniform.
- ☐ Before serving foods from a crockpot, always make sure internal temperature is a minimum of 160°F.
- ☐ Let microwave foods sit for a short time to finish the cooking cycle.
- ☐ Check microwave foods for thorough cooking.
- ☐ Always check internal temperature of meats cooked in microwave to meet the 160°F criterion.

# REALITY CHECK

## E. coli and Children

In 1982 the first outbreak of infection with the *E. coli* bacteria occurred when 47 people in two states got sick from eating contaminated hamburger meat at a fast food restaurant (*E.coli*, 2001). In 1993, a serious outbreak occurred for the same reason, and three children died and many more suffered lifelong disabilities (Evans, 1995). It is

## REALITY CHECK (Continued)

estimated that as many as 20,000 cases of *E. coli* infection appear each year, and as many as 500 people die from it (Cooper, 1995). In the past few years, *E. coli* has been found in unpasteurized fruit juices, and fresh cheese curds, alfalfa sprouts, dry-cured salami, lettuce, raw milk, and game meat (USDA, 2001; Mohle-Boetani et al., 2001). During the years 1996–2003, the incidence of *E. coli* infection has gone down by 42 percent (MMRW, 2004). This is probably due to public awareness and more careful food handling.

*E. Coli* stands for *Escherichia coli,* one of the most abundant species of bacteria in our environment. It lives in the intestines of humans and animals. *E. coli* is common and works with other bacteria within our intestines to enable us to function properly and remain healthy. The problem occurs when the *E. coli* bacteria that are present in animal intestines produce different strains that can be harmful to humans. The rare strain that has occurred recently is referred to as *E. coli* O157:H7; it causes hemorrhaging, blood loss, and dehydration (E. coli infection, 2000).

The *E. coli* O157:H7 bacteria has been infected with a strain of toxin-producing virus. The toxin appears as a protein that causes severe damage to the lining of the intestines. Salt and water are lost in the intestines, and blood vessels are damaged. It can also result in hemolytic uremic syndrome, which can cause acute kidney failure (Held & Griffin, 2000). Young children and elderly persons are the most susceptible to these toxins because dehydration, blood loss, and kidney failure can easily progress to lethal conditions (MMRW, 2004).

Harmful *E. coli* bacteria can be found in a number of foods, the most common of which is ground beef. *E. coli* is commonly found in cattle feces and can be spread by animals and people. This harmful strain is also found in roast beef, unpasteurized milk, apple cider, and municipal water.

The meat inspection system has undergone some radical changes recently, because the most common source of this bacteria is related to hamburger. On July 6, 1996, the U.S. Department of Agriculture announced its new four-step program to revamp the inspection system and to try to reduce the amount of *E. coli* bacteria found in meat products.

Other measures have been taken to protect the public from *E. coli* bacteria. The restaurant industry has adopted the HACCP system and directs restaurants to cook hamburgers to a thermometer-tested 160 degrees Fahrenheit. The federal government has passed measures to regulate fruit juices and sprouted seeds. Healthy People 2010 has an objective to decrease the number of *E. coli* O157:H7 cases by one-half (Healthy People 2010, 2000). An organization called S.T.O.P. (Safe Tables Our Priority) provides information on the *E. coli* bacteria and how safeguards can be practiced to prevent foodborne illnesses (STOP, 2001). Their Web site is located at http://www.stop-usa.org/.

Symptoms of *E. coli* bacterial infection may appear after several hours to several days. In young children, the time period is more likely to be short. In a healthy adult, symptoms may appear and be gone in about a week. In young children, this disease is far more serious and should be reported to the physician immediately if blood is noticed in the diarrhea or if the stools appear watery.

*E. coli* infection can easily be spread from one person to another in early childhood education environments and nursing homes (E. coli infection, 2001). There are specific safeguards the teacher can use to prevent the spread of the *E. coli* bacteria. These include:

- If a child has been infected with the *E. coli* bacteria, he should not be allowed back in care until he has two negative stool cultures (E. coli infection, 2001).

- All meat should be cooked to a temperature of 155°F. The juices should run clear and should not be pink.

- Always clean any surface that has had raw meat on it, including utensils, before another item touches that surface.

- Do not use the plate or tray that the raw meat was on to place the cooked meat on.

*(continues)*

## REALITY CHECK (Continued)

- Always wash hands thoroughly before and after handling meat.
- Do not serve unfiltered apple cider, unpasteurized milk, or fresh cheese curds.

- Always handle diarrhea under strict universal hygiene conditions.
- Wash all fruits and vegetables before eating or cooking (David, 2003).

**CHECK**point: Are you careful when you cook hamburger meat so that it reaches the proper temperature? Do you ever think of this when you go out to eat? What about raw apple juice: Do you drink it, and would you have served it to children before reading this information?

### Key Concept 9.4

### Food Safety

Food safety in the early childhood education environment is essential to prevent the spread of foodborne illnesses. Protecting the early childhood education environment by using safe food practices and strategies will prevent risk. The teacher can use safe, sanitary food-handling practices to better manage food preparation activities to evade bacteria and food spoilage. Using good food-purchasing behaviors helps eliminate foods that may pose risk. The teacher can avoid contamination of foods by understanding how to store foods. The teacher can offer protection from bacterial growth by cooking foods to a minimum of 160°F and checking all cooking methods to be sure they meet this temperature criterion.

## 9.5 IMPLICATIONS FOR TEACHERS

As more children in this country enter early childhood education environments, teachers should understand that they are the people who will be meeting the majority of the nutritional needs for many of these children. The teacher will need to prepare to meet those needs (Fletcher & Branen, 1999).

### *Education*

Familiarity with food programs such as CACFP will help the teacher to access available funds to provide better nutrition for children from low- and limited-income families (Bruening et al., 1999). The teacher can plan nutritious meals by using CACFP guidelines. Other programs provide nutritional training and instructional materials for the children and their parents.

Training for food safety and sanitation is essential for teachers (Kuratko et al., 2000; Briley & Roberts-Gray, 2005). Knowledge is the basis of menu planning. The teacher should know the basics of nutrition, what children's nutritional needs are, and how to use the MyPyramid Food Guidance System and the Dietary Guidelines for Americans to apply that knowledge to create menus that meet those needs. The teacher also should understand the child's developmental stages and how they affect the eating abilities and habits of children. Just as there are health consultants for child early education pro-

With all the appropriate information, the teacher can plan menus considering the child's nutritional needs and developmental level.

grams, there is a trend toward use of dieticians to provide needed information and assistance to these same programs (Padget et al., 2005). A teacher might want to consult with a dietician when doing nutritional planning.

The person in charge of menu planning should have an understanding of accessibility for healthy choices. This understanding allows access to be maximized. Any barriers should be removed. The teacher who plans menus should also do a personal checkup of practices, prejudices, and perceptions that may limit food selection.

The teacher should have knowledge of food safety practices and strategies that protect the food environment in the early childhood education setting. The teacher can prevent waste and risk to health and safety by using good food purchasing, storage, handling, and cooking measures.

**With Children.** The teacher can teach the children better nutritional practices by getting them to try new foods, eat a variety of foods, and consume more fruits and vegetables. Meeting a child's nutritional needs may take more than providing the food and the information. Information about foods is more meaningful, when the actual foods are involved (Fuhr & Barclay, 1998; Brown & Marcotte, 1999). One of the easiest ways a teacher can help to educate children to eat the foods found on the menu is to cook it with them. Having a cooking experience for new foods, culturally diverse foods, and fruits and vegetables is a good way to get children to participate in eating them (Sigman-Grant, 2005; Cason, 2001). Children are likely to eat foods that they helped to prepare. Having at least one cooking experience per week will encourage participation and variety.

Snacks are a fast meal for the children to help prepare. Some children may be able to make their own snacks. Simple items such as rice cakes and peanut butter are a way to begin. Children are capable of this from toddlerhood. More complicated dishes and meals can be made in stages. To prepare soups, for example, vegetables can be cut one day, and the rest of the ingredients prepared and cooked the next.

Another way to educate children is to take them on field trips to the market, vegetable stands, and even farms to see how and where food is grown. There are also excellent videos that provide this information if funding, time, and access prove to be constraints.

Creating opportunities for eating in different ways, like this picnic, is a good way to introduce diversity about ways to eat as well as having foods from other cultures.

There are a number of books that feature foods, many of which involve fruits and vegetables. Having those fruits and vegetables for a snack or meal the same day may encourage children to try new things.

## For Families

Education for the parent is also essential. Good menu planning is not as effective if the parents are not partners. Parents may be relying on the early childhood education environment to be the gatekeeper of their children's nutrition. Parents and teachers need to work together, instead of at cross-purposes (Briley et al., 1999). Posting menus is an easy way for parents to see what foods the child is eating at care. If parents are aware of the menu at school, they can plan to augment the nutritional needs that the early childhood education program has provided. Cooking and tasting demonstrations and videos are other choices for education of parents. When the parents are more educated, they are more willing to participate in planning and encouraging their children to try more variety and new foods.

Another form of education that the teacher may provide to the parents is how to access supplemental foods. Many families have limited or low incomes, and food selections may be limited because of cost. Helping these families access food programs in order to provide them with better food at home may have a positive effect on the early childhood education environment. Children who have well-balanced meals all the time are healthier and more ready to learn.

Information on food safety should also be provided to parents. This information may help the parent avoid foodborne illnesses and prevent the spread of infectious disease in the early childhood education environment. Modeling these food safety behaviors is a good way to educate the parents. Handouts and workshops are another way.

## Cultural Competence

A child's culture is not only the foods served; it is also the setting, what is served within a meal, and the rules that govern the meal (Brannon, 2004). Each culture has food preferences, and some of these may be based on certain food restrictions that may be religious or traditional. As mentioned in Chapter 6, Georgia State University has a Web site that is a wealth of information for different cultures and foods in the format of a pyramid. This site can be accessed at http://monarch.gsu.edu. This might be helpful in menu planning for the different cultures in care. Another helpful vehicle for understanding about other cultures in relation to foods is called The Nutrition Traveling Trunk: Exploring Cultural Differences through Food (Hollingsworth, 2003) which is available at http://www.nfsmi.org.

Cultural competence needs to be practiced in menu planning. The teacher should understand the daily and special event eating patterns of the diverse children in their care. Often the foods themselves are not different from the ones used in the early childhood education environment. However, the names, recipes, method of preparation, and condiments used may make the food appear very different (Block et al., 1995).

The teacher can ask families to share their recipes and talk to them about food. This may be a way to discover the daily and special event choices. It is also a way to determine how food is served at home and how this environment is different from care (Kaiser et al., 1999; Shankar et al., 2001). Adjustments may be made to accommodate these differences. Parents may also be involved in the planning of the menu. Another way to break any barriers to food selection is to have a potluck several times a year, so families can bring a favorite dish that represents their culture. Using their recipes for menu selections is another way to have the children try new foods and have parents feel respected. Foods from other cultures can be included and introduced at snack time, as a beginning. They can later be incorporated into breakfast or lunch.

Hispanic children and other ethnic groups may have a difficult time meeting their MyPyramid Food Guidance System guidelines for fruits and vegetables. Only 8 percent of a group studied for whether or not they met their nutritional needs in an early childhood education environment ate an adequate amount of vegetables and fruits (Padget et al., 2005). Using a variety of fruits and vegetables may help. One reason for lacking fruits and vegetables may be the access to food purchasing due to a lack of funds. The teacher may want to make sure these families get connected to some food program for resources to meet their children's needs.

## Supervision

If the early education program is involved in a food program, it is up to the designated teacher to make sure that all rules, regulations, and guidelines are met. If training or instructional materials are supplied by food programs, it is up to this person to make sure this information is used properly and dispensed to the staff, children, and parents.

Supervision plays a key role in menu planning and food safety. Being able to make sure that these items are handled correctly and are properly supported is important. If the teacher is also the menu planner, this offers checking and balance to the processes. Using the checklists for menu planning and food safety can ensure these processes are carried out properly.

It is up to the teacher to supervise the children's reaction to the menu and observe whether they are eating what was prepared. This supervision may lead to more frequent review and revision. It is important that the guidelines and nutritional needs of the children are being met.

## Key Concept 9.5

### Implications for Teachers

The teacher needs to meet the nutritional and developmental needs of the child. Using guidelines and information from supplemental food programs may help. The teacher needs to be educated in how to apply this knowledge to menu planning and breaking down any barriers that may prevent healthy food choices. Education also helps the teacher to plan for safe food practices. Educating children through cooking and other methods can help them eat a greater variety of foods and try new foods. Families can learn more about nutrition and better food selection at home. Cultural sensitivity provides information as well as help to remove barriers to both food selection and trying new foods. Supervision provides the method to ensure that proper menu planning and food safety are carried out.

## CHAPTER SUMMARY

More than 5 million children are eating meals in early childhood education environments on a daily basis. Nutrition and food safety have been found to be inadequate in many early education programs. It is up to the teacher who plans, and/or prepares meals to be adequately trained or work with a dietician for help. There are a number of nutritional programs that offer assistance in early childhood education environments by providing funding or educational information.

The teacher should know how to select healthy foods, plan adequate menus, and prepare food that is safe. Understanding the importance of breakfast, snacks, and lunch helps the teacher to plan more carefully to meet the needs of the children present. Protecting the early childhood education environment by using safe food practices and strategies will prevent risk.

The teacher can use education, cultural sensitivity, observation, supervision, and work with families to ensure that the early childhood education environment is providing for the nutritional needs of the children present.

## TO GO BEYOND

In this section you will find a number of activities that you can use to apply and improve your knowledge of this chapter. There are also thorough online resources that accompany this text that can be found at http://www.early childed.delmar.com (see description at end of this chapter).

## Chapter Review Critical Thinking Applications

1. Discuss the importance of menu planning in the early childhood education environment. What are the components that a teacher must consider when planning a menu? How might these affect menu planning?

2. Examine the ways a teacher could connect to resources for help with nutrition and menu planning.

3. Discuss the CACFP program. How can it help an early childhood education environment provide better food and nutrition to children?

4. Examine how a best practice checklist might help all area of keeping quality standards for nutrition.

## As an Individual

1. Observe children eating at a fast food restaurant. How much food do they appear to be eating? What types of food do they appear to favor? Record your observations and bring to class to share with other students.

2. What food safety and storage practices have you observed in a fast food or other type of restaurant? What types of these practices have you observed in the home? If you have observed these practices in an early childhood education facility, list them also. Compare the three. How might these practices be improved?

3. Watch parents and children in a checkout line of a supermarket for at least one-half hour. What types of food are they buying? Record your findings and be able to discuss what you found in class.

## As a Group

1. In small groups, plan one week's menu for an early childhood education center. Be sure it is balanced nutritionally and culturally representative of your local area. Compare it to the menus of other groups. Have the menus duplicated and distributed to the class. Evaluate the menus.

2. Divide up into groups and have each group go to two or three fast food restaurants to obtain nutritional information. Create a scale that includes (1) how easy the information was to obtain; (2) whether lighter foods were offered?; and (3) what "hook" was used to influence children? Rate the restaurants using this scale.

3. How would you help a child select better menu items for nutrition at (1) a fast food restaurant; (2) an early childhood education center; (3) a school lunch program; and (4) home?

4. Survey the community for information about food programs that offer help to early childhood education programs. Compile the information and distribute it to the class.

## Case Studies

1. You are a teacher in a large early childhood education program. You have noticed some unsanitary practices occurring both in the

kitchen and in the serving of food. The teacher in charge also happens to be the director's best friend. What steps should you take to ensure better sanitation and safety for your early childhood education environment?

2. The director at the early childhood education program that you work at has realized that the center has been repeating the same menus for a long time. She would like the six teachers at the center to work on putting together a menu that could change frequently. She asks each teacher to prepare a week's menu that includes snacks, breakfasts, and lunches. She also asks that you consider the cultural groups that are represented in your care. These include children of Hispanic, Asian, Southeast Asian, Caribbean-African, and European extraction. Plan a week's menu based on this information.

## Chapter References

American Academy of Pediatrics (AAP). (1998). *Pediatric Nutrition Handbook.* Elk Grove Village, IL: American Academy of Pediatrics Committee on Nutrition.

American Academy of Pediatrics Policy Statement (AAP). (2001). The use and misuse of fruit juice in pediatrics. *Pediatrics, 107*(5), 1210–1213.

Aumann, M., Briggs, M., Collett, M., Corrigan, K., & Hart, P. (1999). Cuisine for kids: A nutrition and culinary course for child nutrition program staff. *Journal of Nutrition Education, 31*(1), 119B.

Block, G., Norris, J., Mandel, R., & Disogra, C. (1995). Sources of energy and six nutrients in diets of low-income Hispanic-American women and their children: Quantitative data from HHANES, 1982–1984. *Journal of the American Dietetic Association, 95*(2),195–208

Brannon, C. (2004, November). Cultural competency: Values, tradition and effective practice. *Today's Dietician,* 14–21.

Briley, M., Jastrow, S., Vickers, J., & Roberts-Gray, C. (1999). Can ready to eat cereal solve common nutritional problems in child care menus? *Journal of the American Dietetic Association, 99*(2), 341–342.

Briley, M., McBride, A., & Roberts-Gray, C. (1997). Banking on nutrition. *Texas Child Care, 21*(3), 2–5.

Briley, M., & Roberts-Gray, C. (1999). Nutrition standards for child care programs—Position of ADA. *Journal of American Dietetic Association, 99*(6), 981–988.

Briley, M., & Roberts-Gray, C. (2005). Position of The American Dietetic Association: Benchmarks for nutrition programs in child care settings. *Journal of The American Dietetic Association, 105*(6), 979–986.

Brown, J., & Marcotte, L. (1999, January/February). Nutrition and cognitive development in children. *Early Childhood News,* 13–17.

Cason, K. (2001). Evaluation of a preschool nutrition education program based on the theory of multiple intelligences. *Journal of Nutrition Education, 33*(2), 161–164.

Cooper, J. (1995). Like your burgers on the raw side? E. coli may give you a raw deal: Death. *The Medical Reporter, 1*(1). Retrieved October 26, 2005, from http://medicalreporter.health.org/tmr0495/tmr0495.html.

David, P. (2003). Stomach virus or food borne illness? *Healthy Child Care, 6*(3). Retrieved October 26, 2005, from http://www.healthychild.net/articles/na33virus.html

E. coli: Preventing a common type of food poisoning. (2001, January 16). Retrieved October 26, 2005, from http://www.mayoclinic.com/invoke.cfm?objectid=BDB021C8-95E8-46AD-BF44C4C204478DE

E. coli infection. (2000, April). American Academy of Family Physicians. Retrieved October 26, 2005, from http://familydoctor.org/handouts/242.html.

Evans, E. (1995, January 17). U.S. moves to update meat inspect tests two years after fatal E. coli outbreak. *San Diego Union-Tribune,* C-3.

Evers, C. (1999, February/March). Food moods. *Healthy Kids,* 75–82.

Federal Register. (2004). Center for Nutrition Policy and Promotion; notice of proposal for food guide graphic presentation and consumer education materials; opportunity for public comment. *Federal Register, 69*(133), 42030–42033.

Food and Nutrition Service (FNS). (2001). *School meals.* U.S. Department of Agriculture. Retrieved October 26, 2005, from http://www.fns.usda.gov/cnd/.

Food and Nutrition Services Online (FSNO). (2004). Facts about the . . . Child and Adult Care Food Program. Retrieved October 26, 2005, from http://www.fns.usda.gov/cnd/Care/CACFP/cacfpfaqs.htm

Fox, M., Glanz, F., Endahl, J., & Wilde, J. (1997). *Early childhood and care study.* Alexandria, VA: U.S. Department of Agriculture.

Fuhr, J., & Barclay, K. (1998). The importance of appropriate nutrition and nutrition education. *Young Children, 53*(1), 74–80.

Hayden, J. (2002, May). Nutrition and child development: Global perspectives. *Child Care Information Exchange,* 38–41.

Healthy People 2010. (2000). Healthy People 2010—Summary of objectives: Food safety. Retrieved October 26, 2005, from http://web.health.gov/healthypeople/Document/HTML/Volume1/10Food.htm.

Held, T., & Griffin, K. (2000, July 26). E. coli sickens children, one critically. *Milwaukee Journal Sentinel.* Retrieved October 26, 2005, from http://www.jsonline.com/alive/family/jul00/coli26s1072500.asp.

Hollingsworth, M. (2003). *Nutrition traveling trunk: Exploring cultural differences through food.* University, MS: National Food Service Management Institute.

Kaiser, L., Martinez, N., Harwood, J., & Garcia, L. (1999). Child feeding strategies in low-income Latino households: Focus group observations. *Journal of the American Dietetic Association, 99*(5), 601–603.

Kunitz, J. (2003). Keeping the kitchen clean. *Child Care Health Connections Newsletter, 16*(6), 3.

Kuratko, C., Martin, R., Lan, W., Chappell, J., & Ahmad, M. (2000). Menu planning, food consumption and sanitation practices in day care facilities. *Family and Consumer Sciences Research Journal, 29*(1), 81–91.

McConahy, K., Smickilas-Wright, H., Mitchell, D., & Picciano, M. (2004). Portion size of common foods predicts energy intake among preschool-aged children. *Journal of the American Dietetic Association, 104*(6), 975–979.

Messina, V., & Mangels, A. (2001). Considerations in planning vegan diets: Children. *Journal of the American Dietetic Association, 101*(6), 661–669.

Mohle-Boetani, J., Farrar, J., Werner, S., Minassian, S., Bryant, R., Abbott, S., Slutsker, L., & Vugia, D. (2001). Escherichia coli 0157 and Salmonella infections associated with sprouts in California, 1996–1998. *Annals of Internal Medicine, 135*(4), 239–247.

Morbidity and Mortality Weekly Report (MMWR). (2004, April 16). Preliminary Food Net data on the incidence of infection with pathogens transmitted commonly through food—Selected sites, United States, 2003. *Morbidity and Mortality Weekly Report, 53*(16), 338–343. Retrieved October 26, 2005, from http://www.cdc.gov/mmwr/preview/mmwrhtml/mm5316a2.htm

Nicklas, T. (2001). Consider nutrition when choosing day care. *Nutrition and Your Child, 2,* 1, 3.

Nicklas, T., Elkasabany, A., Srinivasen, S., & Berenson, G. (2001). Trends in nutrient intake of children in the past two decades. *American Journal of Epidemiology, 153*(5), 969–977.

Nicklas, T., & Johnson, R. (2004). Position of the American Dietetic Association: Dietary guide for healthy children ages 2 to 11 years. *Journal of the American Dietetic Association, 104*(4), 660–677.

Nicklas, T., O'Neil, C., & Myers, L. (2004). The importance of breakfast consumption to nutrition of children, adolescents and young adults. *Nutrition Today, 39*(1), 30–39.

Oakley, C., & Carr, D. (2003a). *Steps to nutrition success checklist: Child care centers best practices for quality nutrition.* University, MS: National Food Service Management Institute.

Oakley, C., & Carr, D. (2003b). *Steps to nutrition success checklist: Family care homes best practices for quality nutrition.* University, MS: National Food Service Management Institute.

Padget, A., Briley, M., Gillham, M., Peterson, F., & Willis, R. (2005). Dietary intakes at childcare centers in Central Texas fail to meet Food Guide Pyramid recommendations. *Journal of The American Dietetic Association, 105*(5), 790–793.

Report on Preschool Programs (RPP). (2004). More centers, but fewer homes gain access to CACFP services. *Report on Preschool Programs, 36*(9), 69.

Safe Tables Our Priority (STOP). (2001). Why are people still dying from contaminated food? Retrieved October 17, 2005 from http://www.safetables.org/pdf/STOP_Report.pdf.

Shankar, A., Gittelsohn, J., Stallings, R., West, K., Gynwali, T., Dhungel, C., & Dahal, B. (2001). Comparison of visual estimates of children's portion sizes under both shared-plan and individual-plate conditions. *Journal of the American Dietetic Association, 101*(1), 47–52.

Sigman-Grant, M. (2005). Snack time and food memories. *Healthy Child Care 8*(1). Retrieved October 26, 2005, from http://www.healthychild.net/articles/na43snacks.html

Skinner, J., & Carruth, B. (2001). A longitudinal study of children's juice intake and growth: The juice controversy revisited. *Journal of the American Dietetic Association, 101*(4), 432–437.

Skinner, J., Carruth, B., Moran, J. III, Houck, K., Schmidhammer, J., Reed, A., Coletta, F., Cotter, R., & Ott, D. (1998). Toddlers' food preferences: Concordance with family members' preferences. *Journal of Nutrition Education, 30*(1), 17–22.

Spark, A., Pfau, J., Nicklas, T., & Williams, C. (1998). Reducing fat in preschool meals: Description of the foodservice intervention component of Health Start. *Journal of Nutrition Education, 30*(2), 170–177.

Stang, J., & Beyerl, C. (2003). Position of the American Dietetic Association: Child and adolescent food and nutrition programs. *Journal of the American Dietetic Association, 103*(4), 887–893.

Tate, M., & Patrick, S. (2000). Healthy People 2010 targets healthy diet and healthy weight as critical goals. *Journal of the American Dietetic Association, 100*(3), 300.

U.S. Department of Agriculture (USDA). *Escherichia coli O157:H7.* October 26, 2005, from http://www.cdc.gov/ncidod/dbmd/diseaseinfo/escherichiacoli_g.htm.

Wohlleb, K. (2004). Hardin county students gobble up 'handy' meals. Kentucky School Boards Association. Retrieved October 26, 2005, from http://www.ksba.org/KSA1003HardinCo.htm

Additional resources for this chapter can be found by visiting the Online Companion™ at http://www.earlychilded.delmar.com. This supplemental material includes extensive chapter quizzes, PowerPoint® outlines, Web links, and various other activities to help better utilize the material in this chapter. The site is updated regularly, so you may check back often to receive the latest information about the subjects in each chapter.

## NUTRITION CURRICULUM SUPPLEMENT

Sample lesson plans and topic maps for subjects that concern nutrition and food safety are provided in the next few pages for the teacher to help reinforce the information that is being modeled by teachers and learned by the children in the early education environment. In addition to the sample curriculum, there is a list of children's books and sources for further information. Some of this information may include songs or finger plays. This sample group is presented to help the teacher design his or her own curriculum by adding to the information provided.

**LESSON**plan
CHAPTER **9**

### LESSON PLAN 1

**Unit:** Nutrition

**Suggested Themes:** MyPyramid Food Guidance System, Fruits and Vegetables, Milk and Milk Products, Strong Bones and Teeth, How Food Helps Us Grow, Where Do Foods Come From, and Breads and Grains.

**Theme:** Grains.

**Objectives:** Children will understand how breads and grains fit into the MyPyramid Food Guidance System and how they help them grow and have energy. They will be able to identify foods that fit into this category.

**Materials:** Examples of fresh bread, bagels, rice, cereals, pasta and other grains or a poster of the MyPyramid. Magazine pictures of grains including numerous breads and grains. An empty poster board, and glue or paste.

**Lesson:** Read the book *Bread, Bread, Bread*. Have children name all the different kinds of breads they can think of. Talk about how bread helps children grow and have energy. Show children examples of other foods that fit into the breads and grains categories. Have them select and cut out pictures of this category from magazine pictures of foods. Using glue sticks, have all children glue their pictures of these foods on a large poster board, creating a collage of breads and grains.

**Follow-Up:** Snack and lunch items will feature bread and cereal group foods such as cereal, spaghetti, tortillas, pancakes, and rice cakes. Read the book *On Top of Spaghetti, Pancakes for Breakfast,* or *Strega Nona.* If children bring their lunches, have all children participate in identifying the bread or grain food group items.

**Age-Appropriate:** Preschool-age children will be able to identify these foods.

**LESSON**plan
CHAPTER **9**

### LESSON PLAN 2

**Unit:** Nutrition

**Suggested Themes:** Junk Foods, Television Ads Influence Food Choices. Learning to Feed Ourselves (for Toddlers), and Exercise Our Bodies.

**Themes:** Exercise Our Bodies.

**Objectives:** Children will understand how exercise makes their bodies strong and healthy.

***Materials:*** A flannelboard and flannel cutouts. An exercise video. Balls, trikes, and a whistle.

***Lesson:*** Explain the importance of exercise to children. Have them give examples of what they think is exercise, clarifying as you go. Tell a flannelboard story about a little boy who didn't exercise and how it made him unhealthy and how he felt after he started exercising. Put on an exercise video and have everyone participate. Take a walk and walk at different speeds from slow to fast. Read the book *Willie Takes a Hike.*

***Follow-Up:*** Plan some organized exercises for the rest of the week. Include foot races and trike races; play Red Light, Green Light, and Simon Says. Use exercise video for kids again. Read books like *Too Much Junk Food, Too Much T.V.,* and *I Went Walking,* and discuss how these might affect children and their exercise effort and time.

***Age-Appropriate:*** Preschoolers will enjoy using their energies in this lesson.

LESSON*plan*
CHAPTER **9**

### LESSON PLAN **3**

***Unit:*** Nutrition

***Suggested Themes:*** Breakfast Starts My Day, Lunch Helps Me Grow, Snacks are Important, and Good Fast Food Selections.

***Theme:*** Lunch Helps Me Grow.

***Objectives:*** Children will learn how to make good selections for lunch box meals.

***Materials:*** Labels from typical convenience foods such as Lunchables and snack items often packed in lunches. Lunch snacks, breads, condiments, meats, cheese, peanut butter and jelly, chips, veggies, juices, sodas, junk food selections. Magazine pictures of foods, paper, scissors, and glue or paste.

***Lesson:*** Show children labels from typical lunch and snack foods. Help them learn how to look at the labels to see what is healthy and what is not. Talk about good selections for a lunch box. Read *Lunch Boxes.* Have children discuss how many different items from different cultures are healthy lunch selections. Have children practice good selections by choosing lunch items from magazine pictures and pasting them on paper. Have children select their own lunch items and make their own lunches. Talk about their selections, and help them make better choices, if necessary.

***Follow-Up:*** Send home a handout of good lunch box selections and those foods you do not want to see in the early childhood education environment (such as candy and soda). Read *What's on My Plate?, Lunch,* and *Gregory, the Terrible Eater.* During lunch time for the rest of the week, read labels from children's lunch box selections. Have children discuss their food choices.

***Age-Appropriate:*** Preschoolers and school-aged children are most likely to be receptive to this information.

LESSON*plan*
CHAPTER **9**

LESSON PLAN **4**

*Unit:* Nutrition

*Suggested Themes:* Healthy Foods, Food Groups, Cooking Healthy Food, Making Good Choices with Food.

*Theme:* Food Groups from MyPyramid.

*Objectives:* Children will learn about each food group and good healthy choices with each food group.

*Materials:* Flannelboard with pictures of each of the food groups found on MyPyramid Food Guidance System, plastic food from each food group for the children to sort the food. Magazines and scissors to make a collage of each food group. Present sliced apples and crackers and milk for a healthy snack.

*Lesson:* Flannelboard will display the five food groups to be used as a discussion topic. Each food group and what foods are healthy will be talked about, and the children will give examples as to what they think is healthy. Children can cut pictures of foods from different magazines to make a collage sorting by groups. At snack time, the children can have the healthy snack in the materials provided above. During the snack, the teacher can talk about the snack and MyPyramid Food Guidance System.

*Follow-Up:* Provide books and magazines that talk about the different food groups such as *Good Enough to Eat: A Kids Guide to Food and Nutrition, Eat Healthy, Feel Great, Alphabite! A Funny Feast from A to Z* and *The Very Hungry Caterpillar*. A letter will be sent to the parents explaining the theme and ask them to donate magazines or books about nutrition. If there is a computer in the environment, find the MyPyramid site and show children the interactive site by groups. This is more likely to be a one-on-one or one-on-two activity. Parents will be sent home handouts and a newsletter with good nutrition information including the URL for the MyPyramid Web site.

*Age-Appropriate:* Preschool and kindergarten children will be able to group the foods.

**LESSON**plan
CHAPTER 9

**LESSON PLAN 5**

*Unit:* Nutrition

*Suggested Themes:* Taking Care of our Teeth, What Food Labels Mean, How Our Bodies Grow, Why We Drink Water, What Vegetables Do.

*Theme:* Taking Care of Our Teeth.

*Objectives:* Children will understand what teeth are important for, how to take care of them, what happens at the dentist's office.

*Materials:* Toothbrushes (one for each child), play and sing along to the song *"Brush Your Teeth"* by Raffi. Small mirrors, magazine pictures of good and bad food for teeth, scissors, glue sticks, paper. A small chicken bone, a clear cup large enough to completely hold the bone and a can of a cola soft drink.

*Lesson:* Talk about teeth, how important they are to keep healthy. Place chicken bone into cup, completely cover with soft drink. Allow to sit for a few days. Observe changes and discuss the changes to the bone due to the sugars in the soda and the discoloration and how it would be similar for teeth. Explain proper ways and how often to brush teeth. Do activity with children sitting in a circle, brushing teeth with water. Pass mirrors around the circle so the children can look inside their mouth while brushing. Sing song, and read one of the books. Have a discussion about foods that are good for your teeth, and the ones that are not. For art, let children cut out magazine pictures of good foods for teeth, and paste on paper.

*Follow-Up:* During the rest of the week, have children brush teeth after lunch. Make "Fruit Faces" by having the children spread cream cheese or peanut butter on toast or a rice cake then add pre-cut fruit shapes to make faces; pineapple, orange, strawberry, grapes. You could also use vegetables such as carrots and celery. Talk about how fruit and vegetables help our teeth stay strong. Talk about how sugars don't help our teeth and look at the discoloration on the bone and discuss it. Send home information sheet about teeth, and what was discussed in class. Sing the song several times during week, and read *Going to the Dentist, The Crocodile and the Dentist, Your Teeth, Critter Goes to the Dentist,* and *How Many Teeth?* Have some dentist props such as a white coat, small mirror, masks for mouth, napkins for patients chest. Put them in the dramatic play area, and let the children be creative. Place dolls and tooth brushes in dramatic play area, also to re-inforce lesson.

*Age-Appropriate:* Preschool-age children will be able to brush their teeth.

LESSON*plan*
CHAPTER 9

LESSON PLAN **6**

*Unit:* Nutrition

*Suggested Themes:* Strong Bones and Teeth, Dairy Products, Where Do Foods Come From, Vitamins and Minerals.

*Theme:* Dairy Products.

*Objectives:* The objective for this is for children to learn what dairy products are and what they do for their bodies. They will be able to identify those products that fit into this category.

*Materials:* Have books out that have to do with dairy products and where they come from. Many "pretend" plastic foods that represent dairy products in the house area that they could interact with and familiarize themselves with. Have pictures of cows, dairies, and foods that come from them. Paper, scissors.

*Lesson:* Field trip to a dairy or a supermarket. Video about cows and dairies might supplement this or substitute if field trips are unlikely. Read *Milk: From Cow to Carton*. The process of getting milk from a cow should be discussed so children have an understanding how it occurs. Snack would come from dairy group. Children could draw pictures of their favorite dairy food or cut out a picture of a cow and surround it with products that come from it.

*Follow-Up:* Play a reminder game about dairy products with plastic foods from dramatic play area and ask, "What is your favorite dairy product?" Read *Milk to Ice Cream, Big Cheese for The White House: The True Tale of Tremendous Cheddar, Milk Makers,* and *Two Cool Cows.* Feature dairy products in meals and snacks and discuss them each time they appear. One day make pudding from scratch and have them watch milk turn into pudding. Making butter or ice cream would work too. Talk about how dairy products help build strong bones and teeth. Put down a piece of butcher paper and have child lay down and help draw an outline of the child. Have the child "put" in bones where they think they go.

*Age-Appropriate:* Children aged three to five years and older can identify dairy foods, and older children can understand the process more.

Topic Map for Food Groups from MyPyramid

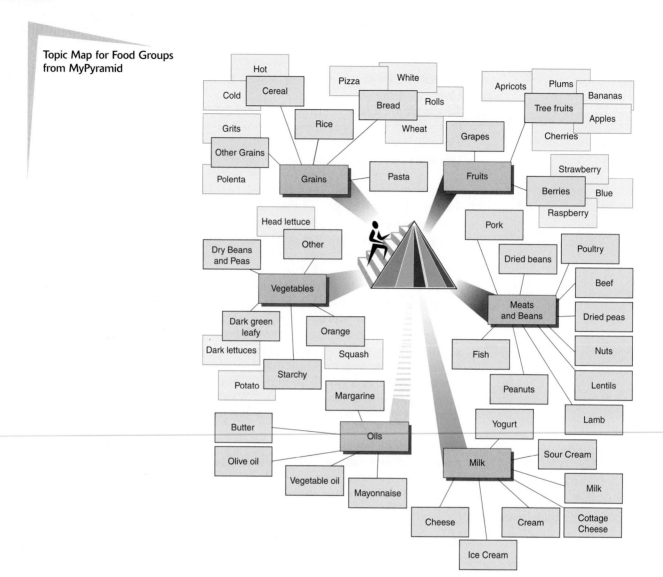

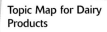

Topic Map for Dairy Products

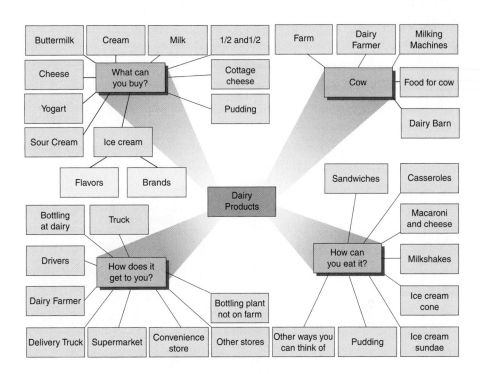

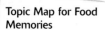

Topic Map for Food Memories

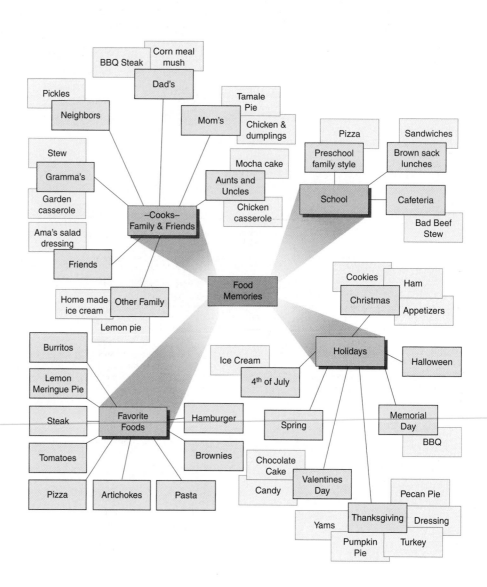

## Children's Books on Nutrition Subjects

Barrett, J., & Nelson, M. (2000). *Food (Elmo's World)*. New York: Random House (Merchandising). Elmo learns that food helps him to grow big and strong.

Berenstain, S., & Berenstain, J. (1985). *Too Much Junk Food*. New York: Random House.

Berenstain, S., & Berenstain, J. (1984). *Too Much T.V.* New York: Random House.

Brown, M. (1986). *Stone Soup*. New York: Macmillan.

Canizares, S., & Chanko, P. (1998). *Water*. New York: Scholastic. Describes liquid, solid, and frozen forms of water.

Canizares, S., & Chessen, B. (1999). *In the Kitchen*. New York: Scholastic. Exploring what happens in the kitchen.

Carle, E. (1987). *The Very Hungry Caterpillar*. New York: Philomel Books.

Chanko, P., & Berger, S. (1999). *Markets*. New York: Scholastic. Exploring things that can be found in markets.

Coplans, P. (1993). *Spaghetti for Suzy*. New York: Houghton Mifflin.

Dahl, M., Farm, S., Kesselring, S., & Ouren, T. (2004). *From the Garden: A Counting Book About Growing Food (Know Your Numbers)*. Minneapolis, MN: Picture Window Books.

dePaola, T. (1989). *Tony's Bread*. New York: Putnam.

dePaola, T. (1988). *Strega Nona*. New York: Simon & Schuster.

dePaola, T. (1978). *Pancakes for Breakfast*. San Diego: Harcourt Brace Jovanovich.

Eagan, R. (1997). *From Wheat to Pasta*. New York: Children's Press.

Ehlert, L. (1989). *Eating the Alphabet from A to Z*. San Diego: Harcourt Brace Jovanovich. Fruits and vegetables from A to Z.

Ehlert, L. (1987). *Growing Vegetable Soup*. San Diego: Harcourt Brace Jovanovich.

Erlich, F. (1991). *Lunch Boxes*. New York: Puffin Books.

Feldman, H. (2000). *My Breakfast: A Book About a Great Morning Meal*. New York: PowerKids Press.

Fleming, D. (1992). *Lunch*. New York: Holt.

Fowler, A. (1995). *Corn On and Off the Cob*. Chicago: Children's Press.

French, V. (1995). *Oliver's Vegetables*. New York: Orchard Books. A boy learns about fresh vegetables in the garden.

Glazer, T. (1995). *On Top of Spaghetti*. Chicago: Good Year Books.

Golden, B. (2001). *A Mountain of Blintzes*. San Diego: Gulliver Books.

Gomi, T. (1991). *Who Ate It?* Brookfield, CT: Millbrook Press.

Gross, R. (1990). *What's on My Plate?* New York: Macmillan.

Haduch, B. (2001). *Food Rules!* New York: Puffin Books.

Hoban, R. (1964). *Bread and Jam for Frances*. New York: Harper and Row.

Julius, J. (2001). *I Like Berries*. New York: Children's Press.

Julius, J. (2001). *I Like Cereal*. New York: Children's Press.

Julius, J. (2001). *I Like Juice*. New York: Children's Press.

Julius, J. (2001). *I Like Potatoes*. New York: Children's Press.

Kottke, J. (2000). *From Seed to Pumpkin (Welcome Books)*. Connecticut: Children's Press.

Krauss, R. (1944). *The Carrot Seed*. New York: Harper and Row.

Kubler, A., & Formby, C. (1995). *Come Eat with Us*. Swindon, England: Child's Play. Multicultural foods and eating methods.

Landau, E. (1999). *A True Book of Apples*. New York: Children's Press.

Landau, E. (2000). *A True Book of Tomatoes*. New York: Children's Press.

Levenson, G., & Thaler, S. (2002). *Pumpkin Circle: The Story of a Garden*. Berkeley, CA: Tricycle Press.

Lord, J. (1987). *The Giant Jam Sandwich*. Boston: Houghton Mifflin.

Lottridge, C. (1986). *One Watermelon Seed*. London: Oxford University Press.

McCloskey, R. (1976). *Blueberries for Sal*. New York: Penguin.

Morris, A. (1989). *Bread, Bread, Bread*. New York: William Morrow.

Morris, J. (1999). *More Cheese, Please: A Book About Trying New Foods*. Pleasantville, NY: Reader's Digest Association.

Napoli, D., & Tchen, R. (2001). *How Hungry Are You?* New York: Simon & Schuster. Two friends try to plan a picnic.

Nechaev, M. (1998). *Apron Annie's Pies.* Cypress, CA: Creative Teaching Press.

Numeroff, L. (1985). *If You Give a Mouse a Cookie.* New York: HarperCollins.

Oda, M. (1984). *Happy Veggies.* Boston: Houghton Mifflin.

Passen, L. (1991). *Fat, Fat Rose Marie.* New York: Holt.

Preiss, L. (1990). *The Pig's Alphabet.* Boston: David R. Goding.

Pruemin, M. (1994). *How to Make an Apple Pie and See the World.* New York: Alfred Knopf.

Rand, G. (1996). *Willie Takes a Hike.* San Diego: Harcourt Brace Jovanovich.

Schwartz, D. (1998). *Plant Fruits and Seeds.* Cypress, CA: Creative Teaching Press.

Seuss, Dr. (1960). *Green Eggs and Ham.* New York: Random House.

Sharmat, M. (1987). *Gregory, the Terrible Eater.* New York: Macmillan.

Sinykin, S. C. (1990). *Come Out, Come Out, Wherever You Are.* Hazeldon, MN: Hazeldon Educational Materials. Story about an overweight girl and her changing perception of herself.

Smalls-Hector, I. (1992). *Apple Picking Time.* New York: Crown Publishing. American tradition of picking apples.

Smith, N. (2002). *Allie the Allergic Elephant: A Children's Story of Peanut Allergies.* San Francisco: Jungle Communications Inc.

Snyder, I. (2003). *Beans to Chocolate (Welcome Books: How Things Are Made).* Connecticut: Children's Press.

Snyder, I. (2003). *Milk to Ice Cream (Welcome Books: How Things Are Made).* Connecticut: Children's Press.

Snyder, I. (2003). *Tomatoes to Ketchup (Welcome Books: How Things Are Made).* Connecticut: Children's Press.

Stevens, J. (1995). *Tops and Bottoms.* San Diego: Harcourt Brace and Co. Bear and Hare learn about plants that grow on top of the ground and under the ground.

Willems, M. (2004). *The Pigeon Finds a Hot Dog!* New York: Hyperion.

Williams, B. (1978). *Jeremy Isn't Hungry.* New York: Penguin Books. Older brother tries to feed Jeremy, but he wants to feed himself.

Williams, R. (1996). *Oranges for Orange Juice.* Cypress, CA: Creative Teaching Press.

Williams, S. (1989). *I Went Walking.* San Diego: Harcourt Brace Jovanovich.

Wood, D., & Wood, A. (1984). *The Little Mouse, The Red Ripe Strawberry, and the Big Hungry Bear.* Swindon, England: Child's Play.

# SECTION IV
# Health in Early Childhood Education Environments

This section discusses four areas that deal with health:

In order to properly cover these expansive topics we will relate them to basic health policies that work well in early childhood education environments: These policies connect health promotion and risk management tools to each chapter's focus.

## CHAPTER 10

# Promoting Good Health for Quality Early Childhood Education Environments

**After reading this chapter, you should be able to:**

### 10.1 Health Policies

Define and discuss health policies and their use as a tool for health prevention, protection, and promotion.

### 10.2 Children's Health Records

Discuss the contents and importance of health records, including up-to-date immunizations.

### 10.3 Staff Health

Discuss the importance of health policies for staff, including staff health records and promoting staff health.

### 10.4 Providing a Mentally Healthy Environment

Indicate the importance that stable, responsive, and consistent caregiving has on providing a child with an optimum environment for good mental health.

### 10.5 Implications for Teachers

Discuss the importance of parent and child education, role modeling positive health actions, and supervision for providing optimum health.

## 10.1 HEALTH POLICIES

● **Health policies**
*framework for ensuring health and well-being in early childhood education settings*

**Health policies** help the teacher manage risks to good physical and mental health that might be found in the early childhood education environment. These policies provide the framework for providing protection and prevention. A teacher who has health policies can improve the care of children. The following information indicates the need for improving the care of children:

- The overall quality of early childhood education programs is not good (Greenspan, 2003; Ghazavini & Mullis, 2002).

- Children of poor or low-income families are more likely to experience substandard care (Loeb et al., 2004; Guendelman & Pearl, 2001).

- At least one in every five children has not received one or more of the vaccinations to prevent childhood diseases and this can lead to epidemic levels of illness (Santoli et al., 2004). The national goal is for 90 percent of children to be immunized. It is important that an early childhood education environment have a policy for children present who are not immunized (Salmon et al., 2005).

- Rates of illness for children in early childhood education environments were higher than rates of illness for children at home for the first two years of life (Silverstein et al., 2003).

- As many as 4 out of 10 preschoolers exhibit one or more problem behaviors, and approximately 1 in 10 children are at risk for their mental health (Collins et al., 2003).

- Teachers often overlook their own health needs while taking care of children in early childhood education environments (Hamre & Pianta, 2004).

Keeping the early childhood education environment healthy takes the cooperation of everyone, including the people who help keep it clean.

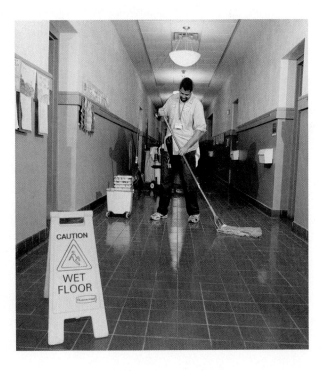

## *Designing a Health Policy*

Health policies should be developed and directed toward the children and staff. They should promote healthy practices for the child, the teacher, and the family. Basic health policies lay the foundation for the atmosphere of the early childhood education environment.

Teachers need to take responsibility for providing the healthiest environment possible in the early childhood education setting. Teachers also need to provide examples of healthy practices and illness prevention strategies and model them for children and their families.

The first part of the process for designing a health policy is to understand the health risks present in the early childhood education environment. Common infectious diseases, healthy practices for sanitation, and records for health for both children and providers are good beginning points. As the environment is examined for the risks to health, needed policies should be listed.

When the policies listed are created, they should be clearly written and include guidelines, limitations, and suggested methods of communication for each topic. Health policies help the teacher develop proper practices based on the knowledge of health promotion, protection, and disease prevention.

Health policies should incorporate the six major goals of high-quality child care (Figure 10-1):

- maximizing health status
- minimizing risk
- using education as a tool
- recognizing the importance of guidelines
- practicing cultural competence
- developing partnerships with families to provide a caring community

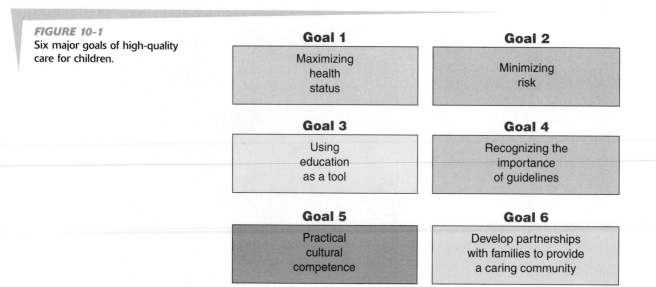

**FIGURE 10-1**
Six major goals of high-quality care for children.

**Goal 1**
Maximizing health status

**Goal 2**
Minimizing risk

**Goal 3**
Using education as a tool

**Goal 4**
Recognizing the importance of guidelines

**Goal 5**
Practical cultural competence

**Goal 6**
Develop partnerships with families to provide a caring community

Basic health policies for promoting good health should cover:

1. *Health Records:* specific records for the child to be accepted and stay in care
2. *Staff Health:* using staff health and health records to promote health and protect the environment
3. *Protective and Preventive Practices for a Mentally Healthy Environment:* specific practices for creating a proactive and interventive environment for good mental health
4. *Implications for Teachers:* strategies and practices for health education, cultural sensitivity, role modeling, working with families, and supervision in early childhood education environments.

### *Key Concept 10.1*

#### Health Policies

Basic health policies should be designed to provide protection, prevention, and promotion of good health in early childhood education environments. These policies should include guidelines, records, and checklists. The health policy should define what is to be done and then outline the process for doing it. It should also define who is responsible and provide for follow-through. When time parameters are critical, the health policy should address them. Good health policies should address the basics of children's health records, staff health, providing a mentally healthy environment, and implications for teachers that provide for education, role modeling, cultural sensitivity, and supervision.

## 10.2  CHILDREN'S HEALTH RECORDS

Increased risk for poor health and mental health is often associated with group care (Ahnert & Lamb, 2003). To help reduce this risk, teachers should create a health policy for children's health records that covers certain basic information regarding each child's health and should include guidelines for all children. The contents of each child's preadmission health history form are listed in Table 10-1. Table 10-2 lists the records that are kept for all children.

 **Orientation**
*meeting or discussion of a child new to care regarding health, special needs, and developmental history*

Guidelines for this health policy should include an **orientation** with the teacher for each child. Good-quality teachers are more likely to ask detailed questions about a child's health. This may determine whether the early childhood education environment is a good match for the child and vice versa (Los Angeles County Child Care Directory, 2001). This orientation would cover the special developmental needs of the child, dietary restrictions, and any special health or nutritional needs. Teachers should have a developmental health history in order to know the child and provide for a holistic approach to care.

**TABLE 10-1**
*Checklist for Child's Health History*

### ✓ CHECK FOR:

- ☐ Name, address, and phone number
- ☐ Physician's name, address, and phone number
- ☐ Emergency numbers (two minimum)
- ☐ State of child's health
- ☐ Record of immunizations
- ☐ Dietary restrictions
- ☐ Allergies and other conditions that may require medication
- ☐ Any condition that requires special consideration for care
- ☐ Any special problems or fears
- ☐ TB test for children older than one year of age
- ☐ Any previous major illness or injury
- ☐ An emergency release form signed by the parent
- ☐ Any emergency instructions from family
- ☐ Any current medications the child is taking
- ☐ Child's health insurance information
- ☐ Duplicate emergency form for field trips
- ☐ Authorization to release child to people other than custodial parent

**TABLE 10-2**
*Records to Keep for Each Child*

### ✓ CHECK FOR:

- ☐ Health history and preadmission exam form
- ☐ Up-to-date immunization records
- ☐ Injury reports
- ☐ Assessment and screening results
- ☐ Medication log and permission slips, where applicable. Some states do not allow teachers to administer medication.
- ☐ Health communication history between parents, staff, and health provider
- ☐ Reports of all illnesses that have occurred while in care
- ☐ Growth chart
- ☐ Any update to the health history as it occurs
- ☐ Known allergies and emergency procedures to follow

● **Confidential**
*keeping information private*

Although the information found in health records is very important to the teacher, it must be a policy that this information remain **confidential** and not be discussed with anyone but the parents of the child, members of the staff, or the child's health care professional, if permitted. The parents should provide the teacher with a release to discuss medical information with the child's doctor. Discussion among staff should remain at a professional level.

Parents should provide the teacher with a release to discuss medical information with the child's doctor. What information should be included on these forms?

Jon, a two-year-old boy, was new to the early childhood education facility. The facility director read Jon's history, but Amanda, his primary teacher, never saw it. In his second week at school, Amanda gave Jon sliced bananas and a cup of raspberry yogurt for morning snack. In a short time, Jon broke out in hives and then went into anaphylactic shock. The early childhood education center called an ambulance immediately. His records were provided to the emergency care technician, who noticed that Jon was allergic to bananas. The director had failed to pass on the information to Amanda. Jon recovered, but the incident frightened everyone involved with the early childhood education facility, including all the children who witnessed it and the parents who heard about it. The center immediately changed its policy to require that all possible teachers for each child must review the child's health history and any specific dietary information must be posted on the refrigerator, in the kitchen, and by each food serving station as a reminder. Information on other allergies was also posted in the corner of the room as a reminder to the teachers.

Certain information in the developmental history could lead to labeling a child; the professionally competent teacher understands the need for discretion and confidentiality.

It is important to have a review procedure included in the health policy. Keeping records current allows for periodic review to look for specific warning signs, normal development rates, and immunization.

*Pause for Reflection*

Are you up-to-date with all your immunizations? If not, why not? What would you do if you worked in an early education environment that did not keep track of immunizations?

As parents drop off children, informal quick health assessment may be made by the teacher. Is the child lethargic and listless? Does the child look flushed or pale?

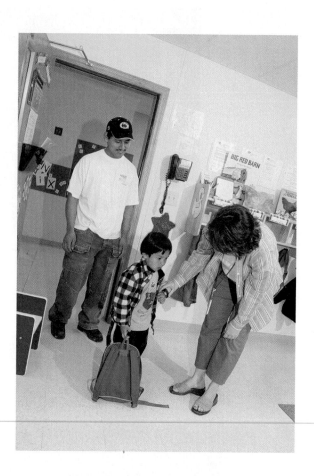

How can preventive and protective measures by the teacher help ensure a healthy environment?

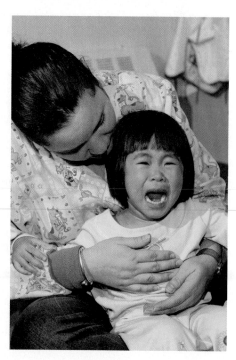

## Key Concept 10.2

### Children's Health Records

Health policies created for the health records of children are vitally important for the prevention of diseases and the protection of everyone involved in the early childhood education environment. Health histories that include currency in immunizations, special considerations, and special needs of children can prevent the spread of infectious disease as well as alert staff to possible health-related problems that may occur in the early childhood education environment. Procedures for orientation of new children in care, as well as the management of communications and confidentiality, give the teacher guidelines for conduct.

Potential teachers should have a complete physical, including a general health evaluation and a review of immunizations, before working with children.

## 10.3 STAFF HEALTH

● **Infectious diseases**
*diseases capable of invading the body and causing an infection to occur; may or may not be contagious*

The health policy that covers staff health records and health care is of primary importance. The teacher usually cares for a number of young children and the potential for spreading **infectious diseases** to other children, other employees, and her own family is great. Other occupational health hazards will be discussed later. Every teacher should be able to comfortably perform the duties of the job. The policy for health records and health care for staff should reflect preventive and protective measures. The health policy should apply to all staff members, including volunteers.

### Staff Records

Before any teacher is hired or considers beginning a career working with children, he or she should have information available to complete a staff health record. The teacher's health history should include the information listed in Table 10-3.

**TABLE 10-3**
*Checklist for Teacher Health History*

✓ **CHECK FOR:**

☐ Name, address, and phone number

☐ Physician's name, address, and phone number

☐ Pre-employment examination that includes an evaluation of general health, the physical ability to perform job duties as outlined, and any condition that would create a hazard to children or other staff

☐ Immunization records including currency in all necessary immunizations and history of childhood diseases

☐ TB screening

☐ Hearing and vision screening

Other items that might be included in an adult health history are limitations in common situations, such as allergies to art materials, medications, and the general health status of family members residing in the household. Any problems with the respiratory system, such as allergies or asthma, should be reported. Some states have mandated forms that will be provided.

Before a potential teacher cares for children, a complete physical should be given. The potential teacher should be checked for musculoskeletal problems such as arthritis or lower back pain that might limit his or her activity or ability to perform the job (Sutton, 2003). This pre-employment health examination will evaluate general health and physical condition. It will also provide the opportunity to complete the schedule of immunizations if any of the required immunizations are missing.

After employment, regular health checkups will evaluate maintenance of good health. An orientation for the new teacher should include procedures to reduce risk for exposure to illness, including hand washing, universal precautions for bloodborne pathogens, and proper sanitation practices (Calder, 2000).

## Maintaining Staff Health

A teacher should protect the health of children and should also be a role model for good health. Maintaining the health of a teacher can be challenging because of the following occupational hazards:

- exposure to infectious diseases
- stress
- risk for back injury
- potential exposure to environmental hazards

***Exposure to Infectious Diseases.*** All teachers should have up-to-date immunizations for or have natural immunity to:

- Tetanus (booster every 10 years)
- Hepatitis A
- Hepatitis B

- Polio
- Measles, Mumps, and Rubella
- Varicella (chicken pox)

If the teacher has had the disease, a natural immunity will have developed. Immunizations and occurrence of infectious disease should be thoroughly checked before employment. If the measles vaccine was given before the age of fifteen months, a booster should be given to an adult, especially if the adult is a female of childbearing age.

The teacher (Zamani, 2003) should also be immunized for:

- Influenza (while working with young children)
- Pneumococcal virus
- Meningococcal virus

The Centers for Disease Control and Prevention also recommends that a potential teacher be screened for tuberculosis (TB). The American Academy of Pediatrics suggests that this test should be given within one year before employment or within one week after employment. If the screening is negative, it is not necessary to periodically repeat it, unless the teacher shows signs of the disease such as chronic coughing, coughing up blood, or more than two weeks with a fever (Kunitz, 2004).

Special safeguards should be in place for pregnant teachers or women with childbearing potential. Unborn children may acquire certain infectious diseases in the early childhood education environment that can cause birth defects and, in some cases, miscarriage. Five of these infectious diseases that can be prevented by proper prepregnancy immunization are measles, mumps, rubella, chicken pox (varicella), and hepatitis B. Other occupational health hazards include herpes, cytomegalovirus (CMV), parvovirus, and AIDS.

Hand washing is the number one defense a teacher uses to avoid the spread of infectious disease. Wearing non-latex gloves helps support the check of disease. Special care should be made to follow all sanitary procedures, especially those that deal with children's mucous secretions, blood, and urine and bowel movements. Teachers should wear gloves each time a child's nose is wiped, after dealing with a cut or injury, for assisting in

Staff meetings are an excellent forum for discussing the occupational health hazards that can affect teachers.

Early childhood education can be highly stressful and often results in job burnout. What measures can teachers take to cope with stress and avoid burnout?

toileting or diaper changing, and before food is handled. Use of latex gloves is not suggested because of possible allergic reactions to the teachers or children. Hands should be washed immediately after removing gloves.

If a teacher becomes ill, a sick day should be taken. Unfortunately, too many teachers go to work while they are ill because they feel they cannot afford not to, without recognizing their part in the spread of infectious diseases. A staff health policy should include a substitute list of teachers for the protection of the children and the rest of the staff. There should also be substitutes or backup teachers if a family child care provider or nanny becomes ill. A family child care provider may have to send the children to another provider's home. This backup care must be arranged in advance so that parents will not have to arrange for another form of care for a day or two.

*Stress.* Caring for children is a rewarding profession, but it has the potential for **stress**. There are a number of reasons why the potential for stress is present in early childhood education:

- Isolation from other adults. This is more likely to occur in family child care and nanny care.

- Long hours and hard work. Working with children and needing to be constantly aware can be stressful. Breaks may be rare.

- Trying to do too much in too little time. Packing the day with too many activities or expectations of yourself or the children in care

- Balancing work and the rest of life. This may include family, roommates, or school.

- Low wages and lack of recognition. Children and those who care for them are not adequately valued in our society.

- Lack of training. Teachers with more training have coping skills, organizational skills, and increased knowledge of appropriate activities for children that help them get through the day with less stress.

- Dealing with parents and respecting their needs

- Dealing with individual children with a variety of needs

● **Stress**
*nonspecific response of the body to any demand put on it*

● **Job burnout**
*inability to perform job due to excessive stress*

**Job burnout** is one reaction to too much stress in life. Burnout is the combination of emotional and physical feelings of not being able to function. It is a result of the accumulation of stress, and is a hazard for teachers and others who work directly with children (Kreisher, 2002). Studies show the job burnout rate for teachers in center-based care is 43 percent per year (University of Colorado at Denver et al., 1995). That means that, for every 100 people who begin the year as a teacher, only 57 are still on the job a year later. A major contributing factor to the significant turnover rate is too much stress.

It is important for the teacher to learn the warning signals and signs of stress (Crute, 2004; Ghazavini & Mullis, 2003). A teacher needs to take care of her own stress level before she can really be of help to children. Awareness of stress is the first step in preventing it and protecting the teacher. Stress is the body's response to a threat. A biochemical reaction occurs within the body whether the threat is real or imagined. Stressors are people, places, or events that an individual perceives as a threat. What may be a stressor to one person may not be a stressor to another person. Causes of stress and reactions to it are unique to the individual (Table 10-4).

A person can learn how to cope with stress and may be able to reduce or eliminate it. Changing one's perception and reaction to the stressor is one way to deal with stress. Another way is to eliminate or reduce the cause or source of stress. Time management is also a helpful tool to eliminate stress.

It is important for the teacher to deal early with stress and to find the best personal coping mechanisms. If a teacher does not deal with the stress, it can lead to depression. A recent study found that about 9 percent of teachers had significant levels of depression (Hamre & Pianta, 2004). Teachers were more likely to be depressed if they worked in family child care or if they had little training or spent more time without other adults in the environment.

There are several techniques for changing perception and reaction to stressors. Sharing stress with others helps one see the problem from another person's point of view. Just talking about it with a friend or family member may reduce the level of stress or even the perception that stress exists. A person who learns to recognize limitations can help reduce stress and possibly

**TABLE 10-4**
*Stress Warning Signal Checklist*

## ✓ CHECK FOR:

- ☐ Persistent feelings of anxiety, nervousness, or depression
- ☐ Fatigue
- ☐ Frustration, moodiness, or irritability
- ☐ Difficulty in concentrating or forgetfulness
- ☐ Loneliness
- ☐ Perfectionism
- ☐ Restlessness
- ☐ Eating too much or too little
- ☐ Sleeping too much or not being able to sleep
- ☐ Job dissatisfaction
- ☐ Absenteeism

- ☐ Procrastination
- ☐ Interpersonal conflicts with adults or children
- ☐ Frequent headaches
- ☐ Neck and backaches
- ☐ Asthma
- ☐ Muscle tension and/or spasms
- ☐ Indigestion, diarrhea, or constipation
- ☐ Infections or skin rashes
- ☐ Lowered immunity to illness
- ☐ Sexual problems
- ☐ Increased smoking, use of alcohol or drugs

A child's schedule may not always agree with the teacher's schedule, causing daily stress for both.

Marcus had a difficult time with transitions, especially at lunch and snack time. First Marcus had to settle down and then he ate very slowly. His teacher, Lavonne, worked hard to follow a scheduled routine each day. She tried to get Marcus to eat faster, but he still dawdled at each meal. Lavonne's feelings of resentment toward Marcus and frustration that she was not meeting her own expectations were causing her stress. She went to Anita, her director, to discuss her feelings. They came to several conclusions. Marcus's behavior of transitioning might always be difficult at mealtimes. Lavonne would continue to try different strategies, but they agreed that in the meantime, she would try not to react to that behavior. In addition, Anita would try to give Lavonne some relief during this stressful time.

Lavonne realized that she could not fix everything, and that gave her the sense of freedom to accept the way Marcus acted at mealtime. Anita tried to provide someone to help Lavonne with the end of lunchtime as often as possible. This left the other teacher with Marcus while Lavonne was free to continue with her plan of activities. Anita and Lavonne discussed what would happen if no one was available to help relieve Lavonne at lunchtime. They agreed that Lavonne's expectation that a schedule should be or could be followed rigidly was unrealistic. Lavonne learned to be more flexible and to not feel bad if everything did not go according to her plan. Lavonne was much happier in her work and the atmosphere of the early childhood education environment was less stressful for everyone concerned.

understand why stress exists in certain situations. A person who realizes certain situations are not within his control should accept the fact that the situation cannot be changed. Instead, the person should take time to recognize what situations can be changed. At this time it is within the power of the individual to change the circumstance in order to reduce or eliminate stress.

Learning to manage time can also help reduce stress. Many people try to do too much. The pressure of having expectations of what can be accomplished in a certain time frame can lead to stress. To change perception about time, there are several positive techniques found in Table 10-5.

**TABLE 10-5**
*Time Management Checklist*

## ✓ CHECK FOR:

- ☐ Do only one thing at a time. Some people try to manage three or four activities at a time. Early childhood education is an activity that almost demands that, but one can learn to try not to do too many things at one time.

- ☐ Slow down.

- ☐ When several children ask for help at the same time, find ways for them to help each other or explain your need to finish with another task first.

- ☐ Learn to say no to activities or events that are not productive or enjoyable.

- ☐ Make a "to do" list every morning or afternoon for the following day. Allow time for this activity. Prioritize the items that must be done, and eliminate those that can be done later.

- ☐ Try not to be a perfectionist. Use the worst case scenario for trying to reduce perfectionism. Ask "what's the worst that can happen" if something is not done up to the self-enforced standard.

- ☐ If you are stuck in a line or traffic, realize it is out of your control. Try relaxing or do deep breathing exercises.

- ☐ Do not try to do everything yourself. If someone offers to help, let them. If help is needed, ask for it.

A number of other strategies are available to help reduce or eliminate stress as it occurs. These methods include both physical and mental coping skills. Some of the things one can do physically are to increase physical activity, eat a balanced diet, and get enough sleep. Exercise is particularly important. Exercising vigorously for 20 minutes, three times a week, can be a major reducer of stress. Hormones are released during exercise that help the body cope with stress. Eliminating sugar and caffeine in the diet can also help to relieve stress because both have physical side effects that may allow stress to occur more easily. Eating healthy foods, including lots of fresh fruits and vegetables, can help the body be more resilient to stress (Kunitz, 2001).

People who care for others often find it difficult to care for themselves. Making more time for leisure, daydreaming, crying when it is needed, and learning to relax are ways that help a person's mind adjust to stress. Some people find it difficult to relax. Learn to schedule a quiet time each day to relax and reflect. Personal reflection is an excellent tool to learn about yourself and can teach you what you should recognize about your own stress. Reading, taking a bubble bath, or watching television may be relaxing. Other leisure activities such as hobbies may be more physically active, but they can be equally relaxing. Do not try the activity at a fast pace nor focus on its competitive nature. This may eliminate the stress reduction quality of the leisure activity. Instead, focus on the enjoyment and relaxation benefits of the activity.

When stress is present, try deep breathing exercises. Breathe in slowly, hold the breath for 1 or 2 seconds, and then let it out slowly. This helps the body to come to a more neutral point. Relaxation response techniques such as holding a group of muscles taut, then allowing them to relax may also help. This process usually involves the entire body, starting with the head and moving down to end with the feet.

Unlike this example, teachers should bend at the knees, not at the waist, when working with children, to ensure proper teacher-child interaction and to reduce the risk of back strain.

*Pause for Reflection*

Do you ever feel under stress? What types of reactions do you have? Are they physical, emotional, or both? What types of steps do you take to relieve your stress? Are there more things you could do to relieve stress before it piles up?

***Back Injury.*** Back problems are very common. Most people experience back pain at one time or another. Teachers may be called upon to lift and carry children many times in a day. They also bend over to play, change diapers, and feed children. Lifting, bending, twisting, and sitting are frequent normal daily activities for the teacher. If these tasks are done correctly, problems with the back can be minimized. However, if they are done incorrectly, serious back problems can result. Many teachers are not as careful as they need to be; therefore, back injury is considered an occupational hazard (Calder, 2000).

It is important for the teacher to learn how to correctly bend, lift, and sit. Lifting should be done by bending at the knees, not the waist. Bending at the knees can help relieve some stress from the back; bending at the waist adds stress to the back. When the knees are bent, the legs carry most of the load. If the waist is bent, the back carries the load. Whatever is being lifted should be kept close to the body, not held away from it. A firm footing is the first step to lifting. Feet should be kept apart, with one near the child and the other a little behind it (Back injuries are preventable, 1999). During lifting, move the feet as needed but do not twist the body (Figure 10-2). Stabilize your body against a wall or other stationary object (Kunitz, 2003). If possible, do not lift or pull heavy objects that need to be moved. Instead, push the object so that the stress on the back is lessened.

Bending over to talk to a child or to perform other common activities should also be done from the knees, not the waist. Getting at the child's level is important, but it can be done in less physically stressful ways. Position can be shifted from bending at the knees to kneeling, sitting in a chair, squatting, or even sitting cross-legged on the floor (Figure 10-3).

FIGURE 10-2
How to lift a weight

FIGURE 10-3
Sitting on a chair or on the floor at a child's level is crucial for effective teacher-child interactions, but it can result in daily back strain. To relieve pressure on the back, bend from the knees when sitting or standing and hold onto something stationary.

Surprisingly, sitting down is more stressful on the back than standing or walking. If sitting is necessary, be sure to maintain good posture and try to sit in a way that supports the curve of the back (Figure 10-4). When bending to sit or to stand from a sitting position, it is better to hang on to something stationary to help remove stress from the back. Teachers often sit in child-sized chairs. This is acceptable as long as it is comfortable, but it should be avoided if it causes back pain or discomfort. If the teacher is holding or rocking a child, this should be done sitting down in an adult-sized chair with good back support.

Just as exercise can relieve stress, it can also build protection for the back. Regular exercise can strengthen the back muscles to support the spine (Figure 10-5) (Crocker, 2003). This will help the back withstand the daily routine of the teacher.

***Exposure to Environmental Hazards.*** There are numerous environmental hazards in child care (PAAAP, 2003). The most common hazards are arts and crafts materials, cleaning supplies, and pesticides. All arts and crafts materials should be examined, and labels should indicate that they are non-

**FIGURE 10-4**
Correct body alignment when sitting.

Arts and crafts materials are some of the most common environmental hazards in early childhood education environments. Good ventilation is essential when working with these materials.

toxic. Throw away any materials that are not labeled nontoxic. If there are any questions, call the local Poison Control office. Some paints or other craft items can cause a harmful reaction. For example, several years ago, some early childhood education programs stopped using shaving cream as an art supply because of the rashes it caused. Others continued using it, because it did not cause rashes. If any materials are found to be harmful to the children or teachers, their use should be discontinued. It is also important to always maintain good ventilation when working with arts and crafts materials.

Cleaning supplies should also be nontoxic. Cleaning supplies may be strong enough to cause skin irritation, so gloves should be worn when using them. The room should be ventilated and air kept circulating during cleaning. This will help lessen any irritation to the nose, lungs, and eyes. If there should be lingering odor, continue with ventilation and air circulation until the odor lessens.

Whenever possible, it is important to use natural pesticides that are nontoxic to people (Walker, 2004). If, for more effectiveness, pesticides

**FIGURE 10-5**
Exercises for the back.

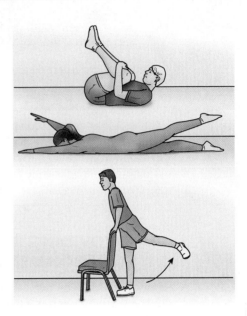

*Lower-Back Exercises*

1. A. Lie flat on your back. Hug your knees to your chest and at the same time, bring your chin to your chest. Repeat twice, holding for 15 seconds each.

   B. Begin on your hands and knees. Simultaneously raise and straighten your right arm and left leg until they are parallel to the ground. Hold for 2 seconds and come back slowly to a starting position. Repeat with left arm and right leg, alternating 10 times.

2. C. Lie facedown, arms extended overhead, palms on floor. Simultaneously raise your right arm and left leg as high as comfortably possible. Hold for 10 seconds and slowly return to start. Repeat with left arm and right leg, alternating 10 times. Gradually build up to 20 times.

   D. Lie facedown, arms at your side and place heels under couch. Slowly raise chest off the floor as high as you comfortably can. Hold for 2 seconds and return to start. Gradually increase to 20 times.

   Strong lower-back muscles and abdominals work together in maintaining a pain-free and healthy back. These exercises will help strengthen the muscles of the lower back, but it is important that you begin your exercises slowly and increase levels gradually. Always begin any exercise program with stretching. Talk to your doctor before attempting any exercises, especially if you are already experiencing back pain.

3. Stand behind a chair with your hands on the back of the chair. Lift one leg back and up while keeping the knee straight. Return slowly. Raise other leg and return. Repeat five times with each leg.

need to be toxic, use products that say "caution" instead of those that issue a warning of danger. Try not to store any pesticides at the early education program site, but if they must be stored, keep them up and under lock and key. When dangerous or restricted-use pesticides are necessary, they should be applied by a professional exterminator when children are not present. The area that the pesticide is applied to should be well ventilated after the application. A teacher should be present and watch the application to make sure that the pesticide does not get on food, food preparation areas, or play areas. If minor use of pesticides, such as spraying for ants, is done by the teacher, the same rules should apply. Gloves should be used and discarded. These cautions will help prevent skin, nose, and lung irritations.

## Key Concept 10.3

### Staff Health Requirements

Staff health is an important factor in the prevention and protection of health in the early childhood education environment. All personnel should have a pre-employment physical examination and should meet health record requirements. Staff health should be maintained by keeping up immunizations and by washing hands frequently. The teacher should employ practices that help avoid stress, back pain, and exposure to hazardous environmental materials.

## 10.4 PROVIDING A MENTALLY HEALTHY ENVIRONMENT

Mental health is an area of health promotion that may be overlooked. One in every 10 children is at risk for mental health difficulties (Collins et al., 2003). Early childhood mental health is related to a child's well-being in relation to social and emotional development (Silverstein et al., 2003). The importance of providing a consistent, loving, and protective environment cannot be stressed enough. Warm, responsive, one-on-one care is essential to providing a good mentally healthy environment (Honig, 1993; Raikes, 1996; Collins et al., 2003). Consistent routines allow children the feeling of security and a sense of trust. Children need an atmosphere where they feel that they belong. Each child needs to feel unique and have a sense of power. The child also needs to feel the freedom to express himself through play, talk, and action. Feeling comfortable enough to express negative emotions may allow the child to work through these types of emotions. The ability of a child to deal with both positive and negative emotions may help the child deal better with life (Bowling & Rogers, 2001).

When a health policy is being developed for mental health, several considerations need to be included. Attention to a child's family situation and cultural background is essential for developing a rapport with the child. Some caution signs for stressful environmental factors that a child may have and that may negatively affect health are found in Table 10-6. Another factor to consider is the child's temperament and physical attributes (Zenah et al., 2005).

● **Self-esteem**
*positive sense of self*

**Self-esteem** in a child is the general product of a mentally healthy environment. When a child has a sense of self-esteem, that child feels both lovable and capable. A child's self-esteem evolves primarily through the quality of relationships with people in her life. Responsiveness in caregiving enables the child to feel good about herself. A teacher offering emotional security and encouragement can provide the foundation for success in later life. The quality of the relationship between the child and teacher can offer the child protective factors for later development (Zenah et al., 2005).

Teacher behaviors that promote a mentally healthy environment can not only provide this in the moment, but can alleviate past problems and

A primary teacher or care-giver for an infant or toddler provides emotional security through an atmosphere of caring and trust. This security is an important foundation for self-esteem.

**TABLE 10-6**
*Caution Signs for Environmental Factors Affecting Mental Health*

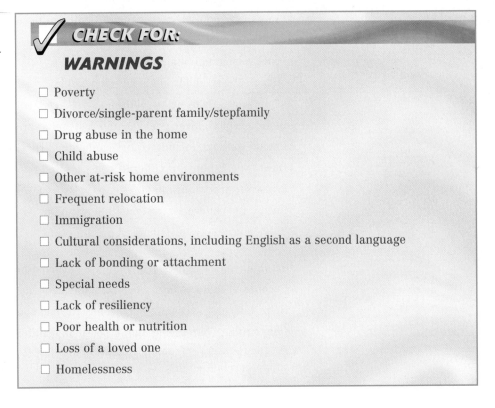

## ✓ CHECK FOR:
### WARNINGS

- ☐ Poverty
- ☐ Divorce/single-parent family/stepfamily
- ☐ Drug abuse in the home
- ☐ Child abuse
- ☐ Other at-risk home environments
- ☐ Frequent relocation
- ☐ Immigration
- ☐ Cultural considerations, including English as a second language
- ☐ Lack of bonding or attachment
- ☐ Special needs
- ☐ Lack of resiliency
- ☐ Poor health or nutrition
- ☐ Loss of a loved one
- ☐ Homelessness

may help the child in the future. Table 10-7 outlines teacher behaviors that are useful in providing a mentally healthy environment.

The health policy for mental health should include a provision for a primary teacher or caregiver for each child. Each child should have one special person to bond with and form a healthy attachment. The primary teacher can create an atmosphere of caring and trust for the child. This offers the child a sense of stability and consistency. A child who is at risk for mental health difficulties may recognize positive qualities in the teacher and may be able to seek those same qualities in other adults in the

**TABLE 10-7**
*Providing a Mentally Healthy Environment*

## ✓ CHECK FOR:

- ☐ Establish a good relationship with parents, including respect and mutual communication.
- ☐ Respond with consistency, predictability, and regularity.
- ☐ Establish daily routines for a sense of security.
- ☐ Provide support and emotional assurance for the child, including attention, affection, respect, and mutual communication.
- ☐ Allow children to safely explore and master the environment.
- ☐ Help children to express and identify emotions.
- ☐ Redirect anger and aggression through play and discussion.
- ☐ Provide a quiet area so the child can remove himself from stimulation when needed.
- ☐ Value each child's uniqueness, including cultural considerations.
- ☐ Promote responsive caregiving for staff and parents.
- ☐ Be flexible and reasonable in expectations.
- ☐ Provide unconditional love
- ☐ Converse with children whenever possible
- ☐ Listen carefully to what children say
- ☐ Be aware of children's moods and respond appropriately
- ☐ Extend comfort, including physical holding, rocking, and soothing
- ☐ Have expectations for children's success and opportunities to succeed
- ☐ Praise for accomplishment
- ☐ Encourage children to try new things, and to do them with minimal help
- ☐ Provide access to unstructured art materials so that children can express themselves whenever they need to
- ☐ Provide opportunities for meaningful participation
- ☐ Encourage children to use problem-solving skills
- ☐ Help children to accept responsibility for behaviors and consequences
- ☐ Offer primary caregiving and, if possible, continuity of care
- ☐ Create a pleasant, homelike environment that promotes interactions and supports relationships

future. If it is at all possible, providing continuity of care is the ideal (Edwards & Raikes, 2002). This means that the teacher would follow the child as he or she ages from group to group through care. For example, a child begins care in the infant group, and when the group moves to toddler care, the teacher also goes with them; then when these children move to preschool, the teacher also follows. When that group leaves care to enter kindergarten, the preschool teacher would revert back to infant care and follow another whole group throughout their time in care. This not only helps children feel safe and secure, but it gives families a sense of continuity, knowing the teacher will remain the same. This is a good feature of family child care, but may be more difficult to attain in center-based care. When there is a goodness of fit between the child and the teacher, the child will feel a greater sense of well-being (DeSchipper et al., 2004). Stability, understanding, and consistency in the early childhood education environment may help the child to become more **resilient** in this environment (Werner & Smith, 2001). (See Realty Check on resiliency in Chapter 14.)

● **Resilient**
*having the ability to recover after being exposed to risk*

*Text continues on p. 393*

Lauren, a withdrawn three-year-old child whose parents had recently divorced, lived with her father, Jim. Jim hired Julie, a live-in nanny, to help care for Lauren. Jim often traveled, sometimes with little notice. Lauren was not allowed to visit her alcoholic mother due to a court order. Julie was there for Lauren whenever a change or an unexpected event happened. Although Lauren's world seemed to have turned upside down, Julie offered comfort and security. Whenever Jim traveled, Julie stayed with Lauren, and she took Lauren home with her on her days off. Julie understood Lauren's need for stability and she was willing to make sacrifices to ensure that Lauren knew she could depend on Julie. Julie was Lauren's nanny for almost two years. Jim remarried when Lauren was ready to attend kindergarten. Today, Lauren is a happy, outgoing seven-year-old who still occasionally talks to Julie on the phone.

## *Key Concept 10.4*

### Mentally Healthy Environment

Many children are at risk for poor mental health. Providing a stable, responsive, and consistent environment can help children acquire protective tools that will help them become more resilient to environmental factors that negatively affect mental health. Providing a primary teacher for each child in care will help to ensure that the child can form a relationship that will provide those protective tools. A teacher who regards a child as unique, understands the child's temperament, and is aware of the family helps to individualize the care and provide the optimum environment for good mental health for each child.

# REALITY CHECK

## Children with Stress

Children today are dealing with many stressful events and life changes. Losses, events, or lifestyles that make the child feel she has no control may cause stress. Today, it appears that children have less time to relax and more time involved in some sort of planned activity. In addition to those risks to mental health mentioned in Table 10-6 the following items may also cause stress in a child's life:

- Birth of a sibling
- Separation anxiety
- Loss of a pet
- Too many scheduled activities
- A new care situation
- A friend leaves the early childhood education environment
- Financial problems at home
- Fears, real or imagined
- Observing violence, in the home, neighborhood, or other real situation
- Peer pressure
- Too little privacy

Children's reaction to stress may be visible in physical, emotional, or behavioral responses. Children have a limited understanding and a good imagination. When life feels out of control, the child may magnify the significance of the stressor. Children do not have the same coping skills as adults, so their reaction to stress may be somewhat different.

Some children may react more to stressful situations than others. If a child is oversensitive or tends to worry, he may experience stress more easily. When a child tends to please others or does not seem to be able to assert himself, stress may have a greater impact (Foxman, 2004). When children are too young to express themselves, they may be more vulnerable to stress. Even securely attached infants and toddlers have been found to have higher levels of cortisol, the stress hormone, when adjusting to a new care situation (Ahnert et al., 2004). Children 24 to 36 months of age were also found to have greater elevated cortisol levels when in all-day care (Macoby & Lewis, 2003). The teacher needs to realize that stress may be part of everyday life for some children. The awareness of this may help the teacher discover ways to help manage the environment to lessen stress for the children present.

Children who react physically to stress may have headaches, stomachaches, or bouts of diarrhea. They may not have their regular appetites and may either not eat or constantly be eating. Children who have normal language may have some language difficulties, such as rapid speech or stuttering. Children with allergies or asthma may have reactions that appear more often.

The emotional reaction to stress can be expressed in a number of ways. The spectrum of behaviors ranges from regressive to aggressive. Children may show regressive behaviors in forms such as withdrawing or having toileting accidents. Children may become clingy and too dependent. They may be unable to make simple decisions, such as with what and whom to play. Children who are stressed may not laugh or smile and may cry more than usual. They may appear to escape into fantasy by constantly daydreaming or watching television. Children may appear fearful and nervous. Children may also become depressed. Five percent of children show signs of depression (Herbst, 1999).

Aggressive emotional behaviors are exhibited by acting out. This might range from throwing a tantrum to more violent behavior. Stressed children may bite or hit other children or adults. Children who use aggression to cope with stress may vandalize toys, equipment, or art of their own or others. They might have difficulty with social interactions. Children under stress may become easily frustrated and use colorful language to express their anger.

Regardless of how it is expressed, teachers need to be alert to the fact that stress can be an important factor in children's behavior. If a child abruptly changes behavior or is a constant source of regressive or aggressive behavior, stress may be a factor. If the teacher helps the child manage her stress, it will lower the risks for later physical or emotional problems (Foxman, 2004). The best way to do this is to structure the environment so that it supports the child. Allow the child to express concerns, listen to what she says, and respond in supportive ways (NCCCH-SRC, 2004). The environment should be protective and prevent more stress to the child. Zenah et al. (2005) suggests that the teacher should have four tools to help maintain a supportive mentally healthy environment. The first is an adequate knowledge of socioemotional development, in order to recognize the emotions of children. The second is a positive relationship with families for clear and open communication to work together for the benefit of the child. The third tool is predictable times to play, eat, and rest, and the fourth is age-appropriate behavior management techniques for children when they have problems. These factors allow children to feel secure, have a sense of control, and to be more able to cope with stress and fears. The environment should be protective and prevent more stress to the child.

Providing structure through a predictable routine allows the child the comfort of understanding what comes next. The teacher can improve the quality of interaction with children by being consistent and reliable. The teacher who forms an attachment to children helps them learn to trust the teacher and the care environment (Gunnar, 2005). This gives some children a feeling of safety and stability that they may not otherwise have.

The teacher can provide children under stress a sense of security in other ways. Some

children under stress may need a quiet place to go to be free of stimulation. Providing a corner of a room that is not decorated and has a comfortable place to sit helps achieve this. Sometimes going from one activity to another can cause a child more stress. The teacher can help children in their transition from one activity to another to reduce stress.

The teacher also needs to help children under stress learn to identify and express their emotions. Role modeling, dramatic play, reading books, and discussions with the child help. A teacher can support children by redirecting their anger, frustration, and aggression. Activities such as rocking horses, swings, and punching bags can alleviate anger. Water play and sand play are soothing and may help dissipate anger. A withdrawn child can be stimulated to act out emotions through play. Providing materials for unstructured art may help children express their emotions (Gross & Clemens, 2002). A child who feels more in control will be able to cope with stress under other situations.

A teacher who listens to children and responds with positive action and words allows them the opportunity to express problems and get in touch with feelings. The teacher should reinforce positive behaviors and reward them with at least a positive comment. A teacher who allows children choices where appropriate can help teach decision-making and problem-solving skills. Those actions show children that the teacher respects them, and children who feel respected have a sense of self-worth.

Each child should be treated as an individual with his own strengths and vulnerabilities (Collins et al., 2003). Using the context of the whole child and considering the family, the home environment, and culture is necessary to really provide the type of environment that will support good mental health and reduce stress for all children in care.

The team approach of the teacher and a parent working together can also be helpful with stress. A parent may be a source of stress for the child and may choose not to participate, although most parents will be cooperative. Some parents

*(continues)*

## REALITY CHECK (Continued)

who are under stress themselves may welcome the teacher's help. The teacher can set up times with the parent to discuss the child. The teacher should show the family respect. Being consistent and predictable in all dealings with the parent can build trust. The teacher can also provide opportunities for the parent under stress to find additional help through counseling.

Employ cultural competence and acknowledge the family's feelings. By being sensitive to different values, beliefs and expectations can assist the teacher to build better relationships with family partners for each child, no matter what his background (Edwards & Raikes, 2002; Zenah, 2005). When the teacher is consistent and predictable in all dealings with the family,

trust can be built. When families are under stress and circumstances are not optimal, children may be more likely to respond to stress with acting out behaviors (Greenspan, 2003). The teacher can provide opportunities for the family under stress to find additional help through counseling and other community resources. When the early childhood education environment is sensitive to the needs of children and their families, the quality of care is improved. The better the quality and the more sensitive the care, the less likely a child will react in an aggressive or assertive manner to the stress he may be feeling (NIH, 2003). The more stable the care, the less stress for the child and the better the environment for the child's social development (Loeb, et al., 2004).

**CHECK**_point:_ What types of things do you think that the children you know stress about? Does this Reality Check reflect what you have observed? What types of things would you add to the stressors listed?

This child may react differently to stress in her life than other children.

Stress may exhibit itself in aggressive behavior.

- ● **Role modeling**
  *setting a behavioral example*
- ● **Cultural competence**
  *perceptive, responsive behavior to cultural differences*

## 10.5  IMPLICATIONS FOR TEACHERS

Children's attitudes and behavior in relation to health are affected by the adults they observe. The well-being of children is influenced by teacher training and good practices (Greenspan, 2003). Teachers can use **role modeling**, **cultural competence**, education, and supervision to influence health.

### Role Modeling

A health policy for role modeling should reflect practices that will affect the actions of children through their observation of their teachers. Good role modeling includes exhibiting the knowledge and practice of healthy behaviors. Teachers should display good personal grooming and hygiene and face each day with a positive mental attitude.

Good modeling uses reinforcement through observation and discussion with children. A teacher who teaches children to use healthy practices and models those behaviors can also help the parent learn. Seeing the child and teacher modeling healthy behavior may encourage the parent to adapt a healthy practice.

A teacher's actions set the stage for children to learn from those actions (Zenah, 2005). If a teacher encourages children to wash their hands a certain way but does not do it in the same manner, the children will not readily adopt those hand-washing techniques. If the teacher comes to work ill, the children will wonder why they should stay home when not feeling well. Children often act as a video camera by repeating what they see and hear.

Haim Ginott (1972) described the effect that a teacher's actions can have on a child:

> I have come to a frightening conclusion. It is my personal approach that creates the climate. It is my daily mood that makes

The teacher and parent should always work together for the benefit of the child.

A teacher who can give her total attention to children can create an atmosphere of positive feelings for them.

the weather. As a teacher, I possess tremendous power to make a child's life miserable or joyous. I can be a tool of torture or an instrument of inspiration. I can humiliate or humor, hurt or heal. In all situations it is my response that decides whether a crisis will be escalated or de-escalated, a child humanized or dehumanized. (p. 15)

Because children view the teacher as a role model, under no circumstances should smoking be permitted at anytime in the early childhood education environment. Smoking is a definite health hazard and

# REALITY CHECK

## Secondhand Smoke

Smoking has long been an acceptable behavior in our culture. For the last 30 or so years, medical research on the effects of smoking has found that smoking can lead to certain cancers, lung diseases, and heart disease. In the United States, 350,000 deaths occur every year because of tobacco use. Cigarettes, cigars, and tobacco carry warning labels about these facts. It has only recently been concluded that secondhand smoke may cause health problems for those exposed to a smoker's environment. Approximately 4000 chemicals, 250 of which are toxic or carcinogenic, have been found in secondhand smoke (US DHHS, 2004b)

Children of smokers have a greater risk for health problems (Klerman, 2004). Low birth weight in newborns may be caused because the mother smoked during pregnancy. If smoking were eliminated, it is estimated that there would be 25 percent fewer low-birth-weight infants. The U.S. Surgeon General also estimates that there would be a 10 percent reduction in infant deaths if smoking ceased. Recent studies have shown that the secondhand smoke of the pregnant mother's coworkers or family may pass bloodborne chemicals to her unborn child. These chemicals have been found to be a prelude to childhood leukemia and other cancers (Husted, 1996).

Approximately 38 percent of children between the ages of two months and five years are exposed to secondhand smoke, also known as environmental tobacco smoke, while in their own homes (Emmons et al., 2001). One quarter of these children are also exposed to smoke while in their mother's wombs. An estimated 8000 to 26,000 new cases yearly of asthma in children are related to secondhand smoke (CDC, 2004b). Between 150,000 and 300,000 cases annually of bronchitis and lower respiratory tract infections in infants and children younger than 18 months of age have been found to be related to secondhand smoke. Children from low-income, less educated families are more likely to be exposed to secondhand smoke. Children can also be exposed to secondhand smoke away from home. More than one-third of children who were not exposed at home were exposed to secondhand smoke by other people. Most exposure to secondhand smoke came from grandparents (Hopper & Craig, 2000). Some exposure to secondhand smoke may come from teachers.

It has been estimated that exposure to secondhand smoke can account for $4.6 billion in medical expenses to treat children (Aligne & Stoddard, 1997). Secondhand smoke is responsible each year for up to 40 percent of the cases of sudden infant death syndrome (SIDS), 20 percent of lower-respiratory tract infections of children under five, and up to 13 percent of otitis media cases (Greider, 1998). Chances for otitis media increase greatly if the mother smoked during pregnancy (Stathis et al., 1999). Where asthma occurs as a result of secondhand smoke, there is an increased risk for a greater number of episodes, as well as school absences and emergency room visits (Emmons et al., 2001). More than 350,000 cases of respiratory disease are found in children each year that are directly related to secondhand smoke (Males, 1995).

Other common childhood health issues of secondhand smoke are

- pneumonia
- bronchitis
- asthma
- middle-ear effusion (hearing loss)
- more difficulty getting over colds
- reduced lung function
- allergic complications
- behavioral problems

*(continues)*

## REALITY CHECK (Continued)

The American Academy of Pediatrics Committee on Substance Abuse has called for a tobacco-free environment for all children (AAP, 2001; AAP, 2002). The policy statement concludes that tobacco smoke has harmful effects to the health and psychosocial well-being of children and adolescents. The policy also calls for a ban on all advertising for tobacco products. It calls on parents and health professionals to be good role models who do not use tobacco products. Because a major health function of a teacher is role modeling, smoking is a behavior that should be avoided.

Secondhand smoke has also been linked to vitamin C deficiency. Lower levels of vitamin C increase the risk for cancer, respiratory illness, and heart disease. The connection to heart disease may also come from smoking households that tend to watch more television, eat less healthy diets, and are less physically active (Burke et al., 1998). Inhaling tobacco smoke may also have harmful effects on cognitive development (Park, 1999). Secondhand smoke exposure has also been related to negative behaviors in toddlers (Brook, et al., 2000).

Secondhand smoke may be considered an environmental issue that goes beyond the home. Elevated levels of cotinine, a biomarker for nicotine, were found in 85 percent of children in one study (Mannino et al., 2001). Children between the ages of four to six years were the hardest hit by the exposure. They were five times more likely to have asthma than children who were not exposed. Many of these children came from nonsmoking homes.

Children have also been known to eat cigarettes or cigarette butts. This can cause low blood pressure and seizure disorders (Mannino, 2003). It is important for teachers to provide a smoke-free environment. Teachers can also help to educate parents about the hazards of exposing their children to secondhand smoke.

**CHECK***point:* Why would smoking in an environment where children are present offer such risk? What should a teacher do to prevent this risk in the early childhood education environment?

teachers should be good role models for health. Many states do not allow smoking on the premises of early childhood education programs. Secondhand smoke has a detrimental effect on children, so they should be isolated from it as much as possible (see Reality Check: Secondhand Smoke). A family child care provider might consider not smoking or giving up the profession to prevent these effects from harming the children in care (Figure 10-6).

### Cultural Competence

Our country's increased cultural diversity is reflected in the early childhood education environment. It is important for the teacher to be sensitive to the needs of children and families concerning health, safety, and nutrition. The teacher needs to learn more about the cultures of children in care. People from diverse cultural backgrounds may have different views and responses to situations concerning health (Zamani, 2000b). These beliefs are an integral part of cultural expression (Anderson, 2000). When health behaviors are viewed in the context of culture, they may be more easily explained. When cultures are not understood, there may be barriers to communication.

Health issues may be critical, and there should always be a clear path for communications. Conflicting cultures can make immigrant and refugee children prone to psychological problems, and they may have a difficult

**FIGURE 10-6**
Cigarette companies often appear to target children.

# Philip Morris Can't Be Trusted With America's Children

**When Philip Morris looks at its future, it sees our children.** Only kids can replace the 3,000 adult smokers who quit or die every day.

Now Philip Morris executives have launched a slick ad campaign claiming they don't want kids to smoke. Yet they also claim tobacco doesn't cause disease, advertising doesn't influence children and nicotine isn't addictive.

If tobacco companies *really* didn't want kids as customers, they would:

- Tell children that tobacco causes addiction and death.
- Stop fighting effective laws to protect children from tobacco.
- Stop spending billions on youth-oriented advertising, event sponsorship and merchandise that kids love.

**Don't trust tobacco companies with our children.** Tell your elected officials and candidates we need action to protect kids from tobacco marketing.

To contact your Members of Congress or to learn more, call **1-800-284-KIDS.**

**CAMPAIGN for TOBACCO-FREE Kids**

time forming a self-identity or feeling a sense of self-esteem (Carballo & Nerukar, 2001; Duarte & Rafanello, 2001). These children may also be at much greater risk for illness due to their living conditions. By using a bias-sensitive curriculum and understanding cultural values and traditional backgrounds, the teacher can help provide children with the tools to maintain their health and feel good about themselves (Zamani, 2000a).

## For Families

An open line of communication about all health issues should be set up upon the entrance of the child into the early childhood education environment. Families should provide a health history, immunization records, and all other health

Culturally diverse early childhood classrooms provide additional challenges for teachers. It is crucial to understand critical values and traditional backgrounds to develop a bias-sensitive curriculum and effectively communicate with the children and their families.

information needed to protect the child from risk. The teacher should be provided with this information during an orientation for the child and her family.

Families should be offered information on health matters on a regular basis. Handouts on children's stress and stress in adults will help provide useful information for the families. Teachers and families should work together if a child shows signs of stress. Offering information about creating good, mentally healthy environments may help them to provide this at home.

## Education

Education is a tool that can be used to promote health. Education for current needs and new developments in health and early childhood education will help teachers maintain a healthy environment. Teachers should have the ability to understand the importance of health records for children and staff. Sound training will offer preventive measures to avoid risk to staff health. Teachers who understand the importance of a mentally healthy environment can develop policies that provide it. Teaching children how to recognize their own feelings can help them to be better able to cope when problems occur.

## Supervision

Supervision is an important tool for teachers to maintain healthy environments. Supervision includes the maintenance of health records for both children and staff. In situations where the teacher is in charge of staff, supervision should be used to prevent stress, eliminate environmental hazards, and prevent backaches. Gentle reminders may help the staff to alter behaviors.

Supervision is also necessary to ensure the maintenance of a mentally healthy environment. Behaviors of children and teachers should be monitored. Children may be at risk due to certain environmental factors, and a teacher who notices this early can help provide intervention. The teacher should be providing consistent, responsive care.

## CHAPTER SUMMARY

Health policies help the teacher manage the environment for good physical and mental health. These policies should reflect the high quality of the early childhood education environment. Accurate child and staff health histories should be maintained, including immunization records. Staff should model and maintain good health by avoiding exposure to infectious diseases, stress, back injury, and environmental hazards. Teachers need to be warm and responsive and give consistent care. These factors allow the teacher to provide a mentally healthy environment for children and protect children against stress. Teachers can affect the health environment of the early childhood education program by role modeling, using cultural competence, providing education, working with families, and using supervision.

## TO GO BEYOND

In this section you will find a number of activities that you can use to apply and improve your knowledge of this chapter. There are also thorough online resources that accompany this text that can be found at http://www.early childed.delmar.com (see description at end of this chapter).

### Chapter Review Critical Thinking Applications

1. Discuss how health policies affect the early childhood education environment.

2. What general health policies should be considered in the early childhood education environment? List and evaluate them.

3. Request health policies from local early childhood education programs and family child care sites. Examine and discuss the elements found in these policies. Interview teachers from these programs to determine the impact of these policies.

4. What is the interrelationship between the teacher's actions and a mentally healthy child care environment?

### As an Individual

1. How do you as a person respond to stress? Identify your responses to stress. Identify your particular stressors.

2. List and discuss the coping mechanisms that you have to deal with stress and your stressors. How could they be improved?

3. How would you deal with a child who is distressed or suffering from outside stresses? What practices would improve the help offered to children who are feeling this way in an early childhood education environment?

4. Compare your family of origin practices at mealtime to the rules found in an early childhood education environment. Compare and contrast their similarities and differences.

## As a Group

1. Observe multicultural approaches in a preschool setting that support a bias-sensitive curriculum. Discuss how that might differ from other curriculums found in the same setting.

2. In small groups of four or five students, compare cultural health practices that may be present in your community. List those practices and cultural origins. As a class, compare the lists and create a master list. How might these practices affect an early childhood education environment?

3. How might stress be reduced in an early childhood education environment? Discuss coping skills that might be used to reduce stress in this environment.

4. What policies might an early childhood education environment have about teacher injury prevention, stress, and burnout? In small groups, design a policy for each item that the class considers important.

## Case Studies

1. Molly and Margaret are teachers who work at the same center. They both are in school part-time and are single mothers whose children are in elementary school. They get along well together, although they work in different classrooms and with different age groups. Both are suffering from stress, on and off the job. What coping skills would you suggest for them. How might they help each other?

2. Mark comes from a home in which his parents just divorced and his mom is about to have a new baby. He was a happy, well-adjusted three-year-old until these events occurred. Now he is angry and aggressive. What can you do to help him?

3. Erica is a parent in your family child care program. Her son Ronnie is 8 1/2 months old. Erica smokes heavily, and Ronnie is having problems with colds and ear infections. How would you handle this?

## Chapter References

Ahnert, L., & Lamb, M. (2003). Shared care: Establishing a balance between home and child care settings. *Child Development, 74*(4), 1044–1049.

Ahnert, L., Gunnar, M., Lamb, M., & Barthel, M. (2004). Transition to child care: Associations with infant-mother attachment, infant negative emotion, and cortisol elevations. *Child Development, 75*(3), 639–650.

Aligne, C., & Stoddard, J. (1997). Tobacco and children: An economic evaluation of the medical effect of parental smoking. *Archives of Pediatrics and Adolescent Medicine, 151*(6), 648–653.

American Academy of Pediatrics (AAP) (2002). *Promoting optimal health for American children: A summary report 1997–2001.* Elk Grove Village, IL: Healthy Child Care America.

American Academy of Pediatrics (2001). Tobacco's toll: Implications for the pediatrician. *Pediatrics, 107*(4), 794–798.

Anderson, B. (2000). School health education in a multicultural society. [ERIC Digest] Champaign, IL: Eric Clearinghouse.

Back injuries are preventable. (1999). *Healthy Child Care. 1*(2). Retrieved October 28, 2005, from http://www.healthychild.net/articles/hy2back.html

Bowling, H., & Rogers, S. (2001). The value of healing in education. *Young Children, 56*(2), 79–81.

Brook, J., Brook, D., & Whiteman, M. (2000). The influence of maternal smoking during pregnancy on toddlers negativity. *Archives of Pediatric Medicine, 154*(4), 381–385.

Burke, V., Gracey, M., Milligan, R., Thompson, C., Taggart, A., & Beilan, L. (1998). Parental smoking and risk factors for cardiovascular diseases in 10 to 12 year old children. *Journal of Pediatrics, 133*(2), 206–213.

Calder, J. (2000). Oh my aching back . . . and other caregiver health challenges. *Child Care Health Connections, 13*(3), 10–11.

Carballo, M., & Nerukar, A. (2001). Migration, refugees and health risks. *Emerging Infectious Diseases, 7*(3), 556–560.

Children's Foundation. (2000). *2000 Child care center licensing study.* Washington, DC: Children's Foundation Cost, Quality, and Child Outcomes Study Team.

Clements, D., Zaref, J., Bland, C., Walter, E., & Coplan, P. (2001). Partial uptake of varicellas vaccine and the epidemiological effect on varicella disease in 11 day-care centers in North Carolina. *Archives of Pediatrics and Adolescent Medicine, 155*(4), 455–461.

Collins, R., Mascia, J., Kendall, R. Golden, O. & Schock, L. (2003, March). Promoting mental health in child care settings: Caring for the whole child. *Zero to Three,* 39–45.

Crocker, A. (2003). Preventing back pain. *Healthy Child Care, 5*(6). Retrieved October 28, 2005, from http://www.healthychild.net/articles/hy30backpain.html.

Crute, S. (2004). Stressed out. *NEA Today.* Retrieved Nov. 3, 2005 from http://www.nea.org/neatoday/0401/stressed.html.

De Schipper, J., Tavecchio, L., Van Ijzendoorn, M., & Van Zeijil, J. (2004). Goodness-of-fit in center day care: Relations of temperament, stability and quality of care with the child's adjustment. *Early Childhood Research Quarterly, 19*(2), 257–272.

Duarte, G., & Rafanello, D. (2001). The migrant child: a special place in the field. *Young Children, 56*(2), 26–34.

Edwards, C., & Raikes, H. (2002). Extending the dance: Relationship-based approaches to infant/toddler care and education. *Young Children, 57*(4), 10–17.

Emmons, K., Wong, M., Hammond, S., Velicer, W., Fava, J., Monroe, A., & Evans, J. (2001). Intervention and policy issues related to children's exposure to environmental tobacco smoke. *Preventive Medicine, 32*(2), 321–331.

Foxman, P. (2004). *The worried child.* Alameda, CA: Hunter House Publishers.

Ghazavini, A., & Mullis, R. (2002). Center-based care for young children: Examining predictors of quality. *Journal of Genetic Psychology, 163*(1), 112–125.

Ginott, H. (1972). *Teacher and child.* New York: Macmillan.

Greenspan, S. (2003). Child care research: A clinical perspective. *Child Development, 74*(4), 1064–1068.

Greider, K. (1998, November). Secondhand smoke: risks to kids range from ear infections to SIDS. *Parent's Magazine,* 42–45.

Guendelman, S., & Pearl, M. (2001). Access to care for children of the working poor. *Archives of Pediatrics and Adolescent Medicine, 155*(6), 651–658.

Gunnar, M. (2005). How young children manage stress: Looking for links between temperament and experience. University of Minnesota, College of Education and Human Development. Retrieved on 11/3/05 from http://education.umn.edu/research/ResearchWorks/Gunnar.html.

Hamre, B., & Pianta, R. (2004). Self-reported depression in nonfamilial caregivers: Prevalence and association with caregiver behavior in child care settings. *Early Childhood Research Quarterly, 19*(2), 297–318.

Herbst, A. (1999, September). What's wrong with our children? *Parents Magazine,* 108–115.

Honig, A. (1993). Mental health for babies: What do theory and research tell us? *Young Children, 48*(3), 69–76.

Hopper, J., & Craig, K. (2000). Environmental tobacco smoke exposure among urban children. *Pediatrics, 106*(4), e47.

Husted, A. (1996, April 23). Secondhand smoke can hurt unborn babies. Retrieved October 28, 2005, from http://www.fensende.com/Users/swnymph/refs/smoke.html.

Klerman, L. (2004). Protecting children: Reducing their environmental tobacco smoke exposure. Nicotine and Tobacco Research. Retrieved 11/3/05 from http://www.ntrjournal.org/klerman.pdf

Kreisher, K. (2002, July/August). Burned out. *Children's Voice Article.* Children's Welfare League of America. Retrieved October 28, 2005, from http://www.cwla.org/articles/cv0207burnedout.htm.

Kunitz, J. (2001). Provider health: Caring for ourselves. *Child Care Health Connections, 14*(1), 10.

Kunitz, J. (2003). Staff immunizations. *Child Care Health Connections Newsletter, 16*(3), 3, 9.

Kunitz, J. (2004). Proper lifting and carrying. *Child Care Health Connections Newsletter, 17*(6), 3, 11.

Loeb, S., Fuller, B., Kagan, S., & Carrol, B. (2004). Child care in poor communities: Early learning effects of type, quality and stability. *Child Development, 75*(1), 47–65.

Los Angeles County Child Care Directory. (LACCD). (2001). *What is quality child care.* Los Angeles, CA: Author. Retrieved October 28, 2005, from http://www.childcare.co.la.us/qualitycc.cfm.

Maccoby, E., & Lewis, C. (2003). Less care or different day care? *Child Development, 74*(4), 1069–1075.

Males, M. (1995, September, 9). It's the adults, stupid: A flawed war on drugs and smoking. *New York Times,* 50179.

Mannino, D., Albalak, R. Grosse, S. & Repace, J. (2003). Second-hand smoke exposure and blood levels in U.S. children. *Epidemiology, 14*(6), 719–717.

Mannino, D., Moorman, J., Kingsley, B., Rose, D., & Repace, J. (2001). Health effects related to environmental tobacco smoke exposure in children in the United States. *Archives of Pediatrics and Adolescent Medicine, 155*(1), 36–41.

National Institutes of Health (NIH). (2003, July 16). Child care linked to assertive, noncompliant and aggressive behaviors: Vast majority of children with normal range. NIH News Release. Retrieved October 28, 2005, from http://www.nichd.nih.gov/new/releases/child_care.cfm.

North Carolina Child Care Health and Safety Resource Center (NCCCHSRC). (2004). Helping your child manage stress. *North Carolina Child Care Health and Safety Bulletin, 4*(5), 5.

Park, A. (1999, August 9). Your health: Bad news. *Time Magazine.* Retrieved from http://www.time.com/time/magazine/archive/.

Pennsylvania Chapter American Academy of Pediatrics (PAAAP). (2004). When parents won't immunize their children. *Early Childhood Health Link, 14*(4), 1–2.

Raikes, H. (1996). A secure base for babies. *Young Children, 51*(4), 59–67.

Salmon, D., Omer, S., Moulton, L., Stokley, S., deHart, M., Lett, S., Norman, B., Teret, S., & Halsey, N. (2005). Exemptions to school immunization requirements: The role of school-level requirements, policies and procedures. *American Journal of Public Health, 95*(3), 436–440.

Santoli, J., Huet, N., Smith, P., Barker, L., Rodewald, L., Inkeias, M., Olson, L., & Halfon, N. (2004). Insurance status and vaccination coverage among US preschool children. *Pediatrics, 113*(6), 1959–1964.

Silverstein, M., Sales, A., & Koepsell, T. (2003). Health care utilization and expenditures associated with child care attendance: A nationally representative sample. *Pediatrics, 111*(4), 371–375.

Stathis, S., O'Callaghan, M., Williams, G., Najman, J., Anderson, M., & Bor, W. (1999). Maternal cigarette smoking during pregnancy is an independent predictor for symptoms of middle ear disease at five years postdelivery. *Pediatrics, 104*(2), e16.

Sutton, A. (2003). Physicals and immunizations. *Healthy Child Care, 6*(2). Retrieved September 19, 2004 from http://www.healthychild.net/articles/hy32physicals.html.

Unimmunized children in child care settings. (2003, December). San Francisco: Child Care Law Center. Retrieved October 28, 2005, from http://www.childcarelaw.org/Publications/Summer2003-corrected.pdf

University of Colorado at Denver, University of California at Los Angeles, University of North Carolina, & Yale University. (1995, January). *Cost, quality, and child outcomes in child care centers* [Executive Summary].

U.S. Department of Health and Human Services (2004). *The Health Consequences of Smoking: A Report of the Surgeon General.* U.S. Department of Health and Human Services, Centers for Disease Control and Prevention, National Center for Chronic Disease Prevention and Health Promotion, Office on Smoking and Health.

Walker, K. (2004). Pesticide use in child care. *Child Care Health Connections Newsletter, 17*(5), 4, 10.

Wallach, L. (1993). Four ways to help children cope with violence. *Education Digest, 59*(2), 29–32.

Werner, E & Smith, R. (2001). *Journeys from childhood to midlife: Risk, resilience, and recovery.* Ithaca, New York: Cornell University Press.

Zamani, R. (2000a). Diversity: Facing the diverse needs of all children. *Child Care Health Connections, 13*(6), 8.

Zamani, R. (2000b). Traditional practices can affect the health of children. *Child Care Health Connections, 13*(5), 9.

Zamani, A. (2003). Vaccines: Not just for children. *Child Care Health Connections Newsletter, 16*(6), 5.

Zenah, P., Stafford, B., Nagle, G., & Rice, T. (2005, January). *Addressing social-emotional development and infant mental health in early childhood systems.* Building State Early Childhood Comprehensive Systems Series, No. 12. Los Angeles, CA: National Center for Infant and Early Childhood Health Policy.

Additional resources for this chapter can be found by visiting the Online Companion™ at http://www.earlychilded.delmar.com. This supplemental material includes extensive chapter quizzes, PowerPoint® outlines, Web links, and various other activities to help better utilize the material in this chapter. The site is updated regularly, so you may check back often to receive the latest information about the subjects in each chapter.

## CHAPTER 11

# Tools for Promoting Good Health in Children

**After reading this chapter, you should be able to:**

### 11.1 Health Policies

Define and discuss health policies for appraising, screening, and assessment.

### 11.2 Recording Health Status of Children

Describe and detail the process of recording appraisals, screening, and assessment.

### 11.3 Assessing a Child's Health Status

Summarize the components of a child's health and how they are assessed.

### 11.4 Implications for Teachers

Relate the importance of education, observation, working with families, and the use of appraisals, screening, and assessment.

## 11.1  HEALTH POLICIES

Children grow and develop at different rates. They also have different levels of health and well-being. Each child must be looked at individually for accurate health assessment. Forming a health policy for appraising, screening, and assessing a child's health is a major task of the teacher. A child's health is a very significant factor in her overall well-being. The following indicators show the need for creating and implementing policies for observation, record keeping, and assessment:

- All teachers should have good tools to assess a child's development (APHA & AAP, 2002; Helms, Clifford, & Cryer, 2004).
- Teachers should be able to recognize developmental delay, signs of maltreatment, disabilities, and other possible health problems (Collins et al., 2003).
- Failure to evaluate and assess a child's progress may deprive the child of needed intervention and corrective measures (Allen, 2004a).
- A teacher should be aware that development takes place in a holistic manner, so that all the contexts are considered. Observation helps meet the needs of children from all backgrounds (Edwards & Raikes, 2002).
- Observations about the child's health, habits, and behaviors help in the early detection of problems (Allen, 2004b). Many types of technology can be used to help the teacher record observations (Nilsen, 2005).

Using health policies for observing, recording, and evaluating a child's health will allow for uniformity in how **appraisals** and **screenings** are carried out. These policies will provide information for **early intervention**, if necessary, and will help protect other children from contagious situations. **Assessment** provides a multitude of tools and procedures that are used to support the child's healthy development and to signify difficulties as they occur.

According to standards of the National Association for the Education of Young Children (NAEYC), a well-prepared teacher should understand the reason for assessment. This knowledge will allow the teacher to use effective assessment strategies (Hyson, 2002). The teacher is often the **primary health assessor**. In an early childhood education center, the director and aides may also contribute to the assessment of the child's health. Creating open lines of communication with the parent is essential to the evaluation of a child's health status. Successful communication begins before issues of concern appear (Dailey, 1999). If there is observation or other information that indicates a child needs screening and **referral**, a discussion with the parent can clarify information and a decision about the next step can be made. Some families coming into care may need more services than a teacher can provide (Politis, 2003). If the decision is for referral, then other professionals such as a speech therapist or audiologist will contribute to the overall assessment and any resulting intervention. Teachers who do not have training in how to handle specific health issues may not be able to meet the needs of a child with a chronic illness (Cianciolo et al., 2004).

There are professional health consultants available for early childhood education environments. These are often nurses or public health nurses who will help both to create policies and to assess a child's health if problems appear (Alkon et al., 2002; Cianciolo et al., 2004).

- **Appraisals**
  *regular process of evaluation of a child's health or developmental norms*
- **Screenings**
  *to select or evaluate through a process*
- **Early intervention**
  *decision to modify a child's at-risk behavior or condition in an early stage in order to lessen the impact of the behavior or condition on the life of the child*
- **Assessment**
  *in-depth appraisal to determine whether a particular health or developmental condition is occurring*
- **Primary health assessor**
  *teacher who knows the children very well and can observe for health and well-being*
- **Referral**
  *sending a child for further testing or screening and making available resources that will intervene and avert risk that is posed to the child*

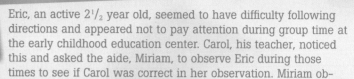

Eric, an active 2¹/₂ year old, seemed to have difficulty following directions and appeared not to pay attention during group time at the early childhood education center. Carol, his teacher, noticed this and asked the aide, Miriam, to observe Eric during those times to see if Carol was correct in her observation. Miriam observed Eric for several weeks and documented what she observed. She agreed with Carol that Eric had attention problems. Carol discussed the situation with Eric's father, Joe, and asked Joe to watch Eric at home. Joe agreed to do this, but he seemed to think that Eric's problem might be related to a recent divorce and living in a single-parent family situation. Joe reported to Carol after a weekend of observation that Eric did seem to have attention problems in certain circumstances. Carol, Joe, and Raoul, the director, met to discuss the situation.

Raoul suggested that they begin with a hearing assessment. Eric went to his physician, who felt further tests were needed and sent Eric to a hearing specialist. The specialist concluded that Eric had a hearing deficit that had gone unnoticed during language development but was serious enough to cause problems at his present age.

Eric was fitted for a hearing aid, and the difference in his attention was remarkable. No one had realized how much Eric had done to compensate for his problem. Now that he could hear, he was like a sponge, trying to soak up information. He asked many questions and was involved in the learning process. Eric's father was grateful that Carol had noticed Eric's problem and had pursued it.

The teacher, as the primary health assessor, is responsible for ongoing observations of the health status of each child in his care. Recorded observations are an additional benefit of presenting a complete picture of a child's health status to parents and can aid doctors in diagnosing health problems.

It is important to understand that, as a primary health assessor, the teacher is a participant observer (Collins et al., 2003). In the early childhood education environment, the teacher rarely has the opportunity to stand back for long periods of time and either casually or formally observe children without interruption. In addition, the teacher brings her own perspective as an assessor. The teacher's temperament, ethnicity, culture, gender, and experience will affect how she assesses a child's health and development (Caufield & Kataoka-Yahiro, 2001).

All of the preceding factors contribute to the need for definite policies to evaluate a child's health status. These health policies include:

- *Record Keeping:* specific objectives and methods of recording health information
- *Assessing a Child's Health Status:* procedures for translating and evaluating information to form assessment; includes using indicators of health difficulties
- *Implications for Teachers:* specific practices for observation, education, working with families, cultural sensitivity, and supervision

## Key Concept 11.1

### Health Policies

Specific health policies for appraising, screening, and assessment are necessary to enable the teacher, as the primary assessor, to accurately evaluate the health status of children. These policies include record keeping and assessing health status. Implications for teachers include practices for observation, education, cultural competence, and supervision.

## 11.2  RECORDING HEALTH STATUS OF CHILDREN

**Observation** helps present a specific picture of an individual child's health status as well as his temperament, personality, behavioral characteristics, and abilities. What a teacher considers significant and what needs further deliberation depends on the individual's insight and intuition. These insights from observation are included in the child's permanent health record.

- **Observation**
  *primary means of data gathering in order to understand children's development and behavior*

### Record Keeping Management Tools

Health policies for record keeping should consider what may be implied as a result of what has been observed. Care should be taken to be as accurate as possible when taking notes and recording information (Nilsen, 2005). Teachers should remember that they are making observations, not diagnoses. A number of different types of record keeping management tools can be used to decrease bias and to present a more accurate picture of the health status of the child.

*Precise Words.* The first of these tools is the use of precise words to describe the condition or event that is observed. For example, "Joey has a snotty nose" might be better recorded as "Joey's nose is constantly oozing yellow-green mucus." Children can get runny noses from colds, allergies, changes in temperature, communicable diseases, and so forth. The fact that the mucus is yellow-green and constantly oozing might infer something more serious than sniffles. If Joey's nose runs often, a comparison between more precise descriptions might show a pattern for an allergy or a more serious problem. Using adjectives that clearly describe what was observed can be a way to increase perceptions about the children in care (Cartwright, 1994).

*Type of Record.* The next health management tool for record keeping is the type of record that will be kept. There are a number of different types of records that are helpful, and there are advantages and disadvantages for each type. Table 11-1 indicates the major types of records for observing health status and the conditions in which each type would be most accurate.

An early childhood education center might use checklists as a major source of record keeping due to the number of children assigned to each teacher. There also may be more need for **time sampling** and **event sampling** due to the number of children involved. **Anecdotal** and **running records** would be used occasionally as time permits or as a situation demands. The use of conversation to mentally or even physically record the level of a child's speech and language is a good developmental tool. A teacher in an early childhood education program at a center would be the most likely to use all types of record keeping.

A family child care provider would more likely use a combination of anecdotal records and checklists as the major source of record keeping. A family child care home usually has children of mixed ages, so the provider has a wider age range to observe. A running record would be used only as necessary, and there probably would be little need for time sampling or event sampling unless a condition or behavior were serious enough to merit their use.

A nanny or in-home care provider would rely mostly on anecdotal records. A nanny should keep a daily log that records the child's health and developmental milestones or difficulties. A running record may be used if the nanny or parents have a specific concern about the child. Because the nanny usually has fewer children to care for and usually spends more time with each child than other types of caregivers do, there would be little need for time sampling or event sampling because the behavior recurrence or conditions leading to behavior would probably already have been noted. A nanny might use a checklist for the daily quick health check, but she would be more likely to do it mentally than to record any significant factors in the daily log.

- **Time sampling** *occurs when an observer records a particular behavior over a specific period of time*
- **Event sampling** *occurs when an observer records a specific preselected behavior as it occurs, every time it occurs*
- **Anecdotal** *a brief narrative account that describes a child's behavior that is significant to the observer*
- **Running records** *a detailed narrative account that describes a child's behavior in sequence, as it occurs*

*Pause for Reflection*

Have you ever had any experience using any of the assessment tools listed? If yes, was a more accurate picture provided with the use of something this formal? What tools do you think would be most useful to you in the future?

*How to Keep Records.* The type of record keeping used usually determines how the record will be kept. Anecdotal notes can be kept in the child's health record, on file cards, or in a notebook and later placed in the child's health file. Running records are usually recorded on separate sheets of paper and then filed. Checklists and time and event samples are usually printed forms that can be added to the child's file.

**TABLE 11-1**
*Types of Health Assessment Records*

| Type of Record | Definition | Best Used For | Limitations |
|---|---|---|---|
| Anecdotal | Brief narrative accounts that describe health conditions and behavior | Daily open-ended observation | Relies on memory of observer, can be out of context |
| Running Record | Detailed narrative account in sequence of health status conditions and behaviors | More comprehensive and keeps better track over time | Time consuming; teacher must have time apart from children to record |
| Checklist | Lists of specific health status, communicable diseases, absence of sign, symptom; monthly, quarterly, and yearly growth and development observations | Daily scan | Specific traits and behaviors; does not describe |
| Time Sampling | Records frequency of health status condition or behavior occurrences | Good for over time, takes less time; objective and controlled | Does not describe condition or behavior |
| Event Sampling | Waits for health condition or behavior to occur, then records specific behaviors | Reoccurring problem; objective and defined ahead of time | Misses details of condition or behavior |

*Adapted from: Observing the Development of Young Children,* by Janice J. Beaty, 2002, *New York: Macmillan,* and *Week by Week Documenting the Development of Young Children,* by Barbara A. Nilsen, 2005, *Clifton Park, NY: Thomson Delmar Learning.*

A teacher might use a tape recorder, digital camera, or video recorder for anecdotal notes, running records, time sampling, or event sampling. Video recordings might also be used for checklists. It is important that permission be obtained for any audio, photographic, or video record to be placed on file before these technologies are used (Nilsen, 2005). The advantages of a digital camera are that film does not need to be developed and a record can be kept conveniently on a compact disc (CD) for further use.

The child's health record file should include all observations made. The file will give a view of the child's health status, conditions, and development over time and may be invaluable to a health professional if a child has warning signals for specific problems. The health file is also a tool for creating good two-way communication with the parent about the child and his development. The health file can be used as part of the regular parent/teacher conferences to discuss the child's overall development. The health record file might be kept on a CD to save room and for greater convenience. If a scanner is available, all records can be scanned and added to the CD. Technology can be very useful in observing children and promoting good health policies and practices.

The type of record keeping tool used for health observation differs depending on the type of care. For example, a teacher in this small classroom with few children may be able to use both checklists and anecdotal notes.

## Key Concept 11.2

### Health Records

Record keeping is a good tool for health management. The wording used to record what is observed should be accurate and descriptive. The type of record that is kept will depend on the care situation as well as the conditions or behaviors that are being recorded. The records that are kept are a valuable tool for communicating with parents and for providing information to health professionals. Technology can be a great assistance in observing and recording behaviors that may be a risk to health and in keeping health records.

## 11.3 ASSESSING A CHILD'S HEALTH STATUS

Appraising a child's health and well-being, screening for **developmental norms**, and evaluating the information obtained allow the teacher to assess a child's health status. This is done at several levels, including the following:

● **Developmental norms**
*Developmental norms statistically average ages which children demonstrate certain developmental abilities and behaviors*

- a daily quick health check
- a general health appraisal
- screening for growth and developmental norms
- a mental health appraisal
- a nutritional assessment

Recorded health observations should be accurate and informative. It is important that teachers realize they are presenting observed behaviors, not diagnosing a problem.

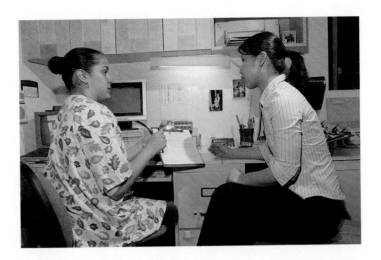

Raphael, a fifteen-month-old active toddler, was being dropped off at the family child care home by his mother, Anna. Frances, the teacher, noticed that Raphael was not his normally happy self and that he appeared to be feverish. Anna explained that she had taken Raphael to the doctor for a checkup the day before and he had received his current series of immunizations. Anna told Frances that the doctor had said that Raphael might be cranky and have a slight fever for 24 hours. Armed with that information, Frances said good-bye to Anna and kept a close watch on Raphael. He played quietly and did not eat as much as normal, but he did not have any other symptoms.

Frances was glad to have the information because when she had first started her child care business, a mother had dropped off a child whose fever had become elevated later in the day. Frances had not been able to reach the mother and had been worried for several hours until the child's doctor returned her call. The doctor told Frances that the girl had had an immunization the day before and that the girl's reaction was normal.

## Daily Quick Health Check

The teacher needs to determine on a daily basis whether a child who is ill or has a health condition that may put other children at risk should be excluded from care. The health policy for daily appraisal is an important tool for preventing the spread of illness and disease.

It is done rapidly and is often referred to as a quick health check. The child's health condition is appraised daily when the child enters care. Table 11-2 shows the signs to watch for while performing the daily quick health check observation.

If a child exhibits any of the signs listed in Table 11-2, the teacher should inform the parents and discuss the observations with them immediately.

**TABLE 11-2**
*Daily Health Checklist*

☑ CHECK FOR:

☐ Activity level
☐ Severe sneezing or coughing
☐ Discharge from nose, eyes, or ears
☐ Breathing difficulties
☐ Sores
☐ Swelling or bruises
☐ Rashes or unusual spots
☐ General mood and behavior
☐ Skin color (pale or flushed)

However, if the symptoms are included in the child care exclusion policy, the parent should take the child home. If the observation is of something vague, the teacher and parent will need to discuss how the child should be managed that day and at what point the teacher will contact the parent. The discussion could reveal a simple explanation of the problem and may alleviate the teacher's concerns.

Figure 11-1 shows the signs that the teacher should be on alert for throughout the day as well as over time if there is a more serious problem.

## General Health Appraisal

A general health appraisal is used when warning signs of questionable health or illness are observed. It can also be used to track the recurrence of illness or health conditions. This appraisal goes into more depth as to the signs of health and illness the teacher might observe in the children in care.

If the teacher notices frequent recurring conditions or that a child is not acting normally, the teacher may want to take a closer look at the child's health. Recurring physical problems such as frequent colds or ear infections may indicate that a child has an allergy or other health problem that needs to be evaluated by a physician. The frequency of a condition will be noted in the child's health record. The parent should be consulted about the frequency before further information is gathered.

If the teacher feels more information is needed, he should seek the help of a health consultant with the parent's permission. That person can help the teacher decide whether the child needs to be seen by a physician or community health clinic. Discussions with the health consultant can assist the teacher in being better prepared to seek further cooperation with the parent about the child's specific health concern.

It is also helpful if a child has a **medical home**. This medical home partnership unites the parents, teachers, and health professionals to ensure that all health and developmental needs are met (Reeves, 2002). The American Academy of Pediatrics (AAP) suggests that the medical home should be family centered and culturally effective. Evaluation of a child's development and needed early intervention can be coordinated through the medical

● **Medical home**
*a partnership of the family, the teacher, and a medical practitioner that ensures that all health, psychosocial, and educational needs of a child are met*

**FIGURE 11-1**
Daily health check.

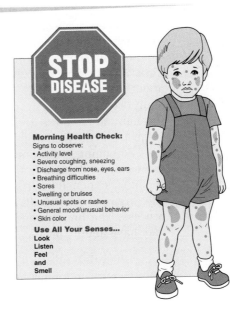

**Morning Health Check:**
Signs to observe:
• Activity level
• Severe coughing, sneezing
• Discharge from nose, eyes, ears
• Breathing difficulties
• Sores
• Swelling or bruises
• Unusual spots or rashes
• General mood/unusual behavior
• Skin color

**Use All Your Senses...**
Look
Listen
Feel
and
Smell

home (AAP, 2002). More information on the medical home can be found in Chapter 16.

## Screening for Growth and Developmental Norms

Screening for growth and development is an essential component of the health status assessment process (Allen, 2004b). Screening identifies whether growth and development fall into the normal pattern and can indicate a potential problem or impairment. An observer should have some knowledge of the normal range of age expectations for developmental milestones (Katz, 1997). Summaries of milestones for development are listed in this section, as are assessment tools, where applicable.

An alert teacher can help detect whether a child falls within the normal range for growth and development. This could be vital in the child's future health status (Lyles, 2003). A child who is small and light for her age may have a growth abnormality and should see a physician, and perhaps a dietician. A child whose speech is garbled at two-and-a-half may need a therapist or audiologist. Many different conditions that can be corrected may be uncovered through careful observation and recording. It is also important to be able to recognize the red flags for developmental norms that are not met (Allen, 2004a). A policy of quarterly screening for developmental norms can aid in this process.

A change in a child's behavior or a child with behavioral difficulties may indicate mental health risk, a nutritional deficiency, child maltreatment, or a physical health impairment. Appraising a child's physical and mental health and nutritional intake will enable discussions with parents to help determine whether a referral should be made. If child maltreatment is suspected, reporting the observation and showing the records that have been kept to proper authorities will be necessary. A health policy for appraisals and consequent discussion or referral is necessary to allow the process to run smoothly.

The American Public Health Association (APHA) and the AAP suggest that teachers have some form of a health consultant on whom to call when they need a resource for assessing health and well-being. The consultant can be a physician, a pediatric or family nurse practitioner, or a registered nurse (APHA & AAP, 2002). The consultant should have some knowledge about nonparental child care, the community, and available resources. Many communities in this country have health consultants available through the resource and referral network or the medical community. This subject is dealt with at greater length in Chapter 13.

Screening is routinely done in early childhood education centers and can easily be done in family child care homes or in the child's own home. It is neither expensive nor sophisticated. Screening takes a closer look at specific areas and can add important information to the overall assessment process. The health consultant can assist with any questions the teacher may have about specific screening methods. Screening is used to

- measure height and weight
- appraise motor development
- check vision
- appraise hearing
- evaluate speech and language
- assess nutritional intake and deficiencies
- appraise mental health

Periodic height and weight checks are exciting for the children and foster a knowledge of pride in their own bodies. The height and weight assessment can be incorporated into the classroom curriculum by visually representing each child's height and weight (on a wall or piece of posterboard) at regular intervals.

Karla, a healthy three-and-a-half-year-old, was very self-confident. She enjoyed having her family child care provider measure her and liked to get on the scale and see how much she weighed. Martine, the teacher, had a special place on her family room wall that was used to measure the height of children in her care. Every two months, Martine would bring out the scale and let the children stand against their spot on the wall to measure them so they could see how they were growing. One day when the children went through this process, Karla could not wait to tell her mother, "I'm three-and-a-half, and three (feet tall), and I weigh 34 (pounds)." She looked forward to these screening opportunities, and they helped her be more comfortable when she had to go to the doctor.

● **Failure to thrive**
*failure of a child to grow physically and develop mentally according to the norms. This condition may occur because of organic defects or lack of emotional bonding*

Infancy is a period of dramatic weight and height gains. Infants should be weighed regularly to ensure that they are growing at a normal rate. The presence of a weight and height below the normal range for the infant's age could indicate a condition called *failure to thrive*.

*Measuring Height and Weight.* Children of all ages fall into a range of normal heights and weights that are calculated on a growth chart. Growth charts are easy to follow and are used to direct attention to body size for age that is not the norm. These growth charts are also available on the Web site of the National Centers for Health Statistics branch of the Centers for Disease Control and Prevention (CDC). The address is: http://www.cdc.gov/growthcharts/. Physicians routinely use these charts to detect problems or abnormalities in a child's growth.

Recording a child's height and weight is part of the normal screening process that a teacher performs on a quarterly basis. It helps familiarize children with their bodies and helps them to better understand the screening process in the doctor's office. Children enjoy knowing how tall they are and how much they weigh. Even though they do not understand what the numbers mean, children seem to gain a sense of self-identification from them.

If a child seems unusually small, thin, obese, or tall for his age, there may be a good reason to compare his height and weight to the growth chart. These conditions may indicate poor nutrition, a hormonal imbalance, or a disease that causes retarded or accelerated growth. Sometimes children exhibit a condition called **failure to thrive** that indicates they are below the normal height and weight range for their age. Other children may be overweight for their height. Screening and early intervention may help prevent obesity. The results of the chart comparison should be discussed with a parent. If there is an indicator for further examination, a referral course should be planned. A discussion with the health consultant would be helpful at this point. The most common starting point for a referral of this sort is the child's own physician. If the child does not have a primary physician, a community health clinic would be the next most likely source that the teacher could recommend to the family.

If changes in diet are indicated, the teacher can support those changes. The teacher will need to be informed by the parent or health professional what should be done to help the child. The teacher could turn to the health consultant for further assistance.

*Appraising Motor Development.* As a child develops, her ability to perform physical activities and use acquired motor skills is one of the most evident areas in growth and development. It is easily observable and is fairly easy to screen. A child should be able to perform the gross motor skills and fine motor skills that are normal for her age range. A certain degree of co-ordination should also be present. Table 11-3 indicates the developmental motor skill norms for the first two years of life.

For children older than two years of age, there are other motor skills and degrees of coordination that should be present. Between ages 2.5 and 3.5 years, a child should be able to perform the gross motor and fine motor skills listed in Table 11-4.

When a child does not appear to be following the development norms for his age, there are usually caution signs present. The warning signals for motor development difficulties are included in Table 11-5.

Some assessment tools that can be used to further evaluate a child's motor skills are The Denver Developmental Screening Tool, The Mullin Scale, The Hawaii Early Learning Profile, the Bayley Assessment Tool, and the Gessell Assessment Tool. A health consultant could help the teacher decide which developmental tool would be most appropriate and might also

**TABLE 11-3**
*Developmental Norms for Gross Motor Skills in Infants*

| Motor Skill | Month at which 90% of Infants Master Skill |
|---|---|
| Lifts head up while lying on stomach | 3.2 |
| Sits with head steady | 4.2 |
| Rolls over | 4.7 |
| Sits alone | 7.8 |
| Stands holding on | 10 |
| Walks holding on | 12.7 |
| Stands alone steadily | 13.9 |
| Walks well | 14.3 |
| Walks up stairs with help | 22.0 |
| Kicks ball forward | 24.0 |

*Reprinted with permission of DDM. © 1969, 1989, 1990 W. K Frankenburg and J. B. Dodds © 1978 W. K. Frankenburg.*

**TABLE 11-4**
*Developmental Norms for Motor Skills of Children 2.5 Years to 3.5 Years*

| Gross Motor Skills | Fine Motor Skills |
|---|---|
| Walk well with a normal gait | Use eating utensils well |
| Run in a straight line | Copy a circle |
| Jump in the air with both feet | Scribble |
| Throw a ball | Stack blocks |
| Reach for objects with one hand | Manipulate large puzzle pieces |
| Climb | Smear paint |
| Hang by both hands | |

**TABLE 11-5**
*Caution Signs for Motor Development*

Throwing a ball in the air is an example of a gross motor skill that children normally master between 2.5 and 3.5 years of age.

✓ **CHECK FOR:**

## WARNINGS

☐ Has difficulty judging distances in relation to himself

☐ Lacks large muscle control and appears clumsy and uncoordinated

☐ Has difficulty pointing out or locating parts of the body

☐ Lacks small muscle control in things like cutting and coloring

☐ Lacks steady hand or arm when reaching or stacking; arm or hand appears to tremble

☐ Has difficulty walking or walks exclusively on the toes

☐ After walking has been mastered, falls frequently or has difficulty using stairs

☐ At the age of 3 years has difficulty building a tower of more than four blocks or cannot copy a circle

assist in the administration of the assessment tool or refer the teacher to a source for help. These tools are not commonly administered by the teacher because they require specialized training.

If it is determined that a child appears to have a motor skill problem, the teacher and a parent should discuss the referral procedure. If the child has a medical home and the team is already working together, referral would be an easy procedure. If there is no medical home, then the child's physician, a community health agency, or a **regional center** is a good starting point. Physical activities may be prescribed to help the child learn to cope with the motor skill difficulties. The teacher will be a source of support for both the child and the parent during this period.

*Checking Vision.* Children use vision to take in information about the world around them, sort it, and then make sense out of it. Visual difficulties should be caught as early as possible for correction and treatment. Children are normally screened for vision during their regular checkups with a physician. If there appears to be a problem, the physician will refer the child to an eye specialist to determine whether there is a visual deficiency. Some children may not have regular physical checkups, so vision problems may not be caught. Vision difficulties can appear over time or rapidly. The signs indicating that a child may have hidden eye problems or visual perception difficulties are listed in Table 11-6.

If the teacher observes any of the conditions listed in Table 11-6, the concerns should be discussed with a parent. The parents may have noticed the same conditions or may already have the child in care for that condition. If that is the case, it is important for the parent to share the information. If the child is not under care, it is important for the parent to understand the potential seriousness of an eye condition and refer the child to his physician or local health clinic.

There are three common eye conditions found in children: nearsightedness, strabismus, and amblyopia. **Nearsightedness**, the inability to see distant objects clearly, is the most common visual problem in young children.

● **Regional center**
*a center in a particular geographic area dedicated to helping families that have children with special needs. The center acts as a resource, a referral agency, and a source of support for families.*

● **Nearsightedness**
*lack of ability to see well, other than close up*

**TABLE 11-6**
*Caution Signs for Vision Problems*

✓ **CHECK FOR:**

## WARNINGS

**Eye Problems:**

☐ Persistent redness, swelling, crusting, or discharge in eyes or eyelids

☐ Excessive tearing

☐ Frequent squinting

☐ Eyes that look crooked or crossed or that do not move together

☐ Head held in a tilted position

☐ Drooping eyelids

☐ Continuous rubbing

☐ Eyes that wander

☐ Inability to see objects unless holding them close

**Visual Perception Difficulties:**

☐ Short attention span

☐ Visually distractible

☐ Unable to visually sequence

☐ Difficulty with color vision

☐ Inability to follow objects with both eyes, near and far ranges

# REALITY CHECK

## *Effects of Lead Poisoning on Children*

It was estimated that almost one million children had lead poisoning in 2004 (CDC, 2004). Although these figures were down from record highs in the early 1980s, it still affects a significant number of children. It is a serious environmental health problem that could be prevented (Mulroy et al., 2004). Twenty-five percent of the housing in the United States contains significant amounts of lead in lead-based paint and lead dust. Lead poisoning affects all families, but African-American and inner city children are most likely to be affected. Twenty percent of African-American children are believed to have some degree of lead poisoning (CDC, 2004). In California, Hispanic children represent more than 80 percent of those found with elevated blood lead levels (Schilling, 2004). Lead poisoning has been called the number one environmental threat to children for many years (Jaroff, 2001).

Children younger than six years of age are especially vulnerable to the effects of lead poisoning because their bodies, including the nervous system, are still developing (Environmental Protection Agency [EPA], 2004). The AAP has even considered lowering the acceptable blood lead levels because there appear to be problems in children who have blood levels lower than what was previously considered acceptable. Lead poisoning can cause mild to severe lasting effects on children. It can affect all systems in the body and does not always show definite symptoms (CDC, 2001). Even low levels of lead are harmful and are correlated with decreased intelligence, affect the development of the nervous system and brain,

## REALITY CHECK (Continued)

and can retard growth (EPA, 2004). Low levels of lead can also be associated with behavioral problems (Mulroy et al., 2004). The effects of damage to the nervous system and brain may manifest themselves as cognitive deficits, lack of ability to concentrate, or even inability to learn (Ryan et al., 1999). Reading, writing, math, visual abilities, and motor skills may be affected. Signs that children may have elevated levels of lead include irritability, insomnia, colic, hearing difficulties, lack of eye-hand coordination, and anemia. If blood levels are high enough, a child could go into seizures and even die from the elevation of lead in the blood.

Lead poisoning has been found to cause learning difficulties and behavior problems. Children with high levels of lead are six times more likely to have reading disabilities. Some experts believe that lead poisoning can contribute to aggression and antisocial and delinquent behaviors (AAP, 1998). One study found that there is a relationship between lead exposure and violent behavior in the commission of homicide (Stretesky & Lynch, 2001).

Many children younger than six years of age live in homes that have peeling lead paint or lead dust in the environment. Families from these houses are almost equally divided between lower and middle/upper incomes. Renters and homeowners are equally likely to have this problem. Children affected by lead poisoning come from all cultural and racial groups (Jaroff, 2001).

More than 80 percent of houses built before 1980 have lead-based paint (NSC, 2004). Lead-based paint was banned in 1978. Lead was removed from gasoline in the 1980s. This has helped to reduce lead levels, but it has not removed it as an environmental hazard to children (Environmental health issues, 1999).

Lead poisoning is most likely to occur if leaded dust or lead paint chips are swallowed. Lead dust is the primary pathway to lead exposure. Children are especially susceptible to lead poisoning because they put many objects in their mouths. They may play in dirt that contains toxic levels of lead, then put contaminated fingers and toys in their mouths. Children

encounter lead chips or dust on window sills, door jams, railings, radiators, and near baseboards. Lead is also found in paint on old toys and furniture and in some jewelry.

Lead is also found in other sources. It has been found in food prepared or served in pottery that contains lead. It can be found in several types of Mexican candy and other traditional snack foods found in Oaxaca and other parts of Mexico that might be brought in or brought back to this country (McKim et al., 2004; August & Brooks, 2005). Brightly colored ethnic home remedies for illness, such as azarcon, may contain lead. Crayons manufactured outside the United States that are particularly bright may contain lead. Secondhand smoke has also been found to contain lead (Mannino et al., 2003).

Lead is absorbed into the bloodstream, then, like calcium, is absorbed by the bone. Lead can accumulate through life. It can be stored in the bone and then return to the bloodstream at any time (Jaroff, 2001). Children's bodies are inclined to absorb more lead, especially if there is an iron deficiency.

The NAEYC recommends a number of protective practices to keep children safe from lead poisoning (Kendrick et al., 1999), including screening children, paint, water, and soil for lead levels. If lead is found, deleading should be done very carefully, and professional assistance may be required. The Department of Health will provide the teacher with this information.

Mulroy et al. (2004) suggested that providing an iron- and calcium-rich diet and washing fruits and vegetables may be preventive measures. Frequent washing of hands, toys, and floors can cut down on lead levels, if present. Thorough housecleaning was found to correlate with reducing blood levels of lead. When houses were cleaned thoroughly 20 or more times per year, children experienced a 34 percent decrease in lead blood levels (Rhoads et al., 1999). For further information the National Lead Information Web site can be accessed at: http://www.epa.gov/lead; this organization may be called at 1-800-424-LEAD.

**CHECK***point:*  What items would you first look for to determine if lead is present in the environment where children are present? What dangers might these items pose? What could be done?

- **Strabismus**

  *a condition that occurs in children that causes one or both eyes to appear crossed*

- **Amblyopia**

  *an unequal balance of a child's eye muscles often referred to as "lazy eye." Condition is improved through the use of eye patch to enable the weaker eye to strengthen with greater use*

It may not be readily detected before the age of two, but corrective lenses will enable the child to see normally. **Strabismus** is the misalignment of the eyes, which occurs because of an imbalance in the eye muscles. It becomes difficult for the eyes to focus on the same point at the same time. Corrective lenses, eye exercises, eyedrops, and sometimes eye surgeries help to correct this problem. **Amblyopia**, also called "lazy eye," occurs when one eye does not see well or is injured, and the other eye takes over almost exclusively. Treatment of this condition is most successful when it is caught before the age of three years. The child wears a patch to prevent vision in the good eye, thereby forcing her to use the inactive eye.

Aaron, two-and-a-half years old, was found to have amblyopia in his right eye. The doctor prescribed glasses with a patch on the right lens. The first day at the early childhood education center, Aaron felt awkward and embarrassed. The other children were curious; some appeared to be fearful and did not understand why Aaron had the patch. At circle time, Regina, the teacher, talked about it with the children. They talked about eyes and how it felt to see things with two eyes and how different it would be to have to use just one eye to help make the other eye see better.

After hearing the comments and questions of the children and sensing Aaron's discomfort, Regina had the children make their own patches and decorate them. Regina, and the children who wanted to, wore the patches tied with yarn during afternoon snack. They were all excited and felt rather glamorous, like a group of pirates. By the end of snack the children with patches could grasp that it was not as easy to see and coordinate with one eye. They all talked about this and asked Aaron questions. These children became helpers to Aaron and their concern restored Aaron's confidence. Regina helped defuse a difficult situation for Aaron.

Vision screening is normally done during a child's regularly scheduled physician visit. However, centers and schools that have a nurse on staff may conduct this screening on site.

Caring for a child with any of these eye conditions will take patience and assistance on the part of the teacher. A child may become easily frustrated or embarrassed over the visual difficulties she is having. It is important that other children understand and not make fun of the child.

*Appraising Hearing.* Hearing loss is caused by a number of factors. For example, a mother may have had an illness while pregnant, or there may have been a genetic factor that caused an abnormal development. Or a child may have been born prematurely or may suffer from recurrent ear infections, allergies, or colds. It is not always easy to detect a hearing loss, but the teacher may notice some caution signals. Table 11-7 contains the ages and questions recommended by the National Association for Speech and Hearing to help the teacher detect whether the child may have a hearing problem.

If a child's responses are not developmentally appropriate, the teacher should discuss with a parent what has been noticed and decide with the parent what action to take for a referral. A conference with the health consultant would help the teacher and the family know how to proceed. Early detection of a hearing problem can help a child learn to cope and adapt to hearing loss or possibly have the hearing repaired.

If a hearing referral is necessary, there are several places to send the child. A visit to the family physician is a good start. Other sources would

**TABLE 11-7**
*Developmental Hearing Norms*

### CHECK FOR:

| | |
|---|---|
| Birth to 3 months | ☐ Does the child listen to speech? |
| | ☐ Does the child cry or startle at noises? |
| 3 to 6 months | ☐ Does the child smile when spoken to? |
| | ☐ Does the child try to turn toward speaker? |
| | ☐ Does the child seem to recognize mother's voice? |
| 6 to 9 months | ☐ Does the child respond to his name? |
| | ☐ Does the child turn head toward where the sound is coming from? |
| | ☐ Does the child notice and look around for source of new sounds? |
| 9 months to 1 year | ☐ Does the child listen to people talking? |
| | ☐ Does the child look up when you call? |
| | ☐ Does the child look around when hearing new sounds? |
| 1 to 2 years | ☐ Can the child follow two requests such as "go to the kitchen and get your cup?" |
| 2 to 4 years | ☐ Can the child point to pictures in a book upon hearing the object named? |
| | ☐ Does the child understand conversation easily? |
| | ☐ Does the child hear the television or music at the same loudness level as everyone else in the room? |
| | ☐ Does the child notice normal sounds like the phone, the doorbell, or a dog's bark? |
| | ☐ Does the child hear you when you call from another room? |

Adapted from Developmental Norms for Speech and Language by the American Speech-Language-Hearing Association © 2005.

Teachers are a good source for observations regarding a child's hearing. It is essential that the teacher be aware of the developmental norms for speech development, which can be an identifier of hearing problems. Teachers may also have access to resources to help parents identify the proper type of specialist to test the child's hearing.

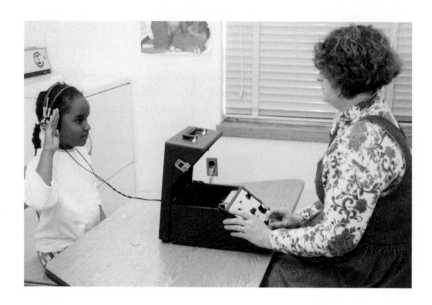

● **Audiologist**

*person trained to identify types of hearing losses, to interpret audiometric tests, and to recommend equipment and procedures to assist the hearing impaired*

include an **audiologist**, a speech language hearing clinic, or a community health agency. Often, school districts have a speech-language and hearing program that will help children in that district before they enter school.

If a hearing loss is detected, the teacher can help the child adapt by speaking slowly and directly at the child, using hand gestures when applicable, and demonstrating more complex instructions where appropriate. Other children in care should be taught these same methods of communicating with the child who has a hearing loss. The teacher can also help to educate and support the parent in the use of these communication methods.

*Evaluating Speech and Language.* Speech and language acquisition come at varying ages in children. Girls tend to verbalize earlier than boys. Children in bilingual households may acquire speech more slowly (Bialystok, 2001). Some children do not acquire speech and language as rapidly as might be expected. These are normal speech and language patterns for children (Perry, 2003). Table 11-8 can help the teacher notice how children use expressive language and if they have the ability to understand at the developmental level given. If a child does not follow this pattern, then the teacher should check the list of warning signals found in Table 11-9.

If a child exhibits any of the caution signs listed in Table 11-9 or is not at the appropriate developmental level, the teacher should discuss this with the parent to determine if the parent agrees that a problem may exist. A discussion with the health consultant may help the teacher and the parent determine the best course of action. The child may have to be referred to a physician or other specialist such as a speech therapist.

A child who has a speech or language problem will need much patience and understanding. The teacher can help the child by allowing her time to speak clearly. The teacher can offer encouragement and reward the child's effort. The child needs caring and warmth. By the teacher's modeling these supportive actions, other children will begin to imitate these actions. This support will make it easier for the child with the problem to practice for success. A child with a good sense of self will be less hesitant or

**TABLE 11-8**
*Normal Speech and Language Developmental Patterns*

| Age | Expressive Language | Ability to Understand |
|---|---|---|
| 3 to 6 months | Babbling, vocalizing pleasure | Smiles in response to speech; seeks sound source; recognizes familiar people and objects |
| 7 to 9 months | Consonants—b,d,m,t,p,z; babbling; imitates speech sounds | Responds to gestures and "no"; can play peek-a-boo, pat-a-cake, and bye-bye |
| 10 to 12 months | First true word may appear; intonations begin; uses all sounds in vocal play | Relates object and name; can follow simple body action commands; always responds to own name |
| 1 to 1½ years | Uses 3 to 20 single words; uses gestures | Follows simple commands; recognizes some body parts and names for objects |
| 1½ to 2 years | Uses 20 to 60 words; combines two words in sentences; 65% speech intelligible | Understands 200 to 300 words; can answer simple yes or no questions |
| 2 to 3 years | Uses 200 to 500 words; three- and four-word sentences; grammar emerges; 70 to 80 percent of speech intelligible | Understands 800 to 900 words; what, why, where questions; can listen to short stories |
| 3 to 4 years | Uses 800 to 1500 words; four- and five-word sentences; asks questions | Understands 1200 to 1500 words; can compare (up and down); responds to two-part commands |
| 4 to 5 years | Uses 1500 to 2000 words; very intelligible speech; eight-word sentences; can tell long stories | Understands 2500 words; answers complex questions; has some color and number concepts |

**TABLE 11-9**
*Caution Signs for Screening and Referral for Speech and Language Development*

## ✓ CHECK FOR:
# WARNINGS

☐ No intelligible speech by two years of age

☐ Voice is monotone, too loud or soft, or of poor quality

☐ Difficult to understand after age three

☐ Nasal quality to voice

☐ Speech too fast or too slow

☐ Difficulty in expressing self, organizing thoughts

☐ Makes very few or no attempts to speak

☐ Inability to produce all speech sounds interfering with communication

☐ Difficulty following directions at appropriate developmental language level

☐ Difficulty in engaging in verbal activities with other children

☐ Stuttering

☐ After the age of four years, inability to communicate in sentences with more than three words or to use "me" or "you" appropriately

Peer interaction during playtime is an ideal time to observe children's speech patterns.

Richard, a bright, cheerful three-year-old, attended a campus early childhood education center three mornings a week. Two full days a week he attended a special school for children with developmental difficulties. Richard was born with a problem with his tongue that was not detected until he was almost two years old. Surgery and the school helped Richard begin to learn how to verbalize. He attended the campus early childhood education center to help him acquire language from his interaction with other children who had good language skills. In the beginning, Richard was hesitant to speak and was somewhat withdrawn. Cathy, his teacher, read several books to the children that dealt with characters who were different. These books helped bring about a dialogue that concluded that there were more similarities than differences among these characters. After this, Richard seemed less hesitant to speak and began to relate to the other children. The children observed how Cathy listened to and spoke with Richard. They began to follow her lead. The inclusion was a success for both Richard and the other children. Richard's language became more intelligible, and the other children learned that differences are not threatening.

self-conscious, enabling her to attempt to use speech and language at every opportunity.

*Mental Health Appraisal.* During observation, the teacher should be aware of at-risk indicators and other behavioral characteristics that may indicate poor social, emotional, or mental health. Table 11-10 shows a number of characteristics that may indicate the child is at risk. Collins et al. (2003) noted that partnerships between early childhood education and mental health professions are essential to provide support for early childhood mental health services that meet the needs of young children.

There are many behaviors that may be annoying to adults but are perfectly normal and a part of a child's development between the ages of

**TABLE 11-10**

*At-Risk Indicators for Children's Vulnerability to Poor Mental Health*

## ✓ CHECK FOR:

### WARNINGS

☐ Aggression or acting out behaviors, without provocation

☐ Passivity, lack of response, or totally withdrawn

☐ Disorganized behavior socially or in play

☐ Poor or inappropriate attachment patterns

☐ Low self-esteem

☐ Easily overstimulated

☐ Unresponsive to verbal cues or affectionate overtures

☐ Clingy, dependent

☐ Hypersensitive

☐ Unable to make decisions or solve problems

☐ Temper tantrums or very irritable

☐ Mood swings with no explanation

☐ Lack of attention or ability to focus

☐ Easily frustrated

☐ Overreaction or inappropriate response to everyday events

☐ Inability to transition easily

☐ Indifference to parent

☐ Avoids eye contact

☐ Anxiously follows teacher everywhere

☐ Little or no interest in others

one-and-one-half and four years of age. Children often do not pay attention and do not do what they are asked. They can be hard to reason with sometimes and may sulk or cry easily. They may not be able to sit still. Some may boss other children around and try to show off.

Younger children may not want to share and will say "no" often when requested to cooperate. They may grab toys, hit, shove, or attack others who have what they want.

It is not uncommon for some children to whine and complain. Other children may have a special blanket or suck their thumbs. Some children are shy and afraid of unfamiliar people and situations. It is not unusual for children to make up stories and tell them as truths.

These typical behaviors are not necessarily indicators of risk for mental difficulties. Behaviors that may indicate children are at risk for problems in mental health are found in Table 11-10. Observing children and identifying warning signals may suggest need for outside intervention (Collins et al., 2003).

When a child shows a number of disturbing behaviors, especially with increasing frequency, it is a good idea to discuss the child's behavior with a parent. If there is no explanation or if the parent expresses concern, the

Identifying at-risk indicators and behavioral characteristics that may indicate a child's poor mental health is an important part of early intervention. It is important for teachers to recognize that normal behaviors, such as crying or shyness, do not necessarily indicate a problem and may instead be just a normal aspect of the child's personality.

# REALITY CHECK

## *Poverty and Childhood*

Approximately 12 million children live in poverty. This represents slightly more than 16 percent of children. Children younger than six years of age are more vulnerable to poverty and its effects. More than 18 percent of children under six live in poverty. If they live in single-parent families, almost one-half will be feeling the effects of poverty on their childhood (National Poverty Center, 2003). These figures indicate a slight increase from the 2000 poverty levels. Although the figures are down from the early 1990s, they are still higher than they should be. The poverty rate in the United States is often two to three times higher than in other Western industrialized countries (NCCP, 2001). Poverty is more likely to affect children of color. Thirty-seven percent of African-American children younger than six years of age live in poverty. Thirty-one percent of Hispanic children live in poverty, while the figure for white children is at about 10 percent (NCCP, 2001). A correlation with the rise of poverty from the 1970s to the 1990s is the significant rise in the number of single-parent families, which has doubled during that period. In total, approximately 28 percent of children live in single parent homes. Almost 50 percent of children from single-parent families live in poverty, compared to less than 15 percent of children from two-parent families.

There are many contributing factors to poverty, including family composition, parent

# REALITY CHECK (Continued)

education, and family income (Nelson, 2000). Although there is a higher total number of Caucasian children living in poverty, the percentage of African American and Hispanic and other children living in poverty is at a higher level. Thirty percent of black children live in poverty, as do 28 percent of Hispanic children and more than 11 percent of Asian and Pacific Islander children. This compares to less than 10 percent of non-Hispanic white children (NCP, 2003). Children living in urban areas represent one-third of the children living in poverty. Children who live in rural areas represent 26 percent of children living in poverty. Children living in suburban areas represent 17 percent of children living in poverty (NCCP, 2002).

Children from families in poverty make up the largest growing segment of the homeless. More than 40 percent of the homeless are families with children (NMHA, 2005). Families with children are the largest growing segment of the homeless population. The risk to children due to poverty is even greater for homeless children because of their lack of housing.

Impoverished living conditions can result in poor health, lack of safety, and poor nutrition. Poor families are six times more likely to report that their children are in poor or fair health than families that have adequate income. Evans (2004) found that the physical environment of housing quality, noise, crowding and air pollution effects children's health and well being. Health problems are reflected in lower blood iron levels and higher levels of vision, hearing, and dental problems. Blood levels of lead are also higher for children living in poverty. Children in poverty have more frequent, more severe, and longer lasting infectious diseases (Brooks-Gunn & Duncan, 1997). Families in poverty may seek primary medical attention in the emergency room (Nelson, 2000). Homeless children are at an even higher risk. Because of living conditions, these children are more likely to have higher levels of respiratory infections and food-borne infections.

Another effect of poverty on children is that they are less likely to participate in and to receive quality early childhood education (Loeb et al., 2004; Evans, 2004). Poor families are more likely to select family child care, and many of these family child care sites are unlicensed and do not follow standards of care that promote optimum growth for children. Children in poor-quality care are less likely to have optimum brain development and more likely to have numerous other health issues. Quality early childhood education is correlated with positive outcomes for poor children. Poor children who are in quality early childhood education programs may experience an improvement in their lives (NICHD, 2001).

Children in poverty are also more likely to have developmental difficulties, which may be related to poor or nonexistent prenatal care for the mother. The difficulties may also relate to being born to teenage mothers. Health conditions are more likely to go untreated for these children.

Poverty appears to contribute to emotional and behavioral problems for children (NMHA, 2005). Children living in poverty are more likely to be affected by substance abuse and child maltreatment, which lead to increased risk for mental health problems that result in emotional and behavioral problems. Homeless children are even more likely to suffer from emotional and behavioral problems. These children are more likely to have frequent changes of residence, be at risk for safety, and suffer from domestic conflict (Burg, 1994).

Children living in poverty are more likely to be at risk for safety in their living conditions (Shonkoff & Meisels, 1998). Poor housing conditions can lead to higher levels of lead and unsafe neighborhoods. The economic stress of living at the poverty level causes higher levels of domestic abuse, including neglect and physical, sexual, and emotional maltreatment.

Income level affects food consumption practices. Financial resources help families meet basic food needs. The less income, the less

*(continues)*

## REALITY CHECK (Continued)

likely the basic needs for nutrition will be met (OSUE, 1998). Children living in poverty are far less likely to have their needs for fruits and vegetables met. Inadequate nutrition can affect cognitive development and behavior (Kleinman et al., 1998). Pollitt (1994) reported that worldwide research shows three conditions correlated with poverty and poor nutrition:

1. effects of poor nutrition and illness on school performance
2. relationship between poor motor and mental development and anemia
3. positive effects of supplemental food programs

Recent evidence has shown that children need enough protein, calories, vitamins, and minerals to prevent malnutrition. Homeless children may be at greater risk for nutritional deficits because their basic food needs may depend on food programs that are not geared to children.

Teachers can have a profound effect on the lives of poor children. They are in the position to provide an environment for a significant portion of the day that will offer children greater physical safety and good nutrition (Greenspan, 2003). Teachers can help improve the health of children through good screening and sanitation practices. They can also help families access health care and nutritional supplement programs. Teachers can offer children emotional stability that may help to counteract the problems that poverty brings to their lives (Werner & Smith, 2001; Grotberg, 2003).

**CHECK***point:* How does poverty relate risk to a child's health and well-being? What efforts might a teacher use to help lessen these risks?

teacher, with the parent's permission, may want to contact the health consultant or a medical home physician. Many conditions that cause a great deal of stress for a child may be at the root of the problem. Collaboration on the part of the teacher, the family, and a health professional, as in the medical home partnership, may detect the problem and enable early intervention to alleviate the difficulty. Identifying mental health issues is less likely done by the physician alone, because most parents may not realize that there is an issue (Horwitz et al., 2003). That is why the collaboration is important. A referral to a physician or mental health counselor or psychologist may be necessary if the difficulties are not easily solved.

*Nutritional Assessment.* Assessment of a child's nutritional status may be warranted for a child whose growth is different from the norm, such as children who appear obese, who have a food intolerance, or who show an increased susceptibility to infections or illness. Assessing a child's food intake pattern may be very helpful in determining if there is a physical or organic difficulty that is affecting a child's growth, health, or well-being. The types of foods a child eats, how much food is eaten, and when and where the child eats may be pertinent information. If necessary, the teacher and the parent can work together to provide this information for a health professional who may further assess the child's condition.

The nutritional assessment will help reveal

- what types of foods the child eats
- how much food the child eats
- when the child eats

- under what circumstances the child eats
- adequacy of nutrition provided to the child
- parental knowledge of nutrients offered to child
- adequacy of the child's diet
- why the child eats what she eats
- why the child refuses to eat certain foods

Nutritional screening is usually accomplished in several ways. The first is the 24-hour dietary recall method. This information is relatively easy to obtain and can be done in several ways. With this method, the parent and teacher create a list of foods eaten, including an estimate of how much food is eaten. This can be done for either a one-day or a three-day period. Because any one day may not reflect the child's normal diet, a three-day record may be more beneficial. Some difficulties with this method are that the estimates may not be accurate, and gaining the cooperation of the parent to record more than one day's intake may be difficult. The recall method may reveal potential patterns of consumption that put the child at risk for nutritional deficiency. See the sample in Table 11-11.

As far as diets for children are concerned, the sample given in Table 11-11 might be a typical diet for a three-year-old. If one were to compare this sample diet to the MyPyramid Food Guidance System and the recommended daily allowances, there are definite indicators that the diet is lacking in grains, vegetables, and fruits and that there is overconsumption in the milk and milk product category.

Another method of nutritional assessment is the food frequency questionnaire (see Table 11-12). This tool will show how often foods are consumed

**TABLE 11-11**
*24-Hour Dietary Recall*

**Name: Dane Leonard**     **Age: 3 years, 2 months**

G = Grains, bread, and cereals     MM = Milk and milk products
V = Vegetables     M = Meat     F = Fruits

*Breakfast*

$\frac{1}{2}$ cup sugared cereal (1 G)
1 cup milk (1 MM)
1 banana (1 F)

*Lunch*

1 corn dog (1 M)
chips
punch
$\frac{1}{2}$ cup pudding (1 MM)

*Dinner*

1 chicken leg (1 M)
peas (1 V)
mashed potatoes (1 V)
1 cup milk (1 MM)

*Snacks*

1 apple (1 F)
2 chocolate chip cookies
1 cup grape juice (1 F)
1 cup milk (1 MM)

*How many servings of each in one day?*

Grains, Breads, and Cereals
(G)—1
Fruits (F)—3
Vegetables (V)—2
Milk and Milk Products (MM)—4
Meats (M)—2

**Assessment:** Low on grains, breads, and cereals; high on milk and milk products in the four food groups plus the "other" group in the period of one week. This questionnaire relies on the parent for recall, but it might be an easier tool to use to find out if the child is lacking in or excessively consuming certain food groups. This tool may also establish a cultural or ethnic eating pattern that may put the child at risk for nutritional problems.

Both of the nutritional assessment tools require understanding and cooperation between the parent and the teacher. Working together to establish what the child's eating patterns are and making changes to help the child follow the recommended diet pattern can be an effective method for establishing respect and forming an alliance between the teacher and the parent. Discussing the dietary pattern with the health consultant or a dietician might be helpful, if a problem is indicated. A referral to the child's physician or local health clinic may be recommended.

**TABLE 11-12**
*Food Frequency Questionnaire for Children*

Name _____ Age _____

Indicate how many times on average your child eats the following foods in a week by marking down the number of times in the category that most describes your child's eating pattern.

D = Daily      O = Often      S = Sometimes      R = Rarely

| Food | Frequency | | | |
|------|---|---|---|---|
| | D | O | S | R |
| Milk and milk products: cheese, milk, yogurt, ice cream, and pudding | ☐ | ☐ | ☐ | ☐ |
| Meat, meat products, and meat substitutes: beef, chicken, pork, lamb, fish, egg, lunch meat, bacon, dried beans, peas, and peanut butter | ☐ | ☐ | ☐ | ☐ |
| Grains, breads, and cereals: rice, pasta, tortillas, grits, breads, cereals | ☐ | ☐ | ☐ | ☐ |
| Fruits and vegetables | ☐ | ☐ | ☐ | ☐ |
| Other: fats, oils, sweet bakery goods, fast foods, and candy | ☐ | ☐ | ☐ | ☐ |

What type of milk does your child drink?

| skim | 1% lowfat | 2% lowfat | whole | formula | breast |
|------|-----------|-----------|-------|---------|--------|
| ☐ | ☐ | ☐ | ☐ | ☐ | ☐ |

How many meals, including snacks, does the child eat in one day? _____

Also, explain the child's eating habits: _____

_____

_____

Are there any dietary restrictions or limitations practiced by your family? If yes, please explain. Yes ☐      No ☐

_____

_____

*Pause for Reflection*

If you were to do a 24-hour dietary recall right now, how would you do? Would you have met your dietary needs, or would you need to change some things?

## Key Concept 11.3

### Health Status Assessment

Assessing a child's health status is a major task for the teacher. Daily health checks, general health appraisals, screening for developmental norms, screening for good mental health, and assessment of nutrition are the tools that the teacher can use to detect any problems or deficits that a child may have. Early detection may lead to early intervention to correct the problem.

## 11.4  IMPLICATIONS FOR TEACHERS

Teachers are a key link in establishing the promotion of good health for children. Teachers have the opportunity to contribute to the health and well-being of children in care. These areas include observation, education, cultural sensitivity, and supervision.

### *Observation*

Observation of children is a significant portion of a teacher's job because it allows a teacher to get to know and understand a child's temperament, personality, abilities, and limitations. When the teacher is specifically observing a child's health and well-being, there are several goals to keep in mind.

***What Is Going to Be Observed?*** The first goal is to decide what is going to be observed. Is the child being observed for physical well-being, how she performs physically, or acts emotionally? Is the teacher specifically looking for a particular health condition or communicable disease? Has the parent indicated a problem he may have observed? What is the age of the child being observed? A three-year-old has different physical and emotional capacities than a two-year-old. Some other considerations that may affect the observations follow:

- Are there cultural differences?
- Is the child at risk?
- Does the child have special needs?
- Has there been a recent event in the child's life that may affect her well-being or behavior (e.g., birth of a baby, loss of a pet, a move)?

These factors will influence what is observed.

***How Will the Observation Take Place?*** A second goal is to understand how the observation will take place. The teacher needs to be aware that his own childhood, feelings, and experiences will affect the interpretation of what is observed and how it is translated. Lakin (1994) suggests that the observer go through stages of observation.

- to act like a scientist and observe physical data
- to be the inspector and sort out feelings from the physical data
- to behave as an advocate and look at the situation from the child's point of view and consider why the child acted in a certain manner
- to act as an artist and use what is observed to take action to support the development and interests of the child (this method enforces a holistic approach to observation)

The "how" of observation also includes what was physically done to carry out the observation. In order to be accurate in the first stage of observation of a child's health and well-being one needs to use all of the physical senses. The teacher will need to:

- look
- feel
- listen
- smell

Looking at the child includes all physical aspects of the child as well as how the child is acting. Listening to the child involves hearing what the child sounds like, as well as what the child says and how it is said. Feeling the child involves touching the child to see if she is feverish, clammy, or has swollen glands or other physical symptoms so that a touch could help determine if a problem exists. Smelling a child would make the teacher aware concerning personal hygiene as well as toileting accidents.

***When to Observe?*** The teacher should also know when the appropriate time to observe is. It is very important that a health check be made daily when the child first enters the early childhood education environments. This quick check should be done before the parent leaves the child. If the child is ill and must be excluded from care, it should be done before other children are exposed.

It is at the drop-off time that the parent may share any particular concerns she has about the child's health or well-being. This helps the teacher to be on the alert for observation of that concern.

In addition to the daily quick check, a child should be observed for physical and mental health on an ongoing basis. If there has been an outbreak of an infectious disease, special care should be taken to observe for that particular disease.

A plan and health policy for monthly, quarterly, and yearly observations for health in regard to assessment and screening for growth and developmental norms should be created and carried out.

## *For Families*

Assessment is a helpful communication device between the teacher and the parent and can lead to collaborative practices that involve all factors of the child's environment: the child, the teacher, the parents, the school, and the community. Information about the child's growth and development is collected and recorded at certain intervals. It is important that the teacher be trained and have a base of knowledge to perform basic assessments. Another good practice is to discuss concerns with a health consultant before talking to the parent so that you are better informed as to the implications of those concerns. The health consultant can also be a source for referrals for the child if there is a difficulty.

The daily appraisal need not be discussed unless there is a problem or concern. All other forms of assessment should be discussed thoroughly with the parent. The parent may need to be educated as to the importance of any assessment. Any difficulty with the child's health and well-being should be addressed early in the process.

When a referral is made, the teacher should follow up. If there is a problem, the teacher should be aware of it and should be given instructions on how best to help the child cope with any difficulty. A discussion with the parent and the person to whom the child was referred would be most helpful to give the child the continuity of care that he might need.

## Education

The use of assessment tools can help provide the children in the early education environment an opportunity to lessen risk to development. The teacher needs to be educated in the use of these tools and to learn to work with a health consultant to provide as much information as possible to promote intervention when it is needed.

## Cultural Competence

A child whose first language is not English may appear not to follow developmental norms. A child who is exposed to two languages may have difficulty switching from the home language to the language used in the early childhood education environment. Patience and understanding are important. It is helpful to have a teacher or someone that the teacher can call upon who speaks the same language as the child to make the shift between the two languages easier.

If the teacher notices real difficulties in hearing, speech, or language, she might want to discuss it with the parent to see if the child seems to have these same difficulties in the native language. If the child seems to have a problem, discussions with the parent and then referral should be approached with cultural sensitivity. Many cultures view any problem with a child as an imperfection that is a source of guilt and shame for the parent. An understanding of the child's native culture helps the teacher relate better with the parent.

Dietary patterns are greatly influenced by cultural and ethnic considerations. Certain cultures such as Southeast Asians and Indochinese rarely consume milk products. Other cultures may not have a varying menu that allows for the meats or fresh fruits and vegetables that a child needs in his diet. When assessing the child's diet, it is extremely important to have some knowledge of the family's customs. This will allow the teacher to be culturally sensitive when talking to the parent. A health consultant, dietician, or family member who speaks both the child's and the teacher's languages can help alleviate any problems that a language barrier might cause. It may be a challenge to help a family from a different cultural background adjust to dietary allowances recommended for the child. A medical home that is headed by a culturally competent physician could prove to be an invaluable source of support for both the teacher and the family.

## Supervision

The teacher needs to supervise the early childhood education environment to make sure that record keeping and assessments are carried out on a regular basis. A director in an early childhood education center usually supervises the assessments and makes sure that the records are kept up to date. In family child care or in-home care situations, there may be only one teacher present. It is up to this teacher to make sure that children's health is supported through regular use of record keeping and assessment.

A communication system also needs to be established within the early childhood education environment. Teachers need to work together and collaborate on promoting the good health of the child. A family child care provider may have an aide or a substitute who could assist in appraisals and assessment. In an early childhood education environment, the child may see several teachers and aides in one day, as well as the director and perhaps a kitchen helper. All of the staff should be trained to cooperate and help in appraising and assessing a child's health status.

### Key Concept 11.4

#### Implications for Teachers

The teacher needs to promote the good health and well-being of the children in care. The teacher does this by using observation, working with families, education, cultural competence, and supervision as tools to promote health and prevent risk.

## CHAPTER SUMMARY

Children must be observed as individuals to assess their health and well-being. Teachers can appraise and assess children for physical health, mental health, and nutrition. They can screen children for growth and developmental norms. Teachers can document their observations through several forms of records. If there appears to be a difficulty in any area, they can discuss it with the parents and offer a referral, if necessary. Teachers need to employ observation, communication with families, education, cultural competence, and supervision to provide adequate assessment measures for children in care.

## TO GO BEYOND

In this section you will find a number of activities that you can use to apply and improve your knowledge of this chapter. There are also thorough online resources that accompany this text that can be found at http://www.early childed.delmar.com (see description at end of this chapter).

### Chapter Review Critical Thinking Applications

1. Explain the interrelationship of assessment and early intervention.

2. Compare the differences between observing children and diagnosing them. Discuss how to observe without making judgments or diagnoses.

3. Discuss how homelessness can affect a preschool-age child. What benefits would that child receive if he or she attended a preschool? What local resources in your community might help this happen?

4. How might technology help in observing, assessing, and recording the development of children?

### As an Individual

1. Assess your own physical health by self-observation. Record how you feel physically for a period of three days. Be sure to use precise words. When you are done, evaluate whether you have been observing or diagnosing your health.

2. Observe two children in an early childhood education situation, if possible. If that is not available to you, go to a local playground or park. Use the anecdotal type of record to document your observations. Write two paragraphs explaining how you felt documenting and what you learned from it.

3. Find two articles on lead poisoning and compare and contrast them. Be able to report on these articles in class.

### As a Group

1. Bring several two-year-olds to class. Provide a number of toys and books for them. Watch them and observe their actions and interactions. Compare these observations for developmental norms for speech, language, and gross motor skills. Discuss how each child develops at his or her own rate.

2. Examine mental health indicators that put children at risk. Select the indicators that are most likely to prelude mental health risk. How could a teacher help to ameliorate these risks?

3. In small groups of four or five, go out into the community and collect resource information that offers help to those people in poverty. Share the resource information in a class discussion. Why does poverty greatly affect the development of children?

## Case Studies

1. Steve has observed three-year-old Jerrod having a difficult time during circle time. He seems to fidget, play around, and not really pay attention, especially if he sits farther away from Steve. Bridget, the assistant, notices that Jerrod is more attentive if he sits closer to Steve. She thinks that it might be that Jerrod has trouble with his hearing. What would be the next step that Bridget and Steve should take? If they feel Jerrod does have a hearing difficulty, what should they do?

2. Emma has been in your care since she was 8 months old. She was happy and loved to explore. She is now 13 months old but does not seem to be growing as fast as she should and seems more listless than she used to be. Her mother doesn't want Emma to get too fat, so she has replaced milk in her bottle with half apple juice and half water. She wants Emma to have as much juice as she wants, not only at meals but at naptimes. How would you handle this?

3. Jose is a quiet two-and-a half-year-old boy. He uses a few garbled words and seems hesitant to speak. His family speaks only Spanish at home, but you are not sure that is why he does not talk much at school. You are concerned that he may have a language difficulty that is not tied to English being his second language. What course of action do you take?

## Chapter References

Alkon, A., Sokal-Guiterrez, K., & Wolff, M. (2002). Child care health consultation improves health knowledge and compliance. *Pediatric Nursing, 28*(1), 61–65.

Allen, S. (2004a). Child development red flags. *Healthy Child Care, 7*(3). Retrieved October 31, 2005, from http://www.healthychild.net/articles/sh39redflag.html.

Allen, S. (2004b). Healthy development milestones. *Healthy Child Care, 7*(1). Retrieved October 31, 2005, from http://www.healthychild.net/articles/mc37develop.html

American Academy of Pediatrics (AAP). (1998). Screening for elevated blood lead levels. *Pediatrics, 101*(6), 1072–1078.

American Academy of Pediatrics (AAP). (2002). *Promoting optimal health for American children: A summary report 1997–2001*. Elk Grove Village, IL: Healthy Child Care America.

American Public Health Association & American Academy of Pediatrics (APHA & APA). (2002). *Caring for our children: National health and safety performance standards: Guidelines for out-of-home care*. Washington, DC: American Public Health Association.

August, K., & Brooks, L. (2005). State health department advises consumers about lead in seasoning imported from Mexico. California Department of Health Services. Retrieved 11/4/05 from http://www.applications.dhs.ca.gov/pressreleases/store/PressReleases/04-42.html

Bialystok, E. (2001). *Bilingualism in development: Language, literacy and cognition*. Cambridge, England: Cambridge University Press.

Brazelton, T. (1992). *Touchpoints: Your child's emotional and behavioral development*. Reading, MA: Addison-Wesley.

Brooks-Gunn, J., & Duncan, G. (1997). The effects of poverty on children. *The Future of Children 7*(2), 55–71.

Burg, M. (1994, May). Health problems of sheltered homeless women and their dependent children. *Health and Social Work, 19*(2), 125–131.

Cartwright, S. (1994, June). When we really see the child. *Child Care Information Exchange*, 5–9.

Caufield, R., & Kataoka-Yahiro, M. (2001). Health training needs of child care professionals. *Early Childhood Education Journal, 29*(2), 119–123.

Centers for Disease Control (CDC). (2001). *CDC's lead poisoning prevention program*. National Center for Environmental Health. Retrieved May 15, 2002, from http://www.cdc.gov.nceh/lead/factsheets/leadfcts.htm.

Centers for Disease Control and Prevention (CDC). (2004, September 16). What every parent should know about lead poisoning. Retrieved October 31, 2005, from http://www.cdc.gov/nceh/lead/faq/cdc97a.htm

Cianciolo, S., Trueblood-Noll, R, & Allingham, P. (2004). Health consultation in early childhood settings. *Young Children 59*(2), 56–61.

Collins, R., Mascia, J., Kendall, R. Golden, O., Schock, L., & Parlakian, R. (2003, March). Promoting mental health in child care settings: Caring for the whole child. *Zero to Three,* 39–45.

Dailey, L. (1999). Communicating health, safety and developmental concerns to parents. *Child Care Health Connections, 12*(5), 4.

Edward, C., & Raikes, H. (2002). Extending the dance: Relationship-based approaches to infant/toddler care and education. *Young Children, 57*(4), 10–17.

Environmental health issues. (1999). Retrieved May 15, 2002, from http://kidshealth.org/parent/safety/environ.html.

Environmental Protection Agency (EPA). (2004). Lead in paint, dust and soil: National Lead Poisoning Prevention Week. Retrieved October 31, 2005, from http://www.epa.gov/lead/lppw.htm

Evans, G. (2004). The environment of childhood poverty. *American Psychologist 59*(2), 77–92.

Greenspan, S. (2003). Child care research: A clinical perspective. *Child Development, 74*(4), 1064–1068.

Helms, T., Cliffor, R., Cryer, D. (2004). Early childhood environment rating scale. New York, NY: Teachers College Press.

Horwitz, S., Gary, L., Briggs-Gowan, M., & Carter, A. (2003). Do needs drive services use in young children? *Pediatrics, 112*(6), 1373–1378.

Hyson, M. (2002). Preparing tomorrow's teachers: NAEYC announces new standards. *Young Children, 57*(2), 78–79.

Jaroff, L. (2001, June 24). Lead poisoning poses the biggest environmental threat to children. *Time Magazine.*

Katz, L. (1997). A developmental approach to assessment of young children. [ERIC Digest] Champaign, IL: Eric Clearinghouse.

Kendrick, A., Kaufman, R., & Messenger, K. (Eds.) (2002). Healthy young children: A manual for programs. Washington, D.C. National Association for the Education of Young Children.

Kleinman, R., Murphy, J., Little, M., Pagano, M., Wehler, C., Regal, K., & Jellinek, M. (1998). Hunger in children in the United States: Potential behavioral and emotional correlates. *Pediatrics, 101*(1), e3.

Loeb, S., Fuller, B., Kagan, S., & Carrol, B. (2004). Child care in poor communities: Early learning effects of type, quality and stability. *Child Development, 75*(1), 47–65.

Lyles, K. (2003). Infant development milestones. *Healthy Child Care, 6*(6). Retrieved October 31, 2005, from http://www.healthychild.net/articles/sh36develop.html.

McKim, J., Keith, S., & Heisel, W. (2004, April 25). Hidden threat: Part one. *Orange County Register.* Retrieved 11/4/05 from http://www.ocregister.com/investigations/2004/lead/part1_printable.html

Mannino, D., Albalak, R., Grosse, S., & Repace, J. (2003). Second-hand smoke exposure and blood levels in U.S. children. *Epidemiology, 14*(6), 717–719.

Mulroy, M., Bothell, J., & Gaudio, M. (2004). First steps in preventing childhood lead poisoning: The role of childcare practitioners. *Young Children, 59*(2), 20–26.

National Center for Children in Poverty (NCCP). (2002). Early childhood poverty: A statistical profile, March 2002. Retrieved November 19, 2004 from http://www.nccp.org/media/ecp02

National Center for Children in Poverty, (NCCP). (2001). Children poverty fact sheet: June 2001. Retrieved May 15, 2002, from http://cpmcnet.columbia.edu/dept/nccp/ycpt/html.

National Institute of Child Health and Human Development (NICHD) Early Child Care Research Network. (2001). Before Head Start: Income and ethnicity, family characteristics, child care experiences and child development. *Early Education and Development, 12,* 545–576.

National Mental Health Association (NMHA). (2005). Children without homes. Retrieved April 11, 2005 from http://www.nmha.org/homeless/children homlessnessfact.cfm.

National Poverty Center (NPC). (2003). Poverty facts. Retrieved 11/10/04. Available online: http://www.npc.umich.edu/poverty/

National Safety Council (NSC). (2004). *Lead poisoning fact sheet.* National Safety Council Fact Sheet Library. Retrieved November 19, 2004 from http://www.nsc.org/library/facts/lead.htm.

Nelson, D. (2000). Connections count: Alternative framework for understanding and strengthening America's vulnerable families. *Young Children 55*(6), 39–42.

Nilsen, B. (2005). *Week by week, documenting the development of young children.* Clifton Park, NY: Thomson Delmar Learning.

Ohio State University Extension (OSUE). (1998). Poverty facts about children. Retrieved May 15, 2002, from www.ag.ohio-state.edu/~online/hyg-fact/5000/5704.html.

Perry, B. (2003, March). Young Children and Language. *Scholastic Early Childhood Today,* 18–19.

Politis, C. (2003, November/December). Discussing developmental delays. *Scholastic Early Childhood Today, 14.*

Pollitt, E. (1994). Poverty and child development: Relevance of research in developing countries to the United States. *Child Development, 65*(2), 283–295.

Reeves, D. (2002). A medical home for every child. *Healthy Child Care, 5*(4). Retrieved October 31, 2005, from http://www.healthychild.net/articles/mc28medhome.html.

Rhoads, G., Ettinger, A., Weisel, C., Buckley, T., Goldman, K., Adgate, J., & Lioy, P. (1999). The effect of dust lead control on blood lead in toddlers: A randomized trial. *Pediatrics, 103*(3), 551–555.

Ryan, D., Levy, B., Pollack, S., & Walker, B. (1999). Protecting children from lead poisoning and building healthy communities. *American Journal of Public Health, 89*(6), 822–824.

Schilling, J. (2004, May/June). Eliminate childhood lead poisoning by 2010. Unversity of California Cooperative Extension. *Nutrition Perspectives 29*(3), 1–2.

Shonkoff, J. P., & Meisels, S. J. (1998). Early childhood intervention: A continuing evolution. In J. P. Shonkoff & S. J. Meisels (Eds.), *Handbook of early childhood intervention,* 2nd ed. (pp. 3–34). Cambridge, England: Cambridge University Press.

Shonkoff, J., & Phillips, J. (Eds.), & The Committee on Integrating the Science of Early Childhood Development. (2000). *Neurons to neighborhoods.* Committee on Integrating the Science of Early Childhood Development, Board of Children, Youth and Families. Washington, DC: National Academy Press. Retrieved October 31, 2005, from http://www.nap.edu.

Stretesky, P., & Lynch, M. (2001). The relationship between lead exposure and homicide. *Archives of Pediatrics and Adolescent Medicine, 155*(5), 579–582.

Werner, E. & Smith, R. (2001). *Journeys from childhood to midlife: Risk, resilience and recovery.* New York: Cornell University Press.

Additional resources for this chapter can be found by visiting the Online Companion™ at http://www.earlychilded.delmar.com. This supplemental material includes extensive chapter quizzes, PowerPoint® outlines, Web links, and various other activities to help better utilize the material in this chapter. The site is updated regularly, so you may check back often to receive the latest information about the subjects in each chapter.

## CHAPTER 12

# Prevention of Illness in Early Childhood Education Environments Through Infection Control

After reading this chapter, you should be able to:

### 12.1 Health Policies for Infection Control
Define and discuss health for the prevention of childhood infectious diseases.

### 12.2 Mechanisms of Infectious Disease Spread
Explain the mechanisms of communicable disease spread.

### 12.3 Immunizations for Disease Prevention
Relate the importance of immunizations in the prevention and reduction of communicable diseases.

### 12.4 Universal Sanitary Practices for the Early Childhood Education Environment
Summarize sanitation methods used in the prevention of spread of disease in the early childhood education environment.

### 12.5 Environmental Quality Control for Disease Prevention
Discuss factors in the environment that quality control can help to curb the spread of disease.

### 12.6 Implications for Teachers
Describe the importance of education, supervision, working with families, and role modeling in the prevention of communicable diseases.

## 12.1  HEALTH POLICIES FOR INFECTION CONTROL

Policies for **infection control** are essential to maintain the health and prevent serious illness of children. Children in early childhood education environments are more likely to become ill than children who stay at home. **Immunization** and **hygiene** can provide barriers to the spread of infectious diseases and illness of children who are in early childhood environments. The need for these policies is reinforced by the following:

- ● Infection control
  *control of infectious agents by sanitary practices*
- ● Immunization
  *vaccines given in order to protect individuals through the development of antibodies against specific infectious diseases*
- ● Hygiene
  *protective measures and sanitary practices to limit the spread of infection and help to promote health*

- Early childhood education centers that have detailed routines to clean and disinfect can significantly cut the number of illnesses reported because the cycle of germ transmission is interrupted (Report on Preschool Programs, 2004).

- Children in early childhood education environments who are younger than three years of age are more vulnerable to disease than are older children (Samuels et al., 2004). Children in infant and toddler care may be more vulnerable to infections because children put almost everything in their mouths (Smith, 2003).

- Children in group care have higher rates of repeat infections (NACCP, 2001; Pellman, 2002). Policies for the control of the spread of illness should be developed (NCCCCHSRC, 2004).

- Eleven percent of all children in the United States, or 8.4 million children, do not have health insurance (NCHC, 2004). Preschool children without health insurance or public health insurance are less likely to be up-to-date with their vaccinations (Santoli et al., 2004).

- Twenty percent of teachers are not comfortable managing communicable diseases (Caulfield & Kataoka-Yahiro, 2001). Teachers should receive training in infection control for early education environments (American Academy of Pediatrics [AAP], 2003)

- In order to protect all children in care and prevent illness, the child care day should start with a health check (APHA & AAP, 2002).

Developing health policies is essential for the control of infection and the spread of diseases. Even more important is communicating these policies to teachers and parents. The distribution of written policies, meetings to articulate and reinforce the written policies, and new staff and parent training sessions are ways to communicate health policies.

The key tools of risk management for health are prevention, protection, and promotion. In order to utilize these tools properly, there must be an understanding of how disease is spread and how it is controlled. It is also important to know that educating teachers, parents, and children can help prevent the spread of disease.

As discussed throughout this text, protection is an important key for the management of risk and the greatest degree of well-being. Keeping healthy includes protective measures such as getting enough sleep, exercising often, eating well and lessening stress levels can help both children and adults optimize their health so risk is lessened.

There are many people involved in the early childhood education environment, both directly and indirectly. The potential for the spread of infectious diseases is increased as these numbers increase. There are the teachers, the children, and the families whose interactions with each other make them more vulnerable than the general population. An added risk is present for a teacher who is pregnant. A fetus is particularly vulnerable to certain infectious diseases. Health policies for the control of infectious diseases are critical for all people involved in the early childhood education environment. These health policies should include:

1. *Mechanisms of Communicable Disease Spread:* understanding the mechanisms that spread disease and practices that will prevent it

2. *Immunizations for Disease Prevention:* understanding the importance of immunizations for protection and prevention and implementing strategies to be sure that children and adults are properly immunized

3. *Sanitation for Disease Prevention:* practices for sanitation, hygiene, and cleanliness that offer protective and preventive measures

4. *Environmental Quality Control for Disease Prevention:* strategies that help prevent the spread of disease in the rest of the early childhood education environment

5. *Implications for Teachers:* methods and practices that provide minimum risk and maximum health protection for the early childhood education environment

## Key Concept 12.1

### Health Policies for Infection Control

Health policies for the control of infection and the spread of disease are essential in early childhood education environments. These policies should cover the mechanisms of disease control, the immunizations, and sanitation needed for disease prevention. Health policies should also address environmental quality control and education for disease prevention. The teacher needs to understand the methods and practices that provide protection and prevention.

## 12.2 MECHANISMS OF INFECTIOUS DISEASE SPREAD

To many people, the early childhood education environment is thought of as a barrier to health. Infectious diseases are common there. Some teachers often complain about frequent illnesses. What most people do not understand is that the frequency of infectious diseases and the potential for disease spread can be greatly reduced through use of sanitary practices.

In order to place barriers against infectious diseases and to try to control them in the early childhood education environment, one must fully understand how disease is spread. It does not matter whether in child care, in an office, or in a home, **germs** are always present. The fact that they cannot be seen does not mean they are not there.

There are several major reasons why the spread of infectious diseases is more likely in the early childhood education environment. The young children present have not yet learned good hygiene practices, and germs multiply in warm, moist places. The early childhood education environment and the children present offer germs many warm, moist places in which to grow. Diseases are spread through the air and by person-to-person contact.

Certain practices or lack of practices in the early childhood education environment greatly contribute to the spread of infectious diseases. Table 12-1 lists those practices.

For greater understanding of why the practices in Table 12-1 are so careless, it is helpful to know exactly how germs are spread to cause infectious diseases. There are four basic ways diseases are spread:

1. respiratory tract transmission
2. fecal-oral transmission
3. direct contact transmission
4. blood contact transmission

● **Germs**
*microscopic organisms*
*that can cause disease*

Early childhood education environments present a challenge for germ control. The frequent exchange of toys among children who have not yet mastered personal hygiene is one example. Important prevention measures include regularly disinfecting mouthed toys and frequent hand washing.

## WARNINGS

- ☐ Failure to wash hands as needed
- ☐ Presence of children in diapers who put toys in the mouth
- ☐ Mixed ages where older children play with children in diapers
- ☐ Large numbers of children present, especially if within a contained area
- ☐ Improper diaper-changing procedures, including disposal and cleanup
- ☐ Staff who have dual duties, such as preparing food and working with children
- ☐ Lack of facilities, such as not enough bathrooms, small rooms, or diaper area not separated from rest of care
- ☐ Water tables or wading pools that are not sanitized or do not have the water changed frequently
- ☐ Pets in the environment that are handled by children or teachers
- ☐ Not requiring or checking immunization records for completion or update for all children in the early childhood education environment
- ☐ Not requiring or checking immunization records for all staff
- ☐ Failure to perform daily health check
- ☐ Not excluding ill staff
- ☐ Not having a good backup substitute list for replacing ill teachers
- ☐ Not having a policy for exclusion of ill children
- ☐ Not properly informing families when the children are exposed to a communicable disease
- ☐ Lack of proper sanitation and cleaning, especially of toys and food preparation, bathroom, and sleeping areas
- ☐ Improper storage of food
- ☐ Lack of hygiene in food handling
- ☐ Inadequate circulation of air
- ☐ Children sharing sleeping space or equipment
- ☐ Failure to have a policy for unimmunized children
- ☐ Lack of multiple sinks for different tasks to prevent cross-contamination

## Respiratory Tract Transmission

● **Respiratory tract transmission**
*germs that are passed through the air from the respiratory tract of one person to another person*

**Respiratory tract transmission** is perhaps the most common method of disease spread in the early childhood education environment. Tiny droplets from the eyes, mouth, or nose get into the air when a child sneezes, coughs, drools, or even talks, and these droplets are transmitted to another person through the air they breathe. This is referred to as "droplet spread," and it is the main way that these illnesses are spread (CDC, 2004a). These droplets can also land on toys, food, and other things in the environment. Germs can live for many hours and activate once they come into contact with the mouth, nose, throat, lungs, or eyes of an uninfected person. When germs come into contact with an uninfected person, they can multiply and cause illness. Colds occur more often in the winter when children spend more time in a confined environment, and the cold germs are spread by sharing of tissues, food, and cups. They can also be spread by coughing or sneezing without covering the mouth. The common cold accounts for 75 percent of all infant illnesses (Pellman, 2002). The most common infections in early childhood education environments are colds and flu (AAP, 2000).

The best ways to prevent germs from spreading are to disinfect toys that are put in the mouth often, wash hands at appropriate times (see Table 12-4), and teach children to protect others when they cough, sneeze, or blow their noses. The number of active germs on a surface can be reduced by 80 to 90 percent if a child sneezes into a tissue instead of in the open or on his arm or shirt (Tierno, 2003). It is important to remember to throw the tissue away after it has been used. Even sneezing or coughing into the crook of an arm is better than sneezing or coughing into the open. Many teachers have found it easy to teach children to do this when coughing, instead of coughing into their hands, which, if not washed, can easily spread the disease (see Figure 12-1). Children under the age of three are more likely to have respiratory tract infections, and they are also more likely to mouth toys and other objects.

**FIGURE 12-1**
Cover Your Cough.

## Fecal-Oral Transmission

- **Fecal-oral transmission** *passing of germs from an infected person's bowel movement via the hand into another person's system via the mouth*

**Fecal-oral transmission** occurs when the germs from one person's feces get into another person's mouth and then are swallowed and introduced into the digestive tract of that person. The most common way for germs to spread is when hands are not washed after toileting, before eating, or before preparing food. Diseases that are spread by fecal-oral transmission can affect a number of children. Rotavirus is a type of fecal-oral disease that is commonly found in the early childhood education setting (CCCHP, 2003).

- **Sanitized** *removal of bacteria, filth, and dirt that makes transmission of disease unlikely*

In the early childhood education environment, another common way that these germs are spread is in the water. Water tables that are not **sanitized** and do not have the water changed frequently are hosts to germs that are transmitted from unwashed hands. The APA and AAHA do not recommend water tables in the early childhood education environment for this reason. However, many teachers feel that the benefits of having a water table outweigh the risks. Therefore, special care must be taken to maintain these water tables so they are not good hosts to germs and do not encourage the spread of disease. This includes washing hands before and after water play. If a child has a runny nose, an open sore, a rash, or diarrhea, he should be given an individual water bin and should not share with others (NCCCCHSRC, 2004). Water tables should be cleaned and sanitized after use.

These germs are also found on rugs, furniture, tables and toys. Hand washing at proper times, proper care of a water table, and proper food safety can help obstruct the spread of disease through the fecal-oral route.

## Direct Contact Transmission

- **Direct contact transmission** *passing of germs from one person's body or clothing to another person through direct contact*
- **Secretions** *saliva, mucus, urine, and blood produced by the body for specific purposes*

**Direct contact transmission** occurs when one person has direct contact with **secretions** from an infected person. Secretions can be left on toys, doorknobs, or other objects that come in direct contact with the uninfected person. Direct contact transmission also occurs when a person picks up parasites from infested objects such as bedding, toys, clothing, or combs. Diseases can spread easily through direct contact among children and teachers in an early childhood education environment if precautions are not taken to curb them. Good hygiene, including hand washing, sanitizing, and proper food handling, can help block the spread of disease through direct contact.

## Blood Contact Transmission

- **Blood contact** *passing of germs through the blood from one person's circulatory system to another person's circulatory system*

Transmitting disease through **blood contact** occurs when the infected blood of one person enters the bloodstream of another person. The infected blood can be transmitted and absorbed easily. For example, spread can occur when an infected person has a cut, scraped skin (such as from a skinned knee), or a bloody nose and is treated by a person with a hangnail, chapped hands, or a small cut. Spread also can occur when mucous membranes such as the inside lining of the mouth, eyes, and nose come in contact with another person's blood through a broken surface. The major risk for this would be child-biting. Teachers should wear non-latex

# REALITY CHECK

## The Issue of Head Lice in Early Childhood Education Environments

Head lice infestation among children between the ages of three and twelve years is common in the United States. It is estimated that there are between six and twelve million cases of infestation every year (Frankowski & Weiner, 2002). Lice are small parasitic insects that are spread through direct contact. Historically, the appearance of head lice on a person has been associated with lack of cleanliness and low socioeconomic class. This is one of the reasons that parents get offended and defensive when their child appears with a lice infestation. Because of these historical connotations, parents whose children have lice often feel guilty or embarrassed. Head lice are common among all socioeconomic levels. Because children are more frequently affected than adults, head lice can have a significant effect on the early childhood education environment. Communication is the key to keeping this situation and the emotional reactions to it in a manageable form, where directors, teachers, and parents work together to solve the problem.

Head lice survive by feeding on a person's blood via the scalp and cannot survive for more than 24 hours without access to it. It takes eight days for a single louse to hatch from the egg and that louse begins to feed somewhere around 10 days after hatching. Each fertile female egg can lay as many as 100 eggs over a period of more than a month. Left unchecked, this can cause a major infestation, which can spread to others via *direct contact.*

More than anything, a head lice infestation is annoying. It is not life-threatening, nor does it carry disease. But it can cause a lot of itching, and if that itching is out of hand, an infection from it may occur. The biggest threat to a person with head lice is the overexposure to the toxic substances used to eliminate them (Pollack, 2000).

Most early childhood education centers and elementary schools in this country have a "no-nits" policy which states that, if children are found to have an active sign of head lice infestation, they will be sent home and must not return until all signs of infestation are gone. The Harvard School of Public Health has found that, although these policies are helpful in principle, they present problems (Pollack et al., 2000). The American Academy of Pediatrics (AAP) and the National Association of School Nurses (NASN) have moved to discourage a "no-nits" policy (Child Health Alert [CHA], 2003a). Frankowski and Weiner (2002) found that, of 1700 children with lice, the ones that had only nits were only 20 percent likely to develop mature head lice. A "no-nits" policy is by no means a guarantee of stopping outbreaks of lice. Most schools lack expertise and tools to distinguish an active from an inactive infestation. Many inactive or nonexistent infestations have been erroneously found to be "active."

Others have found that information about head lice was based on anecdotal evidence, not scientific principle (Figueroa, 2000). In fact, many researchers have found the surrounding hysteria much more disturbing than the infestation itself. A child who has a head lice infestation is more than likely to have had it for at least one month (AAP, 2002). Lice cannot hop or jump around from person to person. Most transmission occurs by direct contact of one person's head to another's. The AAP and NASN have agreed that after proper treatment a child should be allowed to return to school.

Recently, the "no-nits" policy has hit another road block, which is that many products that are supposed to get rid of lice seem to be ineffective. It has been suggested that head lice may have developed an immunity to those products (Frankowski & Weiner, 2002). Overuse of such products can have toxic effects, so other ways to rid a child of head lice have been studied. The general guidelines to eradicate head lice are

## REALITY CHECK (Continued)

- use a shampoo that contains active ingredients that will kill the lice; pemethrin has been found to be the most effective (AAP, 2002)
- use a special lice comb to remove lice after shampooing
- machine wash all possibly infested items using hot water
- all nonwashable items go into dryer for 20 minutes
- vacuum surroundings and throw away the bag
- soak combs and brushes in a bleach solution for one hour and then clean
- items such as stuffed animals should be placed in sealed plastic bags for a period of 3 to 4 weeks
- do not use spray-on lice killers, because the toxicity cannot be controlled

If a parent has followed the above guidelines and head lice are still found on the child, frustration begins. Many directors and teachers have become very discouraged because they have complied with all guidelines and nits remain. Some researchers have suggested applying isopropyl (rubbing) alcohol so that the hair is wet, then rubbing with a white towel for about 30 seconds (CHA, 2003b). The lice will become intoxicated, release the hair shaft and show up on the towel. A number of home remedies have been presented, but none is "scientifically" effective, and some may actually be very toxic. The only home remedy that may be effective, according to the Harvard School of Public Health, is the use of olive oil, which they do not endorse because of lack of scientific evidence. Some early childhood education center directors and teachers have found that this treatment seems to be effective in those cases that appeared to be resistant to the "normal" head lice shampoos.

Another solution is the use of a really good lice comb to examine for nits thoroughly, instead of a visual examination, which may not be as accurate (Mumcuoglu et al., 2001). Still another suggestion has been the use of a nontoxic lotion,

*Nuovo*, which is a lotion that is placed in the hair and then dried with a hair dryer (Pearlman, 2004). The cure rate for this product has been found to be 96 percent though other health professionals question this product and method.

Directors and teachers have often been at odds over the "no-nits" policy. In many cases, teachers trying to follow the exclusion policy for lice have tried to send the child home, or not allow the child to return if head lice or nits (even dead ones) were found. Directors, understanding the parent's frustration, have tended to be more lenient and allowed the child to stay in school. There are a number of factors against a "no-nits" policy. These include (1) a child without a live infestation may be unnecessarily excluded; (2) families that cannot comply may be penalized; and (3) exclusion can cause stigma or hysteria (Dailey, 2000).

The AAP and NASN suggest removal of a "no-nits" policy. It is best for each early childhood education environment to make its own determination. It is also suggested that children not be excluded immediately or sent home early (DHHS, 2003). Parents should be informed that their child needs to be treated properly before returning the next day.

It is best that each early childhood environment evaluate whether to enact a "no-nits" policy. A "no-nits" policy puts the responsibility for removal of nits on the parents. Another guideline for exclusion could be the degree of risk, using a scale to determine whether the risk is high or low (Richardson et al., 2001). This issue should be discussed at length, and a consensus among teachers should be reached so that everyone is comfortable.

Communication and consensus on the issue is critical. It is important that the teacher provide accurate information on the treatment and prevention of head lice. This should be done for all children in the environment, so the information may need to be translated into the languages of all children present. Translators may be available through the local health department.

**CHECK***point:* Why might the "no-nits" policy for early education environments be changing? With all the information at hand, would you have a policy like this in your early childhood education environment?

disposable gloves when caring for a child with an open wound and any secretions. Any child-biting should be handled immediately (see Table 3-9 in Chapter 3).

Following guidelines set up in the remainder of this chapter, the teacher should be able to forestall or deter the spread of disease in the early childhood education environment as shown in Table 12-2. Figure 12-2 shows the five most effective ways to prevent the spread of disease in the early childhood education environment.

**TABLE 12-2**

*Infectious Disease Spread in the Early Childhood Education Environment*

| Method | How Spread | Diseases |
|---|---|---|
| Respiratory tract | Infectious droplets from the mouth, nose, and eyes get in air via talking, sneezing, coughing, and blowing nose. | Colds<br>Strep throat<br>Meningitis<br>Chicken pox<br>Measles<br>Respiratory syncytial virus (RSV)<br>Flu, Hib flu<br>Tuberculosis<br>Whooping cough<br>Ear infections<br>Fifth disease<br>Sixth disease |
| Fecal-Oral | Germs from stool of one person get in mouth of another person and are swallowed. Not washing hands after toileting, before preparing food, before eating, and not disinfecting toys that have been put in the mouth. Also handling pets such as birds, snakes, and lizards can spread bacteria from salmonella. | Hepatitis A<br>Giardia<br>Shigella<br>Salmonella<br>Diarrhea |
| Direct Contact | Infected articles or secretions from infected area. Spread through touching toys, faucets, food, tables touched by infected person. By parasites through bedding, clothing, shared hats, combs, brushes, or dress-up clothing. | Impetigo<br>Lice<br>Scabies<br>Cold sores<br>Pink eye<br>Cytomegalovirus (CMV) |
| Blood | Infected blood from one person entering bloodstream of another person. Infected blood can come in contact through cuts, chapped hands, a hangnail, and other broken skin, or lining of mouth, eyes, nose, and rectum. In the early childhood education environment, common transmitters are child biting, bloody noses, and skinned knees. | Hepatitis B<br>HIV-AIDS |

**FIGURE 12-2**
Five fabulous forestallers of disease spread in early childhood education environments.

Five Fabulous Forestallers

1 Keep immunization requirements and records up to date.

2 Use proper hand washing.

3 Use universal sanitation procedure for diapering.

4 Bleach with hypochlorite.

5 Carry out daily health check.

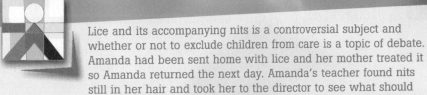

Lice and its accompanying nits is a controversial subject and whether or not to exclude children from care is a topic of debate. Amanda had been sent home with lice and her mother treated it so Amanda returned the next day. Amanda's teacher found nits still in her hair and took her to the director to see what should be done. Sherry, the director in the college laboratory school where Amanda attends, felt that, since head lice was not life-threatening, and Amanda's mother desperately needed the support of the early childhood education program to stay in school and work, she was willing to bend. Without communication, this situation could have created real animosity among staff. If the teachers were trying to enforce the "no-nits" policy and Sherry was allowing the child to stay in care, they would not present a united front. What Sherry and the teachers at this center did was to sit down and review the policy and make some changes.

Amanda's mother had had a very difficult time getting rid of the head lice. Through cooperation, either Sherry or a teacher, Damaris, would spend 10 minutes at the beginning of each day with a lice comb and comb through Amanda's hair as she played a computer game in the director's office. After three weeks, the lice were eradicated and Amanda's family and the early education center had developed a trust that still exists to this day. Amanda has graduated from the center but her parents still come by to volunteer and to help in any way to support this early childhood education program.

## *Key Concept 12.2*

### Mechanisms of Disease Spread

Infectious diseases are common in the early childhood education environment. In order to protect children's health, barriers must be in place. The teacher must understand how diseases spread. The four methods of transmission are respiratory tract, fecal–oral, direct contact, and blood. This knowledge will provide a foundation for the teacher to construct barriers to disease spread.

## 12.3 IMMUNIZATIONS FOR DISEASE PREVENTION

- **Communicable disease**
  *a disease spread from one person to another through means of respiratory spray or infected body fluids*
- **Vaccinations**
  *inactivated, dead, or weakened live organism of infectious diseases to which the body builds resistance*

One of the major deterrents of **communicable disease** spread is immunization against those diseases. Immunizations can protect children from diseases that cause epidemics. These outbreaks could make children violently ill, disable them, and even kill them. Through medical science, a number of these diseases have been controlled by a regular schedule of immunizations for children at particular ages (see Table 12-3 for an immunization schedule).

Immunizations or **vaccinations** are available for a number of diseases that are associated with children and early childhood education environments. Diseases that can be prevented include measles, mumps, rubella, whooping cough (pertussis), diphtheria, Hib (Haemophilus Influenza type B—Meningitis), chicken pox, hepatitis B, and influenza. The recommendation for influenza vaccine was expanded in 2004 (Walsh, 2004). Immunizations for these diseases are recommended by the American Academy of Pediatrics (AAP) and are required for entrance into elementary schools. There is also a vaccination available for hepatitis A, and it is suggested for inclusion to a child's immunization schedule in certain areas (CDC, 2004b). Ask your local health department if your area is one of the recommended places that should include it. The AAP is now also recommending a pneumococcal conjugate vaccine that can prevent meningitis, pneumonia, and serious infections transferred by the blood (AAP, 2001a).

Immunizations against disease are effective as a preventive measure only if they are administered according to schedule. Parents do not always realize that many serious childhood diseases can still pose threats and they need to prevent those threats through immunization. In recent years, whooping cough and measles have greatly increased because enough children have failed to be vaccinated against them (APA, 2004). Adult teachers need to make sure that boosters are administered as scheduled.

With funding from the U.S. Department of Health and Human Services, the AAP and Healthy Child Care Pennsylvania have created a software tracking system for immunization records to be used in early childhood education environments, called *WellCareTracker*. This risk reduction tool allows teachers to keep track of immunizations and screening tests. It flags missing immunizations and continues to check for updates. This allows teachers lead time to notify families when children need an update to their immunizations. This is a Web-based service (https://www.wellcaretracker.org, with continuous updates as needed. At the time of publication of this text, the service was available for $1 per year per child in care, plus a $25 one-time setup fee.

**TABLE 12-3**
*Recommended Childhood and Adolescent Immunization Schedule United States • 2005*

| Vaccine ▼ / Age ▶ | Birth | 1 month | 2 months | 4 months | 6 months | 12 months | 15 months | 18 months | 24 months | 4–6 years | 11–12 years | 13–18 years |
|---|---|---|---|---|---|---|---|---|---|---|---|---|
| **Hepatitis B**[1] | HepB #1 | HepB #2 | | | HepB #3 | | | | | HepB Series | | |
| **Diphtheria, Tetanus, Pertussis**[2] | | | DTaP | DTaP | DTaP | | DTaP | | | DTaP | Td | Td |
| ***Haemophilus influenzae* type b**[3] | | | Hib | Hib | Hib | Hib | | | | | | |
| **Inactivated Poliovirus** | | | IPV | IPV | | IPV | | | | IPV | | |
| **Measles, Mumps, Rubella**[4] | | | | | | MMR #1 | | | | MMR #2 | MMR #2 | |
| **Varicella**[5] | | | | | | Varicella | | | | Varicella | | |
| **Pneumococcal Conjugate**[6] | | | PCV | PCV | PCV | PCV | | | PCV | PPV | | |
| **Influenza**[7] | | | | | | Influenza (Yearly) | | | | Influenza (Yearly) | | |
| **Hepatitis A**[8] | | | | | | | | | | Hepatitis A Series | | |

Vaccines below red line are for selected populations

This schedule indicates the recommended ages for routine administration of currently licensed childhood vaccines, as of December 1, 2004, for children through age 18 years. Any dose not administered at the recommended age should be administered at any subsequent visit when indicated and feasible.

▓ Indicates age groups that warrant special effort to administer those vaccines not previously administered. Additional vaccines may be licensed and recommended during the year. Licensed combination vaccines may be used whenever any components of the combination are indicated and other components of the vaccine are not contraindicated. Providers should consult the manufacturers' package inserts for detailed recommendations. Clinically significant adverse events that follow immunization should be reported to the Vaccine Adverse Event Reporting System (VAERS). Guidance about how to obtain and complete a VAERS form is available at **www.vaers.org** or by telephone, **800-822-7967**.

▓ **Range of recommended ages**  ░ **Only if mother HBsAg(−)**
▓ **Preadolescent assessment**  ▓ **Catch-up immunization**

**DEPARTMENT OF HEALTH AND HUMAN SERVICES**
**CENTERS FOR DISEASE CONTROL AND PREVENTION**

The Childhood and Adolescent Immunization Schedule
Advisory Committee on Immunization Practices    www.cdc.gov/nip/acip
American Academy of Pediatrics    www.aap.org
American Academy of Family Physicians    www.aafp.org

Completion of the immunization schedule for both children and teachers is essential. Children who come to the early childhood education program after receiving their immunization shots may exhibit a low-grade fever or sleepiness

This is an inexpensive way to keep track of immunizations for children in care and keep them up to date.

Children in early childhood education environments need protection not only from the classic childhood diseases, but also from those diseases that seem to flourish in early childhood education environments if proper precautions are not practiced. Recent outbreaks of childhood diseases seem to be traced to child care situations (AAP, 2004; Samuels et al., 2004). These outbreaks include hepatitis B, hepatitis A, and Hib, which is a flulike form of meningitis. Vaccines available for each of these diseases will help protect children in care. Table 12-3 shows the recommended immunization schedule that was most current when this text was submitted for publication. The CDC now updates this chart twice a year. For the most current schedule go to www.cdc.gov/nip to link to the most current immunization schedule for children and adolescents. This page will also link you to the latest adult schedules for the teachers working in the early childhood education environment.

Children in care who are not immunized can jeopardize others who have been immunized or are too young to have received the immunization (PAAAP, 2003). Diseases that can be prevented with immunizations remain a threat, can be difficult to treat, and can be deadly if there are children in early childhood education programs that have not followed the immunization schedule. As a teacher, it is imperative to protect the children and everyone else in the early childhood education environment by requiring the completion of the immunization schedule (Spence, 1999). Parents must provide an immunization record filled out by a physician or local health clinic on the form provided by the state in which the child resides. A copy of this record should be on file with each child's health record and should be periodically updated if the child is in the process of receiving a series of vaccinations. Better still, the teacher can have Well-CareTracker software, at a minimal price, that will provide this information on an ongoing basis. In addition, the teacher should provide information to all parents about the importance and benefits of immunizations (see Reality Check: At Risk for Preventable Disease). Handouts and articles for parents is a good way to keep the importance of immunization in everyone's thoughts.

Children who have not followed the immunization schedule and have missed a particular vaccination will not be protected from that particular disease. If a child has not met all of the requirements of an immunization schedule, he must do so immediately (see Table 12-3). A quarterly check of children's records can help keep them up to date. To simplify record keeping, the teacher can place a "red flag" or special sticker on the file of each child who must still complete the immunization schedule.

If a child in the early childhood education environment has not completed the schedule and the parents do not have any plans to complete it, the child should be excluded from care until the process of immunization is resumed. An exception to this would be a child who, for medical reasons, religious or personal beliefs may be exempt from the immunizations. For example, child with a medical reason such as an allergy to eggs would be exempt. In some states, those with religious or personal beliefs that are documented can be refused enrollment (PAAAP, 2003); in other states, children of parents with a religious or personal belief must be admitted (CCHP, 2004). The early childhood education program should be familiar

# REALITY CHECK

## At Risk for Preventable Diseases

Table 12-3 shows the recommended childhood schedule of immunizations to protect children from communicable diseases. Recent studies show that large numbers of children are at risk for these preventable diseases because they have not been immunized. There has been an increase in reported cases of measles and mumps and, more recently, an outbreak of whooping cough was seen (AAP, 2004). It was thought that whooping cough had been eradicated, but that is obviously not the case. Since 1993, the number of cases of whooping cough has been growing.

The Centers for Disease Control and Prevention (2004b) reported that in 2003 the vaccination coverage for children was at an all-time high. This reflected a strong increase in the pneumococcal and varicella (chicken pox) vaccines and the increased availability of other vaccines. Beginning in 2000 and continuing through 2002, there was a shortage of DTP (diphtheria, tetanus, and pertussis), MMR (measles, mumps, and rubella) and VAR (varicella) vaccines. Up to May 2003, there was a shortage of the pneumococcal vaccine (CDC, 2004b). In 2004, there was a shortage of the influenza vaccine, so that only children between 6 and 23 months were eligible. One finding from the most recent vaccination cover study was that the fourth dose of DTP seems to lag behind, reducing the coverage factor for those children not having this vaccination. Even though there has been an increase, we are still lower in vaccination coverage than the Healthy People 2010 national health objective for 90 percent of the children in the United States to be vaccinated. There may be several reasons for this.

The first reason is that some children have less access to immunization coverage than others. Santoli et al. (2004) found that children with private insurance were more likely to be up to date in their immunizations than those with public insurance or no insurance. Access to immunization may be more difficult for some families. There is now a Vaccines for Children Program, which is a partnership between health care providers and public health agencies that provides uninsured children and those who are in Medicaid with vaccination coverage. More information from the CDC about this program can be found at http://www.cdc.gov/nip.

The second and more controversial reason for some children not having their immunizations up to date is the alleged relationship between an increase in autism and the MMR and DTP vaccinations, which has caused concern among parents in both the United States and Great Britain. This has led to a fall in vaccine coverage in Great Britain (Smeeth et al., 2004). The controversy is due to the inclusion of thimerosal, which is a derivative of an ethylmercury compound, into the vaccines as a preservative. Some studies have shown a link between these vaccinations and autism. The CDC reported that in some areas of the United States the rate for pervasive developmental disorders or autism has been as high as 1 of every 150 children (Parker-Pope, 2004). Twenty years ago, that figure was 1 child in 2500. However, several recent studies have proved no relationship between autism and vaccinations (CHA, 2004; Smeeth et al., 2004). Other researchers are not convinced and are continuing to study this controversy (Parker-Pope, 2004). The U.S. Congress is studying the relation between thimerosal and autism, even though most childhood vaccines have removed thimerosal as the preservative (Groppe, 2004). It has been suggested that there may be a genetic link and that genetically susceptible children, when exposed to thimerosal, may develop autism. Researchers at Columbia University Mailman School of Public Health are

(continues)

## REALITY CHECK (Continued)

close to having a blood test for autistic children to determine whether there is any such genetic susceptibility (Parker-Pope, 2004). Thimerosal is still being used in influenza vaccine for both children and adults. This is considered a potential barrier for some families, but few physicians have concerns about the safety of the influenza vaccine (ORR, 2004).

Vaccines rarely cause life-threatening or life-changing reactions (Sachs, 1999). A child is at far greater risk if she is not immunized properly (CDC, 2002). Risk ranges from common and minor effects to less common and severe effects that can even be life-threatening. Benefits to immunization include protection from illness, prevention of disease outbreaks, and prevention of death. It has been found that, when more children were vaccinated with the

varicella vaccine, fewer children in early childhood education environments without the vaccination actually got chicken pox (Clements et al., 2001). A child who has not followed the schedule for MMR vaccination is 35 times more likely to have measles and spread them than is a vaccinated child (Salmon et al., 1999). Teachers can help eliminate these childhood diseases by requiring immunization schedules be up-to-date before children enter care. They should track the children's records for immunizations that need to be updated for compliance to the immunization schedule. The *WellCareTracker,* discussed in the text, is an effective tool. Teachers should also have a policy for excluding children from care who are not exempt from immunization.

**CHECK***point:* **Why might children be at risk for preventable diseases?**

with state requirements. A medical release form must be on file and kept confidential (CCHP, 2004). If the state allows a religious or personal belief exemption, then an affidavit of religious or personal belief must be on file and kept confidential. This allows the teacher to identify these children without immunizations so they can be quickly excluded if an outbreak of a disease occurs. This exclusion policy should be made clear to the parents of the unimmunized children. Other parents in care should be notified that there is or may be an unimmunized child in care, without revealing that child's identity. This information may be included in the parent's handbook if one is available at the early childhood education program (CCHP, 2004). The Pennsylvania Chapter of the American Academy of Pediatrics (PAAAP, 2003) suggests grouping unimmunized children together and away from the infants in care that are too young for immunizations and from toddlers who may not have finished their immunization schedule. Parents of unimmunized children should be told of this policy if the early childhood education environment decides to follow this recommendation.

The more children in the early childhood education environment who are properly immunized, the less the risk for the spread of those childhood diseases. Teachers also need to verify their own immunity to childhood diseases and should follow the vaccination schedule for Hib, hepatitis A, and hepatitis B. See Chapter 10 for further details on teacher immunizations that are needed.

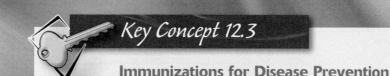

## Key Concept 12.3

### Immunizations for Disease Prevention

Immunizations are a major deterrent to disease. In order to be effective, they must be administered according to schedule. Both the children and the teachers in the early childhood education environment should meet the immunization requirements.

## 12.4  UNIVERSAL SANITARY PRACTICES FOR THE EARLY CHILDHOOD EDUCATION ENVIRONMENT

- **Sanitary practices**
  *practices that remove bacteria, filth, and dirt to cut down on disease transmission*
- **Viruses**
  *a small microorganism that is produced in living cells and that can cause disease*
- **Otitis media**
  *infection of the middle ear*
- **Disinfecting**
  *procedures to eliminate all germs through use of chemicals or heat*

One of the most effective tools you have to create a healthy environment for the child is to incorporate universal **sanitary practices** to keep the environment as clean and germ-free as possible. These protective and preventive actions can greatly reduce risk for infection or disease. Proper sanitary practices can help prevent the spread of **viruses**, bacteria, parasites, respiratory diseases, and **otitis media**.

Cleaning, sanitation, and disinfection procedures should be the main points of a health policy for a sanitary environment. These procedures should include

- hand washing
- diapering
- toileting
- cleaning and **disinfecting**

It is very important that a written explanation of the sanitary practice policy be sent home with children, so that parents understand that an effort is being made to keep the environment healthy and germ-free. Cooperation may also be elicited to encourage children to use these sanitary practices in the home by providing parents with a flyer on correct hand washing procedures.

### Hand Washing

Washing the hands is perhaps the single most important thing the teacher can do to prevent illness personally and to keep it from spreading to the children in care (Aronson, 2003) (see Table 12-4). Handwashing can help to interrupt the germ transmission cycle. The use of antibacterial soap has been found to produce a 50 percent decline in both absenteeism and respiratory illness. The use of antibacterial soap does not appear to be harmful nor to make bacteria resistant with its use (Tierno, 2003). It is essential that the teacher develop the habit of frequent hand washing. Often when the pace of life is hectic, it is easy to forget that hand washing should be done. If it is developed into a routine and becomes a habit, hand washing will be second nature and will be done regardless of the pace.

Teachers can model correct handwashing procedures to the children even as they go about their regular duties.

Routine hand washing should be a part of training in the early childhood education center for any child. It is important to have sinks at a child's level, or safe footstools, so the child can comfortably wash.

The times for routine hand washing shown in Table 12-4 reflect when the teacher should wash hands and help the children wash their hands. By observing this modeling of hand washing behavior, the children can easily follow the teacher's direction. Teacher hand washing should be part of training as well as monitoring the environment. The combination of training and monitoring leads to a very significant decrease in diarrhea in children in early childhood education environment (Aronson, 2003). Another issue that could be looked at from a hand washing viewpoint is the presence of long or artificial nails in the early childhood education environment. Nurses with long or artificial nails were found to cause illness in young babies that they worked with; after they got rid of the nails, the rate of infection and illness decreased (Moolenaar et al., 2000). It has also been suggested that elaborate wrist and hand jewelry should not be used in the early childhood education environment, because it too could harbor germs that good hand washing will not catch (Aronson, 2003). It has been found that rings can hide bacteria

**TABLE 12-4**
*Universal Sanitary Hand
Washing Practices*

**When:**

**Both the Child and the Teacher**

- Upon arrival at child care
- Before eating or drinking
- After touching a child who may be sick
- After using the toilet or changing diapers
- After sneezing, coughing, or using a tissue
- Before and after playing in water that is used by more than one person
- Before and after playing in sandboxes
- After handling pets

**Teacher**

- After handling body secretions (vomit, mucus, and so forth)
- Before and after handling or preparing food
- After cleaning
- Before and after giving medication, if applicable
- After cleaning and handling garbage
- After helping a child use the toilet
- After handling toys that have been mouthed
- After moving from one care group to another

**How:**

- Before starting make sure there is a clean, disposable paper towel available
- Use running water that drains. Do not use a stoppered sink or container.
- You must use soap. Liquid soap is preferable, because germs can grow on soap bars.
- Use **friction**. Rub hands together for germ removal for at least 10 seconds. Rub between fingers and around nails. It has been suggested that children sing the song "Happy Birthday" twice while washing their hands so enough time elapses for good cleaning.
- Rinse thoroughly in running water.
- Turn off faucet with paper towel. Touching the faucet can recontaminate your hands.

● **Friction**
*rubbing together*

*Adapted from* Control of Communicable and Infectious Diseases: A Manual for Child Care Providers, *California Child Care Health Project.*

that cause disease (Trick et al., 2003). Removal of rings should be considered when working in an early childhood education environment.

In 2002, the CDC published recommendations for hand hygiene in health care. These can be translated to the early childhood education environment (Aronson, 2003). The recommendations advocate the use of alcohol-based hand sanitizers in health care. This is less ideal in the early child education environment because of the ingredients in the sanitizers. The use of these types of products will cut down on disease spread, but care should be taken if they are used. These hand sanitizers should be used only in areas where they are inaccessible to children. If they are in an area used by children, they should be used only if sinks are not available. These sanitizers should be used according to the manufacturer's instructions, and the dispenser systems should be checked on a regular basis (Aronson, 2003). They should be stored carefully, because they are flammable.

> *Pause for Reflection*
>
> Do you always wash your hands when you should? If not, why? What could you do to encourage yourself and others you know to wash hands when needed?

### Diapering

● **Fecal contamination**
*contamination occurring through exposure to feces*

**Fecal contamination** in the early childhood education environment leads to the spread of infection from the carrier to others. Containment of fecal matter, use of disposable changing table pads, proper hand washing, and use of disposable gloves are protective measures that control this spread. These measures manage the risk of contamination and spread of disease. Bacteria can also be spread through urine, and the same protective measures help to manage this risk. Gloves may have small defects, so it is important that hands be washed after changing a diaper, even though gloves may be worn (Aronson, 2003; Lyles, 2003). Using a baby wipe is less than ideal because, although it cleans, it does not stop the transmission of disease. Therefore, it is important to remember to wash hands, not just use a baby wipe. This is also true for the children. Use of gloves helps to prevent hands from being soiled with urine and fecal matter, but it does not prevent contamination. Teachers should remember that whatever they handle with these gloves could be contaminated by those same gloves.

The area where diapering occurs should be isolated and equipped for cleanliness and safety (Table 12-5). A correct procedure for changing diapers should be developed and placed above the diaper changing area. Maintaining the procedure as well as a clean and sanitary area to change diapers greatly reduces risk (see Table 12-6).

Proper diapering procedures should be followed to avoid the spread of infection. A sanitary diapering area and the use of disposable gloves are examples of proper diapering procedures

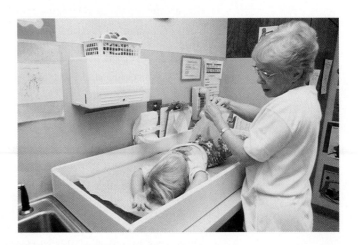

**TABLE 12-5**
*Creating a Sanitary
Diapering Environment*

- Use area for diapering only.
- Provide running water to wash hands before and after diapering.
- Put the diapering area as far away from food preparation area as possible.
- Surface should be flat, safe, and preferably three feet off the floor.
- Make sure surface is clean, waterproof, and free of cracks. Use disposable covers such as squares, rolls of paper, paper bags, or used computer paper. Throw away immediately after use.
- For safety, keep all lotions out of the reach of children. Restrain child. Never leave child unattended.
- Remember, before handling clean diapers or other items, that the gloves are soiled and therefore could contaminate the clean diaper or other objects

*Adapted from* Control of Communicable and Infectious Diseases: A Manual for Child Care Providers, *California Child Care Health Project.*

**TABLE 12-6**
*Universal Sanitary
Diapering Procedures*

- Have area and supplies ready.
- Put on disposable gloves.
- Pick up child. If diaper is soiled, hold child away from you.
- Lay child down on diapering surface. Remove shoes and socks if necessary to prevent their contamination.
- Remove soiled or wet diaper. If clothes are contaminated, remove them.
- Place disposable diapers in a plastic bag and then throw it away in a lined, covered trash can.
- Clean child's bottom with moist disposable wipes. Wipe from front to back, using towelette. Use another towelette if needed.
- Pat dry with paper towel.
- Dispose of towelette and towel in lined, covered trash can with lid.
- Wipe your hands with moist towelette and dispose of in lined, covered trash can with lid.
- Diaper child and dress.
- Wash the child's hands.
- Remove disposable covering from diaper surface.
- Wash area and disinfect with bleach solution.
- Remove disposable gloves.
- Wash your own hands thoroughly.

*Adapted from* Control of Communicable and Infectious Diseases: A Manual for Child Care Providers, *California Child Care Health Project.*

If a child uses cloth diapers, the diapers should be placed in a second plastic bag and sent home with the child. There is too much risk of spreading disease by rinsing or laundering diapers at an early childhood education environment.

If an infant has more than three episodes of diarrhea in one day or if blood or mucus is present, the parent should be notified and a physician should be consulted (Lyles, 2003). Having a medical home for a child makes this a much easier task. When a policy for diapering provides a safe and sanitary method, then illness and disease spread can be reduced.

### Toileting

Toileting in a center is easier to control than toileting in a family child care home or the child's own home. The toileting area should be conveniently located to both indoor and outdoor play space (Gonzalez-Mena, 2004). It should include child-sized toilets and access to sinks with running water. Most centers have child-sized toilets that need to be cleaned and sanitized daily. If the toilet is contaminated with diarrhea, it should be cleaned and sanitized immediately. When training children to use the toilet they should be taught about the importance of washing hands. Instruction in hand washing should be given before and after toileting. Observing the children when they wash their hands will help to know which children need assistance in thorough hand washing. Miller (2003) suggests that the use of a hand-washing song to help children wash their hands for the minimum of 10 seconds that is necessary. This makes the event more fun, and it helps reduce the spread of disease if the hands are washed properly.

Toileting in a family child care home environment often involves a potty chair. The U.S. Department of Health and Human Services (DHHS, 2003) and the U.S. American Academy of Pediatrics (AAP) indicate that the use of potty chairs should be discouraged. Ideally, if they are used, each child learning to toilet should bring his own potty chair to the provider, because it decreases

Toileting is a good opportunity to teach children about the importance of hand washing. Some states require that teachers use disposable gloves when helping children with toileting.

the risk of spreading germs. The potty chairs should be stored clean and kept out of the reach of children and away from other surfaces that may have germs. Table 12-7 reviews sanitary procedures for potty chair use.

The use of disposable gloves is necessary to reduce the risk of spreading disease. It is necessary for the teacher to understand that this is just a stopgap measure and is not a substitute for washing hands. Teachers should check the requirements of their state licensing agencies, as some require the use of disposable gloves for helping with toileting.

## Cleaning and Disinfecting

The first line of defense against germs in the early childhood education environment that involve spills of body fluid, drainage from wounds, changing tables, counter tops, floors and other surfaces is cleaning with soap and

**TABLE 12-7**
*Sanitary Procedures for Potty Chairs*

- Use gloves.
- Wash child's hands.
- Empty contents into toilet.
- Rinse with water. This should be in a sink used for no other purpose. If it is used for hand washing of the child, clean and sanitize sink after toileting.
- Wash chair with soap and water. Empty into toilet.
- Rinse again and place contents in toilet.
- Spray with bleach solution.
- Air dry.
- Wash hands.

*Adapted from* Control of Communicable and Infectious Diseases: A Manual for Child Care Providers, *California Child Care Health Project.*

It is a good idea to record information about a child's progress during diaper changing or toileting so the parents can be informed. By the way, what is wrong with this picture?

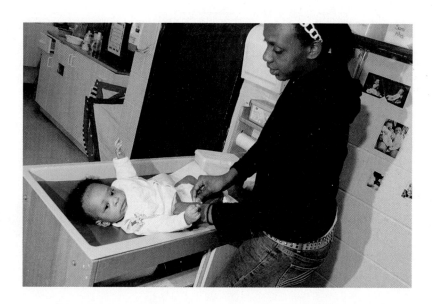

water followed by the disinfecting process (Palmer, 2002). The best way to stop the spread of germs is to both clean and disinfect. Neither is adequate alone. Cleaning gets rid of dirt and some surface germs, while disinfecting rids the surface of the remaining germs through the use of a sanitizing solution. In child care, the most common effective and least expensive sanitizing solution is bleach. According to the CDC's latest standards, liquid bleach should contain a 5.25% hypochlorite solution for maximum sanitizing (Palmer, 2002; Hendricks, 2003).

Several strengths of the sodium bleach solution are necessary for disinfecting different surfaces or contaminants. Figure 12-3 shows a general purpose sanitation mix.

The solution is placed in spray bottles and used in the bathroom, kitchen, and diapering area and on other surfaces and toys. This solution

**FIGURE 12-3**
General purpose cleaning solution used in the bathroom, in the kitchen, in the diapering area, and on toys.

1/4 cup bleach with hypochlorite

1 tbsp. bleach

1 gallon water    1 quart water

### Cleaning and Disinfecting Sanitizing Solution

• Mix 1/4 cup bleach with hypochlorite in 1 gallon of water or mix 1 tablespoon bleach in 1 quart of water.

• Place in labeled spray bottles out of reach of children in the bathroom, the diapering area, and the kitchen.

• Wash surfaces first with soap or detergent and water.

• Spray on sanitizing solution and allow to air dry.

• Replace solution daily.

A standard solution of bleach and water should be used to clean and sanitize the classroom, toy surfaces, and floors. What other surfaces should be sanitized?

is also used on floors and to clean sleeping mats. See Table 12-8 for frequency of cleaning and disinfecting needed in the early childhood education environment.

One area of concern to researchers who observed early childhood education programs in four states was the lack of sanitation in sinks, which allows germs to thrive (Thornburg et al., 2002). It was found that sinks were used for multiple purposes, such as diapering, toileting, washing hands, food preparation, and brushing teeth. The recommended practice is to have multiple sinks—one for each purpose in each area (such as the kitchen, the bathroom, and the program area).

**TABLE 12-8**
*Cleaning and Disinfecting Guidelines*

- Clean objects and surfaces with detergent and water first.
- Next apply bleach solution by spraying from bottle or dipping object in bleach solution and allowing it to air dry.

**Cleaning and Disinfecting Schedule:**

| Object or area | Frequency |
| --- | --- |
| Diaper changing area, toilets, and potty chairs | Clean after every use. Spray with sanitizing solution after cleaning. |
| Bathroom | Clean thoroughly one or more times daily. |
| Kitchen | Clean thoroughly one or more times daily. |
| Play Areas | Mop or vacuum daily. Remove litter or food immediately. For carpet, vacuum daily For flooring, mop, cleaning first, then rinsing and sanitizing |
| Cribs and Cots | Change linen when wet or soiled; otherwise, weekly Disinfect weekly. |
| Toys | Clean and sanitize all mouthed toys after each use. Machine wash stuffed toys and all play items at least once a week and when visibly soiled. Sanitize water tables and wading pools after each use. Throw away mouthed play dough or clay immediately. Change frequently. Dress-up clothes in the dramatic area should be laundered weekly Books, headphones, and computer keyboards should be quickly wiped with an alcohol-based wipe (not a baby wipe) as needed/used. |

*Cleaning:* All-purpose liquid detergents and water are used to remove dirt, urine, or vomit by washing and scrubbing.

*Sanitizing:* Soap, detergents, and abrasive cleaners are used to remove filth, soil, and a small amount of bacteria. To be considered sanitary, surfaces must be clean and germs must be reduced to a level at which disease transmission is unlikely.

*Disinfecting:* A solution of bleach and water is used to eliminate practically all germs from surfaces. For normal disinfecting, a general-purpose solution is used. When working with blood or stools from bowel movement, a contamination solution is used.

For cleaning more infectious items such as blood, blood spills, and body fluids, including vomit, a stronger solution is needed. This stronger solution is shown in Figure 12-4. The contamination cleaning solution is also used for regular cleaning when outbreaks of infectious disease occur.

When a child has soiled her clothing with fecal or bodily fluid, the item should be removed immediately and placed in a plastic bag for the parent to take home and launder. Parents should be informed of this policy when the child enters care. A reminder note should be attached to the soiled clothing bag. Younger children in early childhood environments should always have an extra set of clothes in their cubbies for times like this.

Clothing and hats used for dress-up in play areas should be laundered frequently with bleach. Hats should be sprayed frequently with a disinfectant such as Lysol. If an outbreak of lice or a skin infection such as scabies occurs, these clothes should be temporarily removed, laundered, and placed in airtight plastic bags for at least two weeks.

Toys that children have mouthed should be picked up immediately after they are discarded or dropped and placed in a container that is out of children's reach (Smith, 2003). These toys should be later sanitized before going back into the children's toy environment. The teacher should always wash hands after handling mouthed toys.

Each child should use his own bedding only. These items should be stored separately in bins or boxes labeled with the child's name. Regular weekly laundering can keep bedding fresh and clean. If it becomes contaminated with mucus, feces, urine, vomit, or blood, send it home with the child to be washed.

When soiled or contaminated items are sent home with the child, a reminder note accompanying the items is an effective communication tool. It will explain to the parents why the item was not rinsed and alert them that they should closely observe their child for illness. The prevention, protection,

**FIGURE 12-4**
Contamination cleaning solution. Use to clean blood, body fluids, and vomit.

## Contamination Cleaning Solution

1 tablespoon of bleach with hypochlorite
3/4 cup of water

and control of infectious disease are not always easily understood, but they are very necessary in maintaining a sanitary environment.

It is possible to sanitize the early childhood environment without using bleach (Calder, 2004). Some teachers prefer not to use bleach because they are bleach sensitive or because the solution must be made daily. Alternative solutions include alcohols, phenols, and quaternary ammonium compounds. It is best to read labels as to application and contact time needed to kill germs and for the safety of the product in relation to children. The teacher should consider the safety aspects of using the product on items children may mouth, and also whether the product would be effective against bloodborne diseases.

Good hand washing and disinfecting of commonly touched surfaces has been proven to greatly reduce illness and promote safety in the early childhood education environment (Report on Preschool Programs, 2004).

### Key Concept 12.4

### Universal Sanitary Practices

Universal sanitary practices are some of the most effective risk management tools a teacher can employ to create a healthy environment. A clean, sanitary environment will help curb the spread of germs and infectious diseases. Proper techniques for hand washing, diapering, toileting, cleaning, and disinfecting are the main tools the teacher uses to provide a healthy environment.

## 12.5  ENVIRONMENTAL QUALITY CONTROL FOR DISEASE PREVENTION

There are certain other areas of the early childhood education environment that may contribute to the spread of disease. These special areas of consideration include water play, play dough, air quality, and contamination.

### Water Play

Water play occurs in a container that, if not properly cleaned, can be an environment where germs multiply. If the water becomes warm, it offers a warm, moist place where germs thrive and rapidly multiply. For optimal use of a water table in the early childhood education environment, follow the water table health tips found in Table 12-9.

### Play Dough and Clay

Play dough and clay are also good hosts for germs because they are moist and get warm through frequent contact with children's hands. Safety tips for having play dough and clay in the early childhood education environment are included in Table 12-10.

Water play is an engrossing and enjoyable activity for young children, but a playing field for germs is opened up if the table or container is not properly cleaned.

**TABLE 12-9**
*Water Table Health Guidelines*

- Clean and sanitize the water table with the general purpose sanitation mix daily.
- Change water at least daily; more frequently, if it gets warm (over 72°F). Use fresh, cool water.
- Children should wash hands before and after playing in water table.
- Wash water-play toys daily either with general purpose solution or in the dishwasher.
- Use plastic throwaway items when possible.
- Use an individual water bin for any child with a condition, such as a runny nose, that might spread germs.

**TABLE 12-10**
*Play Dough and Clay Health Guidelines*

- Children must wash hands before and after playing with the play dough.
- Do not use scents in play dough, because it encourages mouthing.
- Replace play dough frequently and always throw it away if it has been mouthed or appears dirty.
- Store play dough in the refrigerator.
- Keep clay in a cool, dry place and make sure it is well covered.
- Clean and sanitize tables before and after play dough or clay is used.
- Allow only a small amount of clay at a time so it can be replaced more often and the expense will not be as great.
- Do not use play dough or clay for a day or two if a fecal-oral disease has been identified in the environment.

Play dough is a classroom staple, but health precautions should be taken to make this fun, manipulative molding clay germ-free and safe for children.

During naptime, at least 3 feet of space should be maintained between cribs and cots. That does not always occur.

## *Air Quality*

Air flow in the early childhood education environment is especially important to help control the spread of germs. Crowding of children contributes to poor air quality (Aronson, 2000). If the air is not moving or if there are too many children in one area, the air will not flow as well as it should, resulting in a better environment for germs. Air fresheners do not help air quality but merely mask odors. They may also pose a threat to some children with allergies or asthma and may trigger a reaction. To avoid poor air quality, follow the air quality health guidelines in Table 12-11. If the air in the early childhood education environment is dry and hot due to heating, everyone in care may be more vulnerable to colds and other respiratory problems. Placing a cool air humidifier or vaporizer adds moisture to the air and can reduce the likelihood of illness (Ware, 2004). Air should be kept as free of triggers for asthma as possible.

## Contamination in Child Care

Special precautions should be taken to minimize the effects of contaminants such as blood, vomit, urine, and loose stools or diarrhea in the early childhood education environment. For proper health precautions see Table 12-12.

**TABLE 12-11**
*Air Quality Health Guidelines*

- Keep air temperature cool; under 72°F helps prevent disease spread.
- Circulate fresh air as much as possible—open windows as daily weather permits.
- Make sure children get outside to breathe fresh air daily, weather permitting.
- Heating and cooling equipment should be checked several times a year and should be cleaned every three months. Any filters should be replaced when serviced to prevent buildup of molds and dust.
- Arrange your environment so that there is plenty of open space. This discourages the spread of germs.
- Keep at least 3 feet of space between cribs and cots in the sleeping area.
- Follow guidelines of indoor space per child so that there is no crowding.
- When placing children on cots, alternate placing head and feet toward the front. This helps avoid airborne transmission.

**TABLE 12-12**
*Health Guidelines for Disease Prevention*

- Minimize the number of people who handle contaminated materials.
- Use disposable gloves and paper towels to clean up spills from diarrhea, blood, urine, or vomit.
- Clean and disinfect surfaces involved with contamination sanitation mix.
- Dispose of cleanup materials, disposable gloves, and so forth in a plastic bag that is covered, tied, and placed in an outside trash can immediately.
- If any contaminated materials soil the child's or teacher's clothes, they should be changed immediately.
- Wash hands immediately.
- Place contaminated clothing in a plastic bag with tie. Double-bag it in another plastic bag and send home with child or teacher to be laundered at home.

## Key Concept 12.5

### Environmental Quality Control for Disease Prevention

There are special areas of need for environmental quality control for infectious disease spread found in the early childhood education environment. These areas include water tables, play dough and clay, air quality, and contamination. Using preventive strategies and techniques for these items can help the teacher control the spread of infectious disease.

## 12.6 IMPLICATIONS FOR TEACHERS

Teachers must use a number of tools to prevent the risk of infectious disease spread. These tools include education and role modeling, cultural competence, and supervision to make sure protective measures are carried out.

### Education and Role Modeling

Education is one of the best preventive tools a teacher has to help control the spread of infectious disease in the early childhood education environment. The effort to prevent the spread of germs and disease needs to be a cooperative venture. Teachers need to model proper health behaviors. Children need to be taught to perform proper health practices. Parents need to understand the need for these practices and help children remember to carry these out at home so they get into the habit of good hygiene.

Children need to focus on several things to play their role in prevention. Good hand washing techniques at the right times is the most important tool for children to prevent the spread of disease. This can be done in a number of ways. Modeling the hand washing techniques is important.

Modeling hand washing should include

- showing
- helping
- telling
- feedback

When the teacher is washing her hands or helping a child to wash his, the teacher should talk about what is happening and why. Reinforcing the conversation and hand washing method with feedback is important for the teacher to see that the child is grasping (1) why hands are being washed; (2) when hands should be washed; and (3) how hands should be washed.

Reminders should be given throughout the day at times when hand washing is a must. A poster or line drawing showing proper hand washing procedures placed by the hand washing sink offers a visual reminder when the teacher is not present.

Hand washing at scheduled intervals throughout the day can be a fun activity and teaches the children good hygiene.

To ensure a healthy environment, one of the teacher's most important tasks is to help children form the good hygiene habit of hand washing. If hand washing is made a fun task, the children will more likely participate and remember when and how to use the hand washing techniques. Teachers who develop or use songs that focus on hands while in circle groups or at the sink at hand washing times may make it easier for some children to grasp good hand washing behaviors. Using books that focus on hands or good hygiene will also help.

### For Families

Parents have a significant degree of responsibility in preventing the spread of disease in the early childhood education environment where their children attend. Parent education is critical in the prevention of outbreaks such as chicken pox, Hib, and meningitis. Parents can make sure their children are immunized according to schedule. They can reinforce the hygiene practices that children learn at school, and they can make sure not to send their children to school when they are ill. Some of the supportive behaviors that are essential on the part of the parents may need some special effort on the part of the teacher.

### Cultural Competence

Cultural competence may be needed, especially when dealing with the issue of immunization. A parent may be unaware of the need for immunizations or may lack access to immunizations. Recent immigrant families may not be aware of the need for immunization or may even feel it is unnecessary. Some children from culturally diverse or immigrant, low-income working families may not have ready access to health care (Guendelman & Pearl, 2001). These families have higher rates of infectious diseases as well as chronic illnesses (Duarte & Rafanello, 2001). Resistance to participation in immunization and screening may also result from culturally defined acceptable behavior or language difficulties (Carballo & Nerukar, 2001). It is important for the teacher to help the parents understand how vital it is to follow the immunization schedule and get regular health care for their children. Teachers can provide resources to help these families connect with public funds for low-cost health insurance for low-income families. It is important for the teacher to help the parents understand how vital it is to follow the immunization schedule. Following this schedule is vital to the child's own health as well as the early childhood education environment.

## Supervision

Children from many different backgrounds may come to the early childhood environment. It is up to the teacher to supervise the environment so that children come into the program as risk-free as possible. There are five basic commandments for infectious disease control that must be monitored by the teacher.

- prevent the spread of disease
- require and monitor immunizations
- report some illnesses to public health officials and to parents
- exclude some children
- be prepared to deal with an ill child, if necessary

### Key Concept 12.6

### Implications for Teachers

The effort to prevent the spread of infectious disease is a cooperative venture. The teacher can educate and model behaviors to the children. Modeling will also help the parent reinforce these behaviors at home. The teacher must be especially culturally sensitive about the need for immunizations and help the parents understand the necessity of a current immunization schedule for children. The teacher must supervise the early childhood education environment to make sure sanitary practices are carried out.

## CHAPTER SUMMARY

Health policies for infection control maintain health and prevent some illnesses in children and adults present in the early childhood education environment. Two practices that contribute to this are good hygiene and sanitary practices. Checking the immunization schedule is another preventive practice. Food safety and storage are other practices that help manage the spread of disease. The four methods of infectious disease spread should be understood and proactive measures taken to reduce the spread.

## TO GO BEYOND

In this section you will find a number of activities that you can use to apply and improve your knowledge of this chapter. There are also thorough online resources that accompany this text that can be found at http://www.early childed.delmar.com (see description at end of this chapter).

### Chapter Review Critical Thinking Applications

1. Discuss the four methods of transmission of infectious diseases. Relate these methods of transmission to sanitary practices that could be performed to prevent spread.

2. Debate the question of whether children with lice should be allowed to stay in care or should be excluded from care.

3. Examine the importance of immunization schedules. How much have these schedules changed in recent years, compared to when the students were young children?

4. Discuss how a teacher would handle the acceptance of a child into care who has not been immunized.

### As an Individual

1. Observe hand washing practices in an early childhood education environment. Next, observe hand washing practices in a public restroom. Compare and contrast these two environments. Were universal hand washing procedures used at appropriate times? Record your observations.

2. Research and report on the programs in your state and local area that help low-income children and their families gain access to health care.

### As a Group

1. Discuss environmental quality control in the early childhood education environment. What further measures might be taken to improve the health of that environment? Discuss the impact of children's cots or sleeping pads being placed so close together.

2. In small groups of four to five students design health policies for (1) lice, (2) long nails on teachers, and (3) hand washing.

3. Research the topic of the present controversy over immunizations. Divide the class in half and debate the issue. What are your conclusions? Should a child be allowed in care without immunizations?

4. Discuss how diversity in early childhood education environments might affect health policies or health practices. List measures that may help culturally diverse families understand these policies and practices.

### Case Studies

1. Chloe came into care on an emergency basis, and her parents did not fill out the health history completely. She has been in care for a month and the family child care provider still does not have the immunization record. What should be done?

2. As a teacher, you have been trying very hard to keep your environment as healthy as possible. You try to wash your hands at the appropriate time, change diapers properly, and clean on schedule. You notice, however, that the two-year-olds seem to be passing colds back and forth and there have been several cases of scabies. What might you be overlooking?

3. You work in an early childhood education facility that has several rooms. During waking hours, the children are spread throughout the center. However, during naptime they are placed on cots in the largest room for convenience purposes. There is hardly any room between the cots to even walk. How would you approach your director about this issue and how it affects air quality?

## Chapter References

American Academy of Pediatrics (AAP). (2000). Controlling illness in child care programs. Retrieved 11/19/04. Available on: http://www.medem.com/MedLB/article_detaillb_for_printer.cfm?article_ID=ZZZN7CDTA7C&sub_cat=13.

American Academy of Pediatrics (AAP). (2001a). *Immunizations and your child.* AAP Parent Pages (a brochure). Elk Grove Village, IL: American Academy of Pediatrics.

American Academy of Pediatrics (AAP). (2002). New head lice statement: AAP discourages "no-nit" policies for return. Retrieved October 31, 2005, http://www.aap.org/advocacy/archives/septlice.htm

American Academy of Pediatrics. (2003). *Red Book: 2003 Report of the Committee on Infectious Diseases.* Pickering L. (Ed.). Elk Grove Village, IL. AAP.

American Academy of Pediatrics (AAP). (2004, November 1). Whooping cough outbreak. Retrieved October 31, 2005. http://www.aap.org/family/whooping-cough.htm.

American Academy of Pediatrics and American Public Health Association, (APA & APHA). (2002). *Caring for our children: National health and safety performance standards: Guidelines for out-of-home care.* Washington, D.C.: American Public Health Association.

Aronson, S. (2000, January). Environmental health in child care settings. *Child Care Information Exchange, 35.*

Aronson, S. (2003, March). 2002 Update on hand hygiene in child (day) care settings. *Child Care information Exchange,* 58–62.

(Staff Writer) California Childcare Health Program (CCHP). (2004, May). Unimmunized children in the child care setting. *Childcare Healthline,* Health and Safety Notes, 1–2. Retrieved 11/4/05 from http://www.ucsfchildcarehealth.org/pdfs/healthandsafety/unimmunizeden050604.

Calder, J. (2004). Sanitizing without bleach. *Child Care Health Connections Newsletter, 17*(6), 2, 9.

Carballo, M., & Nerukar, A. (2001). Migration, refugees and health risks. *Emerging Infectious Diseases, 7*(3), 556–560.

Caufield, R., & Kataoka-Yahiro, M. (2001). Health training needs of child care professionals. *Early Childhood Education Journal, 29*(2), 119–123.

Centers for Disease Control (CDC). (2004a, October 15). Fact sheet: Stopping the spread of germs at home, work and school. Department of Health and Human Services, Washington, D.C.. Retrieved October 31, 2005, from http://www.cdc.gov/flu/protect/stopgerms.htm.

Centers for Disease Control (CDC). (2004b, July 30). National, state and urban area vaccination coverage among children aged 19–35 months, United States, 2003. *Mortality Morbidity Weekly Report, 53*(29), 658–661. Retrieved October 31, 2005, from http://www.cdc.gov/mmwr/preview/mmwrhtml/mm5329a.htm

Centers for Disease Control (CDC). (2002). Guideline for hand hygiene in healthcare settings: Recommendations of the healthcare infection control practices advisory committee and the HICPAC/SHEA/IDSA Hand Hygiene Task Force. *Mortality Morbidity Weekly Report, 51*(16), 1–45.

Child Health Alert (CHA). (2004, May 1). MMR vaccine and autism: A New Study. *Child Health Alert, 22,* 3.

Child Health Alert (CHA). (2003a, September 1). Dealing with head lice- how times have changed? *Child Health Alert, 21.*

Child Health Alert (CHA). (2003b, October 1). Finding hard-to-find lice. *Child Health Alert, 21,* 1.

Dailey, L. (2000). Is that nit dead or alive—or does it matter? *Child Care Health Connections, 13*(6), 4.

Duarte, G., & Rafanello, D. (2001). The migrant child: a special place in the field. *Young Children, 56*(2), 26–34.

Department of Health and Human Services (DHHS). (2003). *Stepping stones to using Caring for Our Children* (2nd ed.). Rockville, MD: Author. Retrieved October 31, 2005, from http://nrc.uchsc.edu/STEPPING/SteppingStones.pdf

Figueroa, J. (2000). Head lice: Is there a solution? *Current Opinion in Infectious Diseases, 13*(2), 135–139.

Frankowski, B., & Weiner, L. (2002). Head lice. *Pediatrics, 110*(3), 638–643.

Gonzalez-Mena, J. (2004). *Infants, toddlers and caregivers.* New York: McGraw-Hill.

Groppe, M. (2004, September 9). Burton leads mercury inquiry. Indiana Star, INDYSTAR.com. Retrieved 9/19/04. Available online (ID: ind65959747): http://nl.newsbank.com/nl-search/we/Archives?s_site=indystar&f_site=indystar&f_sitename=Indianapolis+Star%2FNews%2C+The+%28IN%29&p_theme=gannett&p_product=IN&p_action=search&p_field_base-0=&p_text_base-0=Burton+leads+mercury+inquiry&Search=Search&p_perpage=10&p_maxdocs=200&p_queryname=700&s_search_type=keyword&p_sort=_rank_%3AD&p_field_date-0=YMD_date&p_params_date-0=date%3AB%2CE&p_text_date-0=-3qzM

Guendelman, S., & Pearl, M. (2001). Access to care for children of the working poor. *Archives of Pediatrics and Adolescent Medicine, 155*(6), 651–658.

Hendricks, C. (2003). Floor care. *Healthy Child Care, 6*(1). Retrieved October 31, 2005, from http://www.healthychild.net/articles/mc31Floors.html.

Lyles, K. (2003). Diapering—Safety and sanitation. *Healthy Child Care, 6*(6). Retrieved October 31, 2005 from http://www.healthychild.net/articles/sf36diaper.html.

Miller, S. (2003). Tips for toileting. *Early Childhood Today, 18*(2), 6.

Moolenaar, R., Crutcher, J., San Joaquin, V., Sewell, L., Hutwagner, L., Carson, L., Robison, D., Smithee, L., & Jarvis, W. (2000). A prolonged outbreak of *pseduomonas aeruginosa* in a neonatal intensive care unit: Did staff fingernails play a role in disease transmission. *Journal of Infection Control and Hospital Epidemiology, 21*(2), 80–85.

Mumcuoglu, K., Friger, M, Ioffe-Upensky, I., Ben-Ishai, F., & Miller, J. (2001). Louse comb versus direct visual examination for the diagnosis of head louse infestations. *Pediatric Dermatology, 18*(1), 9–12.

National Association of Child Care Professionals (NACCP). (2001, December 30). Higher rates of repeat infections occur among children in group care. *Medical Letter on the CDC and FDA,* 15.

National Coalition on Health Care (NCHC). (2004). Health insurance coverage. Author. Retrieved October 31, 2005, from http://www.nchc.org/facts/coverage.shtml.

North Carolina Child Care Health and Safety Resource Center (NCCCHSRC). (2004). Managing water outdoors. *North Carolina Child Care Health and Safety Bulletin, 6*(3), 3.

Orr, L. The doctor's view of flu vaccines for infants and toddlers. EurekAlert (EA) Retrieved 11/4/05 from http://ww.eurekalert.org/pub_releases/2004-09/uorm-tdv090304.php

Palmer, D. (2002). Universal (or standard) precautions. *Healthy Child Care, 5*(1). Retrieved October 31, 2005, from http://www.healthychild.net/articles/sh25universal.html.

Parker-Pope, T. (2004, September 7). Study reignites debate on autism, childhood vaccines. *The Wall Street Journal.* Retrieved 9/19/04. Available on: http://www.sfgate.com

Pennsylvania Chapter American Academy of Pediatrics (PAAAP). (2004). When parent's won't immunize their children. *Early Childhood Health Link, 14*(4), 1–2.

Pearlman, D. (2004). A simple treatment for head lice. Dry on, suffocation-based pediculicide. *Pediatrics, 114*(3), 275–279.

Pellman, H. (2002). Day cares and colds. *Pediatrics for Parents, 20*(4), 5.

Pollack, R., Kiszewski, A., & Spielman, A. (2000). Overdiagnosis and consequent mismanagement of head louse infestations in North America. *The Pediatric Infectious Disease Journal, 19*(4), 689–694.

Pollack, R. (2000). Head lice information. Harvard School of Public Health. Retrieved October 31, 2005, from http://www.hsph.harvard.edu/headlice.html.

Richardson, M., Elliman, D., Macguire, H., Simpson, J., & Nicoll, A. (2001). Evidence base of incubation periods, periods of infectiousness and exclusion policies for the control of communicable diseases in schools and preschools. *The Pediatric Infectious Disease Journal, 20*(2), 380–391.

Sachs, J. (1999, March). Vaccines: The real risks and benefits. *Parenting Magazine,* 113–118.

Salmon, D., Haber, M., & Cangarosa, E. (1999). Consequences of religious and philosophical exemptions from immunization laws. *Journal of the American Medical Association, 292*(1), 47–53.

Report on Preschool Programs (RPP). (2004). Strict cleaning routines promote child health, safety, study says. *RPP, 36*(7), 55.

Samuels, M., Lu, N., Shi, L., Baker, S., Glover, S., & Sanders, J. (2004). Child day care risks of common infectious diseases revisited. *Child Care Health and Development, 30*(4), 361–368.

Santoli, J., Huet, N., Smith, P., Barker, L., Rodewald, L. Inkeias, M., Olson, L., & Halfon, N. (2004). Insurance status and vaccination coverage among US preschool children. *Pediatrics, 113*(6), 1959–1964.

Smeeth, L., Cook, C., Fonbonne, E., Heavey, L., Ridrigues, L., Smith, P., & Hall, A. (2004). MMR vaccine and pervasive developmental disorders: A case-control study. *Lancet, 364*(9438), 963–969.

Smith, C. (2003). Toy cleaning. *Healthy Child Care, 5*(4). Retrieved 9/19/04. Available online: http://www.healthychild.net/volume6.html

Spence, A. (1999, February/March). Hot shots. *Healthy Kids Magazine,* 42–50.

Thornburg, K., Cable, S., Scott, J Mayfield, W., & Watson, A. (2002). Recommended sanitation practices in early childhood programs. Midwest Child Care Research Consortium: University of Missouri-Columbia, Columbia, MO. Retrieved April 4, 2005 from http://www.missouri.edu/~cfprww/recpracsanitary.pdf

Tierno, P. (2003). Preventing the spread of germs. *Scholastic Parent and Child, 11*(2), 44.

Trick, W., Vernon, M., Hayes, R., Nathan, C., Rice, T., Peterson, B., Segreti, J., Welbel, S Solomon, S., & Weinstein, R. (2003). Impact of ring wearing on hand contamination and comparison of hand hygiene agents in a hospital. *Clinical Infectious Diseases, 36*(6), 1383–1390.

Walsh, E. (2004). New recommendations for the influenza vaccine. *Child Care Health Connections Newsletter, 17*(6), 1, 9.

Ware, S. (2004). Respiratory hygiene in child care. *Child Care Health Connections Newsletter, 17*(2), 4.

Additional resources for this chapter can be found by visiting the Online Companion™ at http://www.earlychilded.delmar.com. This supplemental material includes extensive chapter quizzes, PowerPoint® outlines, Web links, and various other activities to help better utilize the material in this chapter. The site is updated regularly, so you may check back often to receive the latest information about the subjects in each chapter.

# Supportive Health Care in Early Childhood Education Environments

**After reading this chapter, you should be able to:**

### 13.1 Health Policies

Describe and discuss health policies for the identification and management of childhood communicable diseases.

### 13.2 Identification of Infectious Diseases

Describe the methods and means of identifying childhood infectious diseases for early interventions and prevention of disease spread.

### 13.3 Managing Infectious Diseases

Describe the methods and practices for managing childhood infectious diseases for early identification and prevention of disease spread.

### 13.4 Managing Care for Mildly Ill Children

Summarize and indicate the importance of policies and protocols for care of mildly ill children in early childhood education environments.

### 13.5 Children with Chronic Illnesses

Describe and discuss special considerations for caring for children with chronic illnesses.

### 13.6 Optimizing Health in Early Childhood Education Environments

Describe and discuss the inclusion of a health consultant in the early childhood education program and the advantages of having a medical home for every child.

### 13.7 Implications for Teachers

Indicate the need and importance of education, observation, and supervision for early intervention to manage childhood communicable diseases in the early childhood education environment.

## 13.1  HEALTH POLICIES

Policies for health care in early childhood education are essential to keep children as healthy as possible, to prevent disease spread, and to care for mildly ill children. The following are indicators of the need for good health care policies for child care:

- Children under the age of three years are more vulnerable to infectious diseases because their immune systems are not fully developed (NICH, 2001).

- The chances of diseases being transmitted depend on three things: (1) the characteristics of the children in the group; (2) the nature of the disease; and (3) the health policies and practices of the child care facility (Kendrick, Kaufmann, & Messenger, 2002).

- Children in early childhood education environments are more likely to have a respiratory illness than those children who are at home. But by the age of three years the rate of illness was found to be the same in both settings (Pellman, 2002).

- As many as 10 percent of children in early education environments are infected with pinworms (Palmer, 2003).

- Skin rashes occur often in children; although many cases are mild, others are very contagious and may require exclusion (Moss, 2003). Early childhood education environments should have an exclusion policy and know the difference between what should be excluded and what should not (Dailey, 2002).

- If the state allows medication to be administered in early childhood education environments, there should be a plan to ensure that medications are given safely and correctly (Calder, 2004).

A program's health policy should specify that, if a child exhibits signs and symptoms of a contagious disease or infection, the parents must be notified and an authorized person contacted to come pick up the child.

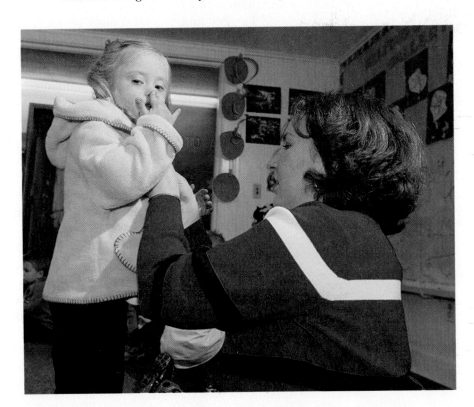

- Accepting a child with a chronic condition into care requires planning by the family and teacher so that the child's needs will be properly met and risk will be reduced (Alexander, 2003). Allergen levels in early childhood education environments may actually contribute to problems (Do child care centers contribute, 2002). Teachers often serve as gatekeepers of children's health (Sailors, 2004).

- Dealing with health in early childhood education is complex, and a health consultant could help a teacher optimize management of the health of children in care (Cianciolo et al., 2004; NAEYC, 2004; Caufield & Kataoka-Yahiro, 2002). A medical home for all children in care could also be beneficial (American Academy of Pediatrics [AAP], 2002).

Health care in early childhood education environments is a complex issue, and many considerations have to be made. A teacher must be able to identify the signs and symptoms of illness and parasite infestations. The identification process helps put an exclusion policy into operation. The exclusion policy enables the teacher to separate those children who are very ill or who are contagious and need to leave the early childhood education environment from those children who are not contagious or very ill and may remain. The exclusion policy should include how to communicate with parents. If children are not excluded from the early childhood education environment, the teacher needs to manage the care for mildly ill children without putting others at risk. Chronic illness in children requires continued treatment and vigilance for things that might trigger responses or cause symptoms to worsen. Children with special health care needs such as those with chronic illness need to have policies created for them that provide the most protective and healthy environment.

Parents and teachers need to work together to help identify and manage risks to the health of the children in care. When a teacher uses a health consultant and encourages a medical home for every child, the health environment in care will be optimized. Teachers need to supervise the environment to intervene and minimize risk and to help maintain the health of all of the children in their care.

To provide the early childhood education environment with the optimum health care, there should be policies for the following:

- *Identification of Childhood Infectious Diseases:* practices for recognizing signs and symptoms of infectious disease for early intervention

- *Management of Childhood Infectious Diseases:* practices for managing childhood infectious diseases, including exclusion

- *Managing Care for Mildly Ill Children:* strategies and practices for managing the care of mildly ill children

- *Children with Chronic Illnesses:* understanding coping skills and strategies needed to provide the most protective and preventive environment for these children in early education programs.

- *Optimizing Health Care in Early Childhood Education Environments:* rationale for using a health consultant and encouraging a medical home for all children in care to maximize the health of everyone in the early childhood education environment.

- *Implications for Teachers:* methods and practices to provide minimum risk and maximum protection for health in the early childhood education environment through education, observation, working with families, and supervision

### Health Policy

Managing health care in the early childhood education environment may be a challenge to the teacher, because it includes a number of aspects. The teacher must learn how to identify infectious diseases and know when to exclude children from care. The teacher must understand how to prevent the spread of infectious disease and protect the health of the children in care. The teacher needs to be prepared for dealing with chronic illness. The use of a health consultant and the encouragement of a medical home for all children will help optimize health in early childhood education.

## 13.2 IDENTIFICATION OF INFECTIOUS DISEASES

The first line of defense for illnesses in the early childhood education environment is the control of infectious diseases through good hygiene and sanitary practices.

### Identifying Infectious Diseases and Illness in Children

The second line of defense is the teacher's ability to identify illness as quickly as possible (Bradley, 2003). Many illnesses may be present several days before signs or symptoms appear. Guidelines for helping a teacher recognize signs and symptoms provide a barrier to the spread of an infectious disease.

*Signs and Symptoms of Illness.* Children may show few signs of illness, then suddenly appear to be ill. The teacher needs to observe for certain signs and symptoms that will help identify an ill child (Figure 13-1). Observation can help determine whether the illness is the type that may spread rapidly and necessitate excluding a child from care. Some signs and symptoms are serious, and others need special consideration because they might signify an oncoming illness.

Conducting a daily health check as the child arrives is the first point of the day to watch for caution signs for health or illness. The health policy for the early childhood education environment should state that any child who exhibits infectious disease signs and symptoms be excluded. This should be strictly enforced. (Table 13-5 presents the conditions for exclusion.)

The child who appears to be below the normal level of mood or activity should be monitored for further symptoms. Signs or symptoms may not be exhibited in the first stages, yet the child may indeed be ill.

FIGURE 13-1

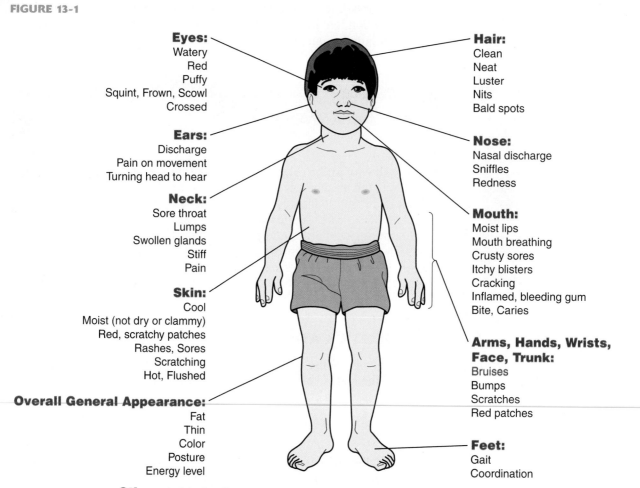

**Eyes:**
Watery
Red
Puffy
Squint, Frown, Scowl
Crossed

**Ears:**
Discharge
Pain on movement
Turning head to hear

**Neck:**
Sore throat
Lumps
Swollen glands
Stiff
Pain

**Skin:**
Cool
Moist (not dry or clammy)
Red, scratchy patches
Rashes, Sores
Scratching
Hot, Flushed

**Overall General Appearance:**
Fat
Thin
Color
Posture
Energy level

**Hair:**
Clean
Neat
Luster
Nits
Bald spots

**Nose:**
Nasal discharge
Sniffles
Redness

**Mouth:**
Moist lips
Mouth breathing
Crusty sores
Itchy blisters
Cracking
Inflamed, bleeding gum
Bite, Caries

**Arms, Hands, Wrists, Face, Trunk:**
Bruises
Bumps
Scratches
Red patches

**Feet:**
Gait
Coordination

**Other:**  Activity level/lethargy, Failure to urinate, Severe coughing, Vomiting, Fever, Seizure

The following are some common primary indicators of whether a child is ill:

- unusual crankiness or listlessness
- complaint of sore throat or difficulty swallowing
- runny nose (clear discharge indicates allergies; green or yellow indicates infection)
- complaint of stomachache or cramping
- diarrhea
- complaint of headache or earache
- red, watery, or draining eyes
- unusual rashes or spots
- infected skin lesions

More serious indicators of illness that need *immediate attention* include the following:

- fever
- vomiting
- severe coughing
- breathing problems
- urine with a strong odor
- unusual drowsiness
- excessive crying
- neck pain or stiff neck
- seizure for the first time

The teacher must determine whether the child is just under the weather or is ill and may have an infectious disease. The teacher can identify illness with the signs and symptoms listed in Tables 13-1 through 13-4.

**TABLE 13-1**
*Identification and Management of Diseases Transmitted Via the Respiratory Tract*

| Disease | Signs/Symptoms | Teacher's Role |
|---|---|---|
| Colds | Sneezing, runny nose, stuffy nose, watery eyes, sore throat, fever<br>Most contagious 2 to 3 days before and 3 to 5 days after symptoms appear | Wipe runny noses; use gloves.<br>Wash hands often.<br>Do not share food, drink<br>Disinfect mouthed toys.<br>Teach children to cover mouth when coughing. |
| Influenza | Fever, chills, headache, drowsiness, muscle aches, nausea, vomiting | Wipe runny noses; use gloves.<br>Wash hands often.<br>Do not share food, drink<br>Disinfect mouthed toys.<br>Call parent if fever or vomiting is present. |
| Strep Throat | Painful, scratchy throat, tender/swollen glands, fever, spots on throat | Wash hands often.<br>Do not share food, drink.<br>Disinfect mouthed toys.<br>Call parent if fever is present or child is unable to swallow.<br>Notify all parents if strep throat is present.<br>Be alert to outbreak.<br>Exclude child from care until 24 hours after antibiotic treatment has begun and no fever is present. |
| Scarlet Fever | Same as above<br>Red, sandpapery rash on trunk, neck, groin<br>Red tongue, flushed cheeks | Wash hands often.<br>Do not share food, drink.<br>Disinfect mouthed toys.<br>Call parent if fever is present.<br>Be alert to outbreak.<br>Exclude child from care.<br>Notify all parents. |

*(continues)*

**TABLE 13-1 (Continued)**
*Identification and Management of Diseases Transmitted Via the Respiratory Tract*

| Disease | Signs/Symptoms | Teacher's Role |
|---|---|---|
| Chicken Pox | Fever, runny nose, blistery rash, cough | Exclude if chicken pox is suspected until doctor confirms. Readmit after the sixth day or after rash is crusted and dry Follow procedures listed under Colds. Children in care should be immunized. |
| Fifth Disease (Parvovirus) | Headache, body ache, sore throat, fever, chills, lacy rash | Follow procedures listed under Colds. If pregnant, report to doctor. |
| Sixth Disease (Roseola) | High fever, lacy rash | Follow procedure listed under Colds. |
| Meningitis | Fever, lethargy, poor feeding, fine red rash, stiff neck, headache, irritability | Exclude if suspected. Report to local health department. Notify all in contact with child immediately. Those in contact begin rifampin antibiotic treatment in 24 hours. See doctor immediately if symptoms appear. Follow procedure listed under Colds. |
| Hib (Haemophilus Influenza type B) | Same as meningitis, earache, rapid onset of difficult breathing, red/swollen joints, red/purple area of skin | Follow procedure listed under Meningitis. All should be immunized. See doctor immediately if symptoms appear. |
| Measles | Brownish/red rash beginning on face, fever, white spots in mouth, runny nose, cough | Exclude if suspected. Allow to return 6 days after rash appears. Report to public health. Notify parents. Wash hands often; use gloves. Do not share food, drink. Disinfect mouthed toys. All children in care should be immunized. |
| Rubella (German Measles) | Joint pain, red rash, enlarged lymph glands | Follow procedure listed under Measles. If teacher is pregnant, notify doctor. All children in care should be immunized. |
| Mumps | Fever, at least one swollen salivary gland near jaw, earache, headache | Exclude if suspected. Allow to return after 9 days. All children in care should be immunized. |
| Whooping Cough | Coughing spells with whoop sounds, vomiting, runny nose | Exclude if suspected. Notify local health department. Notify parents. Allow to return 5 days after antibiotic therapy has begun or 3 weeks after onset of cough. Do not share food, drink. Disinfect mouthed toys. Wash hands often; use gloves. All children in care should be immunized. |

**TABLE 13-1 (Continued)**
*Identification and Management of Diseases Transmitted Via the Respiratory Tract*

| Disease | Signs/Symptoms | Teacher's Role |
|---|---|---|
| Otitis Media (Ear Infection) | Fever, difficulty hearing, pain, drainage from ear | Wash hands often; use gloves.<br>Do not share food, drink.<br>Children with frequent ear infections should be monitored for speech or language difficulties. |
| Tuberculosis | Cough, fever, weight loss, or no symptoms present | Exclude anyone with active TB.<br>Allow to return when no longer contagious.<br>Notify the health department.<br>Notify parents.<br>All children in care should be tested before entrance to care, then every two years. |
| RSV (Respiratory Syncytial Virus) | Runny nose, fever, cough (often severe), bronchiolitis, wheezing, rapid breathing<br>Children with asthma may be more prone to this disease<br>Can lead to pneumonia<br>Most contagious one or two days before symptoms appear and as long as two weeks after | Exclude only if child does not feel well.<br>Infection spreads rapidly, so use procedures listed under Colds.<br>Disinfect toys child has played with. |

Infectious diseases are spread through four methods of transmission: respiratory tract, fecal-oral, direct contact, and blood contact. The signs and symptoms that diseases exhibit may directly relate to the method of transmission.

## Infectious Diseases Transmitted Via the Respiratory Tract

Respiratory tract infectious diseases range from a mild cold to bacterial meningitis, which can be life-threatening. Many of these diseases affect all age groups. Other diseases are more common in children, such as Haemophilus Influenza Type B (Hib). Table 13-1 describes the identification of and management methods for respiratory tract transmitted diseases.

Whooping cough is on the rise and should be kept in mind, although it is not common (AAP, 2004).

## Infectious Diseases Transmitted Through the Fecal-Oral Route

Diseases spread by the fecal-oral route are caused by bacteria, parasites, and viruses that grow and spread in the intestines. The stool is the main vehicle of disease spread to others. Early childhood education environments that have infants and toddlers in diapers are especially at risk for these types of diseases. The best course for preventing the spread of disease is to

# REALITY CHECK

## *Otitis Media in the Early Childhood Education Environment*

Ear infection, or otitis media, is the most frequently diagnosed childhood disease for children that visit the doctor when they are sick (Chronic or recurring ear infections, 2003). These are probably the most common bacterial infections found in children. It is estimated that as many as 50 percent of cases are missed because they have no symptoms (Pettigrew et al., 2004; Zeisel et al., 2002). Children in an early childhood education environment are more likely to have these ear infections than children who are cared for at home. Otitis media is continuing to increase among preschool children and is more likely to occur if the child is poor (Auinger et al., 2003). Boys are more often affected with otitis media than are girls (Zamani & Shaw, 2001). Children under three years are the most susceptible to otitis media (CHA, 2004).

More than 85 percent of children have experienced at least one episode of otitis media (Poole, 2001). By the age of three years, 35 percent of children will have had repeated episodes, which can be termed chronic otitis media (ASHA, 2000). One association with repeated episodes of otitis media is the use of a pacifier (Warren et al., 2001; Hanafin & Griffiths, 2002).

Otitis media is an infection in the middle ear, which is directly behind the ear drum. The ear infection commonly begins as a cold. It is suspected that children in early childhood education environments are more likely to get otitis media because of the number of colds found in those environments. Several environmental factors associated with early childhood education settings include close contact with other children who may have respiratory infections, pets present, or a carpet present near the sleeping area (Celedon et al., 1999).

The bacteria and virus germs move up the eustachian tube, which is a passageway between the throat and the middle ear. If the bacteria settle in the middle ear, pus forms and pressure develops. This causes the pain that is experienced. If left unchecked, the infection can spread to the bone behind the ear and cause a condition called mastoiditis. Fluid from otitis media may remain in the ear for months after the infection is gone. This condition can cause hearing loss for the child.

Otitis media is diagnosed by a physician and treated with antibiotics. The medication should work within several days. For children with chronic otitis media, antibiotics may not be as effective. In these cases, children may require surgery for placement of small tubes to allow the fluid to drain. Children who have received the recommended vaccine that prevents pneumonia and meningitis can decrease their incidence of otitis media because of decreased respiratory infections due to the flu or other illnesses.

It is important for the teacher to recognize symptoms of otitis media so that treatment can be begun early. Signs of otitis media include fever, irritability, ear pain, hearing loss, loss of appetite, and ear discharge. Nonverbal children often pull their ears or cry (ASHA, 2000). Lack of attention during story or group time may also be a sign that the child has an ear infection. It has been found that a high-quality early childhood education program with a low teacher–child ratio may cushion the effects of these ear infections (Feagans et al., 1994). It is important for the teacher to alert the parent to these conditions. Children who develop otitis media early in life may be especially vulnerable for impairments in receptive language and verbal cognition (Paradise et al., 2000). The teacher may need to recommend a referral for hearing or speech problems.

## REALITY CHECK (Continued)

The teacher can help reduce otitis media in the early childhood education environment by washing hands, keeping toys clean, not propping bottles for babies, and teaching children to cover their mouths with a disposable tissue when they cough or blow their nose (CDC, 1997). Also, the teacher should never use cotton swabs on children's ears and should watch for any sign of hearing or speech problems (Zamani & Shaw, 2000).

Ear infections are not contagious and children can stay in care if they are comfortable. If allowed, the teacher may administer medication. The teacher may try to reduce the distractions and sound level for a child with an ear infection (Watt et al., 1993).

**CHECK*point:*** List five protective factors that a teacher can provide to help prevent otitis media in early education environments.

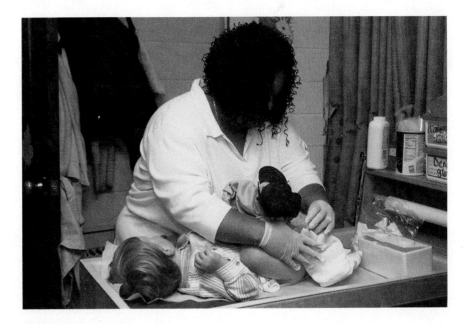

A clean and sanitary diapering area, as well as disposable gloves, is essential in preventing fecal-oral transmission of disease.

always use special precautions. Table 13-2 relates how to identify and manage diseases transmitted through the fecal-oral route. Hepatitis A is a good example of a fecal-oral disease that has appeared linked to child care (MLCF, 2002).

### Infectious Diseases Transmitted by Direct Contact

Diseases transmitted by direct contact are spread from the secretions of one person that penetrate through the skin or mucous membranes of another person. These germs may be in the form of bacterial infections, parasites, or viral infections. Contact may be made directly through the infected or infested skin areas or by touching an infested article of clothing, a brush, or bed linens. The teacher should provide protective measures to prevent the

**TABLE 13-2**

*Identification and Management of Diseases Transmitted Through the Fecal-Oral Route*

| Disease | Signs/Symptoms | Teacher's Role |
|---------|----------------|----------------|
| Giardia | Diarrhea, gas, poor appetite, weight loss, cramping, bloating | Frequent hand washing according to schedule. Use sanitary procedures and gloves during diapering and toileting and before handling food. Exclude if diarrhea is uncontrolled. Allow return once diarrhea is gone. |
| Shigella | Diarrhea, fever, pain, mucus or blood in stool, vomiting, headache, convulsions | Wash hands following schedule. Use sanitary procedures and gloves during diapering and toileting and before food handling. Exclude if fever is present. Call parent immediately if convulsion occurs. |
| Salmonella | Stomach cramps, diarrhea, fever, fatigue, poor appetite | Wash hands following schedule. Use sanitary procedures and gloves during diapering and toileting and before food handling. Notify local health department and all parents. See doctor if diarrhea occurs. |
| Hepatitis A | Fever, jaundice, nausea, poor appetite, dark-brown urine | Wash hands following schedule. Use sanitary procedures and gloves during diapering and toileting and before food handling. Exclude; allow to return one week after onset if fever is gone. Notify local health department and all parents. All exposed persons should have immune globulin treatment. |
| Campylobacter | Fever, vomiting, stomach cramps, diarrhea or severe bloody diarrhea | Wash hands following schedule. Use sanitary procedures and gloves during diapering and toileting and before handling food. Notify local health department and all parents. See doctor if diarrhea occurs. |
| *E. coli* | Diarrhea or bloody diarrhea | Wash hands following schedule. Use sanitary procedures and gloves during diapering and toileting and before handling food. Cook all hamburger meat to 155°F. Notify local health department and all parents. Exclude until diarrhea is gone and stool specimen is negative. |
| Cocksackie virus (Hand, foot, and mouth disease) | Fever, stomach pain, sore throat, rash with tiny blisters on hands, feet, and mouth, diarrhea | Wash hands following schedule. Use sanitary procedures and gloves during diapering and toileting and before handling food. Notify parents. Notify staff. |
| Pinworms | Anal itching, worms that crawl out during sleep or no symptoms present | Follow procedure listed for Cocksackie virus. Each child should have own crib, mat, or cot. Exclude until first dose of medicine has been given; check with family to make sure second dose is taken in two weeks. |

**TABLE 13-2 (Continued)**
*Identification and Management of Diseases Transmitted Through the Fecal-Oral Route*

| Disease | Signs/Symptoms | Teacher's Role |
|---|---|---|
| Rotavirus | Fever, nausea, vomiting, and watery diarrhea<br>Fever and vomiting usually stops after two days<br>Diarrhea may continue for five to seven days | Exclude if diarrhea cannot be contained by diaper or toilet use.<br>Child can return after diarrhea stops.<br>Notify parents.<br>Notify health department only if there is an outbreak.<br>Wash hands following schedule.<br>Follow universal/standard precautions for diapering and toileting.<br>Clean and disinfect surfaces. |

After diapering, both the teacher and the child should wash their hands to prevent the spread of infectious disease. It is good to start the hand washing routine with young toddlers, who are at a higher risk for infectious disease due to mouthing and diapering/toileting activities.

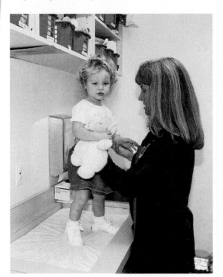

spread of these diseases. Two methods of protection are offered through identification and management, as shown in Table 13-3.

## Bloodborne Infectious Diseases

Infectious diseases are spread through the blood when blood containing the infectious organism in one person enters the bloodstream of another person. This usually occurs if the infected blood comes in contact with broken skin or mucous membranes such as the inside of the nose, mouth, eyes, anal area, or sex organs. The two diseases that are transmitted in this manner

TABLE 13-3
*Identification and Management of Infectious Diseases Transmitted by Direct Contact*

| Disease | Signs/Symptoms | Teacher's Role |
|---|---|---|
| Conjunctivitis (Pinkeye) | Mucus in eye, watery eyes, red/pink eyes, painful eyes, red eyelids, itchy eyes | Keep eye wiped free of discharge. Always wash hands after wiping. Teach children to wipe eyes and wash hands. If child's eyes come in contact with any toys, clean them well. Have child see doctor. Exclude only if white or yellow discharge is present. Allow to return 24 hours after start of antibiotics. Notify parents and staff. |
| Impetigo | Red/cracking/oozing pimples, scaly rash, often on face or a sore that will not heal | If suspected, wash and cover rash with a bandage or gauze. If child scrapes or cuts another area, clean thoroughly. Follow good hand washing procedures. Have child see doctor. Exclude until oozing stops. Follow sanitary cleaning schedule. Notify parents and staff. |
| Ringworm (Tinea) | Flat, growing ring-shaped rash, often scaly, may be in between toes, on scalp, or on body | Keep environment clean, cool, and dry. Wash hands thoroughly. Follow sanitary cleaning schedule. Have child see doctor. If more than one case in care, notify parents and staff. |
| Head Lice (see Reality Check on page 446) | Lice (sesame seed-sized insects) on scalp or hair, nits (eggs) behind ears or nape of neck | Learn to identify nits and regularly check near scalp of children for them (see Figure 13-2). Notify parents with handout concerning procedures. Machine wash all possibly infested items using hot water. All nonwashable items go in dryer for 20 minutes. All other items placed in sealed plastic bags for 30 days. Soak all combs and brushes for one hour in bleach solution. Vacuum rugs, furniture, and mattresses; then throw away vacuum bag. |
| Scabies | Very itchy red bumps or blisters, often between toes or fingers, head, neck, feet | Wash and dry all items contacted by the child 72 hours before outbreak; use hot cycle wash and dry. Vacuum as for ringworm. Have child see doctor. Child may return after treatment. If a serious problem exists, all children and teachers need treatment. Notify parents. |

**TABLE 13-3** (Continued)
*Identification and Management of Infectious Diseases Transmitted by Direct Contact*

| Disease | Signs/Symptoms | Teacher's Role |
|---------|---------------|----------------|
| Cytomegalovirus (CMV) | Often no symptoms, fever, swollen glands, fatigue, jaundice | Always wash hands after contact with urine, saliva, or blood. Do not share food or drinks. Do not share utensils or glasses. Do not kiss children on mouth. Have child see doctor. Can cause problems for pregnant teachers; notify doctor if pregnant. |
| Herpes Simplex (Cold Sores) | Fever, painful, small blisters on lips, mouth, or gums; may ooze | If blisters are oozing and child bites or is drooling, exclude until sores are crusted over. Do not share food, utensils, or glasses. Do not kiss children on mouth. Wash hands often. Follow sanitary cleaning schedule. |

**FIGURE 13-2**
Cycle of head lice treatment (see Reality Check on Head Lice in Chapter 12).

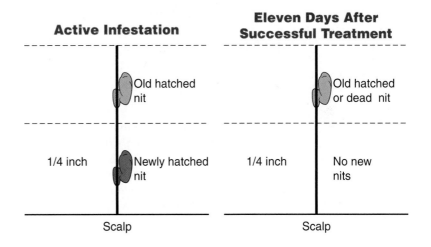

are hepatitis B and HIV/AIDS. These viruses may be present without any symptoms. It is important that all blood and body fluids contacted in the early childhood education environment be treated as if they were contaminated. Prevention of these diseases is critical. All blood spills should be cleaned up immediately and the area disinfected.

All surfaces should be thoroughly disinfected with the bleach solution for contaminated items. If the teacher is aware that another adult or child in the early childhood education environment has hepatitis B or HIV/AIDS, then the stronger solution should be used in all cleaning and disinfecting tasks. Table 13-4 lists bloodborne infectious diseases.

***Disease Note:*** Another childhood disease, Kawasaki disease, should also be recognized. No cause has yet been related to this disease (Burns,

**TABLE 13-4**

*Identification and Management of Bloodborne Infectious Diseases*

| Disease | Signs/Symptoms | Teacher's Role |
|---------|----------------|----------------|
| Hepatitis B | Fever, loss of appetite, nausea, jaundice, pain in joints, skin rash | All present in care should be immunized. All blood and bodily fluids should be cleaned up immediately and treated as if contaminated. All disposable items with blood should be thrown out in plastic bags, then placed in covered trash cans. Everyone washes hands often. Do not share personal items that could be contaminated. Send home contaminated personal clothing with instruction for parents to wash them with bleach and hot water. Discourage aggressive behaviors. Children infected with hepatitis A who demonstrate behaviors such as biting, have no control over bodily secretions, and exhibit other risky behaviors will need to be supervised closely. If this is not possible, the child may have to be excluded from the early childhood education environment. Consult with health department and health consultant. If someone is bitten by an infected person, contact doctor. |
| HIV/AIDS | Failure to grow and develop, enlarged lymph and gland, frequent infections, illness | Follow procedures as in hepatitis B except for immunization. Protect those with HIV or AIDS from infectious disease outbreaks by exclusion; allow to return when outbreak is over. Maintain confidentiality of child with HIV or AIDS. Provide staff with information. |

2001). Signs and symptoms include: a fever that lasts five or more days, redness of the eye, mouth, throat, tongue, and lips, swollen glands, and extreme irritability (Preidt, 2004). This disease is the number one cause of acquired heart disease in children. One in four children who have it develop permanent damage to the coronary arteries (Burns, 2001). It is important to pass this information on to parents whose child may be showing symptoms, so that the child is seen by a physician before the disease progresses.

## Key Concept 13.2

### Identification of Infectious Disease

It is an important task of the teacher to be able to identify infectious diseases. Teachers must have a base of knowledge to recognize signs and symptoms of infectious diseases. They must be able to identify symptoms that are serious for the child and that indicate the presence of a contagious disease.

**A. Impetigo. B. Ringworm. C. Scabies. D. Herpes simplex I (cold sore).** (Courtesy of Robert A. Silverman, MD, Clinical Association Professor, Department of Pediatrics, Georgetown University.)

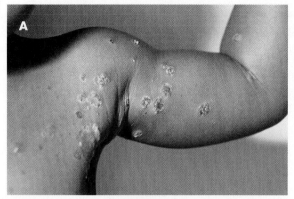
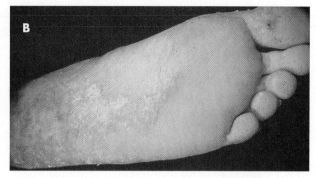
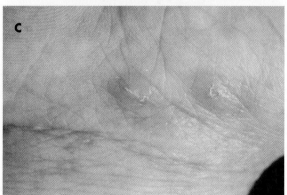
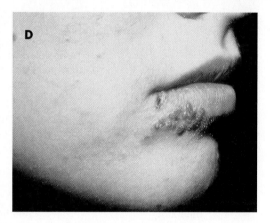

## 13.3 MANAGING INFECTIOUS DISEASES

Teachers who use universal sanitary practices and can recognize and identify signs and symptoms of illness protect the environment and prevent disease from spreading. An additional way to provide management of infectious diseases is to require that everyone involved in the early education program be immunized for those infectious diseases that have vaccines and immunization schedules (see Table 12-3 in Chapter 12). Children's records should be kept current and checked for compliance on a regular basis. The same process should be performed for staff. No one should be hired or should care for children if they do not comply with all of the required immunizations (see Tables 13-1 and 13-4).

Certain symptoms in children, such as fever, may not necessarily indicate an illness. A fever may be a result of too much activity, warm weather, teething, or the body overheating due to other circumstances. If the child does not appear to be ill, a fever may not be a problem. The teacher needs to learn how to take a temperature, how to read it, and how to evaluate whether it is a serious indicator of illness (see Figure 13-3).

The teacher who recognizes serious symptoms knows when to call a parent and when to exclude the child from the early childhood education environment. The ability to identify serious symptoms will help the teacher

**FIGURE 13-3**
Guide to thermometers.

| Mercury | Digital | Tympanic |
|---------|---------|----------|
| 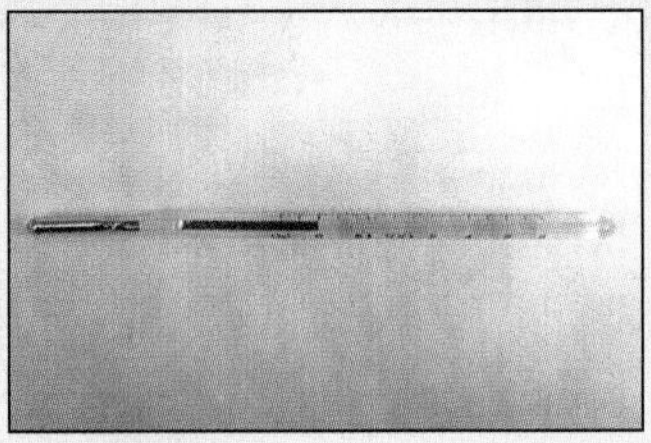 | 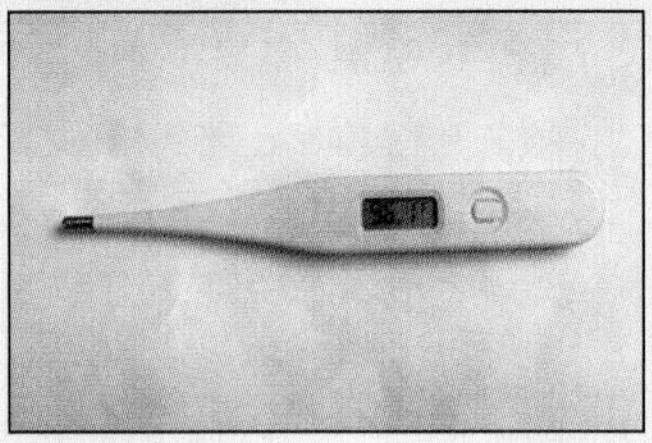 | 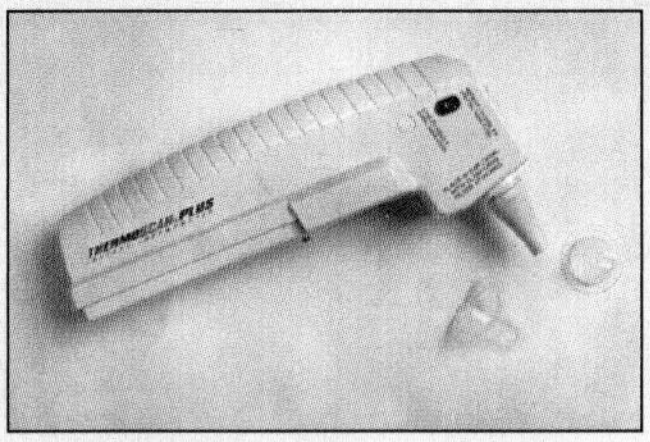 |
| ✓ **Positives**<br>• Lowest cost<br>• Accuracy | ✓ **Positives**<br>• Easy to read<br>• Beeps when ready<br>• Temperature reading is recorded digitally | ✓ **Positives**<br>• Quick reading<br>• Easy to use with fussy children |
| ⚠ **Cautions**<br>• Hard to read<br>• Delicate<br>• Child must be still | ⚠ **Cautions**<br>• Child must be still<br>• Battery powered | ⚠ **Cautions**<br>• Must be placed correctly in ear canal for accurate reading<br>• Battery powered<br>• Highest cost |
| **Methods**<br>A. Shake until mercury line falls below 96° F (30.6°C).<br>B. Clean with soap and water or alcohol. Rinse with cool water.<br><br>**Rectal:** (children under 3 yrs)<br>1. Coat bulb with petroleum jelly.<br>2. Place child stomach down.<br>3. Insert bulb end first 1 1/2 inches into anal canal.<br><br>**Oral:** (children 5 and older)<br>1. Slowly insert thermometer under tongue.<br>2. Child closes lips for 2–3 minutes.<br><br>**Underarm:** (any age, any type—oral or rectal)<br>1. Snugly bury bulb under armpit for 3–4 minutes. | **Methods**<br>A. Clean with soap and water or alcohol. Rinse with cool water.<br>B. Switch on (it beeps at child's highest temperature).<br><br>**Rectal:** Use with nonpetroleum lubricant (K-Y jelly).<br><br>**Oral:** Place far under tongue for one minute.<br><br>**Underarm:** Keep tight under arm. | **Methods**<br>A. Place new plastic covering over end.<br>B. Set for rectal or oral temperature equivalent.<br>C. When small window reads "ready," position the end gently into the ear canal and press the start button.<br><br>After one second, a digital readout of the child's temperature will appear on the small window. |

Sick children who are isolated from the group need a comfortable place to rest and, if possible, the company and reassurance of a teacher until the child's parents or emergency contacts arrive.

know when to notify parents that children in care have been exposed to an infectious disease. Parents can monitor children for further signs and symptoms. Children who need medical attention should go to the doctor immediately. Certain infectious diseases must be reported to the local public health department. This information is available at the health department that has jurisdiction over the area in which the early childhood education environment is located.

When a child shows some signs of illness, the teacher should observe the child and write down the symptoms. Do not draw conclusions. Report measurable facts, such as "Joanna has a temperature of 101°F and looks flushed." If the symptoms are mild and do not affect the child's ability to participate, continue observing the child, and go on with regular activities.

## *Exclusion*

An exclusion policy should be carefully created for the early childhood education environment. This policy should be given to both teachers and parents and should also be posted. It is much easier to enforce a policy that is widely known beforehand. One of the reasons for exclusion would be that the early childhood education environment cannot provide the care and comfort an ill child would need. A child also might not feel well enough to engage in normal activities. And any child who shows symptoms that are on the list of reasons for exclusion should be sent home (AAP & APHA, 2002).

Of special note is the fact that many children have been unnecessarily excluded (Pappas et al., 2000; Skull et al., 2000). This is primarily due to the part of a policy that would exclude children who have fevers but do not show any other symptoms. Fever by itself is rarely a condition for exclusion (AAP & APHA, 2002). The exception to this would be infants from seven weeks to four months of age with a rectal temperature of 101°F or a temperature taken in the armpit of 100°F (Aronson, 2000; Sears, 2003). Any child with a fever of 105°F should have the parents called and see a physician immediately (APHA & AAP, 2002). Use of newer types of thermometers,

Teachers should have the training and proper equipment to take a child's temperature if necessary.

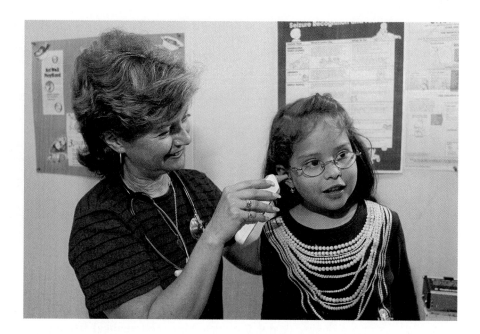

such as a tympanic thermometer that measures temperatures in the ear, can be a more accurate tool for taking a temperature. Figure 13-3 shows these types of thermometers. If a child has a fever with no other signs, the parent should still be notified. The decision as to what to do should be made with the parent (Aronson, 2000).

If a child shows symptoms that are serious or that might be highly contagious, the child should be isolated from the rest of the children in care (Sailors, 2004). The teacher needs to have an area set aside that will allow for isolation. Once serious symptoms are recognized, the parents should be notified immediately (Dailey, 2002). If the parents cannot be reached, there should be backup or emergency contacts in the permanent health file for who to call next. The teacher should ask the parent on a regular basis whether the emergency information is still current. While the child waits for the parent or other emergency contact person, it is important to reassure the child.

In addition to any serious signs or symptoms of illness, conditions such as uncontrolled diarrhea, a yellowish tint to the skin, and discharge of the eyes also indicate the need to immediately isolate the child and call the parent.

Table 13-5 indicates the guidelines for exclusion of ill or infected children. It relates the type of illness or disease, gives the signs and symptoms, and describes the conditions for return to the early childhood education environment. These guidelines are a major tool for the teacher to help manage the spread of infectious disease in the early childhood education environment and are the basis for the health policy for exclusion.

Another important consideration for exclusion is the adults in the early childhood education environment. If a teacher has any of the signs or symptoms in Table 13-5, he or she should also be excluded from participating in care and not return until the conditions for return are met.

When a child is excluded from care, there are several things the teacher needs to do. The parents should be provided with information on the infectious disease that caused the child to be excluded. This is usually

**TABLE 13-5**
*Guidelines for Exclusion of Ill or Infected Children*

| Illness or Infection | Sign or Symptom | Return |
|---|---|---|
| Temperature | Oral temperature of 101°F or more; rectal temperature of 102°F; should be accompanied by behavior changes or other symptoms | Until doctor releases child to return to care |
| Symptoms of severe illness | Unusual lethargy; irritability; uncontrolled coughing; wheezing | Until doctor releases child to return to care |
| Uncontrolled diarrhea | Increase in number of stools, water, and/or decreased form that cannot be contained in a diaper or underwear. | Until diarrhea stops |
| Vomiting illness | Two or more episodes in 24 hours | Until vomiting stops and child is not dehydrated or doctor determines illness not infectious |
| Mouth sores with drooling | — | Until condition is determined to be noninfectious |
| Rash | Rash accompanied by fever or behavior change | Until doctor determines it is noninfectious |
| Conjunctivitis | White or yellow discharge in eye(s) accompanied by eye pain and/or redness around eyes | Until 24 hours after treatment has begun |
| Head lice, scabies, or other infestations | Infestation present | Until 24 hours after treatment has begun; no remaining lice on hair or scalp |
| Tuberculosis | Cough; fever; chest pain; coughing up blood | Until doctor or health official allows child to return to care |
| Impetigo | Rash-blister to honey-colored crusts; lesions occur around mouth, nose, and on chin | Until 24 hours after treatment has begun |
| Strep throat | Fever; sore throat; throat drainage and tender nodes in lymph | After cessation of fever or 24 hours after antibiotic treatment |
| Chicken pox | Sudden onset of slight fever, fatigue, and loss of appetite followed by skin eruption | Until 6 days after eruption of rash or until blister eruption has dried and crusted over |
| Whooping cough | Severe, persistent cough | Until 5 days after antibiotic treatment to prevent infection |
| Mumps | Tender/swollen glands and/or fever | Until 9 days after onset of gland swelling |
| Hepatitis A virus | Fever, fatigue, loss of appetite, abdominal pain, nausea, vomiting and/or jaundice | Until 1 week after onset of illness or as directed by local health department; immune serum globulin should be administered to staff and children who have been exposed |
| Measles | Rash, high fever, runny nose, and red/watery eyes | Until 6 days after onset of rash |

*(continues)*

**TABLE 13-5 (Continued)**
*Guidelines for Exclusion of Ill or Infected Children*

| Illness or Infection | Sign or Symptom | Return |
|---|---|---|
| Rubella | Mild fever, rash, swollen lymph nodes | Until 6 days after onset of rash |
| Unspecified respiratory illness | Severe illness with cold, croup, bronchitis, otitis media, pneumonia | Until child feels well enough to participate |
| Shingles | Lesions | Until doctor allows child to return to care or if child can wear clothing that covers lesions |
| Herpes simplex type 1 | Clear, painful blisters | Until lesions that ooze, involving face and lips, have no secretions |

in the form of a letter or handout. The information includes the exclusion policy for that disease, the period of time the disease lasts, and the conditions for return to the early childhood education environment. The teacher should remove and sanitize any toys the ill child has been playing with or mouthing. Make sure hands are carefully washed and that the hand washing policy is strictly enforced. The illness and teacher actions should be documented and added to the child's health record (Dailey, 2001).

Information on how to care for the disease or condition should also be included. For example, if the child has lice, the information given to the parent would include consulting the physician for the type of shampoo to use, how often to use it, and what else needs to be done to rid the child's home of lice so that the process does not repeat itself.

The teacher should discuss the return to care policy for that particular disease or condition at the same time. Parents like to know the time parameters of a child's illness, if possible, so that necessary work or backup care arrangements can be made.

## Notification of Public Health Officials

A number of infectious diseases must be reported to the local health department so that they can track the disease for patterns of outbreak. This helps to prevent the spread of infectious illnesses in the community. The types of disease typically requiring reporting are those that can spread rapidly and may cause serious illness. Table 13-6 gives a list of infectious diseases that most health departments want reported. It is also a good idea to notify the health department if a large number of cases of an infectious disease not requiring reporting occurs at the early childhood education site.

The teacher should be familiar with the reporting procedures of the local public health department. The teacher who is the health advocate on site should be the person to contact the health department.

**TABLE 13-6**
*Checklist of Commonly Reported Childhood Infectious Diseases*

## ✓ CHECK FOR:

- ☐ Chicken pox
- ☐ *E. coli*
- ☐ Giardia
- ☐ Hepatitis
- ☐ Hib (Haemophilus influenza type B)
- ☐ Measles (rubeola)
- ☐ Meningitis
- ☐ Mumps
- ☐ Polio
- ☐ Rubella (German measles)
- ☐ Salmonella
- ☐ Shigella
- ☐ Tuberculosis
- ☐ Whooping cough (pertussis)
- ☐ AIDS

## Notification of Parents

It is important to notify all families in case of infectious disease occurrences that will cause exclusion or will need a follow-up by the parents. This notification provides them with information such as signs, symptoms, and incubation period (Figure 13-4).

Letting parents know ahead of time about exclusion policies, such as placing them into the parent handbook, is also beneficial. It is much easier to handle the management of ill children if these communication guidelines are in place (Sailors, 2004).

If the infectious disease is serious and is one that has preventive measures, such as hepatitis A, the teacher should notify the parents. This will allow the parents to take the child in care to the family physician, who may administer a course of treatment. It is critically important for the parent of a child exposed to a serious infectious disease to understand the need for taking the child to a physician. The teacher needs to make sure that parents understand the role they play in the prevention of disease and preserving the child's health.

*Pause for Reflection*

How would you handle a situation in which a parent shows up with an obviously ill child and tells you that she has to go to work because she has a presentation to give that her job depends upon?

**FIGURE 13-4**
Sample notice to parents.

**NOTIFICATION**

A case of strep throat was identified in the center today. If your child develops any of the symptoms below, you will be called by a staff member to take him/her home. Please make arrangements to pick up your child immediately for the safety of other children/staff and the comfort of your child.

- Painful, scratchy throat

- Tender, swollen glands

- Fever

- Spots on the throat

Please do not return the child to the center until your doctor advises you in writing that it is safe to do so.

Thank you for your cooperation.

Sincerely,

Maria Anderson

1553 Winding Way Drive
(555)444-8888

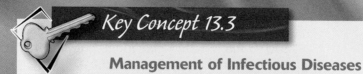

## Key Concept 13.3

### Management of Infectious Diseases

The role that the teacher plays in managing infectious diseases must be clearly perceived. The first line of defense is the use of sanitary procedures for hand washing and the use of gloves. The next step is to make sure immunizations are current for everyone in the early childhood education environment. The teacher must understand the procedures and policies for exclusion from and return to the early childhood education environment. The teacher must recognize when to notify the public health department and when to notify the parents of children in care.

## 13.4 MANAGING CARE FOR MILDLY ILL CHILDREN

The teacher has a number of tools that will help make the decision as to whether to care for a mildly ill child. The most effective tool for managing care for mildly ill children is a series of three questions that the teacher should ask (APHA & AAP, 2002) (Figure 13-5).

### Three Questions

The first question a teacher should ask is: *"Is the child's infectious disease highly infectious or communicable at this time?"*

There are certain childhood infectious diseases that do not pose a health threat. Some of these may be viral diseases that are no longer contagious once the symptoms appear or the infectious disease might be one that is not highly contagious. For example, colds are very common in young children (Zamani, 2005). Most children average six to ten colds in the period of a year. Ear infections are not easily spread and therefore should not cause a child to be excluded from care. The teacher needs to be familiar with those diseases that are not easily spread and that will allow the child to participate in care.

**FIGURE 13-5**
**Medication safeguards.**
(Adapted from the California Childcare Health Program, Judith Calder, Author.)

**Three Questions**

1. Is it a highly infectious or communicable disease?
2. Does the child feel well enough to participate?
3. Can the teacher provide the mildly ill child adequate care?

The teacher must decide whether to keep the mildly ill child in care, based on the risks to the child, the staff, and the other children in care and the ability of the teacher to provide care to the ill child.

The decision-making process proceeds to the next step once it has been established that the infectious disease is not highly communicable or does not pose risk to others in care. The question, *"Does the child feel well enough to participate in the early childhood education environment?"* addresses the issue of whether the child feels well enough to be in care.

Families are busy, and parents may have deadlines or have difficulty missing work. It may be tempting to take a child who is ill but not contagious to school. The daily quick health check is an effective tool for the teacher to help prevent this from happening. Parents need to understand their responsibility to keep a child who does not feel well at home.

The final question in the decision-making process is, *"Can the teacher provide the mildly ill child adequate care?"* This question addresses several issues:

- Is there a place for the child to rest or play quietly?
- Is there a teacher who can be responsible for caring for the mildly ill child?
- If not, are the parents willing to pay extra for care so that the teacher can hire a helper?

There may be a number of additional tasks that have to be performed, and the teacher should agree to provide care for the mildly ill child only if the quality of care is consistent with that usually provided in the early childhood education environment.

If the answers to any of the three questions indicate that the teacher would have difficulty caring for the child, the parent must take responsibility for caring for the ill child. There may be an alternative care site that specializes in caring for mildly ill children. Contact the local resource and referral agencies for information.

A child centered approach focuses on the child's individual needs.

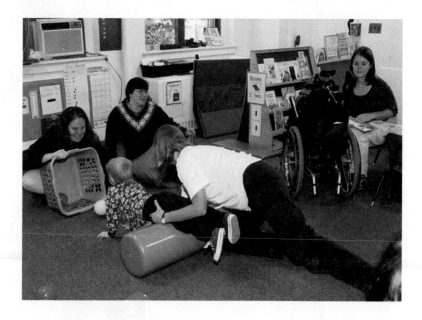

## Special Considerations for Care of Mildly Ill Children

If the decision to care for the mildly ill child is made, the teacher should be prepared to provide the degree of care needed. Table 13-7 provides a checklist of strategies that will help the teacher meet the needs of the mildly ill child.

If the illness requires the administration of medications, there are special procedures that should be followed. In some states, administering medication is prohibited. Teachers should check with the local licensing agency. Figure 13-6 has the basic reminders about medication administration, and Table 13-8 gives specific instructions that should be followed (Palmer, 2005). The most common errors with medications in the early childhood education environment are missing the dose and medication's not being brought back to the care site so that it can be administered after the first day (Sinkovits et al., 2003). The most common medications given in early childhood education environments are

- Antibiotics
- Acetaminophen, such as Children's Tylenol (fever reducer)
- Cold medications
- Analgesics/antihistamines (for allergies)
- Bronchodilators, including inhalers and nebulizers
- Decongestants
- Medications for chronic conditions

Antibiotics top this list. Parents often ask physicians for these medications even if the child has a virus that is not helped by the use of antibiotics (NCCCHSRC, 2005). Antibiotic resistance appears to be occurring among children who are given too many antibiotics (Calder, 2004). It is more common for parents to pressure physicians for antibiotics than it is for teachers

**TABLE 13-7**
*Care Checklist for the Mildly Ill Child*

### ✓ CHECK FOR:

☐ Observe the child for signs and symptoms of the illness. Share this information with the parents at a midday phone call and when the child is picked up.

☐ Record the signs and symptoms.

☐ Frequently check with the child to provide the extra attention and care she may need while ill.

☐ Provide quiet activities that will hold the interest of the child, such as tapes, videos, books, stories, and artwork.

☐ Set aside a quiet corner or separate space for the child to be quiet, rest, or nap.

☐ Administer prescribed medication as directed, if allowed.

☐ Supply foods and beverages that provide good nutrition and follow guidelines as indicated by illness or recommended by a physician.

**FIGURE 13–5a**

### Remember the Five C's

**Correct Medication** given to the **Correct Child** using **Correct Amount**
at the **Correct Time** given by the **Correct Method**

Adapted from the California Childcare Health Program, Judith Calder, Author

**FIGURE 13-6**
Children can very easily mistake medication for candy. Medications should be stored in a locked cabinet at all times. (Courtesy of Payless Drug Store.)

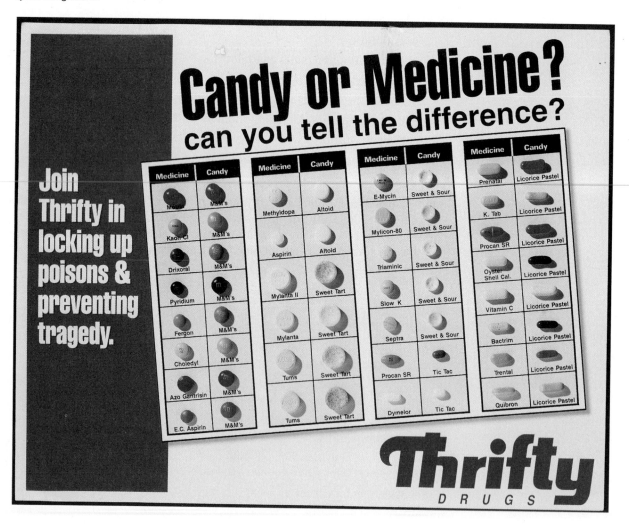

**TABLE 13-8**
*Procedures for Administering Medication in Early Childhood Education Environments*

- It is a good idea to have one teacher per group of children to be the consistent administrator of medicine. This person should be the most knowledgeable about how to do this and should be known to the child.

- Any medication, whether over-the-counter or prescribed, must have the child's name on it with the date and be clearly labeled.

- All medications should be in original containers and not transferred to other containers.

- Medications should be administered according to the label direction.

- Parents must include a written note for permission and the instructions and dose for each medication.

- The medication label and parent's instructions should not conflict. The instructions should be photocopied and one set placed in the child's folder. The other set of instructions should be kept with the medication.

- Use accurate medical measuring devices, such as dosage cups or vials, when administering medicine. Do not use common kitchen utensils such as a teaspoon. This can affect proper dosage.

- Parents' instructions should be provided every time a child is ill or a new prescription is provided for a chronically ill child.

- Always wash hands before and after administering medication.

- Explain to the child what medication you are giving and why. NEVER refer to medicine as candy (see Figure 13-7).

- Teachers should administer medication exactly as prescribed. This includes method, dose, time, and frequency prescribed. If the prescription says to give it until medication is gone, as with antibiotics, then this should be done regardless of how the child feels. There is a reason for dosage dates.

- Teachers should always keep an accurate written record of medication given, including time and dosage, in a medication log. This way other teachers in the environment can check and not repeat a dose unnecessarily. Copies of the medication log for the child should be provided to the parent whenever medication is given, even if on a daily basis.

- Medications should be kept at proper temperatures, as directed on the label. If the medication needs refrigeration, it should be kept in a plastic zip bag to keep it away from food items.

- Always watch for reactions. Have a list of possible side effects for each medication given.

- Store all medications out of the reach of children, preferably in a locked cabinet, on a high shelf, or in the back of the top shelf of the refrigerator.

# REALITY CHECK

## Special Care for Mildly Ill Children

Many companies experience high absenteeism rates from their employees because their children are ill. A child's illness causes missed deadlines, parents who feel guilty, and coworkers who must do extra work because of the absent worker (Sears, 2003). This situation can cause many problems for the parents and discomfort for the child. Children are most comfortable in a familiar setting with familiar people when they are ill. This familiarity offers emotional support for the ill child. It is not always possible to provide this familiar comfort, so parents may have to settle for physical care alone.

Care for mildly ill children may take place in several ways.

- care in the child's own center, family child care setting, or in-home care
- family child care homes or centers that specialize in caring for mildly ill children
- corporate on-site care for ill children of employees
- in the child's home by specialized teachers
- At a hospital site that contracts with corporations and/or the general public

Many centers and family child care homes provide this care within their regular programs. Most states permit early childhood education centers to offer get-well care for mildly ill children. Some centers provide a designated teacher to care for these mildly ill children. Some teachers specialize in the care of mildly ill children.

To address this situation, many corporations are cooperating by providing care for mildly ill children. One example of this is TLC for Mildly Ill Children, which is located in the Virginia Mason Hospital in Seattle, Washington.

It contracts out with local corporations and business and also provides services to the public (Virginia Mason Team Medicine, 2004). University of Illinois employees can use home-based care provided especially for their mildly ill children (Unger, 2004). Another example is the Chicken Soup Room at the ABC Child Care in Temecula, California, for children who are already in care at the site. Johnson and Johnson provides on-site care for mildly ill children at their headquarters in New Brunswick, New Jersey. This is offered at their early childhood education center in an infirmary.

There are centers specifically designed for the care of mildly ill children. These centers must meet licensing standards that are more stringent than those for regular care sites. They must also be very careful to prevent the spread of infectious diseases. The AAHP and APA suggest that these special centers have the following for each child:

- information concerning the diagnosis and the attending physician's name
- prognosis for illness, including activity level, diet, and so forth
- health care plan
- open communication line with parents

Caring for mildly ill children can be challenging (Polyzoi & Babb, 2004). Mildly ill children can still be relatively active. Care should include provision of toys, games, and other activities that provide these children stimulation as needed.

The licensing regulations should be determined for the local area and state where the care will take place, if the teacher intends to provide this type of care for mildly ill children.

**CHECK**point: Does your local area have a "chicken soup" child care facility for mildly ill children? If not, what special regulations do you think your local area would have to meet to establish a care center for mildly ill children? Would these regulations be so prohibitive that it would be impossible to have this type of facility?

to ask parents to get them, because parents often believe that antibiotics will speed up their child's return to care (Friedman et al., 2002).

There should always be a policy on administering medication, and it should be shared with the parents if it is appropriate in the state where care is taking place. If the parent asks for herbal remedies or other natural medicines to be given to the child, it is a good idea to ask the parents to give these to the children at home because they are not regulated.

## *Key Concept 13.4*

### Special Considerations for Care of Mildly Ill Children

Taking care of mildly ill children is not something all teachers or early childhood education situations are prepared to do. Determining the ability to handle this type of care will be based on three questions:

1. Is the infectious disease contagious or will it put others at risk?
2. Is the child able to participate in care?
3. Can the teacher accommodate the needs of the mildly ill child?

When the determination is made, the teacher will need to understand the issues of the special care he or she will be providing for the child. One of the special considerations is the administration of medication. The teacher should follow exact procedure for this.

## 13.5 CHILDREN WITH CHRONIC ILLNESSES

- **Chronic illnesses**
  *medical conditions requiring continuous treatment*

**Chronic illnesses** or conditions affect between 15 and 18 percent of the population younger than eighteen years of age (Laundy & Boujaoude, 2004). A chronic illness requires continuing treatment. The range of the condition can be from mild to severe. Teachers are most likely to be confronted with children who have a mild or moderate form of a chronic illness.

Each chronic illness has its own unique causes, indicators, and medical responses. Most chronic illnesses have organizations that can provide the teacher with a wealth of resources. The following chronic illnesses are covered in this text: allergies, asthma, diabetes mellitus, HIV, seizure disorders, and sickle cell anemia. These are the most common chronic illnesses found in early childhood education environments. Whatever chronic condition presents itself, the teacher should gather as much information and resources on the condition as possible (Alexander, 2003). Know what constitutes an emergency for that condition, and be prepared to act in an emergency. Practice for that emergency can reduce stress and help actions if the emergency occurs.

The following information should help a teacher provide care for a child who has one of these chronic illnesses. Each chronic illness description provides the definition, significance, and how the disease occurs. This gives the teacher a background in order to understand the rest of the information. The remaining details inform the teacher about triggers, identifiers, and strategies for care of a child with the particular chronic illness. It is important to note that some states do not allow teachers to administer

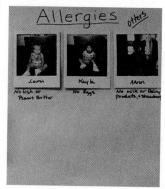

Teachers need to be aware of allergies or potential allergies for all children in their care.

● **Triggers**
*substances or conditions that activate a response*

medication. If this is the case, a health professional should be close by if help is needed, or the family of the child with a chronic illness should make provisions for emergencies.

## Allergies

***Definition.*** An allergy is a heightened response to a substance.

***Significance.*** Some children have known allergies; many others may have undiagnosed allergies. Symptoms depend on the organs that are affected (Williams, 2002).

***How Does It Occur?*** The person who is allergic to a substance is exposed to it by ingestion, touch, or breathing.

***When Does It Occur?*** It occurs when the person is exposed to a substance that causes the response. Common allergy **triggers** are

- foods such as peanut butter, nuts, wheat, chocolate, milk, fish, and citrus
- pollen from flowers, grasses, hay, weeds, or trees
- mold spores
- dust
- animal fur, feathers, or dander; this may be on a live animal, feathers in a comforter, or an animal skin on a wall
- insects, including stings or parts from dead insects such as cockroaches

***Identifiers of Reaction.*** Allergic reaction may take the form of sneezing, hay fever, asthma, swelling/hives, eczema, or cold-like symptoms when the respiratory system is affected. Digestive tract symptoms may include nausea, vomiting, and diarrhea.

***Support.*** Be alert to the signs of allergic reactions of children in care. Discuss any allergies with parents, and avoid those triggers that are observed to cause a response. It is very important to work hard to keep the early childhood education environment or family child care home clean and free of dust mites and other allergens. Forty percent of early childhood education environments have been found to have levels of allergens high enough to cause a reaction in an allergic child (Do child care centers contribute, 2002). For more serious allergic reactions, the child may need medication administered. If an epinephrine instrument such as an EpiPen is needed, there should be written permission from the parent for a teacher to administer it. It would be most helpful for the teacher to be able to work with a health consultant and the child's physician to be better prepared to do this.

## Asthma

***Definition.*** Asthma occurs when there is a narrowing of the small airways in the lungs called bronchi and bronchioles. Muscles around the airways tighten and, when mucus clogs these airways, breathing difficulty results.

*Significance.* Asthma effects about 6.3 million children younger than eighteen years of age (Getch & Neuharth-Pritchett, 2004). Rates of asthma are continuing to rise rapidly (NCEH, 2005).

*How Does It Occur?* Most asthmatics have persistent bronchial irritation. Environmental irritants trigger reactions that lead to an attack or episode.

*When Does It Occur?* The asthma episode or attack may occur if the child is exposed to one or more of the following triggers:

- the same items found on the allergy list
- household products—vapors, deodorants, sprays, cleaning solvents, paints
- dust from clothes, broom, furniture, or filters on furnaces and air conditioners
- weather—humidity, cold, wind
- exercise—overexertion
- infections such as colds, bronchitis, or other viruses
- smoke—cigarette, pipe, or cigar
- strong emotions—fear, laughing, crying, anger
- aspirin
- at the end of the day when tired and lying down and mucus accumulates

*Identifiers of Reaction.* Tightening of airways and muscles causes difficulty breathing. In addition to shortness of breath, an increase in breathing rate can occur, and the child may be either irritable or listless. The child may also have a more rapid speech pattern, dark circles under the eyes, and a fever (Getch & Neuharth-Pritchett, 2004). Wheezing, coughing, and spitting up of mucus may also occur.

*Support.* Be aware of asthmatic reactions, especially after exercise, emotional display, or exposure to allergens. The teacher should keep the child free from infection by providing a healthy, safe environment. It might be helpful for the teacher to use "A Checklist for Parents and Providers" available at www.asthmaandallergies.org. This comprehensive list would be extremely helpful in providing the healthiest environment for a child with asthma or even allergies. In addition you may want to use the Child Care Asthma Action Card, which can be downloaded, from http://www.schoolasthmaallergy.com as a further tool. The Action Card should be filled out by the health professional and the parents as part of the asthma control team that must be put in place. If an inhaler or nebulizer is to be used for the child, the directions found in Table 13-9 should be followed. A teacher may not be totally comfortable handling an asthma emergency (Getch & Neuharth-Pritchett, 2004). If there is ever any question about a child's ability to breathe comfortably, emergency services should be called. If an episode does occur, the teacher should make sure the child is sitting up and is calm, and encourage the child to focus on slow, deep breathing. Follow procedures if medication should be given.

**TABLE 13-9**
*Administering Inhaled Medications in Early Childhood Education Environments*

Contact your local licensing agency to determine if you are allowed to administer inhaled medication for the children that need it. If you are allowed, then the following should be done for each person who may administer the medication to the child:

- Obtain written permission from parent or guardian to administer the medication via the inhaler or nebulizer.
- Obtain written permission from parent or guardian to contact the child's physician. If the child has a medical home, this relationship will already be established.
- Contact the child's physician and get written instructions on what the specific child needs with the administration of the medication.
- Obtain training from the parent or guardian or health consultant on how to administer the inhaled medication.
- Keep a written record in the medical log each time this type of medication is administered. Prepare a copy for the parents whenever the child had the medication administered, even if on a daily basis.

Adapted from "Administration of Inhaled Medications in Child Care," available through the Child Care Law Center, San Francisco, CA.

## Diabetes Mellitus

**Definition.** Diabetes mellitus occurs when insulin is not produced in the pancreas at the rate the body needs it. Insulin is involved in the process that stores and uses glucose for energy. There are two types of diabetes: type I, which is insulin dependent, and type II, which is noninsulin dependent.

**Significance.** Type I diabetes is often referred to as juvenile-onset diabetes; it is the most common type among children. Approximately 125,000 American children have type I diabetes (American Diabetes Association [ADA], 2003). This type of diabetes requires insulin injections at least twice daily. Food and exercise levels must be controlled, and blood sugar needs to be tested several times throughout the day.

**How Does It Occur?** Because adequate insulin is not present, the body cannot absorb excess glucose. Glucose levels build in the blood and spill into the urine. Sugar not used for energy is stored in fats; when broken down, the resulting chemicals, ketones, can poison the blood if they are allowed to accumulate.

**When Does It Occur?** Diabetes reaction is triggered when there is

- too much exercise
- not enough food
- too much sugar
- too much insulin

*Identifiers of Reaction.* Lack of insulin can cause numerous reactions. Among them are

- disorientation, confusion, blurred vision
- excessive sweating
- dizziness, poor coordination
- irritability, behavior change
- excessive thirst or sudden hunger
- coma

*Support.* The teacher will need to be educated and trained in what to watch for and provide and how to handle emergencies when caring for the diabetic child (Sutton, 2002). Glucose levels are affected by diet and exercise, so those activities should be carefully monitored. Children aged four years and younger are not usually capable of being involved in their own care and treatment. The ADA (2003) suggests that a child in care have a Diabetes Health Care Plan. This plan should be individualized for the child and should be prepared by the parents working with the teacher as a team effort. This process is simplified if there is a health consultant available or if the child had a medical home. These entities can also be involved in the plan.

The family should provide the materials, equipment, and training necessary for diabetes care tasks. The family should also discuss the diet and meal schedule of the child with the teacher. In addition to their own telephone numbers, the family should provide emergency numbers for the child's diabetes care team so that they can be contacted if necessary.

There should be at least one teacher and one backup adult on site who is trained to perform the fingerstick blood glucose monitoring and record the results. They should also be able to test urine or blood for ketones. These teachers should know how to react to the results, if necessary. The early childhood education environment should provide an area where there will be privacy for the child to be tested and to have insulin administered, if necessary. The child's diet should be carefully tracked and recorded.

A diabetic child may also have episodes of hypoglycemia, and the same basic tenets of the teacher's being trained on how to handle an episode and the parents' providing the proper supplies would hold true for this as well.

## HIV/AIDS

*Definition.* Human immunodeficiency virus (HIV) infection is a viral infection that threatens the immune system's ability to fight off infection. It can lead to acquired immunodeficiency syndrome (AIDS), which is a combination of illnesses that may become life threatening.

*Significance.* Ninety-one percent of children with HIV/AIDS had it passed from mother to child. HIV/AIDS in children in the United States has declined from 1800 new cases yearly in 1996 to only 150 new cases yearly in 2000 (CDC, 2002). Even with this decline, the seriousness of this bloodborne disease should not be minimized. The teacher should be aware of the implications and protect all children in the early childhood education environment from this risk.

*How Does It Occur?* The methods of transmission that affect children are in utero transmission via blood from a mother who has the disease; breast milk from HIV-positive mother; sexual abuse by a person with AIDS; and exposure to blood or blood products from an infected person through a cut or sore.

*When Does It Occur?* Exposure to infection or normal childhood diseases can trigger an immunosuppressed response. Chicken pox is especially dangerous.

*Identifiers of Reaction.* Some symptoms found in children with HIV/AIDS are

- multiple bacterial infections
- enlarged spleen and liver
- abnormal growth patterns
- frequent illnesses

*Support.* There are two areas of support that a teacher needs to give. The first area is protecting the child with HIV/AIDS from exposure to childhood diseases, especially chicken pox. The second is to protect all other children and teachers from HIV/AIDS. Universal precautions should be followed. These include hand washing and sanitary procedures and wearing gloves when in contact with blood or other bodily fluids. Everyone with sores, scratches, or lesions should keep them covered. The teacher should also attempt to prevent and handle immediately any biting by any child in the early childhood education environment.

## Seizure Disorders

*Definition.* Seizure disorders is another term for epilepsy and febrile seizures. Twenty types of seizure disorders may occur when there is temporary overactivity in the electrical impulses in the brain.

*Significance.* One in every 100 persons has some form of seizure disorder on the continuum from rare to frequent displays.

*How Does It Occur?* Seizure disorder can result from head injuries, infections, high fevers, or lead poisoning, or it may be hereditary.

*When Does It Happen?* Possible triggers include

- fast-rising fevers
- fatigue
- disorientation from outside source, such as flashing lights or rapid movement

*Identifiers of Reaction.* Because there are twenty different types of seizure disorders the reaction range is wide. The following list demonstrates the range:

- dazed behavior
- unusual sleepiness and irritability
- unexplained clumsiness, falls
- feeling strange, disoriented
- rapid eye movements, eyes rolling up
- head appears to move involuntarily
- involuntary, unnatural movements of body
- unconsciousness, drooling at the mouth

*Support.* The first thing a teacher should do is to become familiar with the type of disorder the child has and how to handle the reaction of that disorder. When the reaction occurs, remain calm. If a child is having a seizure that includes unconsciousness, place the child on the floor and turn him on his side. Place something soft under the child's head. Patiently wait until the seizure has finished, and then help the child in the transition to normal activity. If the seizure lasts longer than 10 minutes, call the parents or physician.

## Sickle Cell Anemia

*Definition.* Sickle cell anemia is a hereditary disease that affects the red blood cells. It is most often found in African-American children and young adults.

*Significance.* Sickle cell anemia occurs in 1 of 400 African-Americans.

*How Does It Occur?* An abnormality in the red blood cells causes them to change shape and decrease the amount of oxygen that they deliver to all parts of the body. When this causes blockage to tissues of an organ or joint, this leads to pain and may be damaging to the tissues in that location.

*When Does It Happen?* Sickle cell anemia can be triggered by

- fatigue
- overexertion from exercise
- stress

*Identifiers of Reaction.* There may be no apparent triggers. When a reaction happens, there may be intense pain in arms, legs, back, or chest.

*Support.* A teacher should be aware of the disease and watch the child for shortness of breath and fatigue. If a crisis occurs, the teacher should remain calm, call the parents, and support the child until she is picked up. A preventive measure would be to protect the child from infection by offering a sanitary environment.

### Working as a Team

Many of the issues that occur when caring for a child with a chronic illness are similar to those of a child with special needs. Some children with a chronic illness qualify as children with special needs under the Americans with Disabilities Act. Regardless of whether the child qualifies, using the strategies developed for children with special needs will help the teacher meet most of the needs of the chronically ill child.

The team for a chronically ill child may consist of the parent, the physician, and the teacher. This supports the idea of a "medical home" for the child. The teacher needs to ask questions and access any other resources available (such as a health consultant), to help support the care for the child. The teacher should have a plan for care for each child with a chronic illness if a reactive or crisis episode should occur. It is vital that the teacher learn to recognize and identify reactions that may lead to crisis and be prepared to handle an emergency that may result from the crisis. This includes understanding what constitutes an emergency that requires outside help. The teacher who possesses the knowledge of how to handle a crisis can remain calm and do what needs to be done.

## Key Concept 13.5

### Chronically Ill Children

Many teachers will find themselves caring for one or more children with a chronic illness. A teacher needs general knowledge of the chronic illness—especially the reactions leading to a crisis episode. She should also have understanding of what to do should this occur. Many of the strategies used for children with special needs can be applied to the child with a chronic illness.

## 13.6 OPTIMIZING HEALTH IN EARLY CHILDHOOD EDUCATION ENVIRONMENTS

As has been mentioned frequently through this chapter and the other chapters in this section, the use of a health consultant and the encouragement for every child to have a medical home can optimize the health environment in early childhood education programs. The health consultant can provide training, information, and resources the teacher may otherwise not have available. The medical home can provide a natural team effort for each child.

### Child Care Health Consultants

It is difficult to assume that each teacher will know how to handle every health issue that may come up (Cianciolo et al., 2004). A teacher can easily provide comfort, but she may not always know how to handle chronic illness or emergencies that deal with health. The idea of a child care health consultant originated in the late 1990s in the Maternal and Child Care Bureau, and support of this issue has been continued by the American Academy of Pediatrics (HCCP, 2001). Child care health consultants can provide assistance in a number of areas (Aronson, 2002; Alkon et al., 2002). See Table 13-10 for some of the ways that a health consultant might provide help.

A health consultant for the early childhood education environment may be a public health nurse, nurse, nurse practitioner, or other health professional. The health consultant should have specialized training for the early childhood education setting. A National Training Institute for Child Care Health Consultants has been federally funded at the University of North Carolina (Cianciolo et al., 2004). The use of health care consultants is Action Step Nine of the Healthy Child Care America arm of the AAP. Both entities see the health consultant as a positive step to provide the maximum environment for good health and safety in early education.

The health consultant may be provided through a local resource and referral agency, a health clinic, health agency, or children's hospital. If none of those provide health consultation for the local area, the teacher might try contacting the AAP representative in the state in which care is performed. The map for this information can be obtained through Healthy Child America and is available online at http://www.healthychildcare.org

## A Medical Home for Every Child

As described in Chapter 11, a medical home is a partnership of the family, the teacher, and a medical practitioner that ensures that all health, psychosocial, and educational needs of a child are met. This care should be provided in a culturally effective way to remove any barriers that might be present (Cooley & McAllister, 2004). As a child enters care, she needs

**TABLE 13-10**
*Duties of Health Care Consultants*

- Train teachers on health and safety issues
- Perform on-site assessments of health and safety in the early childhood education environment
- Provide technical advice on improvements for health and safety
- Work with teachers to provide families with information on health and safety issues and concerns
- Help create policies for health, safety, nutrition, and food safety
- Provide telephone consultation to teachers as issues arise
- Help link teachers, families, and medical home for greatest communication on issues of health
- Help link teachers, families, and children to community resources
- Provide referrals for families and children who need services
- Review staff and children's health records
- Support the idea of a medical home
- Provide assistance, training, and information for managing care of children with chronic illnesses and/or special needs

to have her immunizations up-to-date. This is the first contact that the teacher has with the child and the family about health. It would be a good time to ascertain whether the family has a regular health care provider. If the family does not have one, then the teacher can encourage the family to find one (AAP, 2002).

A number of families do not have a single source of medical care, and some lack access to medical care altogether. This lack of consistent medical care can result in delays in diagnosis and treatment, missed immunizations, and trips to the emergency room that may not have been necessary (Reeves, 2002). In turn, this situation has an affect of the health of the children in these families. When these children are in early childhood education programs, it can also affect the health of everyone in that environment.

Lack of insurance may be one barrier to a consistent source of medical care. Families with insurance are more likely to have a medical home (Starfield & Shi, 2004). Today, many states offer free health insurance through Medicaid or low-cost health care plans to families that qualify. Other barriers include location, cultural practice patterns, and other social forces. The teacher can assist families in finding a medical home by providing information about access to no-cost or low-cost medical insurance and to the possible sources of medical care. Medical homes may be private physicians, hospital outpatient clinics, public health services, community health centers, public health departments, health maintenance organizations, and even school-based clinics or clinics linked to schools.

If the barrier of access is removed, families are more likely to have regular medical care. When the health provider is more culturally competent, all families are more likely to use services. A child with a medical home is more likely to be provided care on a consistent basis, including intervention if needed. Children with chronic illnesses and special needs, in particular, need a medical home (Cooley & McAllister, 2004). The teacher who is caring for a child with a chronic illness or special needs will feel greater support if a medical home is present. A team consisting of the family, the teacher, and the health care provider can promote better health for all children in care and optimize the environment for health, safety, and well-being.

## Key Concept 13.6

### Optimizing Health

The use of a health consultant and encouraging each child to have a medical home will optimize the environment for health and safety. A health consultant can provide training, assist in creating policies, and provide assistance in many other ways. A child with a medical home can have consistent medical care and can have intervention done as soon as it is needed. Having a team of the family, the health care provider, and the teacher can promote better health for children in care.

## 13.7 IMPLICATIONS FOR TEACHERS

Teachers need the tools of observation and supervision in order to provide and maintain a healthy environment. Education and cultural competence also help them to manage the spread of disease as well as to manage care of the mildly ill child. This endeavor can be aided by the use of a health consultant and the provision of a medical home for each child.

### *Observation*

Observation provides the teacher the ability to recognize any symptoms of infectious disease early. The daily quick health check allows the teacher to monitor the health of a child on a regular basis. Recording any signs, symptoms, or irregular behaviors can give the teacher indicators of illness. When a child is observed, the question "Is the child able to participate?" can be answered more readily. A teacher who knows a child well will recognize whether the child is acting in a normal enough manner to be in the early childhood education setting.

### *Supervision*

Supervision is a powerful tool that helps the teacher to manage health care in the early childhood education environment. Supervising the setting for proper immunizations and sanitary hand washing and cleaning procedures can reduce the amount of infectious diseases seen. Supervising for exclusion and return policies help keep contagious diseases away from the early childhood education environment.

Notifying the public health department allows the teacher to help manage the spread of infectious diseases both in and out of the early childhood education environment. When the health department is able to track infectious diseases, another child care setting may benefit from the notification. This may prevent further outbreaks.

Teachers need to notify all parents when a child in care has an infectious disease that is highly contagious and/or can cause serious problems. The parents can observe for the signs and symptoms and can prepare for follow-up care after exposure to the infectious disease.

### *Education*

Education provides a wonderful tool for the promotion of healthy habits and the prevention of disease. All participants in the early childhood education environment should be educated to avoid exposure to and reduce the spread of infectious diseases.

Education offers teachers the base of knowledge and training needed to carry out their daily task of creating a healthy environment. Teachers who have the ability to identify the signs and symptoms of infectious diseases protect the environment against any further spread of these diseases.

Education for children in early childhood education environments incorporates several things. The first educational tool the teacher will use is to share the importance of hand washing along with the "how-tos" and "when tos." Teaching children to recognize when they feel ill may help the teacher identify an infectious disease before outward symptoms appear.

This may provide another level of protection for all of the children in care. Teaching children at their own level about an infectious disease that is present in the early childhood education environment may reinforce the information sent home concerning that disease.

## For Families

Working with families in the early childhood education environment is essential to maintain health and well-being of children at all times. Education for parents allows them to work with the teacher as a team. It also allows the family to offer a more protective environment in the home. Teaching parents about hand washing and the importance of immunizations will help them understand their own responsibility to protect their children and to prevent disease. Parents who understand proper procedures for the care of a child with an infectious disease may be able to reduce the seriousness of the disease.

It is suggested that every child should have a medical home. This is a primary health care provider who takes care of both well care and screening measures as well as treating illnesses (Sokol-Gutierrez, 2000; Lombardi, 1999). A medical home allows for regular visits and should help prevent serious health problems. Today, most children are eligible for some type of health care insurance. A Web site to check is http://www.insurekidsnow.gov. A teacher should cooperate with parents by providing information about medical homes and available resources so that each child can have a medical home.

## Cultural Competence

The teacher needs to understand that early access to health care for ill children is perhaps the major issue for cultural competence. This may be especially true for recent immigrants. Certain cultures may have had little access to health care. Parents of these children may not understand the importance of early health care for children. For example, there appears to be a pattern of delayed care for Latin American children (Zambrana et al., 1994). Emergency medical services appear to be the primary care for many of these children (Carballo & Nerukar, 2001).

Parents may not have children immunized because of fears, cultural beliefs, or lack of understanding of the importance of immunizations. Although teachers need to respect the beliefs of different cultures, the "No immunization, no care" rule must be enforced to protect all children in care.

When a child becomes ill, the teacher may have to help the parent access health care. Many cultures use the emergency room as their first contact of care. This is dangerous for the child and it is not protective for the early childhood education environment. It may take extra effort on the part of the teacher to help parents from other cultures provide the health care needed for these children (Sokol-Gutierrez, 2000). This is one of the reasons that a medical home for a child can be a boon to early childhood education environments. The medical home should be culturally effective (Cooley & McAllister, 2004).

Immunization may be another culturally sensitive issue. Many families do not understand the need for immunization. If the child is from a country where immunizations are not readily available, the thought of having a child stuck with needles may be fearful (Gonzalez-Mena, 2004). The need for immunization should be dealt with when the child enters care. The rule, "No immunization, no care," must be understood by both the teacher and the parents. No exceptions should be made. The teacher may need to educate parents who want to enter their child in care about the need to adhere to the immunization schedule. When a child is in care, it is up to the teacher to follow up and make sure that immunizations occur.

The teacher should understand the sanitary habits of the various cultures that are represented in care. The teacher may have to provide extra education or acquire interpreters to inform parents of their responsibility in keeping their children well. This task can be greatly assisted if there is a health care consultant for the early education environment.

> ## Pause for Reflection
>
> Are there any superstitions related to health from your own culture or others you are familiar with that might be helpful to know so that you are more culturally competent? How might you work with a parent with one of these superstitions?

## Key Concept 13.7

### Implications for Teachers

The implications for the teacher are the tools of observation, supervision, education, working with families, and cultural competence that help the teacher create the holistic approach needed to deal with the many issues raised. Observation can identify infectious diseases early and thus provide some protection for others in care. Supervision will give the teacher the tools needed for exclusion and notification. The teacher must be educated, and must educate parents and children in methods that will forestall the spread of infectious diseases. Teachers should work cooperatively with families to provide healthy environments both at home and at school. Cultural competence should be practiced to help the teacher include all children and parents in providing the best preventive environment possible. The use of a health consultant and provision of a medical home for the children in early childhood education programs could optimize the health environment.

## CHAPTER SUMMARY

Teachers need to prevent disease spread and to care for mildly ill children. They need to form exclusion policies and understand reporting procedures. Teachers need to determine whether they have the ability to care for children who become ill and are not contagious as well as chronically ill children. Observation and supervision will help the teacher identify and manage infectious diseases and chronic illnesses. Education will help to teach healthy habits to children and their parents. Working with families and using cultural competence the optimal health environment is possible.

## TO GO BEYOND

In this section you will find a number of activities that you can use to apply and improve your knowledge of this chapter. There are also thorough online resources that accompany this text that can be found at http://www.early childed.delmar.com (see description at end of this chapter).

### Chapter Review Critical Thinking Applications

1. Discuss the identification and management of infectious diseases. How should these be applied in early childhood education situations?

2. Describe the particular skills needed to manage infectious diseases. How well prepared are you for these skills? What could you do to improve these skills?

3. How might early childhood education in your area be improved if there were a facility that specifically dealt with mildly ill children?

4. Discuss the presence of children with chronic illnesses in the early childhood education environment. Should a teacher have more qualifications to work with these children?

5. Examine how a health consultant and a medical home for all children can affect a teacher's job.

### As an Individual

1. Obtain the local licensing guidelines for exclusion. Compare and contrast those with the ones in this text. Should they be more thorough?

2. Describe the type of early childhood education environment you intend to participate in, then ask the three questions about caring for ill children. How do they relate to the particular care situation you have in mind?

### As a Group

1. Discuss exclusion policies. In small groups, design an exclusion policy for center-based care and one for family child care. How are they different? Why?

2. Examine the idea of "medical home." Does this make sense, or are there other solutions that might better help keep children well? How does this work in your own community?

3. In small groups, design a center for mildly ill children. Describe what this type of center would look like and what type of training might be necessary to run it. Is this a possibility for your own community?

## Case Studies

1. Charley has arrived at school and seems to have a runny nose. Upon further inspection, since the mucus is clear, Lauren, his teacher, allows him to stay. She keeps a careful eye on him and notices at about 11:00 A.M. that he seems to be feverish. By noon, Lauren notices a blistery rash on his torso. She immediately suspects chicken pox. What actions should she take?

2. Kevin and Kyle, three-year-old twins, were rubbing their eyes a great deal. Kevin also had a white discharge coming from his left eye. Donna, their family child care provider, noticed this and suspected that both boys had conjunctivitis (pink eye). She informed the boys' mother when they were picked up. The next morning, Donna woke up with red, watery eyes. How should Donna proceed with the day? If Kevin and Kyle arrive at care that morning, should she let them stay? How would you handle this?

3. Four-year-old Taylor did not eat much of her lunch. Connie, her teacher, noticed that this was unusual behavior for Taylor. She decided to keep an eye on Taylor. Within an hour, Taylor began to have diarrhea, shortly after that she began vomiting. How should Connie proceed? What should she do for Taylor?

4. Paula is a four-year-old who has diabetes. Her diabetes is controlled by insulin injections. The diabetes is pretty well under control, because her urine is tested several times a day when she is in your care. She still needs help to test it. A few of the other children in your class are very curious about this. How should you handle this situation in a way that will assist Paula as well as answer the curious children?

## Chapter References

Alkon, A., Sokal-Guiterrez, K., & Wolff, M. (2002). Child care health consultation improves health knowledge and compliance. *Pediatric Nursing, 28*(1), 61–65.

Alexander, L. (2003). Chronic conditions in classroom. *Healthy Child Care, 6*(4). Retrieved October 31, 2005, from http://www.healthychild.net/articles/shllchronic.html.

American Academy of Pediatrics (AAP). (2004, November 1). Whooping cough outbreak. Retrieved October 31, 2005, from http://www.aap.org/family/whoopingcough.htm.

American Academy of Pediatrics (AAP). (2002). *Promoting optimal health for American children: A summary report 1997–2001.* Elk Grove Village, IL: Healthy Child Care America.

American Academy of Pediatrics (AAP). (2000). Controlling illness in child care programs. October 31, 2005, from http://www.medem.com/MedLB/article_detaillb_for_printer.cfm?article_ID=ZZZN7CDTA7C&sub_cat=13.

American Academy of Pediatrics & American Public Health Association (AAP & APHA). (2002). *Caring for our children: National health and safety performance standards: Guidelines for out-of-home care.* Washington, DC: American Public Health Association.

A sick child and a demanding job. Have a backup plan. Retrieved December 28, 2005, from http://www.mayoclinic.com/invoke.cfm?id=WL00006.

American Diabetes Association (ADA). (2003). Care of children with diabetes in school and day care setting. Position Statement. *Diabetes Care, 26*(1), S131–S135.

American Speech and Hearing Association (ASHA). (2000). Questions and answers about otitis media, hearing and language development. Retrieved May 15, 2002, from http://www.kidsource.com/asha/otitis.htm.

Aronson, S. (2002). *Healthy young children: A manual for programs.* Washington, DC: National Association for the Education of Young Children.

Aronson, S. (2000, November). Exclusion of children with fevers from child care. *Child Care Information Exchange,* 88–89.

Auinger, P., Lanphear, B., Kalkwarf, H., & Mansour, M. (2003). Trends in otitis media among children in the United States. *Pediatrics, 112*(3), 514–520.

Bradley, R. (2003). Child care and common communicable illnesses in children ages 37 to 54 months. *Archives of Pediatric and Adolescent Medicine, 157*(2), 196–200.

Burns, J. (2001). Kawasaki disease. *Advances in Pediatrics, 48*(2), 157–177.

Calder, J. (2004). Medication administration in child care programs. California Childcare Health Program. Retrieved 11/4/05 from Program http://www.ucsfchildcarehealth.org/pdfs/healthandsafety/medadminEN102004.pd

Carballo, M., & Nerukar, A. (2001). Migration, refugees and health risks. *Emerging Infectious Diseases, 7*(3), 556–560.

Caufield, R., & Kataoka-Yahiro, M. (2001). Health training needs of child care professionals. *Early Childhood Education Journal, 29*(2), 119–123.

Celedon, J., Litonjua, A., Weiss, S., & Gold, D. (1999). Day care attendance in the first year of life and illnesses of upper and lower respiratory tract in children with a familial history of atopy. *Pediatrics, 104*(3), 495–500.

Centers for Disease Control (CDC). (2002). Diagnosis and reporting of HIV and AIDS in states with HIV/AIDS surveillance—United States, 1990–2000. *Morbidity and Mortality Weekly Report, 51*(27), 595–598. Retrieved October 31, 2005, from http://www.cdc.gov/mmwr/preview/mmwrhtml/mm5127a3.htm.

A "new" virus that commonly causes respiratory infections in children. (2004, March 1). *Child Health Alert, 22.* Chronic or recurring ear infections (otitis media). Retrieved October 31, 2005, from http://www.itonsil.com/itonsil_why_adenoid_otitis.html.

Cianciolo, S., Trueblood-Noll, R., & Allingham, P. (2004). Health consultation in early childhood settings. *Young Children, 59*(2), 56–61.

Cooley, W., & McAllister, J. (2004). Building medical homes: Improvement in strategies in primary care for children with special health care needs. *Pediatrics, 113*(5), 1499–1506.

Dailey, L. (2001). Excluding children due to illness: Four steps to a healthier program. *Child Care Health Connections, 14*(4), 6–7.

Dailey, L. (2002). Excluding children due to illness. *Healthy Child Care, 5*(6). Retrieved October 31, 2005, from http://www.healthychild.net/articles/sh30illness.html.

Do child care centers contribute to allergy problems? (2002, March). *Child Health Alert, 20*(3).

Feagans, L., Kipp, E., & Blood, I. (1994). The effects of otitis media on the attention skills of day-care-attending toddlers. *Developmental Psychology, 30*(5), 701–708.

Friedman, J., Lee, G. Kleinman, K., & Finklestein, J. (2002). Acute care and antibiotic seeking for upper respiratory tract infections for children in day care: Parental knowledge and day care center policies. *Maternal and Child Health Journal, 6*(3), 189–193.

Getch, Y., & Neuharth-Pritchett, S. (2004). Asthma management in early care and education settings. *Young Children, 59*(5), 34–41.

Gonzalez-Mena, J. (2004). *Infants, toddlers and caregivers.* New York: McGraw-Hill.

Hanifin, S., & Griffiths, P. (2002). Does pacifier use cause ear infections in young children? *British Journal of Community Nursing, 7*(4), 206, 208–211.

Healthy Child Care Pennsylvania (HCCP). (2001). How to choose and use a child care health consultant-trainer. Retrieved 11/4/05 from http://www.ecels-healthychildcarepa.org/content/11-04%20Choose-Use%20%20Health%20 Consultant.pdf

Kendrick, A., Kaufman, R., & Messenger, K. (Eds.). (2002). Healthy young children: A manual for programs. Washington, D.C. National Association for the Education of Young Children.

Laundy, J., & Boujaoude, L. (2004, August). Children with chronic conditions. University of Michigan Health System. Retrieved October 31, 2005, from http://www.med.umich.edu/1libr/yourchild/chronic.htm.

Lombardi, J. (1999). Viewpoint: child care is education . . . and more. *Young Children 54*(1), 48.

Lucarelli, P. (2002). Raising the bar for health and safety in child care. *Pediatric Nursing, 28*(3), 239–242.

Hepatitis A epidemic linked to child care facilities. (2001, December 9). *Medical Letter on the CDC & FDA (MLCF), 7.*

Moss, K. (2003). Fifth disease: Not just another rash. *Healthy Child Care, 6*(1). Retrieved October 31, 2005, from http://www.healthychild.net/articles/ sh31Fifth.html.

Mullihill, B., Shearer, D., & Van Horn, L. (2002). Training, experience and child care providers' perceptions of inclusion. *Early Childhood Research Quarterly, 17*(2), 197–215.

National Association of Child Care Professionals (NACCP). (2001, December 30). Higher rates of repeat infections occur among children in group care. *Medical Letter on the CDC and FDA (MLCF).* 15.

National Association for the Education of Young Children (NAEYC). (2004, March). Child care health consultants and trainers. *Beyond the Journal, Young Children on the Web.* Retrieved October 31, 2005, from http://www.journal.naeyc.org/btj/ 200403/HealthConsultants.pdf

National Center for Environmental Health (NCEH) (2005). National asthma control program: 2002 at a glance. Retrieved 11/4/05 from http://www.cdc.gov/nceh/ airpollution/asthma/aag02.htm.

National Institute of Child Health and Human Development (NICCHD). (2004). Growing up healthy: An overview of the national children's study. Retrieved October 31, 2005, from http://www.nationalchildrensstudy.gov/get_involved/learn_more/ growing_up_healthy.cfm.

National Institute of Child Health and Human Development Early Child Care Research Network (NICH). (2001). Child care and common communicable illnesses. *Archives of Pediatrics and Adolescent Medicine, 155*(4), 481–488.

North Carolina Child Care Health and Safety Resource Center (NCCCHSRC). (2005). Will antibiotics help? *North Carolina Child Care Health and Safety Bulletin, 5*(2), 5.

Palmer, D. (2005). Administering medications in childcare. *Healthy Child Care, 8*(2). Retrieved October 31, 2005, from http://www.healthychild.net/articles/ mc43givemeds.html.

Palmer, D. (2003). Pinworms. *Healthy Child Care, 6*(5). Retrieved October 31, 2005, from http://www.healthychild.net/articles/sh35pinworms.html.

Pappas, D., Schwartz, R., Sheridan, M., & Hayden, G. (2000). Medical exclusion of sick children from child care centers: A plea for reconciliation. *Southern Medical Journal, 93*(6), 575–578.

Paradise, J., Dollaghan, C., Campbell, T., Feldman, H., Bernard, B., Colborn, D., Rockette, H., Janoksy, J., Pitcairn, D., Sabo, D., Kurs-Lasky, M., & Smith, C. (2000). Language, speech sound production and cognition in three-year-old children in relation to otitis media in their first three years of life. *Pediatrics, 105*(5), 1119–1130.

Pellman, H. (2002). Day cares and colds. *Pediatrics for Parents, 20*(4), 5.

Pettigrew, M., Gent, J., Triche, E., Belanger, K., Bracken, M., & Leade, B. (2004). Association of early-onset otitis media in infants and exposure to household mould. *Paediatric Perinatal Epidemiology, 18*(6), 441–447.

Polyzoi, E., & Babb, J. (2004). The challenge of caring for mildly ill children: A Canadian national child care study. *Early Childhood Research Quarterly, 19*(3), 431–448.

Poole, J. (2001). Ear infections. *Healthy Child Care, 4*(2). Retrieved October 31, 2005, from http://healthychild.net/articles/sh20ear.html.

Preidt, T. (2004, October, 25). New guidelines for Kawasaki disease issued. Health-Central. Retrieved October 25, 2005, from http://www.healthcentral.com/news/NewsFullText.cfm?id=521928.

Reeves, D. (2002). A medical home for every child. *Healthy Child Care, 5*(4). Retrieved October 31, 2005, from http://www.healthychild.net/articles/mc28medhome.html.

Strict cleaning routines promote child health, safety, study says. (2004). *Report on Preschool Programs (RPP), 36*(7), 55.

Sailors, J. (2004). Ill children in child care. *Healthy Child Care, 7*(6). Retrieved 11/4/05 from http://www.healthychild.net/articles/sh42ill.html.

Sears, W. (2003). Too sick for daycare? Retrieved October 31, 2005, from http://www.askdrsears.com/html/8/T085300.asp.

Sinkovits, H., Kelly, M., & Ernst, M. (2003). Medication administration in day care centers for children. *Journal of the American Pharmaceutical Association, 43*(3), 355–356.

Skull, S., Ford-Jones, E., Kulin, N., Einarson, T., & Wang, E. (2000). Child care center staff contribute to physicians visits and pressure for antibiotic prescription. *Archives of Pediatrics and Adolescent Medicine, 154*(2), 180–183.

Sokol-Gutierrez, K. (2000, January). Partners in health: Helping families advocate for their children's health. *Child Care Information Exchange,* 51–53.

Starfield, B., & Shi, L. (2004). The medical home, access to care and insurance: a review of evidence. *Pediatrics, 113*(5), 1493–1498.

Sutton, A. (2002). Dealing with diabetes. *Healthy Child Care, 5*(4). Retrieved October 31, 2005, from: http://www.healthychild.net/articles/ny28diabetes.html.

Unger, J. (2004, September 23). Home-based care to be offered for mildly ill children of eligible U. of I. Employees. News Bureau, University of Illinois at Urbana-Champaign. Retrieved October 31, 2005, from http://www.news.uiuc.edu/news/04/0923sickchild.html.

Virginia Mason Team Medicine. (2004). Corporate benefits of Tender Loving Care—Daycare for mildly-ill children. Seattle, WA: Virginia Mason Medical Center. Retrieved October 31, 2005, from http://www.vmmc.com/dbChildrens/sec2778.htm.

Warren, J., Levy, S., Kirchner, H., Nowak, A., & Bergus, G. (2001). Pacifier use and the occurrence of otitis media in the first year of life. *Journal of Pediatric Dentistry, 23*(2), 103–107.

Watt, M., Roberts, J., & Zeisel, S. (1993). Ear infections in young children: The role of the early childhood educator. *Young Children, 48*(11), 64–72.

Williams, P. (2002). Allergies in children. *Healthy Child Care, 5*(2). Retrieved October 31, 2005 from http://www.healthychild.net/articles/sh26allergies.html.

Zamani, R., & Shaw, P. (2000). Ear infections (otitis media) and hearing loss in young children. Retrieved May 15, 2002, from http://ericps.ed.uiuc.edu/cchp/factsheet/earinfection.html.

Zamani, A. (2005). Runny noses in your program and how to deal with them. *Connections, 3*(2), 17–19.

Zambrana, R., Ell, K., Dorrington, C., Wachsmur, L., & Hodge, D. (1994). The relationship between psychosocial status of immigrant Latina mothers and use of emergency pediatric services. *Health and Social Work, 19*(2), 98–102.

Zeisel, S., Roberts, J., Burchinal, M., Neebe, E., & Henderson, F. (2002). Longitudinal study of risk factors for otitis media in African American children. *Maternal Child Health, 6*(3), 189–193.

Additional resources for this chapter can be found by visiting the Online Companion™ at http://www.earlychilded.delmar.com. This supplemental material includes extensive chapter quizzes, PowerPoint® outlines, Web links, and various other activities to help better utilize the material in this chapter. The site is updated regularly, so you may check back often to receive the latest information about the subjects in each chapter.

## HEALTH CURRICULUM SUPPLEMENT

Sample lesson plans and topic maps for subjects that concern health are provided in the next few pages for the teacher to help reinforce the information that is being modeled by teachers and learned by the children in the early education environment. In addition to the sample curriculum, there is a list of children's books and sources for further information. Some of this information may include songs or finger plays. This sample group is presented to help the teacher design his or her own curriculum by adding to the information provided.

**LESSON***plan*
CHAPTER **13**

### LESSON PLAN **1**

***Unit:*** Health

***Suggested Themes:*** My Family, Myself, Being a Friend, Showing and Sharing My Feelings.

***Theme:*** Showing and Sharing My Feelings.

***Objectives:*** Children will develop an understanding of the feelings they experience. They will learn ways to express their feelings.

***Materials:*** Marking pens and paper. Books. Magazines. Finger paints and paper. Paints and paper. Play dough. Cut out cardstock circles 3 to 4 inches in diameter.

***Lesson:*** Talk with children about feelings. Read book *Feelings: Inside and Outloud Too.* Discuss book. Have children practice feelings on their faces as you read the book. Talk about ways to verbalize feelings like singing, yelling, and so forth.

Talk about positive ways that children might express anger (punching bag, play dough, painting, and so forth). Talk about inappropriate ways to express emotions (biting, kicking, hitting, and so forth). Show pictures from magazines or books and have children identify feelings. Let children have free time to express a feeling they have had. This can be done by drawing a happy picture, drawing or painting faces to match moods, picking out a magazine picture, or making a finger paint to match a mood. Some children may have difficulty with this concept, while others will easily be able to do it.

***Follow-Up:*** Provide more books on feelings for children to read. When reading any book and a feeling is shown, note that feeling and the expression or ask children to tell you what it is. Have materials available for children to make a mobile with circles that they can draw or cut out faces with feelings that express a range of emotions. Learning card given to parents to explain the importance of encouraging children to express their feelings in socially accepted ways.

***Age-Appropriate:*** Preschoolers. If handled correctly even toddlers can benefit.

LESSON*plan*
CHAPTER **13**

**LESSON PLAN 2**

*Unit:* Health

*Suggested Themes:* Hearing, Smelling, Seeing, Tasting, Doctor Checkups, A Visit to the Dentist, My Body and Its Parts, How Tall Am I and What Do I Weigh?

*Theme:* A Visit to the Dentist.

*Objectives:* Children should understand the importance of healthy teeth and who can help them keep healthy.

*Materials:* A new toothbrush for each child (supplied by dentist). Clothing for the dramatic play area to emulate dentist uniform. Books. Bulletin board on dental health.

*Lesson:* Have a dentist come visit children. A toothbrush is given to teach child. Dentist explains how to brush teeth. Children do a "dry" run with toothbrushes. Dentist talks about what he/she does when children visit. After dentist leaves, children brush teeth with water in bathroom. Reinforce proper toothbrushing techniques. Put each toothbrush in baggy and place in each child's cubby.

*Follow-Up:* Read *Doctor De Soto* about a mouse who is the dentist to a number of different animals. Talk about how different the teeth are. Talk about how they would brush teeth. Discuss other ways to help keep teeth healthy, such as good diet. Watch dramatic play for reinforcement. Give parents information sheet provided by dentist or create one on proper brushing. Play the song "Brush Your Teeth" by Raffi.

*Age-Appropriate:* Toddlers and preschoolers.

LESSON*plan*
CHAPTER **13**

**LESSON PLAN 3**

*Unit:* Health

*Suggested Themes:* What is a Germ? Wash Those Germs Right Off of Your Hands! Keeping Food Safe. What Is an Immunization?

*Theme:* Wash Those Germs Right Off of Your Hands!

*Objectives:* Children should know how and when to wash their hands.

*Materials:* Plaster of Paris. Magazines. Books. Sink, liquid soap. Bulletin board on hand washing procedures with pictures of when to wash.

*Lesson:* In circle or group time. Discuss germs. Read *Germs Make Me Sick!* Discuss the importance of hand washing and the occasions that hands should be washed. Demonstrate how to wash hands. Have children show you how to wash hands. Move into bathroom area with sinks. Show children how you wash your hands. Sing "This is the Way We Wash our Hands" ("All Around the Mulberry Bush" tune) as children show the teacher how hands should be washed. Correct if needed. Query as to when hands should be washed.

*Follow-Up:* Make plaster of Paris handprints for children to take home. Wash hands at appropriate times. Have children wash hands at appropriate times. Do several finger plays including "My Hands" (Herr & Libby,

1995). This makes children more aware of their hands. See if they can add a line to the finger play that indicates hand washing and the importance of it. Hand out parent information sheet or learning card so parents are aware of correct procedures and times for children to wash their hands.

*Age-Appropriate:* Toddlers and preschoolers. Toddlers may not understand but they are sensory and will wash hands properly with encouragement and reinforcement.

## LESSONplan
## CHAPTER 13

### LESSON PLAN 4

*Unit:* Health

*Suggested Themes:* Keeping My Body Healthy, Getting Enough Sleep, Taking Care of Myself When I Am Sick, How Do I Feel?

*Theme:* Taking Care of Myself When I Am Sick.

*Objectives:* Children should be able to help themselves get well.

*Materials:* Blankets and pillows, doctor kit, and so forth, for dramatic play area. Books. Paints, pens, and paper.

*Lesson:* Have a nurse visit to explain what a child needs when she is sick. Talk about rest, drinking liquids, and taking the medicines the doctor gives. Discuss ways to rest, what drinks might be appealing, and how you never take medicine unless the doctor says you should. Also talk about preventing other people from getting sick by washing hands and not sharing cups.

*Follow-Up:* Read *Sick in Bed.* Let children play patient and nurse or doctor. Have children draw picture of things they could do for themselves to make them well. Put a note on the bulletin board to parents on what was discussed today.

*Age-Appropriate:* Preschoolers.

Topic Map for Teeth

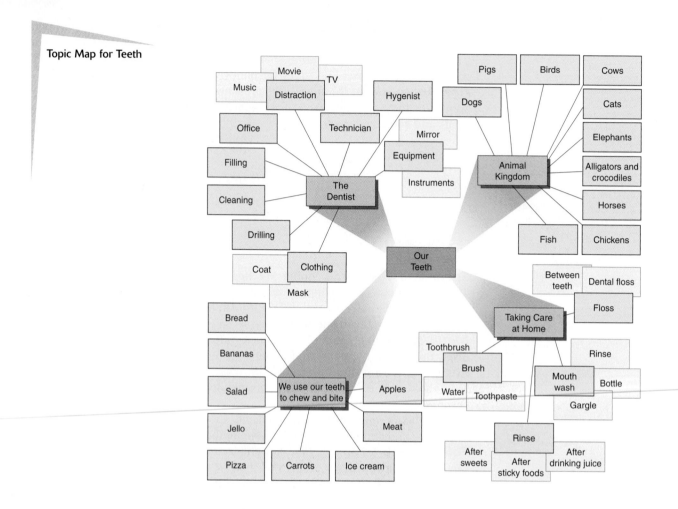

Topic Map for Our Bodies

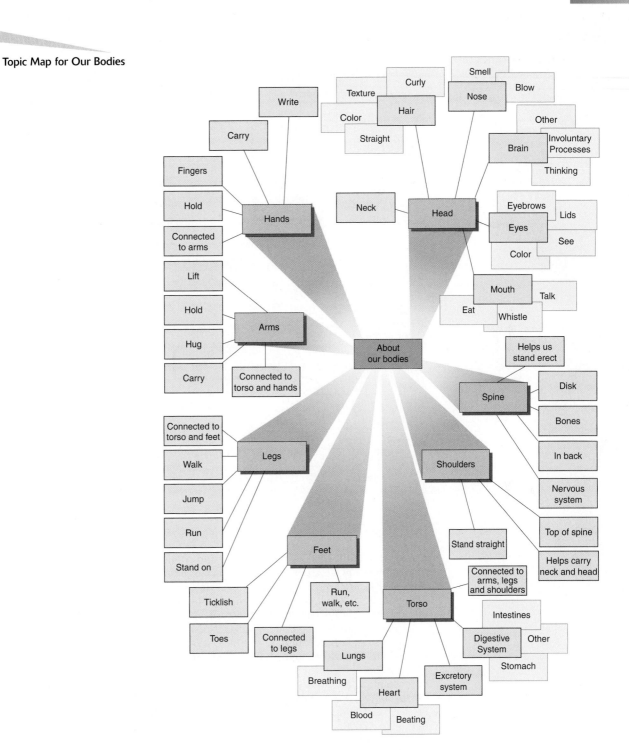

Topic Map for Germs Can
Make Us Sick

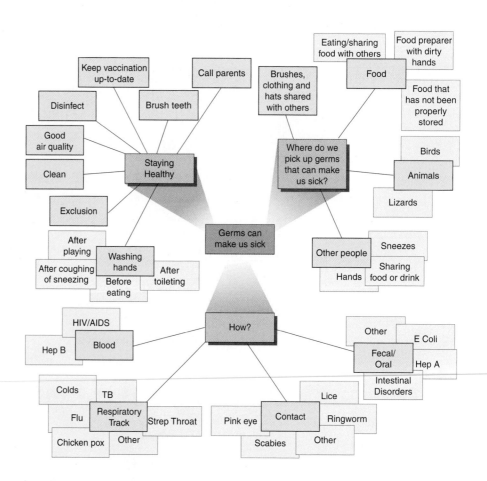

## Children's Books on Health Subjects

Agassi, M. (2000). *Hands Are Not for Hitting.* Minneapolis: Free Spirit Publishing.

Aliki. (1992). *I'm Growing.* New York: HarperCollins Publishers.

Aliki. (1984). *My Five Senses.* New York: HarperCollins Publishers.

Allington, R., & Kriell, K. (1985). *Hearing.* Milwaukee: Raintree.

Berenstain, S., & Berenstain, J. (1999). *The Magic School Bus Inside Ralphie: A Book About Germs,* Eddy, TX: Sagebrush.

Berenstain, S., & Berenstain, J. (1988). *The Bad Dream.* New York: Random House.

Berenstain, S., & Berenstain, J. (1988). *Ready, Set, Go.* Exercise. New York: Random House.

Berenstain, S., & Berenstain, J. (1983). *The Messy Room.* New York: Random House.

Berenstain, S., & Berenstain, J. (1981). *Visit to the Dentist.* New York: Random House.

Berger, M. (1995). *Germs Make Me Sick!* New York: HarperCollins Publishers.

Berger, M. (2000). *Why I Sneeze, Shiver, Hiccup, & Yawn (Let's-Read-and-Find-Out Science 2).* New York: HarperTrophy.

Brandenburg, F. (1979). *I Wish I Was Sick, Too!* New York: Mulberry Books.

Bridwell, N. (1996). *Clifford's Sports Day.* New York: Scholastic Books. About exercise during a sports day.

Charlip, R., & Supree, B. (2001). *Mother Mother I Feel Sick Send for the Doctor Quick Quick Quick.* Berkeley, CA: Tricycle Press.

Cole, J. (1994). *You Can Smell Forever with Your Ear.* New York: Grosset and Dunlap. Five senses.

Collins, R. (2004). *Germs.* New York: Bloomsbury USA Children's Books.

Creative Group at PSS! (1996). *The Boo Boo Book.* New York: Putnam and Grosset.

Demuth, P. (1997). *Achoo!: All About Colds.* New York: Grosset & Dunlap. A children's story that explains how germs spread diseases such as colds.

Dunn, S. (1994). *Keeping Fit.* Chicago: Good Year Books.

Durant, A., & Gliori, D. (2004). *Always and Forever.* About grief and death and how to deal with it. San Diego: Harcourt Children's Books.

Fowler, A. (1991). *Feeling Things.* Chicago: Children's Press.

Fowler, A. (1991). *Hearing Things.* Chicago: Children's Press.

Fowler, A. (1991). *Seeing Things.* Chicago: Children's Press.

Fowler, A. (1991). *Smelling Things.* Chicago: Children's Press.

Frandsen, K. (1987). *I'd Rather Get a Spanking Than Go to the Doctor.* Chicago: Children's Press.

Henkas, K. (2004). *Kitten's First Full Moon.* A story of frustration for a kitten trying to get milk from the full moon and how the problem is solved. New York: Greenwillow.

Katz, B. (1996). *Germs! Germs! Germs!* New York: Cartwheel Books. A children's story about germs, from the germ's point of view.

Leonard, M. (1988). *Getting Dressed.* New York: Bantam Books.

Leonard, M. (1988). *Taking a Bath.* New York: Bantam Books.

Little, J., & Plecas, J. (2003). *Emma's Strange Pet.* About a little girl and her allergy to most pets and the new pet that her brother is jealous of and wants one too. New York. HarperCollins.

Numeroff, L. (1995). *Chimps Don't Wear Glasses.* New York: Simon & Schuster.

Oremerod, J. (1983). *Be Brave Billy.* London: J.M. Dent and Sons Ltd. Being brave about going to doctor and dentist.

Oxenbury, H. (1983). *The Check-up.* New York: Penguin Books.

Page, R., & Jenkins, S. (2003). *What Do You Do with a Tail Like This?* Goes through the body parts of different animals and explains how those parts function. New York: Houghton Mifflin.

Payne, L. M. (1994). *Just Because I Am.* Minneapolis: Free Spirit Publishing Inc.

Polland, B. K. (1975) *Feelings: Inside and Outloud Too.* Berkeley, CA: Celestial Arts.

Ready, D. (1998). *Dentists.* Mankato, MN: Capstone Press.

Reasoner, C. (1995). *Little Box Book's First Aid Kit.* New York: Putnam and Grosset. Four small books including Stethoscope, Cough Syrup, Adhesive Tape, and First Aid Kits.

Rey, H. A. (1973). *Curious George Goes to the Hospital.* Boston: Houghton Mifflin.

Rice, J. (1997). *Those Mean, Nasty, Dirty, Downright Disgusting but Invisible Germs.* Saint Paul, MN: Redleaf Press. A little girl gets germs off her hands by washing them down the drain.

Rice, J., & Stricklin, A. (1997). *Those Icky Sticky Smelly Cavity Causing But . . . Invisible Germs.* St. Paul, Minnesota: Redleaf Press.

Rockwell, A. (1982). *Sick in Bed.* New York: Macmillan.

Rogers, F. (1989). *Going to the Dentist.* New York: G.P. Putman and Sons.

Rogers, F. (1986). *Going to the Doctor.* New York: G.P. Putnam and Sons.

Romanek, T., & Cowles, R. (2003). *Achoo: The Most Interesting Book You'll Ever Read About Germs (Mysterious You).* Tonawanda, New York: Kids Can Press.

Ross, T. (2000). *Wash Your Hands!* La Jolla, CA: Kane/Miller Book Publishers.

Schweibert, P., & DeKlyen, C. (2001). *Tear Soup.* Book about loss and how to deal with it. Portland, OR: Grief Watch.

Sesame Street. (1985). *Sign Language ABC with Linda Bove.* New York: Children's Television Workshop, Random House.

Silverstein, A., Silverstein, V., & Nunn, L. (1999). *Allergies.* New York: Grolier Publishers.

Simon, N. (1974). *I Was So Mad.* Morton Grove, IL: A. Whitman.

Steig, W. (1982). *Doctor De Soto.* New York: Farrar, Straus & Giroux. Mouse dentist works on all kinds of animals.

Weigelt, U., Kadmon, C., Kadmon, K., & Kazeroid, S. (2003). *Bear's Last Journey.* Norway: Nord-Sud Verlag.

Wells, R. (1995). *Edward's Overwhelming Overnight.* New York: Penguin Books. Edward the unready bear has fears about spending the night with a friend.

Ziefert, H., & Smith, M. (1988). *What Do I Hear?* New York: Bantam Books.

Ziefert, H., & Smith, M. (1988). *What Do I See?* New York: Bantam Books.

Ziefert, H., & Smith, M. (1988). *What Do I Smell?* New York: Bantam Books.

Ziefert, H., & Smith, M. (1988). *What Do I Taste?* New York: Bantam Books.

Ziefert, H., & Smith, M. (1988). *What Do I Touch?* New York: Bantam Books.

# SECTION V
# Current Issues in Early Childhood Education Safety, Nutrition, and Health

This section discusses four areas that deal with current issues.

14.  Child Maltreatment

15.  Children with Disabilities or Other Special Needs

16.  Creating Linkages

These topics will prepare the teacher to deal with sensitive issues; create linkages with children, families, and the community; and develop curriculum for safety, nutrition, and health in the early childhood education environment.

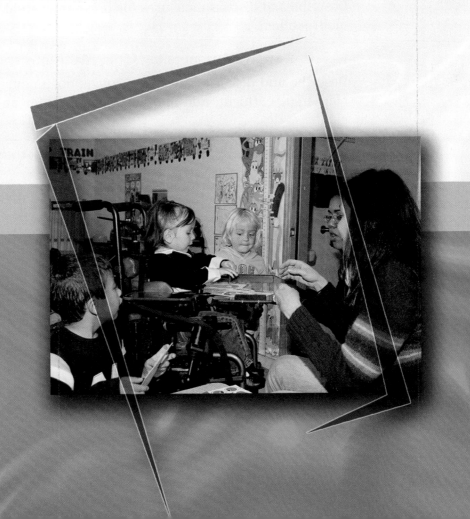

# Child Maltreatment

**After reading this chapter, you should be able to:**

## 14.1 Policies for Child Maltreatment

Define and discuss policies for child abuse that may affect the early childhood education environment.

## 14.2 Preventive Measures for Child Maltreatment

Describe and discuss measures for preventing child maltreatment.

## 14.3 Protective Measures for Child Maltreatment

Describe and discuss how to recognize, document, and report child maltreatment, and methods for caring for an abused child.

## 14.4 Working with Children from Substance-Abusing Families

Describe and discuss the common problem and their solutions that may arise in early childhood education environments when working with children from drug-abusing families.

## 14.5 Implications for Teachers

Describe and discuss the importance of education, observation, role modeling, and supervision in dealing with special topics issues.

## 14.1  POLICIES FOR CHILD MALTREATMENT

A teacher may encounter a child who has been maltreated in some way. Child maltreatment is defined as "all intentional harm to or avoidable endangerment of anyone under 18 years of age" (Berger, 2005). This includes neglect, physical abuse, sexual abuse, and emotional abuse. Child maltreatment is a serious threat to the health, safety, and well-being of children in this country. It is up to the teacher to offer preventive and protective measures to all children in the early childhood education environment. The following issues show the need to create policies that deal with child maltreatment (see Figure 14-1):

- Almost 3 million cases of child maltreatment, involving 5.5 million children, were reported in 2003. More than 1 million incidents of child maltreatment were substantiated (U.S. Department of Health and Human Services [HHS], 2005).
- Children younger than six years of age are the most at risk for being abused and neglected. The greatest percentage of victims are younger than one year (NAIC, 2004; HHS, 2005).
- Seventy-six percent of abuse and neglect fatalities are younger than four years old (CDC, 2004). Forty-four percent of the fatalities are children younger than one year (HHS, 2005).
- Helping parents recognize behaviors that may develop into abusive behaviors and can produce positive parent–child relationships instead of the cycle of abuse (CPPS, 2004; Olson & Hyson, 2003).
- A supportive adult can make a difference in the life of a child who is in an abusive family (Groves et al., 2000; Kersey & Malley, 2005; Werner & Smith, 2001).
- Eighty percent of perpetrators were found to be parents (HHS, 2005). Approximately one-half of all cases of child abuse and neglect involved the substance abuse of the parents (ChildHelp USA, 2004).
- Children over the age of three years can learn abuse prevention concepts (Crosson-Tower, 2002).

**FIGURE 14-1**
Child maltreatment statistics, 2003 (HHS, 2005).

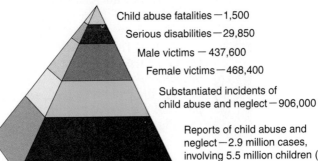

**Deaths Aren't The Whole Story**
The toll of child abuse and neglect

In addition to the estimated 1,500 children who die from abuse or neglect each year, tens of thousands more are seriously injured and many are left with lifelong disabilities.

Child abuse fatalities—1,500
Serious disabilities—29,850
Male victims — 437,600
Female victims—468,400
Substantiated incidents of child abuse and neglect—906,000
Reports of child abuse and neglect—2.9 million cases, involving 5.5 million children (2003)

The teacher should provide an environment that supports the children's well-being. The environment and the actions of the teachers must be beyond reproach. Methods of practices for preventing accusations must be used.

The teacher should learn to recognize any indicators that a family may be at risk for maltreatment of the children. Intervention methods and strategies should be used when necessary. The teacher is mandated to report any maltreatment that may be observed. He should learn to recognize the signs and symptoms of maltreatment. The teacher needs to know how to document and report any indicators of maltreatment that have been observed (Nunnelley & Fields, 1999). Teachers should know the methods and strategies used to provide for the well-being of a child in care who has been maltreated.

The following are areas in which policies should be created for child maltreatment prevention and protection:

1. *Preventive Measures:* understanding how to prevent accusations and how to intervene to protect children in care from maltreatment

2. *Protective Measures:* practices to recognize, document, and report all forms of child maltreatment and methods for working with abused children

3. *Working with Children from Substance-Abusing Families:* Understanding the common problems and their solutions that may arise in early childhood education environments when working with children from drug-abusing families

4. *Implications for Teachers:* practices that use the tools of education, cultural sensitivity, observation, and supervision to provide children with protection and prevention from harm and to offer an environment that fosters well-being

## Key Concept 14.1

### Policies for Child Maltreatment

Child maltreatment affects as many as 5 million children annually. Teachers should learn preventive, protective, and promotional measures that will help provide for the well-being of children. Policies should be created to help the teacher provide intervention and prevent accusation. These policies should offer the teacher methods and practices needed for recognition, documentation, and reporting of child maltreatment. The teacher should understand protective strategies to provide the child who has been maltreated with an atmosphere of support and a sense of trust in the teacher. The teacher should understand the effects that substance-abusing families have on children and how to help them.

## 14.2 PREVENTIVE MEASURES FOR CHILD MALTREATMENT

Child maltreatment is a very sensitive issue that needs to be carefully handled. Child maltreatment can be complex when it surfaces as an issue in early childhood education environments. The teacher has a number of responsibilities for handling this issue. Prevention, protection, and promotion of child safety are essential. Children should never be harmed (NAEYC, 2004). Prevention of child maltreatment can be effective and is less costly in terms of human suffering as well as financial cost needed to remedy it (Donnelly, 1992).

Teachers can offer preventive measures by cooperating with their state licensing agency. Many states screen teachers for a history of child maltreatment. The director or teacher who employs others can make sure all prospective employees are screened for child abuse and neglect and conform to the licensing regulations (Palmer & Smith, 2002a). This screening would include teachers, janitors, secretaries, cooks, substitutes, and volunteers. If it is difficult to get local licensing or screening information, NAEYC recommends using the screening decision model developed by the American Bar Association (Wells et al., 1995). This instrument is very thorough (NAEYC, 1997). Other screening methods might include checking with the state department of motor vehicles for driving records, running a credit check, and obtaining educational transcripts. It is important that at least three professional and personal references be checked.

In addition to the licensing process, each prospective employee should be carefully interviewed, and all referrals from previous employment

A good policy for hiring new teachers is to carefully screen them, including an in-depth interview and checking all references.

should be checked. Table 14-1 lists a sample of questions the teacher might ask prospective employees. If there are any doubts about the person after the interview, the teacher should listen to her intuition. There is no room for doubt when it comes to the safety of children in care. New employees should go through a probationary period so that the employing teacher may carefully observe them as they relate to the children. If the new teacher does not meet the standards of behavior on or off the job, a policy should be in place to terminate him.

Proper teacher–child ratios also act as a preventive measure. If the ratio is followed, teachers are able to best meet each child's individual needs. Check your state for regulations on ratios. If your state does not have them, NAEYC accreditation suggests the following:

- 1:6–8 for infants
- 1:8–12 for toddlers
- 1:14–20 for preschoolers
- 1:16–20 for kindergartners
- 1:20 for primary grades

Preservice orientation and inservice training should be given to keep teachers up to date about child maltreatment in a group setting. This should include the definition of child maltreatment, identification of signs of maltreatment, and how to document and report child maltreatment. Many cases of maltreatment are either erroneously reported or go unreported because the teacher does not understand what constitutes maltreatment and how it should be reported (Nunnelley & Fields, 1999).

Another preventive measure is to set up the early childhood education environment so that children and teachers are never isolated from view of others (Palmer & Smith, 2002b). Some centers use video equipment that promotes high visibility for the parents to see all angles of the early childhood education environment. Restrooms should have an open door policy that require the door to remain open so that there is no opportunity for privacy. Supervision should be provided to support this. Establish policies to discourage maltreatment, such as never using physical punishment even if the state in which the early childhood education program is located allows

**TABLE 14-1**
*Sample Interview Questions to Screen for Abuse Potential*

- Why do you want to work with children?
- How would you describe your own childhood?
- What is your viewpoint on discipline?
- Do you believe in corporal punishment (hitting a child)?
- Does child behavior ever make you angry?
- How do you express your anger?
- A series of "What would you do if?" questions that relate to anger, discipline, etc.
- What are some coping skills you have to alleviate stress?

it. Understand what emotional maltreatment entails, and be aware of it so that it does not occur. For example, never belittle a child. If the teacher feels angry and may hurt a child, he or she should take a break and have a coworker take over, or at least talk to someone.

## Preventing Accusations

Teachers should inform parents who sign their children up for care that there is a policy that covers child maltreatment. The teacher needs the parent to understand that any suspected maltreatment must be reported. All states and U.S. territories **mandate** that teachers report any suspected child maltreatment. Approximately 50 percent of the substantial cases in 2002 were reported by mandated reporters such as educators, child care providers, and social workers (CDF, 2004). The parents should also be informed of the steps the teacher uses to prevent maltreatment from occurring in the care situation. The teacher should make sure the parents understand the philosophy of discipline, guidance, and child care.

Routine quick health checks should be done daily. During this time, in addition to observing for health, take time to observe bruises, scratches, or any other injuries that you note. If the child comes to care with an unexplained bruise or physical injury, the teacher should ask the parent about it. The report of the bruise and the explanation should be recorded and added to the child's file. Use injury incident reports any time an accident or injury occurs in your care. Discuss these daily with the parents as they pick up the children. Save a copy of the report in the child's file to document each accident or injury. Any injury incident report should include the date, time, nature of the injury, and any comments by the parent. Documentation is the teacher's best defense (Figure 14-2). Visitors to the early childhood education environment should be required to sign in and out. A clear directive should be given by parents concerning who is allowed to pick up their child or children in care. If a substitute or new volunteer is present or will be coming later in the day, the

● **Mandate**
*an order by law*

Teachers are in a good position to identify possible maltreatment. In most states, they are mandated to report suspected abuse.

**FIGURE 14-2**
*Injury Incident Report*

# Injury Incident Report

Child's name: _____

Date: _____ Time: _____

Where did the incident take place? _____

Description of incident: _____

_____

_____

_____

Teacher's initials: _____

Action taken by teacher: _____

_____

_____

_____

Observations of behavior changes, if any: _____

_____

_____

_____

Parent notified: _____

Teacher's initials: _____

Teacher's signature _____ Parent's signature _____

parents should always be informed before they leave children in care (NAEYC, 1997).

## Intervention

Intervention strategies such as observation, discussion, and action may prevent maltreatment. The teacher should learn to identify when parents or their children are under stress. The teacher should work closely with parents to establish a good, communicative relationship (NAEYC, 2004). NAEYC suggests that the teacher take an active part in preventing abuse and neglect. The Center for the Study of Social Policy (CPPS, 2004) suggests that the use of a teacher is a new, effective, and affordable strategy that may help to prevent child maltreatment. They noted that teachers can offer five protective factors (see Table 14-2). Developing trust and respect keeps the line of communication open between teacher and parent. The teacher may observe a parent or child under stress over a period of time. Talking with the parent may help to relieve the stress or open up other avenues to relieve stress. The teacher can inform the parent that there may be coping skills or outside help for this stress. Information regarding stages of child development and effective ways to handle guidelines and discipline should be made

**TABLE 14-2**
*Five Protective Factors for Helping Families Prevent Child Maltreatment*

1. Establish trusting relationships with families in order to provide the parents greater resilience. Teachers that are trained to look for early warning signs of distress can be better able to intervene if they have positive relationships with families.

2. Help to provide a sense of community for the families in care through social events, potlucks, cultural competence, and other measures.

3. Pass along knowledge of child development and parenting through daily communication, newsletters, handouts, libraries, and support groups.

4. Respond to family crises by offering real support and connections to resources for families. Families may be suffering from unemployment, illness, or housing difficulties and may not have the coping skills or strategies to seek the help they need.

5. Offer children support so that they can develop their social and emotional competence. Providing protective measures, helping children identify their feelings, and teaching problem-solving strategies will make the children more resilient. This, in turn, may help parents look at their children in a more positive light.

Stress is a major factor in abusive situations involving parents and children. Training is available for teachers to learn sensitivity to these areas and provide resources for parents.

available to families. Children from the age of three years can be taught preventive strategies and concepts. They can easily learn about what abuse is, what the body parts are, and the types of touching (Crosson-Tower, 2002). This may provide the action needed to impede the progress of maltreatment.

Table 14-3 relates some factors that may exhibit potential for abuse. These behaviors may be exhibited to greater extent when a parent is under stress.

A child's behavior may not always be consistent, due to temperament and developmental changes. The teacher will, however, probably be able to find a pattern of behavior for most children. When a child begins to exhibit increases in poor behavior or appears sad or withdrawn, he may be experiencing stress in his life. The teacher can talk with the child about his feelings, and alert a parent to these changes. Children can also use coping skills to relieve stress.

---

*Pause for Reflection*

Have you ever been a victim of child maltreatment, or do you know someone who has? What are some of the effects of maltreatment on children? Do you feel you could help a child who has been maltreated?

---

**TABLE 14-3**
*Factors That May Lead to Abusive Behaviors*

- Significant changes in lifestyle: death of family member, divorce, unemployment, marital difficulties, or a recent move.
- Poor knowledge of child development and unrealistic expectations of the child's capabilities (e.g., the child is a little adult).
- Isolation from support; little or no contact with extended family, neighbors, and friends.
- Low self-esteem.
- Few coping abilities.
- Poor impulse control. Gets angry for even minor things.
- Questionable communication behaviors. May appear to feel threatened or defensive when ordinary questions are asked concerning the child or children.
- Lack of bonding or attachment to a child or children.
- Appears to be under the influence of alcohol or drugs.

## Key Concept 14.2

### Preventive Measures

Preventive measures such as screening teachers and having an open door policy can help prevent undue accusations against responsible teachers. Teachers should always document any accident, injury, or illness that a child has while in care. The teacher should be aware of the indicators of social circumstances and behaviors of children and parents that could escalate into child maltreatment. Intervention may help prevent maltreatment from occurring.

## 14.3  PROTECTIVE MEASURES FOR CHILD MALTREATMENT

It is imperative that every teacher be aware of the physical and behavioral indicators of maltreatment. Child maltreatment can be defined as "harm or neglect of a child by a parent, relative, babysitter, caregiver, or any other adult" (Seattle-King County Department of Public Health, 1991).

### *Recognition*

A teacher needs to know how to recognize the indicators of child maltreatment. Child maltreatment is divided into four categories: physical, emotional, sexual, and neglect (CDC, 2004). Each type of abuse has signs and symptoms that may indicate that child maltreatment has taken place. A child may suffer from maltreatment in one or more areas.

It is essential that the teacher have an awareness of the indicators of maltreatment. All states mandate that people who care for children are to report suspected abuse. In most states, failure to report brings penalties, including a monetary fine. Some teachers may feel reluctant to report because they believe that the parents may retaliate or that their relationship with the parents may be compromised. Regardless of reluctance or feelings of guilt, a teacher who suspects child maltreatment must report it. The report may make a lasting difference in a child's life. It may prevent death or injury and may help the family to access resources and assistance. In some states, the only follow-up to the maltreatment report may have to come from the early childhood education center unless the children were removed from parental custody. This places the teacher in an awkward situation. All states protect teachers from criminal or civil liability due to reporting of maltreatment.

Each type of abuse has signs and symptoms that a teacher should be on the lookout for.

*Physical Abuse.* Physical abuse is any act that results in a nonaccidental physical injury. This type of maltreatment may result from severe corporal punishment or from intentional injury by deliberate assault. Table 14-4 includes many physical and behavioral indicators of physical abuse.

*Emotional Abuse.* Emotional abuse includes placing unrealistic demands, excessive yelling, and unnecessary criticism that results in emotional harm or mental suffering. It is perhaps the most difficult type of child maltreatment to prove, but it may be observed when the interaction between a child and parent is seen. See Table 14-5 for a list of indicators of this type of abuse.

*Sexual Abuse.* Child sexual abuse can be sexual exploitation as well as sexual assault upon the child by an adult or older child. Sexual exploitation includes fondling, mouth to genital contact, exhibition, and showing or using the child for obscene materials. The offender is known to the child in 76 percent of the cases of child sexual abuse (HHS, 2005). Sexual maltreatment is a reality in the United States. It is estimated that as many as one in five adult women were abused as children. Table 14-6 includes indicators of sexual abuse.

**TABLE 14-4**
*Indicators of Physical Abuse*

A consistently vacant, withdrawn, or detached child may be a victim of emotional abuse.

**Physical**

- Bruises—in linear markings, clusters, on several different areas at a time, and at various stages of healing. May appear after absence, weekend, or vacation.
- Burns—cigarette or cigar, immersion burns (on buttocks and genitalia), patterns (iron, grid), rope or infected burns for which treatment may have been delayed.
- Unexplained bite marks.
- Lacerations or abrasions—typically around mouth, eyes, and external genitalia and may be in various stages of healing.
- Internal injuries.
- Head injury or whiplash—from shaking the child, known as shaken baby syndrome.

**Behavioral**

- Tells you parents or other adult hurt him.
- Overcompliant.
- Poor self-concept.
- Wary of adult contact, may be frightened of parent or parents or other adults.
- Does not want to leave the early childhood education environment.
- Extremes in behavior.
- Feels deserving of punishment.
- Vacant, withdrawn, or detached.
- Indiscriminately seeks affection.
- Chronic ailments—stomachaches, headaches, vomiting.

TABLE 14-5
*Indicators of Emotional Abuse*

**Physical**
- Failure to thrive.
- Withdrawn or depressed.
- Disruptive or hyperactive.
- Speech or language disorders.
- Repetitive rhythmic movements.
- Little facial affect—no signs of emotional response.
- Bedwetting or toileting accidents for older children.

**Behavioral**
- Rigid in conformity to authority.
- Parent is demanding and unrealistic about the capabilities of the child.
- Destructive or antisocial.
- Sleep disorders.
- Unusual fears.
- Behind in mental or emotional development.
- Aggressive or compliant behavioral extremes.

TABLE 14-6
*Indicators of Sexual Abuse*

**Physical**
- Torn, stained, or bloody underclothing.
- Pain, itching, or swelling in genital areas.
- Bruises, lacerations, or bleeding in genital, vaginal, or anal area.
- Discharge in vaginal/genital area.
- Venereal disease.
- Difficulty in walking or sitting.
- Pain when urinating or defecating.

**Behavioral**
- Withdrawn, fantasy, or infantile.
- Poor self-esteem and self-image.
- Poor peer relationships.
- Depression.
- Abrupt changes in behavior such as eating, sleeping, or school performance.
- Excessively clingy or inappropriate attachment.
- Exceptional fear of a person or place.
- Draws scary pictures that include plenty of black and red coloring.
- Inappropriate sexual knowledge or behavior.

# REALITY CHECK

## Shaken Baby Syndrome

Shaken baby syndrome is a form of child maltreatment involving forceful or violent shaking of a child from birth to five years of age (National Institute of Neurological Disorders [NINDS], 2004). More than 50,000 children in the United States are forcefully shaken every year (Zamani, 2003). It is the leading cause of death and accounts for the majority of permanent damage or disability to infants and children who are physically abused (Carbaugh, 2004a). Approximately 15 percent of child maltreatment deaths are due to shaking, and it is possible that another 15 percent may be due to shaking (Massey-Stokes, 2003). It is often difficult to believe that children are maltreated, and especially by shaking a baby (Reece, 2004). It most commonly occurs in children under two years of age, especially those between six and eight months of age (Palmer, 1998).

Children up to the age of five years have been known to have been violently shaken and to have shaken baby syndrome (Zamani, 2003). It is much more common for males to be shaken than females, perhaps due to societal expectations of males (Carbaugh, 2004a). Children with disabilities are more likely to be shaken than those without disabilities. Shaken baby syndrome can also occur as a result of tossing a small child into the air. This type of shaking makes infants and young children especially vulnerable to injury because their heads are larger, their neck muscles are not well developed, and their brain and surrounding tissues are very fragile. The violent shaking of the baby is usually done in anger and frustration. When this type of shaking occurs, it multiplies the force to between five and ten times that which occurs when a child trips or falls. Anyone who might witness this type of force could easily see how the child would be in a life-threatening situation (AAP, 2001). The sudden movements occurring with this type of

force can cause some parts of the brain to pull away. The result is torn brain cells and blood vessels (AHA, 2001b). Babies' brains have a high water content, and the nerve cells in their brains are less likely to have a high level of myelination. Often a young child's brain rotates much more than an adult's brain would.

Shaken baby syndrome does not occur with short falls, seizures, or because a child has been vaccinated. It only occurs through violent shaking, which does not have to last more than 20 seconds or 40–50 shakes to do damage that can be fatal (NCSBS, 2000). Twenty-five to thirty percent from babies who die from child maltreatment die of being shaken. The common triad of injuries for shaken baby syndrome is water on the brain with swelling and subdural and retinal hemorrhages (Harding et al., 2004). These are commonly accompanied by other injuries such as broken ribs. One baby in four dies as a result of shaking. Very few babies escape permanent injury, and most survivors suffer brain damage (AHA, 2001b). Permanent injury for the majority of these babies can range from partial to complete blindness and hearing loss, as well as seizure disorder, cerebral palsy, developmental disabilities, autism, behavior problems, and sucking and swallowing disorders. It can also result in a permanent vegetative state.

Adult males in their twenties who are the father of the child or the boyfriend of the mother are the most common perpetrators of shaking a baby (Carbaugh, 2004a). Estimates that adult males are the perpetrators range from 65 to 90 percent. Often they are involved in domestic violence and substance abuse (AAP, 2001). The most common risk factors for shaken baby syndrome are the following (NCSBS, 2005a; Carbaugh, 2004a):

- Depression, anxiety
- Substance abuse

# REALITY CHECK (Continued)

- Low income
- Social isolation or lack of social support
- Diminished satisfaction with relationship
- Poor family function
- Loss of perceived control, feelings of frustration

Females who shake babies are more likely to be baby-sitters or teachers than mothers. Several recent sensational cases across the nation have focused on teachers who were accused of shaking a baby and causing death or permanent damage.

Immediate medical help can reduce the impact of shaking. Many people who do shake an infant put the child down, thinking he or she will sleep and later wake up and be fine (AAP, 2001). Any opportunity for recovery may be lost during this time. People who shake an infant often claim to have no knowledge of how the child got injured. This claim prevents vital care, because medical tests that take a great deal of time are used to determine the cause of the injury before proper care may be initiated.

Babies who have been shaken exhibit signs that may indicate they have been seriously shaken (Carbaugh, 2004b). These include:

- Poor feeding
- Hard to wake up
- Throwing up
- Breathing problems
- Pooling of blood in the eye
- Weakness
- Seizures
- Coma

When a child is brought to the emergency room with these symptoms and no other apparent reason for this condition, there will always be an investigation by the social agency in charge of child protection (Blumenthal, 2002).

Frustration with a crying child seems to be the biggest cause of the act of shaking. Most people are unaware that this type of shaking can cause permanent damage or death to a child. A normal baby spends between two and three hours a day crying. Approximately one-fourth of infants cry much longer than that. There may be no apparent reason for the crying. Infants in the one- to four-month-old range are most likely to display this excessive crying (NCSBS, 2000). Recently, Dr. Ronald Barr described his discovery called "The Period of PURPLE Crying" (NCSBSb, 2005). He found that babies may tend to cry more and more from birth until about 2 months of age. There is no pattern to the crying, and when the baby cries he may resist any effort at soothing. The infant may look as if he is in pain, even if he isn't. This type of crying typically occurs in the late afternoon and evening and may last at least a half-hour or more. For more information about this type of crying, as well as more links for teachers, visit the Web site, http://www.dontshake.com. This information may make someone who is with a crying infant feel better knowing that it is normal.

A teacher who is easily frustrated or angered may respond by shaking in an attempt to get the baby to stop crying. Shaking may stop the crying, but it may also kill the baby or injure her to the extent that she will never fully recover. It is very important for teachers of young children to understand this and never, ever, shake a baby.

Some methods have worked to help stop a baby from crying. The first step would be to calm down and try to figure out what is making the baby cry. Is the baby crying because she is hungry, wet, too hot, too cold, or over-tired? Does the baby have a fever or is she in pain? The next step is to try to help the baby to relax (Carbaugh, 2004b). Running a vacuum cleaner near the baby, giving her a pacifier, or cuddling the child gently may help to alleviate the crying (AHA, 2001a). Swaddling a baby or rocking him gently, turning down the lights, or even playing some calming music might help. If none of those suggestions work, realize that a baby can be left in a safe place to cry. Walk away after putting the baby in a safe place. This third step keeps the baby safe. Listen to music or call someone for support or advice. If the crying continues, call the doctor. After you have

*(continues)*

## REALITY CHECK (Continued)

calmed down, resume trying to help the baby (Palmer, 1998). If you become desperate, call the parents to come get the child and then call CHILDHELP (800-4-ACHILD) to talk to someone while you wait for the parent. If crying is difficult for you to hear, you may want to consider working with older children, who may be less frustrating for you, or not working with children at all.

Parents should also be educated about shaken baby syndrome (Massey-Stokes, 2003). When parents are educated, the incidence of shaken baby syndrome can be significantly reduced (Dias et al., 2005). Obtain brochures to hand out, and put up a poster warning about shaken baby syndrome. These can found by visiting the National Center on Shaken Baby Syndrome at http://www.dontshake.com, or by faxing 801-627-3321. This will help the parent to better understand and prevent shaking at home. It will also help the parent to understand that it is best for the teacher to call the parent when help is needed. As an infant or very young child enters care, have a handout for the family on how to cope with crying babies. Display this handout on the bulletin board.

**CHECK***point:* What are the steps to take if a baby has cried and cried and you can't seem to stop it and you are getting frustrated?

Children who are unsupervised for long periods of time (a sign of neglect) are at a higher risk for death than children who are physically abused.

***Neglect.*** Neglect causes death more frequently than any other type of child maltreatment (CDF, 2004). Approximately 36 percent of fatalities due to child maltreatment were found to be from neglect in 2003 (HHS, 2005). Neglect of a child includes depriving the child of food, shelter, medical care, supervision, or education. Negligence occurs both in actions and in failure to act on behalf of the child. Severe neglect includes intentional failure to provide and allowing danger to the child's person or health. Table 14-7 includes the indicators of neglect.

**TABLE 14-7**
*Indicators of Neglect*

**Physical**

- Always hungry, dirty, or inappropriately dressed.
- Lacks medical or dental care.
- Lack of supervision, especially for long periods of time.
- Unsanitary home.
- Abandonment.
- Underweight, poor growth.
- Consistently absent from school.
- Signs of hunger.
- Fingernails are long and dirty.

**Behavioral**

- Stealing or begging for food or money for food.
- Parent brings child early and picks up late.
- Inappropriate attachment or affection.
- Shows or expresses no emotions.
- Parent abusing drugs or alcohol.
- Overly responsible; assumes adult role.

## Documentation

If the teacher suspects or has reason to believe that maltreatment is occurring, then it must be reported. The teacher does not have to personally witness the maltreatment or have positive proof that it occurred. Teachers need to understand how to document suspected child maltreatment and how to report it (Palmer & Smith, 2002a).

Observing children is one of the major jobs of a teacher. The teacher needs to be aware of the indicators of maltreatment that may be observed in order to notice a problem. The teacher should observe the child at different times of day and in different settings and record the observations in note form.

The teacher should record behavior, conversation, and physical signs. This type of anecdotal record may signify a pattern that indicates maltreatment is present. It may also indicate that there is no pattern present and what the teacher noticed about a bruise and limp might have been a result of a fall. The records should be kept in the child's health record in case there is need to refer to them again. If a teacher is still uncertain, he or she should talk to others on the staff to see what they think. In the end, if the teacher reasonably suspects that maltreatment has occurred, it must be reported.

## Reporting

If the teacher needs to report child maltreatment, the reporting process should be clear. In most states there is a Child Welfare Office or Child Protective Services. If the teacher is unsure, the local Department of Social Services or law enforcement agency should be contacted, well before any suspected maltreatment is observed. There may be forms that the teacher needs to keep on hand. The teacher should also inquire whether there is a 24-hour hotline so the number may be posted.

When a report is filed, the child's name, address, and age must be included. The parents' names and address or addresses (if they have separate homes) should also be given. The teacher's name and address should also be given. Anonymity for the teacher will be provided. The teacher must realize that the parents might be able to tell who reported the maltreatment, because it is likely that the teacher has more information about the child than anyone else.

The teacher may want to talk to the parent before reporting the maltreatment. Some parents may be relieved that help is available, although anger and hostility are another common reaction and may result in the parents' removing the child from the early childhood education environment. If the teacher decides to tell the parents before the report, once again, she should explain the requirement to report any suspected maltreatment. As difficult as it may be to tell the parents before reporting the suspected maltreatment, it may be better that they still have trust in the teacher for her honesty. The best course is for the teacher to plan to help the parents through the process. Supporting the family after reporting maltreatment is often a center-based responsibility and includes referrals to meet the needs of the family.

A roadblock that a teacher may run into is reluctance to report maltreatment. Human emotions enter into matters that are this grave. Reluctance may be based on the teacher's personal background, lack of support from supervisory personnel, or family rights issues. In some cultures, a family's rights over their children are deeply held beliefs (Zamani, 2000). The teacher may feel nervous or emotional about this because of her own family experiences. She may fear that the parents will retaliate or that they will pull their child out of the early childhood education environment. The teacher may even fear that she will lose her job. Often, the teacher may feel she is betraying the child and the family by reporting suspected maltreatment (Nunnelley & Fields, 1999). "Knowing how, when and what to report about child abuse and neglect may make a life or death difference for a child" (AHA, 2001a).

## Caring for the Maltreated Child

If maltreatment is blatant and puts the child in real danger, the child may be removed from the family. If this is the case, the courts, foster families, or other family members who gain custody of the child may wish to continue to keep the child in the early childhood education situation, so as to maintain some consistency in the child's life.

> *Pause for Reflection*
>
> Could you easily report suspected child maltreatment, or would that be a roadblock for you?

Domestic violence is a problem for families of all languages and cultures.

Teachers need to understand how to support a child and her family or custodian after maltreatment has been established. The first step in this process is for the teacher to examine her confidence level, her knowledge of human development, and how she feels about the maltreatment. How the teacher feels about herself will affect whether she can offer support. If the teacher has a low confidence level, it will be difficult to help the child raise his.

The teacher needs to determine her level of understanding about what is normal behavior. She needs to understand what behaviors need to be redirected. These factors will determine the skill level the teacher has to do the job. The child may need to address factors of his social and emotional development process. Can the teacher help a child learn to trust and live within safe boundaries? Judging the maltreatment can impede the teacher's ability to perform. Placing blame and being angry will not help the teacher perform her job.

It is estimated that one of every three women was sexually abused as a child (Stith, 1998). If the teacher has personally suffered from abuse in some form as a child, there may be unresolved feelings. Will these feelings hinder the relationship with the child or parent?

If the teacher determines that she is capable of helping and supporting a maltreated child, there are several critical things that he or she can provide:

- trust
- predictable routines
- consistent behavior
- safe boundaries
- confidence
- good communication skills

These will offer the child the sense of well-being needed to progress beyond the maltreatment.

# REALITY CHECK

## Domestic Violence and Its Effect on Children's Lives

The home can be a more dangerous place than the streets. Women are nine times more likely to get hurt in the home than on the streets. Three-quarters of domestic violence occurs in the home (Children's Defense Fund, 2004). Domestic violence usually involves a pattern of assaultive and/or coercive behaviors toward an intimate partner. This can be physical, sexual, or emotional abuse (NAIC, 2004b). It is estimated that between 25 and 30 percent of women have been beaten at least one time in an intimate relationship. Studies indicate that the number of children that witness domestic violence and the maltreatment of their mothers ranges from 3.3 to 10 million (Family Violence Prevention Fund [FVPF], 2004). Witnessing maltreatment can include hearing it, seeing it, and knowing about it. A child may not have seen or heard the act occurring, but he or she may indeed be able to see the results by observing cuts, bruises, and broken bones. Maltreatment ranges from insults to beatings to homicide (Osofsky, 1999). Experts believe that domestic violence is the single major precursor that leads to child abuse and neglect. Studies have found that in homes where domestic violence is present, children are 15 times more likely to be physically abused or neglected. It has been estimated that in 60 to 75 percent of homes where the mother is battered, the children are also battered. (Osofsky, 1999).

Changes that have occurred in family systems in recent decades have led to greater stress in families. Some of these changes include poverty, social isolation, low educational levels, marital discord, and lack of coping abilities. All of these can lead to child maltreatment. Families are no longer like those that were portrayed on television in the 1950s and 1960s. Divorce affects almost one in two families, and more than one in four families are headed by a single parent. Parents may not be able to stay at home with children due to economic stresses, so younger children may be in nonparental care and older children may become latchkey children. More families with children live in poverty, and there is a greater degree of drug and alcohol abuse than we have previously seen in this country. All of these factors contribute to stress that can manifest in domestic violence.

Domestic violence occurs at every socioeconomic level and in every racial, cultural, religious, and ethnic group. Men are more likely than women to commit domestic violence. Men who had witnessed domestic violence in their homes as they were growing up were found to be twice as likely to abuse the women in their life as men who had not (FVPF, 2004). Women who commit domestic violence usually do so in self-defense or in retaliation for abuse.

Even if children themselves are not maltreated, witnessing abuse can have traumatic effects on them. Witnessing violence may lead to fear, discipline problems, depression, poor social interaction, and drug abuse among children (FNMPD, 2001). Long-term effects may include posttraumatic stress disorder and personality disorders (Groves, 2003). Physical problems can be present as well as cognitive developmental delays (NAIC, 2004b). Witnessing violence may lead to children's performing violent acts as they get older (Garbarino, 2001).

It has been reported that 79 percent of children in institutions for violent behavior have witnessed violence. Boys who witness violence are more likely than girls to act out. They are three times more likely to become abusive to their domestic partners later in life. Girls are much more likely to allow abuse to occur to them as women. Both behaviors perpetuate domestic violence.

## REALITY CHECK (Continued)

Many professionals believe that witnessing domestic violence is the most harmful type of violence that a child could experience (Groves, 2003). When children see violence in their own homes with their own families, they realize that they have no safe place. Even a child under the age of one year can still have memory of when domestic violence or child maltreatment occurred (Gaensbauer, 2004). If a child cannot feel safe at home, he is less likely to develop trust and later explore his environment. Without trust and exploration, achieving autonomy as a normal course of development is difficult. Children may also feel guilty that they could not prevent the act or that they did something to trigger the act (FNMPD, 2001). Children who witness domestic violence may become anxious and fearful under most conditions.

Children who have an adult they can trust are likely to cope better. Frequent positive inter-actions can help a child feel safe (ACT, 2001). The most protective factor for a child who does not feel safe at home is the existence of a strong, positive relationship between the child and a competent and caring adult (Kersey & Malley, 2005). Teachers can provide this type of relationship and can develop trust between themselves and the children in their care. Teachers can help to foster resiliency and teach children conflict resolution. Providing these types of supportive relationships for vulnerable children is being encouraged for inclusion in the early childhood education environment (Kersey & Malley, 2005).

Teachers can model prosocial behaviors and help children have a greater sense of acceptance and self-esteem. Children can be praised and recognized for good behaviors and redirected away from aggressive behaviors. Teachers can also provide a safe haven from a difficult home life for a few hours a day.

**CHECK***point:* **What protective factors could a teacher provide for a child who has witnessed domestic violence?**

## Key Concept 14.3

### Protective Measures for Child Maltreatment

Protective measures such as recognition of maltreatment, documentation, and reporting give teachers the tools needed to protect children from maltreatment. The teacher should be able to recognize the physical and behavioral indicators of physical abuse, emotional abuse, sexual abuse, and neglect. The teacher should understand the procedures for documenting and reporting maltreatment, and know the practices and strategies that will offer care to a maltreated child.

## 14.4  WORKING WITH CHILDREN FROM SUBSTANCE-ABUSING FAMILIES

It is estimated that 30 percent of drug abusers are women of childbearing age. As many as 24 percent of children in this country may have been pre-natally exposed to harmful substances (NIDA, 1998). Prenatal exposure to drugs can cause developmental difficulties in several areas:

- Children may be unable to organize their own play.

- Sporadic mastery is common.
- Learning strategies and problem solving may be hindered by a lack of organization of inner states.
- Communication and language development may be impaired by delayed acquisition of words and gestures, inability to express feelings, and speech difficulties.
- Difficulty with motor skills may be exhibited in both gross and fine motor skills.
- Acquiring a sense of self may be hampered by lack of attachment or inconsistent or negligent care.

All of these vulnerabilities can be assessed through observation and the use of assessment tools. Women who enter drug treatment programs often have custodial children and few economic resources (Hanson, 2002). Approximately 80 percent of the perpetrators of child maltreatment are parents (HHS, 2005), and almost one-half of parents who maltreat children have some substance abuse problems (ChildHelp USA, 2004). These families may present a great challenge to the teacher. The families may be represented in several ways:

- the recovering family, who may be feeling vulnerable
- the addicted family living in chaos, who may be emotionally unavailable or negligent
- the foster family or kinship caregiver (related to the child), who may feel overwhelmed

**FIGURE 14-3**
**Downward Spiral of Addiction**

Distrust

Unhappiness

Denial

Irritability

Loss of interest

Self-defense

Depression

Self-neglect

Loss of self-respect

Dishonesty

Isolation

Indefinable fears

Hostility

Blames others

Escape

Chronic depression

Increased drug use

Suicide attempts or admits defeat

Bottoming out and into recovery or death

## *The Recovering Family*

The recovering family may be in or out of a recovery program. The parent or parents may have few coping skills. The parents may be developmentally "frozen" at the stage where they were in their own development when they began abusing drugs. They may be emotionally unavailable and struggling with attachment issues. They may be struggling to remain clean. The environment may be chaotic. The parents also feel aware for the first time in a long time, especially if they have been in recovery for a while. This may make them feel ashamed and guilty for what they have put their children through. Many of these parents could use the role modeling from a teacher to understand what is the way to treat children. The teacher should try to create a sense of trust so that information about parenting can be passed along through conversation and other measures found in Table 14-2.

## *The Actively Abusing Family*

The addictive family brings a whole series of problems. As people who abuse drugs go through the cycle of abuse, there is a tendency to get hostile when dealing with people in authority. Figure 14-3 shows the feelings that the downward spiral of addiction can cause in an active substance-abusing family.

Substance-abusing families live in an extremely chaotic environment. Children from this environment may have difficulty getting their physical needs met. There may not be food or clean clothes available for them. They may suffer great stress from negligent or inconsistent care at home. It is estimated that in 50 percent of cases where parents maltreat their children, substance abuse is involved (ChildHelp USA, 2004).

It is very difficult for a child to be able to count on a substance-abusing parent to meet the child's needs. Behavioral problems with a child may directly relate to active drug use in the home (Delaney-Black et al., 2000). An active substance abuser may have sudden mood swings that display the person as being either really up or really down and depressed. It is difficult to predict whether the person will show up when expected for appointments, including bringing the child to care. An addict may lose track of time or suffer from a hangover. Another common characteristic of an active abuser is the avoidance of contact with concerned persons. "Isolation is the core of addiction" ("The Battlefield," 1993, p. 37). A parent who is actively abusing drugs or alcohol may have difficulty forming a bond of trust with anyone and may be emotionally unavailable to the child or the teacher. Abusing families put their children at risk. They may fear that if help is sought, the child will be removed from the home. The family addictive system may discourage any behavior changes.

---

*Pause for Reflection*

Do you know the statistics for substance abuse in your community? Do you know the drug most commonly abused? Have you ever known someone with a substance abuse problem? Can you relate to the section on "The Actively Abusing Family"?

---

## The Foster or Kinship Family

Foster families or kinship families in which the caretaker is a relative may have their own difficulties. Legal custody of the child may be in flux. The parents may still have legal custody. The circumstances that led the child to this caretaker situation may have an effect on the caretakers. They may be sad, angry, depressed, or overwhelmed. If the parent of the child is around and wants to participate in the child's life, that can cause difficulties. There may be legal boundaries that have been or need to be mandated. The teacher will need to be aware of these or any other legal custody issues. Teachers can also assist these families by recognizing that extra help may be needed both in the early childhood education environment and in the home. Teachers can help the family access social services to support them through the difficulties they may encounter.

## Establishing a Relationship with the Family

Establishing a relationship with the family is a crucial step in the intervention process to help a child from a substance-abusing family. Providing a safe and secure environment for the parent and family is almost as critical as providing that type of care for the child. As difficult as it may be, the teacher should try to establish communication with the parent concerning the child. The teacher should be consistent and predictable in this relationship, and should use cultural competence if applicable. The

Many grandparents are actively involved in their grandchildren's lives. As many as 10 percent are helping to raise these children, and the majority of these children have at least one parent with a substance abuse problem.

teacher who tries to show respect to the family is more likely to be accepted by them.

According to the 2000 U.S. Census, approximately 4.5 million children in this country are living in households headed by grandparents. Almost one-half of those children are there because of their parents' substance abuse. More than 50 percent of these children are younger than six years of age (EAAA, 2004). Regardless whether the family is a foster family or a kinship family such as grandparents raising grandchildren, legal custody of the child may be in flux. Becoming a kinship family usually happens in one of three ways. The most common way is for families to take the children in without reporting the parents to a child protective service and avoiding the court system. Parents can also "drop off" their children for a visit and not return for months or years. Both of these situations usually help the children, but they do offer some legal issues for both the teacher and the kin that will need to be addressed. The third way is for kin to be given guardianship through the juvenile or dependency court system. In this case, they do have custody, so there are no legal issues.

Many teachers try to avoid difficult situations involving parents. They may also avoid difficult parents (Boutte et al., 1992). Children in this situation need the support of the teacher. The teacher should avoid arguing with the parent, getting angry, being taken in by the parent's defensiveness and becoming an enabler. The teacher should model good coping skills, be flexible, remain calm and nonjudgmental, and be culturally competent. It might help the teacher to practice possible parent responses and be prepared to answer them. If none of these suggestions work, respect the limitations of your abilities (Gonzalez-Mena & Stonehouse, 2000). You may need outside help in the form of a counselor or drug counselor in your area.

### *Working with the Children*

The teacher needs to provide a safe and protective environment. Good child development techniques are essential. A child at risk can be a challenge. The teacher may need to add some protective and facilitative factors to his skills. The best thing that the teacher can do is to provide consistent, predictable, and reliable care. These measures can improve the quality of interaction with the child and help to form an attachment bond.

The child at risk may need to be protected from overstimulation. The teacher can help the child by creating a quiet, safe place to retreat. Transition times may stress the child at risk. The teacher can provide structure and clear limits to help make the transition more manageable. These measures also allow the child to understand boundaries and acceptable behaviors. Recent studies have shown that if the child at risk is able to find someone with whom to develop a secure attachment, that child is likely to be able to overcome nonmedical behavioral, and developmental difficulties (Groves, 2003). A child at risk from a substance-abusing environment will have to find reliable bonds with other people. The teacher who helps a child in this way may give the child the tools needed to find other adults to rely on.

If the situation at home is intolerable, the teacher may have to report the situation to the local Child Protective Services office. If the child or children are removed from the home environment, it is possible that Child Protective Services will work with the foster family or relative caring for the children to continue in the early childhood education situation. The consistency of the teacher and the early childhood education environment will be a very important source of support to the child.

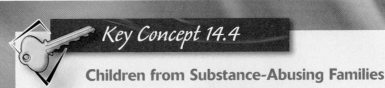

### Key Concept 14.4

### Children from Substance-Abusing Families

Many teachers may find themselves working with children from substance-abusing families. They should learn to recognize the indicators for this condition. Teachers who understand the family situation are more likely to be able to help. Families may be in recovery, may be active abusers, or may be a foster or kinship family that has complex issues to address. Teachers can work more productively by developing good communication and trust with these families and their children.

## 14.5  IMPLICATIONS FOR TEACHERS

Teachers need to see that a policy is created for child maltreatment. The policy should include the processes needed to help prevent child maltreatment and protect the children in care. These methods and strategies should include education, working with families, cultural competence, observation, and supervision. Education for the teachers, as well as the parents and children, offers prevention and protection. Cultural competence is crucial, because in some cultures child maltreatment may not be seen as a problem but a parental right. Observation helps the teacher to recognize and document maltreatment. Supervision maintains a set of checks and balances to provide protection for the children in the early childhood education environment and prevent some maltreatment from occurring.

## Education

It is essential that the teacher understand what child maltreatment is and how to recognize it. Awareness and familiarity with the indicators of abuse in four areas—physical, emotional, sexual, and neglect—can help a teacher observe for them. Teachers need to understand the process to report maltreatment because they are the mandated reporters of child abuse. The teacher must know how to report maltreatment, and in order to do so he or she must know how to document for accuracy and support.

*With Children.* The teacher can help to educate the child about what is and what is not acceptable behavior between the child and an adult. The teacher can promote safety from sexual abuse from an early stage. At eighteen months, children can learn about body parts. From three to five years of age, they can learn about the body parts and what parts are unacceptable for others to touch. At each age and stage, there is something children can learn to identify "bad touches" to avoid. A child who learns to use the word "no" will be empowered to help protect herself.

A child who learns to achieve mastery in her life by making choices may be more prepared to act if she is abused. A teacher can provide opportunities that allow the child choices.

A teacher can model self-control, verbalize feelings and fears, and provide a predictable, stable environment. These actions will offer the child a protective environment where she feels safe enough to talk. A child who experiences this environment may be more willing to share difficulties in her life.

## For the Families

Education can also be a tool to help the teacher to prevent maltreatment. Having methods and strategies for working with children and parents can help the teacher offer greater protection for the children. The teacher can

Cultural competence and good communication skills will assist a teacher in dealing with children and their families to help prevent child maltreatment and protect the children in their care.

educate the parents and children to help prevent maltreatment. Parents can be educated about normal child development and the behaviors that can be expected at that point of development. Parents who have an understanding of the capabilities of their children may have more realistic expectations. The teacher should keep an open line of communication with the parents. They can share common concerns about the child or about stress in the family environment. This can help to form a partnership. The teacher can also support the parent during times of stress or other difficulties by providing referrals or resources. Teachers may help reduce the likelihood of child maltreatment by family members. Working with families and giving them support may help to break the cycle of abuse (NAEYC, 1997).

## Cultural Competence

- **Immigrant**
  *one who leaves a country to settle in another*
- **Migrant**
  *a transient who travels from place to place to find work*

Cultural competence is a preventive measure. The process of childrearing may be culturally defined. What is normal and acceptable in one culture may not be considered normal or acceptable in another. The United States has large **immigrant** and **migrant** populations that are ever increasing. A teacher who cares for children from a culture other than his own should try to learn about the childrearing practices and behavior of that culture. Some of the diverse cultural practices that may be seen as child maltreatment include female circumcision, coining, cupping, scarring, and burning of the skin; and use of poisonous herbal remedies (Zamani, 2000).

The family's view on discipline and punishment may be in conflict with the laws of this country. Some cultures believe in corporal punishment as a consequence for violating a rule of unquestioning obedience and unrealistic expectations. The teacher can ask a family about their cultural customs. This is a good way to understand if this is the case. If it is the case, the teacher may need to begin a dialogue with the family. The teacher should show respect about differing cultural beliefs of the family, but should also clearly inform them about the law (Gonzalez-Mena, 1997).

Families who recently immigrated or migrated may have experienced a great deal of stress (Duarte & Rafanello, 2001). Stressful events related to the relocation of families may affect their psychological well-being. Strange customs, lack of support networks, and inability to speak English may all contribute to the stress of a child and family.

## Observation

Observation is the most important tool that a teacher has to protect a child from maltreatment. The observation for signs and symptoms of child maltreatment can make the teacher aware of the possibility that the child's safety and well-being are in jeopardy. Observation is also the key tool for documentation of suspected maltreatment. A good observer will use the tools of the senses to report what was seen, heard, felt, and smelled.

Observation also plays a part in preventing maltreatment. It is important to observe the early childhood education environment for practices that offer prevention from maltreatment. The teacher may also observe for the stressors and behaviors of families, because the teacher can intervene before maltreatment takes place.

# REALITY CHECK

## Helping Vulnerable Children to Become Resilient

Some children manage to thrive despite much stress and turmoil in their lives. Other children who have very little stress and turmoil in their lives may not manage as well. According to researchers, the terminology for these two circumstances is referred to as a child's resiliency or vulnerability (Osofsky, 1999).

A child who is vulnerable may be so due to a variety of factors. These factors may be inborn and include genetic abnormalities, malnutrition, preterm birth, prenatal stress, or drug exposure. Temperament may also be a factor. Difficult children have a harder time adapting and getting into a rhythm in life. Parents may have a more difficult time coping with and attaching to a difficult child.

Outside circumstances that may make a child more vulnerable are usually related to significant relationships. The bonding process is extremely important. Children who are insecurely attached may be more vulnerable to outside environmental stresses such as poverty, abandonment, or chaotic living. A child whose physical circumstances may make him vulnerable can have that vulnerability lessened by having a secure attachment to a significant person in his life (Osofsky, 1999). First-born children who begin life with no physical difficulties and who are easy in temperament are thought to be most resilient (Werner & Smith, 2001).

Child abuse or neglect can also be a major factor in making a child vulnerable. We know that resiliency can be fostered and that there is no special timeline for it. Children don't become resilient on their own. They must have a connection to someone who has faith in them (Breslin, 2005). They need to feel good about themselves and their capabilities.

There are protective factors that can foster resilience in children. These include having caring and supportive relationships, positive and high expectations, and opportunities for meaningful participation (Kersey & Malley,

2005). Grotberg (1999) has described a resilient child in the framework of three factors:

1. I HAVE (strong relationships, structure and rules at home, role models, encouragement, access to services)
   Building block = TRUST
2. I AM (lovable and my temperament is appealing, proud of myself, a person who has hope and faith, cares about others)
   Building block = AUTONOMY, IDENTITY
3. I CAN (manage my feelings and impulses, seek trusting relationships, communicate with others, solve problems)
   Building block = INITIATIVE, INDUSTRY

Breslin (2005) also identified four major characteristics that resilient children appear to have: heightened sensory awareness; high, positive expectations; a clear and ongoing understanding of one's strengths and abilities; and a well-developed sense of humor. Armed with this knowledge, Breslin believes that those particular resilient behaviors can be enhanced and supported by a teacher.

Emmy Werner and Ruth Smith (2001) have done a 40-year study on resilience in children as they grow into adulthood. They have found that children who begin life as vulnerable can be helped to become resilient. The most important factor they found was that, if a child has one significant, trusting relationship with an adult, he or she will be able to seek out that type of relationship with others. If that trusted person can help foster social competence, the child will be more likely to have the ability to communicate, to respond with caring, to have a sense of humor and the ability to attract others, and to identify those who can be resources. A trusted person can help a child learn problem-solving skills, foster imagination, and teach about initiative. A child with those abilities will have the ability to organize and have a greater degree of

# REALITY CHECK (Continued)

coping skills. A trusted person who gives a child a sense of autonomy can help the child have a healthier sense of self-esteem and feel more under control about life. This can give a child a sense of purpose and optimism for the future.

Resilient children find it much easier to develop key trusting relationships with an adult. This adult can be a parent, grandparent, other relative, or a teacher. This relationship allows the resilient child the freedom to know that she is significant. As long as the resilient child has someone who cares for her, she can handle almost any situation that comes along.

Both vulnerability and resiliency are significant to the teacher. The teacher may watch a vulnerable child who is insecurely attached have great difficulty coping with life. She may observe a resilient child cope with problems that seem insurmountable. The more supportive the environment is for either of these children, the less the stress.

The vulnerable child may need extra support from the teacher through responsive and stimulating care (Levin, 1999). He may need the teacher to adapt to his needs. The vulnerable child will definitely benefit from a secure attachment with the teacher. This factor can help the child deal with other factors in his life.

The teacher can help to foster resiliency in the vulnerable child by providing:

- Unconditional love
- Comfort, including physical holding, rocking, and soothing
- Consistency
- Clear limits
- Stability
- Security
- Expectations of success and opportunities to succeed
- Praise for accomplishment
- Encouragement to try new things and to do so with minimal help
- Opportunities for meaningful participation
- Acknowledgment and labeling of the child's feelings so that he or she can identify those feelings and be able to recognize them in others
- Encouragement to use problem-solving skills
- Support for increasing persistence
- Help for children to accept responsibility for behaviors and consequences
- Acceptance in times of error, behavior difficulties
- Materials that allow the child to use and develop her imagination
- Materials and opportunities to explore new things

The teacher can also model confidence and optimism, good self-esteem, and flexibility. By communicating verbal expressions of caring and calming and by sharing positive feelings, a teacher can reassure the child of her value.

The resilient child will need the care and support of the teacher, much as a cheerleader helps a team play a game. Although this child is already equipped for success, he will need the secure attachment of an adult to remain successful. If a secure attachment with an adult is unavailable elsewhere but is found at the early childhood education environment, the child may retain his resiliency to the problems and stresses that life may bring (ACT, 2001).

It is important to remember that dealing with a vulnerable child is not easy. The teacher needs to remember not to get enmeshed in the family's life while helping the child. Not everything can be easily fixed. The teacher should accept what is not in his control and learn to only control that which can be controlled. He should share feelings with others and not bottle up frustration, anger, or sadness that might come when working with a child who is vulnerable. If outside help is needed, then resources should be used. The teacher needs to remember to take time each day for himself so that he does not become vulnerable to the situation.

**CHECK***point:* Name what you consider to be the five most protective factors you could offer to a child who might be vulnerable.

### *Supervision*

Everyone in the teacher's employ must be trained to recognize, document, and report maltreatment. Employees should learn to recognize their own stress. The teacher should supervise the early childhood education environment to prevent any situation or practice that does not offer protection from, and prevention of, child maltreatment. Discipline should be supervised to make sure it is correct and that all teachers offer good guidance and discipline and do not cross the line into punishment.

The teacher should supervise to make sure all protective measures such as recognition, documentation, and reporting of child maltreatment are done when necessary, in the right way, and in a timely manner. It is important for the teacher to supervise the care of a maltreated child and to make sure the child is being offered a supportive environment. The teacher should make sure the child's health, safety, and well-being are promoted by healthy interactions.

## Key Concept 14.5

### Implications for Teachers

The teacher can promote a safe environment by using tools that prevent and protect children from child maltreatment. The tools of education, working with families, cultural competence, observation, and supervision can help the teacher to offer a safe environment for the well-being of the children in care. Education helps the teacher recognize abuse-related behaviors and the four types of abuse. It helps the teacher understand how to document and report maltreatment. Education gives the teacher strategies to help the maltreated child. Cultural competence may offer an intervening measure to prevent children from being maltreated. Observation is the major tool used to recognize, document, and report maltreatment. Supervision provides the necessary checks to make sure the environment is offering protection and prevention of abuse.

## CHAPTER SUMMARY

Considering the large number of children who are abused or neglected each year, teachers should learn preventive, protective, and promotional measures that will help provide for children's well-being. Policies should be created that will help the teacher ensure preventive measures such as freedom from accusation and the ability to intervene. Protective measures such as recognizing maltreatment, documentation, and reporting give teachers the tools needed to protect children from maltreatment. The teacher should know the practices and strategies that will offer care to a maltreated child. The tools of education, working with families, cultural competence, observation, and supervision can help the teacher to provide an environment that offers safety and well-being to the children in care.

## TO GO BEYOND

In this section you will find a number of activities that you can use to apply and improve your knowledge of this chapter. There are also thorough online resources that accompany this text that can be found at http://www.early childed.delmar.com (see description at end of this chapter).

### Chapter Review Critical Thinking Applications

1. Define and discuss the different forms of child maltreatment.
2. Describe some of the factors that are involved in child maltreatment, including what might lead an adult to abuse a child.
3. Explain how child maltreatment is recognized.
4. Describe how a teacher would report child maltreatment.
5. Explain how you would prevent shaken baby syndrome.

### As an Individual

1. Collect information about child abuse services available in your community.
2. Research shaken baby syndrome, finding at least two articles on the topic. Write a one-page paper on the subject and be prepared to discuss it in class. Why is it important to understand this topic?
3. List ways that cultural differences might affect child maltreatment. Be prepared to discuss in class.

### As a Group

1. Watch a film or video that describes child maltreatment. Compare the film with the reality of child maltreatment. Was the film/video realistic?
2. Invite a speaker from the local child abuse hotline to talk about reporting child maltreatment.
3. Invite a local physician who deals with child maltreatment in the emergency room to speak and describe what he or she sees occurring in your own community.
4. Examine some factors in today's society that might lead to child maltreatment. Especially discuss domestic violence and its effect on the family.
5. Discuss the conflicting feelings that a teacher who suspects abuse has in making the decision to report. What should be done to ensure the right decision is made?
6. Create a policy for child abuse reporting for child care.

### Case Studies

1. Thomas, a three-year-old, bites Lordes when she won't give him the ball she is playing with. Angela, the lead teacher at your site, grabs Thomas by the arm and, while she is screaming and yelling

at him for having bitten Lordes, she bites Thomas and says "Here, let's see how you like it when someone bites you!" Of course, Thomas starts to cry then Angela yells, "Stop it right now, you big baby, or I'll really give you something to cry about!" With that, Angela storms off the playground and leaves you with this situation. What will you do now and what will you do later?

2. The D'Amigo family has a new baby daughter. Their three-year-old, Emilio, is in your class. Emilio used to be a happy, outgoing little boy but now he is withdrawn and anxious. He clings to you every day when his father drops him off, and he cries when it is time to go home. He seems to be exhausted and each day sleeps soundly at naptime. What do you think?

3. One day while you are observing during free play, Duran, Micah, and Devonne are in the dramatic play area. Devonne and Duran are twins. Devonne is pretending to be the mom and Micah is the child and Duran is the dad. You hear Devonne say, "Micah you are a bad little boy and I am going to send you to bed without any supper." Duran then says, "Come here, you bad boy, I am going to give you a whipping." At that point, Duran takes a belt and pretends to hit Micah with it. How should you proceed?

## Chapter References

Adults and Children Together (ACT). 2001. Violence prevention for teachers of young children. Retrieved May 15, 2002, from http://www.apa.org/pi/preventviolence/act.html.

American Academy of Pediatrics (AAP). (2001). Shaken baby syndrome: Rotational cranial injuries—technical report. Committee on Child Abuse and Neglect. *Pediatrics, 108*(1), 206–210.

American Humane Association (AHA). (2001a). America's children: How are they doing? Retrieved May 15, 2002, from http://www.americanhumane.org/children/factsheets/amer_child.htm.

American Humane Association (AHA). (2001b). Shaken baby syndrome. Retrieved May 15, 2002, from http://www.americanhumane.org/children/factsheets/shake.htm.

The Battlefield of addiction. (1993, July 19). *Maclean's.* Special report. 36–39.

Blumenthal, I. (2004). Shaken baby syndrome. *Postgrad Medical Journal, 78*(926), 732–735.

Breslin, D. (2005). Children's capacity to develop resiliency—how to nurture it. *Young Children, 60*(1), 47–58.

Carbaugh, S. (2004a). Understanding shaken baby syndrome. *Advances in Neonatal Care, 4*(2), 105–114.

Carbaugh, S. (2004b). Understanding shaken baby syndrome. *Advances in Neonatal Care, 4*(2), 188–119.

Center for the Study of Social Policy (CPPS). (2004). A new, effective and affordable strategy for child abuse and neglect prevention. Retrieved October 31, 2005, from http:///www.cssp.org/uploadFiles/brochure.pdf

ChildHelp USA (CHU). (2004). National child abuse statistics. Retrieved October 31, 2005, from http://www.childhelpusa.org/abuseinfo_stats.htm#substance

Children's Defense Fund (CDF). (2004). Domestic violence and its impact on children. Retrieved November 26, 2004 from http://www.childrendefense.org/childwelfare/domesticviolence/factsheet.asp

Crosson-Tower, C. (2002). *Understanding child abuse and neglect.* Boston, MA: Allyn and Bacon.

Delaney-Black, V., Covington, C., Templin, T., Ager, J., Nordstrom-Klee, B., Martier, S., Leddick, L., Czerwinski, R., & Sokol, R. (2000). Teacher-assessed behavior of children prenatally exposed to cocaine. *Pediatrics, 106*(4), 782–791.

Dias, M., Smith, K., Deguehery, K., Mazur, P., Li, V., & Shaffer, M. (2005). Preventing abusive head trauma among infants and young children: A hospital based, parent education program. *Pediatrics, 115*(4), 470–477.

Donnelly, A. (1992). Healthy families in America. *Children Today, 21*(2), 25–26.

Duarte, G., & Rafanello, D. (2001). The migrant child: A special place in the field. *Young Children, 56*(2), 26–34.

Egyptian Area Agency on Aging (EAAA). (2004). Statistics for grandparents raising grandchildren. Retrieved October 31, 2005, from http://www.egyptianaaa.org/GRGstatistics.htm.

Family Violence Prevention Fund (FVPF) (2004). The facts on children and domestic violence. Retrieved October 31, 2005, from http://endabuse.org/resources/facts/Children.pdf

Fantuzzo, J., & Mohr, W. (1999). Prevalence and effects of child exposure to domestic violence. Center for the Future of Children: The David and Lucille Packard Foundation. *The Future of Children, 9*(3), 21–32.

Farmington, New Mexico Police Department (FNMPD). (2001). How domestic violence affects children. Retrieved May 15, 2002, from http://www.farmington.nm.us/dept/police/domesticviolence/affectchildren.html

Florida is using day care workers to monitor kids in state custody. (2004). *Child Protection Report, 30*(3), 19.

Fullwood, C. (2002). *Preventing family violence: Community engagement makes the difference.* San Francisco: Family Violence Prevention Fund. Retrieved October 31, 2005 from http://endabuse.org/programs/children/files/Preventing.pdf.

Gaensbauer, T. (2004). Telling their stories: Representation and reenactment of traumatic experiences occurring in the first year of life. *Zero to Three, 24*(5), 25–31.

Garbarino, J. (2001). Violent children: Where do we point the finger of blame? *Archives of Pediatrics and Adolescent Medicine, 155*(1), 13–14.

Gonzalez-Mena, J. (1997). *Multicultural issues in child care.* Mountain View, CA: Mayfield Publishing.

Gonzalez-Mena, J., & Stonehouse, A. (2000, January). High-maintenance parents. *Child Care Information Exchange,* 10–12.

Grotberg, E. (1999). A guide to promoting resilience in children: Strengthening the human spirit. In B. Cesarone (Ed.). *Resilience Guide: A Collection of Resources on Resilience in Children and Families.* Champaign, IL: ERIC Clearinghouse on Elementary and Early Childhood Education Retrieved October 31, 2005, from http://resilnet.uiuc.edu/library/grotb95b.html

Groves, B. (2003). *Children who see too much: Lessons from the child witness to violence project.* New York: Houghton Mifflin.

Groves, B. (2001). Children who witness violence. Family Communications. Retrieved October 31, 2005, from http://www/fci.org/early_care/violence_witness_article.asp.

Groves, B., Lieberman, A., Osofsky, J., & Fenichel, E. (2000, April/May). Protecting young children in violent environments: A framework to build on. *Zero to Three, 5.*

Hanson, G. (2002, May). In drug abuse, gender matters. In *National Institute of Drug Abuse Articles that Address Women and Gender Differences 17*(2). Retrieved from http://www.drugabuse.gov/PDF/NNCollections/NNWomenGender.pdf

Harding, B., Risdon, R., & Krous, H. (2004). Shaken baby syndrome. *British Medical Journal, 328*(3), 700–721.

Kersey, K., & Malley, C. (2005). Helping children develop resiliency: Providing supportive relationships. *Young Children, 60*(1), 53–58.

National Association for the Education of Young Children (NAEYC). (2004). Where we stand on child abuse prevention. Retrieved 11/6/05 from http://www.naeyc.org/about/positions/pdf/ChildAbuseStand.pdf#xml=http://naeychq.naeyc.org/texis/search/pdfhi.txt?query=Position+Statement+on+Child+Abuse&pr=naeyc&prox=sentence&rorder=750&rprox=500&rdfreq=1000&rwfreq=1000&rlead=1000&sufs=2&order=r&cq+&id=42ea282a81

Levin, D. (2003b). *Teaching young children in violent times: Building a peaceable classroom* (2nd ed.). Cambridge, MA: Educators for Social Responsibility.

Levin, D. (1999). Changing needs, changing responses: Rethinking how we teach children. *Child Care Information Exchange, 99*(7), 46–49.

Massey-Stokes, M. (2003). Shaken baby syndrome. *Healthy Child Care, 6*(2). Retrieved October 31, 2005 from http://www.healthychild.net/articles/mc25/shakenbaby.html

Meltz, C. (2004, September 16). Validating fears helps students to face them. Boston Globe. Retrieved 10/14/04. Available online: http://www.boston.com/yourlife/family/articles/2004/09/16/validating_fears_helps_students_to_face_them/

NAEYC. (1997). NAEYC position statement on the prevention of child abuse in early childhood programs and the responsibility of early childhood professionals to prevent child abuse. *Young Children, 52*(3), 42–46.

National Center on Shaken Baby Syndrome (NCSBS). (2000). Shaken baby syndrome questions. Retrieved May 15, 2002, from http://www.dontshake.com/sbsquestions.html.

National Center on Shaken Baby Syndrome. (2005a). Please don't shake me. Retrieved on 11/6/05 from http://dontshake.com/.

National Center on Shaken Baby Syndrome. (2005b). Important update about the period of PURPLE crying program. Retrieved 11/6/05 from http://dontshake.com/Subject.aspx?categoryID=13&PageName=UnderstandInfantCrying.htm

National Clearinghouse on Child Abuse and Neglect Information (NAIC). (2004a). *Child maltreatment 2002: Summary of key findings.* Retrieved October 31, 2005, from http://www.acf.hhs.gov/programs/cb/publications/cm02/index.htm

National Clearinghouse on Child Abuse and Neglect Information (NAIC). (2004b). *Children and domestic violence: State Statutes Series 2004.* Retrieved October 31, 2005, from http://nccanch.acf.hhs.gov/general/legal/statutes/domviol.cfm#backnsix

National Institute on Drug Abuse (NIDA). (1998). *Pregnancy and drug use trends.* National Institutes of Health. Retrieved 11/6/05 from http://www.nida.nih.gov/Infofax/pregnancytrends.html

National Institute of Neurological Disorders. (2004, October 26). NINDS Shaken baby syndrome information page. Retrieved November 24, 2004 from http://www.ninds.nih.gov/disorders/shakenbaby/shakenbaby_pr.htm

National Organization on Fetal Alcohol Syndrome (NOFAS). (2004). Frequently asked questions at NOFAS. Retrieved October 25, 2005, from http://www.nofas.org/faqs.aspx?ID=5.

Nunnelley, J., & Fields, T. (1999). Anger, dismay, guilt, anxiety—The realities and roles in reporting child abuse. *Young Children, 54*(5), 74–79.

Office of National Drug Policy. (ONDP). (2004, Oct. 26). Drug Facts: Women and Drugs. Retrieved October 31, 2005, from http://www.whitehousedrugpolicy.gov/drugfact/women/

Olson, M., & Hyson, M. (2003). Supporting teachers, strengthening families: A new NAEYC Initiative. *Young Children, 58*(3), 74–75.

Osofsky, J. (1999). The impact of violence on children. *The Future of Children, 9*(3), 33–49.

Palmer, D., & Smith, C. (2002a). Preventing abuse in your childcare center. *Healthy Child Care, 5*(5). Retrieved October 31, 2005, from http://www.healthychild.net/articles/sf29abuse.html.

Palmer, D., & Smith, C. (2002b). Recognizing and reporting abuse. *Healthy Child Care, 5*(6). Retrieved October 31, 2005, from http://www.healthychild.net/article/sf30preventabuse.html.

Palmer, D., & Smith, C. (2000). Violence prevention: What childcare providers can—must!—do about it. *Healthy Child Care, 3*(6). Retrieved October 31, 2005, from http:// www.healthychild.net/articles/sf18prevent.html.

Palmer, S. (1998). Shaken baby syndrome. The Arc. Retrieved May 15, 2002, from http://www.thearc.org/faqs/Shaken.html.

Reece, R. (2004). The evidence base for shaken baby syndrome. *British Medical Journal, 328*(5), 1316–1317.

Seattle-King County Department of Public Health. (1991). *Child care health handbook.* Seattle, WA: Washington State Department of Social and Health Services.

Shaken baby syndrome. (2003). Retrieved October 31, 2005, from http://www. mayoclinic.com/invoke.cfm?id=AN00668

Stith, A. (1998, July). Recognizing child abuse: The first step toward preventing false reports. *San Diego Family Magazine, 32–34.*

U.S. Department of Health and Human Services (HHS). (2005). Child maltreatment 2003. Washington, DC: Retrieved October 31, 2005, from http://www.acf.hhs. gov/programs/cb/publications/cm03/cm2003.pdf

Wells, S., Davis, N., Dennis, K., Chipman. R., Sandt, C., & Liss, M. (1995). *Effective screening of child care and youth service workers.* Washington, DC: American Bar Association Center for Children and the Law.

Werner, E., & Smith, R. (2001). *Journeys from childhood to midlife: Risk, resilience, and recovery.* Ithaca, New York: Cornell University Press.

Zamani, R. (2003). Fact sheet for families: Never shake a baby. *California Child Care Health Program.* Retrieved 11/6/05 from http://www.ucsfchildcarehealth. org/pdfs/factsheets/nevershakebabyen042505.pdf

Zamani, R. (2000). Traditional practices can affect the health of children. *Child Care Health Connections, 13*(5), 9.

Additional resources for this chapter can be found by visiting the Online Companion™ at http://www.earlychilded.delmar.com. This supplemental material includes extensive chapter quizzes, PowerPoint® outlines, Web links, and various other activities to help better utilize the material in this chapter. The site is updated regularly, so you may check back often to receive the latest information about the subjects in each chapter.

## CHAPTER 15

# Children with Disabilities or Other Special Needs

**After reading this chapter, you should be able to:**

## 15.1 Policies for Children with Disabilities or Other Special Needs

Define and discuss policies for children with disabilities or other special needs that may affect the early childhood education environment.

## 15.2 Inclusion of Children with Disabilities and Other Special Needs into Early Childhood Education Environments

Describe and discuss the process of including children with disabilities or other special needs into the early childhood education environment.

## 15.3 The Team Approach

Describe and discuss the forming of a team to create an optimal environment for a child with disabilities or other special needs.

## 15.4 Supporting the Child with Disabilities or Other Special Needs

Describe and discuss the best practices for the support of children with disabilities or other special needs.

## 15.5 Supporting Families Who Have a Child with Disabilities or Other Special Needs

Describe and discuss the best practices for the support of families with children with disabilities or other special needs.

## 15.6 Implications for Teachers

Describe and discuss the importance of education, observation, role modeling, working with families, cultural competence, and supervision in dealing with children with disabilities or other special needs.

## 15.1  POLICIES FOR CHILDREN WITH DISABILITIES OR OTHER SPECIAL NEEDS

Policies need to be developed for children with disabilities or other special needs that may be included in the early childhood education environment. The teacher may deal with numerous issues presented by accommodating a child with disabilities or other special needs and should be prepared to do so. These issues should be examined in order to provide the maximum protection, risk prevention, and well-being of these children in the early childhood education environment. The following are reasons for development of policies for children with disabilities or other special needs:

- Children who have disabilities and are in early childhood education programs with nondisabled children show more advanced play than if they were in special care for disabled children alone (Diamond et al., 1994).
- For children with disabilities or other special needs, inclusion is meant to allow them to participate fully and actively, not just to be present (Brault, 2004a).
- In 2000, at least 600,000 preschool children received special education services in preschool because of a disability. Support and training should be provided for preschool teachers to promote integration of service providers into the early childhood education setting (Legal Update Newsletter, 2004).
- The Americans with Disabilities Act requires that all public accommodations, including family child care homes and early childhood education programs, must provide access to children with disabilities (CCLC, 2001).

All children can benefit from play in an inclusive environment.

- Children with disabilities or special needs are children first, and therefore each is unique regardless of the presence of any disability (Shaw, 2003).

- Almost 13 percent, or one in eight children in the United States, have special health care needs (USHRSA, 2004). Boys were 50 percent more likely to have special health care needs (van Dyck et al., 2004). One in six children may need more specialized care than children who follow developmental norms (Aronson, 2000).

Some children may come to the early childhood education environment with no issues that affect their health, safety, and well-being. Preventive measures can help these children remain risk-free in care. Other children may have disabilities or other special needs that affect them and their care (HRSA, 2004). An individual with a disability is defined as "a person who has a physical or mental impairment that substantially limits one or more major life activities" (USDOJ, 2002). Quality early education environments respond positively to differences in children's abilities (Child Care Aware, 2003). In order to provide the most protective and healthy environment, policies need to be created to deal with some of the issues that might arise when caring for children with disabilities or other special needs. The issues that are most likely to emerge as the teacher performs care are

1. *Inclusion of Children with Disabilities or Other Special Needs:* Teachers should understand the effects of accommodation on early childhood education environments.

2. *The Team Approach:* Caring for the child with disabilities or other special needs should not be done alone, but requires help and support. Strategies for creating a team need to be used.

3. *Supporting the Child with Disabilities or Other Special Needs:* Each child with a disability or other special needs has differing abilities. The teacher can use strategies to successfully include these children.

4. *Supporting Families Who Have a Child with Disabilities or Other Special Health Care Needs:* Families who have a child with disabilities or other special needs may have needs of their own that the teacher can help them to address.

5. *Implications for Teachers:* A teacher may take care of children with disabilities or other special needs. These children need a holistic approach to care using education, cultural competence, and supervision.

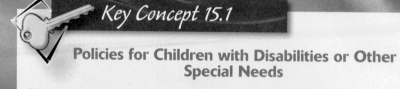

### Key Concept 15.1

### Policies for Children with Disabilities or Other Special Needs

Many children in care have no special issues in their lives that will affect the early childhood education environment. However, the teacher who accommodates children with disabilities or other special needs may have to deal with a number of issues. The teacher needs policies that will help maximize the care environment for those children.

## 15.2 INCLUSION OF CHILDREN WITH DISABILITIES OR OTHER SPECIAL NEEDS INTO EARLY CHILDHOOD EDUCATION ENVIRONMENTS

The Federal Americans with Disabilities Act (ADA) of 1990 was enacted to protect people with physical or mental disabilities from discrimination. If a person has a physical or mental impairment that limits how he lives his life, he is considered disabled. The ADA defines disability as "a physical or mental impairment that substantially limits a major life activity." Title III of this act states that public accommodations must make reasonable modification to accommodate people with disabilities. Under the law, privately operated early childhood education environments are considered public accommodations. Under Title III, a public accommodation must comply with basic requirements that do not allow discrimination in excluding, segregating, or unequally treating a person with a disability. This act also applies to transportation services that are provided. Title III allows for reasonable accommodation to be made to policies, practices, and procedures of the entity (early childhood education program). Barriers in architecture that are inexpensive or easy to change must also be removed or altered (USDOJ, 2002). Title II of the ADA applies to early childhood education programs that are operated by state or local government agencies such as school districts or municipalities. These programs fall under not only ADA but also the Individuals with Disabilities Education Act (IDEA), which was originally passed in 1975 (CCLC, 2004). This act was recently renewed (NICHCY, 2004).

The ADA basically applies to all early childhood education situations except for a nanny caring for children in their home and church-operated programs. A teacher cannot discriminate against a child because of a disability. This nondiscrimination policy might be included on any promotional literature the teacher offers and should be included in the teacher's health care policies. A teacher should be willing to make reasonable adjustments or adaptations in order to accept a child with special needs into care. Any teacher who does not attempt to make these adjustments or adaptations can be held liable for nonaccommodation and may be at risk for a lawsuit from the Department of Justice. The determination of whether the teacher has made a reasonable effort to accommodate the child may be found by following the chart in Figure 15-1, which was created by the Child Care Law Center.

The first step is to determine whether a child's condition poses a direct threat to the early childhood education environment. If this threat cannot be eliminated through reasonable accommodation, then the child cannot be accommodated. If there is no direct threat posed, then the teacher would identify how she might accommodate care to the needs of the child. Other considerations include removing barriers, using auxiliary aids and services, and modifying policies, practices, and procedures. Thorough investigation should occur so that, at the end of this investigation, it is clear either that the child can be accommodated or that, as of this point, the early childhood education environment cannot accommodate the child. If this is the case, then it is possible to set long-term goals to accomplish the accommodation of children with disabilities or other special needs. Figure 15-2 makes this process easy to understand. The ADA does not require any "undue burden" (significant difficulty or expense) on the part of the accommodator.

The IDEA may also affect public schools, but in a different way. It is used to determine whether a child has a disability and then to learn what

**FIGURE 15-1**

When Are You Required to Admit a Child with a Disability? The Evaluation Process Under the ADA, Title III: Public Accommodations. (Copyright © 1995, 2002 Child Care Law Center. Reprinted with permission.)

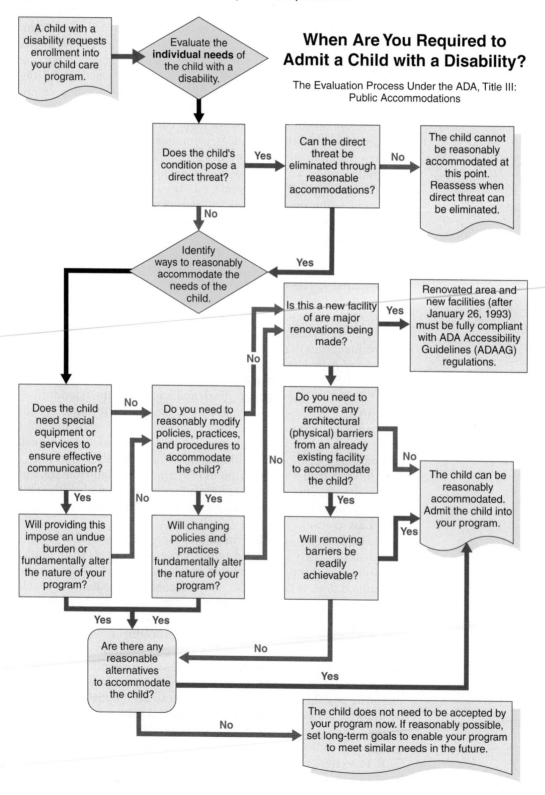

# The Americans with Disabilities Act (ADA)
## *A New Way of Thinking: Title III*

**ADA GOAL:**

To *make reasonable accommodations for* individuals with disabilities in order to *integrate* them into the program to the extent feasible, given *each individual's* abilities.

**ADA PRINCIPLES:**

- INDIVIDUALITY
  the abilities and needs of *each* individual;
- REASONABLENESS
  of the modification to the *program* and to the *individual;*
- INTEGRATION
  of the individual *with others* in the program.

**TYPES OF MODIFICATIONS:**

- AUXILIARY AIDS AND SERVICES
  special equipment and services to ensure effective communication;
- CHANGES IN POLICIES, PRACTICES AND PROCEDURES;
- REMOVAL OF BARRIERS
  architectural, arrangement of furniture and equipment, vehicular.

**REASONS TO DENY CARE:**

- ACCOMMODATION IS UNREASONABLE, and there are no reasonable alternatives.

  ☐ For **auxiliary aids and services,** if accommodations pose an ***UNDUE BURDEN*** (will result in a significant difficulty or expense to the program) or will fundamentally alter the nature of the program;

  ☐ For **auxiliary aids and services,** or **changes in policies, practices or procedures,** if accommodations ***FUNDAMENTALLY ALTER*** the nature of the program;

  ☐ For **removal of barriers for existing facilities,** if accommodations are ***NOT READILY ACHIEVABLE*** (cannot be done without much difficulty or expense to the program). Childcare facilities built after January 26, 1993 must comply with ADA Accessibility Guidelines (ADAAG)

- DIRECT THREAT
  The individual's condition will pose or does pose a significant threat to the health or safety of other children or staff in the program, and there are no reasonable means of removing the threat.

the special needs are (NICHCY, 2002). Once these needs are determined, special educational intervention would occur. This intervention is usually accomplished by local education agencies (LEA), such as a school district. If a particular school district does not have the ability to provide the special education intervention needed, an interdistrict transfer to a school that can handle the special needs of the child may occur.

Children from birth to age two years may need this early intervention because they experience delays in

- Cognitive development
- Physical development, including vision and hearing
- Communication development

- Social or emotional development
- Adaptive development
- or because they have a diagnosed mental or physical condition that will probably result in developmental delays

Those same categories apply to children ages three through nine; for these children, one is allowed to use the term "developmental delay" without specifying which area of delay is involved. These delays are defined by states and must be measured by appropriate diagnostic procedures and instruments. If a child age three years or older has been previously diagnosed with one of the following conditions, he or she would be eligible for services (NICHCY, 2002):

- Autism
- Deaf-blindness
- Emotional disturbance
- Hearing impairment (including deafness)
- Mental retardation
- Multiple disabilities
- Orthopedic impairment
- Other health impairment
- Specific learning disability
- Traumatic brain injury
- Visual impairment (including blindness)

The concept of IDEA is to include these children in a program that is designed to help them to be educated, from kindergarten on, at the greatest level possible in a public school. Before that, for children under school age, intervention and special educational services may be offered on site at a public state preschool or may be offered to an individual child at the early childhood education environment, depending on the LEA plan. Special education professionals work directly with the teacher to offer intervention to the children who need it. The impact of the ADA on the IDEA is that children are now included within the same classroom as children without disabilities or other special needs, and special education services are delivered in that venue. There are many benefits to inclusion.

## Benefits of Inclusion

The ADA legislation was created to encourage acceptance and lessen discrimination. Some children with disabilities or other special needs can easily be accommodated into care, whereas others may require some adaptation. Some children may have disabilities that are beyond the teacher's abilities to accommodate. These decisions should never be made automatically. Rather, a decision as to whether a child can be reasonably accommodated needs to be made on a case-by-case basis. Including children with special needs in the early childhood education environment has many benefits to everyone involved (NCCCHSRC, 2005).

For the child with special needs, the early childhood education environment offers opportunities to play and grow. These children make better developmental progress when they are mainstreamed with children with no

When children with and without disabilities or other special need are accommodated together in the same setting, they learn acceptance and self-esteem.

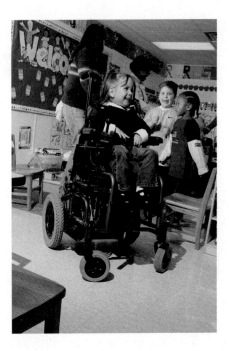

disabilities or other special needs. Their play is more advanced (Brault, 2004a). Children with special needs learn better interaction skills and become more self-reliant. Being included allows the child with disabilities or other special needs to learn to cope and figure out appropriate social skills. This allows the opportunity to make friends and build a positive self-concept (Buysee, et al., 2003).

Children with no disabilities or other special needs benefit from being around children who have them. They can learn empathy and can see that diversity is not so scary. The children with disabilities are more like them than they are different (Olson et al., 1999). Opportunities for interaction between children with disabilities or other special needs and other children reinforce this concept. Children can gain an awareness of how to express compassion, concern and care (Brault, 2004b). Children may actually help the adults in the environment reach a good comfort level with children with special needs. Children usually ask a few questions about a disability, then focus on the child and not the disability (Grechus, 2000). Teachers can learn from them.

Teachers can also benefit by realizing that all children are more alike than different. By focusing on the child's strengths, not weaknesses, a teacher can be more successful. The teacher working with a child who has a disability or other special needs will learn patience and self-confidence in his ability to care for the child. The teacher can learn techniques for supporting a child with disabilities or other special needs with individualized activities (Brault, 2004a). Children have the same basic needs, and every teaching skill that is strengthened is shared with all the children in care.

The parents may learn that the child with special needs is more like other children than they expected, and this awareness may allow them a comfort they had not experienced before. The parents of children with disabilities or other special needs will receive support from the teacher to carry on everyday life. When they share the responsibility with the teacher to help the child learn, families are expanding their own understanding. The family that has their child in early childhood education can become aware of more resources and can experience a connection to a caring community.

## Key Concept 15.2

### Inclusion of Children with Disabilities or Other Special Needs into the Early Childhood Education Environment

Children with disabilities or other special needs may be included in the early childhood education environment. The Americans with Disabilities Act (ADA) discusses public accommodations. The Individuals with Disabilities Education Act (IDEA) provides the intervention. Teachers should be aware of these laws and how to determine whether they are able to take a particular child with disabilities or other special needs into the early childhood education environment. While doing so, they should consider the potential benefits for everyone.

## 15.3 THE TEAM APPROACH

Caring for a child with disabilities or other special needs should not be done without help and support. The parents who approach a teacher about providing care for their special child should provide contact to a number of professionals who are dealing with the child. Some typical members of this group might be a physician, an audiologist, an occupational therapist, a nutritional consultant, a speech pathologist, and a counselor.

The Health Resources and Services Administration of the Maternal and Child Health Bureau are working in conjunction with Healthy People 2010 to support children with special health care needs. They suggest that care be coordinated through a medical home (see Chapter 13). They also suggest children be screened early and often so that, if intervention is needed, it can be given immediately. A major goal is a community-based service system where families, teachers, health practitioners, and other community resource people work together for the benefit of the child. The timeline for this to be in place is by 2010 (AAP, 2002). Olson et al. (1999) suggest that an inclusive community such as this empowers parents, gives teachers the training and support they need, and provides necessary support services.

Each child has unique needs, and the people who will help the child are selected to meet those needs. In the classroom, additional assistance may be needed depending on the particular needs of the child. For example, a child with a hearing impairment may need a sign language translator; or a child with cerebral palsy may need an occupational therapy technician to visit regularly to help the child reach her maximum potential for physical movement and coordination.

The IDEA was passed in 1990 and renewed in 2004. It provides special education and other services related to disabilities or developmental delay in children. It offers the means to create a team for each child with disabilities or other special needs (CCLC, 2004). This team approach supports the child and offers everyone involved a common sense of purpose. Everyone on the team works together to help the child reach her maximum potential developmental growth level. It is essential that those involved participate in the team on an equal level.

# REALITY CHECK

## *Attention Deficit/Hyperactivity Disorder (AD/HD)*

Attention deficit/hyperactivity disorder is a condition that has two basic symptoms: inattention and a combination of hyperactivity and impulsive behaviors. It is estimated to affect between 3 and 10 percent of children in the United States (Shaw, 2003). The behavior patterns that typify AD/HD usually begin appearing between the ages of three and five years. Most children of this age are more active, more impulsive, and less able to focus their attention than are adults. Children are also more likely to be unaware of time and future events in comparison to here-and-now wants and desires. If these behaviors seem to be out of hand or occurring more often in one child in comparison to others, that child may be exhibiting the beginning behaviors of AD/HD. Boys are at least three times more likely to exhibit these behaviors than girls. In fact, some studies show that boys may be as much as nine times more likely to exhibit these behaviors because they are more likely to be genetically linked to nervous system irregularities than are girls (Shaw, 2003).

Typical AD/HD behaviors listed by the American Psychological Association (Nadeau & Dixon, 1994) include:

- failure to give close attention to details of "work" at school or other activities
- difficulty in focusing attention on play activities or tasks
- difficulty in listening when spoken to
- apparent inability to follow through on instructions
- difficulty in transitioning from one activity to another
- avoidance of activities that call for concentrated mental activity
- apparent inability to organize himself/herself for activities or tasks

- easily distracted by stimuli in the environment
- talks when inappropriate, often interrupts conversation
- easily loses things and seems forgetful
- difficulty in awaiting his or her turn for activities
- difficulty sitting still, squirms with hands or feet
- leaves group when expected to remain
- runs around excessively at inappropriate times
- difficulty participating in quiet activities
- talks excessively
- appears to be active at all times

Not all children who have some or many of these symptoms have AD/HD. There are other conditions and problems that may cause these behaviors. It is very important to have the child diagnosed, so that corrective measures can take place to assist the child in coping and overcoming some of the obstacles of this condition. If a child in care is exhibiting a significant number of these behaviors, the parent should be asked to have the child screened for this condition. Careful consideration should be made in discussing this with the parents. Historically, it was believed that this condition was caused by dysfunction in the home. Another belief for the cause of AD/HD has been that the child's diet was high in sugar and food additives. Recent studies have shown that neither of these items is related to AD/HD, so parents may feel relieved to know that their parenting is not the cause for the child's condition.

What has been found to be linked to AD/HD are connections and chemicals found in the brain. In new research, lower levels of

*(continues)*

# REALITY CHECK (Continued)

attention activity and glucose have been found in the brains of people with AD/HD.

Other studies have been investigating neural connections and causal factors for interruption. These factors have included genetics and prenatal exposure to chemicals, drugs, alcohol, and tobacco. Brain cells developed during pregnancy enable the transmission of neural signals from the eyes, ears, and skin and allow for the control of responses to the environment. Some research has focused in the direction of vision problems affecting information that is taken in and organized. A recent study looked at the correlation between television watching and later attention problems (Christakis et al., 2004). The researchers felt that this activity might shorten children's attention span. The conclusion was that 10% of children studied had problems with attention. The fact remains that it is not known what causes AD/HD.

For a child to be diagnosed, there are several areas that will be checked. First, the child has a physical examination that includes a thorough family medical history. The parents and perhaps the child's teacher are interviewed and complete a behavior rating scale. The child is observed in several situations, and a variety of psychological tests may be given. If the parents cannot afford this type of diagnostic screening, the early childhood education center should help the parent link to helpful community resources. Often, a child's school district may be of assistance, even before the child enters kindergarten. Many school districts feel that early diagnosis of conditions such as AD/HD will help them manage the situation for the school-age child.

Teachers and directors can help these children even before a diagnosis is made by controlling and monitoring the environment so that the child can be more successful (Shaw, 2003). Some of these helping strategies developed for the U.S. Office of Special Education, U.S. Department of Education include:

- Anticipate events, and help with transition from one event to another. This includes informing the child of the change before and during the transition.
- Break tasks down into smaller, more manageable steps.
- Use immediate rewards for completed tasks and positive behaviors, which should always include praise for a job well done. This might include a special chart for this child and the use of stickers to show the child how well he is doing. You might want to focus on a few tasks at a time, in order to allow the child greater success.
- Keep this child near you when working on tasks so that you can maintain eye contact.
- Use gestures to emphasize directions.
- Eliminate unnecessary materials, so that the child can focus on the task at hand.
- Provide a quiet area for the child to go to if he is feeling overloaded. Distractions can cause the overload and exacerbate the problem.
- Have a special place for the child's belongings and tools and ask the parents to do the same for the child at home.
- When speaking directly to the child, use his name and focus attention, including eye contact with the child, until the signal to communicate has been received.
- Communicate often with the parent as to how the child is doing in the early childhood education environment, and inquire about behavior at home so that a partnership in helping the child is created.
- Establish clear rules with immediate consequences, so that the child understands that the behavior exhibited is not acceptable. This might included a time-out area for the child to go to when he cannot control his behavior.

**CHECK***point:* List five protective strategies you might use for a child with AD/HD in your classroom.

Each professional may have ownership in part of the process and may tend to see that part as the most significant. Each member of the team has a key ingredient to help the child. Often, when a professional works with a teacher, she gets a greater understanding of child development (Brault, 2004a). With this knowledge, when she sees children in groups and how they interact, she may have a better grasp on how to help a child with disabilities or other special needs. Each player on the team must contribute his unique ingredient and cooperate to make this holistic approach work.

● **Individualized family service plan**
*plan that coordinates services to meet the needs of the child with special needs and his or her family*

*The Individualized Family Service Plan.* The team should work together to prepare what is called an **individualized family service plan** (IFSP). The IFSP provides for an organized goal and delivery of services to the child and the family. The plan should be made up of measurable outcome objectives, which help guide the team to provide what the child needs. It is much easier to assess the success of a plan based on whether the objectives have been met.

Usually one person is designated as the coordinator of the service plan. This is often the representative of the group that has financial responsibility. It can be a professional who represents the Department of Health or the Department of Education and varies from state to state.

There should be one contact person who coordinates the care of the child with special needs in the early childhood education situation (Allred et al., 1998). For a center, it might be the director or the child's primary teacher. In a family day care home, it would most likely be the care provider. In an in-home care situation, it would be the nanny who has agreed to care for the child with special needs.

Families are also an integral part of the IFSP. They know their children best and can help by sharing knowledge and information (Vakil, 2003). The IFSP is based on the unique needs of each child. Families play an important role because they are the bridge between the child, the early childhood education community, and all the service providers.

The cooperative team should work together, each bringing to the system their unique expertise to benefit the child.

If a child with disabilities or other special needs is accepted in to the early childhood education environment, the teacher should be prepared to accept the responsibilities that go along with caring for that child. The team effort continues at the early childhood education site. All people involved in the care of the child should be privy to what is planned for the child. The IFSP should be shared and the objectives should be reviewed to identify the progress of the child. If any training is needed to provide care for the child, all members of the caregiving team should receive it. The early childhood education program that accepts a special needs team should provide the skills necessary to help the child reach maximum potential (CCLC, 2004).

## Key Concept 15.3

### The Team Approach

Children with disabilities and other special needs may be included in the early childhood education environment. The Individuals with Disabilities Education Act provides the intervention and means to create a team. The individualized family service plan (IFSP) is the vehicle for the team. The teacher is an integral part of this team that works to support the child with disabilities or other special needs.

## 15.4  SUPPORTING THE CHILD WITH DISABILITIES OR OTHER SPECIAL NEEDS

Each child with a disability or other special need has his or her own particular needs requiring support. Support can be offered to all children with special needs in some general ways. The teacher and the special needs team should develop goals that match the needs and abilities of the child. The teacher is the one who will carry out these goals on a daily basis and should be involved in the process.

*The Environment.* Adjusting the physical environment to adapt to whatever special needs are present is a good starting point. Removing obstacles assists children who are visually impaired or who have physical disabilities that may require a walker or a wheelchair. For children with emotional disabilities, the teacher may need to provide a quiet corner. The area needed for adaptive equipment should be in a place that does not interfere with other activities.

The toys that are present in the environment should be safe and durable for the sake of all children. They should provide opportunities for learning, interaction, exploration, and engagement. Modifying toys as needed may help the child with special needs use the toy for its intended purpose. As an example, the ring in a ring toss game may need to be cut larger for the child with special needs to feel successful. After a child with special needs has been in care for a while, the teacher may notice what types of toys that child is most likely to choose and use. Selecting new toys that have similarities will offer new challenges or things to explore. Table 15-1 includes strategies for the successful inclusion of children with differing abilities in the early childhood education environment. Whatever goals are

**TABLE 15-1**
*Strategies for Inclusion of Children with Disabilities or Other Special Needs*

**Instructional Adaptation**

- Establish realistic goals
- Describe task or activity
- Model task or activity
- Adapt task or activity to child's ability for time allotted
- Give child time to practice new things that he is learning
- Teach in small segments
- Sit close to child or stand near to provide assistance
- Plan for transition times
- Provide visual clues by labeling pictures and objects
- Be clear when giving directions using descriptive language
- Encourage sensory experiences such as tasting, touching, smelling

**Physical Adaptation**

- Learn to position a child in the most comfortable way for him to work and play (this may take the help of a physical therapist)
- Clear pathways
- Organize access and physical spaces as needed
- Keep doors shut, if needed
- If adaptive equipment is needed, provide and use
- Know about and use assistive technology as needed
- Promote health and safety—adapt for activities like hand washing, as needed

**Communication**

- Address child directly so that he knows you are speaking to him
- Be a good listener and observer
- Use everyday activities like books, music, and play to foster language development
- Expand language by repeating what the child said and then extending it with other words
- Model correct language and pronunciation
- Make directions easy to understand
- Praise child for attempts at communication, even if not perfect
- Facilitate play in developmentally and age-appropriate activities
- Teach children to understand nonverbal responses of child with a disability or other special needs
- Use assistive technology where applicable

**Social Interaction and Peer Support**

- Teach peers to assist friends
- Encourage peer partnerships (i.e., "buddies")

*(continues)*

**TABLE 15-1** (Continued)
*Strategies for Inclusion of Children with Disabilities or Other Special Needs*

### Social Interaction and Peer Support (Continued)

- Encourage interaction and meaningful participation
- Teach peers to understand nonverbal responses
- Teach peers to repeat or rephrase words for better understanding
- Answer peers' questions honestly
- Model respect
- Model warm and accepting manner

### Environmental Support

- Be familiar with IFEP or IDEA for child
- Utilize support of other team members of the IFEP or IDEA when needed
- Have clear line of communication with family including suggestions or information that may help child adapt
- Recognize the child's strengths
- Create and maintain setting for children of all abilities to thrive and develop
- Model desired behavior
- Support child with organized schedule and structure in a safe, nurturing environment and allow for flexibility
- Provide time and support for transition with clear and consistent signals
- Provide realistic, reasonable consequences for unacceptable behaviors
- Use visual cues such as on cubbies, equipment and materials
- Provide positive support for persistent attention
- Ensure health and safety

### Emotional Support

- Recognize each child's uniqueness
- Recognize the similarities among all children
- Show respect, acceptance and warmth
- Help children to learn to express feelings in acceptable ways
- Establish a positive relationship with families

chosen for the IFSP should be incorporated with routine care. To help reinforce this, signs might be posted as reminders (Allred, 1998). Daily routines help reinforce the skills and competencies of a child with special needs. When you create a nurturing, supportive environment, all children will benefit (Greenspan, 2003; Bakley, 2001).

Flynn and Kieff (2002) suggested three guidelines for promoting outdoor play. The first is to consider the quantity and quality of the multisensory activities available for children. These involve moving, hearing, tasting, touching, and seeing. The second is to promote independence for all children. By considering a child's abilities and needs, modifications of activities and materials can be made. The final guideline is to use cooperative learning groups, in which a few children work together in a meaningful way. This promotes positive interaction and allows for communication (Hess, 2003). It is this type of strategy that also supports the creation of friendships (Buysee et al., 2003).

Assistive technology can also be used to support the participation of children with disabilities or other special needs (Mulligan, 2003). Table 15-1 indicates some recommended practices for use of assistive technology developed by the Division for Early Childhood (DEC) of the Council for Exceptional Families (Mulligan, 2003).

Music is also a tool that can be used in the inclusive environment to get children to participate (Moore, 2004; Humpal & Wolf, 2003). It is a fairly unrestricted part of daily activities and can offer a host of experiences for all children, especially those with disabilities or other special needs. The level of engagement in music activities can vary from child to child and can range from observation to complete participation. Music can open doors to social experiences, teach social skills, and help facilitate friendships.

Sandall et al., (2002) proposed that there are eight types of modifications that can be made for children with disabilities or other special needs to optimize the early childhood education environment. These modifications are

1. Environmental support
2. Materials adaptation
3. Simplification of the activity
4. Using a child's preferences (materials, activity, person)
5. Special equipment
6. Adult support
7. Peer support
8. Invisible support (naturally occurring events)

Adapting the environment for the child with disabilities or other special needs by using this list, providing opportunities with music, and using

A least restrictive environment should be provided for all children with disabilities or special needs.

the specific strategies found in Table 15-1 will help the teacher maximize the environment for optimal development.

*Intervention.* If the teacher observes that the child is having difficulty playing with certain toys, games, and other materials, she may need to intervene. The teacher may help the child learn how to play with a toy or adapt the toy to play. She may have to show the child how to use or adapt for use other play materials. Modeling appropriate play behavior may help the child learn how to be a player.

The teacher may also encourage other children to assist the child. The children who are not disabled may need help in learning how to understand and accept the child with a disability or other special needs. The teacher may teach specific skills such as eye contact or appropriate language. The children in the group can learn to help the child with a disability or special need to accomplish tasks on her own when capable, as well as specific helping behaviors when appropriate. The teacher can also model acceptance and show understanding. Her actions and words with the child with special needs are the most effective tools she has to teach the other children about interaction. The nondisabled child can role model and provide opportunities for positive interaction with the child with special needs.

> *Pause for Reflection*
>
> How might you use assistive technology and music to help children with disabilities? Which appeals to you more, and why?

- **Activity based**
  *activities that promote adaptive behavior*
- **Functional skills**
  *skills that allow children to adapt to their environment*
- **Generalizable skills**
  *common skills that can be practiced and used in different settings*

Teacher intervention should be **activity based** and occur in a natural manner. Opportunities for this type of intervention occur in everyday activities. The objective of activity-based intervention is to help develop two different skills for the child with special needs (Vakil et al., 2003). The first skill is referred to as **functional skill** and offers the child opportunities to adapt to the physical and social environments in care. The child receives personal satisfaction and a sense of accomplishment that helps her gain confidence.

The other type of skill is referred to as **generalizable skill** and transfers from one setting to another. An example of this would be a child with a

Tamara, an autistic child, was acquiring some sign language capabilities. She spent part of her morning in a special school and then went to Kate's family day care before lunch. Her favorite food was watermelon, and whenever Kate served Tamara watermelon she could sign the word *more*.

Kate felt that there was an opportunity for learning here, so she went to the special education teacher at Tamara's school and learned how to sign the word *watermelon*. She used it at every opportunity she could when she gave Tamara watermelon for lunch or snack. Eventually, Tamara learned how to sign the word. Her mother was very excited when she informed Kate several days later that Tamara had asked through signing for watermelon for dinner. It was a real milestone in Tamara's limited language.

# REALITY CHECK

## Autism

Autism is a disorder that has a wide range of symptoms and characteristics that can range from mild to severe. Autism is typically thought of as a disorder that presents difficulties in verbal and nonverbal communication, as well as an inability to carry out normal social interactions and play activities (Leekha, 2000). Each child, as well as adult, can exhibit unique combinations of these behaviors in various degrees of severity. Many children are diagnosed as having Asperger syndrome, which is a form of autism in which the person is high functioning in most ways. People with this condition are quite verbal and intelligent but can be self-absorbed.

Many researchers today believe that the major defect or deficit in autism has to do with theory of mind. In normal development, by the age of four years, theory of mind is present in children. This gives each of us the understanding that we have our own thoughts, perceptions, and emotions, but so do others. We grasp the fact that, when we interact with others, we may not share the same perceptions, but we are able to adapt and adjust. The autistic child appears to not have this same capability. Self-absorption and the inability to consider others are major characteristics in most autistic people. This factor may also account for the fact that autistic children do not imitate others as normal children do, which offers the foundation for much of a child's learning process.

Problems beyond communication and social difficulties found in autistic children include sensory disturbances, gastrointestinal problems, depression, food allergies, AD/HD, and obsessive-compulsiveness. The latest research appears to connect these characteristics with the genes that may be causing the major defects (Nash, 2002).

Why has concern about autism appeared to increase? Until recently, it was believed that only 1 child in 10,000 might have this rare disorder. The latest research concludes, however, that as many as 1 in every 150 children younger than 10 years of age may have some form of autism or a related disorder (Nash, 2002). If adults are included, as many as 1.5 million people in the United States may be afflicted with an autistic disorder, which makes this condition five times more common than Down syndrome. The incidence of autism appears to be increasing at an annual rate of 10 to 17 percent (ASA, 2002). In April, 2002, a U.S. congressional committee declared autism a national health emergency.

To understand the difference between a normally developing young child and a child with autism, look at some of the following characteristics from the National Institutes of Mental Health brochure on Autism (1999):

### A Normal Child

Studies mother's face and interacts through smiles, etc.
Hears normally, reacts to sounds
Learns to speak and gains in vocabulary
No apparent attachment to anyone
May get frustrated when hungry or tired
Has normal social interaction with others
Moves from activity to activity
Uses body with normal motor skills
Explores toys and plays with them in a normal manner
Enjoys pleasure, avoids pain

### An Autistic Child

Avoids eye contact and has little interaction, if any
No reaction or hyperreaction to sounds, smells, textures, or tastes
Begins to develop language, then abruptly ceases development
Attached and may cry when mother leaves child's presence
May be overly aggressive with no reason
Zoned out/tuned out—little interaction
Fixates on an activity and is repetitive
Strange motor actions such as flapping, rocking, and banging head
Licks, sniffs, or mouths toys beyond toddlerhood
Self-inflicts pain

(continues)

## REALITY CHECK (Continued)

Autism appears to have no specific single cause. In many families, there seems to be a genetic link, because there is a pattern of autism in the family. No particular genetic link has been found as yet. A number of researchers believe it is a combination of genes—as few as 3 or as many as 20—that may yield this condition. It is suspected that some of the genes regulate neurotransmitters and/or control brain development.

Another belief, which has been highly publicized in Britain, is that autism is caused by the measles, mumps, and rubella (MMR) combination vaccination (Smeeth et al., 2004). (See Reality Check: At Risk for Preventative Disease in Chapter 12, for more information.) These vaccines in the past contained thimerosal, a mercury-based preservative (AAP, 2004). Many parents of children who later developed autism have reported that their child was normal before this vaccination and then began having problems that were later diagnosed as autism. This link is unsubstantiated, and no evidence has been found to explain how these vaccines might cause autism (CHA, 2004; Smeeth et al., 2004). Even though there has been no concrete evidence, there is a major debate over whether this vaccination may, in fact, be linked to autism, or whether there is no link at all (Park, 2002). Congress is in the process of investigating to see whether any link may actually exist (Groppe, 2004). In the meantime, manufacturers of most vaccines have removed thimerosal from the vaccines. The one exception is the influenza vaccine, which the AAP recommended that all children receive between 6 and 23 months of age as an annual vaccine (AAP, 2004).

The University of California at Davis is studying concentrations of mercury, PCBs, and other heavy metals to see whether they may be causing autism. These researchers believe that some children are more genetically susceptible to these and other agents. The University of Rochester is investigating how ingestion of certain teratogens might lead to autism. They are specifically looking at a gene that is turned on only briefly during the first trimester of life. The premise is that a teratogen at this time may affect the developing brainstem.

There is no basic medical testing for autism. Accurate diagnosis of autism is generally based on intense observation of a child's communication, developmental level, and behaviors. This would include input from parents and a developmental history of the child. Behaviors found in autism are also often found in other medical disorders, so medical tests for those behaviors may be possible to rule out autism. In an ideal world, diagnosis should be made by a multidisciplinary team that may include a speech/language therapist, a psychologist, a neurologist, a developmental pediatrician, and any other professional with expertise in autism and its characteristics (Autism Society of America [ASA], 2002).

One thing is certain, that early diagnosis is critical, because the sooner intervention and treatment occur, the better chance the child has of functioning at the highest level possible. A number of successful approaches can result in great differences in children before and after assistance. Emphasis to help autism always includes early intervention. If interventions occur at the stages where normal children pick up their learning skills, it is much more helpful to autistic children than "catching up."

Developmental appropriateness, a great degree of structure, behavior-based interventions, and training of parents and others to work with children are the most successful foundations for helping an autistic child. With proper intervention strategies, many autistic children can grow up to lead productive lives.

Dr. Temple Grandin (2001), an autistic adult, has shared how the world is viewed by an autistic person. She suggests using the following as keys to help understand the autistic child and creating strategies to help that child:

- Autistic people think in pictures, not in language. Pictures are their first language; words are their second language.

- Avoid long strings of verbal language. Make language short and succinct.

## REALITY CHECK (Continued)

- Many autistic children are good at computer skills, drawing, and art. Encourage these skills.
- Use fixations to teach. If a child likes trains, use trains to teach him how to count or to read.
- Use visual objects and other visual methods to help teach a child about numbers and number concepts.
- Be sensitive to sounds in the surrounding environment; many autistic children and adults are sound sensitive.

- Some autistic children are bothered by fluorescent and other types of lighting, so be aware of this.
- Some autistic children sing better than they speak, so singing instructions to them may improve their understanding.

Teachers can use this list to offer more measures and strategies in order to help the autistic child in the early childhood education environment.

**CHECK***point:* What are five strategies to use to assist a child with autism?

speech or language disorder learning how to name a particular object. A ball is a ball whether it is at the early childhood education environment, at home, or in the park.

The teacher should recognize the strengths in all children in care. The holistic approach to early childhood education focuses on the whole child. Activities and opportunities that focus on strengths, support, and minimize difficulties should be provided. All children want to feel capable, successful, and confident. A teacher who is aware of this can easily provide the environment a child needs.

Intervention may also include the teacher being able to identify a child who is already in care. Some children may have special needs that have not been detected and need to be addressed. The teacher should look for help to identify the behaviors or characteristics that appear to indicate a special need. Regional centers, maternal and child health services, and other resources are helpful sources for this information.

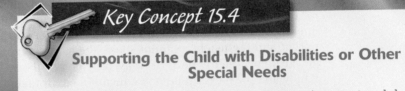

### Key Concept 15.4

### Supporting the Child with Disabilities or Other Special Needs

The teacher should provide a safe, protective environment and do whatever possible to both challenge and support the child with disabilities or other special needs. Through modification and intervention, the teacher can provide the help these children need.

## 15.5 SUPPORTING FAMILIES WHO HAVE A CHILD WITH DISABILITIES OR OTHER SPECIAL NEEDS

Families who have a child with disabilities or other special needs will come to the early childhood education environment with an extra set of issues that other families do not have (Gonzalez-Mena, 2004). Some parents are in denial that their child has a disability. Other families may feel guilt. Cultural issues may affect both of these if the family is from a culture that does not easily accept children with exceptionalities or does not perceive them as healthy. It is important that there be a plan for special care and that the teacher work closely with the family to create that plan (Walsh, 2005).

Children living in poverty are at the greatest risk for disabilities or other special needs (Peterson et al., 2004). These families may have less perceived access to intervention services or lack of awareness in regard to developmental delays in their children. The degree of knowledge that a family has about their child's special needs can range from being almost an "expert" to very little. Regardless of where the family is on this spectrum, they are going to need a greater degree of support than many families in care (Legal Update Newsletter, 2004).

Parents whose child is developing in an atypical manner may be surprised to see what typical development is and may feel saddened to realize that their child is so far behind or will never be at that point in his or her development. It is important for the teacher to offer these families the ability to come and participate if they choose. Fathers in particular may find it difficult to relate to their children with disabilities or other special needs. One of the reasons for the IFSP is to involve the entire family (Rump, 2002). An environment that is welcoming for fathers allows them to get more involved with their children and to observe how to successfully nurture them. In any communication that is sent home to the families, be sure to include fathers as well, if they are present.

Families' parenting skills may be limited if they spend a great deal of time providing physical care for their children with disabilities or other special needs. As their children participate in the early childhood education program and they observe the role modeling of the teacher, they can hone their parenting skills and feel more like typical parents than they may have previously felt. Families provide the emotional connection to the children that can help the teacher interact at a greater degree with both the children and the families. Teamwork and cooperation are essential to provide the greatest number of opportunities for these children to grow and develop to their highest potential (Walsh, 2005).

Cultural differences must be addressed (Legal Update Newsletter, 2004). As much as possible, it is important to accept how the families care for their children with disabilities or other special needs. It is crucial to keep lines of communication open and to remove language as a barrier. If the parent and the teacher cannot speak the same language, it is important to get an interpreter. The IFSP may provide for those services for both the family and the early childhood education environment. In general, communication is a vital link uniting all segments of the team effort. It is useful for both the teacher and the family to look at their own differences. They may have different communication styles, and they may process information differently (Greenspan, 2004). Understanding this helps them to appreciate their differences and to empathize with their child who is also different in his or her own way.

Strategies to optimize communication in the early childhood education environment are found in Chapter 16. Programs that are culturally competent and communicate effectively with families can offer the greatest degree of support.

## Key Concept 15.5

### Supporting Families Who Have a Child with Disabilities or Other Special Needs

Supporting families who have children with disabilities or other special needs is challenging because these families have more issues as their children enter care. Providing access and support that includes both parents, if present, is vital for the child. Modeling parenting skills, being culturally competent, and communicating effectively are other strategies to use to support these families.

## 15.6  IMPLICATIONS FOR TEACHERS

The teacher needs to understand that some children in the early childhood education environment have disabilities or other special needs that can be challenging. Children with disabilities or other special needs may have special circumstances. The teacher needs to use tools such as education, supervision, working with families, and cultural competence to help these children and their families by providing an environment that will support the safety, nutrition, health, and well-being of the child.

### Education

When children with disabilities or other special needs are included in care, some modifications to the early childhood education environment may be necessary. These may include toys, equipment, or nutritional requirements. Teacher intervention may be needed to help the child interact and engage in exploration of the environment. The teacher may need to use natural situations for activity-based learning. All of these situations require teacher knowledge and awareness. The teacher may need special training by the other IFSP team members in order to be fully able to support the child.

There may be times when children with disabilities and other special needs need one-on-one help. This boy with Down syndrome is picking out a book to be read by his teacher to help settle him down for a nap.

Inclusion of children with special needs has many benefits.

It is important for the teacher to remember that he or she is not alone in dealing with these issues. Outside support and resources are available from local and national organizations and agencies. Child care resource and referral services might be a good source of support. Another source would be professionals in the community, who are often willing to help by discussing issues and solutions. Local early childhood education organizations can offer support and may even have a support network in place.

## For Families

The teacher should try to do whatever is possible to support the family of a child with disabilities or other special needs. A team needs to be created, and a clear line of communication needs to be in place. It is important to help parents access any resources they may need, and to cooperate with the resources they bring with them. The teacher can model parenting skills and cultural competency.

## Cultural Competence

If the child with disabilities or other special needs is from a different cultural background, the teacher may need an additional tool, which is cultural competence. Many cultures have the tendency to either ignore or deny that a child has a problem. Other cultures may focus on the problem to such a degree that it becomes an obsession. Values, childrearing practices, family roles, and outside support may all have an effect on how a disability is perceived. State departments of maternal and child health, departments of social services, and regional centers may be good resources for this information. The reactions and tendencies on the part of families whose children have disabilities or other special needs may also be true of families with chronically ill children.

# REALITY CHECK

## Children with Fetal Alcohol Syndrome (FAS)

Fetal Alcohol Syndrome (FAS) is a spectrum disorder that is characterized by growth retardation, facial anomalies, and problems with the central nervous system (Sokol et al., 2003). The growth deficiencies and central nervous system damage and dysfunction are conditions that are lifelong and will affect the child in many different ways (Astley & Clarren, 2000). FAS is the leading preventable cause of birth defects and developmental disabilities (Chesnoff et al., 2005).

FAS is caused by a mother drinking alcohol during her pregnancy. The physiological mechanism that makes it unsafe for the fetus is not yet understood (Eustace et al., 2003). It is unknown whether it is the timing, the amount of alcohol, the mother's genetic predisposition, or some other factor that causes one child of a mother who drinks to be affected and another child not to be. Mothers whose children had FAS were likely to have fewer prenatal visits, more pregnancies, more mental health problems, and more injuries (Kvigne et al., 2003). They were also more likely than other mothers to drink heavily and to binge drink. Until the entire situation with pregnancy and alcohol is understood, pregnant women are counseled to stay away from alcohol to prevent FAS (Sharpe et al., 2004).

Another condition caused by a mother drinking alcohol during pregnancy is alcohol-related neurodevelopmental disorder (ARND). Children with ARND may demonstrate behavioral problems and learning disabilities similar to those of children with FAS (CDC, 2004).

Harwood and Kleinfeld (2002) presented the following list of behaviors or factors that may be evidence of central nervous system damage from either FAS or ARND:

- Developmental delays
- Poor impulse control
- Inconsistent knowledge base/sporadic mastery
- Difficulty grasping concepts
- Problem with perception, sensory integration, and tactile defensiveness
- Hyperactivity
- Learning disabilities
- Distractibility
- Head circumference below the third percentile

As the list indicates, an FAS child in the early childhood education environment may challenge the teacher with erratic behaviors and learning difficulties. The first step may be to get the child identified by connecting her with a medical home and requesting the assistance of a health consultant. If the mother is still actively using alcohol, she may not be able to understand or may be in denial about her child's problems. The next step is to plan strategies to help the child. A child with FAS or ARND may have a difficult time learning how to play and may not be able to focus. Transitioning from one activity to another may also be hard for the child.

The teacher can use some of these strategies that help with FAS/ARND children:

- Provide a team for working with the child.
- Build on the child's strengths.
- Provide a routine and organized schedule, so that the child understands the environment.
- Offer opportunities for success.
- Try to avoid outbursts by offering adequate time for vigorous play with lots of movement.
- Connect with occupational therapy if it is needed.
- Give the child options for play and learning.

*(continues)*

## REALITY CHECK (Continued)

- Practice patience.
- Help the child with memory by repeating, repeating, repeating.
- Offer social reminders.
- Be aware of the child's bodily needs—many of these children need oral stimulation, so they may be putting fingers or hands in mouth.
- Keep instruction concrete and understandable.

- Give directions in a short, direct, and calm manner.
- Provide visual cues.
- Use music as a behavior modification technique.

This is a challenging yet preventable disorder. The teacher may also post information in the classroom for pregnant mothers to read so they can better understand what they might be preventing by abstaining from alcohol.

**CHECK***point:* What is meant by "building on the child's strengths?" Why would that be important for learning how to work with a child with FAS or ARND?

Katy went to a special school that mainstreamed healthy children with children with chronic diseases. Both she and her friend, Paul, had diabetes that required urine testing and shots of insulin as needed. Many of the other children watched as Katy and Paul and their teacher, Charles, tested the urine to find out the condition of each of their systems for insulin. This process evolved into an activity for all the children. They would all gather around, and most could identify what the insulin test result was. They often watched Katy and Paul get shots. Everyone was involved so there was nothing really "different" about Katy and Paul that the other children considered to be a problem.

## Supervision

The teacher who care for a child with disabilities or other special needs must carefully supervise the early childhood education environment, because these children are more at risk for health and safety issues as well as nutritional well-being. It is up to the teacher to observe these children with a holistic approach. The teacher may need to observe more often, to make certain that the child's special needs are met and relief is offered through supportive behaviors.

Medication and nutritional needs must be maintained through careful supervision. The timing and frequency of medication administration for a child with disabilities or other special needs may be critical. These needs may have to be met by an outside source if the teacher lives in a state where he is not allowed to offer medication. Nutritional needs may also be significant. In addition, the teacher will need to supervise any team created for a child from the early childhood education viewpoint in order to reinforce that child's goals.

## Key Concept 15.6

### Implications for Teachers

A teacher may take care of children who have disabilities or other special needs. These children need a holistic approach to their care and education. The tools that the teacher will use are education, working with families, cultural competence, and supervision. The teacher needs a knowledge base for these. Children who do not have these special circumstances may need to be taught to understand and support the children who do. Cultural competence needs to be practiced because of the actions and reactions of other cultures to children with disabilities or other special needs. Supervision will provide an environment that offers maximum well-being for all children.

## CHAPTER SUMMARY

Some children in care may have disabilities or other special needs that affect the early childhood education environment. If these children are included, the teacher should work as part of a team with the families and service providers who are part of the child's special care plan. Teachers can help support the child by using strategies that maximize the child's abilities while in the early childhood education environment. Teachers can support the family by keeping a clear line of communication and by understanding cultural issues. Teachers need to be prepared to offer stability and support to all children in the environment. Teachers are most effective in meeting children's needs when they use a holistic approach that includes education, working with families, cultural competency, and supervision.

## TO GO BEYOND

In this section you will find a number of activities that you can use to apply and improve your knowledge of this chapter. There are also thorough online resources that accompany this text that can be found at http://www.early childed.delmar.com (see description at end of this chapter).

### Chapter Review Critical Thinking Applications

1. How does the Americans with Disabilities Act affect early childhood education environments? Describe the process of accommodating children with disabilities or other special needs.

2. Describe and discuss the Individuals with Disabilities Education Act and how it offers a team approach.

3. Describe and discuss autism and its implications for early childhood education environments.

4. Describe and discuss fetal alcohol syndrome and its implications for a teacher.

## As an Individual

1. Research children's books that deal with the issues discussed in this chapter. Create a list of 10 "special subjects" books and report to class on one of these books. These lists will be collated, duplicated, and distributed to the entire class.

2. Examine how individualized family service plans (IFSP) are handled in your community. List the agencies that handle the IFSP and deliver the services needed for the family and the child with disabilities or other special needs. Do these agencies offer any type of support to teachers who care for the child with special needs?

## As a Group

1. Divide the class into small groups and send them into the community to gather information on what help is available for children with disabilities or special needs. Collate the information, distribute it to the class, and discuss your findings. Was there any specific help available for teachers of these children?

2. Discuss how cultural differences might affect working with families who have children with disabilities or other special needs. List measures that would help the teacher bridge these differences.

3. In small groups of four or five, create a policy for an emergency situation related to a child's disabilities or special needs. Evaluate what extra support might be needed for this type of an emergency.

4. Discuss AD/HD and how a child with this condition might affect the early childhood education environment. What measures could a teacher use to support a child with AD/HD?

## Case Studies

1. Mimi is a three-year-old who is hard of hearing and has limited speech. She has recently joined Lin's family child care. What steps could Lin take to help Mimi transition into the care environment? What should Lin do to help the other children help her to support Mimi?

2. Kamryn is new to the early childhood education center, and Mandy is her teacher. Kamryn is two years old, and her mother has recently been told that she has autism. The mother has not yet contacted the school district. How would you help her to get an IFSP started for Kamryn?

3. Malin has come to care with some serious vision difficulties. He is almost three and has great physical control. What could you do to help him adjust to your center and maximize the environment for him?

## Chapter References

Allred, K., Briem, R., & Black, S. (1998). Collaboratively addressing needs of young children with disabilities. *Young Children, 53*(5), 32–35.

American Academy of Pediatrics (AAP). (2002). *Promoting optimal health for American children: A summary report, 1997–2001.* Elk Grove Village, IL: Healthy Child Care America.

American Academy of Pediatrics (AAP). (2004). What parents should know about thimerosal. Retrieved April 10, 2005 from http://www.cispimmunize.org/fam/thimerosal.htm

Aronson, S. (2000, September). Updates on a new vaccine, TB screening and inclusion of children with special needs. *Child Care Information Exchange,* 78–80.

Astley, S., & Clarren, S. (2000). Diagnosing the full spectrum of fetal alcohol-exposed individuals: Introducing the 4-digit diagnostic code. *Alcohol and Alcoholism, 35*(4), 400–410.

Autism Society of America (ASA). (2002). What is autism? Retrieved 11/27/04 from: http://www.autism-society.org/site/PageServer?pagename=whatisautism

Bakely, S. (2001). Through the lens of sensory integration: A different way of analyzing challenging behavior. *Young Children, 56*(6), 70–75.

Brault, L. (2004a). Inclusive early care and education program for children with disabilities and other special needs. *CAEYC Connections, 33*(1), 17–19.

Brault, L. (2004b). Music activities for children with disabilities and other special needs. *CAEYC Connections, 33*(1), 22–23.

Buysee, V., Goldman, B., & Skinner, M. (2003). Friendship formation in inclusive early childhood classrooms: What is the teacher's role? *Early Childhood Research Quarterly, 18*(4), 485–501.

Chasnoff, I., McGourty, R., Bailey, G., Hutchins, E., Lightfoot, S., Pawson, L., Fahey, C., May, B., Brodie, P., McCulley, L., & Campbell, J. (2005). The 4 P's Plus screen for substance use in pregnancy. Clinical applications and outcomes. *Journal of Perinatology, 25*(6), 368–374.

ChildCareAware (CCA). (2003). Why is quality child care important for my child with special needs? New York, NY: Author.

Child Care Law Center (CCLC). (2001, October 30). Questions and answers about the Americans with Disabilities Act: A quick reference (information for child care providers). Retrieved November 26, 2004 from: http://www.childcarelaw.org/Publications/ADA%20QA.pdf

Child Care Law Center (CCLC). (2004, October 20). Questions and answers for parents about the IDEA & preschool in California. San Francisco: Author. Retrieved on November 27, 2004 from: http://www.childcarelaw.org/Publications/Q%27s%20%20A%27s%20about%20IDEA%20%20Preschool.11-04%20final1.pdf

Christakis, D., Zimmerman, F., DiGiuseppe, D., & McCarty, C. (2004). Early television exposure and subsequent attentional problems in children. *Pediatrics, 113*(4), 708–713.

Centers for Disease Control (CDC). (2004, July 26). Living with fetal alcohol syndrome. Author. Retrieved 11/24/04 from http://www.cdc.gov/ncbddd/factsheets/FAS_living.pdf

Child Health Alert (CHA). (2004, May 1). MMR vaccine and autism: A New Study. *Author: 22,* 3.

Diamond, K., Hestenes, L., & O'Connor, C. (1994). Integrating children with disabilities in preschool: Problems and promise. *Young Children, 49,* 68–79.

Eustace, L., Kang, D., & Coombs, D. (2003). Fetal alcohol syndrome: A growing concern for health care professionals. *Journal of Obstetric, Gynecologic, and Neonatal Nursing, 32*(2), 215–221.

Flynn, L., & Kieff, J. (2002). Including everyone in outdoor play. *Young Children, 57*(3), 20–26.

Gonzalez-Mena, J. (2004). *Infants, toddlers and caregivers.* New York: McGraw-Hill.

Grandin, T. (2001). Teaching tips for children and adults with autism. Retrieved 11/26/04 from http://www.autism.org/temple/tips.html

Grechus, M. (2000). Who's challenged? Children with special needs or their caregivers? *Healthy Child Care, 3*(3). Retrieved May 15, 2002, from http://www.healthychild.net/Articles

Greenspan, S. (2001, May). Working with the hearing impaired child. *Scholastic Early Childhood Today,* 20–21.

Greenspan, S. (2003, November/December). Working with the child who has difficulty communicating. *Scholastic Early Childhood Today,* 28–29.

Greenspan, S. (2004, April). Working with parents of children with special needs. *Scholastic Early Childhood Today,* 20–21.

Groppe, M. (2004, September 9). Burton leads mercury inquiry. Indiana Star, INDYSTAR.com. Retrieved September 19, 2004 (ID: ind65959747): http://nl. newsbank.com/nl-search/we/Archives?s_site=indystar&f_site=indystar&f_site-name=Indianapolis+Star%2FNews%2C+The+%281N%29&p_theme=gannett &p_product=IN&p_action=search&p_field_base-0=&p_text_base-0=Burton+ leads+mercury+inquiry&Search=Search&p_perpage=10&p_maxdocs=200&p_ queryname=700&s_search_type=keyword&p_sort=_rank_%3AD&p_field _date-0=YMD_date&p_params_date-0=date%3AB%2CE&p_text_date-0=3qzM

Harwood, M., & Kleinfeld, J. (2002). The value of early intervention for children with fetal alcohol syndrome. *Young Children, 57*(4), 86–90.

Hess, K. (2003). Keep the change: A hard-earned success. *Young Children, 58*(4), 30–32, 44.

Humpal, M., & Wolf, J. (2003). Music in the inclusive environment. *Young Children, 58*(2), 103–107.

Kvigne, V., Leonardson, G., Borzelleca, J., Brock, E., Neff-Smith, M., & Welt, T. (2003). Characteristics of mothers who have children with fetal alcohol syndrome or some characteristics of fetal alcohol syndrome. *Journal of the American Board of Family Practitioners 16*(4), 296–303.

Legal Update Newsletter (2004, Summer). Making inclusion a part of planning for universal preschool. San Francisco: Child Care Law Center. Retrieved November 27, 2004 from: http://www.childcarelaw.org/Publications/Summer% 202004Final.pdf

Moore, T. (2004). Providing music and movement for children with disabilities. *CAEYC Connections, 33*(1), 11–13.

Leekam, S., Lopez, B., & Moore, C. (2000). Attention and joint attention in preschool children with autism. *Developmental Psychology, 36,* 539–547.

Mulligan, S. (2003). Assistive technology: Supporting the participation of children with disabilities. *Young Children, 58*(6), 50–51.

Nadeau, K., & Dixon, E. (1997). Learning to slow down and pay attention: A book for kids about ADD. Washington, DC: ADA-Magination Press.

Nash, J. (5/6/2002). The secret of autism. Time Magazine. Retrieved September 19, 2004 from Internet path: http://www.time.com/time/covers/1101020506/ scautism.html

National Dissemination Center for Children with Disabilities (NICHCY). (2004, November 17). The latest scoop on IDEA reauthorization. Retrieved November 27, 2004 from http://www.nichcy.org/reauth/scoop.htm

National Dissemination Center for Children with Disabilities (NICHCY). (2002). General information about disabilities: Disabilities that qualify infants, toddlers, children, and youth for services under the IDEA. Retrieved November 27, 2004 from: http://www.nichcy.org/pubs/genresc/gr3.htm

National Institute of Mental Health (NIMH) (1999). *Autism.* NIH Publication No. 97-4023. Bethesda: MD.: National Institute of Mental Health.

North Carolina Child Care Health and Safety Resource Center (NCCCHSRC). (2005). Parents are partners in planning. *North Carolina Child Care Health and Safety Bulletin, 7*(2), 5.

Olson, J., Murphy, C., & Olson, P. (1999). Readying parents and teachers for inclusion of children with disabilities: A step-by-step process. *Young Children, 54*(3), 18–23.

Park, A. (5/6/2002). Vaccines: Are the shots safe? Time Magazine. Retrieved November 26, 2004 from: http://www.time.com/time/covers/1101020506/scvaccine.html

Peterson, C., Wall, S., Raikes, H., Kisker, E., Swanson, M., Jerald, J., Atwater, J., & Qiao, W. (2004). Early Head Start: Identifying and serving children with disabilities. *Topics in Early Childhood Special Education, 24*(2), 76–88.

Sandall, S., Schwartz, I., Joseph, G., Chou, H., Horn, E., Liever, J., Odom, S., & Wolery, R. (2002). *Building blocks for teaching preschoolers with special needs.* Baltimore: Paul H. Brooks Publishing Co.

Sharpe, T., Alexander, M., Hutcherson, J., Floyd, R., Brimacombe, M., Levine, R., Mengel, M., & Stuber, M. (2004). Report from the CDC. Physician and allied health professionals' training and fetal alcohol syndrome. *Journal of Women's Health, 13*(2), 133–139.

Shaw, P. (2003, April). Including children with special needs: Tips for child care providers. California Child Care Health Program. Retrieved November 26, 2004 from http://www.ucsfchildcarehealth.org/webpages/pdftext/healthsafety/inclen081803.pdf

Smeeth, L., Cook, C., Fonbonne, E., Heavey, L., Ridrigues, L., Smith, P., & Hall, A. (2004). MMR vaccine and pervasive developmental disorders: A case-control study. *Lancet, 364*(9438), 963–969.

Sokol, R., Delaney-Black, V., & Nordstrom, B. (2003). Fetal alcohol syndrome disorder. *Journal of the American Medical Association, 290*(22), 2996–2999.

Vakil, S., Freeman, R., & Swim, T. (2003). The Reggio Emilia approach and inclusive early childhood programs. *Early Childhood Education Journal, 30*(3), 187–192.

vanDyck, P., Kogan, M., McPherson, M., Weissman, G., & Newacheck, P. (2004). Prevalence and characteristics of children with special health care needs. *Archives of Pediatrics and Adolescent Medicine, 158*(9), 884–891.

Walsh, E. (2005). Partnering with parents to create a special care plan. *Child Health Care Connections Newsletter, 18*(3), 8.

U.S. Department of Health & Human Services (HRSA). (2004, September 7). New national survey finds one in eight U.S. children has special health care needs. Washington, DC. Author. Retrieved September 8, 2004 from: http://newsroom.hrsa.gov/NewsBriefs/2004/specialneedsurvey.htm

U.S. Department of Justice (USDOJ). (2002, May). A guide to disability rights laws. Washington, DC: Author. Retrieved November 27, 2004 from: http://www.usdoj.gov/crt/ada/cguide.htm

Zamani, R. (2000b). Diversity: Facing the diverse needs of all children. *Child Care Health Connections, 13*(6), 8.

Additional resources for this chapter can be found by visiting the Online Companion™ at http://www.earlychilded.delmar.com. This supplemental material includes extensive chapter quizzes, PowerPoint® outlines, Web links, and various other activities to help better utilize the material in this chapter. The site is updated regularly, so you may check back often to receive the latest information about the subjects in each chapter.

# Creating Linkages

After reading this chapter, you should be able to:

### 16.1 Policies for Creating Linkages

Describe and discuss policies for creating linkages for better health and well-being within the early childhood education environment and the community.

### 16.2 Toward Better Communication Skills

Describe and discuss how to develop good communication skills for working with parents, children, and coworkers.

### 16.3 Cultural Competency

Describe and discuss the importance of understanding issues regarding diversity and how they may affect safety, nutrition, and health in early childhood education.

### 16.4 Accessing Community Resources

Describe and discuss the importance of accessing and developing community safety, nutrition, and health resources for helping the teacher, the child, and the parents.

### 16.5 Developing Effective Advocacy

Describe and discuss the advocacy role the teacher plays in linking the child, the family, the community, and beyond.

### 16.6 Creating a Caring Community for Families

Describe and discuss how to create a caring community environment that provides the maximum protection for a child's health and well-being.

● Linkages
*connections that unify the teacher, child, family, and community*

## 16.1  POLICIES FOR CREATING LINKAGES

**Linkages** should be formed within and without the early childhood education environment in order to offer the maximum in protection and prevention for issues dealing with children's safety, nutrition, and health. The teacher needs to secure the cooperation of coworkers, parents, and community resources to create these linkages. The following indicators reflect reasons for linkages to offer support to the child care environment:

- More frequent communication between teachers and families may facilitate a greater knowledge for both sides and improve the care given to the children in the early childhood education environment (Ghazvini & Mullis, 2002).

- Communication skills that are well developed and backed by knowledge of one's own perspective and those of other cultures can help the teacher negotiate conflicts based on culture (Obegi & Ritblatt, 2005). There are 47 million people in the United States who speak a language other than English at home (ECT, 2004a)

- Teachers who are culturally competent have the ability to value diversity, know what their own cultural perception is, can manage the differences between the two, and can adapt to the cultural context of the community they serve (Burchenal & Cryer, 2003; NCCC, 2003).

- If the language and culture of a community is valued, families are more likely to become involved with their children's school (Riojas-Cortex et al., 2003).

- Early childhood education programs are becoming family-centered organizations that reflect the changes going on in society (Hamilton et al., 2003).

- The biggest challenge that teachers have in trying to make sure good public policy for early childhood education environments exists is to be "at the table" and advocate for what is good care for children (CCW, 2002).

- Teachers and parents who work together as a caring community can improve the quality of child care (Collins et al., 2003).

Communicating with the child is the first step toward learning how to communicate with parents, coworkers, and directors regarding a child's safety, nutritional, and health needs.

● **Synergy**
*combined effort
or action*

**Synergy,** or combined effort, is much more effective than individual effort. This is especially true in the early childhood education environment. Policies should be in force to help develop approaches using synergy as often as possible. The holistic approach to early childhood education allows the teacher to understand that one person would be less effective than a combined effort. A teacher is called upon to be many things to a child. The physical, emotional, and cognitive care and education of a child is a very large task. Most teachers are involved in this task on a daily basis for a number of children.

The teacher can help make this job easier. The teacher who learns to communicate about the child's safety, nutritional, and health needs can be more proactive in the care of children. This effort will involve communicating to the parent as well as all those present in the early childhood education environment. Coworkers, directors, assistants, and food preparers should all be involved in the effort to promote and protect the health and well-being of children in care. An important part of this communication is to let the parents know, in advance, what the policies are for safety, nutrition, and health (Lucarelli, 2002).

The communication effort helps the transition from the early childhood education environment to the home environment so that the child can feel the sense of well-being as a constant. Many parents do not realize how much they can actively affect their own environment. A teacher who passes on knowledge about safety, nutrition, and health can help parents create a better environment at home.

A teacher who is culturally competent is more effective in preventing problems and protecting the well-being of the child. The many cultures, races, and other diverse conditions of people in this country are rapidly causing change, and this diversity should be understood instead of ignored. The teacher who learns to celebrate the differences and understand the similarities will be more effective in offering the children in care an optional environment. The teacher who approaches situations from a broad viewpoint will be more likely to pick up nuances of how families approach safety, nutrition, and health. A teacher should be comfortable knowing his limitations (Gonzalez-Mena & Stonehouse, 2000).

This parent board shares information about many community resources.

In addition to the parents and families, the teacher also needs to seek help from outside the early childhood education environment. A teacher is rarely a qualified health or nutrition professional. There will probably be instances when the teacher will need to call on outside resources and professionals to deal with a situation that presents a challenge.

It is getting more difficult to remain in the early childhood education environment without acknowledging that the teacher be an advocate for the health, safety, and well-being of children. This not only occurs within the environment and to the parents, but in the greater community. The difficulties that communities are seeing with violence, poverty, homelessness, child maltreatment, and other family situations may have a residual effect in the early childhood education environment. The teacher may feel the need to take a leadership role to help improve the community or the situation.

The best way to provide families with a caring community is to use the synergistic approach. A team can be created when working with people within the early childhood education environment, with parents, and in the greater community. A teacher who makes the most of the people and the resources available will offer the children in the early childhood education program the best environment possible.

In order to provide the maximum benefit to the child, there should be policies that include the following:

1. *Communication Skills:* practices for supporting better communications among teachers, parents, children, and others

2. *Cultural Competency:* understanding diverse cultures, races, and health conditions in order to recognize differences and similarities that will help maintain the well-being of children

3. *Accessing Community Resources:* understanding how to recognize and access community resources that will help the teacher be more effective in providing for safety, nutrition, and health

4. *Developing Effective Advocacy:* understanding the importance of advocacy and how to perform it

5. *Creating a Caring Community for Families:* understanding that, when families are more involved in the early childhood education environment, the quality of health and well-being of children will be improved

### Key Concept 16.1

### Policies for Linkages

Early childhood education is an important part of many children's lives. Its quality is greatly improved if there is good communication with parents and if cultural competence is practiced. The quality of care is promoted by accessing and using community resources. The teacher who is an advocate for the child with the parents, others, and the greater community is offering maximum protection and prevention. Creating a caring community for families uses synergy for greater safety, nutrition, and well-being both at the child care site and for the families at home.

## 16.2 TOWARD BETTER COMMUNICATION SKILLS

Development of good communication is critical for the early childhood education environment. Families come in many different forms. There may be two parents present, or only a single parent. There may be two parents present where one of them is a stepparent. Grandparents, aunts, uncles, and foster parents are becoming increasingly responsible for raising children. Mutual communication with the parent or guardian concerning the child should show respect and acknowledge feelings about certain situations. This helps both parties feel more comfortable. Keeping parents informed about the child's activities and any concerns you have helps families learn how to trust you and provides a basis for communication (Honig, 2002; Gonzalez-Mena, 2004).

### *Developing Trust and Respect*

The teacher who is consistent and predictable in the relationship with parents helps develop a bond of trust. If the teacher shows the child and the family respect, they are much more likely to be responsive and to participate actively in the safety, nutrition, and health of the child (Figure 16-1).

The teacher should be supportive and responsive to concerns about a child. This should be established at the beginning of the relationship with the child and parent or guardian and should be continued on a daily basis. Establishing and continuing the communication relationship is often a matter of common sense, as listed in Table 16-1.

Make sure that you do not make any assumptions about the child or the family culture (Shaw, 2000; Gonzalez-Mena, 2004). Ask questions and, where applicable, be aware of cultural issues. If culture may be a part of the issue and a relationship has already been established, you might want to ask direct but sensitive questions about the culture or ethnicity to help you to understand (Kaiser & Rasminsky, 2003). Before you begin, you should become aware of your own culture so you can understand your own behavior and interactions with others. There may be communication barriers on both sides—not created by language, necessarily, but by cultural differences (Obegi & Ritblatt, 2005). There may also be a language barrier that should be addressed. With the help of the health consultant or other parents in care,

A bond of trust between teacher, parent, and child can be formed by consistency and respect.

**FIGURE 16-1**
The Five Cs of Parent Relations.

Confidentiality    Consistency

Common Sense

Communication    Caring

**TABLE 16-1**
*A Dozen Ways for a Teacher to Successfully Communicate*

- Show a genuine interest in the child, and ask the parent to share feelings and concerns about the child.

- Encourage the parent to ask questions, visit the early childhood education environment, and participate whenever possible. Seek input whenever possible.

- Be an active listener. Focus on the parent or guardian, not on how to respond. Assume nothing. Clarify any confusion or misunderstanding by repeating what was heard.

- Provide parents with verbal and written information about the child and the concerns or information that will help address the safety, nutritional, and health needs of the child.

- Think before speaking. What is it that needs to be communicated? What is the best way to do it? Practice through role play if you need to.

- Any concern about the child should be dealt with immediately and not allowed to go unchecked. Never discuss a child in front of other children or adults.

- Be positive and discuss good behaviors and accomplishments as well as problems.

- Be flexible. Each family is unique and has different needs. Be aware of the family situation, the cultural background, and the child's home environment.

- Be a good observer. Often it is what is not said or done that may be significant. Learn to read nonverbal cues such as body tension, avoidance of contact, a sense of chaos, or other vulnerabilities.

- Never compare the child or situation with others. This never accomplishes anything and can cause resentment and guilt.

- Always keep whatever is communicated in confidence. Use the information to help the child and family find resources or get any help necessary.

- Remain calm; do not argue or be defensive. Model good coping skills.

a translator can be found to help, if that appears to be a barrier to communication between families and teachers about the needs of a child.

Remember, when you are engaging in communication with parents, you should make sure to respect their comfort zone, as well as your own. Be sure to communicate thoroughly and ask questions about anything that might be relevant to the issue at hand. It is important to realize that "one size" or one solution does not fit all situations and people. Each child, each family, and each issue is different, and the teacher should be considerate of that fact (Kaiser & Rasminsky, 2003; d'Entremont, 1998). You can ask parents for their opinions and ask them to clarify what they have said. A family's values should be supported, but both the teacher and the family should realize that there are different perspectives. Always keep in mind that the goal is the well-being of the child (Gonzalez-Mena, 2004). Without clear discussion, communication may break down, and both the parent and the teacher may become frustrated. Clear communication must occur in order to understand differences, whether they be cultural, religious, or socioeconomic. Gonzalez-Mena and Bhavnagri, (2001) suggested that, when you are trying to communicate about a practice or policy that the family may not understand or agree with, some questions should be asked. Those questions are found in Table 16-2.

## Developing a System of Communication in Early Childhood Education Environments

Good communication skills are necessary for the early childhood education staff. It can affect the quality of care (Lucarelli, 2002). During a day, the same child may have more than one teacher. These teachers need to communicate with each other as to the child's safety, nutritional, and health needs. The quality of any interactions concerning the child affect the care of the child. Children need to feel that their environment is constant and that the care is consistent. The degree of communication among staff members can affect the morale of the early childhood education environment. There can be problems if any one person feels that she is not being heard or her opinion is not respected. When the communication within the early childhood education environment is consistent, the children can also learn to communicate at a higher level.

Communication is most effective when it is verbal and face to face. However, the nature of the early childhood education environment may not always

TABLE 16-2
*Questions for the Teacher to Clarify Perspective*

1. Is the family's cultural perspective on this issue different from mine?
2. How does the family's cultural perspective relate to its care practices for their children?
3. What goals do the family have for the child, and how do those goals relate to the cultural perspective of the family?
4. Are the policies of care particularly suited to one culture and not all?
5. Have I attempted to understand the family's perspective and the complexity of the issues that may be present?
6. Have I tried to explain to the family my own rationale based on my perspective, and have I looked at my own perspective and how culture may have affected it?
7. What are some creative ways to address both perspectives and solve the problem?

Face-to-face verbal communication between teachers and supervisors is the most effective way to monitor situations and identify problem areas and training possibilities.

offer the opportunity. A system of communication through notes, after-hours telephone conversations, and regular staff meetings can help to maintain an open line of communication about concerns and issues concerning the well-being of the children in care. If the early childhood education environment includes a director, he or she should model good communication and help others on the staff to resolve any conflicts that may be present.

Another area that might be further developed in the early childhood education environment is communication with preverbal infants and toddlers. Recent research has shown that very young children can reduce their communication frustration level by learning simple signs to represent language (SC, 2000). Early childhood education centers all over the United States and Great Britain are employing this method of communication for the preverbal children in care (Signs of the times, 2004; Fawcett, 2001; Meller, 2001). The idea is that children know what people are saying to them before they can talk, but they cannot reciprocate in spoken language (Helms, 1999). Children younger than 12 months are capable of learning and mastering simple signs (Baca, 2001; Fiedler, 2002). Signing can encourage communication at least six months before children begin to form basic words (Goodwyn et al., 2000). The ability to learn to communicate gives preverbal children the opportunity to participate and decreases their frustration level. Signing has been found to be a major source of reducing tantrums and stress for very young children. Another benefit has been that children who use signs at this early stage of development can increase their cognitive abilities (Goodwyn et al., 2000). Communication like this has also shown to increase the bonding level of the child and the person communicating with the child. In fact, when babies communicate by using signs, they are much more likely to engage those they are communicating with to form a reciprocal relationship (Moore et al., 2001). Children who engage in reciprocity through language develop the ability to become more rational in their thinking, can problem-solve both on their own and with others, and can learn to be more reflective (Greenspan, 2003a).

Opinions differ as to which signs should be used with preverbal children. Some believe that using American Sign Language (ASL) is the best way. Others have been successful in making up signs that, when consistently used, seem to work fine. Videos such as *Baby Signs* and *Sign with Me* are available to help parents and teachers understand this important communication pattern. Good communication between the child and the teacher can affect the child's cognitive and language development (Loeb et al., 2004). The quality of communication between a child and a teacher affects the overall quality of care. A teacher who gets down to the child's eye level when talking or listening is more attentive to the child's needs (Sherry, 2004). When a child feels that someone is listening to what he says and cares about it, he is better able to develop a sense of self (Greenspan, 2003b). A teacher who creates activities or has available materials that encourage interactions among children in care will also foster language between children. Using stories to engage children in conversation can be beneficial (Whaley, 2002). It can help children to interact with each other, the teacher, and the story. Storytelling can help extend the language of the children.

### Key Concept 16.2

## Good Communication Skills

Communication is a key factor in the success of an early childhood education environment's effort to provide for the safety, nutrition, and health of the children present. Communication with the families of the children is vitally important and should be a priority. Asking for input and listening to parents are key to consistency and optimum care. Communicating with others who participate in the early childhood education environment allows protection and prevention to be at their highest level.

● **Diversity**
*differences; variety often related to culture*

## 16.3  CULTURAL COMPETENCY

Culture is defined as parameters of behavior. Regardless of the culture of a home environment, when one steps into the outside world, **diversity** is everywhere. The increasing population of different cultural groups has had an impact on the United States (Lundgren & Morrison, 2003). The society we live in is multicultural and multifaceted. Being culturally sensitive is no longer enough. To be a successful, effective teacher, one must be culturally competent (Obegi & Ritblatt, 2005; Kaiser & Raminsky, 2003).

Everyone should learn how to handle this diversity, and this is especially true for people who care for children. The teacher has the opportunity to teach children positive values about gender, race, ethnicity, class, and disabling conditions. The teacher will also be dealing with families of children who may represent differing cultures, social class, ethnicity, and other variations of background and experiences.

Creating a cultural consistency between the home environment and the environment in care is important (Gonzalez-Mena, 2004). If there is no representation for a child's culture in toys, language spoken, language in books, foods, or other people around her, then she is likely to feel that she is in "stranger" care (Cronin & Jones, 1999). Children who are uncomfortable in care are less likely to play and learn and more likely to be at risk for safety, nutrition, and health problems. When a child is exposed to diversity in culture and cultural practices, she is more likely to become comfortable and to see differences as normal (Gerstenblatt, 2000). When a child is comfortable in care he is more likely to develop a sense of identity (Crockenberg, 2001; Gonzalez-Mena, 2000). The awareness of cultural diversity and differing values has the potential to greatly improve the early childhood education environment. It will also allow the teacher the ability to best meet the needs for safety, nutrition, and health for all children in care.

## Preparing for Cultural Competence

Cultural competency is about how we learn to value diversity in many ways and how we come to situations with open minds about other cultures and diverse backgrounds. Valuing this diversity is the first step in the process of building a framework for cultural competency (NCCC, 2003). The second step is for the teacher to recognize her own cultural background, attitudes, beliefs, and guidelines for behavior (Obegi & Ritblatt, 2005; Huber, 2004). People can break down barriers to accept those who are different if they understand their own biases and ways of operating. Figure 16-2 shows the Cultural Competency Continuum and a teacher can place himself or herself on the continuum

**FIGURE 16-2**
Cultural Competency
Continuum

### CULTURAL COMPETENCY CONTINUUM

Cultural Destructiveness
(Intentionally deny, reject, or outlaw any other culture)
↓
Cultural Incapacity
(Accept the existence of other cultures but unable to work effectively with other cultures)
↓
Cultural Blindness
(Assume that all people are basically alike; universal approach and services for all people)
↓
Cultural Precompetence
(Willing to learn about and understand other cultures)
↓
Cultural Competency
(Able to work effectively in cross-cultural situations; develop standards, policies, practices and attitudes that value diversity)
↓
Cultural Proficiency
↓
(Proactive in promoting cultural diversity; seeks opportunities to improve cultural relationships)

Reprinted with permission by Carol Ann Brannon, MS, RD, LD "Dietetic Diversity" a Continuing Education Course published by Nutrition Dimension, Inc. April, 2005. (www.nutritondimension.com)

Diverse classrooms present the immediate need of understanding and nurturing diversity. Teachers play an important role in creating an antibias environment in which children can grow and learn about their own and others' uniqueness.

when looking at biases and methods of operating. Each person should appreciate his or her own uniqueness as well as similarities to others.

The next step is to create a balance within the dynamics of difference. Today, early childhood programs of all kinds reflect the cultural, ethnic, and racial differences found in the greater society (DiNatale, 2002). There is the early childhood education environment and the home environment. Duarte and Rafanello (2001) suggested that "best practices recommend that environment and instruction practices reflect the language and culture of the children they serve." Teachers must work actively to get families involved so that there are no barriers between the two environments and children will be able to get the best possible care and education from both of them. Families from other cultures may want and need help with parenting skills and other care issues (Bornstein & Cote, 2004). Routines, practices, and procedures in care may be unfamiliar to or misunderstood by families (Walker-Dalhouse & Dalhouse, 2001). Teachers may be happy to provide information and would appreciate it if this type of consistency between the two environments could be created. Working towards this balance enables the teacher to create an environment where all children are able to accept who they are and value their backgrounds (Keiffer, 2001; Marshall 2001). The teacher next needs to seek to acquire and increase knowledge about other cultures. This also entails cultural sensitivity. When learning about another culture, one should recognize subtleties that may not be apparent and should accept a person from another culture in the many ways he may express his cultural background. One should take care not to apply a group label and make the assumption that all individuals within a group are alike (Early Childhood Teacher, 2004a). For example, Asians are not all alike. China, Japan, Vietnam, Maylasia, and the Philippines may all be classified as Asian, but their cultures are very diverse. Cultural competence is something

The teacher can gain insight into diversity issues by talking with parents individually or in groups.

that is gained in informal and natural ways by observing, asking for, or seeking out information and by being involved with the children and families in care (Moore, 2003, Moore 2004). A teacher cannot know everything about all cultures, but knowledge about one culture at a time can be acquired through exploration of that culture (Huber, 2004). Some techniques for developing cultural competence can be found in Table 16-3.

This approach should cover more than just how different cultures celebrate holidays or the foods they eat. A teacher who is trying to understand diversity should learn how families behave on an ongoing and everyday basis (see Table 16-3). Values and beliefs regarding items such as family roles, child-rearing practices, gender differences, and communication styles are reflected in how families live their lives on a daily basis (Huntsinger et al., 2000).

## Personal Interactions

Personal interactions are the best way to adapt to the issues of cultural diversity (Okagaki & Diamond, 2000; Burchenal & Cryer, 2003). As diversity is explored and understood it allows the teacher to be more able to communicate, more sensitive, and more willing to change and adapt (Seefeldt, 2002). Having an open dialogue can break down misconceptions and fears on the parents' part and help to establish trust.

In some cultures, there are distinctive differences that can be observed for, and communication style can be adjusted. In low-context cultures such as Western Europe and the United States, great value is put on independence. Communication is precise, direct, and logical. In cultures that are high-context, such as Latino, African-American, Asian, Native American, and Southern European cultures, interdependence is valued. Communication is more likely to include nonverbal cues, and tradition, history, and social status play a great role (Kaiser & Rasminsky, 2003).

**TABLE 16-3**
*Techniques for Developing Cultural Competence*

- Develop a dialogue with parents about their own cultures. Invite them to share their culture with others in the early childhood education environment. Express a desire to learn from the parents. Ask for their opinions, and encourage them to participate. This might include having them help plan curriculum and participate in activities.

- If language barriers exist, try to find someone who can translate and break down any barriers to teacher–parent communication.

- Have family evening potlucks where families bring dishes representing their backgrounds and share some of their histories with other families.

- Research games, songs, and so forth, from other cultures in books on child care curriculum and histories. If there are children in care who have disabilities, this can also be researched. Incorporate these into the curriculum.

- Attend cultural fairs to get a greater understanding about the cultures represented in the early childhood education environment. Learn everything you can about a child's home culture.

- Create a support group with other teachers. Use this collaborative effort to share information, resources, and hold open discussions. This is a good way to remove barriers that the teacher may have.

- Observe children who are from diverse cultures, socioeconomic levels, or abilities. Watch the child with parents and family members. Do this without judgment. Watch how they communicate on verbal and nonverbal ways.

- Talk to others in the community who represent the diverse group to find out about the group.

- In larger early childhood education situations, encourage the hiring of diverse staff.

- Acknowledge with parents that a topic may have many points of view and, when necessary, reach a consensus for the well-being of the child.

- Create a family book where families of the children in care talk about the people in their families, their customs, their home, and their lives. Have pictures to go with these—if the family has no camera, have the children help draw the pictures to go into the book. If the care environment has a digital camera or video recorder available, it could be checked out to families to accomplish this task.

- Create a regular time every week or two to invite parents to sing songs from their culture or share stories. Have them talk about cultural traditions. If needed, try to have a translator.

- Put up pictures of famous buildings or places around the world, and of children and families from all over the world.

- With prior parental permission, use digital cameras and video recorders to take pictures of the children to place on the wall.

- Provide some distinctive cultural clothing and props, such as product boxes, for the dramatic play area.

- Provide children's books about other cultures and in the prevailing language. A number of books from many cultures are now available.

- Incorporate storytelling from other cultures into activities. If possible, bring in bicultural storytellers.

- Incorporate music from other cultures.

- Plan cooking projects for foods from other cultures, maybe even recipes brought in by children to represent their family's culture.

An understanding of different cultural backgrounds provides a deeper understanding of parenting strategies. Socioeconomic differences are also an important factor.

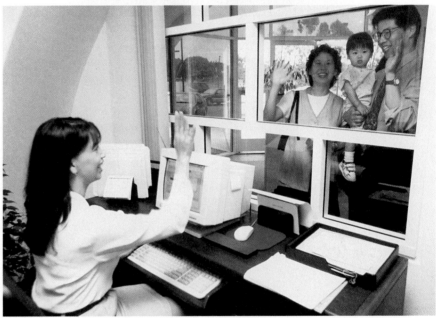

There are other indirect ways to communicate as well, such as pauses and silences. See Table 16-4 for some strategies to help with cross-cultural communication.

Differences in backgrounds may elicit necessary responses in order to maintain the safety, nutritional well-being, and health of the children in care. Parents develop their philosophy of how to parent based on their own culture, socioeconomic background, personality, and family experiences.

Studies have shown that, even though parents may come from diverse cultural backgrounds, it is the socioeconomic level that most greatly affects parenting styles (Julian et al., 1994). These and other studies have found few differences in parenting based on culture alone. Low income status may bring with it emotional stress and decreased abilities of parents and families to provide the necessary support for the children (Reynolds, et al., 2000). Social conditions such as large households, lack of access to health care, and unemployment were found to have an effect on the health of children of Mexican immigrants (Duarte & Rafanello, 2001).

**TABLE 16-4**
*Keys to Cross-Cultural Communication*

- Be open, honest, and respectful.
- Understand and respect personal space. Individuals of different cultures have varying degrees of comfort about the amount of personal space between them and another person.
- Establish a rapport in the common interest of the child.
- Express interest and pay attention by listening carefully.
- Respect silence. It may be a cultural norm or the result of taking time to understand what is being said in a nonnative language.
- Watch how, when, and if eye contact is made. In some cultures making eye contact shows lack of respect.

Diversity can be incorporated into any type of activity simply by presenting different types of people, food, or landscapes that encourage discussion of those differences.

The realization by the teacher that families are more alike than different breaks down further barriers to providing care. The effects of low income may be more easily understood than a cultural difference. As the teacher recognizes the similarities to families of other cultures, the ability to discern differences may increase.

## Understanding Family Actions

● **Acculturated**
*adopting attitudes and beliefs*

There may be cultural differences that account for the actions of families. These are most likely to occur in families who are less **acculturated** to the social values commonly accepted by American society. Families who perceived difficulties in adapting to the patterns of social integration were more likely to place greater demands on children and were found to practice more strict control over them (Julian et al., 1994). Families that operate from the viewpoint of their own culture alone are more likely to have bicultural conflicts. These conflicts may include how children are expected to behave, how health is perceived, whether safety is seen as an issue, and how children are fed (Gonzalez-Mena, 2004; Zamani, 2000; Keiffer, 2001).

## Integrating Diversity into the Early Childhood Education Environment

It should be understood that differences may present themselves between the early childhood education environment and the home environment. Children develop their attitudes and identity through experiences in their environments and with their bodies as they pass through developmental stages. When children are infants and toddlers, they become self-aware. As they grow and explore their world, they begin to identify differences as well as similarities. They will also begin to question differences. Teachers should be able to respond appropriately. For example, color is an integral part of a person, and children of color should be made to feel that who and what they are is good (Moore, 2003).

A teacher should show appreciation for diversity and be aware of the dynamics involved when diverse cultures interact. She should be sensitive to group differences but should not stereotype or minimalize the differences. This can lead children to form prejudgments (West, 2001; CCHP, 2001; Wardle, 2001). A teacher should teach respect and tolerance for everyone in the early childhood education environment. Tolerance should include people who are diverse culturally, racially, ethnically, or in abilities. Biracial, biethnic children may need extra support in this respect (CCHP, 2001). Children with racial or ethnic differences should be empowered to stand up for themselves (Wardle, 2001).

The best way to manage diversity is on an ongoing basis. The teacher should continually interact with children and other adults with diversity in mind. The early childhood education environment should integrate diversity into all aspects of providing for the safety, nutrition, and health of children.

Children who learn about diversity in a positive manner are less likely to develop biases as adults (Derman-Sparks, 1999). Children learn from what the people around them think, say, and do. Table 16-5 offers some suggestions to help integrate diversity into the curriculum for safety, nutrition, and health.

### Key Concept 16.3

#### Cultural Competency

A teacher needs to manage diversity on an ongoing basis. Children in early childhood education environments represent a wide array of family structures, ethnic and cultural backgrounds, and experiences. The teacher who employs techniques that encourage understanding of diversity is better prepared to interact with children and their parents. This is essential for the teacher who wants to offer an environment that provides the best in safety, nutrition, and health for the child. The teacher can initiate activities that promote the integration of diversity into the early childhood education environment.

**TABLE 16-5**
*Activities that Integrate Diversity*

- Create a nonjudgmental atmosphere. Avoid isolating any child.

- Focus on the diversity of the children in your own early childhood education environment. This includes not only culture, but also lifestyle and socioeconomic differences.

- Weave different cultures into the curriculum themes. This allows for greater depth of understanding.

- Provide materials that depict diverse images. This might include pictures on the wall of children from all backgrounds, toys that are nonsexist and representative of the different cultures in your early childhood education environment. Dolls should be anatomically correct. Books and stories should be from a cross-section of society, including those in different languages that represent children in your care.

- Include staff from diverse backgrounds at all levels of responsibility. It is important to have this representation reflect the diversity of children in your care.

- Actively involve parents. Have parents and teachers from diverse cultures share their knowledge of their home cultures.

- Encourage participation by community helpers from diverse backgrounds for special circle times or programs that deal with safety, nutritional, or health issues. A visiting nurse may be Filipino, a police officer may be African-American, and a dietician may be in a wheelchair.

- Initiate activities that help provide self-esteem, self-identity, and well-being for mental health. Help children learn to value the differences and similarities among themselves. This will help break down stereotypical viewpoints that may impair how a child feels about himself or others.

- Encourage children to develop critical thinking skills to resist prejudice and develop acceptance.

- Respond positively to children's questions about issues concerning diversity. A child who asks about a disabled person should be answered instead of being ignored or having the question sidestepped. What is not discussed becomes the foundation for bias. These are the times for the teachable moment.

- Discuss and try to find ways to support the differing values of the families in your care.

*Pause for Reflection*

What cultures are you personally familiar with? Are you from a distinct culture that is different from the "American" culture of the early settlers from Europe? What might you do to become more culturally competent about a culture you are not familiar with?

## 16.4  ACCESSING COMMUNITY RESOURCES

The teacher may need to access a host of resources to help in meeting the safety, nutritional, and health needs of the children in care. The number of resources available may depend on the type of community where the care is provided. With any type of care, if there is a health consultant available, that person can act as a key or conduit to all available resources. The same is true for the medical home of each child. These health professionals can connect the teacher with a myriad of resources. If neither of these is available, then the community would have to be surveyed to find them.

### Surveying the Community for Resources

Larger urban communities such as major cities are more likely to have a number of resources that the teacher can access. Smaller urban or suburban communities may offer a more limited number of resources, and rural communities may have even fewer. This is only one determining factor. The teacher will have to attempt access to resources to determine the number available in the local community.

Another factor is the degree of commitment that the local governments have to the well-being of children. Some cities, counties, and states have a higher degree of commitment and therefore have more resources available for teachers. An example would be those cities that have a specialist on staff to help the area organize for early childhood education programs. However, other states and counties and cities may have less commitment or fewer of their own resources, which limits the information that they might otherwise provide.

Child care resource and referral agencies are a good source for parents to find quality, licensed child care that meets their individual needs.

# REALITY CHECK

## Bananas—A Few People Can Make a Difference

In 1973 in Oakland, California, three women organized a support group for other mothers who did not have extended families in their area. Originally, they wanted to exchange care and information, form a play group, and relate their childrearing concerns. They called themselves "Bananas," which referred to how they were feeling as well as what was present in their lives at this point—children who were at the banana eating and squishing stage. They felt that this name would make them more accessible and would be easy to remember. Some mothers in the group were looking for nonparental early childhood education environments so they could work outside the home. At about the same time, the state government was wondering if the expenditure of public monies for child care was really necessary. These women were afraid that the already scarce care available would become nonexistent, so they became politically active. They organized a survey and found that money for care was needed, especially for the care of infants. These women began a campaign to change the situation. They motivated legislators to introduce and pass the legislation that created the first resource and referral network in the nation.

Bananas found themselves in business as they became the first resource and referral agency in the country. They worked as volunteers for the first year or so and later found that there was enough money coming in that there could be some paid positions. They began offering teacher workshops and classes, and organizing support groups for parents and teachers.

Today, Bananas has evolved into one of the most effective linkages in the nation. They employ more than 30 people, with volunteers still donating their time and effort. Their mission is to help parents in any way that they can. They help find child care of all types. From experience in their area, they know that the preferred care for infants is an in-home nanny who is shared by two families. They help create these family-family links through interviews and questionnaires. Bananas also helps families access needed resources and gives workshops for parents.

For 15 years they employed a nurse to handle health and safety issues. She not only interacted with the parents but also created informational handouts on health and safety issues. Bananas entered new territory when an out-of-state move turned one woman from an employee to a health consultant who writes a column for their newsletter.

Bananas offers teachers a place where they can link with families that need care, find information they need, and participate in teacher training workshops. Bananas offers classes and workshops on site, and they have created a linkage with the Peralta Community College District. They teach classes at Merritt College, and the college gives credit for some of the classes held at Bananas.

Bananas is still actively involved in affecting legislation. One of its major achievements is the creation of TRUSTLINE, an 800 hotline number for parents to check the backgrounds of license-exempt caregivers such as nannies. This hotline has found a number of individuals who had criminal backgrounds or who were registered as sex offenders and were trying to care for children.

Bananas has formed another organization that shares their space and deals with children who have special needs. This organization offers services to families, teachers, and children. It organizes teams that include the family, the teacher, and health and nutrition professionals, and offers support and access to resources and referrals.

## REALITY CHECK (Continued)

None of the original founders of Bananas remain involved. Arlyce Curry joined Bananas when it was six months old and at the volunteer stage. For many years she has led Bananas to bigger and greater goals. Bananas is a shining example of what a few people can do to make a difference in the care of children. Check out the Bananas Web site at http://www. bananasinc.org/; it has many great resources in various languages.

**CHECK***point:* What is the name and history of your local child care resource and referral agency?

Many states, counties, and cities have community child care resource and referral agencies. These agencies provide much-needed information that the teacher should attempt to access.

The federal government provides many resources that the teacher can access. Government agencies such as the U.S. Department of Health and Human Services and the U.S. Department of Agriculture provide a great deal of information to promote safety, nutrition, and health. The information is readily available to all consumers and is easy to access through mail or the Internet. Some information may be available locally at government offices or through programs such as the Women, Infants, and Children program (WIC) and Head Start.

Many national organizations have offices that provide information to promote the health and well-being of children. All of them have a national office and some have state and local affiliates that provide easier access to information. Examples of these are the American Red Cross and the American Cancer Society.

Colleges and universities are resources for information. The departments most likely to have important information are child development, nutrition, human services, family studies, nursing, and schools of medicine. Both public and private institutions of higher learning are usually happy to share their information. Some might even be willing to share expertise, if time permits. Many child care health consultants come from this resource. Some universities offer extension services that are excellent sources of all types of information concerning children, families, nutrition, and health. Pennsylvania State University and Iowa State University are good examples of this type of support.

Hospitals, clinics and health centers, and poison control centers may also be good resources. They have information readily available that concerns the health, safety, and well-being of children. These types of facilities may also offer speakers for specific information such as immunizations. These speakers can be used for special topic programs that the teacher provides for families. Also remember the health consultant and medical home as previously discussed in several chapters. These are both excellent resources for you to tap into to get many services or other needs met for the children in your early childhood education environment (Cianciolo et al., 2004; Alkon et al., 2001).

Many common local resources exist for teachers regardless of their location. These resources are included in Table 16-6.

**TABLE 16-6**
*Common Local Resources for Safety, Nutritional, and Health Information or Assistance*

- Department of Public Health
- Hospitals, children's hospitals
- Health centers and clinics
- Fire and police departments
- Child care licensing/foster care licensing
- Child care resource and referral agencies
- Children's protective services
- Gas and electric companies
- Colleges and universities
- Medical societies (e.g., American Academy of Pediatrics)
- Local chapters of national organizations such as American Red Cross, American Dietetic Association, Girl Scouts, American Cancer Society, American Heart Association, and March of Dimes
- Poison control centers
- Libraries
- Head Start
- Department of Social Services
- Dental societies
- Family day care associations
- State and local affiliates of the National Association for the Education of Young Children (NAEYC)
- Schools and school districts (for screening, school nurses, and special education resources)
- Humane societies
- County extension services
- WIC
- Visiting Nurses Associations
- Department of Parks and Recreation
- Pharmacies and pharmacists
- Department of Environmental Protection
- Associations for cultural and ethnic affiliations

## Organizing and Using the Resources

It is vitally important that the teacher have resources organized should need for access occur. The American Public Health Association and the American Academy of Pediatrics recommend that a teacher create a community resource file that includes written information on a number of topics dealing with safety, nutrition, and health. These resources are for the teacher and the parents of children in care. If the information is available in the parent's native language, it should be provided; as an alternative, a translator should be used, whenever possible. These organizations also recommend that the teacher use consultants from local available resources. Consultants might include people from the fields of health care, nutrition, safety, mental health, or child abuse prevention. Because the teacher's time is often taken up with the business of care, the consultants can offer an invaluable service.

Prominent health organizations recommend that teachers create a community resource file that includes written information on different topics dealing with safety, nutrition, and health.

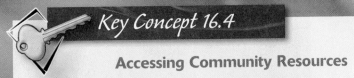

## Key Concept 16.4

### Accessing Community Resources

Access to community resources is very important for the teacher. Having a health consultant or health professional from the medical home act as a key conduit to resources is a great help. The teacher should be prepared with a number of local resources for the safety, nutritional well-being, and health of the children in care. These resources include written information and people who might consult. Resources should be surveyed and organized so that the teacher is prepared to use them if the need arises.

● **Advocate**
*to support or speak on
behalf of another*

## 16.5 DEVELOPING EFFECTIVE ADVOCACY

The majority of people who become teachers do so because of care and concern for children and their welfare. Regardless of the type of care the teacher is supplying, opportunity may present itself to **advocate** on behalf of a child. It is an inherent part of the job of a teacher to make sure the children in care are supported for optimum health, safety, and well-being. This may require the teacher to talk to parents, health professionals, and other sources of community resource and support. There are organizations that can help a teacher get involved and learn to advocate (CCW, 2002). The Center for Child Care Workforce (CCW), The National Association for the Education of Young Children (NAEYC), and the National Association for Family Child Care are just a few that could help the teacher to get involved, learn to advocate, and gain leadership skills.

### For the Early Childhood Education Environment

Center-based care may already anticipate this need. It may even be part of a director's job description. Teachers in center care may need to advocate to the director about problems or issues about children or the environment of care. In turn, directors may represent the early childhood education center to the parents and others. Directors should be prepared for this through their education, training, and experience. They should help the teachers in their facilities to learn to do the same. Staff meetings, daily consultation, and mentoring will help teachers learn to best represent the children in care. Education and training will provide added support for teachers.

### For the Family Child Care Provider

New family child care providers may not anticipate the need to intercede on behalf of a child. Veteran providers report a great deal of advocacy on behalf of the children in care. Approaching parents is usually the first line of

Teachers, by the nature of their profession, also become child advocates to make sure that children in care are supported for optimum health, safety, and well-being.

Family child care providers can benefit from contact with other family care providers. This promotes the sharing of information and support that are inherent in a center.

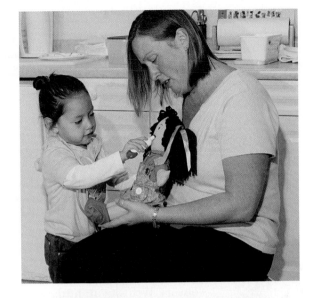

Nannies may find themselves in the awkward position of not being able to communicate effectively with parents about the child because of the employer–employee relationship. Nanny support groups are a good way for nannies to get together and share solutions to these and other common problems.

communication. However, community resources and support may be necessary to help the provider approach a situation with the parents.

Support from others in the same profession might prove to be very valuable to the family day care provider. National organizations have local chapters that may provide this support. Local child care resource and referral agencies may also help the family child care provider to find others to share concerns and solutions. Local licensing may also be a source of connecting with other family day care providers. Education and training facilities are also a source of support and learning to advocate on behalf of children.

### *For the Nanny*

The in-home care provided by a nanny may appear to be an ideal situation. With lower nanny–child ratio, one might think there would be few problems. Very few people performing the job of a nanny are trained, and they may be surprised to find that difficulties are present here too. Two issues raised by many nannies are home safety and nutritional needs. The families that employ nannies are not always aware of what is safe or healthy for children. It may be awkward for the nanny to approach the family because of the employer–employee relationship. Nannies need to understand the importance of advocacy for the children in care. Community resources and support can provide the foundations needed.

Nanny support groups are good sources of resources and solutions for advocacy. Local placement agencies may know of support groups in the area. Placing an ad in the local family press or newspaper to start a nanny support group has been effective in many parts of this country and in Canada. A list of support groups can be found on the National Association of Nannies Web site at: http://www.nannyassociation.com or on the Nanny Network Web site at: http://www.nannynetwork.com.

The American Public Health Association and American Academy of Pediatrics recommends that early childhood education programs designate a "health advocate" to receive additional training in the areas of safety, nutrition, and health.

## *The Health Advocate*

The American Public Health Association and the American Academy of Pediatrics (2002) would like to see health advocacy in early childhood education taken one step further. They recommend that early childhood education facilities and large family child care homes should have one person who is designated as the health advocate. In many cases, this might be the health consultant. In other cases, it would be an assigned teacher. This designated teacher would receive more training in issues concerning safety, nutrition, and health. In cases of small family child care home providers and nannies, the health advocate is usually the teacher (Caufield & Kataoka-Yahiro, 2001). The designated health advocate could also be an outside community resource such as a health professional who is in the facility on a frequent basis and knows the children well. This may be a health professional from a medical home. Many resource and referral networks and agencies have added a health consultant to their staff. These health consultants are generally available to teachers in the local area for questions and can act as a resource. The California Child Care Health Program is a pioneer and innovator in the area of health consultants for child care. They offer a bimonthly newsletter that is available at http://www.ucsfchildcarehealth.org.

## *Leadership*

Leadership may go beyond advocating for the children in the early childhood education environment to the parents and others. Some issues may be of real concern, and the teacher may want to pursue the issue at another level. This may be involvement to make changes at the local level or even more sweeping changes at the state or national level.

Grassroots advocacy or leadership begins at the local level. Local affiliates of national organizations that represent the early childhood education programs or children may be a good starting point. The national office can provide the local contact. Some cities and counties have a child care coordinator. This office may be able to provide good information and may be willing to help change local ordinances, laws, and other matters affecting the care of children.

Another source of help, support, and need for change may be the local health department. Other local places of support for advocacy are children's hospitals, school districts, and medical societies.

Some states and local areas have child law advocacy groups, and some have a child care lobbyist who can provide valuable information and assistance. These can be found by contacting the local or statewide legal societies.

The teacher may have to take a greater leadership role if these types of support for advocacy are not available. Pursuing the issue may call for directly working with townships, city councils, county board of supervisors, or aldermen. If the issue goes beyond local assistance, the teacher may need to contact state legislators, the governor, individual representatives, or senators who represent the area in state or national matters.

Whatever the reason for advocacy or leadership, many teachers feel it is their responsibility to go beyond just providing daily care. The issues involved in safety, nutrition, and health for children have a tremendous impact on the well-being of children and their future.

## Key Concept 16.5

### Advocacy for Children

Teachers may need to advocate for children in care on issues concerning safety, nutrition, and health. The teacher can do this in all areas of child care. Early childhood education centers, family child care homes, and nannies may all need advocacy at some point in time. The advocacy contact may be with parents, community resources, or other sources of support. Some issues may cause the teacher to seek local, state, or national assistance to make changes.

## 16.6 CREATING A CARING COMMUNITY FOR FAMILIES

In order for a caring community to exist, the families in care must be involved. The early childhood education environment should develop a program philosophy or policy that is family-friendly and encouraging of family involvement (Baldwin et al., 2003). We must begin as we did in the first chapter, when we looked at the holistic care of children. Looking at the whole child includes all the aspects, such as historical, cultural, and economic. Families and family systems are an integral part of the lives of children in care (Hamilton et al., 2003). The first objective would be to create a plan as to how the family caring community will evolve (Hurt, 2000).

Teachers must develop mutual trust and understanding to work with families in a partnership. There may be barriers to this that will need to be addressed. There may be barriers of culture, language, or communication style. These may bring with them misperceptions about parental roles (Ahnert & Lamb, 2003). Some teachers may not see parents as partners because they feel they have more knowledge about child development and are therefore the "experts." Parents may lack confidence because they don't believe in their own capabilities. Parents may work and may feel guilty about having their children in care so many hours. Whatever the reason, the barriers must come down. One of the new standards of the National Association for the Education of Young Children (NAEYC) is to "build strong relationships with all families in all communities" (Hyson, 2002). Early childhood education environments that are based upon relationships are of the highest quality. Preschools, public schools, family child care homes, and nannies that generate meaningful family involvement will be able to provide the optimum experience and ensure greater health, safety, nutrition, and well-being of the children. A beginning step is to use communication in many forms to connect with the families. Frequent communication provides more opportunities to create a balance between the early childhood education environment and home environments (Ghazvini & Mullis, 2002). Making communication in all forms an integral part of the plan is a step toward creating a caring community. Using bulletin boards to post information, having a notebook or notepad available to parents to communicate with the teacher, and sending notes home about good things about the child are great ideas (Honig, 2002). In the case of the family child

**FIGURE 16-3**
Creating a Caring Community

**Team Members**

**Family**

**Teacher**

**Community Resource**

care provider or nanny, there could be a daily log used to keep communication lines open. Where appropriate and if possible, provide communication in the parents' native language if the family is unfamiliar with English. A translator could be an older child, friends, or other family members who are native speakers. A newsletter for all parents talking about the early childhood education environment and events could be offered on a regular basis—as frequently as weekly or as infrequently as monthly. Label pictures in the environment to help parents who do not have English as a first language to see the simple words to describe the pictures. Communication is the beginning of collaboration.

The early childhood education program or family child care home should be family-friendly. If there is a comfortable welcoming place provided for the parents to sit and talk with the teacher or with other parents or watch their children, their level of comfort will be high. Before the families and children even enter the early childhood education environment, it would be nice to post "Welcome" signs in all languages represented by the children in care (DiNatale, 2002). Again, the use of translators who are familiar with the families or live in the community could help. When the physical environment is welcoming, it shows a strong sense of respect for the families and the capabilities of the children (Edward & Raikes, 2002). Early childhood education environments that support the families and children to create new friendships and be open to learning about each other will create a safe heaven for all. This safe haven will promote the emotional well-being of all and will support greater interaction and communication.

Family events such as potlucks or field trips can help involve families and make lasting connections with everyone in care, so that a community can be created. If the type of care is one in which education of parents through workshops or classes is available, this too can offer families a sense of community. All early childhood education environments could offer information

Periodic measurements of a child's height is one example of the type of information that might go in a child's safety, nutrition, and health file.

about classes that are available, as well as news articles and magazine articles that deal with child development and parenting. A number of centers in educational systems such as colleges and universities have created "parent rooms," where student parents can go to study, be sociable, and connect with others. Many students have economic difficulties, and some of these centers have even provided mini food banks for the families so that nutrition for the children and their families is consistently healthy.

As a member of a caring community, the teacher represents the issues dealing with safety, nutrition, and health that concern the early childhood education environment. The teacher may have solutions to some of these issues. It is important for the teacher to determine the areas in which she is well-informed, has had experience, and has received specialized training. This will allow the teacher to form the base from which to seek help from outside sources.

Creating a file of safety, nutritional, and health information will allow the teacher to have a great deal of necessary information available as it is needed. Keeping a current list of community resources will also help the teacher function as a team member. Networking with other teachers will also help provide information.

The health records, daily observations, and assessments of a child will help the teacher establish whether the child has an issue or problem that may affect the child's health or well-being. Involving the family in every step of the way will help them to feel a part of the early childhood education environment. In some cases, because of cultural perspectives or denial, the family may not want to discuss certain items. By establishing trust and having the caring community as an integral part of the early childhood education environment it may make it easier for teachers to approach the more delicate matters such as these issues. Parents want to feel a sense of control and if the issue is approached in a manner where the parent feels empowered the family may be more likely to respond to any intervention attempts made to help the child.

*Pause for Reflection*

What might you personally do to see that a caring community is created in your early childhood education environment?

## Providing an Atmosphere for Teamwork

If a teacher connects effectively with families it will be easier to see the goals, hopes and dreams that the families have for their children (Hurt, 2000). Outreach to families is the key to creating caring communities. As a family partner, the teacher represents the issues. The teacher can provide an atmosphere for teamwork that will encourage the parents to participate. Responsiveness to parental concerns, trust, modeling respect, and good communication skills provide the basis for a parent–teacher relationship. Parents appreciate warmth, positive attitudes, and accessibility of the teacher. When this type of climate is available to parents, they are more likely to participate. If parents are comfortable, they may be open to volunteering in care if it is asked of them. The needs and interests of the parents are important. These may be examined through surveys, conferences, parent information centers, parental involvement in the program, and home visits.

The teacher should survey the parents and other adults in the early childhood education environment on a regular basis to find out where help is needed on issues concerning safety, nutrition, and health of the children. Parents often respond to a call for information solicited by the teacher. The survey might form the basis of special topics for newsletters, parent handouts, speakers, videos, or even field trips including both parents and children.

The survey could begin a dialogue between a parent and the teacher relating to a specific issue with a child. Teacher and parent conferences may help to continue this dialogue. For example, one of the answers you may find in your survey is that some families have no access to health care for their children. This also means that there is no "medical home" for those children. A teacher can inform a family about available no- and low-cost public health insurance policies in the local area and can help them navigate the health care system to advocate for their children (Sokol-Guiterrez, 2000). Parents may recognize a problem but be unwilling to admit that it exists if the teacher approaches them first. Asking the parents for input may put the parent at ease and may help the parent to acknowledge the problem. If this approach does not work, soliciting the help of a community resource may be necessary.

Parents may also feel the need for specific help dealing with parenting issues that could affect the health and well-being of children. Posting a list of topics to be considered may help parents decide which issues are most pressing to them, so they can request information. Creating a parent center, even if it is just a tabletop or rack for providing information may help engage the parent in a mutual effort. A parent who is used to accessing information may be better prepared to participate as a team member. If there are a significant number of non-English speaking families in care, the teacher should attempt to provide information in the language of the family. Community support may be needed to accomplish this.

Annie was a family child care provider who was very organized and really tried to help the parents of the children in her care. She printed a weekly newsletter telling parents what the children did that week and reminding them of future events. She included any new safety, nutrition, or health information she received from the local agencies that she was linked to.

One day, a mother came to her, worried and stressed. Lisa, a first-generation Vietnamese-American, was concerned that her extended family wanted to "coin" her son Vu when he was sick. Coining involves placing a hot coin on the child's neck that causes red streaks in this area. Normally, Lisa would have gone along with tradition, but she had read in the paper that this practice was dangerous. She wanted Annie to help her with this problem. Annie called several local health care agencies and confirmed that "coining" was indeed dangerous. The agencies mailed information to her that she gave to Lisa. Lisa was able to go to her family and tell them that although she appreciated their traditions, she could not allow her son to be put in danger with that particular tradition. She told them that whenever Vu was ill, she would take him to the physician for care.

Home visits allow the teacher to view the child in a more holistic manner, with all the environments considered (Shaw & Zehaye, 2000). Some parents and families are more than happy to encourage the teacher to visit their homes, but this may not be possible due to time constraints. However, if an issue is creating difficulties, a home visit may provide a better picture or elicit more cooperation from the parents involved. A home visit should be handled carefully, and it might be a good idea to consult with community resource professionals before visiting the family. Some families may refuse to participate in this strategy. The nanny may have an advantage in creating a partnership based on this aspect, because the care is provided in the family's own home and the teacher is privy to most of what is occurring.

## Providing Linkages to the Community

All of the strategies used to create a caring community in the early childhood education environment may also help to promote the inclusion of a third party, the greater community and its resources. Teachers should have access to a number of people who are resources for community support. Successful early childhood education programs and family child care homes are those that involve community agencies and support networks (Lovejoy, 1998). These people may include health professionals, nutritionists, and those employed in safety professions such as police and firemen. Social workers, occupational therapists, family counselors, speech therapists, and child abuse prevention specialists are all good sources of community support. Partners may also be secured from organizations such as the American Red Cross, Head Start, community health services, resource and referral agencies, and special interest groups such as the March of Dimes.

Prevention is one of the primary goals of the teacher to protect the children's health, safety, and well-being. Providing linkages for families to many of the community resources can help prevent problems concerning these issues. Collaboration with people parents might turn to for guidance might help integrate the information into the early childhood education environment,

The "team" of teacher and parent can also be expanded to include a resource and referral worker.

thus making the information more accessible and saving time in an issue of importance (Lally et al., 2001). These linkages may occur by simply providing brochures and access information, and they can occur by inviting these community resources to speak at special programs the teacher provides for parents. Linkages may also occur through referrals to specific professionals to provide extra help or care to children who may need it. If teachers understand the community system for a specific need of a child, they can help families get needed information and services (Shaw, 2000). A parent must participate for this linkage to be successful. Earlier groundwork for establishing good communication should make getting parent participation easier. A family who is involved in a caring early childhood education community is more likely to be involved. The more the family is involved, the more valuable are all the linkages. This will allow for the greatest protection, prevention, and assurance of well being for the children in care.

## Key Concept 16.6

### Creating a Caring Community

Teachers need the help of parents and community resources in order to provide the optimum environment for good safety, nutrition, and health for children. Providing an atmosphere for a caring community can engage parents and create a linkage between the early childhood education environment and the home environment. Providing families a linkage to community resources can help the teacher to create a team that will help protect and provide the best for the children's health, safety, and well-being in and out of the early childhood education environment. Providing an atmosphere for creating a caring community for families will create a linkage between the early childhood education environment and home environments.

## CHAPTER SUMMARY

A teacher should provide an environment that meets the safety, nutritional, and health needs for the children while they are in the early childhood education environment. Communication with the families is vitally important and should be a priority.

The teacher should practice cultural competency on an ongoing basis. Children in care represent a wide variety of different family structures, ethnic and cultural backgrounds, and experiences. The teacher can initiate activities that promote the integration of diversity and cultural competence into the early childhood education environment. Teachers should access and use community resources that will help provide a greater degree of health and well-being for the children and families they work with.

Teachers may need to advocate for the children in the early education environment on issues concerning safety, nutrition, and health. Teachers need the help of parents and community resources in order to provide a caring community and the optimum environment for good safety, nutrition and health for children.

## TO GO BEYOND

In this section you will find a number of activities that you can use to apply and improve your knowledge of this chapter. There are also thorough online resources that accompany this text that can be found at http://www.early childed.delmar.com (see description at end of this chapter).

### Chapter Review Critical Thinking Applications

1. Discuss the importance of communication in the early childhood education environment. Include all the elements.

2. How does diversity affect early childhood education environments? What steps should be taken to be culturally competent?

3. How would you go about creating a caring community for parents? What would you do to get parents really involved and feeling comfortable?

### As an Individual

1. List the resources in your area that a teacher could use.

2. Research the topic of preverbal communication by finding two articles on signing with infants. Write a two to three paragraph paper and be prepared to discuss in class.

3. Survey the community for culturally diverse health and safety practices. Create a list to share with the class.

4. Go to your local resource and referral agency and find out what measures they are taking to advocate for the children in your community. List these measures and discuss in class. What more might be done to help children in the community?

### As a Group

1. Working in small groups, create a list of resources for the teachers that is compiled from the lists individuals have collected. Do any of these deal with diversity or advocacy?

2. In these same groups, create a team of teachers, parents, and resources. Role play these different roles.

3. Discuss the best methods to create a "cultural consistency" between the early childhood education environment and the home.

### Case Studies

1. You are a new teacher in an inner-city preschool with a number of children from different cultures. You love your job, but you are overwhelmed by the issues that you are facing that seem culturally oriented, particularly communicating with several parents whose first language is not English. What should you do to help manage the diversity in your environment and acquire a greater degree of cultural competence?

2. Cort is a three-year-old boy in Keela's class. He appears to be having some difficulty with his vision. His mother, Janice, is struggling to keep her family clothed, fed, and sheltered and does not have

health insurance. Janice knows Cort has a problem, but she does not have any resources to help him. What steps should Keela take to help Cort and his mother? What resources in the community could she call?

3. Su Yen was opening an early childhood education program in an urban area. She had no worries about the number of children that might attend, because there was a real lack of that type of program in that area. She was concerned about creating a climate in which parents would participate. She wanted to create a caring community that would help to meet children's needs and the parent's needs. How would she go about creating this type of climate at her school? What suggestions might you give her to help her?

## Chapter References

Ahnert, L., & Lamb, M. (2003). Shared care: Establishing a balance between home and child care settings *Child Development, 74*(4), 1044–1049.

Alkon, A., Sokal-Guiterrez, K., & Wolff, M. (2002). Child care health consultation improves health knowledge and compliance. *Pediatric Nursing, 28*(1), 61–65.

American Academy of Pediatrics (AAP). (2002). *Promoting optimal health for American children: A summary report 1997–2001.* Elk Grove Village, IL: Healthy Child Care America.

American Public Health Association & American Academy of Pediatrics, (APHA & AAP). (2002). *Caring for our children: National health and safety performance standards: Guidelines for out-of-home care.* Washington, DC: American Public Health Association.

Baca, M. (2001, July 28). Baby talk: Signals may ease communication between parents and infants. *San Diego Union Tribune,* E1, 4.

Baldwin, V., DaRos-Voseles, D., & Swick, K. (2003). Creating a caring community. The University of Arkansas nursery school experience. *Early Childhood Education Journal, 10*(3), 157–162.

Bornstein, M., & Cote, L. (2004). "Who is sitting across from me?" Immigrant mothers' knowledge of parenting and children's development. *Pediatrics, 114*(5), 557–564.

Brannon, C. (2004). Cultural competency-Values, traditions and effective practice. *Today's Dietician, 6*(11), 14–18.

Burchinal, M., & Cryer. D. (2003). Diversity, child care quality and developmental outcomes. *Early Childhood Quarterly, 18*(4), 401–426.

*Business Week.* (2000, August 14). Look who's talking—with their hands: By signing, even infants can tell you what's on their mind. *Businessweek Online.* Retrieved May 15, 2002, from http://www.businessweek.com/2000/00_33/b3694165.htm?scriptFramed.

California Childcare Health Program (CCHP). (2001). Unique needs of biracial/biethnic children. *Child Care Health Connections, 14*(1), 8.

Caufield, R., & Kataoka-Yahiro, M. (2001). Health training needs of child care professionals. *Early Childhood Education Journal, 29*(2), 119–123.

Center for Child Care Workforce (CCW). (2002). Worthy wage action packet, 2002. Washington, D.C.: Author. Retrieved November 28, 2004 from http://www.ccw.org/pubs/WWday2002actionpacket.pdf.

Cianciolo, S., Trueblood-Noll, R., & Allingham, P. (2004). Health consultation in early childhood settings. *Young Children, 59*(2), 56–61.

Collins, R., Mascia, J., Kendall, R., Golden, O., Schock, L., & Parlakian, R. (2003, March). Promoting mental health in child care settings: Caring for the whole child. *Zero to Three,* 39–45.

Crockenberg, S. (2001). The importance of culturally competent child care.

Cronin, S., & Jones, E. (1999, January). Play and cultural differences. *Child Care Information Exchange,* 46–47.

d'Entremont, L. (1998). A few words about diversity and rigidity: One director's perspective. *Young Children, 53*(1), 72–73.

Derman-Sparks, L. (1999). Markers of multicultural/antibias education. *Young Children, 54*(5), 43.

DiNatale, L. (2002). Developing high-quality family involvement programs in early childhood settings. *Young Children, 57*(9), 90–95.

Duarte, G., & Rafanello, D. (2001). The migrant child: A special place in the field. *Young Children, 56*(2), 26–34.

Early Childhood Teacher (ECT). (2004a, November/December). Profiles in culture. *Scholastic Early Childhood Today,* 46–48.

Early Childhood Teacher (ECT). (2004b, November/December). Early childhood director Desire J. Ford on celebrating compassion and cultures in the classroom. *Scholastic Early Childhood Today,* 51–52.

Edward, C., & Raikes, H. (2002). Extending the dance: Relationship-based approaches to infant/toddler care and education. *Young Children, 57*(4), 10–17.

Fawcett, A. (2001, July 3). Baby talk. *The Atlanta Journal-Constitution.* Retrieved May 1, 2002, from http://littlesigners.com/ajc_babytalk.html.

Fiedler, D. (2002). Talking babies: Using sign language to communicate with your baby. Retrieved 11/19/04 from http://www.parentsknow.com/articles/july02-sign_language.php.

Gann, C. (2001). A spot of our own: The cultural relevancy, anti-bias resource room. *Young Children, 57*(6), 34–36.

Gerstenblatt, P. (2000). Providing culturally sensitive child care environments. *Child Care Health Connections, 13*(1), 8.

Ghazvini, A., & Mullis, R. (2002). Center-based care for young children: Examining predictors of quality. *Journal of Genetic Psychology, 163*(1), 112–125.

Gonzalez-Mena, J. (2004). *Infants, toddlers and caregivers.* New York: McGraw-Hill.

Gonzalez-Mena, J. (2000). *Multicultural issues in child care.* Menlo Park, CA: Mayfield Publishing.

Gonzalez-Mena, J., & Bhavnagri, N. (2000). Diversity and infant-toddler caregiving. *Young Children, 56*(5), 31–35.

Gonzalez-Mena, J., & Stonehouse, A. (2000, January). High-maintenance parents. *Child Care Information Exchange,* 10–12.

Goodwyn, S., Acredolo, L., & Brown, C. (2000). Impact of symbols on early language development. *Journal of Nonverbal Behavior,* 24. Abstract available at: http://www.focusites.com/babysigns/symbolicgesturingarticle.htm.

Greenspan, S. (2004, April). Reciprocity–A two-way street. *Scholastic Early Childhood Today,* 21-23.

Greenspan, S. (2003a). Child care research: A clinical perspective. *Child Development, 74*(4), 1064–1068.

Greenspan, S. (2003b, November/December). Working with the child who has difficulty communicating. *Scholastic Early Childhood Today,* 28–29.

Hamilton, M., Roach, M., & Riley, D. (2003). Moving toward family-centered early care and education: The past, the present and a glimpse of the future. *Early Childhood Education Journal, 30*(4), 225–232.

Helms, A. (1999, November 28). Teaching babies sign language before verbal speech. *Toronto Star.*

Hispanic PR Wire. (Sept 10, 2004). Innovative Spanish language series targeting home-based child care provides to begin airing on PBS stations this week. Retrieved September 19, 2004 from: http://www.hispanicprwire.com/news_in.php?id=2896&cha=8&PHPSESSID=58b7f3732032d412178c73fd2c8cc1d9.

Honig, A. (2002). *Secure relationships: Nurturing infant/toddler attachment in early care settings.* Washington, DC: NAEYC.

Huber, L. (2004, November/December). Making the most of multicultural materials. *Scholastic Early Childhood Today,* 10–12.

Hunt, R. (1999). Making positive multicultural early childhood education happen. *Young Children, 54*(5), 39–42.

Huntsinger, C., Huntsinger, P., Ching, W., & Lee, C. (2000). Understanding cultural contexts fosters sensitive caregiving of Chinese American children. *Young Children, 55*(5), 7–15.

Hurt, J. (2000). Create a parent place—Make the invitation for family involvement real. *Young Children, 55*(5), 88–92.

Hyson, M. (2002). Preparing tomorrow's teachers: NAEYC announces new standards. *Young Children, 57*(2), 78–79.

Julian,T., McKenry, P., & McKelvey, M. (1994). Cultural variations in parenting: Perceptions of Caucasian, African-American, Hispanic-American and Asian-American families. *Family Relations, 43*(1), 30–38.

Kaiser, B., & Raminsky, J. (2003). Opening the culture door. *Young Children 59*(4), 53–57.

Keiffer, V. (2001). The importance of culturally competent child care. *Child Care Health Connections Newsletter, 14*(6), 8.

Lally, J., Lerner, C., & Lurie-Hervitz, E. (2001). National survey reveals gaps in the public's and parent's knowledge about early childhood development. *Young Children, 56*(2), 49–53.

Loeb, S., Fuller, B., Kagan, S., & Carrol, B. (2004). Child care in poor communities: Early learning effects of type, quality and stability. *Child Development, 75*(1), 47–65.

Lombardi, J. (2001). It's time to redesign child care to create 21st century early education. *Young Children, 56*(3), 74–77.

Lovejoy, A. (1998). Components of successful parent education programs. NGA Center for the Best Practices. Retrieved May 15, 2002, from http://www.nga.org/center/divisions/1,1188,c_issue_brief^d_1833,00.html.

Lucarelli, P. (2002). Raising the bar for health and safety in child care. *Pediatric Nursing, 28*(3), 239–242.

Lundgren, D., & Morrison, J. (2003). Involving Spanish-speaking families in early education programs. *Young Children, 58*(3), 88–95.

Marshall, H. (2001). Cultural influences on the development of self-concept: Updating our thinking. *Young Children, 57*(6), 19–25.

Meller, T. (2001, March 18). Looking for signs. *The Journal Newspapers.* Retrieved May 15, 2002, from http://www.signingwithkids.com/swkmedia.htm.

Moore, B., Acredolo, L., & Goodwyn, S. (2001, April). *Symbolic gesturing and joint attention: Partners in facilitating verbal development.* Paper presented at the Biennial Meetings of the Society for Research in Child Development.

Moore, T. (2004, November/December). Encouraging acceptance and compassion through play. *Scholastic Early Childhood Today,* 38–44.

Moore, T. (2003, November/December). Giving children global views. *Scholastic Early Childhood Today,* 41–48.

National Center for Cultural Competence (NCCC) (2003). Conceptual frameworks/models, guiding values and principles. Washington, DC: Author. Retrieved September 16, 2004 from http://gucchd.georgetown.edu/nccc/framework.html.

Obegi, A., & Ritblatt, S. (2005). Cultural competence in infant/toddler caregivers: Application of a tri-dimensional model. *Journal of Research in Childhood Education, 19*(3), 199–213.

Okagaki, L., & Diamond, K. (2000). Responding to cultural and linguistic differences in the beliefs and practices with families of young children. *Young Children, 55*(3), 74–80.

Reeves, D. (2002). A medical home for every child. *Healthy Child Care, 5*(4). Retrieved September 19, 2004 from: http://www.healthychild.net/volume6.html.

Reynolds, A., Miedel, W., & Mann, E. (2000). Innovation in early intervention for children in families with low-incomes—Lessons from the Chicago child-parent centers. *Young Children, 56*(2), 84–58.

Riojas-Cortez, M., Flores, B., & Clark, E. (2003). Los ninos aprenden en casa: Valuing and connecting home cultural knowledge with an early childhood program, *58*(6), 78–83.

Seefeldt, C. (2002, November/December). Linking your program to children's home language and culture. *Scholastic Early Childhood Today,* 18.

Shaw. P. (2000). Discussing provider concerns with parents. *Child Care Health Connections, 13*(1), 9.

Shaw, P., & Zehaye, S. (2000). Do I have the tools? *Child Care Health Connections, 13*(5), 10.

Sherry, C. (2004, September 6). Communication key in search for day care. The Post-Crescent. Retrieved September 7, 2004 from www.postcrescent.com ID: app54447073.

Shpancer, N. (2002). The home-daycare link: Mapping children's new world order. *Early Childhood Education Quarterly, 17*(3), 374–392.

Smilechild.co.uk Magazine (SC) (2004, November). Signs of the times. Author. Retrieved November 29, 2004 from http://www.smilechild.co.uk/magazine/generator.asp?article=67.

Sokol-Gutierrez, K. (2000, January). Partners in health: Helping families advocate for their children's health. *Child Care Information Exchange,* 51–53.

Wardle, F. (2001). Supporting multiracial and multiethnic children and their families. *Young Children, 57*(6), 38–39.

West, M. (2001). Teaching the third culture. *Young Children, 57*(6), 27–32.

Whatley, C. (2002). Meeting the diverse needs of children through storytelling. *Young Children, 57*(2), 31–34.

Walker-Dalhouse, D., & Dalhouse, A. (2001). Parent-school relations: Communicating more effectively with African American parents. *Young Children 56*(4): 75–80.

Additional resources for this chapter can be found by visiting the Online Companion™ at http://www.earlychilded.delmar.com. This supplemental material includes extensive chapter quizzes, PowerPoint® outlines, Web links, and various other activities to help better utilize the material in this chapter. The site is updated regularly, so you may check back often to receive the latest information about the subjects in each chapter.

## CURRENT ISSUES CURRICULUM SUPPLEMENT

Sample lesson plans and topic maps for subjects on current issues related to health, safety, and nutrition are provided in the next few pages for the teacher to help reinforce the information that is being modeled by teachers and learned by the children in the early childhood education environment. In addition to the sample curriculum, there is a list of children's books and sources for further information. Some of this information may include songs or finger plays. This sample group is presented to help the teacher design his or her own curriculum by adding to the information provided.

**LESSON**plan
CHAPTER 16

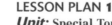

### LESSON PLAN 1

*Unit:* **Special Topics—Child Abuse Prevention**

*Suggested Themes:* I Know My Body, Stranger Safety, Good Touches and Bad Touches.

*Theme:* Stranger Safety.

*Objectives:* To be safe, children are made aware of some of the lures that a stranger may use.

*Materials:* Puppets—an adult and several children. Pictures of child lures strangers use such as candy, emergencies, open car doors, and so forth.

*Lesson:* Using the puppets, depict some of the lures that strangers use that put children's safety at risk. Show children pictures of some of the items or conditions that may occur during a child lure situation. Discuss the use of candy, asking for directions, and the open car door. Talk about safe people to go to for help. Discuss having a password for an emergency lure.

*Follow-Up:* Reminders on the bulletin board. Parent handout on child lures. Have a parent meeting to discuss the importance of training children about child lures.

*Age-Appropriate:* Older preschoolers and school-aged children are able to assimilate this information.

**LESSON**plan
CHAPTER 16

## LESSON PLAN 2

*Unit:* Special Topics—Inclusion, Chronically Ill Children, Children with Stress
*Suggested Themes:* Being Different/Being Alike, How to Help Our Friends, Sometimes I Feel Sad, Sometimes I Feel Angry, Sometimes I Feel Lonely.
*Theme:* Being Different/Being Alike.
*Objectives:* Children learn to recognize that they are more like children with disabilities than different. They also learn to accept differences.
*Materials:* Pictures of children with disabilities. Dolls with disabilities.
*Lesson:* Read *My Buddy* and *In Other Words*. Have a discussion comparing the two themes. Talk about how both boys might feel. Ask children to recognize how both boys are the same, then ask the children to recognize how they are similar to both boys. Have children who are willing to wear a patch over one eye during snack time. Discuss how it felt. Ask them to tell you in what ways they felt similar to when they did not wear a patch. How did the two compare?
*Follow-Up:* Read *Our Teacher's in a Wheelchair*. Ask the children if being the different/same changes when someone is grown up. Place pictures in room of children with different disabilities. Have dolls with disabilities available to play with in dramatic play area.
*Age-Appropriate:* Preschoolers can discern the same and different.

**Topic Map for Stranger Safety**

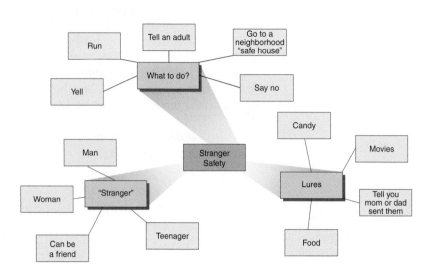

**Topic Map for Different Cultures in our School**

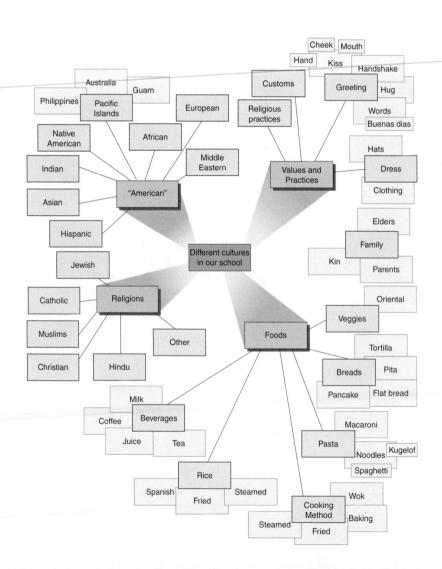

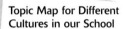

Topic Map for
Communication

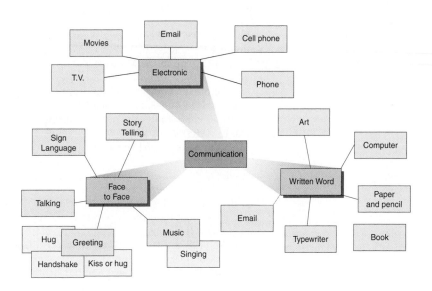

## Children's Books on Current Issues in Early Childhood Education, Safety, Nutrition and Health

Arthur, C. (1979). *My Sister's Silent World.* Chicago: Children's.

Bunnett, R. (1992). *Friends in the Park.* Bellingham, WA: Our Kids Press. A typical day in the neighborhood park with children with varying abilities and diverse cultures.

Carter, A. (1997). *Big Brother Dustin.* Morton Grove, IL: Albert Whitman & Co. A young boy with Down syndrome learns his parents are expecting a baby.

Charlip, R. (1979). *Handtalk: An ABC of Finger Spelling and Sign Language.* New York: Macmillan.

Chodos-Irvine, M. (2003). *Ella-Sarah Gets Dressed.* Explains how everyone else in the family thinks the girl dresses wrong, then her friends come to the door dressed in the same flamboyant manner. San Diego: Harcourt Children's Books.

Cohn, J. (1994). *Why Did It Happen?: Helping Children Cope in a Violent World.* New York: Morrow.

Corman, C., & Trevino, E. (1995). *The Jumpy Jumpy Elephant.* Milwaukee: Specialty Press. A smart little elephant learns he has ADD.

Cowen-Fletcher, J. (1993). *Mama Zooms.* New York: Scholastic. A mother takes her son everywhere in her wheelchair.

Cronin, D., & Bliss, H. (2003). *Diary of a Worm.* Story about a worm who has no hands and how he goes about his daily life. New York: Joanna Cotler Books.

Damrell, L. (1991). *With the Wind.* New York: Orchid Books. A boy who enjoys the freedom of horseback riding just happens to have a disability.

Dwyer, K. (1991). *What Do You Mean I Have a Learning Disability?* New York: Walker and Co. A boy having problems in school is tested and finds out he has a learning disability.

Ely, L., & Dunbar, P. (2004). *Looking After Louis.* A new boy with autism arrives at school and the children help him out. Morton Grove, IL: Albert Whitman & Company.

Emmert, M. (1989). *I'm the Big Sister Now.* Morton Grove, IL: Albert Whitman. A young girl tells the story of her older sister who has multiple disabilities.

Foreman, M. (1996). *Seal Surfer.* San Diego: Harcourt Brace & Co. A boy with a disability learns to surf and enjoy the ocean.

Gordon, S., & Cohen, V. (2000). *All Families are Different.* Comparison of families and how they are different. Amherst, New York: Prometheus Books.

Heelan, J. (2000). *Rolling Along: The Story of Taylor and His Wheelchair.* Chicago: Rehabilitation Institute of Chicago. A young boy with cerebral palsy enjoys his new mobility with his first wheelchair.

Hesse, K. (1993). *Lester's Dog.* New York: Crown. A deaf child overcomes his fear of a dog.

Hoban, T, (1987). *I Read Signs.* New York: Morrow.

Kadohata, C., & Kuskin, J. (2004). *Kira-Kira.* Story about the life of a Japanese girl growing up in the Midwest. New York: Atheneum Books.

Karim, R. (1994). *Mandy Sue's Day.* New York: Clarion Books. A blind girl is more like other children than different.

Kastner, J. (1993). *Naomi Knows It's Springtime.* Honesdale, PA: Boyds Mills. A blind child knows the signs of spring.

Lears, L, (1998). *Ian's Walk: A Story About Autism.* Morton Grove, IL: Albert Whitman & Co. A young girl learns to appreciate the way her autistic brother experiences the world.

Lears, L., & Ritz, K. (2003). *Ian's Walk: A Story About Autism.* Morton Grove, IL: Albert Whitman & Company.

Maquire, A., & Bailey, S. (2000). *Special People, Special Ways.* How people are more alike than they are different, even with disabilities. Arlington, TX: Future Horizons.

Mayer, M. (1983). *I Was So Mad.* New York: Golden Books.

Moore, D., & D'Orazio Adler, M. (2003). *Ethan and Phoebe, A Child's Book About Autism.* A story of a girl and her brother who has autism. Philadelphia: Xlibris Publishing.

Ofosky, A. (1992). *My Buddy.* New York: Henry Holt and Company. About a boy's disabilities.

Peterson, J. W. (1977). *I Have a Sister and My Sister Is Deaf.* New York: Harper-Collins Publishers.

Pitzer, M. (2005). *I Can, Can You?* About infants and toddlers with Down's Syndrome and activities in their daily lives. Bethesda, MD: Woodbine Press.

Polland, B. K. (1975). *Feelings: Inside and Outloud Too.* Berkeley, CA: Celestial Arts.

Powers, M. E. (1986). *Our Teacher's in a Wheelchair.* Niles, IL: A. Whitman.

Rabe, B. (1998). *Where's Chimpy?* Morton Grove, IL: Albert Whitman. A story about a girl with Down syndrome and her father.

Rickert, J. (1992). *Russ and the Fire House.* Bethesda, MD: Woodbine House. A boy with Down syndrome goes "on duty" with his uncle, a fireman.

Rickert, J. (2001). *Russ and the Almost Perfect Day.* Bethesda, MD: Woodbine House. A boy with Down syndrome has a great day going to school and playing with friends.

Robb, D., & Piazza, G. (2004). *The Alphabet War. A Story About Dyslexia.* About a boy struggling with learning ABC's but he has dyslexia so it is hard. Morton Grove, IL: Albert Whitman & Company.

Simon, N. (1974). *I Was So Mad.* Morton Grove, IL: A. Whitman.

Simon, N., & Flavin, T. *All Families Are Special.* Talks about how families are unique and points out differences and similarities. Morton Grove, IL: Albert Whitman & Company.

Thomas, P., & Harker, L. (2002). *Don't Call Me Special: A First Look at Disability* Covers a number of disabilities in ways children can understand. Hauppague, NY: Barron's Educational Series.

Thompson, M. (1996). *Andy and His Yellow Frisbee.* Bethesda, MD: Woodbine House. Kids dealing with autism.

Walker, J. (1993). *In Other Words.* Toronto, Canada: Annick Press. A boy with disabilities imagines what it would be like to live without them.

Watson, E. (1996). *Talking to Angels.* San Diego: Harcourt Brace Jovanovich. Girl who talks to her autistic sister.

Winn, C., & Walsh, D. (1996). *Clover's Secret.* Minneapolis: Fairview Press. Clover attempts to hide family violence.

Woloson, E., & Gough, B. (2003). *My Friend Isabelle.* Story about two close friends who are different but it is not really noticed. Bethesda, MD: Woodbine House.

Woodson, J., & Lewis, E. (2004). *Coming On Home Soon.* Story of a girl separated from her mother, whose mother finally does come home. New York: Putnam Juvenile.

# *Appendix*

## SOURCES OF MATERIALS RELATED TO SAFETY, NUTRITION, AND HEALTH

Abbott Laboratories
100 Abbott Park Road
Abbott Park, IL 60064-3500
http://www.abbott.com

Aetna Life, Casualty and Health Companies
151 Farmington Avenue
Hartford, CT 06156
http://www.aetna.com

Alexander Graham Bell Association for the Deaf, Inc.
3417 Volta Place, NW
Washington, DC 20007
http://www.agbell.org

Alliance for Healthy Homes
227 Massachusetts Avenue
Suite 200
Washington, DC 20002
http://www.aeclp.org

American Academy of Pediatrics
141 Northwest Point Boulevard
Elk Grove Village, IL 60009-1098
http://www.aap.org

American Allergy Association
P.O. Box 7273
Menlo Park, CA 94026

American Alliance for Health, Physical Education,
   Recreation, and Dance
1900 Association Drive
Reston, VA 20191
http://www.aahperd.org

American Automobile Association
1000 AAA Drive
Heathrow, FL 32746
http://www.aaa.com

American Cancer Society
1599 Clifton Road, NE
Atlanta, GA 30329
http://www.cancer.org

American Dairy Association
Dairy Management Inc.
10255 W. Higgins Rd. Suite 900
Rosemont, IL 60018
http://www.dairyinfo.com
http://www.ilovecheese.com

American Dairy Products Institute
116 N. York Street
Elmhurst, IL 60126
(630) 530-8700
http://www.adpi.org

American Dental Association
211 E. Chicago Avenue
Chicago, IL 60611
http://www.ada.org

American Diabetes Association, Inc.
1701 N. Beauregard Street
Alexandria, VA 22311
http://www.diabetes.org

American Dietetic Association
216 W. Jackson Boulevard
Chicago, IL 60606-6995
http://www.eatright.org

American Foundation for the Blind
11 Penn Plaza
Suite 300
New York, NY 10001
http://www.afb.org

American Heart Association
7272 Greenville Avenue
Dallas, TX 75231
http://www.americanheart.org

American Hospital Association
One North Franklin, 27th Floor
Chicago, IL 60606
http://www.aha.org

American Institute of Baking
1213 Bakers Way
Manhattan, Kansas 66505-3999
http://www.aibonline.org
(nutrition education and food safety)

American Insurance Association
1130 Connecticut Avenue, NW
Suite 1000
Washington, DC 20036
http://www.aiadc.org

American Lung Association
1740 Broadway
New York, NY 10019
http://www.lungusa.org

American Medical Association
515 N. State Street
Chicago, IL 60610
http://www.ama-assn.org

American National Red Cross
431 18th Street, NW
Washington, DC 20006
http://www.redcross.org

American Optometric Association
243 N. Lindbergh Boulevard
St. Louis, MO 63141
http://www.aoanet.org

American Printing House for the Blind
1839 Frankfort Avenue
Mailing Address: P.O. Box 6085
Louisville, KY 40206–0085
http://www.aph.org

American Public Health Association
800 I Street NW
Washington, DC 20001–3710
http://www.apha.org

American School Health Association
7263 State Route 43
P.O. Box 708
Kent, OH 44240
http://www.ashaweb.org

American Social Health Association
P.O. Box 13827
Research Triangle Park, NC 27709
http://www.ashastd.org

American Speech-Language-Hearing Association
10801 Rockville Pike
Rockville, MD 20852
http://www.asha.org

The Arc of the United States
1010 Wayne Avenue
Suite 650
Silver Spring, MD 20910
http://www.thearc.org
(services and programs for children with mental
  retardation)

The Arthritis Foundation
1330 W. Peachtree Street
Atlanta, GA 30309
http://www.arthritis.org

Asthma and Allergy Foundation of America
1233 20th Street, NW
Suite 402
Washington, DC 20036
http://www.aafa.org

Childhood and Youth Division
Health Canada
Jeanne Mance Building
9th Floor
Tunney's Pasture
Ottawa, Ontario
K1A OK9 Canada
http://consumerinformation.ca

Children's Defense Fund
25 E Street, NW
Washington, DC 20001
http://www.childrensdefense.org

Committee for Children
2203 Airport Way South
Suite 500
Seattle, WA 98134
http://www.cfchildren.org

Consumer Information Center
Pueblo, CO 81009
http://www.pueblo.gsa.gov

Council for Exceptional Children
Division of Early Childhood
P.O. Box 79026
Baltimore, MD 21279-0026
http://www.cec.sped.org

Cystic Fibrosis Foundation
6931 Arlington Road
Suite 200
Bethesda, MD 20814
http://www.cff.org

Department of Health and Human Services
Food and Drug Administration
5600 Fishers Lane
Rockville, MD 20857–0001
http://www.fda.gov

Easter Seals National Headquarters
230 W. Monroe Street
Suite 1800
Chicago, IL 60606
http://www.easter-seals.org

Environmental Protection Agency
1200 Pennsylvania Avenue, NW
Washington, DC 20460
http://www.epa.gov

Epilepsy Foundation of America
4351 Garden City Drive
Landover, MD 20785
http://www.epilepsyfoundation.org

Federal Emergency Management Agency
500 C Street, SW
Washington, DC 20472
http://www.fema.gov

Feingold Association of the United States
P.O. Box 6550
Alexandria, VA 22306
http://www.feingold.org

Florida Department of Citrus
P.O. Box 148
Lakeland, FL 33801–0148
http://www.floridajuice.com

Food and Nutrition Information Center
National Agricultural Library Room 304
10301 Baltimore Avenue
Beltsville, MD 20705–2351
http://www.nal.usda.gov/fns

General Mills Educational Services
P.O. Box 1113
Minneapolis, MN 55440
http://www.generalmills.com

Health Education Foundation
2600 Virginia Avenue, NW
Suite 502
Washington, DC 20037

Healthy Choices for Kids
P.O. Box 39
Ellensburg, WA 98926
http://www.healthychoices.org

The Huntington's Disease Society of America
158 W. 29th Street
7th Floor
New York, NY 10011–2420
http://www.hdsa.org

International Life Sciences Institute
1126 Sixteenth Street, NW
Suite 300
Washington, DC 20036–4804
http://www.ilsi.org

Johnson & Johnson Family of Companies
One Johnson & Johnson Plaza
Room WH2133
New Brunswick, NJ 08933
http://www.jnj.com

The Joseph P. Kennedy, Jr. Foundation
1133 19th Street, NW, 12th Floor
Washington, DC 20036
http://www.jpkf.org

Kellogg Company
One Kellogg Square
Battle Creek, MI 49016
http://www.kelloggs.com

Learning Disabilities Association of America
4156 Library Road
Pittsburg, PA 15234
http://www.ldanatl.org

Lefthanders International
P.O. Box 8249
Topeka, KS 66608

March of Dimes Birth Defects Foundation
1275 Mamaroneck Avenue
White Plains, NY 10605
http://www.marchofdimes.com

Maternal and Child Health Bureau
Health Resources and Services Administration
5600 Fishers Lane
Parklawn Building, Room 1805
Rockville, MD 20857
http://www.mchb.hrsa.gov

Metropolitan Life Insurance Company
One Madison Avenue
New York, NY 10010
http://www.metlife.com

Muscular Dystrophy Association—USA
National Headquarters
3300 E. Sunrise Drive
Tucson, AZ 85718
http://www.mdausa.org

National Academy of Sciences
National Research Council
Office of News and Public Information
500 Fifth St., NW
Washington, DC 20001
http://www.nationalacademies.org

National Association for Down Syndrome
P.O. Box 4542
Oak Brook, IL 60522
http://www.nads.org

National Association for the Education of Young
  Children
1509 16th Street, NW
Washington, DC 20036–1426
http://www.naeyc.org

National Association for Visually Handicapped
22 W. 21st Street
New York, NY 10010
http://www.navh.org

National Clearinghouse on Child Abuse and Neglect
  Information
330 C Street, SW
Washington, DC 20447
http://nccanch.acf.hhs.gov

National Education Association
1201 16th Street, NW
Washington, DC 20036
http://www.nea.org

National Council on Family Relations
3989 Central Avenue, NE
Suite 550
Minneapolis, MN 55421
http://www.ncfr.org

National Dairy Council
10255 W. Higgins Rd.
Suite 900
Rosemont, IL 60018
http://www.nationaldairycouncil.org

National Fire Protection Association
1 Batterymarch Park
P.O. Box 9101
Quincy, MA 02269–9101
http://www.nfpa.org

National Health Council
1730 M Street, NW
Suite 500
Washington, DC 20036
http://www.nhcouncil.org

National Health Information Center
Office of Disease Prevention and Health Promotion
P.O. Box 1133
Washington, DC 29913–1133
http://www.health.gov

National Hemophilia Foundation
116 W. 32nd Street
11th Floor
New York, NY 10001
http://www.hemophilia.org

The National Dissemination Center for Children with
  Disabilities
P.O. Box 1492
Washington, DC 20013-1492
http://www.nichcy.org

The National Institute of Allergy and Infectious
  Diseases
Office of Communications and Public Liaison
Building 31, Room 7A-50
31 Center Drive MSC 2520
Bethesda, MD 20892-2520
http://www.niaid.nih.gov

National Institutes of Health
Department of Health and Human Services
Bethesda, MD 20892
http://www.nih.gov

National Livestock and Meat Board
444 N. Michigan Avenue
Chicago, IL 60611

The National Pediculosis Association
P.O. Box 610189
Newton, MA 02461
http://www.headlice.org

National Reye's Syndrome Foundation
P.O. Box 829
Bryan, OH 43506–0829
http://www.reyessyndrome.org

National Safety Council
1121 Spring Lake Drive
Itasca, IL 60143–3201
http://www.nsc.org

National Spinal Cord Injury Association
6701 Democracy Boulevard
Suite 300, #300–9
Bethesda, MD 20817
http://www.spinalcord.org

National Sudden Infant Death Syndrome Resource Center
2070 Chain Bridge Road
Suite 450
Vienna, VA 22182
http://www.sidscenter.org

National Wildlife Federation
1400 16th Street, NW
Washington, DC 20036–2266
http://www.nwf.org

Nutrition—Health Canada
A.L. 0900C2
Ottawa, Canada
K1A 0K9
Telephone: (613) 957-2991
Toll free: 1-866-225-0709
http://www.hc-sc.gc.ca

Office of Early Childhood Development
Department of Human Services
John A. Wilson Building
1350 Pennsylvania Avenue, NW
Washington, DC 20004
http://www.dhs.dc.gov

Poison Prevention Week Council
P.O. Box 1543
Washington, DC 20013
http://www.poisonprevention.org

Prevent Blindness America
500 E. Remington Road
Schaumburg, IL 60173
http://www.preventblindness.org

Public Health Services for Children
U.S. Department of Health and Human Services
200 Independence Avenue, SW
Washington, DC 20201
http://www.hhs.gov/kids

Ross Products Division
Abbott Laboratories
625 Cleveland Avenue
Columbus, OH 43215–1724
http://www.ross.com

Sex Information and Education Council of the United States
130 W. 42nd Street
Suite 350
New York, NY 10036–7802
http://www.siecus.org

State Farm Insurance
One State Farm Plaza
Bloomington, IL 61710
http://www.statefarm.com

Unilever Group
Englewood Cliffs, New Jersey
http://www.unilever.com

United Cerebral Palsy
1600 L Street, NW
Suite 700
Washington, DC 20036
http://www.ucp.org

U.S. Department of Agriculture
Agricultural Research Service
14th & Independence Avenue, SW
Washington, DC 20250
http://www.ars.usda.gov

U.S. Department of Education
400 Maryland Avenue, SW
Washington, DC 20202–0498
http://www.ed.gov

U.S. Government Printing Office
Superintendent of Documents
732 N. Capitol Street, NW
Washington, DC 20401
http://www.gpoaccess.gov

Veterans of Safety—Student Chapter
Central Missouri State University
Humphreys #201
Department of Safety Science and Technology
Warrensburg, MO 64093
http://www.safetycenter.cmsu.edu

Vision Council of America
(Better Vision Institute)
1700 Diagonal Road
Suite 500
Alexandria, VA 22314

The World Health Organization
Regional Office of the Americas
525 23rd St., NW
Washington, DC 20037
202-974-3000
http://www.who.int

# *Glossary*

## A

**accident**—unforeseen occurrence that results in injury.

**acculturated**—adopting attitudes and beliefs.

**activity based**—activities that promote adaptive behavior.

**advocate**—to support or speak on behalf of another.

**age appropriateness**—consideration of the developmental abilities of a particular age group in the selection of toys, materials, and equipment.

**agile**—easy, flexible, fast movement.

**amblyopia**—an unequal balance of a child's eye muscles often referred to as "lazy eye." Condition is improved through the use of eye patches to enable the weaker eye to strengthen with greater use.

**amino acids**—organic compounds containing carbon, hydrogen, oxygen, and nitrogen; the key components of proteins.

**anaphylaxis**—sensitivity to an allergen that causes an attack that can result in collapse or death.

**anecdotal**—a brief narrative account that describes a child's behavior that is significant to the observer.

**antibias**—an approach to curriculum that removes all inequities due to race, gender, and abilities.

**antibodies**—proteins produced in the body to react with or neutralize antigens in order to protect the body.

**appraisals**—regular process of evaluation of a child's health or developmental norms.

**assessment**—in-depth appraisal to determine whether a particular health or developmental condition is occurring.

**assimilate**—to absorb and incorporate in order to make alike.

**at risk**—exposed to chance of injury, damage, or hazard.

**attachment**—the bond that develops between a child and another person as a result of a long-term relationship.

**audiologist**—person trained to identify types of hearing losses, to interpret audiometric tests, and to recommend equipment and procedures to assist the hearing impaired.

**autonomy**—a child's quest from ages one to two to develop a sense of self and self-rule.

## B

**baby bottle tooth decay**—tooth decay that results from the remains of milk left on the teeth as a result of drinking from a baby bottle.

**bacteria**—organisms that can survive within or outside of the body, some of which cause diseases.

**basal metabolism**—the amount of energy used by the body while at rest.

**behaviors**—actions or conduct that put safety at risk.

**blood contact**—passing of germs through the blood from one person's circulatory system to another person's circulatory system.

## C

**calories**—the unit of measurement for the energy found in foods.

**cardiovascular disease**—disease resulting from impaired function of the heart and/or surrounding arteries.

**caregivers**—persons who care for children: teachers, family child care providers, nannies.

**cephalocaudal**—development from the top to the bottom of the body or from the head down toward the toes.

**cholesterol**—a steroid or fatty alcohol found in animal fats that is produced by the liver of the animal.

**chronic illnesses**—medical conditions requiring continuous treatment.

**communicable disease**—a disease spread from one person to another through means of respiratory spray or infected body fluids.

**complete protein**—protein that contains all essential amino acids.

**concrete operational stage**—third stage of cognitive development, in which logical ideas can be applied to concrete or specific situations.

**condition**—circumstance or situation in which safety is at risk.

**confidential**—keeping information private.

**contact**—touching.

**conversation**—conversing with a child is a good indicator of speech and language developmental level. It is best used for daily observation and observations over time and may be less useful if the child's first language is not English.

**coronary atherosclerosis**—disease of the heart resulting in the walls of arteries degenerating due to fat buildup.

**coronary heart disease**—disease of the arteries feeding the heart muscle.

**cultural**—related to traits and ascribed membership in a given group.

**cultural competence**—perceptive, responsive behavior to cultural differences.

**curriculum**—course of study that relates to the subject being examined.

## D

**dehydrated**—loss of water in the body that may impair normal bodily functions.

**dental caries**—tooth decay.

**developmental disabilities**—physical or mental incapacities that interfere with normal progress of development.

**developmental norms**—statistically average ages at which children demonstrate certain developmental abilities and behaviors.

**dilated**—pupils of the eye that are enlarged due to shock or injury.

**direct contact transmission**—passing of germs from one person's body or clothing to another person through direct contact.

**disabled**—incapacitated.

**disaster preparedness**—ability to be ready or prepared for any type of disaster that may occur.

**disinfecting**—procedures to eliminate all germs through use of chemicals or heat.

**diversion**—something that changes the focus of attention.

**diversity**—differences; variety often related to culture.

## E

**early intervention**—decision to modify a child's at-risk behavior or condition in an early stage in order to lessen the impact of the behavior or condition on the life of the child.

**ecological**—pertaining to the relationship of the individual to the environment.

**economic**—the satisfaction of the material needs of people.

**emergency contact**—the person or persons to notify in case of an emergency.

**environment**—all of the conditions, circumstances, and influences that surround and affect the development of an individual.

**environmental hazards**—chance for risk resulting from environmental conditions.

**enzymes**—organic substances produced in body cells that can cause changes in other substances through catalytic reaction.

**ethnicity**—relationship to a national, cultural, or racial group.

**evacuation**—removal of persons from a site where a disaster or emergency exists.

**event sampling**—occurs when an observer records a specific preselected behavior as it occurs, every time it occurs.

## F

**failure to thrive**—failure of a child to grow physically and develop mentally according to the norms. This condition may occur because of organic defects or lack of emotional bonding.

**fat soluble**—vitamins that dissolve in fat, but not in water, such as vitamins A, D, E, and K.

**fecal contamination**—contamination occurring through exposure to feces.

**fecal-oral transmission**—passing of germs from an infected person's bowel movement via the hand into another person's system via the mouth.

**feedback**—a technique for encouraging desired behaviors in children through communication.

**fine motor skills**—physical skills related to small body movements, particularly of the hands and fingers, such as using scissors, holding a crayon, or working a puzzle.

**food frequency questionnaire**—an estimate of the frequency of foods eaten during the period of one week.

**food jag**—preference for one particular food over all others, normally occurring during the preschool years.

**friction**—rubbing together.

**functional skills**—skills that allow children to adapt to their environment.

## G

**generalizable skills**—common skills that can be practiced and used in different settings.

**genetics**—the origin of features of an individual.

**germs**—microscopic organisms that can cause disease.

**gross motor skills**—physical skills that use large body movements such as running, jumping, and climbing.

**growth retardation**—the hindering of progress of normal growth and development.

**guidelines**—statements of advice or instruction pertaining to practice.

### H

**health policies**—framework for ensuring health and well-being in early childhood education settings.

**health promotion**—the improvement of health conditions by encouraging healthful characteristics and customs.

**health status**—the condition of health of an individual.

**heredity**—the transmission from parent to child of certain characteristics.

**holistic**—consideration of the whole being.

**hormones**—chemical substances formed in one organ of the body and carried to another organ or tissue where they have specific effects.

**hygiene**—protective measures and sanitary practices to limit the spread of infection and help to promote health.

**hypertension**—very high blood pressure.

### I

**immigrant**—one who leaves a country to settle in another.

**immunization**—vaccines given in order to protect individuals through the development of antibodies against specific infectious diseases.

**inclusion**—to include or integrate.

**indicators**—a sign or characteristic that signifies a problem may exist.

**individualized family service plan**—plan that coordinates services to meet the needs of the child with special needs and assist his or her family.

**infection control**—control of infectious agents by sanitary practices.

**infectious diseases**—diseases capable of invading the body and causing an infection to occur; may or may not be contagious.

**ingestion**—putting into the digestive system through swallowing.

**inhalation**—breathing in through the nose and mouth.

**injection**—the forcing of fluid or poison into the body via a sharp object such as an animal bite or an insect bite.

**injury prevention**—forestalling or anticipating injury risk.

**iron deficiency**—lack of adequate supplies of iron needed for normal growth, development, and production of red blood cells.

**isolation**—situation that causes a person or persons to be set apart or separated from other people.

### J

**job burnout**—inability to perform job due to excessive stress.

### L

**lactose intolerance**—inability to process lactose found in milk and milk products.

**laws**—rules of conduct established and enforced by authority.

**liabilities**—safety risks or hazards.

**linkages**—connections that unify the teacher, child, family, and community.

**low center of gravity toy**—riding toy where the center of weight is low and balanced, making it difficult to tip over.

**Lyme disease**—disease transmitted via the bite of a tick or deer tick.

### M

**macronutrients**—major nutrients needed for the body, such as fats, protein, and carbohydrates.

**malnutrition**—inadequate nutrition as a result of improper diet or lack of food.

**mandate**—an order by law.

**medical home**—a partnership of the family, the teacher, and a medical practitioner that ensures that all health, psychosocial, and educational needs of a child are met.

**metabolism**—chemical changes that take place as nutrients are taken into the blood, processed and absorbed by the blood, or eliminated from the body.

**metabolize**—change occurring by chemical and physical processes in living cells.

**micronutrients**—supporting nutrients, such as vitamins, minerals, and water, needed by the body.

**migrant**—a transient who travels from place to place to find work.

**mobile**—ability to move about easily.

**multi-use facilities**—early childhood education environments that are used for other functions.

## N

**nearsightedness**—lack of ability to see well, other than close up.

**nutrients**—substances found in foods that provide for the growth, development, maintenance, and repair of the body.

## O

**obesity**—condition of overweight to the extent that the body is carrying 20 percent more weight than the normal body for the size and bone structure.

**objectives**—goals; expected outcomes.

**observation**—primary means of data gathering in order to understand children's development and behavior.

**orientation**—meeting or discussion of a child new to care regarding health, special needs, and developmental history.

**otitis media**—infection of the middle ear.

**overnutrition**—excess intake of foods that provide more than adequate amounts of the substances needed for growth, development, maintenance, and repair of the body, often resulting in overweight.

## P

**parasites**—organisms that live off of another organism.

**poison control center**—a resource available through a phone call in case of poisoning.

**positive reinforcement**—reward given in response to a particular behavior that increases the chance of that behavior occurring again.

**preoperational stage**—second stage of cognitive development, in which logic is limited.

**primary caregiver**—the person assigned to be a child's main caregiver throughout the day in order to form a positive attachment bond.

**primary health assessor**—teacher who knows the children very well and can observe for health and well-being.

**profusely**—pouring forth freely or abundantly.

**proximodistal**—development of the body from the inside toward the outside or from the torso through the arms and out to the fingers.

## R

**referral**—sending a child for further testing or screening and making available resources that will intervene and avert risk that is posed to the child.

**regional center**—a center in a particular geographic area dedicated to helping families that have children with special needs. The center acts as a resource, a referral agency, and a source of support for families.

**regulations**—recommendations that are made a requirement by law.

**rescue breathing**—the process of steps to help a person who is not breathing resume normal breathing.

**resilient**—the ability to recover after being exposed to risk.

**respiratory diseases**—diseases of the nose, ears, sinuses, throat, and lungs.

**respiratory tract transmission**—germs that are passed through the air from the respiratory tract of one person to another person.

**risk**—the chance of injury, damage, or loss.

**risk management**—the act of managing risk.

**role modeling**—setting a behavioral example.

**running records**—a detailed narrative account that describes a child's behavior in sequence, as it occurs.

## S

**safety zones**—areas that offer little risk.

**sanitary practices**—practices that remove bacteria, filth, and dirt to cut down on disease transmission.

**sanitizing**—removal of bacteria, filth, and dirt that makes transmission of disease unlikely.

**screening**—to select or evaluate through a process.

**secretions**—saliva, mucus, urine, and blood produced by the body for specific purposes.

**self-esteem**—positive sense of self.

**self-regulation**—to control and direct one's actions.

**sensorimotor cognitive development**—first stage of cognitive development that utilizes motor abilities and senses.

**shock**—an imbalance of the circulatory system as a result of injury that includes a decrease in blood pressure, a rapid pulse, and possible unconsciousness.

**shock absorbers**—materials that lessen the force of a fall.

**staff-to-child ratio**—the number of staff required to provide proper care for the number of children of a certain age group.

**standards**—statements that define a goal of practice.

**strabismus**—a condition that occurs in children that causes one or both eyes to appear crossed.

**stress**—nonspecific response of the body to any demand put on it.

**survival procedures**—preparation and steps to follow to stay in place in case of disaster or weather emergency.

**synergy**—combined effort or action.

### T

**theme**—subject being emphasized.

**time sampling**—occurs when an observer records a particular behavior over a specific period of time.

**topic web**—graphical representations used for organizing and communicating knowledge about a particular topic.

**travel information sheet**—check-off sheet that monitors all conditions for travel safety.

**triggers**—substances or conditions that activate a response.

**24-hour dietary recall method**—record of what was eaten for a 24-hour period that relies heavily upon memory.

### U

**undernutrition**—less than adequate intake of foods that provide the substances needed for growth, development, maintenance, and repair of the body.

**unintentional injury**—physical injury that is the result of an unintentional event.

### V

**vaccinations**—inactivated, dead, or weakened live organism of infectious diseases to which the body builds resistance.

**virus**—a microorganism that is produced in living cells and that can cause disease.

**vulnerability**—inability to protect from risk.

### W

**water-soluble**—vitamins that dissolve in water, such as vitamins B and C.

# *Index*

*Note:* Page numbers followed by a 't' indicate tables; page numbers followed by an 'f' indicate figures.